RISK MANAGEMENT: TEXT AND CASES

Mark R. Greene
Oscar N. Serbein

Reston Publishing Company, Inc.
A Prentice-Hall Company
Reston, Virginia

Library of Congress Cataloging in Publication Data

Greene, Mark Richard
  Risk management.

  Bibliography.
  Includes index.
  1. Risk. 2. Insurance. 3. Insurance, Business.
I. Serbein, Oscar N.   joint author.
II. Title.
HG8053.G78   368   77–26159
ISBN 0–87909–730–2

© 1978 by Reston Publishing Co.
A Prentice-Hall Company
Reston, Virginia 22090

10 9 8 7 6 5 4 3 2 1

Printed in the United States of America.

Contents

Preface

This book is intended as a first course in risk management for those students who wish an introduction to risk and risk bearing as a function of the business firm. The treatment is limited primarily to situations where the happening of a random event will bring about financial loss. The identification, analysis, and measurement of loss possibilities, and the principal methods of managing such contingencies constitute the basic core of the book.

The definition of risk management adopted in the text is broad enough to include some topics not commonly associated with the risk management function. Chapters on estate planning, speculative risk, preretirement counseling, and merger and foreign operations have been included in recognition of the wide range of activity in which a risk manager may be engaged. Estate planning, in particular, should be especially useful to small businesses where business continuation problems may arise, and where the risk manager may also be the owner and general manager of the firm.

Insurance as a major way of managing certain types of risk is considered at some length. The aspects of insurance treated are those that impinge directly on the risk management function. Thus, the emphasis is on insurance markets and products, selecting insurers and insurer intermediaries, the legal framework surrounding the transfer of risk to insurers, pricing of insurance contracts, and the principles followed by insurers in selecting risks. Extensive discussions of the details of insurance contracts and problems in the organization and management of insurers, and other institutional aspects of insurance are beyond the scope of this text and are typically available in specialized insurance courses.

Sufficient materials have been included in the text to accommodate courses of varying lengths and emphasis. No assumptions are made about the extent of the students' prior knowledge of insurance. Thus, the book may be used as the text in an introductory course in risk and insurance, or it may be used in specialized risk management courses where some knowledge of insurance is presumed. In the latter case, the instructor may wish to omit certain chapters devoted mainly to insurance.

Over 200 end-of-chapter questions have been included. Many of these exercises are essentially of the review type, while others require the willingness of the student to seek out the needed information through the use of reference materials. In addition, Chapter 20 contains a set of cases that are designed to be of help to those instructors who wish to use a case as the main vehicle for instruction. In situations where the case method, as such, may not be used, the cases may serve as the basis for extensive written reports.

A number of persons and organizations have been helpful to the authors during the preparation of this text. Although it is not possible to list all of their names, special mention should be made of Professor Harold C. Krogh, Dr. George Head, and Herbert L. Cunningham, who read substantial portions of the text and offered valuable suggestions; of Paul R. Johnson, Peter Lusztig, and Jack Lowe, who participated in the preparation of some of the Stanford cases; and of Carol Corina, Norma Honza, and Rita Plume, who typed much of the manuscript during the period it was being tested in the classroom. It is a pleasure for the authors to extend their thanks to them. Authors would also like to thank the students who helped gather some of the case materials and the risk managers who cooperated with them in supplying information. The authors are also indebted to the American Council of Life Insurance, American Management Association, A. M. Best and Co., Casualty Actuarial Society, Insurance Information Institute, Richard D. Irwin, Inc., Society of Actuaries and Stanford University for permission to reprint certain materials.

Mark R. Greene

Oscar N. Serbein

I

Risk Management
as a Function of
Business Administration

1

The Field of
Risk Management

Although such areas as finance, marketing, accounting, and production have long been considered as functions of business management, it has only been relatively recently that risk and its management has been recognized as a separate function of business requiring knowledge and skill on the part of a corporate officer designated as a risk manager. Risk management may be defined as "the process for conserving the earning power and assets" of the firm (or the individual) "by minimizing the financial effect of accidental losses."[1] The accidental losses that are normally contemplated are those that arise from such occurrences as plant fires, liability suits, and similar events. Considerable uncertainty surrounds when such events will occur and what the magnitude of the loss will be.

Although the risk manager is usually concerned only with pure risks of the type just mentioned, there are a number of techniques available for handling the adverse consequences of speculative risks.[2] Modern concepts of

[1] James Cristy, "Selling Insurance to Risk Managers," *The National Insurance Buyer*, XIII (September 1966), p. 16.

[2] A pure risk is one in which the occurrence of some uncertain event can only result in loss. A speculative risk is one where gain or loss may occur. See Chapter 2 for an extended discussion of risk.

risk management emphasize the wide scope of the risk manager's responsibility. In the future he may well work with speculative as well as pure risks and with a wide variety of risk-bearing techniques.

In this chapter the following topics are considered:

1. Objective of risk management

2. Scope of risk management

3. Organization for risk management

4. Responsibilities of the risk manager
   a. Risk identification and classification
   b. Risk measurement
   c. Methods of handling risk
   d. Record keeping
   e. Cooperation with other departments
   f. Reports
   g. Policy
   h. Office management
   i. Initiative
   j. Maintenance of professional skills

5. Qualifications of the risk manager

6. Evaluation of the risk manager

7. Relationship of risk management to insurance

OBJECTIVE OF RISK MANAGEMENT

The principal objective of risk management has been defined as "the effective planning of resources needed to recover financial balance and operating effectiveness after a fortuitous loss, thus obtaining a short-term cost of risk stability and long-term risk minimization."[3] To achieve such an objective the risk manager must select the method of risk treatment that results in a net economic advantage to the firm. In the top-level management of the firm, there is often "conflict between optimization of return on capital and the increasing demand that waste of human, natural, and financial resources cease."[4] Risk managers can help in the resolution of the conflict through their activities in risk and cost control.[5]

SCOPE OF RISK MANAGEMENT

It is sometimes argued that the management of risk could encompass all of the operations of a business, and that all of the top executives of a firm are in effect risk managers. It is necessary, therefore, to define the scope of the risk management field in order to differentiate it from the total operation of the business enterprise. Historically, the scope of risk management as a separate activity within the business firm was fairly well limited. Typically, the risk manager was essentially an insurance manager whose primary responsibilities centered around

those risks that were amenable to transfer to professional risk takers, primarily property and liability insurance companies. Additionally, the risk manager (or insurance manager) would have some responsibility for safety and prevention. Over time the scope of the risk management function was enlarged to include some nontransfer methods of risk treatment such as planned no insurance, self-insurance, and related procedures. For the most part, the emphasis was on the protection of physical assets rather than on human assets.

An issue often arises about whether the protection of human assets through employee benefit programs, including such areas as group life insurance, group disability insurance, group travel accident insurance, and pensions, is properly within the purview of the risk manager. One of the early studies dealing with this issue was published by the National Industrial Conference Board in 1956, where it was found that 60 percent of the companies surveyed gave the corporate insurance manager the chief responsibility for the administration of employee benefits. A more recent study of this matter was made by *Time* in cooperation with the Risk and Insurance Management Society.[6] Their survey, conducted at the end of 1974, involved a six-page questionnaire that was sent to 1,786 companies and organizations in the United States that were members of RIMS (Risk and Insurance Management Society). Slightly over 50 percent of the questionnaires were returned resulting in a total response of 909 firms. Approximately 53 percent of the full-time risk/insurance managers who responded to the questionnaire were involved in the administration of

[3] Edgard S. Clark, "Financial Officers Change and Risk Management," Address before the Financial Officers of Northern California, January 31, 1973.

[4] *Ibid.*

[5] By risk control is meant those activities, such as prevention, that result in reducing the probability that loss will occur.

[6] "The Future and Changing Roles of Corporate Insurance as Seen by the Risk/Insurance Managers," An Attitudinal Survey sponsored by: *Time* in cooperation with the Risk and Insurance Management Society, 1975.

employee benefit plans, while about 57 percent of the part-time managers had such responsibility. Table 1–1 provides additional details. Although these results show a slight decline in responsibility for employee benefits as compared to 1956, they show an increase over 1966. In the latter year Professor Ivry found that approximately 50 percent of the full-time insurance managers who responded to his questionnaire were involved in the administration of employee benefit plans.[7]

Of the full-time risk/insurance managers in the *Time* study who indicated that they had responsibility for employee benefits, approximately 94 percent said this responsibility was in the health area, 51 percent had responsibility for pensions, and 23 percent for rehabilitation. Other areas mentioned were life insurance, disability, compensation, accident, profit sharing, benefits payment, travel, auto, and safety. Involvement in these other areas was not particularly substantial. The percentage of those having responsibility varied from 1.3 percent to 14.8 percent. These findings do not differ substantially from the results of Professor O'Connell's study, which was published in 1976.[8] He found that approximately 20 percent of the risk managers he surveyed had full responsibility for benefit programs.

Professor Ivry found, as might be expected, that risk/insurance managers who were officers of their companies were more involved in the administration of the employee benefit plans than insurance managers as a whole. Among the insurance managers who were

TABLE 1–1   Involvement of Risk/Insurance Managers in Administration of Employee Benefit Plans 1974

Responsibility for Employee Benefits	Responding Managers	
	Full-time (percent)	Part-time (percent)
Yes	52.5	56.6
No	47.5	43.4
TOTAL	100.0	100.0

SOURCE: *Time* survey, p. 64.

officers, approximately 48 percent were involved in all plans, and some 35 percent were involved in some plans. In cases where corporate insurance managers are in no way involved in employee benefit programs, the reason often is that other structures exist within the firm for the purpose of administering employee benefits. The personnel department is often given the responsibility, which it discharges through a Director of Employee Benefits. A distinction is sometimes made between wage and salaried employees. Administration of benefits for the former group might reside with the personnel department, while the latter would be the responsibility of the insurance department. Sometimes the involvement of the insurance manager in employee benefit plans is chiefly advisory or in some other way a shared responsibility. Ivry found that part-time insurance managers were also involved in employee benefit plans. Approximately 48 percent of this group indicated that they were involved in all plans.

In terms of the attitude of risk managers toward involvement in employee benefit administration, approximately 64 percent of full-time managers indicated that insurance managers should be involved in employee benefits. Of those full-time insurance managers

[7] David A. Ivry, "The Corporate Insurance Manager and Employee Benefit Plans," *The Journal of Risk and Insurance*, XXXIII (March 1966), pp. 1–17.

[8] John J. O'Connell, "Changing Responsibilities and Activities of Risk Managers — 1969 vs. 1975," *Risk Management*, XXIII (January 1976), p. 21.

involved in all employee benefit plans, some 90 percent indicated that they should be involved.

In summarizing his study, Ivry concludes:

It can be argued that the field of employee benefits is so highly specialized today that the insurance manager should confine his activities to the increasingly complex field of exposures in the property-liability area. The ideal arrangement would be for an insurance manager or risk manager to have several subordinates who are specialists in these particular areas. There would be a specialist(s) in the traditional areas of corporate insurance management and a specialist or specialists in employee benefit plans. The insurance manager would rely heavily on the technical skills of his subordinates. He would be himself more a manager than a technician, but there would be centralization of insurance activity in one department. There appear to be advantages to this approach compared with the approach used by some companies that create an employee benefits department completely separate from the insurance department. Often the two managers report to different officials. From an efficiency point of view, this approach can be questioned seriously.[9]

Including employee benefit plans within the scope of the risk management function seems highly logical, particularly so when one considers that most of these plans typically make use of insurance techniques to meet the risks inherent in such plans.

Over the years the scope of the risk manager's activity has broadened considerably. Today it is more common than before to refer to the person in charge of risk management for the business firm as a *risk manager* rather than

an *insurance manager*. Likewise, much more consideration is being given to the noninsurance aspects of managing risk. Insurance is now seen as being only one of a large number of methods for meeting risk. It is possible that in the future the risk manager will not limit his activities to the analysis and meeting of pure risk situations, but will extend his activity to include many aspects of speculative risk. It is possible that such activities as quality control, market research, business forecasting, hedging, and investment will be within the scope of a risk department administered by an officer of the business firm.

ORGANIZATION FOR RISK MANAGEMENT

Once the importance and scope of the risk management function has been recognized, it is necessary to consider where in the organizational structure of the firm to locate the office of risk manager. That no single answer to this problem exists is evident from a survey of the literature on this aspect of risk management.

The National Industrial Conference Board study of risk management published in 1956 showed that 60 percent of the surveyed companies had either a separate insurance department or a full-time insurance manager. Ivry reported that approximately 71 percent of the firms he surveyed had full-time insurance managers.[10] The more recent *Time* study was in substantial agreement with the Conference Board report and showed that approximately 60 percent of the companies that responded accorded their risk/insurance managers

---

[9] Ivry, "The Corporate Insurance Manager and Employee Benefit Plans," p. 16–17.

[10] Insurance manager and risk manager are used interchangeably in this discussion. Historically, the expression "insurance manager" was the more common.

full-time status. This same study showed that in those situations where the risk/insurance manager was part-time, the additional responsibilities involved such things, for example, as finance, taxes, accounting, real estate, legal, safety, purchasing and personnel. The titles of risk/insurance managers, whether full or part-time, vary considerably. The *Time* study found that, for full-time managers, such words as *insurance, manager, director, risk,* to name a few, appeared in the title. Between 3 and 4 percent of the full-time managers had the title of vice-president. A smaller percentage had the titles of treasurer or secretary. Further detail appears in Table 1–2. There was also considerable variation in the titles of executives to whom risk managers report. Approximately 47 percent of the full-time risk managers reported to the vice-president, 39 percent to the treasurer, 16 percent to finance, and 4 percent to the president. Examples of other officers to whom the managers reported are: controller, chairman of the board, secretary, director, and executive.[11] For the most part insurance managers report to officers with responsibilities in the general field of finance, even though insurance is only in part a financial function. Since the function of risk management is not easily categorized in terms of the traditional business functions, one possibility is that it should have its own departmental designation with the head of the department reporting directly to the president.

Ivry's study showed that in the group of firms he studied over 50 percent of the full-time insurance managers were employed by firms having 5,000 or

TABLE 1–2   Titles of Risk/Insurance Department Heads

	Full-time manager (percent)	Part-time manager (percent)
Insurance	74.6	39.0
Manager	62.5	35.3
Director	25.0	15.8
Risk	23.4	7.8
Corporate	20.5	11.4
Assistant	5.1	20.8
Treasurer	1.8	16.1
Vice-president	3.5	12.5
Secretary	1.0	11.4
Administrator	4.1	2.8
Safety	3.4	3.3
Administration	1.0	5.6
Employee Benefits	2.7	2.8
Controller	—	5.6
Finance	0.6	3.2
Supervisor	0.8	3.6
Purchasing	0.6	2.8
Personnel	0.4	2.8
Officer	1.8	0.8
Taxes	0.2	3.6
Loss Prevention	1.2	0.8
Other	8.7	22.5
Total number of respondents	506	403
Number answering question	504	360

SOURCE: *Time survey*, p. 61.

more employees. By contrast, some 87 percent of the part-time insurance managers were employed by firms having under 5,000 employees. Although the majority of full-time insurance managers work in large firms, Ivry found that some firms with fewer than 500 employees had full-time insurance managers.[12] Thus, full-time attention to risk problems is by no means exclu-

[11] For more detailed information see "The Future and Changing Roles of Corporate Insurance as Seen by the Risk/Insurence Managers," p. 62.

[12] Ivry, "The Corporate Insurance Manager and Employee Benefit Plans," p. 4.

sively relegated to very large firms. Ivry's results were in broad outline largely confirmed by the *Time* study. The latter organization found that approximately 75 percent of the full-time risk managers were employed by firms having 4,000 or more employees, while two-thirds of the part-time managers were employed in firms having fewer than 4,000 employees. Further, approximately 5 percent of the full-time managers were in firms having between 1 and 999 employees.

The place assumed by risk management activities on the organizational chart varies considerably among business firms. The complexity of the organizational chart as it relates to risk depends to some extent on the size of firm, the risk philosophy of top management, and the type of business. Figure 1–1 displays the organization of the insurance department of a large integrated oil company. This department is responsible for the full range of insurance needs for the firm, as well as being responsible for certain safety matters, including a safe drivers program. Figures 1–2, 1–3, and 1–4 provide alternative organizational charts for businesses other than oil companies. The type of organization depicted in Figure 1–3 is not typical, but it does show the extent to which the risk function, at least in its insurance aspects, can appropriately be encompassed by the personnel department. All of the illustrations exemplify the diversity that now exists among business firms in their approach to the risk function from a managerial point of view.

Any resolution of the question as to where the risk function should be placed on the organizational chart invariably requires the consideration of certain issues that arise about the philosophical and operational characteristics of a particular firm. The main issues

that need to be considered are (1) the scope of the risk management function, including the integration of property insurance, employee benefits, and preventive activities; (2) the level of responsibility expected of the risk manager; (3) centralization vs. decentralization of risk management activities; and (4) the internal structure of the risk department, including the number of employees. The first two of these issues have been discussed earlier in this chapter. The last two issues need further consideration.

Whether the risk department should be centralized or decentralized will depend to a considerable extent on whether the firm in its overall management policy adopts a stance in favor of centralization or decentralization and whether the firm is geographically dispersed, including foreign operations. Those persons who favor decentralization believe that this approach provides more clarity and greater speed in deciding what to do about risk problems. They would also point to the possibility of better and more direct personal communication in planning for risk, as well as the possibility that resolution of problems after a loss may be more efficient and just. The arguments for centralization include the following points: (1) to the extent that insurance contracts are used to meet risk problems, lower costs may be obtainable through mass purchasing; (2) better insurance coverage may be possible through the use of blanket policies, broad forms, and better engineering and agency service; and (3) the advisability of separating operating management from risk management.

It is likely that for most large firms the conflict between centralization and decentralization will be resolved by utilizing both concepts. Because of the basic characteristics of risk manage-

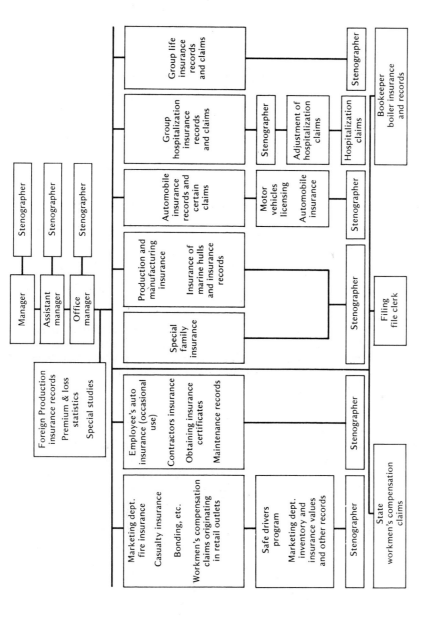

FIGURE 1-1. A Highly Specialized Insurance Department (an oil company with nearly 20,000 employees). Reprinted by permission of the publisher from Albert A. Blum, *Company Organization of Insurance Management*, A.M.A. Research Study Number 49 (c) 1961 by American Management Association.

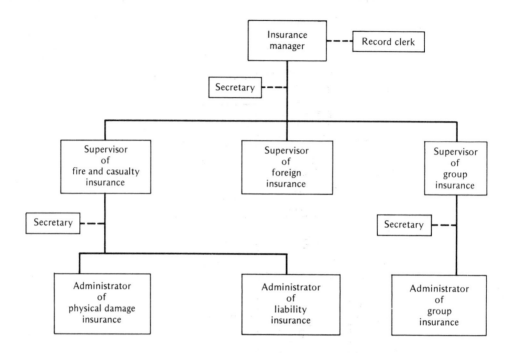

FIGURE 1–2.   The Insurance Department in an Electric Products Company (25,000 employees). Reprinted by permission of the publisher from Albert A. Blum, *Company Organization of Insurance Management*, A.M.A. Research Study Number 49 (c) 1961 by American Management Association, Inc.

ment, such matters as policy, risk methodology, and risk financing are probably best handled centrally, while safety, prevention, and foreign operations are best done on a decentralized basis. One reason for this compromise solution is that in foreign operations in particular, knowledge of local customs and laws plays a large part in determining the feasibility of a particular approach to a risk problem. Similarly, the success of safety and prevention activities, whether the plant is located in a foreign country or in another state in the United States, often depends on cooperation with plant managers and knowledge of specific working conditions and problems.

How large the risk department

should be in terms of number of employees depends on the scope of the activities assigned to the risk department, the level at which it operates in the firm, and the extent to which it operates as a self-contained unit. Existing risk and/or insurance departments tend to be small. Table 1–3 shows the results obtained by *Time* in its survey of department size. Over 60 percent of the insurance departments with full-time managers in the business firms that participated in the survey had 3 or fewer employees.

RESPONSIBILITIES OF THE RISK MANAGER

The duties and responsibilities of the risk manager include risk identification

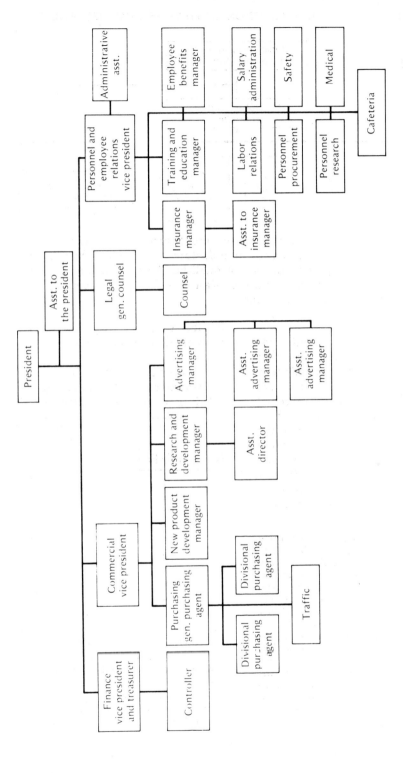

FIGURE 1-3. Insurance as Part of the Personnel Department. (A company engaged in manufacturing and transportation with 4,000 employees.) Reprinted by permission of the publisher from *Company Organization of Insurance Management*, A.M.A. Research Study Number 49, (c) 1961 by American Management Association, Inc.

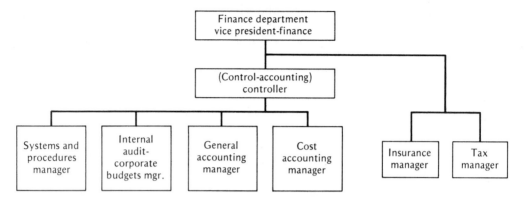

FIGURE 1–4. Reporting Relationship of the Insurance Manager in the Finance Department (a metal products manufacturer with more than 2,000 employees). Reprinted by permission of the publisher from *Company Organization of Insurance Management*, A.M.A. Research Study Number 49 (c) by American Management Association, Inc.

and analysis,[13] risk measurement, risk treatment, record keeping and information analysis, cooperation with other departments, reports, recommendations on policy, office management, initiative and independence, and intellectual growth. A brief description of these items will be included here. Some of the responsibilities, such as cooperation with other departments, will be discussed more thoroughly later in this chapter, while risk identification, measurement, analysis, and treatment will

be the subject matter of subsequent chapters in the book.

TABLE 1–3   Size of Insurance Departments of Organizations with Full-time Insurance Managers, 1975[1]

Number of Employees	Responding Organizations percent[2]
1	22.5
2	23.1
3	18.8
4	13.1
5	6.0
6	5.0
7	2.9
8	2.9
9+	5.7
	100.0

SOURCE: *Time* survey, p. 65.

[1] This tabulation excludes secretarial and clerical personnel but includes the risk manager.

[2] The base to which these percentages apply is 495 full-time risk managers who responded to this question in the survey.

[13] Allen and Duvall have suggested that the risks here considered might well be labeled *manageable risks*. By a manageable risk they mean one that: 1. Arises solely out of the activities of the firm and is incidental to them; 2. Is associated with the occurrence of an undesirable contingency that can only produce an economic loss; 3. Must be identifiable, and to some extent, both the frequency of occurrence and the magnitude of economic loss associated with each calamity must be subject to probability estimates. See Tom C. Allen and Richard M. Duvall, *A Theoretical and Practical Approach to Risk Management*, (New York: American Society of Insurance Management, Inc., 1971), pp. 1–2.

Risk Identification and
Classification

One of the most important duties
of the risk manager is the identification
and analysis of possible sources of accidental loss. Fire, windstorm, flood, and
similar natural phenomena may bring
serious damage and destruction to
buildings and their contents. Also, defalcation by employees, liability suits,
loss of goods in transit, product failure,
changing tastes of consumers, economic
recession, and many other problems
may lead to substantial financial losses
and possibly failure of the business itself. It is the responsibility of the risk
manager to be certain that all potential
sources of accidental loss be identified
well in advance of their possible occurrence. There is no procedure that is recommended as optimal for this purpose.
Three approaches to this problem are
often recommended: (1) use of questionnaires; (2) examination of balance
sheets; and (3) flow charts.[14]
Although identification of all possible risks facing a business firm that
could lead to loss through the happening of a chance event is important, this
task must be accompanied by an analysis of the data that have been collected.
Not all risks are equally serious, nor are
all of them transferable to professional
risk takers. Decisions need to be made
about the appropriate ways of providing against possible financial loss. Risk
classification is often helpful as a preliminary step in deciding on these ways.
The major purpose of risk classification
is to separate risks according to frequency and severity, with the latter

being measured in terms of dollar
magnitude.[15]

Risk Measurement

Once risks have been identified
and classified, the next problem for the
risk manager is to determine an appropriate method of risk treatment. In particular, a decision to transfer a risk or
not to transfer it will often depend on
considerations that are related to the
possible magnitude of the loss, the frequency with which it might occur, and
similar matters. Thus, some means of
adequately measuring the risk is of considerable importance. Probability theory
offers appropriate techniques for making mathematical statements about risk
and thus provides a way to measure
the uncertainties surrounding fortuitous
loss.[16] It is essential for the risk manager to keep adequate loss records for
the purpose of constructing loss distributions. It may be useful to represent
these observed distributions by mathematical functions, which in turn can be
used for the determination of appropriate probabilities.

Principal Methods of Handling
Risk (Risk Treatment)

Once appropriate information is
available about the characteristics of the
risks faced by a business firm, a variety
of techniques are available for meeting
the financial consequences of chance
events. The principal techniques may
be placed into four categories: (1)

[14] For an example of a questionnaire, see
Risk Analysis Questionnaire, (New York:
American Management Association), pp. 3–43.
Use of balance sheets and flow charts is dis-
cussed in Chapter 4.

[15] A detailed discussion of risk classification is contained in Chapter 2.

[16] The use of probability in decision
making will be discussed in Chapter 3. The
purpose of the discussion here is to emphasize
that risk measurement is an important aspect
of risk management.

avoidance, (2) prevention (control), (3) assumption (retention), and (4) transfer. By risk avoidance is meant a technique whereby the business firm does not subject itself to risk through refusing to undertake ventures wherein costs of treating the risk would be great enough to make the venture unprofitable. Risk prevention (control) consists of various methods used to lower the probability that a given event will occur. The principal control technique is prevention, including safety and protective procedures. Risk assumption is a procedure whereby financial losses caused by chance events are met through the financial resources of the firm without recourse to professional risk takers. Included as retention procedures are such items as self-insurance, captive insurers, planned no-insurance, ignoring of risks, and deductibles. By risk transfer is meant procedures for shifting risk to persons or organizations outside the business firm who agree to accept the risks of others. Perhaps the best known transfer procedure is insurance, and insurers are the principal organizations that act as professional risk takers, although they by no means accept all risks. Other examples of transfer are suretyship, hedging (use of commodity markets and puts and calls), guarantees and warranties, type of business ownership; and hold harmless agreements.[17]

[17] Most of the techniques described in this paragraph, as well as additional ones, will be discussed in greater detail in subsequent chapters. A type of business ownership that limits the risk of its owners (stockholders) is the corporation. Hold harmless agreements are contractual arrangements wherein one party to the contract relieves the other party of financial responsibility for certain kinds of loss. For an extended discussion of these agreements, see Harvey W. Rubin and William G. Ziletti, "The Hold Harmless Agreement," *Risk Management*, XXII (December 1975), pp. 41–47.

No responsibility of the risk manager requires more skill or is more important than that of deciding on the appropriate way of planning and providing for the possible financial consequences of various risks. The skill with which the risk manager copes with this problem will often determine the extent to which the function of risk management contributes to the overall profitability of the firm.

Record Keeping

The keeping of appropriate records is essential for the risk department of a business firm primarily for two reasons: (1) these records form the basis for reports emanating from the risk department; and (2) they provide the statistical data needed in the process of deciding on appropriate courses of action in regard to risk treatment.

The types of records kept will depend on the size of the risk department, as well as on the general level of authority granted to it. As a minimum, records need to be kept on amount and location of all assets (including loss exposures to which they are subjected), on losses sustained whether insured or not insured, on treatment procedures including insurance, and on facts about group coverages. Property records should include statements about original cost and current value as well as descriptions of fixed assets and location. Fire maps and property appraisals should also be a part of the record keeping. Insurance records should include a policy register, premium costs, loss and claim data, inspection reports, studies of new coverages, and independent advisory reports. To the extent that group coverages are the responsibility of the risk manager, record cards ought to be kept for individual employees, as well as payroll deduction authorizations, beneficiary designation forms, and group insurance waivers.

Of prime importance even for fairly small risk departments is a risk manual. The purpose of such a manual is to provide policy statement on how the firm views risk and its treatment, to state the risks to which the firm is exposed, to outline and define the responsibilities of the risk manager, to state how various risks are being treated, and to define reporting and record keeping procedures. Although it may not be necessary to distribute the entire manual to all personnel, appropriate parts of it should be distributed to the various departments of the firm. It is the risk manager's responsibility to make certain that an insurance manual is prepared initially and that it is kept up-to-date.[18]

Cooperation with Other Departments

Since risk tends to pervade most of the operations of any business firm, the risk manager must cooperate with other departments of the firm in order to discharge his responsibilities to the firm as a whole. All of the major departments of the typical business impinge on the risk department in some way. However, the departments that are most directly related are legal, personnel, finance, and production. A brief discussion of the types of relationship involved will serve to illustrate the interdependence that exists between risk and other departments.

[18] For additional information see James C. Crisly, *The Essentials of Corporate Insurance Administration* (New York: American Management Association, Insurance Series Number 94, 1952), pp. 14–16, and C. Henry Austin, *Operating Guides for the Corporate Insurance Buyer* (New York: American Management Association, Insurance Series Number 98, 1953), pp. 39–56.

Since the management of risk often involves the use of contracts as a vehicle for risk transfer, the need for cooperation with the legal department of a business firm becomes evident. In terms of insurance contracts the legal department can be of assistance in drafting contracts tailored to a particular risk. It also can draft deviations from standard contracts and help in the interpretation of contract wording. Contracts such as leases and hold harmless agreements may serve to increase, decrease, or create risk, and a careful review of these contractual relationships can be of considerable help in the risk identification and analysis responsibilities of the risk manager. Goods in transit often raise problems about when the title to these goods passes, and thus the question of who is responsible for protecting against the financial consequences of fortuitous loss often becomes a legal one. In a somewhat different area, liability questions can arise in connection with the lending of equipment, manufacture of products, and in other operations of the firm. Advice of counsel may well be necessary in resolving some of the issues involved. Another area in which legal advice is often needed centers around group insurance and other employee benefits. Help in drafting group insurance contracts, as well as determining if employees are entitled to benefits, may well involve legal expertise.

Whether employee benefit plans are supervised by the risk department or by the personnel department, close cooperation is essential to the maximum effectiveness of the various programs that make up the employee benefit package. Where group insurance programs are the responsibility of the risk manager, he must negotiate with insurers and be responsible for collection, disbursement, and accounting for funds, as well as for the overall administration of the program.[19] The personnel department must be involved in determining the magnitude of benefits, questions of eligibility, enrolling of employees in the various plans, and other questions of an essentially nonfinancial type. Interdepartmental cooperation in the operation of employee benefits is often best effected by setting up two committees. James M. Gillen has suggested that one committee might be called "the Employee Benefit Plan Committee" and the other "the Review Committee." The first committee would have the responsibility for developing and designing new plans and for the revision of existing plans. The second committee would interpret the provisions of existing plans and would review the operation of the plans in an effort to assure their satisfactory and uniform administration. The risk manager or his representative might well serve on both of these committees.

The finance department is often directly involved in the operations of the risk manager, since in many firms his immediate supervisor is often one of the financial officers of the firm. Even when this is not the case, the finance department has an interest in knowing how the assets of the firm are being protected from fortuitous loss and whether the protection afforded is adequate. The financial officer is also interested in the adequacy of loss settlements that may occur under insurance contracts and in any financial reporting that may emanate from the risk department. The reason for the interest stems

from the fact that the financial resources of the firm are involved when losses occur, and such losses may have a serious effect on the financial stability of the firm. One way the finance department can cooperate is by actively participating in the preparation of the annual report from the risk department and by assisting with loss adjustments.

In manufacturing firms, production departments are directly concerned with risk, since loss of materials, machinery, and labor can seriously interrupt the operations of the firm with resulting loss of income and assets. Losses from fire and allied perils are of particular concern, as well as lost time from employee accidents and sickness. The risk manager should seek the cooperation of the production department in the preparation of the insurance manual, in matters of safety, and in fire and related loss adjustments. The risk department in turn can be of help to the production department, not only through risk identification and treatment, but also by supplying information on new developments in safety and on the effectiveness of existing protective equipment.

Although the need for the cooperation of all departments of a business firm in the task of risk management is evident, effecting the cooperation involves considerable initiative and effort on the part of department heads. One means of providing the necessary cooperation is through the establishment of an advisory committee to the risk department consisting of the heads of the departments that are most concerned with risk problems. The committee could be chaired by the risk manager and should meet routinely to coordinate risk problems throughout the firm.[20]

[19] The responsibility of the person in charge of employee benefits (and ultimately the firm) has increased considerably as a result of the passage of the Employee Retirement Income Security Act of 1974. For a summary of accounting, reporting, and other requirements associated with benefit plans, see Appendix B.

[20] Material in this section is based on *Coordinating Insurance Buying with Other Departments*. (New York: American Management Association, Insurance Series Number 92, 1952), pp. 3–18.

Reports

The risk manager's responsibility for reports is two-fold: (1) he must prepare reports on the activities of the risk department at least annually for dissemination to top management and department heads; (2) he must receive and review reports from other departments, insurers, and other agencies whose reports are relevant to risk and its management.

Reports from the risk department may vary in content depending on the purpose of the report. Reports to various levels of top management might include recommendations for changes in insurance coverage, information on premiums and losses, budget estimates, information on the financial strength of insurers, data on insurable values, perhaps reviews of special studies, projects, and information on how the risk policy is being carried out. If the report is to go to other departments, it might contain information on inspection reports and recommendations and summaries of claims. A report to the production department, for example, could include summaries of industrial accidents, while a report to personnel might include information on group insurance claims. Reports on the automobile accidents of salesmen might go to sales management. It is not often that risk departments issue reports to employees, although if the department is in charge of fringe benefit programs, it might advise employees about their group insurance coverage, including the amount of retirement income that has been accumulated.

The risk manager must seek reports on the firm's operations including, for example, data on new processes, products, and contracts, as well as information on changes in fire protection, payroll handling, check cashing, accounting and inventory control, real estate bought and sold, building construction, property in transit, and business interruption values. Reports to and from insurers are important. The risk manager will want to inform insurers on changes in exposures, action taken on engineering recommendations, and reports on losses. He will want to receive data on inspection reports, summaries of claims and reserves, and financial reports, as well as other pertinent information. Proper use of reports can greatly aid the risk manager in his communication responsibilities and his duties to keep appropriate persons and departments informed about new developments in the risk field.

Policy

Policy is not solely the responsibility of the risk manager, but its central importance to the risk function is such that the risk manager needs to know in specific terms what the attitude of top management is about risk and should participate with them in the task of drawing up a policy statement.

Although policy statements will differ in terms of inclusiveness depending on the size of firm and the exposure to risk, as a minimum, such a statement should contain a clear assignment of responsibility to a specific department and delegate appropriate authority to a risk manager to act for the top management in matters relating to risk. The scope of the authority and the limitations placed upon it should be clearly stated. In addition, the statement of policy should make clear the position taken by the top management of the firm in such matters as safety and prevention, risk retention, risk transfer, and risk avoidance. Wherever possible the statement should be specific. Thus, dollar amounts might be quoted in statements about retention. The conditions under which risk transfer is to be utilized, such as use of excess insurance and deductibles, should be set forth clearly. It is essential for the risk manager to know whether the firm's management is essentially risk averse or not.

Office Management

The risk manager's role in the business firm is not solely that of a professional adviser in matters involving risk identification, control, and treatment. He is also the head of a department, and has responsibility for managing the affairs of that department. He must determine the best manner in which to carry out his responsibilities as well as the duties of his subordinates, which may include specialists in various aspects of risk management. The size of the department and the complexity of its organization will depend to a considerable extent on the size of the firm and the nature of its activities and on the commitment of top management to the risk function. The risk manager's general administrative object will be to make the greatest contribution possible to the earnings of the firm.

Initiative

Much of the success of the risk management function will depend on the initiative taken by the risk manager and on the independence with which he is allowed to pursue his activities. He must be given the freedom to act independently (but within policy guidelines) on matters involving risk control and treatment. This might well include, for example, freedom to select agents, brokers, and consultants in matters relating to risk transfer. How well the risk manager is able to determine risk situations and to recommend appropriate

treatment will depend primarily on his initiative in seeking out appropriate facts relating to business operations and then using these facts to protect the firm against chance loss.[21]

Maintenance of Professional Skills

The field of risk management, like all professional fields, is not static. The risk manager has the responsibility to keep abreast of new developments in his field, to evaluate these developments, and to implement ideas and procedures that will enhance his department. The task is complicated by the fact that risk management is an area that involves many types of knowledge from fields that are fairly diverse. The risk manager needs to keep up on legal developments not only in the United States but in foreign countries as well. Engineering knowledge and ability is often essential in risk control, and new developments in this field are often important in successfully preventing loss. Other areas of knowledge that are vital to the risk manager, and about which he must keep up-to-date, are accounting, finance, economics, and insurance.[22]

QUALIFICATIONS OF THE RISK MANAGER

Although the idea of risk is not new, the concept of risk management is. There

[21] See Horace P. Liversidge, "What Management Expects of the Insurance Department," published in *The Growing Job of Risk Management*, (New York: American Management Association, Inc., 1962), pp. 45–46.

[22] For a discussion of the concept of professional status for risk management see Wayne Snider, "Reaching Professional Status," *Corporate Risk Management: Current Problems and Perspectives* (New York American Management Association, 1956), pp. 20–35.

are few risk management departments in colleges and universities, and professional societies in this and related fields have not defined the specific educational or experience background needed by the risk manager. There are no licensing requirements specified by the various states or the federal government. One step in the direction of providing a professional background for risk managers was taken in 1965 by the Insurance Institute of America. In that year the Institute established a series of six examinations leading to a diploma in risk management. The subjects covered in the examinations were: (1) General Principles of Insurance; (2) Principles of Fire, Marine, and Allied Lines Insurance; (3) Principles of Casualty Insurance and Surety Bonding; (4) Principles of Risk Management; (5) Practices in Risk Management; and (6) Management and Finance. Currently the Associate in Risk Management Diploma requires passing of examinations in (1) Structure of the Risk Management Process, (2) Risk Control, and (3) Risk Financing.

The risk manager normally has need for background beyond that provided by preparation for specific examinations. During his college years and afterward, the prospective risk manager might well seek educational experience in such academic areas as public speaking, business law, accounting, mathematics, economics, transportation, and insurance. There are subjects not often taught in colleges that are valuable background for the risk manager. Examples of such subjects are fire prevention and safety. Even though these subjects might not be available in many colleges, they often are available in extension programs or in courses offered by professional societies.

Apart from formal educational experience, the risk manager has at his disposal many opportunities to acquire knowledge through participation in the activities of professional societies. The American Management Association for many years has been interested in risk management and insurance and has published a number of research studies and management reports that are valuable to the risk manager. The professional society that is directly related to risk management is the Risk and Insurance Management Society. This organization publishes a magazine entitled *Risk Management,* which contains many articles relating to the theory and practice of risk management. In addition there are many trade groups whose activities bear on problems of interest to the risk manager.

In summary, the risk manager has a need for a technical as well as a nontechnical education, which can be drawn upon in an administrative setting.[23]

EVALUATION OF THE RISK MANAGER

Any evaluation of the performance of the risk manager should depend on the prior establishment of performance standards for the various responsibilities that he assumes. It can be argued that to carry out these responsibilities he will need imagination, perception, a broad understanding of the corporate mechanism, good managerial ability, and technical knowledge either on his own part or on the part of those working with him.[24] His evaluation could depend on how well he has brought

[23] For further discussion see H. Wayne Snider, "Reaching Professional Status: A Program for Risk Management" published in *The Growing Job of Risk Management* (New York: American Management Assoc., Inc., 1962), pp. 301–9.

[24] See Clarke, "Financial Officers," p. 9.

these qualities to bear in the performance of his duties.

RELATIONSHIP OF RISK MANAGEMENT TO INSURANCE

Historically, the risk management function has been closely linked with insurance. Many risk managers have come from insurance companies where they have acquired knowledge about insurer operations. Their role in the firm has often been that of an insurance buyer and their activities have centered around problems of risk transfer and those preventive activities that are closely related to insurance loss experience.

Insurance experience is valuable since insurance companies are the primary example of businesses that undertake the risks of others. In spite of fairly widespread use of risk assumption techniques, insurance contracts remain the principal way of handling risk by many business firms. Thus, any discussion of risk management must treat insurance at some length, including the principles surrounding its purchase.

SUMMARY AND CONCLUSIONS

1. Risk management may be regarded as a function of the business firm in a manner similar to finance, marketing, accounting, and production.

2. In terms of scope of activities, risk managers typically have major responsibility for property and liability insurance and items related to it. Some other areas in which risk managers may be involved are: safety administration, claims handling, prevention, self-insurance, and employee benefits.

3. The specific responsibilities of risk managers involve risk identification and classification, risk measurement, risk treatment, record keeping, cooperation with other departments, reports, and office management. In addition the risk manager needs to cultivate initiative and independence and to grow intellectually.

4. Although there is no governmental licensing of risk managers, it is nevertheless essential that they acquire a professional background. Among the specific subjects to be pursued are the general principles of insurance; principles of fire, marine, and allied lines insurance; principles of casualty insurance and surety bonding; principles of risk management; and the general principles of management and finance. Background subjects should include law, accounting, economics, and transportation.

5. Evaluation of the performance of the risk manager includes forming judgments about his general managerial ability, his understanding of the corporate mechanism, and his technical knowledge of risk management.

6. Insurance is one of the ways of meeting risk, and experience with and knowledge of the insurance mechanism is of value to the risk manager.

QUESTIONS FOR DISCUSSION

1. Many persons believe that the responsibilities of the risk manager will increase over the next five years. Give reasons that would support this viewpoint. What reasons would you cite for the contrary view?

2. Risk management is a relatively new function in the management of business enterprises and was scarcely known twenty-five years ago. Write a brief paper on the history of risk management in the United States. To what do you attribute its principal development?

3. In the *Time* survey approximately 92 percent of the risk managers who responded indicated that their departments were centralized, although only some 66 percent of the firms of which they were a part had centralized company managements. What reasons would you give in trying to account for the difference in policy? Are there situations in which a decentralized risk management department would seem to be desirable? If so, describe them.

4. Discuss the responsibility of the risk manager and describe the ways in which they are typically met.

5. What is meant by risk identification? Describe the principal ways in which risks are identified. What are the advantages and disadvantages of each?

6. Employee benefits are in a number of instances placed under the supervision of the risk manager. Define the expression *employee benefit*. Do you believe the responsibilities associated with these benefits will increase or decrease over the next five years? Give reasons for your answer.

7. What is the relationship between risk management and insurance? Carefully define each term and give examples of activities that might be classified as one or the other or both.

8. What is a risk management policy statement? What purpose does it serve? Discuss the content of a sample policy statement. How would you improve present practice?

9. What type of educational background should a risk manager have? Discuss the present state of education for risk management. What improvements would you recommend?

10. Prepare a solution to the Case Kaiser Aluminum and Chemical Corporation (Organization Case) that is given in Chapter 20.

2

Risk and Risk Bearing
in the Business Firm

Risk is pervasive in society and within the business firm. Man seeks security and yet assumes voluntarily many risks in the hope of profit and in the desire for business and economic development. As John Dewey writes, "Man who lives in a world of hazards is compelled to seek for security. He has sought to attain it in two ways. One of them began with an attempt to propitiate the powers which environ him and determine his destiny. . . . The other course is to invent arts and by their means turn the powers of nature to account; man constructs a fortress out of the very conditions and forces which threaten him."[1]

This chapter introduces some basic concepts in risk and risk bearing, viewing the subject broadly. The attempt here is to enable the reader to gain perspective in analyzing the more specialized applications of risk treatment presented later. The material is presented under the following heads:

1. Pervasiveness of risk in the enterprise

2. Definitions of risk and related terms

3. The law of large numbers

4. Objective vs. subjective risk and probability

5. Pure vs. speculative risk

6. Dynamic and static risk

7. Risk according to loss severity

8. Risk and profit

9. Ways of handling risk

PERVASIVENESS OF RISK IN THE ENTERPRISE

Risk (uncertainty as to loss) pervades the entire enterprise and its scientific management is indispensable to success in the industrialized economy. (The definition of risk is expanded below.) Many failures of management can be traced to failure to recognize or deal with risk. There is a natural tendency for managers to emphasize the profit aspect of enterprise and to subjugate explicit consideration of risk. As discussed below, in most business situations there is a trade-off between risk and return, with expected higher returns being made possible only at the expense of accepting higher risks. In one study, for example, it was discovered that sales managers had a consistent bias in overestimating the expected return from

[1] John Dewey, *The Quest for Certainty* (New York, G. P. Putnam's Sons, Capricorn Books Ed., 1960), p. 3.

new products, which are normally associated with high risk.[2]

Some of the ways in which risk may be recognized throughout the business firm and its operations are illustrated below. Methods of handling some of these risks are presented briefly at this point and are explored in greater depth later on.

Risk aspects of the enterprise may be examined under the following major headings: (1) property and personnel, (2) marketing, (3) finance, (4) personnel and production, and (5) environment.

Property and Personnel Risks

The business firm is confronted constantly by potential loss to property and to personnel through such common perils as fire, explosion, windstorm, flood, theft, business liability damage suits, and death or disability of its personnel. Losses may be direct or indirect; for example, a physical peril may destroy property outright, causing direct loss, or the loss may take the form of reduced income from business interruption, stemming indirectly from the occurrence of some peril. Such risks are often handled through insurance, but other methods of handling them are also employed. These methods are discussed below. Later chapters explore the insurance mechanism in some detail.

Marketing Risk

Marketing has been defined as all of those business activities necessary to move goods from producer to consumer. It does not generally include the production of the goods themselves. The major functions include such activities as buy-

[2] Donald S. Tull, "The Relationship of Actual and Predicted Sales and Profits in New-Product Introductions," *The Journal of Business*, vol. 40, no. 3, July 1959, pp. 233–50.

ing, selling, transportation, and storage. Activities such as standardization and supplying market information and research also are important collateral functions of marketing activities. Some specific examples for illustrative purposes follow:

1. Buying and Selling

Many risks are taken by the business firm in the buying and selling functions. A seller may not be able to sell goods he has bought, thus suffering unexpected price markdowns. Sources of such price risks include changes in consumer style preferences, shifts in the fashion cycle, unexpected weather conditions, inability to hire competent sales personnel, ineffective advertising appeals, inability to extend sufficiently favorable credit terms, poor service by distributors, or international events. The case of the market failure of the Edsel automobile, produced by the Ford Motor Company in the 1960's, has been analyzed extensively. One possible explanation of this market failure, which is reported to have cost at least $250 million, was an unexpected shift in consumer preference toward more conservative automobiles. A possible cause of this unexpected shift was the national concern with the earth orbiting of the "Sputnik" by the U.S.S.R., and the uncertain implications of this advance in space technology to the national security of the United States. This event occurred about the same time as the introduction of the Edsel car, which had been preceded by careful market studies of potential consumer acceptance of the new product.

Other examples of risk characterizing the buying and selling function are improper identification of the class of consumers (market segment) or competition and lack of knowledge of the attitudes of the buying consumer for which a product is designed, with consequent financial losses from improper advertising and promotion and other selling effort. The failure rate characterizing new products is known to be very high, perhaps as high as 90 percent, due to the difficulties and uncertainties in gaining initial market acceptance. American automobile manufacturers, for example, were slow to capitalize on growing consumer preference for smaller, more compact automobiles until foreign competitors had first gained a significant foothold in the U.S. market. Manufacturers of baby food discovered that their product was increasingly in demand by that segment of consumers over age 65 and faced the problem of how best to redirect advertising and promotional efforts to this new consuming group. Finally, sellers have misjudged the mental attitude toward uncertainty of consumers by failing to use devices such as product guarantees as a way to overcome buyer resistance, particularly in some types of sales such as those sold by telephone or by mail order.

Selection or marketing channels constitutes an important risk of loss in the buying and selling function. An interesting example of this is in the area of automobile insurance. Following World War II some insurers known as direct writers began to establish and to expand their own exclusive distribution structures and to abandon the use of agents representing several insurers, usually called independent agents. The movement was similar to the tendency to "circumvent the wholesaler" in many tangible goods fields. Firms such as State Farm Mutual, Allstate, and Nationwide Mutual, using exclusive agents, soon captured a substantial share of the U.S. automobile insurance market which

had formerly been served by insurers using independent, nonexclusive agencies. (Agents of direct writing insurers usually are independent in the sense that they do not have an employer-employee relationship with the insurer they represent.) Among the factors accounting for the success of this "direct sale" movement were the vast increase in sales of automobiles following World War II and the need for more efficient and lower cost insurance distributional systems, the use of marketing research techniques to determine effective psychological appeals to the buyer of automobile insurance, and more effective claims settlement facilities used by the direct writers.

2. Transportation

Goods may be stolen, damaged, or destroyed in transit from perils for which the common carrier is not liable. Goods may be confiscated by others, such as foreign agencies in the case of international sales. Legal disputes over salvage may cause unexpected losses to the shipper. The seller may become liable for freight charges even though goods are not delivered. Delays in shipping may cause loss through spoilage or because of reductions in market price before the goods can be delivered. Unexpected losses may occur because actions by foreign governments prohibit the importation of goods already shipped.

3. Storage

Improper facilities for storage may cause unexpected losses. Normal perils such as fire, explosion, and other perils producing pure risks subject the goods to loss. Unexpected delays in removing goods from storage may cause loss from unusual storage charges. Forgery of warehouse receipts representing goods in storage may result in unexpected crime loss. Owners of storage facilities may suffer unexpected loss due to the nature of goods stored. In one case, a warehouse was completely filled with "prestologs," a product made from compressed sawdust and sold as fireplace fuel. A water leak in the roof caused the product to get wet, which produced expansion in volume of the sawdust, bursting the entire building apart. In another case, an electric utility firm had water stored behind a dam. The dam burst causing a loss of expected sales of electricity from the stored water, a loss about as serious as the damage to the dam itself.

4. Information and Standardization

Failure to have correct market information is an important source of risk in the marketing function. Obviously, the entering of new markets without prior knowledge of consumer attitudes, acceptable prices, expected sales levels, and type of products in demand, greatly increases risk of failure of the product or service to be sold. The cost of obtaining sound market information and research must be considered in the price of risk reduction and weighed against potential gains.[3]

Standardization of parts also may be viewed as a risk reduction device. Standard sizing greatly facilitates mass production and distribution and reduces the cost to the consumer. It minimizes the risk of unsold parts inventories. The mass output it makes possible through lower prices has a similar effect.

[3] See Mark R. Greene, "Market Risk — an Analytical Framework," *Journal of Marketing*, April 1968, pp. 49–56.

Finance Risk

Most firms depend on credit to conduct their operations. Losses may arise both from credit received as well as credit extended. Banks may call or fail to renew loans due to deteriorating business conditions, thus causing financial setbacks in the firm due to curtailed operations. Unexpected increases in interest costs may reduce profits.

Insolvency of customers is another source of financial loss. An example is the recent case of Lockheed Corporation's financial embarrassment due to bankruptcy of a foreign supplier of aircraft engines. Replacement of the engines from other suppliers was impossible without causing very large losses. This unexpected financial loss required U.S. congressional action in 1972 to alleviate this situation in the form of additional loan guarantees of $250 million to banks lending to the firm. In some cases, particularly when the firm depends importantly on a few large customers, insolvency of any one of which would threaten the firm's own solvency, commercial credit insurance is available. Methods to handle these and other speculative risks are explored in Chapter 8.

Financial risk exists in such decisions as to the type of securities employed in providing funds for the business firm, investment decisions, employment of self-insurance funds, and arranging bank financing. For example, the use of bonded indebtedness and bank loans increases the leverage, and potential gains from leverage, at the cost of additional risk. If a firm can borrow at seven percent interest and earn ten percent on these funds, within the business, the return to the owner's capital may be expected to exceed ten percent. Assume that a firm is capitalized at $1 million, of which $500,000 is represented by seven percent debt, $500,000 is represented by the owner's capital, and the firm earns ten percent on its total capital ($100,000). The return to the owner's capital of $500,000, after paying $35,000 in interest (.07 x $500,000), is the ratio $65,000/$500,000, or 13 percent. However, if the firm earns only two percent on its invested capital, its total earnings of $20,000 (.12 x $1,000,000) would be insufficient to meet the $35,000 of interest on its borrowed capital. In this way financial leverage introduces risk into the operation of the business. Earnings (or losses) to the owner are magnified beyond what they would be if leverage did not exist.

Various methods are available to reduce financial risk. For example, subordinated, convertible, or debenture bonds carry less risk to the enterprise than first mortgage bonds. Bonds without sinking fund requirements have less risk than bonds with such a feature. In bank financing, five-year or renewable loans generally carry less risk than short term loans because the payback period may be extended without new approvals from the bank. Selling receivables to the bank without recourse to the seller carries less risk than selling with recourse because if the debtor fails to repay, it is the bank's loss, not the selling firm's loss.

If the firm is making investments in stocks and bonds, such investments obviously carry some degree of risk. This risk can be assessed by objective measurements of standard deviation in dividend returns, market price fluctuations, earnings per share of common stock, or other more sophisticated statistical measures.[4] It will be the task of

management to decide upon both the degree of risk acceptable at each given level of expected return in a given portfolio.

In examination of investment portfolios, for example, it has been found that managers have not analyzed the risk associated with their portfolios which have contained securities yielding small returns and yet were characterized by high risks. Scientific analysis of the risk component brought about an efficient portfolio, *i.e.,* one which maximizes expected return in the portfolio and minimizes risk.[5] Undoubtedly many investment failures can be attributed to failure to take risk into account in a scientific manner.

Personnel and Production Risk

Management decisions in the area of personnel and production involve considerable risk which often is not explicitly recognized. Failure to recognize these risks has caused considerable loss to many business firms. To take a few examples: (1) Paying salesmen on a strict commission basis transfers the risk of "no sales" to the salesman, as compared to a salesman who receives some salary regardless of the amount sold. The employer of the commissioned salesman pays no compensation if sales are not made. In the long run, however, such a policy may cost management dearly in terms of loss of customer goodwill, failure of salesmen to service their territories thoroughly or to cultivate new small firms which could eventually become large volume customers. (2) Placing a person who is essentially a risk averter into a position which involves considerable risk taking. Studies show that such a policy generally results in higher labor turnover,

[4] John L. Evans and Stephen H. Archer, "Diversification and Reduction of Dispersion: An Empirical Analysis," *Journal of Finance,* vol. 23, December 1968, pp. 761–67.

[5] Harry Markowitz, "Portfolio Selection," *Journal of Finance,* vol. 7, March 1962, pp. 77–91.

poor performance, and generally poor morale among the individuals so placed.[6]

(3) Deciding to build a plant with too little capacity or too great a capacity for the size of the expected market. If, for example, a firm overbuilds, as has been true in such industries in the United States as aluminum manufacturers, overhead costs absorb profit margins which tend to be thin anyway due to relatively great supply, when compared to the demand. If the plant has too little capacity potential, business may be lost to competitors, leading to permanent loss of market share.

(4) Another example of production risk lies in the area of inventory control. If inventories are allowed to build up to levels too high for current demand, unacceptably high costs of storage, insurance, obsolescence, and deterioration may result. If inventories are kept too low, orders may be lost due to inability to fulfill customer demand promptly, or extra costs involved in special production runs to fulfill special orders may be incurred.

(5) Failure to plan proper plant layout or to construct plants initially with built-in loss prevention measures (*e.g.,* sprinkler systems) may increase production costs to noncompetitive levels. For example, a sprinkler system in most areas of the United States will repay its costs within five years in reduced property insurance premiums. These personnel and production risks can be reduced only by careful advance planning, much research and study.

Environmental Risk

Environmental risk has assumed great importance for the business firm in recent years for business decisions involving both domestic and foreign activities. It is well recognized that certain inner city areas may present unacceptable levels of risk for business operations, due to the existence of poverty, crime, poor law enforcement, unavailability of insurance, existence of fire hazards, etc. Rising rates of crime, divorce, and other types of social disintegration threaten environmental security, and create new problems for business and for insurers.[7]

International operations often present greater risks than domestic operations due to difficulties in evaluating unfamiliar conditions abroad. F. T. Haner has developed a formal method for quantifying international environmental risk, elements of which are composed of some 15 factors said to produce operational risk for the business firm doing business abroad. Among these factors are political stability, ease of conversion of currency to foreign exchange, internal inflation, attitudes of governmental officials toward foreign investors, rate of economic growth, quality of legal and accounting services, quality of labor supply, stability of labor relations, and quality of communications. Weights are assigned to each factor according to subjective evaluations of the degree of risk present and a composite index prepared to summarize the quality of the international environment of each of the major countries in the world.[8] In this way risk may be given explicit recognition by management before investments are made or operations begun abroad.

[6] J. L. Morris, "Propensity for Risk Taking as a Determinant of Vocational Choice," *Journal of Personality and Social Psychology,* vol. 3, March 1966, pp. 328–35.

[7] Mark R. Greene, "Research Problems for Marketing Insurance in the 1970's," *Annals of Society of Chartered Property and Casualty Underwriters,* December 1971, pp. 293–312.

[8] F. T. Haner, "Environmental Risk Index," *Business International,* (unpublished paper, 1970).

C. A. Kulp[9] analyzed the factors which produce risk according to two sources, those stemming from interactions or conditions affecting society as a whole and those affecting primarily individuals. The first he termed *fundamental hazards*, and the second, *particular hazards*. Uncertainty from fundamental hazards appears to be mainly environmental risks.

Fundamental hazards are defined as those which affect an entire society or a major segment thereof, such as uncertainties in the economic system, major social and political changes, and extraordinary natural disturbances such as earthquakes, tornadoes, and drought. Particular hazards are those affecting mainly an individual or firm such as premature death, fire, and legal liability.

Although he does not say so explicitly, Kulp implies that fundamental hazards are best treated by some sort of governmental action. He also stresses the use of certain techniques other than commercial insurance, such as hedging and use of corporate form of organization. Thus Kulp recognized that commercial insurance is only one of the devices needed to treat risk in society, and that other techniques are needed. The need for developing ways to handle environmental risk has greatly increased the importance of risk management, which takes a broad view of risk and various ways of dealing with it.

SOME DEFINITIONS

Risk

There are many ways in which the word *risk* is used and for that reason there is no single definition of the term which is universally employed. In this

[9] C. A. Kulp, *Casualty Insurance*, 3rd ed. (New York: Ronald Press, 1956), pp. 5–6.

text we use the term mainly to mean the uncertainty of occurrence of economic loss. However, it should be recognized that the term is also used to refer to (a) an insured object such as a home or car, (b) a peril such as fire or earthquake, (c) the probability of an event which may cause loss, (d) the loss itself, or (e) the hazardous condition. Furthermore, risk has been classified differently, such as fundamental or particular, pure or speculative, static and dynamic, objective and subjective, private and social, insurable and uninsurable, and many others. A full development of these concepts will not be considered here, but those of some interest for risk management are explained below.

Loss

In this text, loss refers generally to economic loss. Some types of losses are not easily expressed in economic terms, and an important problem in risk management is to consider the various ways in which this task is accomplished. For example, juries frequently award monetary damages for mental anguish suffered as a result of an accident for which a business firm may be held liable. Although it is difficult to say how much mental anguish may be measured in terms of money, subjective factors operate to influence juries to establish exact sums for such damages. An analysis of subjective risk (see discussion below) may be of some use in understanding this process.

Perils and Hazards

Most students of risk and insurance draw a distinction between risk and such terms as peril and hazard. A *peril* is an event which may cause a loss, such as a fire, windstorm, or explosion. A *hazard* is a condition which affects both the frequency and size of a loss. Hazards may be physical, moral, or morale. For example, frame construction of a building is considered more physically hazardous than brick construction since the loss is likely to be greater to a frame than to a brick building if the perils of fire or windstorm occur. An example of a moral hazard is the mental attitude of persons with criminal records who are more likely to cause loss than those without criminal records. A morale hazard is said to exist when a person has a mental attitude which causes him to suffer more loss than others, perhaps subconsciously — *e.g.*, persons who are accident prone.

Probability

Probability should be distinguished from risk. Some authors have not done so, and as a result the analysis of problems involving both risk and probability are somewhat restricted. Probability may be defined broadly as the chance of loss and, as such, is a concept of an average value. In contrast risk is a concept of variability and reflects the uncertainty of an event rather than its underlying probability. For example, a fair coin may be flipped 100 times, with an underlying probability that heads will result 50 times. The fact is, however, heads may not occur exactly 50 times, but may vary from this number. Risk is the uncertainty that exactly 50 heads will occur and may be measured by some concept in statistical variation such as the standard deviation or coefficient of variation. (These concepts will be expanded in Chapter 3.)

Probability may be expressed in terms of simple frequency of events or in terms of monetary values. It may be estimated subjectively or by observing past history, or both. Thus, if an insurer has 10,000 houses and on the average

100 catch fire each year, the estimated probability of loss in terms of past frequency would be one percent. In the above example, if probability is to be expressed in terms of monetary values, each house would be valued and a sum would be taken, showing the total exposed value of the houses. The average annual value of losses would then be divided by the total exposed value. This percentage would express probability in terms of the monetary value of the loss. Thus if the total exposed value is $2 million and the average annual loss is $400,000, the monetary value of probability would be two percent of exposed value. The percentage chance of loss (probability) multiplied by the total possible dollar loss is known as the *expected loss*. Thus, if a $10,000 building has a 1 percent chance of being destroyed by fire annually, the expected loss is $100.

THE LAW OF LARGE NUMBERS

The *law of large numbers*, stated nontechnically, says that as the number of events increases, the variation in the proportion of actual outcomes from expected outcomes tends to decrease constantly and approaches zero. If one measures risk by this variation, we may say that as the number of events increases, risk decreases. When only few events are under consideration, risk is high, and it gradually diminishes as the number of events under consideration increases. Thus, a manager with 3,000 automobiles being driven throughout the country under various conditions may be able to predict the number of collisions he will experience with much greater accuracy; *i.e.*, less risk, than if he had only ten automobiles, even though the probability of loss through collision may be the same in both cases.

As another example, an insurer insures 1,000 houses and the probability of fire is five percent, he can expect 50 houses to burn. If an extra house burns and 51 losses occur, the variation of actual to expected is only 1/50, or 2 percent. Now, if instead of 1,000 houses, the insurer has 100 houses, he may "expect" five houses to burn. If an extra house burns and six losses occur, the variation of actual to expected is 1/5, or 20 percent. In the second case, the variation is ten times as great, relatively speaking, as in the first case. Thus we may see that the law of large numbers is a powerful tool for predicting the amount of risk that the insurer faces.

OBJECTIVE AND SUBJECTIVE PROBABILITY

It has become commonplace to hear weather reports expressed in terms of probability, such as a 20 percent chance of showers. These expressions represent summaries of large amounts of weather data as perceived and interpreted by the weather forecaster. They are based, in part, on known tendencies of weather patterns and in part on subjective guesses by the forecaster about likely outcomes as a result of these patterns. Such estimates may be termed *subjective probability*. Probability can be also based upon "statistics" or on *a priori* knowledge of the physical nature of an event, such as coin tossing or drawing cards from a well-mixed deck. One may describe this as *objective probability*. The accuracy of probability estimates depends on the knowledge of odds or upon the size and quality of the statistical patterns available for study. To be useful, statistics must be interpreted by someone; various individuals may in-

terpret the same data in such different ways and their conclusions may be directly opposite from one another.[10] It is for this reason that the concepts of subjective and objective risk should be introduced.

OBJECTIVE VS. SUBJECTIVE RISK

Objective risk is that concept of risk discussed above when reference was made to the law of large numbers. Objective risk is the measure of the degree of variation in the proportion of actual from expected events. This proportion declines as the number of observed events increases. Hence, we can say that objective risk defined as a proportion declines as larger and larger numbers of events are involved. Statisticians may express objective risk in terms of statistical error in sampling from a larger universe of events. The statistical error measurement depends on a number of assumptions. Insurers are concerned with reducing or eliminating objective risk they experience in covering the exposures to loss. In reducing objective risk it is necessary to see that all of the statistical assumptions made in its estimation are fulfilled. These will be examined in Chapter 3.

It is obvious that objective risk has little or no real meaning when applied to a single event or even to a small number of events. For example, one cannot state with much certainty how much variation will occur in obtaining heads in six flips of a coin. While three heads are expected (if the experiment were repeated many times) one can easily ob-

[10] Paul Slovic, "Psychological Study of Human Judgements: Implications for Investment Decision Making," *Journal of Finance*, vol. 27, no. 4, September 1972, p. 783.

tain six heads (or tails) in a row in a single experiment. In such a case the analysis of objective risk would be so great as to be virtually meaningless as a basis for decision making.

Where objective risk estimates cannot be made with sufficient accuracy, or where opinions of management differ in interpretation of the data which are available for study, the concept of *subjective risk* may be useful in analyzing the problem. Subjective risk may be defined as the uncertainty of an event as seen or perceived by an individual. This perception depends on the attitudes toward risk of the individual concerned. At one extreme there may be the "risk lover," a person who perceives little danger or uncertainty as to outcome in a situation and in fact prefers a situation with a great deal of uncertainty to those in which the outcome is known or can be estimated with considerable certainty. At the other extreme is the "risk hater," or "risk averter," who may require very high odds for success before he will embark on an adventure of any type. (See Chapter 3 for more discussion of risk profiles.)

In a given situation it is possible, and in fact quite likely, that while objective risk may be low, subjective risk of the decision maker may be high, and *vice versa*. This can occur because the decision maker lacks knowledge of either the probability or the expected variation in a distribution of events. He may be so risk averse that even if he controls such a large number of objects subject to loss that he could predict them with great accuracy and self-insure, he will still seek commercial coverage. On the other hand, a risk lover may perceive little risk even if he controls only a small number of objects in which objective risk is extremely high.

There have been many attempts to measure subjective risk and to predict human behavior from these measurements.[11] Few of these attempts have been conclusive although many different tests have been employed: tests of personality attributes, tests of utility of money to the individual, life experience inventories, gambling behavior in laboratory experiences, subjective assessments by colleagues, etc. Many of the findings of students of the subject have not been in agreement. For example, education and intelligence, contrary to expectations, are not necessarily associated with willingness to take risk, although age and sex appear to be related, with older people and women tending to be risk averters. The influence of group discussion tends to increase the degree of willingness of individuals to make

[11] Mark R. Greene, "Attitudes Toward Risk and a Theory of Insurance Consumption," *Journal of Insurance*, vol. 30, June, 1963; N. Kaas, "Risk in Decision Making as a Function of Age, Sex, and Probability Preference," *Child Development*, vol. 36, 1964, pp. 577–82; N. Kogan and M. A. Wallach, "Risk Taking as a Function of the Situation, the Person, and the Group," in G. Mandler and P. Mussen, eds., *New Directions in Psychology, III*, (New York: Holt, Rinehart and Winston, 1967); A. A. Minkowich, *Correlates of Ambivalence, Risk Taking and Rigidity*, USAF Document 64–1468, 1964; D. Mosteller and P. Nogee, "An Experimental Measurement of Utility," *The Journal of Political Economy*, vol. 159, October, 1951; Y. Rim, "Leadership Attitudes and Decisions Involving Risk," *Personnel Psychology*, vol. 18 (Winter, 1965); Paul Slovic, "Assessment of Risk Taking Behavior," *Psychological Behavior*, vol. 61, 1964, and "Information Processing Situation Specificity, and Generality of Risk-Taking Behavior," *Journal of Personality and Social Psychology*, vol. 22, No. 1, April, 1972, S. Lichtenstein and P. Slovic, "Reversals of Preference Between Bids and Choices in Gambling Decision," *Journal of Experimental Psychology 89* (1971), pp. 46–55; Ralph W. Swalm, "Utility Theory — Insights into Risk Taking," *Harvard Business Review*, Nov.–Dec. 1966.

risky decisions. It has been found that a person who is a risk averter in economic risk may be a risk taker when it comes to social or physical risks, and *vice versa.* There is no general knowledge of just how consistent a person's attitudes toward risk may be over time; *e.g.,* how often he may change his attitudes.

It may be concluded that scientific findings in the area are far from exhausting the subject or in discovering any simple explanation of variations that are apparent in individuals' attitudes toward risk. Enough has been discovered, however, to establish that an examination of subjective risk of an individual may be an important clue to understanding his behavior and, in particular, his economic or business decision patterns. For example, studies by Swalm[12] revealed significant tendencies for managers to make decisions within a given customary financial framework unrelated to the financial ability of the firm as a whole. He found that apparently corporations tend to reward risk averters rather than risk takers, and that risk taking willingness varies greatly among executives. There is the distinct implication that a risk manager in a corporation should attempt not only to measure objective risks faced by his company, but also to consider risk attitudes of himself and of those executives with whom he works, particularly his superiors.

PURE VS. SPECULATIVE RISK

For many years writers on the subject of risk and insurance have made a distinction between pure and speculative risk. *Pure risk* is that risk in which the event which occurs may cause a loss only, while speculative risk involves events

which may produce either a gain or a loss. For example, fire, windstorm, explosion, flood, earthquake, riot and civil commotion, and similar perils generally cause loss, never a gain, and the uncertainty concerning their occurrence may be termed pure risk. On the other hand, most business risks are speculative such as those involving marketing, production, and financial decisions which are taken with the idea of a gain, but in which the possibility of loss is also present.

A business faces both pure and speculative risks. Most, but not all, pure risks lend themselves to handling through insurance, while most speculative risks are not generally handled through commercial insurance. Other methods of handling these risks must be found. Occasionally a risk thought to be speculative may be handled through insurance if certain safeguards are taken. An example is commercial credit risks, the risk that the buyer will be unable to pay for goods bought on open account credit because of some event or condition such as business insolvency, dishonesty, death, or uninsured catastrophe. The risk is speculative because the seller may be induced to sell to individuals with weak credit (thus assuming a higher degree of risk than normal) in the hope of additional profits from the sales thus made. Commercial insurance may be available, however, even though the risk taken is speculative, because such transactions are also subject to pure risk — the events such as dishonesty or death of the buyer or uninsured fire are not within the control of the purchaser of insurance (the seller). The policy contains a substantial deductible both a flat dollar amount designed to exclude the seller's normal bad debt loss from coverage, and also a percentage deductible (known as coinsurance) designed to require the seller to share a

---

[12] Swalm, "Utility Theory," pp. 123–136.

portion of each credit loss equal to or greater than his expected profit on the transaction. With these and other controls (from the viewpoint of the insurer), the speculative risk is minimized and the pure risk accepted for coverage.

Another example of speculative risk in which a type of insurance solution is employed is the risk of loss through strike. The risk occurs because the employer may refuse to grant the union a wage increase or to meet some other demand from organized labor, thus taking the risk that his plant operations, sales, and profits will be interrupted through work stoppage. If the action is successful, from the employer's viewpoint, and the work stoppage is averted without the wage increase or other demand being granted, there is a profit to the employer over what would otherwise be the case. If the action is unsuccessful, the employer may have a serious loss, including a permanent loss of business to competitors. The insurance mechanism has been employed under certain conditions to handle such risk. For example, the Association of American Railroads adopted a strike insurance plan in 1959 to indemnify a struck railroad for certain fixed expenses. The plan is financed by premiums paid by participating railroads and by additional assessments, if necessary, subject to certain limits. If more than 50 percent of the industry is struck at one time, the insurance is not operative, under the assumption that in such a case the loss would be catastrophic in nature, with railroads not struck being essentially unable to pay for losses suffered by struck railroads. In this case, presumably the government would step in with assistance. Other industries such as airlines, newspapers, and building contractors have adopted strike insurance plans under varying arrangements. (See discussion in Chapter 14.)

It is significant that most types of risk facing business firms have some elements of both pure and speculative risk incorporated in them. A fire, normally thought to represent only pure risk, may destroy a building which is uneconomical or was going to be destroyed anyway; thus, actually causing a profit to be made for the owner. A business life insurance policy on the life of a key man who has died after having left his employer may actually bring about a profit to the firm which has maintained the policy on the key man. The risk may have been largely pure at first but may become speculative risk later on if the key man has left. On the other hand, a speculative risk such as the risk that insufficient sales of a product will occur, thus causing a loss of the investment in the product, usually contains elements of pure risk. For example, a manufacturer may stock up heavily on air conditioners only to have a fire destroy his inventory just before the selling season.

DYNAMIC AND STATIC RISKS

Some writers have differentiated between dynamic and static risks. *Dynamic risks* are related to uncertainties produced by an ever-changing society, changes in environment, consumer wants, business organization, and technology. *Static risks* are those which exist even if there were no such changes, and are usually illustrated by pure risks such as fire, flood, windstorm, and explosion.[13] Dynamic risks, on the other hand, are more closely allied to speculative risks.

In the past commercial insurers have tended to ignore dynamic risks to

[13] A. H. Willett, *The Economic Theory of Risk and Insurance* (Philadelphia: University of Pennsylvania Press, 1951).

some extent, basing this on the feeling that there is little or nothing they can do about them. In recent years, however, insurers have taken greater interest in the changes in the environment and have moved vigorously in some cases to alleviate some of these risks.[14] Examples of this action include the allocation of investment funds to rehabilitate slum areas and increased support of research to make automobiles and highways safer. Insurers are increasingly recognizing that it is difficult to separate, or even to distinguish clearly, the problems created by dynamic risks and those created by static risks. For example, the nature of the peril fire, a static risk, is greatly influenced by social conditions in a crowded city, technological advances in building materials, and the attitudes of society toward loss prevention in general.

RISK CLASSED BY LOSS SEVERITY

Bob A. Hedges[15] has suggested that risk may be classified according to loss severity — the risk producer. He recognizes three loss classes, as follows:

Class I: Those losses which do not disturb a firm's basic finances.

Class II: Those losses which would require borrowing or selling new common stock.

Class III: Those losses larger than Class I or II, which might bankrupt the firm.

Tom C. Allen and Richard M. Duvall, developing Hedges' classification,[16] state that the main feature of Class I risk is the small variability (small standard deviation) of losses. Class II risks have a much larger variability, and Class III risks have extreme variability, to the point that once they occur, the firm may not survive. Allen and Duvall argue that Class I and II risks can be handled by various internal methods, but Class III risks should normally be transferred. (See discussion below on handling risk.)

RISK AND PROFIT

Economists have long discussed profit as the reward for risk bearing. This implies that if risk could be eliminated, the need for profit would also be eliminated. The question arises as to whether successful risk management will have the effect of reducing or eliminating profit. For example, this view was stated by F. B. Hawley who argued that if the businessman could eliminate all of his risks through insurance he would have no income left which could not be attributed to management's wages or monopoly gains. In his view, the insurer becomes the true entrepreneur.[17]

Part of this argument may be countered by recognizing that, generally speaking, insurers do not accept *all* of management's risks; rather they attempt generally to limit themselves to pure risk. Pure risks by their nature do not produce a profit, rather only losses to the firm which runs them. Thus,

[14] Greene, "Research Problems," pp. 293–312.

[15] Bob A. Hedges, "Proper Limits in Liability Insurance — A Problem in Decision Making Under Uncertainty," *Journal of Insurance*, vol. 28, no. 2 (June 1961), p. 73.

[16] Tom C. Allen and Richard M. Duvall, "A Theoretical and Practical Approach to Risk Management," (New York: American Society of Insurance Management, 1971), pp. 9–17.

[17] F. B. Hawley, "The Risk Theory of Profit," *Quarterly Journal of Economics*, vol. 7, p. 86.

eliminating or transferring pure risk would not reduce profit for the non-insurance firm; of course, *insurers* may earn a profit from assuming pure risk. Not all of the pure risk can be eliminated through the law of large numbers. Commercial insurers do everything within their power to reduce or eliminate pure risk, and in practice underwriting gains and losses vary substantially. Thus, the profit of the commercial insurer depends in part on the success with which he can eliminate pure risk, leaving a margin which will include both profit and allowances for contingencies. His profit, then, stems from underwriting skills, knowledge of the hazards and perils surrounding the pure risk, investment profits, and managerial efficiency in keeping expenses as low as possible. From the insurer's viewpoint, the pure risk he assumes is actually speculative, since his operations may produce either a profit or a loss.

C. O. Hardy contributed insight to the relationship between risk and profit when he observed that in a purely competitive economic system, profits would tend to disappear if it were not for uncertainty. Other things being equal, people prefer the safe enterprise to the risky enterprise if the probable end result is the same. Thus, "of two opportunities, if one offers a certain return of 6 percent, while the other may yield anywhere from nothing to 12 percent, the former is the more attractive . . . doubtful enterprises do not attract capital in sufficiently large quantity to bring the return in them down to the same average level as safe enterprises, but only down to the level where the most probable difference is sufficient to overcome the disinclination to incur risk. Profit is, therefore, a permanent and necessary part of the social dividend and is accounted for as the only incentive to

render the service of 'uncertainty bearing,' which is as essential a service as that of saving capital or doing work."[18]

Hardy also recognized the role of ignorance as a contributor to risk taking, observing how businesses often enter unprofitable fields characterized by high risk through ignorance: "Men follow each other, like sheep, in flocks, though the sheep are not wise in inferring that wherever there is enough good grass for a few, there must be plenty for the whole flock that goes after them."[19] Clearly it is the *hope* of profit which lures capital, but there is no guarantee that profit will, in fact, result. He also observes that "The only way in which risk enables an individual to secure a profit is by its tendency to keep others out of the field."[20] Profits result mainly in a competitive society from entrepreneurs who enter a field and enjoy some insulation from competitors because of the uncertainty and dislike of risk that exists in their minds and consequent hesitancy, or delay in entering a given business. Risk has in common with monopolistic conditions (such as patent rights) the fact that both factors help reduce the number of potential competitors and thus help account for profit.

The question still remains as to whether the non-insurance business firm would eliminate its profit if it were able to rid itself of speculative risk, as well as pure risk. Speculative risk is closely associated with uncertainty, defined by Frank Knight as unmeasurable

[18] C. O. Hardy, *Risk and Risk Bearing* (Chicago: The University of Chicago Press), pp. 37–38.

[19] Adapted from T. E. C. Leslie, "The Known and the Unknown in the Economic World," *Fortnightly Review*, XXXI (1879), pp. 934–40.

[20] *Ibid.*, p. 40.

risk.[21] Knight argues that speculative risk involved in entrepreneurship "is not and cannot be a known quantity."[22] Knight admits, however, that "unmeasurable uncertainty" (*i.e.*, speculative risk in our terminology) may nevertheless be estimated by an individual and decisions in some cases made upon these estimates. Furthermore, through the process of grouping of decisions there is some tendency for fluctuations to cancel out and for the result to approach constancy in some degree.[23] Thus in some cases uncertainty may indeed be treated as though it is "measurable," even if it, in fact, is not really subject to scientific determination. In any event, individuals have devised ways to handle this unmeasurable uncertainty through such devices as consolidation, diffusion of effort, specialization of effort, and better efforts at prediction and control of future events. As Knight admits, "In any case, we do strive to reduce uncertainty, even though we should not want it eliminated from our lives."[24]

Profit may be viewed as a lure and a reward for assuming "unmeasurable" risk; yet it still appears to be true that management usually tends to do everything possible to minimize risk, as will be amplified below and in Chapter 8. Does this imply that such efforts will reduce profits below what they would otherwise be? In the long run, this would seem to be the case. Various empirical studies have shown that lower profit rates (not necessarily total profits) tend to be associated with "less risky" industries,[25] and *vice versa*. It will generally be necessary to offer a higher reward to induce capital to be committed to the production and distribution of "risky" new, untried products or services. Once committed, the management of such capital, however, generally attempts to reduce both pure and speculative risk as much as possible, usually as a step to maximize and stabilize the expected short-run profits. The more successful this effort is, the more competition is encountered, which tends to reduce prices and profits. Once "proved," the field then contains less risk and attracts capital that formerly was withheld from such ventures.[26]

As Knight states, "with uncertainty entirely absent, every individual being in perfect knowledge of the situation, there would be no occasion for

---

[21] Frank H. Knight, *Risk Uncertainty and Profit* (New York: Harper and Row Torchbooks, 1965). In Knight's book the term risk was used to connote all uncertainty which was measurable, and hence controllable through insurance or otherwise and therefore not reward for profit, but rather just a cost of doing business like any other business cost.

[22] *Ibid.*, p. 44.

[23] *Ibid.*, p. 235.

[24] *Ibid.*, p. 238.

[25] Bank Administration Institute, *Measuring the Investment Performance of Pension Funds* (1968); W. B. Hickman, *Corporate Bond Quality and Investor Experience* (Princeton University Press, for the National Bureau of Economy 1958); Paul H. Cootner and Daniel M. Holland, *Risk and Rate of Return* (Massachusetts Institute of Technology, 1964). Only a few contrary positions on this point have been published. Richard W. McEnally and Lee A. Tavis, " 'Spatial Risk' and Return Relationships: A Reconsideration," *The Journal of Risk and Insurance*, vol. 36, No. 3, September 1972. See, for example, Lemont K. Richardson, "Do High Risks Lead to Returns?", *Financial Analysts Journal*, March–April 1970, and Harold G. Fraine, *Valuation of Securities Holdings of Life Insurance Companies* (Homewood, Ill.: Richard D. Irwin, 1962), p. 46.

[26] C. A. Tisdell, *The Theory of Price Uncertainty, Production and Profit* (Princeton University Press, 1968); see also the review and analysis of this book by N. F. Laing, *Economic Record*, vol. 46, pp. 411–18, Summer 1970.

anything of the nature of responsible management or control of productive activity . . . under conditions of perfect knowledge and certainty such functions would be undertaken by laborers merely, performing a purely routine function, without responsibility of any sort, on a level of men engaged in mechanical operations."[27] Knight points out that while some economists (*e.g.,* J. B. Clark) attribute profit to dynamic changes going on within the economy, this is true only if the nature of the change is unknown, for if the future were known "competition would certainly adjust things to the ideal state where all prices would equal costs."[28] He concludes that the presence of true profit depends on an "absolute uncertainty in the estimation of the value of judgment or upon the absence of the requisite organization for combining a sufficient number of instances to secure certainty through consolidation."[29]

We may conclude that profit is both the lure and the reward for the assumption and bearing of speculative risk. In the short run, successful risk reduction efforts help attain profits which were anticipated when the venture was started. In the long run such efforts bring stability which is associated with lower rates of return. Mankind tends to be a risk averter, however, and to seek security.[30] This is not inconsistent with commonly held assumptions of economists about the role of profit as a reward for risk bearing. Neither pure nor speculative risk can be eliminated completely and in the long run profit tends to vary inversely to the degree of success achieved in eliminating risk.

27 *Ibid.,* pp. 267–68.

28 Knight, *Risk Uncertainty,* p. 37.

29 *Ibid.,* p. 285.

30 Dewey, *Quest for Certainty,* p. 3.

WAYS OF HANDLING RISK

As was noted in the previous chapter, several methods of handling risk, both pure and speculative, are in common use. Generally, these methods are employed in combination with one another. They include (1) assumption, (2) transfer, (3) combination, (4) loss prevention, (5) avoidance, and (6) knowledge and research.

Assumption

Assumption, or retention, of risk is probably the most common way of handling risk. One may argue that this method hardly qualifies as a way of handling risk since under it one essentially does nothing about the uncertainty to which he is exposed. However, it is worthwhile to note that an individual or manager who consciously assumes risk is doing something about it by the very act of being aware of those perils and hazards which may cause loss. Being aware of the risk, he may consciously or unconsciously make adjustments in his operations which will help alleviate the impact of risk, ease its burden, and assist him in using other methods more effectively. Awareness of risk is a significant achievement in better management, while ignorance of risk can result in unpleasant surprises when the loss occurs which will often have far more negative impact on operations than would be the case had the risk been recognized in advance. Indeed, an important job of the risk manager is to recognize sources of risk so that appropriate advance action may be taken, or at least so that management may be prepared mentally for possible losses should the peril occur. Mental attitudes toward risk affect the degree to which risk assumption is used. A risk averting management will usually be less willing to assume risks than a risk loving management.

Transfer

Risk transfer is widely used to handle both pure and speculative risk. *Insurance* is perhaps the most common method of transferring pure risks. Through it the uncertainties imposed by certain events may be shifted to the insurer, leaving management free to devote its full efforts to its normal business. Presumably, generally, management efficiency is thereby enhanced.

Insurance may be defined as a method to reduce risk by combining under one management a group of objects so similar in character and so situated that the total accidental losses to which the group is subject become predictable within reasonably narrow limits. Private insurance is usually effected by legal contract, whose characteristics generally follow the requirements of any binding contract such as offer and acceptance, consideration, legal purpose, and legal capacity to contract. Insurance may exist, however, without such a private legal contract; examples include public insurance programs, certain types of service arrangements, and programs of self-insurance within the business firm, where there is a loss-sharing arrangement but no definite legal contract exists between two or more private parties.

Limits of Insurance as a Transfer Device

There are certain ideal characteristics of insurable risk which should be mentioned for, as mentioned previously, not all risks may be easily transferred to the insurer. These characteristics are as follows: (1) the risk should be accidental or random in nature and the loss-causing event should be outside the control of the insured. Once the loss has

occurred, or is very likely to occur, insurance becomes impractical because the premiums required will be prohibitively high. Insurance is one service which must be purchased "in advance of the need." Once the building is burning, once the dam has burst, it is too late for transfer through insurance. (2) The values exposed to loss should not be arranged in such a way as to be subject to simultaneous destruction. If an insurer's only loss exposure is composed of buildings in a single, congested location, there is no "spread of risk" and a fire could destroy sufficient values to cause bankruptcy to the insurer. For example, many insurers with such an undue concentration of values became insolvent after the San Francisco fire and earthquake of 1906. (3) There should be a sufficient number of exposure units of fairly equal value and nature to allow the law of large numbers to operate. The insurer should be able to predict its total expected losses with reasonable accuracy, and this tends to be very difficult unless there are some minimum number of units of exposed values existing (See Chapter 3). (4) The loss should be measurable and determinable. To meet this requirement, past data on losses to be expected must be reasonably available, the values exposed must be expressable in monetary terms, and methods to estimate the loss must be worked out.

Pure risks generally (but not always) meet the above requirements while speculative risks often do not. Pure risks caused by perils such as fire, windstorm, explosion, and collision are widely covered by insurance; but limitations in the insurance contract are imposed or coverage is denied entirely when the particular conditions of a given applicant for insurance do not fully meet the above conditions. In the case of flood, for example, requirement (2) above has prevented private insurers from offering coverage because of the possibility of simultaneous destruction of all of the exposure units in a given flood plain and also because of the difficulties involved in persuading those not situated in a flood plain to purchase coverage and to contribute to the losses of those who are so situated. Coverage against flood has been made possible through subsidization by the federal government in the United States; in effect, this has accomplished a spread of risk through the mechanism of taxation.

Speculative risks generally do not meet requirements (1), (2), or (4) above. Speculative risks are entered into voluntarily and are often not beyond the control of the insured, and hence not accidental. If the insurer were to cover the risk of failing to make a profit because of inadequate sales, for example, the insured could enter into ill-advised ventures at no risk to himself and collect his "profit" from the insurer. Since bad conditions in one industry tend to spread to all units of the industry, and often to the whole economy, requirement (2) above would fail. The insurer would be subject to catastrophic losses if it had insured many risks within a single industry which suffered losses. Insurers do not have financial ability to withstand losses characteristic of a general business depression. Furthermore, there would be endless difficulties in meeting requirement (4) in deciding how much "profit" was lost and in defining what perils, e.g., what management mistakes, were to be covered.

Very often the transfer method is used to handle speculative risk. Common examples are limiting of liability through formation of the corporation, hedging by dealers in commodities, leasing, and inventory control. Thus a retailer may shift the risks of building ownership to a lessor by renting rather than owning his business structure. An example of handling speculative risk

without insurance is the use of common stock options. An option to buy a stock in the future at some specified price is known as a *call* and a similar option to sell is known as a *put*. In general the price of such options is a small fraction of the price of the stock itself. Thus, if a businessman believes there is a good chance that the price of a certain stock will rise in the near future, he may either invest in the stock at its full price, or he may purchase a call option at a much smaller cost. Now if he is wrong and the price falls instead of rising, the most he can lose is the price of his call option. If the stock rises, as anticipated, he may exercise his option and obtain the expected profit. The risk of loss of price declined has been greatly reduced, without sacrificing the chance of gain. The individual selling the businessman put or call options is a speculator who, in effect, bears the price risk for a price.

Combination

The combination method of handling risk is illustrated by techniques such as insurance, diversification of product line, and formation of holding companies with unrelated lines of business. From the viewpoint of the insurer, the chief technique used is combination of a sufficiently large number of similar objects to make the loss predictable within narrow limits. This is made possible by the law of large numbers (discussed above and in Chapter 3). In a similar manner, speculative risks in industry are minimized through diversification. Thus, if losses in one line occur, they may be offset by profits in another line. A manufacturer may engage in the production of heating and air conditioning units, for example, so that in hot years the profits of selling air conditioners will help offset the losses by reduced sales of heating units. The reverse may occur in cold years.

Loss Prevention

A widely employed method of controlling losses through risky perils is that of taking measures to prevent the loss or to minimize its financial impact. Examples include the use of fire-resistant building materials, industrial accident controls, safer highway and automobile construction, and medical research to prolong life. Loss prevention may eliminate the risk entirely if the possibility of loss is practically eliminated, such as has occurred in some cases; *e.g.*, discovery of polio vaccine. In most cases, loss prevention does not eliminate the risk of loss, however, but reduces its probability, both in terms of frequency and severity, thus reducing the financial impact of the loss when it occurs.

Avoidance

Closely related to loss prevention and transfer is the technique of avoiding situations which have the potential of causing loss to the individual or to the firm. An automobile dealership may avoid the risk of loss arising from lending customers substitute cars by simply not offering that service. Or the firm may transfer the risk by using taxicab companies to take customers to their destinations. A firm may avoid operations in an area known to be subject to some peril such as flood. A person may avoid the risk of loss through crash of airplanes by traveling by train, etc. Insurers may avoid risk of loss by refusing to underwrite in a given area, such as inner city ghettos, in effect transferring the risk to the occupants.

Knowledge and Research

Subjective risk may be reduced through knowledge and research. The more an individual knows about the uncertainties he faces, the less subjective risk he tends to perceive or the greater is his confidence in meeting, handling, or accepting it. A person who knows nothing of the stock or commodities market may not be willing to commit investment funds to those markets; but once he has learned more of the opportunities, as well as the dangers, of these investment media he may be willing to utilize them. Pure risks can also be reduced through knowledge and research. An insurance underwriter may be unwilling to accept particularly hazardous risks; *e.g.*, taxi fleets, until he has discovered ways and means to maintain loss controls and hence lowered his level of perceived risk. A number of insurers have specialized in the so-called hazardous risks and have made satisfactory underwriting gains in fields avoided by other insurers because of their superior knowledge of the experience with the risk.

SUMMARY AND CONCLUSIONS

1. Risk is pervasive in society and within the business enterprise. An overall perspective of risk and risk bearing as it affects all functions of business is helpful to appreciate the nature of and reasons for specialized types of risk treatment as it is discussed in this book. Risk-handling devices may be recognized in various forms in each of the major functional areas such as marketing, finance, and personnel and production management. A more complete analysis of this subject, including ways of handling speculative risk as it appears throughout the business firm, is treated in a later chapter.

2. Risk is differentiated from the concepts probability, peril, and hazard. Risk and probability may be viewed objectively or subjectively. Subjective interpretations of risk and probability are very important since it is basic that decisions are made not necessarily on the facts that exist, in fact, but upon the facts as they are perceived by the decision maker. Objective risk is defined in terms of some concept in statistical variance. Attempts to measure the reliability and validity of subjective risk have not been conclusively successful to this point, although progress is being made. Nevertheless, managers should consider both objective and subjective aspects of risk in their decision-making activities if risk management achieves its full objectives.

3. Business faces both pure risk and speculative risk. Most decisions and events contain aspects of both of these types of risk simultaneously. The risk manager's selection of the method of risk treatment should take into consideration this fact. Increasingly it may be possible for insurers to handle speculative risk, whereas in the past insurers have attempted to confine their activities to pure risk.

4. Profit, viewed as a reward for risk bearing, may in the long run be reduced as management becomes more successful in averting risk; in the short run, however, risk management activities tend to increase profit level and to stabilize them. In the short-run, unexpected and unplanned loss can disrupt operations or even cause bankruptcy. Economic studies point to the finding that lower profit anticipations are associated with new untried industries or products, which by their nature must carry the hope of greater than usual gains in the minds of the entrepreneur if they are to be undertaken initially. It would seem that neither pure nor speculative risk can be eliminated entirely, either in the short or long run.

5. Major ways of handling risk, both pure and speculative, include assumption, transfer, combination, loss prevention, avoidance, and knowledge and research. Ideally, risks must possess certain defined characteristics to lend themselves to transfer through insurance. Since risks seldom possess all of these required characteristics, risk handling methods become complex and risk managers must usually employ some combination of the various methods and will not rely on any one method alone, such as insurance.

QUESTIONS FOR DISCUSSION

1. Some writers treat risk and probability as though they were identical concepts, *i.e.*, the chance of loss. In this chapter, it has been pointed out that risk and probability, measured objectively, vary inversely. Explain the significance of this inverse relationship to the risk manager.

2. (a) A businessman estimates that "there is only a 10 percent chance of success" in a given venture which he is considering. What type of probability concept is illustrated in this statement? (b) A businessman states that, based on the last ten years' experience of his firm, in the average ten percent of his automobile fleet has experienced at least one collision. What type of probability concept is illustrated in this statement? (c) How would you formulate a statement of objective or subjective *risk* in the above cases?

3. A business firm is planning to acquire another company through merger. In the acquisition, a manufacturing plant in another state is being transferred to the firm. Give examples of (a) pure risk, and (b) speculative risk which might be involved in this transaction.

4. Explain how effective risk handling might increase short-run profits, but decrease long-run profits.

5. It has been stated that "planned bankruptcy" is one method of handling risk. What type of risk would bankruptcy solve? How would you classify "planned bankruptcy" as a risk device? What types of losses could not be handled in this manner? Explain.

6. Give examples of speculative risk from each of the following functional areas of business: (a) marketing, (b) finance, and (c) personnel.

7. Patents and trademarks represent a method of reducing risk. Explain what type of risk is involved and how patents would reduce it.

3

Theoretical Concepts and Applications to Risk Management

A theory is a system of explanatory principles which help to form the basis for consistent decision making. In the field of risk management, elements of theory are partly mathematical and partly nonmathematical. Some of these concepts were introduced in the last chapter. In this chapter we will amplify some of the principles and show how they may be applied in examples of practical problems of handling risk in the business firm. Major topics discussed include:

1. Loss prediction

2. Recognition of sources of loss

3. Estimating frequency of loss by probability analysis
   a. Some statistical concepts for risk management
   b. Rules of probability analysis
   c. Applying probability rules

4. Estimating frequency and severity of loss
   a. The expected value approach
   b. Tree diagrams
   c. Expected utility approach
   d. Worry factor analysis
   e. Paired comparison approach

PREDICTING LOSSES

A major challenge in risk management is the scientific approach to loss prediction. Ignoring this problem is to assume implicitly that either no losses will occur or that, if they do occur, they will not be sufficiently serious to cause the firm any hardship. Unless such an assumption is justified (and there are some circumstances in which it might well be justified), the risk manager must grapple with the problem of making the best estimates he can about future loss patterns. The problems can be divided into steps as follows: (1) recognizing the various possible sources of loss, (2) estimating the probable frequency of occurrence of the loss producing peril, (3) estimating the severity of the loss, should the peril occur, (4) determining the financial ability of the firm to withstand the loss. Once these steps are taken, the risk manager is in a good position to decide which of the various methods of handling risk (discussed in Chapter 2) should be employed in each given case.

RECOGNITION OF SOURCES OF LOSS

Various steps in recognizing sources of loss are many and complex. A more detailed treatment of this subject is given in Chapter 5. It may be noted at this point, however, that this first step is a crucial one in effective risk management. To take one example, the peril flood or explosion, while infrequently occurring, often cause catastrophic loss.

Just because a flood, explosion, or other peril has never occurred before is no assurance that it will not happen in the future. Part of the problem here is to define carefully the extent and type of peril and possible resulting loss. For example, some perils often cause large *indirect* loss, as well as direct loss, to a firm by interrupting sales or supplier operations. If this possibility is recognized, steps can be taken in advance to handle the risk, often without undue cost — *e.g.*, lining up alternative suppliers in advance in case a major supplier is crippled due to some cause. Failure to recognize the exposure in advance can produce very serious negative consequences for the firm.

ESTIMATING LOSS FREQUENCIES BY PROBABILITY ANALYSIS

As discussed in Chapter 2, probability can be conceived of subjectively or objectively. People can make estimates of likely outcomes from a subjective analysis of events, both past and present, and these subjective estimates may be the only ones available to the decision maker. Much greater scientific precision can be achieved in the analysis, however, if probability is studied objectively. Objective probability analysis can be based upon historical analogy (sampling from a universe of events) or upon the physical nature of experiments. An example of the latter would be the flipping of a fair coin, or the drawing of cards from a well mixed deck of cards. The nature of the experiment permits one to determine precisely what the measurement of probability is in a given case. Thus, the probability of obtaining heads or tails in a single flip is .50, and the probability of drawing a spade in a deck is .25.

Unfortunately relatively few real-life situations in social sciences permit the assessment of probability from the physical nature of an experiment. The method of historical analogy (*i.e.* sampling) must be used to approximate the probability of most events in which we are interested, such events as the probability of death, fire, windstorm, explosion, or other events which occur more or less randomly. Such estimates are used mainly to predict future events. The discussion below is concerned mainly with the definition, estimates, and analysis of probability using sampling tools.

SOME STATISTICAL CONCEPTS FOR RISK MANAGEMENT

The risk manager should have working knowledge of certain statistical concepts as a basis for understanding risk management theory. The discussion here is not intended to be complete; basic books on statistics should be consulted for a more elaborate treatment.

Probability

Probability is the chance of occurrence of a given event. In insurance situations probability often is expressed as percentage of times which in the long run a loss-producing event will happen. Thus, fire frequency may be stated as a probability of .5 percent per year (.05) in a given territory for a certain type of construction.

Probability Distribution

A probability distribution is a listing of all possible events in a *set* together with the probability that each event will occur. Suppose, for example, we are interested in studying how accidents are distributed in a given plant which employs 1,000 men. From past records over several years, the risk manager discovers that in 60 percent of the years there were no accidents. In 20 percent of the years there was one accident, in 10 percent of the years there were two accidents, in 6 percent of the years there were three accidents, and in 4 percent of the years there were four accidents. A probability distribution describing these findings would appear as follows:

Possible Event (accidents)	Probability of Occurrence
0	.60
1	.20
2	.10
3	.06
4	.04
Total	1.00

Theoretical Probability Distribution

As mentioned in Chapter 2, theoretical probability distributions are those whose shape is established by some mathematical formula. These distributions are useful because they possess known characteristics which can facilitate the analysis of loss frequencies they describe. Examples of theoretical distributions often used in insurance problems are the binomial, the normal, and Poisson. Each of these has complex formulas which will not be given here. Examples of how theoretical probability distributions may be useful follow.

Mean

The *mean* is an arithmetic average of a group of numbers. For example, the mean of a binomial probability loss distribution may be given by the letters np where n is the number of possible events and p is the probability of loss. Thus, if there are 100 automobiles, n would be 100 since it is theoretically possible for all 100 autos to be involved in a loss. If the annual probability of loss is found to be 5 percent, the mean annual loss would be .05(100), or 5 autos.

Standard Deviation

Standard deviation is a measure of dispersion of a probability distribution. It is also the most widely accepted measure of risk. The larger (smaller) the variation of numbers in a probability distribution from the mean, the larger (smaller) will be the standard deviation. For example, if a risk manager learns that each year the number of deaths in a work force of 10,000 is, say, 10 and that this number has never been less than 9 or more than 11, it is obvious that the dispersion, and standard deviation, will be less than if the deaths ranged, say, from 5 to 15, averaging out to be 10.

In actually calculating standard deviation, one proceeds as follows. Assume that for the past five years deaths in a work force have numbered 10, 8, 12, 13, and 7, respectively. The total is 50 and the mean, 10 deaths per year. Now calculate the deviation of each year's deaths from 10 and square the results. The deviations are 0, 2, -2, -3, and 3, and the squared deviations are 0, 4, 4, 9, and 9. Next, sum these numbers, take the average, and extract the square root. The sum is 26, mean is 5.2 (also known as the *variance*), and the square root of 5.2 is 2.28, the standard deviation.

Standard error is the standard deviation of mean values taken from successive samples of data drawn from a given population. (See Table 3–3.)

Coefficient of Variation

A way to gauge the importance of any standard deviation and to compare different standard deviations as a measure of relative risk in different situations is to divide the standard deviation by the mean. This measure is known as the *coefficient of variation*. In the above example the coefficient of variation is the ratio of 2.28 to 10, or .228, or 22.8 percent. A coefficient of variation is also a useful way to express risk (uncertainty) and to compare the risk attaching to different sets of loss exposures. In a typical situation, for example, the risk in automobile liability losses is much higher than the risk in workers' compensation losses because auto liability losses are usually less frequent, but more severe than industrial injury losses.

Confidence Intervals

In theoretical loss probability distributions, the analyst may state in advance the number of losses which are expected to occur within different ranges of the mean — *i.e.*, within so many standard deviations either side of the mean. In the normal distribution, for example, which is bell-shaped, 68.27 percent of all of the numbers in the distribution fall within one standard deviation of the mean, 95.45 percent fall within two standard deviations of the mean, and 99.73 percent fall within three standard deviations of the mean.

When the problem is to estimate the mean number of losses in a "population" using sample information, the concept of *confidence intervals* is useful. The risk manager can select the degree of confidence he wishes in making such estimates. If certain statistical conditions are met in selecting the sample, the risk manager may behave as if the mean number of losses occurring in the sample represents the true mean number of losses in the total population, within a given error range and with a given probability of being correct.

Thus, the risk manager may be able to state, "I can be 95.45 percent sure" that the population mean number of losses will fall within the range of two standard errors from the sample mean. If the mean is 10 losses and the standard error is 1.02 losses, this means that the risk analyst can predict the population mean number of losses will be within the range of 10 plus or minus 2 (1.02) or between 7.96 and 12.04. The probability that he will be right is .95.

Expected Value

One of the most useful statistical concepts in risk management is that of *expected value*, the result obtained by multiplying the value of each possible event times its respective probability and then summing. For example, assume there are only two possible events, "fire" and "no fire" with corresponding probabilities of .01 and .99, respectively. Assume that if fire occurs the loss is $10,000, but if no fire occurs the loss is zero. The expected value of loss by fire is $10,000(.01) + $0(.99) = $100. The expected value is the mean of the above probability distribution. It expresses the average long-run loss which an insurer would have to pay if it insured this event, and thus summarizes the "pure premium" calculation which is the starting point for determining the final premium.

Rules of Probability Analysis

There are certain basic underlying assumptions of probability analysis which should be observed if sampling technique is to be successfully employed in loss prediction:

(a) The sample (or set) from which conclusions are drawn must be *randomly selected* from the larger population comprising the universe of all possible events. If this requirement is not met, in the case of the simple random sample, for example, not all the items have an equal chance of being drawn and generalizations about the larger population of events will not necessarily be true.

(b) All weights assigned to probability statements must be *positive*. Probability is so defined that it cannot be a negative number. Rather, probability is expressed as a number between 0 and 1. Probabilities assigned to a set of mutually exclusive and collectively exhaustive events must total to 1.

Events are mutually exclusive when there is no possibility that if one event occurs, the other can also occur. A set of events is collectively exhaustive if it represents all possible events in the set. We will illustrate this situation below.

(c) If events in the sample occur *independently* of one another and are randomly selected, certain calculations become possible which are of great value in risk management and decision making. Events are said to occur independently of one another if the outcome in one event does not affect the probability of occurrence of another event. Thus, if it may be assumed that because a fire has occurred once, there is no necessary *change* in the probability of having a second (or third) fire; we can say that fire losses are independent of one another.

(d) If we know the probability of an independent event in a set of mutually exclusive and collectively exhaustive events, we may employ certain rules such as the *additive* and *compound probability* rules. Under the additive rule, for example, if the probability of occurrence of four events in such a set is .25 for each event, the probability of occurrence of *either* of two events is .50, (.25 + .25); any three events, .75; and any four events, 1.0. Thus the

probability assigned to all the events must total to 1.

The compound probability rule states that the probability of simultaneous or consecutive occurrence of two or more events in a set of mutually exclusive and collectively exhaustive events is the product of their individual probabilities. For example, assume there are two decks of well-mixed cards and we wish to know the probability of drawing an ace from each deck on the first draw. The events would be independent of each other since drawing an ace from one deck would not influence the probability of drawing an ace from the second deck. The probability of this occurrence would be the product of the separate probabilities, or $4/52 \times 4/52 = 16/2704$. However, if we draw two cards from one deck only, and we obtain an ace on the first draw, the event "draw an ace on the second draw" is not independent of the first, since there are now only 51 cards left to draw from. Accordingly, the probability of drawing two aces from the same deck would be $4/52 \times 3/51$, or $12/2652$. This second example is an example of conditional probability. The probabilities of all possible events in this example must total to 1.0, as shown in Table 3–1.

(e) *Conditional probability* is the probability of some event, *given* the occurrence of some other event or some combination of events. The event in question is no longer independent, but depends on some prior condition being fulfilled. For example, assume that there are four possible events with the probability given in Table 3–2.

Assume that we wish to know what the probability of two or more collisions will be, *if there are any collisions at all*. By the additive rule, we know that the probability of two or more collisions is .10 (the sum of probabilities of events 3 and 4). However, we are redefining events and are imposing a limitation

TABLE 3–1

Event	Probability	
	1st Draw	2nd Draw
Draw two aces	$4/52 \times 3/51 =$	12/2652
Draw no aces	$48/52 \times 47/51 =$	2256/2652
Draw one ace only, 1st draw	$4/52 \times 48/51 =$	192/2652
Draw one ace only, 2nd draw	$48/52 \times 4/51 =$	192/2652
		2652/2652 = 1

that involves only a part of the sample set by the conditions set forth. This part is restricted to the sum of the probabilities involving *any* collision (the sum of events 2, 3, and 4). These probabilities total .30. The denominator of the probability equation is therefore .30 and the conditional probability is the ratio .10/30, or 1/3, that if there are any collisions at all, the probability of two or more collisions is one in three. In symbols,

$$P(E_1) \text{ given } E_2 = \frac{P(E_1)}{P(E_2)} = \frac{.10}{.30}$$

TABLE 3–2

Event	Probability
1. No collisions occur in one year.	.70
2. One collision occurs.	.20
3. Two collisions occur.	.06
4. Three or more collisions occur	.04
Total	1.00

where E_1 is the event, two or more collisions will occur (sum of 3 and 4 above) and E_2 is the event one or more collisions will occur (sum of 2, 3, and 4 above).

APPLYING PROBABILITY RULES

The above rules of probability analysis must be used with care because in actual practice the assumptions on which these rules are based may not be met, or may be met only approximately. Often one of the principal weaknesses of data available to the risk manager is that the data may not be truly representative of the larger population from which they are drawn and thus may lead to inaccurate conclusions. For example, a risk manager may observe accidents in a plant over a period of five years and calculate the mean and standard deviation of losses. From this he reasons that the best single estimate of loss for the next year is the average of the past five years. How might this be misleading? Lack of representativeness may be due to several factors: (1) the sample may not be large enough, (2) the sample may be biased, (3) the sample may not have been drawn at random, or (4) the events may not be independent of one another. In other words, there may be large sampling error which should be recognized in interpreting the results. Sampling error might be caused by generalizing from a sample which is too small and hence unstable. (The number of losses may vary 100 percent from year to year.) The sample may be drawn from a single month, such as January or from a single plant, neither of which may be a typical month for accidents, or a typical plant for working conditions. In some plants losses may be unusually high because they are not independent, *e.g.*, unsafe acts of some workers may be copied by other workers in the plant. Accident frequency may increase over time as long as this condition exists.

The firm may utilize sources other than its own records in order to increase the accuracy of estimates of probability and variation of losses. Insurance industry records, trade association data, governmental studies, etc., are among the sources which might be utilized.

In the absence of objective data on which to base estimates of probability and variance of losses, subjective estimates can be made, based on prior general experience of managers.

Another basic rule of probability, the *central limit theorem*, may be utilized to forecast losses by statistical means.

Forecasting Losses by Statistics

In most risk management problems involving loss estimation, it is not practical to take a large number of samples. Sampling experiments have shown that when a number of random samples are taken from a population, the mean of each sample will vary from the mean of the population. However, if the number of samples taken is large enough, and the sample means are plotted on graph paper, a normal curve of error will result, *i.e.*, it will be bell-shaped. This happens even if the data in the original population, or from a single sample, are *not* distributed normally. This result has been proved mathematically and is the essence of the central limit theorem, of which the law of large numbers is a special case.

Standard Error

The standard deviation of these sample means has a special name, *stan-*dard error*. The standard error is used to draw inferences about the universe. These inferences include (a) the mean of the random samples approaches the mean value of the population from which they are drawn when the number of samples is large enough, (b) one standard error includes 68.25 percent, two standard errors include 95.45 percent, and three standard errors, 99.73 percent of the area under a normal curve.

The formula for standard error is

$$SE = \frac{s}{\sqrt{n}}$$

where n = the sample size and s is the assumed standard deviation of the population. Let us illustrate the use of standard error in the following risk management problem: A risk manager observes a sample of loss data (see below) from a sample of 1,000 workers (n) in one year and he wishes to draw inferences about future losses which might be expected over a large number of years. He calculates the mean (M) and standard deviation (s) of losses in the sample. The risk manager does not know what M and s are for the whole "population," but the mean and standard deviation of his sample is the best single estimate of the mean and standard deviation of all losses in the population — *i.e.*, all losses to be expected in a large number of years in the future. What variation in losses can be expected in all future years? To answer this question, the risk manager first calculates the standard error, by the above formula. The steps are as follows:

Step 1

Calculate the standard deviation(s) of losses in the sample.

TABLE 3–3   Sample Loss Distribution

Dollars of Loss (X)	Number of Workers (n)	Total Loss
$ 0	800	$ 0
110	100	11,000
200	70	14,000
500	30	15,000
	1,000	$40,000
Mean Loss (M)		$40

Calculation of the standard deviation(s) of this sample is:

X − M	(X − M)² × n	Weighted Squared Deviations
$–40	$ 1,600 × 800 =	$1,280,000
70	4,900 × 100 =	490,000
160	25,600 × 70 =	1,792,000
460	211,600 × 30 =	6,348,000
Total	1000	$9,910,000

Mean of squared deviations:[1] $9,910, Standard Deviation $= \sqrt{9910} = \$99.55$

Step 2

Calculate the standard error (SE).

$$SE = \frac{s}{\sqrt{n}} = \frac{\$99.55}{\sqrt{1000}} = \frac{99.55}{31.62} = \$3.15$$

Note that although the standard deviation ($99.55) is relatively large, when compared to the mean loss ($40) the standard error ($3.15) is quite small.

The risk analyst can assume in the

above case that for all possible future periods, the *mean* loss will lie within a known range of $40. Specifically, the risk analyst can be 95.45 percent confident that the mean loss will fall in the range $40 ± 6.30 (two standard errors). At the 99.73 percent confidence level, the mean loss will fall within the range $40 ± $9.45 (three standard errors). Note that in this calculation the risk analyst may draw inferences only about the mean loss for a large number of years. The mean loss for *the next year or any single year* may have a greater variation than that shown above. Thus, in the above example the distribution of losses from 1,000 workers in a single year could look very differently from the above.

Setting Loss Reserves

Using the above analysis and knowing that the firm has 1,000 workers, the risk analyst may predict that the average annual losses will not exceed $49.45 × 1,000, or $49,450, 99.73 percent of the time. Using this information, the risk manager can estimate the size of a loss reserve fund in the event he plans to recommend self-insurance for the risk. In this case, he might recommend a self-insurance fund of $50,000,[2] even though the best estimate of losses for any one year is $40,000.

Rate Negotiation

The risk manager may also use the above analysis in his negotiations with commercial insurers on premium rates. The pure premium, or expected value of the loss, is $40, the relative risk (at the 99.73 percent confidence level) is $9.45/

---

[1] It is common to divide by the quantity n − 1 instead of n (*i.e.*, in this case by 999 instead of 1,000) because the first method eliminates certain statistical bias. For large numbers this bias is negligible, however, and so the simpler method is used here.

[2] For a more complete discussion of this type of analysis, see David B. Houston, "Risk, Insurance, and Sampling," *Journal of Risk and Insurance*, December 1964.

$40, or 24 percent. If the insurer requires an expense loading of 35 percent, the gross premium should approximate $40/(1 − .35), or $61.54, plus whatever charge for risk the insurer might make. Because the risk manager can demonstrate that there is little chance that in the long run the pure premium will exceed the expected by more than $9.45 per worker, the final premium quoted per worker should not exceed $\frac{\$40.00 + \$9.45}{1 - .35}$, or $76.08. Some insurers may quote less than this amount because their aversion toward risk may be less than other insurers. (Measurement of subjective risk attitudes is discussed below.)

Evaluating the Size of the Sample

The validity of the estimate of probability of loss as discussed above may be checked mathematically if it can be determined that the losses of a certain nature are distributed in accordance with some known probability distribution, such as the normal or binomial distribution, events of which fall in accordance to the familiar "bell-shaped curve." To illustrate, suppose that the losses are found to fall in accordance with the binomial distribution. Assume that it is estimated that the probability of loss in a given case, say automobile collisions, is .20 annually. The firm has 1,000 automobiles exposed (assuming losses are random and independent of one another) and thus "expects" 200 collisions annually. How accurate is such a prediction, given the assumptions as to sample size? A simple formula is available which will provide some guidance:

$$N = \frac{Z^2 p(1-p)}{E^2}$$

where N = the number of exposure units

p = the probability of loss

E = the degree of accuracy, or tolerable error, expressed as a percent of permitted error to the total number of exposure units

Z = the number of standard deviations to be used in setting confidence limits

In this problem we are interested in the value of E, the accuracy of the prediction. Some assumption is necessary to make regarding the "confidence level" of the prediction. Suppose that management wants to be "95.45 percent confident" in its prediction. This means that there is only a 4.55 percent chance that the result given by the formula will be due to chance factors or sampling error. In such a case, due to the characteristics of the binomial distribution, the value of Z will be 2, since in such a distribution, 95.45 percent of all occurrences fall within two standard deviations of the mean. If management wished to be "99.73 percent confident" of the results, Z would be 3, etc.

Substituting in the formula, and assuming a desired confidence level of 95 percent, we have as an estimate of accuracy for E.

$$1000 = \frac{2^2 \times .20(1-.20)}{E^2}$$
$$E^2 = .00064$$
$$E = .025$$

The error estimate .025 may be interpreted as follows: Given a binomial distribution of collision losses, 1,000 autos, and an estimated loss probability of 20 percent, there is a 95.45 percent chance (Z = 2) that the actual loss probability will not exceed 22.5 percent, nor fall below 17.5 percent (.20 ± .025).

This result may be understood more fully by the following checking procedure. If the firm has 1,000 autos with probable loss of .20, it expects 200 collisions annually. The standard deviation of the binomial distribution is given by the formula $\sqrt{n\ p\ (1\text{-}p)}$, or in this example $\sqrt{1000\ (.2)(.8)}$, or 12.6. Two standard deviations is 25.2 collisions, which includes 95.45 percent of all expected losses. The ratio of 25.2 to 1000 is .025, the tolerable error. The expected range of loss is thus 200 ± 25.2, which amounts to a 12.5 percent variation from the expected loss ($25/200 = 12.5\%$).

If management is not satisfied with such a wide dispersion of probable losses, it must either have a larger number of exposure units, or reduce the degree of confidence required. For example, if management wants a 95 percent confidence level, but desires to keep the error level to .01 (which would be only 5 percent deviation from the estimated loss), we can determine by the above formula, that the required number of autos would be 6,400, determined as follows:

$$N = \frac{2^2 \times .20(.80)}{(.01)^2} = 6400$$

Any other assumptions are, of course, possible regarding values to be assigned to the four variables in the equation, the value of any one of which can be determined once the other three are known or for which values are assumed.

It should be noted that formulas similar to the ones illustrated are possible only if the distribution frequency of losses being studied fall reasonably close to some mathematical distribution whose mean and standard deviation are known. If losses are not so distributed, the formula will give misleading results.

ESTIMATING THE FREQUENCY AND SEVERITY OF LOSS

To obtain estimates of loss severity, expected value analysis, discussed above, is often helpful. Assume that it has been determined that management has made careful studies of loss exposures and has derived the best estimates of loss from insurable perils. These are shown in Table 3–4.

The maximum *possible* is $6 million. The long run or most *probable* loss (*i.e.*, the expected value of the loss) is $650,000. The minimum possible loss is zero. Management may judge the severity of loss by reference to either or both of these concepts. If the firm cannot stand to lose the maximum possible loss, some type of risk handling, discussed in Chapter 2, must be employed. Given the assumptions, the firm has no choice other than to expect, in the long run, to lose $650,000 each year, on the average, from the perils it faces.

In a given year, the risk of suffering extreme losses can also be judged using expected value analysis. Management may decide subjectively that there is only a small probability of suffering the maximum possible loss (say .001), a somewhat larger probability of suffering a 50 percent loss (say .01), a substantial

TABLE 3–4

Property Exposed	Replacement Cost	Probability of Loss (frequency)	Expected Value of Loss
Building	$1,000,000	.01	$ 10,000
Equipment	2,000,000	.02	40,000
Automobiles and trucks	3,000,000	.20	600,000
Totals	$6,000,000		$650,000

probability of suffering a loss equal to the expected value (say .75) and a modest probability (.239) of having no loss. These judgments are presented in Table 3–5. The represented events, for illustrative purposes, are assumed to be a distribution of collectively exhaustive and mutually exclusive events.

Using expected value analysis, the adjusted measure of loss severity in a given year is expressed in quantitative terms as $523,500.

Probability Trees

Another approach to analysis of the expected value of possible losses and risk management decisions is use of probability tree diagrams, illustrated in Examples 1 and 2 in Figures 3–1 and 3–2. The value of tree diagrams lies in the fact that management may formally consider various decisions about se-

TABLE 3–5

Event	Prob-ability	Expected Value
Suffer total possible loss — i.e., lose $6,000,000	.001	$ 6,000
Suffer a 50% loss — lose $3,000,000	.01	30,000
Suffer expected value of loss — $650,000	.75	487,500
Suffer no loss	.239	0
Expected Value of Loss	1.00	$523,500

quential events which may lead to a loss, assessing the probability of each of these events with greater accuracy separately than would be possible if all of the events had to be considered simultaneously.

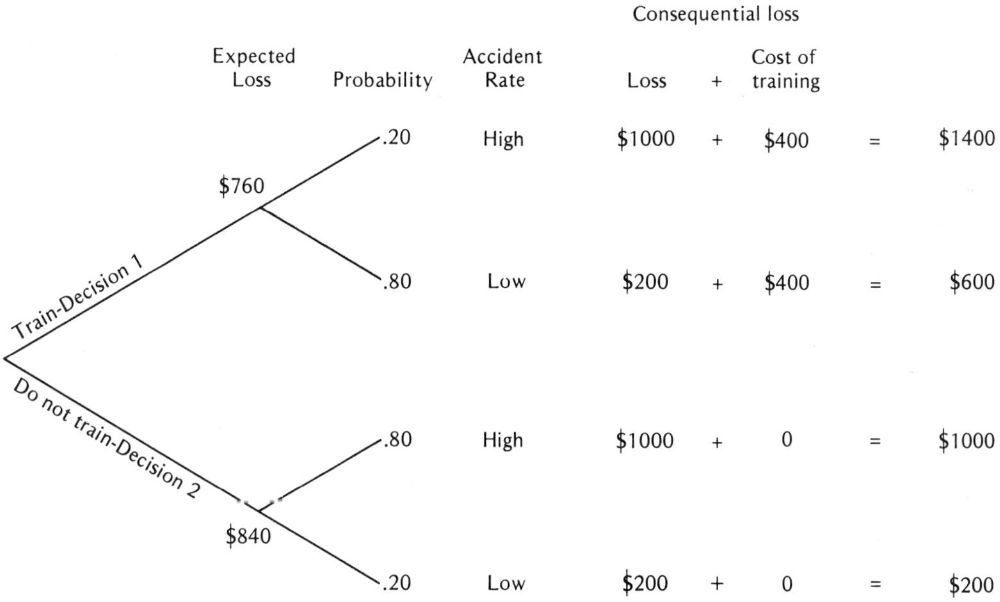

FIGURE 3–1.   Probability Tree to Analyze a Risk Management Decision.

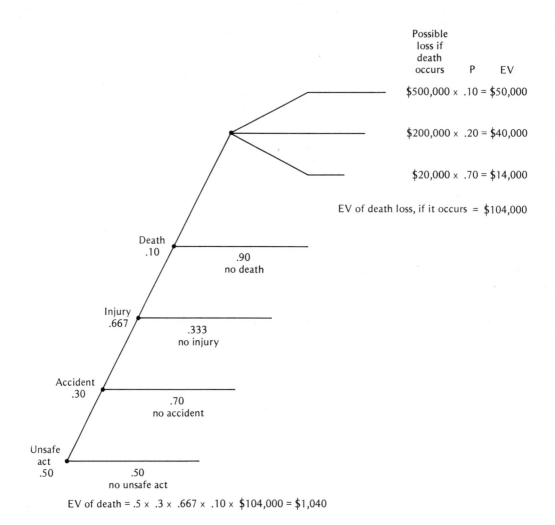

FIGURE 3–2.   Tree Diagram in Risk Management in Industrial Injuries.

Example 1

In the first example, a risk manager is considering two possible decisions as possible reactions to the problem of rising accidents in his plant. Decision 1 is to spend $400 to train workers and decision 2 is to forego training and instead issue only general appeals to workers to be more careful.

He calculates that accident rates will be reduced by training, but that there is a modest probability (20 percent) that accidents will be high even with training since not all workers react favorably. Also, if training is not undertaken, there is also a small probability (20 percent) that accident rates will be reduced due to the favorable reaction to an appeal by management to be more careful. The financial consequence of "high" accident rates is estimated to be a loss of $1,000 per week in workers' compensation costs, while the financial consequences of "low" accident rates is estimated at $200 per week.

The risk manager decides to outline the different decisions and their consequences, together with probability assessments. This is shown in Figure 3–1 which illustrates a probability tree diagram. By examining Figure 3–1, the risk manager may see that the expected loss of decision 1, "train," is $760, compared to an expected loss of decision 1, "do not train," of $840. The expected loss of decision 1 is calculated by the expression $1400(.20) + $600(.80) = $760. The expected loss of decision 2 is $1000(.80) + $200(.20) = $840.

The risk manager would presumably take decision 1 since this act minimizes his expected losses. This is done even though there is a modest probability that even if he spends money for training, it will not be successful. The probability tree helps organize the various possibilities and to arrive at better decisions that might otherwise be the case.

Example 2

In Figure 3–2, a problem of assessing the expected value of an industrial death in a plant is diagrammed. At the extreme right, estimates are made as to the possible ranges of cost of an industrial death. It is assumed that the cost of most deaths which occur will be regulated by an appropriate workers' compensation law, which usually places relatively low limits of liability (in this illustration, $20,000) for which the probability is estimated subjectively to be 70 percent. However, management may recognize that some deaths may involve negligence on the part of the em-

ployer and will result in law suits which may cause much higher losses, in this illustration placed at $200,000 and $500,000, with probabilities 20 and 10 percent, respectively. The expected value (EV) of such losses, *if they occur*, is shown to be $104,000.

However, management recognizes that it has certain control over the working environment which produces unsafe acts. It is also recognized that not all unsafe acts produce accidents, nor do all accidents produce injuries, nor do all injuries produce deaths. In fact, management is able to assess probabilities that under present conditions there is a .50 chance that unsafe acts will occur, a .30 chance that accidents will result from unsafe acts that do occur, that there is a .667 chance that injuries will result from the accidents that occur, and that only 10 percent of all injuries result in deaths. Presumably, if unsafe acts can be reduced, so will the frequency of events that lead up to industrial deaths. Assuming different events occur at random and utilizing the compound probability rule, the expected loss from industrial accidents in Figure 3–2 is: $.5 \times .3 \times .667 \times .10 = .01 \times \$104,000 = \$1,040$.

If monthly meetings of production workers are held and an educational and loss prevention program initiated to reduce unsafe acts, assume that unsafe acts can be reduced by half. If this is possible, the expected value of each industrial death is also cut in half, to $520. Management is now in a position to determine the expected gains from loss prevention. For example, if the employer has 20 employees, he can afford to spend up to 20 × $520, or $10,400, for a loss prevention program which will reduce unsafe acts by one half. If the employer has more than 20 employees, he gains an expected loss reduction of $520 for each additional employee, assuming there is no increase in the total cost of the loss prevention program.

By the use of the tree diagram, management may assess the probabilities of losses more accurately than otherwise might be possible. Management may calculate the changes in expected losses by examination of the changes that occur in each individual probability value in the tree. For example in Figure 3–2 if, through better first aid procedures, the probability of deaths can be reduced from .10 to .05, once the injury has occurred, the expected value of an industrial death is again reduced by half and the amount that can be economically justified in instituting such procedures easily calculated as illustrated above. Similar approaches can be effective in solving other problems involving risk. It is not hard to appreciate that it is easier to make probability estimates of individual events in the tree than it is to make these estimates for the final event singly without considering the intermediate phases. Thus, simple decisions can be made leading to better complex decisions.

The Expected Utility Approach

One limitation in the above analysis is that a loss which is severe to one firm may not be severe to another firm. One management may be more risk averse than another and may perceive losses differently. For example, a loss of $100,000 may bankrupt a small firm, but might hardly be noticed by a larger firm.

Severity of possible losses can be analyzed by what has been termed the expected utility approach to measurement. It assumes that a loss suffered by a poor man causes greater hardship to

him than an equal loss to a richer man. Such a conclusion is based on the *law of diminishing marginal utility,* in which economists have hypothesized that each additional dollar of income, or unit of merchandise, received by an individual has less and less value to him than the preceding unit. It follows that loss of one dollar of income to a rich man will cause less hardship than the same loss to a poor man. A person's *utility curve* is derived in order to determine his attitudes toward money loss. For each sum of money loss to which the person is exposed, a utility value is assigned. These values are multiplied by the probability of loss and a total expected utility of loss is derived. The implications for risk-handling methods are important, and may be illustrated by reference to a decision as to whether or not to purchase insurance.

Risk Profiles

The first step in utilizing the expected utility approach to determining loss severity is to identify management attitudes toward different amounts of loss. There are three general theoretical attitudes to consider: (a) the person who is neutral toward risk, (b) the person who is a risk lover, and (c) the person who is a risk averter. Of course, there are many gradations within these extremes.

(a) The risk neutral person is one who attaches no more significance, relatively speaking, to a $10 loss than he does to a $100 loss. Thus, if he attaches one utility point to a loss of $10, he will attach 10 utility points to $100 of loss, 100 points to a $1,000 loss, 1,000 points to a $10,000 loss, etc. A risk neutral person really uses the expected monetary value approach in viewing risk. A risk-neutral person is one who would pay no more than the expected value of the loss in order to transfer the risk to others. If there is a $10,000 loss exposure subject to a loss probability of .01, the risk neutral person would pay no more than $100 ($10,000 × .01) to avoid the risk. Obviously, such a person would seldom, if ever, be a purchaser of insurance because the insurer would not offer coverage for the expected value of the loss, due to the necessity of charging overhead costs in addition to expected losses.

(b) A risk lover is a person who attaches subjective value to taking risk. If a gamble is offered to a risk lover, he will pay an amount above the expected value of the game in order to play, presumably because of the pleasure he receives from risk taking. Suppose there is a lottery with 1 million tickets outstanding, each selling for $2. The prize is $1 million and there is only one winning ticket. The risk lover may realize that the fair value of each ticket is only $1, but he is willing to pay $2 because $2 may mean little to him and $1 million would mean much to him if he should win, even though the chance is slight. Similarly, if the risk lover faces a risk of losing $2,000 with a probability of .01, he would not be willing to pay the fair value of risk transfer, $20, to avoid the risk even if someone should offer to assume it for that price. Obviously, the risk lover is not a person who would generally be inclined to purchase insurance, the price of which is higher, not lower, than the expected value of the loss.

(c) The risk averter is a person who dislikes risk such that he will be willing to pay more than the expected value of the loss in order to avoid running the risk. As possible losses increase, they have greater and greater negative significance to the risk averter.

Conversely, if the risk averter is offered a $100 lottery ticket with a .01 probability of winning, he would be willing to pay less than $1 for the ticket.

It has been hypothesized by Friedman and Savage[3] that in most cases a person will simultaneously gamble and buy insurance, seemingly inconsistent conduct, because their utility functions have different slopes depending on the amount of money involved. For example, a person may be willing to gamble small sums since these amounts mean little to him, whereas a large sum which might be won would have proportionately more value to him because it would enable him to enjoy an entirely new and higher living standard, at least temporarily. Such an individual therefore may be found to be risk loving within a certain range of monetary values, risk neutral in other ranges, and risk averse in still other ranges.

To illustrate, consider the schedules depicting the maximum transfer fees each of three individuals might be willing to pay to rid themselves of risk of loss of the sums shown in the left column (Table 3–6). These values are plotted in Figure 3–3. They show that the risk-neutral person is always willing to pay the expected value of the loss as a transfer fee to avoid risk, the risk averse person is always willing to pay more, and the risk loving person less, than the expected value of the loss to avoid risk. However, the risk averse person is willing, up to a point (in this illustration, up to $25,000), to pay a constantly rising percentage of the expected value of the loss. Between $25,000

[3] Milton Friedman and L. Savage, "Utility Analysis of Choices Involving Risk," *Journal of Political Economy* (August 1948). See also Mark R. Greene, *Risk and Insurance* (Cincinnati: South-Western Publishing Company, 1977), pp. 38–42.

TABLE 3–6

Expected Value of Loss	Maximum Transfer Fee as a Percent of the Expected Value of the Loss		
	Risk Neutral Person	Risk Averse Person	Risk Loving Person
0	0	0	0
$ 5,000	100	100	100
10,000	100	105	95
15,000	100	110	90
20,000	100	115	85
25,000	100	120	80
30,000	100	127	73
35,000	100	135	66
40,000	100	142	59
45,000	100	146	54
50,000	100	149	51

and $35,000 he is willing to pay a percentage which rises at an increasing rate, and finally above $35,000 a percentage which rises at a declining rate. In this illustration a point is reached at about $50,000 where the risk averse person is willing to pay 149 percent of the expected value of the loss, but no more. In other words, his risk aversion curve is expected to level off once a certain point of monetary loss is reached. This may occur because he lacks resources to transfer risk for losses above some point (in this case $50,000), or because he is unable psychologically to imagine the impact of losses above this point. The risk loving person's attitudes are assumed to be the exact reverse of the risk averting person.

Developing Utility Schedules

The above illustration makes certain assumptions regarding how people with different attitudes toward risk are expected to behave. The question arises, "How can we actually determine the utility schedule of a given individual?"

Many attempts have been made to answer this question, using questionnaire techniques, personality tests, gambling experiments, and others.[4] None of the attempts have been entirely satisfactory for reasons to be discussed later. Even the meaning of utility schedules has been interpreted differently, some holding that utility schedules measure how individuals *do* in fact behave, while others hold that they depict merely how rational people *should* behave. Certainly an individual does not often consciously or explicitly realize what his own utility function is in making decisions under uncertainty. Perhaps the best reason for studying utility schedules is to discover an underlying rationale for complex decision making under uncertainty.

An analogy from the sport of tennis might illustrate the rationale for the above statement. A tennis player seldom is conscious of the operation of physical laws underlying his shots, but he is governed by them just the same. It might be theoretically possible to develop mathematical formulas showing the speed, direction, arch, and angle the ball will take if it is struck with a certain force, under given conditions of play such as wind direction, weight of the ball, air resistance against the fuzz

[4] One of the early attempts to validate risk-taking attitudes by means of utility measurements was conducted by Mosteller and Nogee, whose experiments demonstrated that it was feasible to predict future gambling behavior by utility schedules developed from behavior noted on simple wagers. See F. Mosteller and P. Nogee, "An Experimental Measurement of Utility," *Journal of Political Economy*, vol. 59, 1951, pp. 371–404. For a summary of other experiments see Mark R. Greene, "Attitudes Toward Risk and a Theory of Insurance Consumption," *Journal of Insurance*, vol. 30, no. 2, June 1963, pp. 165–182.

Transfer fee, as a
percent of the expected
value of the loss

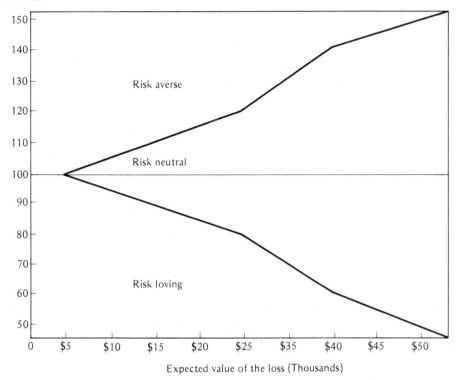

FIGURE 3–3.   Risk Profiles of the Risk Neutral, Risk Averse, and Risk Loving Individuals.

of the ball, etc. With sufficient knowledge and techniques under scientific conditions, it might be possible to develop better tennis-playing ability in the same manner that instruments and techniques have been developed to make very complex calculations necessary for space travel which permits relatively accurate space maneuvers. Thus, the study of utility functions underlying decision making under uncertainty might eventually be of significant value in ensuring more effective and more consistent economic behavior.

A technique to measure a person's utility by a questionnaire method will be illustrated below as a first step in showing how utility schedules, once determined, might be used in making decisions under uncertainty.[5] In this technique the respondent is asked how he would choose between two outcomes, one certain and one involving uncertainty. For example, he would be asked which he prefers, a certain sum of $500 or an opportunity to enter a game in which he has a given probability, say 50 percent, of winning $1,000 and a 50 percent chance of winning nothing. If

[5] See John von Neuman and Oskar Morgenstern, *Theory of Games and Economic Behavior* (Princeton University Press, 1944).

the person chooses the certain sum of $500, the interviewer raises the odds of winning up to a point where the respondent is indifferent between the two alternatives. The experimenter assigns initial arbitrary utility values to two extreme sums and proceeds to solve equations to determine the utility attached by the respondent to each sum.

Utility and the Insurance-buying Decision

Applying this method to an insurance decision, let us assume an arbitrary utility value of 0 to be assigned to zero loss, and 100 to the worst possible loss.[6] Assume that the worst possible loss is $6 million. Ask the respondent how much he would pay to eliminate a risk in which he had to run a .50 chance of losing $6 million or nothing. If he answers $3½ million, the utility assigned to $3½ million would be 50 points. This follows because the individual is apparently indifferent between paying $3½ million and entering a game in which he has a .50 chance of losing $6 million and a .50 chance of losing 0. Since the arbitrary initial utility value assigned to $6,000,000 was 100, by formula we may see

$$.50 \text{ (Utility of } \$6,000,000) + .50$$
$$\text{(Utility of 0)} = \text{Utility of } \$3,500,000$$

or, by substitution,

$$.50 (100) + .50 (0) = \text{Utility of } \$3,500,000$$
$$50 = \text{Utility of } \$3,500,000$$

The quantities on each side of the equation are equal because the subject indicated he is indifferent between either of the two alternatives.

Next ask the individual how much he would pay to avoid a risk in which he has a .50 chance of losing $3,500,000 or nothing. If he answers $2,000,000, the utility of $2,000,000 is 25, determined as follows:

$$.50 \text{ (Utility of } \$3,500,000) + .50$$
$$\text{(Utility of 0)} = \text{Utility of } \$2,000,000$$
$$.50 (50) + .50 (0) = 25$$

In a similar manner utility points can be assigned to all value between zero and the maximum possible loss, using an interpolation procedure for intermediate values. Assume that a person's utility function, using the above method, has been determined and that the probability of each possible loss has been determined in accordance with some of the procedures discussed previously in this chapter. The expected utility and expected value of the loss is shown in Table 3–7.

If the individual purchases no insurance, his expected loss in utility is by running the risk 7.585 points. In order to determine whether or not to pay a transfer fee (insurance premium), the individual decision maker must now find the dollar equivalent to 7.585 utility points. Let us assume that by linear interpolation from the above schedule this dollar equivalent of this utility is $970,000.[7] The decision maker would not be willing to pay more than $970,000 to avoid the risk. If he did so, he would be sacrificing more utility than he would lose by assuming the risk. Note that according to the expected utility criterion, the manager would be will-

[6] See, also, C. Arthur Williams and Richard M. Heins, *Risk Management and Insurance*, 2nd ed., (New York, McGraw-Hill Publishing Co., 1971), pp. 222–23.

[7] Arrived at by solving the following proportion for x:
$$\frac{7.585}{6.25} = \frac{x}{800,000}$$

TABLE 3–7
Expected Utility of Losses

(1) Possible Loss	(2) Utility Points	(3) Probability of Occurrence	(4) Expected Utility of Loss (2)×(3)	(5) Expected Monetary Value of the Loss (1)×(3)
$6,000,000	100.	.001	.1	$ 6,000
3,500,000	50.	.008	.4	28,000
2,000,000	25.	.03	.75	60,000
1,200,000	12.5	.20	2.50	240,000
800,000	6.25	.50	3.125	400,000
500,000	3.12	.20	.624	100,000
300,000	1.56	.05	.078	15,000
200,000	.78	.011	.008	2,200
TOTAL		1.00	7.585	$851,200

ing to pay not more than $970,000 to avoid a risk whose total monetary expected value is $851,200, calculated in Table 3–7 column (5). Apparently, this person is a modest risk averter, because he is willing to pay more than the expected value of the loss to transfer the risk. However, it is doubtful that he would be able in the real world to purchase insurance against a total loss because the commercial insurer would normally require a margin of between one-third and one-half of the premium to cover expenses. This individual is only willing to pay about 17 percent more than the expected value of the loss to transfer the risk, which would give the insurer a margin of only 22 percent of its premium. Yet, paying any more would cause a greater loss of utility to the decision maker than the expected utility lost by running the risk.

If the individual were considering the purchase of insurance with a $500,000 deductible, his total loss of utility by running the remaining risk would be 6.885 (7.585 − .624 − .078 − .008 = 6.885) (from Table 3–7). The dollar equivalent to a loss of utility of 6.885 would be about $880,000, by linear interpolation from Table 3–7. The individual would thus be willing to purchase insurance with a $500,000 deductible for a premium of $880,000. From column (5) of Table 3–7, we can determine that the expected value of losses above $500,000 is $734,000. If the insurer took this risk for the $880,000 premium, his margin would be only about 17 percent of the premium (100 − 734/880 = 16.6). Presumably the insurer would insist upon a higher deductible, or a greater premium, or both.

If the deductible were $800,000, the manager would have an expected loss of utility (from Table 3–7) of 3.76 by running the remaining risk (7.585 − 3.12 − .624 − .078 − .008 = 3.76). A loss of 3.76 in utility has the dollar equivalent (by linear interpolation from Table 3–7) of about $602,500. Thus, the manager would be willing to pay up to $602,500 for insurance with an $800,000 deductible. The expected value of losses above $800,000, from column (5) of Table 3–7, is $334,000. The insurer would probably be willing to accept such a risk at a premium of $602,500, which would give the insurer a margin of 45 percent of the premium for expenses. Thus, the possibility of commercial risk transfer exists during the range of between $500,000 and $800,000 deductible. Alternatively, there may exist some room for reduction in the premium in this range of deductibles because the insurer may be willing to reduce his expense or profit margin below 45 percent of the premium. In this way the limits of bargaining over the price and terms of insurance service may be more scientifically analyzed.

Limitations

Although the basic idea of utility analysis as an explanation of insurance-buying behavior and other risk-taking behavior seems sound, there are several difficulties or disadvantages in its practical application. First, errors may exist in a person's utility schedule derived by asking questions involving hypothetical decisions involving risk. There is a well-known difference between what one answers on a test and what he will do in real life when confronted with a decision. Second, utility has been measured by inference after observing one's behavior on other types of tests (such as the need for achievement (N-ach) or "deterrence of failure" tests), biographical inventories of life experiences, and subjective evaluations by peers. None of these tests, including the method illustrated above, has been developed to the point that they are both reliable and valid indicators of willingness to take risk. Studies have, in fact, determined that the various tests do not agree with one another.[8] Thus, at the present time there seems some doubt that real utility schedules of individuals can be deter-

mined with sufficient accuracy to be entirely satisfactory in making real-world decisions.

Third, little is known about how stable one's attitudes toward risk might be over time. A decision made on the basis of a utility schedule in one month may not be sound for another month. Is it necessary to take continuous tests of utility attitudes? If so, how frequently should they be taken?

Fourth, there is evidence that other types of risk besides financial or economic risk, as measured by attitudes toward wealth, are important factors in decision making. Minkowich, for example, showed that attitudes toward financial risk do not necessarily coincide with attitudes toward social (prestige) or physical risk. In his studies, he discovered that the personality characteristics hostility and ambivalence (feelings of conflict) tend to increase willingness to take financial risk but to decrease willingness to take physical or prestige risks such as might be involved in dangerous sports or in acting in ways unacceptable to one's peers. He also demonstrated that the conditions surrounding the administration of tests of risk attitudes had an important effect on the results.[9] In other words, test results might be unreliable because of distractions involved in testing procedures.

Worry Factor Analysis

The degree of severity of financial loss due to uncertain events has also been measured by a technique developed by Professors Arthur C. Williams, Jr., and Richard Heins called worry factor analysis.[10] The worry factor is the dollar value assigned by the risk

[8] Slovic, "Assessment of Behavior," pp. 220–233.

[9] A. A. Minkowich, Correlates of Ambivalence, pp. 49–61.

[10] Williams and Heins, Risk Management and Insurance, pp. 226–29.

manager to the uncertainty associated with any uncovered dollar losses in a given situation. For example, if the risk manager purchases complete insurance with no deductible, the worry factor is zero because there is no uncertainty as to loss. If the risk manager is considering no insurance at all, or is considering several insurance contracts, with varying amounts of deductibles, the uncovered loss is presumed to be related to the degree of "worry" in the mind of the buyer, and it is assumed that the manager can place a dollar value upon this sum. Suppose the manager is faced with a $6 million total exposure to loss (see Table 3–7), but his firm is so large that a total loss of $6 million is inconsequential. The worry factor would likewise be minimal.

Decisions in the area of insurance are made by adding the premium, the expected value of any uncovered loss, and the dollar value assigned to the associated "worry" produced, and then selecting the alternative producing the least expected loss. To illustrate, assume there are four alternative decisions for the risk manager with $6 million total possible loss, as shown in Table 3–8.

According to the worry factor model in Table 3–8, the decision maker suffers the least total expected loss by taking Decision 3, insurance with $800,000 deductible, although the differences in the loss figures in Column 5 are not great. The manager can easily see that his assessments of worry importantly affect the decision process. For example, if the decision maker's worry is related more with the absolute size of the deductible rather than the expected value of the uncovered loss, the outcome might be entirely different, depending on his degree of risk aversion.

The value of the model is that it forces the risk manager to place some quantitative measure on his subjective assessment of worry. As such, it is similar to the procedure utilized in the

TABLE 3–8
The Worry Factor Model

(1)	(2)	(3) Expected Value of Uncovered Loss (EVUL)**	(4) Worry Factor***	(5) Total Loss (2)+(3)+(4)
Decision	Premium*			
1. Buy total loss coverage ($6,000,000)	$1,702,400	0	0	$1,702,400
2. Accept $500,000 deductible	$1,468,000	$117,200	$ 35,000	$1,620,200
3. Accept $800,000 deductible	$ 668,000	$517,200	$258,000	$1,443,200
4. Buy no insurance	0	$851,200	$681,000	$1,532,200

* Calculated from Table 3 7, Column 5 as twice the expected value of the loss.

** Calculated as follows: For $500,000 deductible take the sum of the expected values of losses of $500,000 or below from Table 3–7, Column 5. For $800,000 deductible, take sum of expected values of all losses of $800,000 or below from Table 3–7, Column 5.

*** Assumed to bear some approximate relationship to the expected value of uncovered losses. In this illustration, the worry factor at $500,000 deductible is about a third of the EVUL, at $800,000 deductible about half of the EVUL, and for no coverage the worry factor is assumed to be 80 percent of the EVUL.

expected utility measure and suffers some of the same weaknesses. For example, the problem of consistency over time exists in making decisions about the amount of dollar value assigned to some degree of worry. On the other hand, the worry factor model has the advantage of forcing the risk manager to make a formal analysis of risk before making decisions.

Paired Comparison Approach

Still another approach to assessing the severity of loss to the risk manager suggested by Williams and Heins[11] is the paired comparison approach. Under this approach it is assumed that the decision maker may find it easier to compare only two things at a time and decide which he prefers, rather than consider simultaneously a whole range of possible decisions.

In a very simple case, for example, suppose the risk manager is considering an automobile insurance deductible problem. A premium schedule is prepared with ascending order of risk (reflected by rising deductibles) as shown in Table 3–9.

The analyst realizes that in Policy 2 he saves $50 by accepting a $100 deductible and saves an additional $40 in Policy 3 by accepting an additional deductible of $400. In Policy 4 the saving is only $30 for an additional deductible of $500. The relative saving declines as risk increases. The decision taken may hinge on whether the additional risk in Policies 2, 3, and 4 is worth it, and this in turn may depend largely on the risk manager's attitudes toward risk and upon his perceptions of the probability of loss of the amounts under the deductible.

In the paired comparison approach

11 Ibid.

TABLE 3–9

Policy	Deductible	Insurance Premium	Saving over Previous Policy
1	$ 0	$200	—
2	100	150	$50
3	500	110	40
4	1000	80	30

the risk manager first compares Policy 1 with Policy 2. If he believes the additional risk is worth $50, he prefers the savings to the risk and chooses Policy 2. Next, he compares Policies 2 and 3. In Policy 3 he realizes a smaller savings for a much larger risk and may decide that he prefers the lower risk of Policy 2. Here the process stops, for Policy 4 involves even greater risk than Policy 3.

In a second example, we shall assume that the risk manager has knowledge of the loss probabilities of additional exposure involved in accepting

TABLE 3–10

Decision	Premium	Saving in Premium Over Prior Decision
1. Buy $6,000,000 of insurance (total loss coverage)	$1,700,000	—
2. Purchase $500,000 deductible insurance	1,500,000	$200,000
3. Purchase $800,000 deductible insurance	700,000	800,000
4. Buy no insurance	0	700,000

higher deductibles. Using the loss distribution in Table 3–7 as an example, let us suppose the manager is presented with the set of alternatives shown in Table 3–10.

The risk manager may have a hard time deciding which of the above decisions to take by considering the entire set simultaneously. Under the paired comparisons approach, the decision maker considers only two decisions at a time. First, he decides whether he prefers Decision 1 to Decision 2. This is accomplished by comparing the savings in premium, $200,000, to the probability of occurrence and amount of additional uncovered losses under Decision 2. Referring to Table 3–7, it can be determined that the probability of additional uncovered losses for each decision in the above problem is as shown in Table 3–11.

In analyzing the two decisions the risk analyst realizes that he saves $200,000 by accepting a $500,000 deductible. This exposure has an expected value of $130,500. To accept the deductible is comparable to a decision to pay $200,000 for insurance on a $500,000 loss exposure whose expected value is $130,500. The premium may appear fairly high to a modest risk taker. If the risk analyst prefers to save $200,000, he

prefers Decision 2 over Decision 1 and the above process is repeated in other decisions involving more risk.

In comparing Decisions 2 and 3, the manager asks whether he prefers a savings of $800,000 to a .50 chance of having a loss less than $800,000, but greater than $500,000, i.e., an *additional* uncovered loss of $300,000, whose expected value is $150,000. Let us say he prefers the savings, meaning that he prefers to run the risk. He then prefers Decision 3 over Decision 2. Otherwise he would be apparently unwilling to take a .50 chance of suffering an additional uncovered loss of $300,000 even though he would save $800,000 in insurance premiums by so doing. It seems unlikely that he would prefer to lose $800,000 for such small additional coverage.

Next, the decision maker compares Decisions 3 and 4. In this case he asks whether he prefers a saving of $700,000 in premium to a 23.9 chance of losing an additional $5,200,000. If he prefers the savings, he decides to run the risk and apparently prefers Decision 4 to Decision 3. This is not a likely outcome because most risk managers would be unwilling to exchange a $700,000 savings for a 23.9 percent chance of losing an additional $5,200,000. In this

TABLE 3–11

Decision	(1) Total Uncovered Loss	(2) Amount of Additional Uncovered Loss Over Prior Alternative	(3) Probability of Occurrence	(4) EV (2)×(3)
1	$ 0	—	—	—
2	500,000	$ 500,000	.261*	130,500
3	800,000	300,000	.50 **	150,000
4	6,000,000	5,200,000	.239***	1,242,800

* From Column 3, Table 3–1, .011 + .05 + .20 = .261

** From Column 3, Table 3–1, (.011 + .05 + .20 + .50) − .261 = .50

*** From Column 3, Table 3–1, 1.00 − .761 = .239

case the premium is less than the expected value of the loss, and insurance would appear to be a bargain. Therefore, the decision maker apparently prefers Decision 3, which most closely expresses his attitudes toward the severity of losses he faces.

Conclusion

In the three examples employing utility analysis, the worry factor model, and the paired comparison approach to decision making, the final decision was similar — purchase insurance with a deductible of $800,000. The outcome could have varied, however, with only slight changes in the assumptions, or in the attitudes toward risk of the decision maker. The value of these models lies in the discipline they enforce in formal consideration of the mental attitudes toward risk of the decision maker and to increase the likelihood of consistent decisions in judging the severity of loss to firms with different sets of risk attitudes.

SUMMARY AND CONCLUSIONS

1. Among the most important problems of risk management which lend themselves to solution, at least in part, by application of theoretical models, are those involving prediction of losses. Included among the problems are estimating both frequency and severity of losses and making decisions under conditions of uncertainty.

2. Probability is defined statistically and the rules of probability analysis may be applied to the problems of predicting losses. Among these are the additive, compound probability, and conditional probability rules. Among the problems to which these rules are applied are those of estimating the minimum size of sample required for given levels of accuracy of loss prediction and for given levels of confidence in the results.

3. In estimating the severity of loss to management, the problems of handling extreme ranges of possible losses and the mental attitudes toward risk are considered. Among the tools to help solve these problems are the expected value approach, tree diagrams, utility analysis, worry factor analysis, and the paired comparison approach.

QUESTIONS FOR DISCUSSION

1. In a six-sided die, what is the probability of throwing a "three" in one toss? A four? Why? What assumptions are necessary for your answer to be correct?

2. A soldier was reported to have made $20,000 over a period of his Army service by standing on the sidelines of dice games and betting even money that the dice thrower would "seven out" before he made his point if it were a six or an eight. What would account for his success?

3. What is the probability of getting three heads in a row in flipping an "honest" coin? What probability rule is involved here?

4. If there is a 90 percent chance that no loss will occur, a 7 percent chance that one loss will occur, and a 3 percent chance that two or more losses will occur, what is the probability that only one loss will occur, if any losses occur at all? What probability rule is illustrated? Explain.

5. A risk manager is employed in a plant with 2,000 employees. The probability of occurrence in this industry of a permanently disabling injury in five years is found to be .10 (200 workers). The risk manager is willing to self-insure the risk if he can be 99 percent confident that over the five-year period the loss will not exceed .11 of the workers (220 workers). Assuming that disabling industrial injuries of a permanent nature are random and independent events and fall in accordance with a binomial probability distribution, does the risk manager have enough employees to self-insure? Show your calculations.

6. In problem 5 above, if the risk manager's required confidence level were reduced from 99 percent to 95 percent, would this change your answer? If so, how? Explain.

7. If there are three ranges of estimated probability of loss, .01, .05, and .10, and management believes that there is a .50 chance that the loss will be .01, .30 chance that the loss will be .05, and a .20 chance that the loss will be .10, what is the expected value of the probability of loss? Show calculations.

8. Explain how tree diagrams can be of assistance in risk management.

9. In using the expected utility approach to solve risk transfer approaches, formulate a decision rule which you believe is rational.

10. Give examples of what you interpret to be economic, physical, and social risk, as mental attitudes.

11. Do you consider yourself to be risk neutral, risk averse, or risk loving? In what situations, financial, physical, or social? Why? Discuss.

12. Consult the article by Ralph O. Swalm, "Utility Theory — Insights into Risk Taking," *Harvard Business Review*, vol. 44, Nov.–Dec. 1966, for the manner in which utility schedules are developed for the subjects in that experiment. Compare with the method used in this text. Which method do you prefer? What are the weaknesses of each? Discuss.

13. In your opinion, can a manager more easily assess a monetary value to "worry" than he can decide the size of probability values required before certain actions would be taken, as utilized in the method of developing utility schedules discussed in the text? Why?

14. Referring to Table 3–8, show how the decision might change if the value assigned to worry were made to equal, in each case, the total uncovered losses.

15. Ask yourself whether you would prefer to save $50 in cash on automobile insurance premiums or run a .30 chance of having a loss of $50. If you prefer the savings, ask yourself the question of whether you would prefer to save $25 in cash for a 10 percent chance of losing $200. If you prefer the savings, ask yourself whether you would prefer to save $100 in cash or run a five percent chance of losing $2,000. Which decision do you prefer? Assess the paired comparison method of reaching a decision on auto insurance.

16. A risk manager draws 90 employee numbers at random from each of the past 10 years. For these employees the average number of yearly work injuries is found to be 9, with a standard deviation of 1.

a) What is the standard error of the sample distribution?
b) At the 95 percent confidence level what will be the best forecast of the highest and lowest future average work injury rates?

17. Referring to Table 3–7, the text states "the dollar equivalent to a loss of utility of 6.885 would be about $880,000, by linear interpolation . . ." Show how such a figure was obtained, and explain why the insurer might not be expected to accept the risk at this premium.

4

Administration of the
Risk Management Function

Management of any function involves planning, organizing, and controlling. In the case of risk management, the administrator must consider problems such as policy formulation, handling risk, how the work will be organized within the firm, at what level decisions involving pure risk will be made, definition of goals and objectives, and setting up of controls to assure adequate discharge of risk management functions and their evaluation. These topics are discussed below under the following heads:

1. Policy formulation

2. Decision flow chart

3. Risk identification
   a. Loss exposure surveys and check-lists
   b. Use of financial statements
   c. Appraisals and valuation

4. Record keeping

5. Value vs. cost in risk management

6. Risk management objectives and evaluation

7. Common errors in risk management

POLICY FORMULATION

One of the first problems facing the risk manager is the definition of risk man-agement policies that he will follow. Before policies can be set, management objectives must be chosen. Obviously, these policies should be formulated with the assistance of top management. As Robert Rennie has observed, ". . . growth is the dominant motivation of modern corporate management . . . it is equally clear that risk and uncertainty are major barriers limiting such growth. The more ambitious the plans for expansion, the greater will be the physical risks and uncertainties of future events."[1] Thus, the function of risk management is closely linked with the basic policies of top management, and careful policy formulation for risk management becomes essential if general management's objectives are to be achieved.

Policies serve as a guide to action. They serve, in a broad way, as a set of rules to follow, and lay out constraints to action. Policies may be broad or narrow, major or minor, short term or long term. Policies are adopted to conserve the time of management so intensive individual consideration does not have to be given to each separate decision involving risk. Risk management policies will also be formed in the light of objectives set down for the risk man-

[1] Robert A. Rennie, "The Measurement of Risk," *The Journal of Insurance*, March 1961, p. 85.

agement department. Typical objectives are discussed later in this chapter.

Examples of general statements of risk management policies are: (1) It shall be the policy of the company to reduce as much as possible the costs of risk of loss to the firm which would have the effect of endangering the solvency of the firm, (2) It shall be the policy of the company to transfer to others the risk of loss to the firm which shall exceed X dollars, and to assume any loss less than this amount, (3) It is the policy of the company to employ the techniques of loss prevention to the maximum extent possible, to set aside reserve funds to meet unexpected losses above X dollars, and to transfer to commercial insurers or to others any losses which may exceed X dollars. Detailed policies are sometimes spelled out in manuals guiding risk management administration.

Effect of Risk Profiles

One factor that will have influence on the type of policy selected by management in the handling of risk is the risk profile of both top management and the risk manager himself. If, for example, subjective risk attitudes are not considered, difficulties in administration may arise. A risk loving management who employs a risk averting risk manager may find it difficult to carry out policies involving high risk retention in certain areas. (See Chapter 3 for a discussion of risk profiles.) On the other hand, a risk loving risk manager working for a risk averse top management may assume risk never intended by his superiors. In formulating sound risk management policy, therefore, one of the first steps which should be taken is to study, either objectively or subjectively, the risk profiles which characterize the firm's managers. Alderson and

Green observed that in one study, if top level managers in a firm had specified that the company goal was to obtain a 20 percent return on new investments, lower level managers tended to attach little significance to rates of return above 20 percent and tended to assign strongly negative utility values to rates of return below 20 percent. Because of differences in risk attitudes, the company ran the risk of losing out on profitable investments above the 20 percent level, even though the risk element was only slightly more in given cases. On the other hand, if the rate of return on a project was below 20 percent, it might be discarded, even though risk was sufficiently lower to justify the project.[2] In risk management decisions, a similar example is found when a risk averse manager insures property whose loss would be relatively inconsequential to the firm, or when a risk loving manager accepts insurance with a deductible account too high considering the limited financial capacity of his firm.

THE DECISION FLOW CHART

In carrying out his functions, as we have seen (see Chapter 2), the risk manager has several tools at his disposal: assumption or retention, insurance, other types of transfer (such as leasing), avoidance of the risk, abatement of the hazard through loss prevention, and diversification. The risk manager will normally utilize all of these methods in varying degrees, depending on the type of loss to which he is subjected, the severity of the possible loss, the types of hazards faced, and the costs involved in utilizing each of these methods. A

[2] Wroe Alderson and Paul E. Green, *Planning and Problem Solving in Marketing* (Homewood, Illinois: Richard D. Irwin, Inc., 1964), p. 165.

chart showing the structure of decision making in risk management is given in Figure 4–1.

Recognition

Some comments about Figure 4–1 may help clarify the procedures it suggests. Recognition of possible sources of loss is perhaps the most difficult and challenging aspect of the job of the risk manager. This task is aided by proper use of surveys discussed below. Obvious sources of loss such as fire, explosion, windstorm, liability suits, loss of key personnel, and interruption of

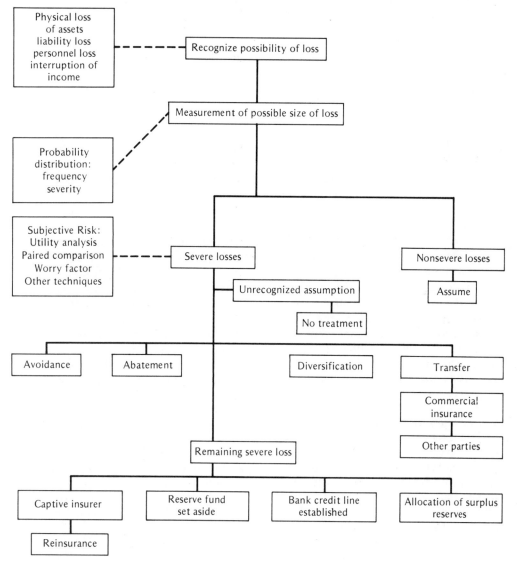

FIGURE 4–1.   A Decision Flow Chart in Handling Risk.

income due to defined perils are usually well known to most risk managers and present few recognition problems. Less obvious are often the ones which produce expensive and often embarrassing losses which no one expected. In one case, for example, a firm acquired the assets of another company and discovered too late that the other management had not carried fire insurance on one of the key buildings, which was destroyed by fire after the acquisition was consummated. The firm brought legal action against its insurance agent for failing to examine the terms of the sale which required the acquiring firm to carry the insurance. In another case a firm relied heavily on loss prevention methods as a substitute for adequate fire insurance. This was carried out through an extensive sprinkler system which management felt virtually guaranteed the safety of the operation. Unfortunately, an explosion cut off the water supply on which the sprinkler system depended and the entire building was destroyed in the ensuing fire. In another case, a resourceful risk manager recognized that the firm's profits on a given export shipment of perishable goods might be lost in the event that some sort of political action of the importing country might delay delivery, thus producing spoilage and loss of the goods. He succeeded in obtaining coverage against such a peril. In another case, an alert risk manager noticed the possible existence of a large, unfunded pension liability in a company being considered for acquisition. Later investigation proved that the pension system indeed had very large unpaid obligations, discovery of which permitted the acquiring firm to reduce the purchase price of the new acquisition by several million dollars.

Measurement

Once the source of loss has been recognized, management must measure its possible size and make an evaluation of its severity. The problem of measuring losses through probability assessments and the development of probability distributions has been discussed in Chapter 3. Additional discussion on the keeping of adequate records and maintenance of property appraisals to assist in this task will be presented below.

Severity

It should be obvious that potential losses which will cause no particular hardship to the firm may be most economically assumed and paid for as they occur out of working capital as a cost of doing business. A common error in risk management is to insure property which no longer exists, which has been sold, or which would otherwise not be worth insuring. In one case, for example, a firm was insuring old rental houses on land scheduled for future plant expansion. These houses were to be demolished; the rental income was not a significant income to the firm, but only covered minimum maintenance costs. If the houses were destroyed, obviously no particular hardship would result, and the property would not be rebuilt. In another case, it was found that insurance premiums were still being paid on rented automobiles even though they had been returned to the rental agency, and forty lawnmowers had been insured on policies with $50 deductibles.[3]

Decisions as to which losses are severe and which are not is not a partic-

[3] "Hot Item in New Jersey City: Insurance Bungles," *Business Insurance*, September 11, 1972, pp. 1–2.

ularly easy problem, as was discussed in Chapter 3. The methods of utility analysis, paired comparison, the worry factor method, or other techniques to measure subjective risk attitudes toward loss are available as formal methods of determining severity. Most commonly, however, the matter of severity will probably be, in practice, a subjective judgment by management without formal analytical tools. A serious problem is that of unrecognized assumption of severe losses, some of which may cause the insolvency of the company. Obviously this is one pitfall which should be avoided completely, if possible. As pointed out above, nevertheless, many firms will assume severe risks without realizing it. Constant vigilance is necessary to ferret out such risks and take action to prevent unrecognized assumption of severe risks.

Standard methods to handle the severe and recognized risk of loss are identified in Figure 4–1 as avoidance, abatement, diversification, and transfer, which were discussed in Chapter 2. Any remaining severe loss exposure that cannot be handled by these methods must nevertheless be considered. One technique to handle these risks suggested in Figure 4–1 is the use of the reinsurance market through a self-owned or captive insurer which does not retain a significant portion of a loss exposure, but instead passes most or all of the risk to a separate reinsurance company. The firm's wholly owned insurer may not only take much of the parent company's risk, but in addition may solicit business of other firms.

Setting aside a reserve fund for losses is another method of handling the risk of remaining severe losses, although it is probably not used widely because it means keeping the funds in savings accounts or other liquid invest-ments which usually produce a rate of return lower than the firm could earn on the same funds invested in its business. Allocation of surplus for contingencies is also a widely employed method of recognizing the risk of severe loss. The difficulty with this method is that it is nothing more than a bookkeeping entry on the balance sheet, removing amounts formerly shown as unassigned surplus, and placing them in specially earmarked accounts for possible losses. If the loss occurs, the surplus account obviously does not provide funds out of which to pay the loss. It may, however, have the effect of warning management of the possible loss and encouraging more conservative dividend policies or other management policies or practices.

Obtaining credit lines at banks for possible losses is also a method of handling the remaining severe loss. If the loss occurs, management has the advantage of having advance assurance from the bank that credit will be available to restore the property. Obviously, this credit would be in the form of a loan which would have to be repaid. Fees for stand-by credit are often very low for firms with good credit ratings. While this method of handling risk is obviously not as secure as the insurance method, it may be superior to doing nothing at all about large loss exposures. If the firm waits until it has had a large loss before seeking credit, its bargaining position for credit terms is usually sharply reduced below what it would be if advance arrangements had been made.

RISK IDENTIFICATION

As noted above, the recognition and identification of sources of loss from unexpected events is one of the prime tasks of the risk manager. The importance of this task can hardly be over-emphasized, since the very survival of the firm as a business enterprise may depend on advance attention given to it. Two major techniques of risk identification are (1) loss exposure surveys and checklists and (2) use of financial statements.

Loss Exposure Surveys and Checklists

One method for developing an orderly review of loss exposures is the loss survey or checklist. Prepared checklists are available, but it is obvious that many items on these lists will not apply to given firms. For example, the American Management Association has prepared a lengthy survey form designed to obtain information on nearly every aspect of the operations of any business firm, large or small.[4] It is organized according to major types of insurance exposures, such as those relating to crime, transportation, physical loss to buildings and contents, business interruption, automobiles, boats and aircraft, plate glass, and others. Questions are developed to elicit information needed to insure the losses and are arranged according to the type of insurance available. In using even a comprehensive checklist it is possible that the risk manager may overlook important exposures. Many exposures that a risk manager must deal with may be unique to his firm. Therefore, the checklist employed in a given case should be tailored specially for a given firm after careful study of the exposures faced by that firm. Once prepared, it should be updated at least annually.

[4] A copy of *Fact Finding Techniques in Risk Analysis* may be obtained by writing to the American Management Association, 135 West 50th Street, New York, N.Y. 10020. See Appendix A.

A checklist for property exposures in a department store is illustrated in Figure 4–2. Separate schedules should be developed showing values exposed, insurance coverage applicable, person responsible for paying premiums, special provisions applicable, etc. Checklists should also be developed by the risk manager for the liability and personnel exposures. Liability checklists, for example, may cover possible liability arising out of losses from use of the premises, elevators and escalators, products sold, professional services rendered, from outside sponsorships of races or other athletic events, new construction, acts of subcontractors, installation work on premises of others, contractual liability assumed, officers and directors liability, and ownership of vacant land. Personnel checklists may cover such items as industrial injuries, dishonesty loss, loss through death or disability of owners or key personnel, loss through medical or hospitalization expense, pension liabilities, liability to personnel arising from union contracts, and others.

A checklist may show as much or little information as desired: specific locations of property; special perils which exist; nature and extent of insurance, if any; and the existence of formal appraisals. Once an appropriate checklist has been developed the risk manager should attempt to identify as closely as he can exactly what loss the firm would suffer if the property were destroyed, how it might be destroyed, what public or employee liability the firm faces in its operations, and how the firm proposes to deal with the situation in each case. In this way the chance of overlooking important exposures is reduced, and the chance of insuring values of an inconsequential nature is also reduced.

An advantage of the checklist is that it warns the management of the firm to study loss exposures or to make

Item	Location	Replacement cost or possible loss	Depreciation applicable	Risk Handling method used
Property:				
1. Buildings				
Main store				
Branch stores (A, B, C, etc.)				
Warehouses (A, B, C, etc.)				
2. Inventories and supplies				
Dept. 1				
Dept. 2				
Dept. 3				
3. Equipment in buildings				
Data processing				
Office machines				
Cash registers				
Boilers or furnaces				
Fixtures and counters				
Air conditioning				
Alarm and detection				
4. Leasehold, improvements				
5. Property belonging to others				
Customers				
Employees				
Owners of concessions				
In branch stores				
In warehouses				
In transit (domestic, foreign)				
6. Other property				
In open storage				
In transit				
Accounts receivable				
Mortgagees' interests				
Leased property				
Value of favorable leases				
Signs				
Insured's personal property				
Especially valuable property (gems, paintings, statues, valuable papers, securities, money, books, records, etc.)				
Safes and vaults				
Information stored in EDP tapes				
7. Powered vehicles				
Autos and trucks, owned and leased				
Other motorized equipment				
Aircraft, boats				
8. Consequential losses				
Profits				
Fixed charges				
Payrolls				
Rental income				

FIGURE 4–2. Property Loss Exposure Checklist for a Department Store.

decisions on matters formerly neglected. For example, in Figure 4–2, the management must estimate the value of the information stored on tapes in the electronic data-processing system, the value of customers' and employees' property, and the value of property in transit. Management must decide upon appropriate risk-handling methods, the size of insurance deductibles, the method of reporting fluctuations in inventory values to the insurer, and the possible loss of profits and fixed charges in case of interruption of business due to some peril.

Risk Identification Using Financial Statements

Analysis of financial statements may be a useful tool in helping the risk manager to identify systematically various company risks and to ensure that important items are not omitted from checklists as discussed above.

The Balance Sheet

Detailed examination of each asset and liability item may produce information relating to risk of loss that might otherwise be overlooked. Examples of such an analysis include the following:

1) Cash. Management of company cash may involve risks of physical loss while cash is being taken to the bank for deposit. The perils of forgery, theft, bank failure, employee infidelity, as well as physical destruction represent sources of possible loss of cash. The management of petty cash as well as bank deposits should be reviewed. Adequacy of safes and internal control procedures should be examined. In one case a bookkeeper stole a large sum of money from a stamp fund over a period of twenty years. The thefts were not detected by normal auditing procedures because each individual theft was small.

2) Securities. Securities may be lost in much the same manner as cash. Some firms keep securities on their premises instead of banks. The risk manager should institute procedures to reduce the risk of loss of securities, after a thorough review of management systems over these assets. In one case the risk manager arranged to have brokers deliver newly purchased securities directly to the bank so as to avoid any risk of loss from internal corporate handling.

3) Accounts receivable. Company assets represented by accounts receivable are subject to loss by many perils other than the obvious bad debt losses. Above-normal loss may stem from destruction of the debtor's plant due to uninsured perils, death or disability of the debtor, dishonesty or business incompetence of the debtor. Accounts may be uncollectible because the debtor has a legal complaint against the seller stemming from misrepresentation of the goods, false advertising, or failure to honor warranties. Finally, accounts may be concentrated among a small number of customers, thus increasing the relative risk of loss due to any of the above perils which happen to any one account.

4) Inventories. The risk manager needs to examine detailed information of the types of inventories used, where they are located, when they are scheduled to be used, the ease and speed with which alternative sources of supply may be arranged, how hazardous inventories are used and stored, who is responsible for the safety of each type of inventory, and the particular hazards that may characterize each class of inventory — e.g., explosive or inflammable items.

5) Buildings and equipment. In risk management audits it is common to find that many building and equipment exposures are either overlooked com-

pletely or carry duplicate insurance coverage. A formal review of all such items carried as assets is necessary for sound risk management. Many of the questions noted above for inventories may be determined for buildings and equipment as well. In addition, buildings in the process of construction, leased equipment and buildings, elevators, generators, boilers, and fuel tanks carry special hazards that usually require the attention of the risk manager. Thus, the firm may wish to insure the builder's risk and to ascertain the continued maintenance of liability and workers' compensation coverage by the builder. Obligations under contracts may expose the firm to certain losses, *e.g.*, a lease or purchase agreement may require assumption of liabilities for negligence of others.

6) Automobiles. Although autos and trucks are not usually identified separately on the balance sheet, most firms have a large exposure to loss from this source which requires sound risk management procedures. Questions are raised as to who drives each car or truck, how distant the operation is from headquarters, the extent to which employee-owned or hired cars are used in company business, extent of liens, replacement costs, etc.

7) Miscellaneous assets. The risk manager must exercise considerable alertness to detect unusual asset exposures. In one case the risk manager of a larger farmers' cooperative realized that the firm had an exposure of loss to catfish grown in farmers' ponds under special contracts. He negotiated insurance coverages against loss by water pollution, forest fire, and other perils. In another case the risk manager of an electrical utility recognized that water behind a dam was in fact an asset subject to loss, since dam breakage would result in loss of revenues from water-powered electric generators. A decision was reached to insure the water against such loss.

8) Accounts or notes payable. An investigation of payables may reveal exposures to loss of concern to the risk manager. For example, if payments must be made in foreign currency, a risk of loss exists from increases in the market price of this currency at the time of payment of the account. As another example, an investigation of a note payable or bonds may reveal that the creditor requires the firm to maintain certain insurance on property purchased with the loan proceeds. Obviously, the risk manager must investigate these matters and see that his firm is in compliance.

9) Financial solvency. The risk manager should be concerned with the ways in which the general financial position of the firm affects pure risk management. Obviously, when there is a weak statement (*e.g.*, large liabilities in relation to assets), the firm's credit at the time of a fire or other catastrophe will be less than it might otherwise be. In some cases, the risk manager may work with the treasurer to arrange standby bank credit as a substitute for insurance.

The Income Statement

Analysis of the income statement can also be of great help in the process of risk identification. The following items are illustrative:

1) Sales. Analysis of the composition and type of sales revenues may answer questions about risks of loss from foreign sales, sales on credit, dependence on a few customers, sales dependent on franchises or licenses which could be lost by failure to meet certain requirements, product liability, seasonality of sales, terms of sale, etc.

The risk manager should ask questions such as these: Do terms of sale require the firm to carry transportation insurance? To what extent will sales be hurt if the manufacturing plant is shut down wholly or partially by fire? How will sales be affected by a shutdown at a supplier's or customer's plant? To what extent will interruption of the business result in permanent loss of customers, and what steps should be taken to minimize this loss?

2) Miscellaneous income. In some cases examination of miscellaneous sources of income may lead to discovery of certain risks. For example, the existence of rental income may point to real estate the firm owns. Is this real estate properly protected? Income from a franchise might point to a liability risk resulting from acts of the franchisee which could cause loss to the risk manager's firm.

3) Expenses. An analysis of expense items can often reveal a host of potential risks. Direct labor expense reflects the industrial accident exposure. Wage agreements will usually contain obligations for insurance coverage on employees and other employee benefits. Analysis of travel expenses can reveal the location and type of travel, including use of employee cars and hired cars, employment of temporary help by salesmen, use of watercraft or aircraft, etc. Rental expense can pinpoint the existence of risks in connection with leased property. Research and development expense may reveal risks in areas outside the normal operations of the firm, and should be examined carefully by the risk manager. Finally, the risk manager can determine the extent of fixed expenses, those which must be met even if the business is shut down by some fortuitous event. In many cases the business interruption loss is greater than direct loss from perils such as fire, explosion, or windstorm.

Appraisals and Valuation

Part of the task of risk identification is not only to identify possible sources of loss, but in addition, to appraise the value of property or determine the income exposed to loss. In general the appraisal of property and income determination for risk management purposes presents different problems than appraisal for tax purposes, or for other financial or accounting purposes. For example, fire insurance policies may state that they will indemnify the insured for the replacement cost of property less an allowance for depreciation, without detailing how these quantities will be determined. The risk manager should give attention to these questions *before* any loss occurs. Additional discussion of the types of records needed by the risk manager for appraisal purposes is given below.

RECORD KEEPING

The risk manager should maintain certain records, or have these records quickly available in other departments, for several purposes:

1. To furnish information on the existence and status of all insurance policies, endorsements, and agreements, including expiration dates, premium costs, policy limits, where responsibility lies for paying the premium, and other information. The availability of such records for proving losses is obvious, but they serve many other collateral purposes as well. For example, year-to-year comparisons of insurance costs in specific areas can reveal trends upward or downward, and can prompt investi-

gations of alternative methods of risk handling if costs rise too much. Such records can help prevent unintended lapsation of coverage, through overlooking expiration dates or failure to pay premiums on time.

It is not uncommon for business firms to toss all insurance policies, premium receipts, endorsements, and other documents relating to insurance in a file drawer, or even worse, in a cardboard box in some dusty corner. Several examples of this have been discovered by students of the authors who were making case investigations of risk and insurance management. Obviously, such a process is not equivalent to proper record keeping, even though all these documents represent the original sources for much of the information needed. Such procedures invite many unnecessary problems. For example, since notice of policy expiration may either be lost or may not be sent at all from the agent or the insurer, coverage may lapse without adequate policy controls. Neither do such methods of record keeping permit effective control over insurance agreements, costs, or coverage.

2. To furnish information on reporting of inventory levels, payrolls, safety inspections, new automobile purchases or sales, and other types of data often required under insurance policies. For example, many business firms have fluctuating inventories and insure them under coverages which require regular reporting to the insurer of the values exposed. Failing to report may reduce or eliminate coverage entirely, or may subject the insured to coinsurance penalties in the event of loss. Periodic payroll audits by the insurer are made to determine workers' compensation insurance premiums. Since different premium rates apply to different occupational classes, efficiency demands that payrolls

be properly classified so that excessive premiums are not being paid on occupational classes no longer existing. In one case, for example, it was discovered that a firm was paying insurance premiums on the payroll of a subcontractor working on a certain project, when in actuality, these costs were being paid by the subcontractor to a separate insurer.

3. To furnish information on losses incurred, losses reimbursed by insurance, losses unreimbursed by others, loss frequency, causes of loss, and other types of information about losses. These data are valuable for many reasons. Complete loss information is invaluable to the risk manager if he wishes to employ competitive bidding for new insurance coverage or to negotiate for lower rates when existing insurance coverage comes up for renewal, or to negotiate for premium refunds under experience or retrospective rating plans. The insurance buyer is the only source for much of this information, since to gather it from insurers is usually difficult, time-consuming, or simply not possible at all because the insurers lack the information. Complete data on loss frequency provides the risk manager with a tool for estimating future losses in his firm, and helps him to make more rational choices as to the various methods of handling risk, as discussed in Chapter 3. Analysis of the causes of loss provide the risk manager with concrete information needed to develop better loss prevention or safety programs. For example, it is well known that sprinkler systems to reduce fire loss have been extremely effective, and usually pay for themselves in a few years by the savings produced in fire insurance premiums. Safety lectures and other procedures to reduce industrial injuries have gradually reduced industrial injuries over the years. Loss cause data

help the firm eliminate obvious sources of loss, such as exposed machinery or inadequate electrical controls.

Another valuable use of loss data is to analyze these losses in terms of size so that insurance deductibles can be selected wisely. If it is discovered, for example, that 80 percent of all collision losses to trucks or other vehicles fall under $250, serious consideration should be given to selecting automobile coverage with a deductible of this amount, rather than a more common deductible of $100. Otherwise, the insured is "trading dollars" with the insurer, whose premium must be high enough to cover the loss plus an additional charge for its overhead of 35 to 50 percent.

4. Another important type of record keeping lies in appraisals of values for insurance purposes. Independent firms such as the American Appraisal Company, or Marshall and Stevens in the United States are often employed to perform this task. Appraisals of property values are necessary in order to prove losses under insurance contracts. They must be kept reasonably current. The Standard Fire Policy, on which most property insurance in the United States is based, places the burden of proving a loss upon the insured. Although the insurer or the loss adjustor may assist the insured in proving amounts of his loss, it is obvious that without adequate records the job cannot be done properly. Regular accounting records usually show only the original cost, the applicable depreciation, and the current book value of the property. This information is of limited value for insurance purposes because under most property insurance contracts the basis for settling claims is the current *replacement cost* of the prop-

erty, less an allowance for depreciation. Often the contract calls for waiving the deduction for depreciation if the coverage is endorsed for replacement cost insurance. Regular accounting records may not be kept so that this information can be conveniently extracted in the form really needed for insurance loss settlement procedures.

The task of proving losses may be doubly difficult if the fire or other peril has destroyed, wholly or partially, the firm's accounting records. This implies that the risk manager should either keep separate records himself, with duplicates stored in an outside safe depository, or arrange with the accounting department to do so. Many risk managers supplement written records with photographs of the property itself. It is significant that a widely sold insurance known as "accounts receivable and valuable papers" is carried precisely for meeting the extra expenses involved in reconstructing destroyed records and in meeting the losses incurred because of inability to collect accounts due to destroyed records evidencing these debts. Such insurance, valuable as it is, is no substitute for prior safeguarding of the records, or providing duplicate records elsewhere.

VALUE VS. COST IN RISK MANAGEMENT

A significant problem for management is to compare the cost of risk handling and risk management with the financial returns of this function. The costs of insurance, loss prevention, transfer fees, and lost opportunities due to the presence of risk can be very substantial. In the United States, for example, it has been estimated that insurance premiums account for about 19 percent of the national income.[5] While many types of risk management costs are, for all practical purposes, compulsory for the firm, many others are discretionary. Intelligent evaluation of the returns on risk management is essential if this function is to be properly controlled. As Rennie has stated,

To the extent that the risk manager can improve his techniques for measuring risk, and to the extent that he can reduce uncertainty, he can extend the growth horizons of the firm . . . If the risk manager shuns this opportunity to broaden his conception of risk management within the firm, he may find that he has become a minor functionary, performing routine tasks developed by other specialists.[6]

Evaluation of the returns to risk management involve more than justifying the risk manager's salary and expenses; rather, it involves a careful analysis of the extent to which risk management covers its cost by expense reduction, profit improvement, and creation of new profit opportunities. A more fundamental problem is the measurement of the cost of risk itself, in order that subsequent reductions in this cost may be compared to the cost of efforts to reduce it.

The Cost of Risk

The cost or burden of risk in the enterprise should be distinguished from the costs incurred through losses themselves. The cost of loss may be the full value of an asset totally destroyed by some peril. The cost of risk is the cost

of bearing the uncertainty of occurrence of the loss. This uncertainty exists in the minds of management's executives and is subjective in nature. The full measure of its cost may never be known exactly because it may be impossible to measure the value of lost profit opportunities which are avoided because of the existence of risk, the loss of executive capacity induced because of worry, or the cost of instability of profits caused by unpredictable losses. (See discussion of ways to measure subjective risk — e.g., the worry factor — in Chapter 3.) Management typically attempts to minimize the cost of bearing risk while simultaneously maximizing returns. The inefficient handling of risk can produce very large losses, even bankruptcy of the firm.

The Cost of Risk Management

The costs of risk management include (a) salary and expenses of the risk manager and his staff, (b) insurance premiums, (c) uninsured losses, (d) the cost of loss prevention activities, and (e) the cost of risk transfers and risk avoidance methods (e.g., lease payment and extra costs of purchasing services from outsiders). Estimates of these expenses can be derived in most firms through some modest amount of cost analysis. It is important to recognize that the cost of risk management is more than the cost of insurance or the risk manager's salary.

How Costs May be Reduced

Methods of reducing the cost of risk and the cost of risk management are sufficiently complex that separate chapters in this book are devoted to them. (See Chapters 6 and 14.) Some illustrative examples are appropriate at

[5] Mark R. Greene, *Risk and Insurance*, 4th ed. (Cincinnati: South-Western Publishing Co., 1977), p. 103.

[6] Rennie, "Measurement of Risk," p. 87.

this point, however. First, appropriate use of deductibles on insurance contracts potentially can save large sums and reduce the cost of risk transfer. For example, suppose that by accepting a $250 deductible (as opposed to $100 deductible) on collision damage to trucks, typical annual premiums can be reduced by $100 per truck. This is equivalent to exchanging an uncertain loss of $150 for a certain saving of $100. Unless the annual probability of collision loss exceeds 66⅔ percent, it would pay to accept the deductible. (See further analysis of this problem in Chapter 3.)

Second, consider the case of a firm launching a new venture under the direction of an executive who has developed the idea and for whom no immediate replacement is available. Assume that a relatively large sum is being invested, say $1,000,000, and that the potential returns are 20 percent, or $200,000 annually. A risk exists that the executive in charge will die or become disabled before the venture is sufficiently established so that it can be maintained with other personnel. If this event occurs, there is a strong probability that 75 percent of the initial investment will be lost. Management may transfer this risk to an insurer through a $1,000,000 short-term life insurance policy endorsed for disability income protection. The cost of the premium on this contract may be far less than the burden of running the risk as perceived by management and by the investors.

Third, suppose an insurer proposes to increase the required deductible or to increase the insurance premium on a certain policy. The risk manager can investigate the reasons for this action and take steps to minimize its impact. In one case an insurer proposed to increase a flood insurance deductible from $25,000 to $100,000 at a certain loca-tion. The risk manager of the firm visited the city where the increased deductible was to be effective and studied the flooding history at that location. It was found that the only recorded flood occurred several years previously when six inches of rainwater flooded the shop, with minimal damage. Confronted with this evidence, the insurer was persuaded that its proposed action was unjustified.[7]

Fourth, by proper planning the risk manager can effect large savings in income tax dollars. A major example lies in arranging pension or profit-sharing contributions so that all of the requirements for tax deductibility are met. If a firm is in the 50 percent tax bracket, $1 paid into a pension fund which is qualified for tax purposes, actually costs the firm only $.50 in after-tax income. Similarly, if a pension fund is made noncontributory (the employer pays all of the cost and the employee pays nothing) substantially more dollars can be paid into the fund than would be the case if the plan were contributory. This occurs because if an employee is first paid $1 and asked to contribute to his own pension fund, he must first pay federal and state income taxes on the $1, netting perhaps $.75, thus reducing his contribution 25 percent. (See Chapter 12 for a fuller discussion of this problem.)

Fifth, it has been shown that loss prevention expenditures often save substantial sums from two major sources: reduction in insurance premiums, and reduction in the cost of uninsured losses. For example, in one study it was reported that in a chain of department stores, some units had sprinkler systems and some did not. The stores with sprinklers had fire loss costs of 7.8 cents per $100 of inventory, compared to 28.5

[7] Edward D. Hansen, "Reducing Insurance Costs Through Risk Management," *Financial Executive*, November 1969, p. 52.

cents for nonsprinklered stores. Fire insurance rates on sprinklered stores were only 30 percent of the rates for nonsprinklered stores.[8]

RISK MANAGEMENT OBJECTIVES AND EVALUATION

It is the function of management to make regular and effective evaluations of executive performance. Without such evaluation, the function of management control cannot be properly discharged. Both strengths and weaknesses of the risk manager and his performance should be analyzed so that improvement can be continually made. Such an evaluation requires that ways be found to determine how well the objectives of the risk management function are being attained. This implies that objectives themselves be clearly set forth at the outset so that the risk manager can see how he will be evaluated and upon what factors his performance will be judged and rewarded.

Various objectives for risk management might be (1) that no "severe" losses disrupt the firm's financial position stemming from insurable risk, (2) that the costs of risk and risk management are kept within reasonable bounds, (3) that constant progress in loss reduction be recorded, (4) that methods be established under which objective analysis of the cost of risk of new projects in the firm can be determined in advance of financial commitments, (5) that long range plans for risk reduction and profit maximization be developed and periodic assessments of progress in fulfilling these plans be made, (6) that constant study be made

of new exposures to potential loss so that effective methods of handling the potential risk can be made.

It is understandable that many risk managers will not be in a position of authority, nor will they be given the responsibility, of meeting all of these objectives. The above list, however, is intended to be a typical, not comprehensive, list which is only suggestive of the objectives risk managers might be expected to meet. The list helps suggest to the risk manager ways and means by which evaluation may be made. For example, it is clear that the risk manager must have the cooperation of many departments, such as accounting and financial management, so that appropriate information is available to him to carry out his functions. It is clear that good record keeping is essential and that systems be established to provide a constant flow of the desired information for control purposes. For example, information on industrial accident frequency and costs must be available if the firm is to have someone be responsible for loss reduction.

In many cases, the managers set their own objectives and they outline how they intend to measure their accomplishments in meeting these objectives. Periodically, they are expected to report to their superiors on their achievements. Thus, the risk managers may frequently have the duty of developing reasonable objectives and measures of their accomplishments in order to assist their superiors in the evaluation process.

COMMON ERRORS IN RISK MANAGEMENT

Risk management shares with other types of management many types of errors which reduce efficiency and

[8] R. M. Duvall, "Should a Property be Sprinkler Protected?," *Risk Management Methodology* (a compendium of articles from the *Journal of Commerce*, 1971), p. 17.

profit. For example, failure to set goals and objectives in sufficient detail, as mentioned above, may result in inability to measure progress, loss of morale, and generally ineffective performance. Failure to keep adequate records is part of this problem. The following discussion, however, is devoted to three general areas in which risk management errors most frequently occur, that of risk exposure recognition, loss abatement, and insurance management.

Errors in Loss Abatement and Risk Recognition

Unless a risk is initially recognized little can be done to solve the problems it may create. This area is frequently neglected.[9] As shown in Figure 4–1, risk recognition is the first step in risk management. Specific examples of this type of error are:

1. Failure to install or maintain loss prevention systems, such as safety meetings for employees, fire-extinguishing equipment, guard rails, machinery shields, adequate lighting, regular cleaning, rubbish elimination, auto safety checks, regular inspection of dangerous equipment such as boilers, enforcement of safety rules and the wearing of safety clothing. One consequence of such failure is to cause insurance premiums to be higher than they might otherwise be, in addition to direct losses caused by accidents or loss of employee efficiency. For example, many firms do not require initial or continuing physical examinations and analysis of employees who are working in positions requiring specific physical health standards. This failure may increase accidents, which may in turn produce partial shutdowns, loss of efficiency by use of substitute

[9] Russell B. Gallagher, "A Practical Approach to Risk Management," *Business Horizons*, vol. 3, no. 2, Summer 1960, pp. 78–86.

personnel, and may cause product liability claims caused by reductions in production-line quality.

2. Allowing employees to change the terms of sale of shipments, leaving merchandise shipments at the risk of the seller, even though title has passed to the buyer. In such a case any transportation insurance which the seller may have would not apply because the seller no longer has an insurable interest in the goods. The buyer may have arranged his insurance to exclude such shipments, believing that the goods are covered by the seller.

3. Salesmen may be allowed to make unsupported claims for products that are not designed to fulfill such claims. In this case, the firm is exposed to product liability suits.

4. Bids on production or construction contracts may be made without including the cost of insurance or other risk abatement or transfer costs in the bid price. In this case such costs must simply be absorbed and may reduce profits below what they would otherwise be.

5. Advertising programs may be designed with the use of copyrighted materials such as books, films, film clips, and articles, without obtaining appropriate releases, or waivers, or without paying the required indemnification from the owners of the copyrights. Such procedures expose the firm to damage suits for infringements.

6. Acquisition of real estate for expansion purposes without studies of subsurface conditions which might later cause loss. In one case a chemical manufacturer purchased some land including an area to be used as a settling basin for pollutants that could not be discharged into streams. It turned out that the subsurface of the land was porous limestone, and within a short period, the pollutants were entering the stream

sources.[10] In setting up new sites, management sometimes forgets to check to see if the available water supply will be sufficient for fire protection, without which physical damage insurance costs may be prohibitively great.

7. Design of plants or buildings without due regard to protection needs against loss or insurance costs. Many firms fail to obtain engineering studies of the consequences of given types of construction and plant layout. The use of sprinkler systems, noted previously, will minimize fire losses and pay for themselves in reduced insurance premiums within a short time. Use of fire resistant materials in the building construction will have similar effects. Designing plants so as to minimize losses by spreading out buildings and installations to prevent the spread of fire, should it occur, will also reduce fire losses should they occur. Locating storage buildings away from production centers will isolate possible fires and reduce their impact upon general operations. Termite protection cost is low when the building is under construction, but can be very costly after the building is in place. Many of these considerations are ignored in the planning stages when their cost can be minimized.

Errors in Insurance Management

Specific examples of errors which frequently occur in insurance management include:

(1) Inadvertent failure to purchase insurance on exposures subject to loss. This type of error often stems from failure to recognize the potential loss initially. For example, business interruption and employee fidelity losses may be overlooked. Loss also may stem from failure to arrange insurance to

cover automatically new property acquired, or in failure to report values to the insurer as required under existing contracts, such as under inventory reporting forms. In one case, just prior to a large explosion which damaged most of the buildings in a small Oregon community, a car dealer had just acquired a stock of parts for a new line of vehicles he was taking on. The excess inventory exceeded the limits of his coverage and also resulted in coinsurance penalties under existing contracts.[11] In another case, involving a merger, the acquiring firm was held responsible for insuring the property of the firm acquired, but had not done so, and a large fire loss was found to be uninsured.

(2) Underinsurance and *coinsurance penalties.* Failure to insure exposures for their full value when the firm cannot afford to self-insure the difference between the coverage actually purchased and the values exposed. In one study of small retailers, it was found that 16 percent of the firms covered less than 50 percent of the sound value of their buildings, loss of which they could ill afford in case of damage greater than 50 percent. In over half of these cases, the same firms had policies with 90 percent coinsurance clauses, in effect requiring the insured to carry 90 percent to value or share a portion of any loss. In these cases, an average of five-ninths of any partial loss would be recovered.[12]

(3) Insuring small potential losses and leaving large potential losses uninsured or underinsured. This type of

[11] Mark R. Greene, "The Effect of Insurance Settlements In a Disaster," *Journal of Risk and Insurance,* vol. 31, no. 3, (September 1963), pp. 384–86.

[12] Donald Watson and A. G. Homan, *Insurance Management Problems of Small Retailers* (Eugene, Oregon: University of Oregon Press, July, 1962), p. 20.

[10] *Ibid.,* p. 81.

error is typical in the field of liability insurance, where inadequate limits of liability are carried. In the small retailer study, about 10 percent of the firms carried bodily injury liability limits of less than $20,000 per accident. Only about 7 percent of the firms carried limits of $100,000/$300,000 or greater. Since the cost of raising liability limits is much less, proportionately, than the increase in limits, greater coverage is economical. The firms studied were in effect self-insuring the large loss, while insuring the relatively small loss. Yet, few obviously had the financial resources to withstand any large suit, such as might occur through product liability, or premises liability.[13] Another common example of this error is insuring property with low, or no, deductibles when large premium savings would be possible with even modest deductibles.

(4) Overinsurance — or insuring loss exposures no longer in existence. It seems surprising that many firms or organizations have such little control over insurance matters that premiums are paid out needlessly for exposures that do not exist, or are relatively small. In one report, for example, a municipality was found to be insuring 56 vehicles not listed on county inventories. Eight vehicles had been insured twice, resulting in premium overpayments of $900 for one year.[14] It is not uncommon to discover that multiple policies are being carried on such risks as medical losses, say by carrying auto-medical payments in addition to a group medical policy on employees and workers' compensation coverage. In the small retailer study,[15] 27 percent of the firms were

carrying plate glass insurance, even though over half of all glass losses falls below $100 and the general maximum exposure to loss was relatively small.

(5) Failure to pinpoint responsibility for insurance management. A common error in insurance management is failure to appoint persons within the firm who are charged with definite responsibility for insurance matters and authority to carry out this responsibility. Either this responsibility is haphazardly assigned to some assistant clerk who does little more than file policies, and deals with one or more insurance agents and brokers; or it is ignored entirely, the decision on insurance being taken by the general manager without particular study, control, or attention.

Another form of this type of error takes place when insurance responsibility is in effect delegated to an outside agent who is expected to make adequate recommendations as to the insurance needs of the firm and to place the appropriate coverage in the insurance market. Unfortunately, it is relatively uncommon for this responsibility to be delegated formally, in writing, so that the agent can be held accountable for results. Even worse, firms very commonly employ two or more agents to handle different insurance needs, with little or no coordination between them. Such practices result in overlapping of coverage, duplication of premiums, lack of control over insurance costs, gaps in coverage, nonconcurrency of coverages placed, and uneconomical purchasing in small quantities rather than the more economical and comprehensive blanket coverages. Seldom is the insurance agent given the type of information he really needs to do a thorough job of risk analysis within the firm. For example, in the study of small retailers, it was discovered that the sample of firms had an average of about two agents, and

13 *Ibid.*, p. 39.

14 *"Insurance Bungles,"* pp. 1–2.

15 Watson and Homan, *Problems of Small Retailers,* pp. 56–57.

nearly 20 percent had three or more agents with whom they dealt. Interviews with the managers showed that among the reasons for this situation were (1) 40 percent of the managers tended to distrust agents and were reluctant to divulge confidential information to them about the firm's business affairs; (2) managers believed that if they gave all of their business to one agent, insurance rates might be higher than before; (3) managers distrusted the "survey approach" presumably because they feared that such a method would disclose important gaps in their coverage, and that they were unwilling to pay out any more for insurance, even if it were demonstrated that increased coverage was needed, i.e., they were afraid of what the survey might reveal. (4) They believed that spreading the business around would encourage more trade with their firms by those affected, i.e., encourage reciprocity.[16]

(6) Failure to compare insurance prices, or to employ competitive bidding. Although the firm may pay great attention to shopping for the best price offered by suppliers in tangible goods and materials, there is a common belief that "insurance costs are all the same," and that it does not pay to employ competitive bidding in the field of insurance. In the small retailer survey,[17] for example, only 20 percent of the firms stated that they shopped for insurance. It has been demonstrated in many instances, however, that sometimes very large differences exist in the price charged for almost identical insurance coverage. In one case, competitive bids for public liability insurance in a small city revealed a price differential of $3,000 annually in the costs. In the small retailer survey a case was found

in which two firms each located in the same city carrying almost an identical policy had storekeepers' liability rates which varied by 100 percent.[18] A competitive bid for student term life insurance on a campus of 20,000 students revealed a price variation on identical coverage of approximately 50 percent. Substantial differentials in price exist even in lines of insurance which presumably are controlled by rating bureaus, such as fire insurance. Many of these differentials are due to differences in subjective underwriting interpretations about the property and its loss potential and characteristics. For example, the occupancy of a building may be classified differently by two different underwriters; in some cases the occupancy may have changed and the insured is entitled to a lower rate, but has not been granted this rate because his agent has not applied for a reduction or is unaware that the occupancy change has occurred, or that the insured is entitled to it. Competitive bidding will often reveal such opportunities for the bidders to reduce the rate. Good insurance cost control requires periodic episodes of shopping the market. Admittedly, more than price enters into the analysis of resulting bids, since other factors such as quality and quantity of insurer and agency services, completeness of insurance coverage, financial solidity of the insurer, loss adjustment policy, and other factors should be analyzed. Nevertheless, even after these and other factors are considered, insurance rates vary widely and it is mainly through competitive bidding that these variations can be discovered.

(7) Failure to review the financial position of the insurer before placing coverage. Although many insurers enter bankruptcy each year with losses to

[16] Ibid., pp. 62–63.

[17] Ibid., p. xix.

[18] Ibid., p. 42.

policyholders in the form of unpaid claims, it is still a common error in insurance management not to examine the financial condition of the insurer in whom the firm's security is entrusted. (See Chapters 15 and 16 for additional discussion.) Quite complete financial data are gathered and reported annually about most insurers, by such firms as A. M. Best Company and Standard and Poors. Annual reports are available in the offices of state insurance commissioners. Financial ratings, and policyholder ratings for each company are issued by Best. These ratings summarize the agency's opinion of the insurer and offer some guidance to the insured in selecting an insurer. In one analysis of these ratings, it was shown that about 25 percent of some 739 stock insurers, 5 percent of 338 mutuals, and a third of 62 reciprocal insurers covered by the rating agency were not rated, indicating generally that the insurer is too new for adequate evaluation. In this study about 1 percent of the stocks, 5 percent of the mutuals, and 3 percent of the reciprocals carried ratings which were generally unsatisfactory from the policyholder's point of view.[19] For most buyers, therefore, perhaps a third of all insurers either carry no ratings, or unsatisfactory ratings, such that it might be unwise to utilize their services unless absolutely necessary.

Unless such a source is consulted, the buyer is forced to rely on the judgment of the agent or broker in placing coverage. However, generally agents or brokers are not bound at law to guarantee the financial solvency of the insurer in which the coverage is placed. The insured therefore has little recourse against his agent if his insurer goes

bankrupt. At the very least, it would appear that the insured should carefully examine (a) the financial and policyholder ratings of the insurer, (b) the balance sheet data of the insurer to determine such standard ratios as net worth to debt, the ratio of sales premiums written to net worth, and (c) the total size of the insurer as measured by assets. It may be discovered, for example, that the insurer is smaller in asset size than the insured and lacks appropriate reinsurance facilities to handle the exposure.

(8) Failure to review insurance programs regularly and keep coverages and provisions updated to fit changing conditions. It is quite common in many firms to wait for insurance agents or brokers to offer to renew existing coverages with little or no revision, when current policies expire. The agent does not ask questions about changed conditions which should require increased or decreased coverage. Because of this, insurance may be carried on property no longer owned, may cover liability on operations no longer performed, and may fail to cover new property acquired, or liabilities assumed since the last renewal. Other errors in insurance coverage discussed above are much more likely to occur when there is no system established to alert the insurance manager that new exposures have been acquired or old ones eliminated, so that he can adjust insurance coverage appropriately.

(9) Failure to keep adequate insurance and loss records. All insurance contracts require the insured to prove claims. If current inventories of property are not available, it is easy to forget the very existence of property lost in a fire, much less permit the insured to establish the value of lost property. (See discussion of record keeping above.)

---

[19] Greene, *Risk and Insurance*, 2nd edition, p. 151.

SUMMARY AND CONCLUSIONS

1. An essential function of the risk manager is policy formulation. Risk management policies must be made up with the assistance and cooperation of top management. The risk-taking characteristics of both the risk manager and top management should be considered in formulating appropriate risk management policies.

2. The decision flow chart is an important tool in the administration of risk management functions. The major elements in the decision process are (a) recognition of the possibility of loss, (b) measurement of the possible size of loss, (c) dealing with risk of severe losses, and (d) dealing with risk of remaining severe losses which cannot be handled by traditional methods of avoidance, abatement, diversification, and transfer.

3. Another significant tool of risk management is the loss exposure survey and checklist. In general these surveys should be tailored to the particular needs of the firm and should be divided in accordance with the major classes of risks faced by the firm.

4. Record keeping is an important function of the risk manager. Very often the records required are not conveniently available from the regular accounting department, but must be kept separately by the risk management department. Among other things, the record-keeping function is necessary to keep track of the existence and status of all insurance records, to furnish information on exposures to loss, to furnish information on losses incurred and losses reimbursed, to assist in the recovery of claims from insurers.

5. In the evaluation of risk management the extent to which the risk manager reduces the cost of risk as well as the cost of performing risk management functions must be calculated. Various methods are available to reduce each of these costs. It is the function of general management to make regular evaluations of the performance of the risk manager.

6. Many unnecessary errors in risk management regularly recur. They include errors in risk abatement, loss recognition, and errors in the management of the insurance program. Common errors in the management of the insurance program include failure to compare prices, failure to pinpoint responsibility for insurance management, overinsurance, underinsurance, subjecting the firm to coinsurance penalties, insuring with financially unstable insurers, failure to review and revise risk programs on a regular basis, and failure to keep adequate insurance records.

QUESTIONS FOR DISCUSSION

1. Why should risk management policies be made and supervised by top management when risk management functions are generally performed at a fairly low level in the organization? Explain.

2. What conflicts may arise in risk management if top management is risk-loving and the risk manager is risk-averting, or *vice versa?*

3. Referring to Figure 4–1, consider the case of a firm which owns vacant land which it is holding for the eventual development of a mountain resort. What problems in loss recognition may arise from such ownership?

4. In handling remaining severe loss (see Figure 4–1): (a) contrast the use of bank credit lines with insurance, and (b) distinguish between setting a reserve fund aside and allocation of surplus reserve.

5. Develop a property loss checklist for a firm with which you are familiar, similar to that contained in Figure 4–2, but with special consideration given to the particular needs of the firm chosen. Which items appear on your list which are not on the list in Figure 4–2?

6. The text lists four major reasons for record keeping by the risk manager. Should the risk manager maintain records, when this function is normally carried out by the accounting department? Explain.

7. Following a severe windstorm and rain in which the insured's house was blown off its foundations and completely destroyed, the insurer denied a claim for loss on the grounds that only a foundation existed and there was no proof that a building was ever on the site. When the insured countered by arguing that he had been paying premiums on the building insurance for some years, the insurer stated that many insureds purchase insurance on sites in which they intended to build, but never completed the building. What type of record keeping might have helped the insured prove his loss to the insurers?

8. Do you think there is any difference between the cost of risk and the cost of risk management? Discuss.

9. An author gave three rules of risk management as follows: (a) Don't risk a lot for a little, (b) Don't risk any more than you can afford to lose, and (c) Consider the odds. Restate these rules in terms of concepts presented in the section common errors in risk management.

10. From an income tax standpoint, why are some risk managers reluctant to set aside reserve funds for losses, and instead prefer the use of insurance?

5

Loss Control

An important responsibility of the risk or insurance manager is that of leadership in the area of loss prevention and control. Loss control itself is an activity which must be carried on throughout the enterprise and on many different levels in the nation, state, and community. The risk manager is not solely responsible for loss control leadership, since this type of management must necessarily affect most executives and supervisors throughout the firm. Yet, because loss control is so important in its effect on the success of risk management, generally the risk manager must take a leading role in the planning, organizing, and controlling of activities that are directed at preventing or reducing losses. An outline of the major types of loss control and prevention, approaches to this activity, and economic aspects of the subject are explored below, under the following headings:

1. Concepts in loss control
   a. Hazard control
   b. The chain concept
   c. Human vs. mechanical concept
   d. Haddon's energy transfer approach
   e. System safety

2. Levels of approach
   a. Federal government
   b. State and local government
   c. Private insurers
   d. Firms
   e. Individuals

3. Rationale of loss control

4. Loss control and insurance

5. Loss control and government — OSHA

CONCEPTS IN LOSS CONTROL

Loss control may be defined as those activities designed to reduce, prevent, or otherwise control accidental events which produce economic or social loss. Loss control is aimed at reducing both the *frequency* and the *severity* of losses. Reducing the frequency of automobile accidents may require one type of approach, and reducing the severity of these accidents may require another approach. For example, employee driver education may be aimed mainly at reducing the frequency of accidents, and fast, emergency first aid service and enforcement of speed laws may be emphasized as important methods of reducing severity of loss from automobile accidents.

Hazard Control

In understanding loss prevention it is important to identify the concepts of physical, moral, and morale hazards. As defined in Chapter 2, a hazard is a condition which affects both the frequency and severity of losses. Physical hazards stem from tangible physical conditions, while moral and morale hazards stem from mental attitudes. Using automobile safety to illustrate, the physical hazards which are significant include vision-restricting weather, poor law enforcement, slick or icy roads, and unsafe vehicles. Moral hazards may be illustrated by allowing automobiles to be driven by those with unstable personalities, those with poor training in proper driving methods, and those whose social and psychological backgrounds lead them to take a definite mental attitude of disregarding the rights of others. Morale hazards are illustrated by allowing automobiles to be driven by those who may subconsciously be accident prone and who may take an attitude of indifference toward loss. In many cases youthful drivers who may possess immature personalities are characterized by the morale hazard, while those with criminal backgrounds often present a moral hazard as well as a morale hazard.

Recognizing that control over physical, moral, and morale hazards presents one approach to effective loss control, risk managers have organized their activities around a hazard control framework. Thus, sprinkler systems may be installed to reduce the physical hazard of fire, and driver training may be used to reduce the moral and morale hazard to automobile accidents. Internal accounting controls are employed to reduce the moral and morale hazards leading to embezzlements. The physical hazards to stealing tools may be reduced by requiring that small tools be checked in and out daily. Safety training programs are aimed at reducing industrial accidents stemming from improper mental attitudes toward safety. Machine guards are installed to reduce the physical hazards to industrial accidents.

The Chain Concept

It is also recognized that loss control may be viewed in a framework of a chain of events leading to loss. Links in the chain are the source of loss, reduction of hazards, minimization of loss, and salvage. Appropriate corrective action may be taken anywhere in the chain. (a) At the first link in the chain, for example, control may be exercised at the source. Thus, buildings may be constructed initially to resist fire; ships may be built to resist ocean storms; automobiles may have shock-absorbing bumper systems; and employee training may improve mental attitudes toward accident prevention. Education to improve the quality of life may be employed to improve health and increase life expectancy. Gun control laws may remove the instrument through which many lives are lost. Guard rails on highways can be buried to make driving safer. (b) At the second link, control may be exercised through continuous inspection and reduction of hazards that exist once the loss exposure already exists. For example, buildings, ships, and vehicles may be inspected regularly for hazards that may cause loss. Employees may be supervised closely to see that safe practices are being followed. (c) At the third link, control may be exercised through minimizing the loss once the accident has occurred. Thus, sprinkler systems may douse fires quickly, seat belts may prevent driver injuries after the collision, lifeboats may save the lives of passengers once the iceberg has been struck, and first aid stations and prompt medical attention may minimize the ultimate loss from industrial injury. (d) Finally, loss control may be exercised through effective salvage operations, once the damage has been done. Thus, physical and vocational rehabilitation can in many cases restore an injured worker to useful employment. Prompt action to sell property damaged by fire can minimize the economic loss that might otherwise result.

Human vs. Mechanical Concept

One philosophy of loss control states that it is most productive to concentrate upon the human being in preventing, avoiding, or reducing the consequences of loss. Another philosophy holds that it is best to concentrate on the mechanical or engineering approach — to make the physical, social, and psychological environment in which the human being operates a safer environment. To illustrate, the human approach to loss control would hold that to reduce industrial accidents it is best to enforce safety rules, help prevent unsafe acts which lead to accidents, and to instill loss prevention consciousness at all levels of management. The engineering approach would hold that it is most effective to concentrate on having safe mechanical conditions in a plant, such as good lighting, foolproof equipment, good housekeeping, and machine guards. This is not to state that either of these approaches should be used exclusively; rather it is a question of which should be emphasized. Often the answer to this question is one of economics, a problem to be discussed later.

An early protagonist of the human approach to loss prevention was W. W. Heinrich. In his studies of industrial ac-

cidents in the United States in the 1920's, Heinrich found that most accidents (about 88 percent) were a result of unsafe acts committed by workers and the remaining were caused by other factors such as defective equipment.[1] He developed the famous "domino theory" in which the accident sequence was seen as a row of five dominoes, as follows: social environment, fault of the person, unsafe act, accident, injury. Each factor produced the condition following it, ending in injury. Heinrich described a typical accidental injury as follows:

Assume that an employee in a manufacturing plant receives a fractured skull as the result of a fall from a ladder. Investigation discloses that he descended the ladder with his back to it, in willful disregard to instructions, and caught his heel on one of the upper rungs. The effort to train and instruct him and to supervise his work was not effective enough to prevent this unsafe practice. Further inquiry also indicated that his social environment was conducive to the forming of unsafe habits and his family record was such as to justify the belief that reckless tendencies had been inherited.

Here is a chain of circumstances and events that tie in with one another in unmistakable fashion. If ancestry and social environment had been free from criticism, it is probable that the injured person might have had a safer and better attitude and would have been more subject to control through supervision. If supervision had been more effective, the employee might not have committed the unsafe act even though he was inherently inclined to be reckless. If the unsafe act had not been committed, assuredly this particular accident would not have occurred, even if all the preceding factors had tended to promote it; and if the

[1] W. W. Heinrich, *Industrial Accident Prevention* (New York: McGraw-Hill Book Company, 1959).

accident had not occurred there could have been no injury.[2]

Heinrich argued that the easiest way to correct the conditions producing industrial injuries was to concentrate upon the unsafe act, since management could probably do little about either social environment or fault of the person. He felt that it was management's duty and responsibility to reduce accidents, and that the key man in this effort is the foreman. Heinrich estimated that management's attention to loss prevention was justified, if for no other reason, by the fact that indirect costs of accidents, such as ruined materials and lost time, amounted to four times the direct costs of worker injuries.

Haddon's Energy Transfer Approach

William Haddon's approach in analyzing the causes of loss[3] offers an interesting risk management guide to developing a formal strategy of loss control. Haddon draws attention to the fact that damages to individuals and property are essentially a result of unplanned, often rapid, releases of energy. Examples include hurricanes, fire, lightning, and vehicles. There are ten strategies in which this energy transfer process may be managed in such a way as to prevent or reduce the resulting damage. An outline of each strategy and an example of its use and effect is shown in Table 5–1.

It will be observed that Haddon's

[2] *Ibid.*, p. 18.

[3] William Haddon, Jr., "On the Escape of Tigers: An Ecologic Note," reprinted by Insurance Institute of America in *Topical Outline, RM 55 Risk Control*, May 1975, from *Technology Review*, May 1970 (Alumni Association of the Massachusetts Institute of Technology, 1970).

energy transfer approach contains some of the elements of both the chain concept and Heinrich's approach discussed above. An important advantage of Haddon's concept is that it focuses on the ways in which a common element or force, namely energy, may be dealt with, no matter what the particular type of loss may be. Thus, the concept can be applied to fire, flood, earthquake, death, disability, and to many other perils which involve energy transfers causing loss to persons or property.

In applying the above strategies, Haddon points out that they need not be employed successively, but rather as many as possible should be applied all at once. A risk manager might employ Haddon's strategies, for example, in a problem of dealing with the peril of fire in a warehouse where fuel supplies are stored. Strategy 1 could not be used unless it was decided not to store fuel on the premises at all, but Strategy 2 could be employed by reducing the amount of fuel, particularly hazardous fuel, stored at any one place or time. Strategy 3 would suggest that fire walls be built around fuel locations, and Strategy 4 might be used by storing fuel in small containers so as to reduce the concentration of burning, if a fire once started. Strategy 5 would suggest that fuel depots be separated from other property to which fire might spread, and Strategy 6 might result in protecting nearby properties with fire retardant or explosion-proof barriers. Strategy 7 might have application in that storage tanks or floors could be padded so as to reduce the chance of sparks which could ignite the fuel. Strategy 8 could result in having nearby buildings or other property made out of fireproof materials and Strategy 9 could suggest that the nearby properties, including the storage warehouse itself, be protected by fire and sprinkler systems. Finally, Strategy 10

TABLE 5–1

Strategy	Illustration
1. Prevent marshalling of energy in the first place.	1. Prevent workers from climbing to high places from which they may fall.
2. Reduce the amount of energy which is marshalled from which accidents may result.	2. Reduce the number of workers permitted to climb to high places.
3. Prevent the release of energy which has built up.	3. Build guard rails to prevent falls from high places.
4. Slow down the release of energy.	4. Reduce the height from which employees must work; slow down the rate at which explosives are permitted to burn.
5. Separate, in space or time, the energy which is released from the object susceptible to injury.	5. Prohibit entry to blasting areas during blasting periods.
6. Place a physical barrier between energy source and the object susceptible to injury.	6. Require workers to use safety helmets, or shoes, or eye glasses.
7. Modify the contact surface by rounding or softening edges.	7. Design cars with padded dashes; build toys without sharp edges.
8. Strengthen the object against damage by energy release.	8. Require fireproof building construction. Require workers to be vaccinated against disease.
9. Mitigate the damage which has not been prevented by above eight measures.	9. Use fire alarm systems, sprinkler systems, energency medical care facilities, storm warning systems.
10. Use rehabilitation and restorative techniques where damage has occurred.	10. Retrain injured workmen with permanent disabilities.

could be followed in case losses occurred by procedures involving adequate salvage development of more efficient rebuilding techniques, or utilization of better replacement materials.

Systems Safety

An approach to loss control which has received increasing emphasis is known as systems safety. Under this concept, a safety engineer conceives of a plant as a total system rather than concentrating on specific loss exposures. System safety was first developed by the U.S. Air Force as an engineering

discipline to assure the successful completion of weapon systems. Systems safety involves simultaneous consideration of each working part of a plant, such as factory layout, lighting, noise, ventilation, security, machinery design, and working rules. Utilizing mathematical techniques, the interrelationships and consequences of possible product defects can also be analyzed and predicted. In this way attention to loss control in a broad context is possible. For example, using systems safety the risk manager can achieve better control over future legal liability suits against the firm for defective products which may be attributed to negligent operations of the plant than would be otherwise possible. It is apparent that the systems safety approach utilizes both human and engineering methods to help prevent loss.[4]

LEVELS OF APPROACH

Loss control and prevention may be approached from several different levels in society: (1) federal government, (2) state and local government, (3) private insurers and insurer-supported associations, (4) firms, and (5) individuals.

Federal Government Activities

Increasingly the federal government has concerned itself with the problem of safety and loss prevention. Perhaps one of the most significant pieces of legislation passed in this field is the 1970 Occupational Safety and Health Act (OSHA), discussed in detail below. This act is sweeping in that it requires employers to maintain a work place free from recognized hazards that can cause death or physical harm to employees. It covers all business firms in interstate commerce except for mining and railroad industries, which are covered by other federal safety laws and programs.[5] Another federal agency under which loss prevention is a major function is the Food and Drug Administration which works toward making safer foods and drugs available. The National Highway Safety Bureau, the Army Corps of Engineers and the Bureau of Reclamation, the Federal Bureau of Investigation, the Federal Aviation Agency, the

National Bureau of Standards, and the U.S. Forest Service are among the other federal agencies working for loss prevention in their respective fields. In a larger sense, hardly an agency of government is not concerned in some way or other with loss prevention. For example, the armed forces have as their main goal the protection of the country and its allies from invasion by hostile forces.

An example of how federal governmental agencies operate is found in the work of the Bureau of Motor Carrier Safety. This agency, part of the Federal Highway Administration, has the responsibility of reducing accidents, injuries, and property losses caused by commercial vehicles. The agency deals with approximately 150,000 shipping firms which operate about 3 million medium and heavy commercial vehicles and employ about 5 million drivers. Road checks of vehicles are made, each requiring from 30 to 60 minutes. If unsafe conditions are found the vehicle can be declared out of service on the spot until deficiencies are corrected. A driver who has worked for more than a specified number of hours can be prohibited from driving any farther until he has rested. Drivers must meet certain medical standards and must carry a doctor's certificate attesting to their physical ability to drive. Seat belts are required on all vehicles operated in interstate commerce.[6]

State and Local Government

Hundreds of state and local agencies carry on loss prevention work. To mention only a few, there are state and local police forces, state fire marshall offices, local fire departments, water and

[4] "Systems Safety Spreads into Industry," *Business Week*, July 17, 1970, p. 57.

[5] Examples are the Federal Coal Mine and Safety Act, the Atomic Energy Act, and the Bureau of Railroad Safety.

[6] U.S. Department of Transportation Federal Highway Administration, *The Bureau of Motor Carrier Safety* (U.S. GPO, 1972).

sewer control agencies, automobile accident prevention agencies, (including statistical gathering groups), industrial accident commissions, building inspectors, public health agencies, and public schools and universities which teach safety training.

A recent example of loss prevention action at the city level is the enactment of building security laws. Under such laws building owners are required to install and maintain safety measures against such losses as burglaries. Such laws are justified as being equally important as laws regulating plumbing and electrical installations in buildings as public safety measures to ensure proper hygiene and protection against fire due to inadequate wiring or other electrical installations. One law, for example, required the use of given types of locks, bars over certain windows, and in some cases, burglar alarms and steel reinforced doors. The goal is to harden the target for burglars.[7] Not only are such measures successful in discouraging burglaries initially, but they allow more time for police to arrive because of the additional time it takes burglars to enter buildings. In one case burglary rates were reduced 33 percent through such measures over a period of about six years.[8]

Private Insurer Organizations

Many insurance companies and large agencies specialize in loss prevention work for their customers. Prominent among these are insurers specializing in given lines of insurance, such as workers' compensation, multiple-peril policies on large risks, credit insurance, glass insurance, surety bonding, boiler and machinery insurance, and health insurance. In many cases, especially where the size of the account is substantial, the insurer or agency will offer specialized loss prevention engineering services to the customer, including driver training, plant safety methods, and fire prevention engineering.

Insurer-supported organizations also perform many loss prevention services. The National Safety Council, for example, compiles highway accident statistics, conducts safety conferences, and performs other services to reduce accidents in public places. Underwriters Laboratories, one of the oldest insurer-supported groups, was formed in 1894 to test for safety in thousands of products produced by manufacturers. This service is performed for a fee to a manufacturer desiring an independent test of his product. If the product is certified as safe, the manufacturer may show this "UL" approval certificate on the label. The National Fire Protection Association is a national insurer-supported group to conduct research and establish standards for fire protection. The American Insurance Association, a successor organization to the National Board of Fire Underwriters, is the agency which classifies all cities and towns in the United States according to its fire protection services, information which is used for fire insurance rate making. This organization also assists state and local agencies in improving their fire prevention services.

An example of an insurer-supported organization which has been attacking the problem of preventing losses on the nation's highways is the Insurance Institute of Highway Safety. This institute has made notable contributions to many parts of the general problem of reducing loss of life and property in automobile accidents through efforts to improve highway safety. Studies by this organization have

[7] *Wall Street Journal*, April 27, 1973, p. 1.
[8] *Ibid.*

identified and measured major factors causing or intensifying the frequency or severity of loss from automobile accidents. For example, among the factors found to be directly associated with severe losses are: lightweight cars, cars without collapsible steering assemblies, state laws which do not require helmets to be worn by motorcycle riders, guardrail ends which are not buried, roadside signs which are not of the break-away type, high speed limits and high speeds, and driving under the influence of alcohol. The Institute has worked to correct these factors through state and federal agencies responsible for highway safety.

In another study the Institute reported that state laws regulating the drunk driver typically require a concentration of alcohol in the blood of .10 percent by weight. In order to reach this level of concentration, a 200-pound person would have to drink about 9.5 ounces of 80-proof liquor during a 1½ hour period following a meal. (A 150-pound person would need about 6 ounces.) A large portion of the persons killed in road accidents had levels of concentration far above the .10 percent level, indicating that they had been drinking heavily before driving. The conclusion is that the drinking-driving problem is not caused principally by the casual one- or two-martini drinker-drivers, but rather mainly by persons who drive after having consumed large amounts of liquor.

About half of all citizens in the United States both drive and drink in combination at least occasionally. Knowing this, Americans have tended to tune out the warnings about driving and drinking, knowing that they have been doing it and have not gotten into accidents. They have not realized that the main problem is with the excessive drinker who also drives. As a result much of the effort to reduce the incidence of driving-drinking has been wasted, dismissed as so much propaganda not based on fact.[9]

In tests of vehicles against solid barriers, the Institute discovered many things about automobile design. Cars were found to be excessively damage-prone, even at low speeds of 5 and 10 miles per hour. In many cases the damage suffered by vehicles was completely unnecessary from an engineering standpoint. For example, in one case in a 10 mile-per-hour crash, a windshield broke on both sides due to mounting brackets which localized the force in such a way as to guarantee breakage.[10]

Firms

Most large business firms sponsor active loss control programs. Among their activities are safety inspections, maintenance of first aid offices, driver training, plant safety education and training, enforcement of safety work rules, installation of safety equipment and devices, and design of machines and production systems to prevent accidents. To illustrate, in one case a plastics plant caught fire and ordinary water spray would not control the blaze. The fire was fed by the burning of plastic pellets used as raw material in the manufacture of plastic articles. The pellets contained a flammable substance which facilitated their handling in fabricating articles, but presented a substantially increased fire hazard. In the fire the pellets burned as if they were fuel for a blow torch. Cooperation between the in-

[9] Dr. William Haddon, Jr., "Alcohol-Baton Rouge Approach," in Charles W. Wixom, (ed.), *Key Issues in Highway Loss Reduction* (Washington, D.C.: Insurance Institute for Highway Safety, 1970), pp. 44–45.

[10] John T. Holloway, "Vehicle Design Loss Factors: The Crash Tests of 1970 Models," in Wixom, *Key Issues*, p. 169.

surance underwriters and the individual firm was successful in installation of appropriate safety measures in order to reduce the hazard and to prevent large increases in insurance rates.

Individuals

Loss prevention is also a responsibility of the individual, who must cooperate in this endeavor for the entire effort to be successful. No matter how careful the design of a plant for safety, how thorough the employee training in safe procedures, how excellent the safety equipment provided, or how meticulous the safety supervision, if the individual employee fails to practice that which he has been taught, the loss prevention effort may fail.

RATIONALE OF LOSS CONTROL

The efficiency of loss control efforts may be judged on at least two different bases: (a) economic, and (b) noneconomic. If the rationale is economic, loss control will be pursued as long as the benefits exceed the costs, expressed in economic terms. Presumably the marginal cost–marginal revenue rule will apply. That is, costs of loss control will be incurred so long as the last dollar of profit resulting from loss control exceeds the last dollar of costs incurred. Noneconomic reasons for loss control imply that the firm should pursue these efforts on humanitarian grounds and that any expenditure for loss prevention is worthwhile if it prevents or reduces loss of life or prevents human suffering brought on by illness and accidents. Most loss control work is undertaken with both motives, economic and noneconomic, in mind.

An example of mainly economic rationale in loss control is illustrated by an installation of a monitoring and control system in a large manufacturing plant. The system cost $160,000 to install but permitted reducing the number of guards to one, effecting a savings of $40,000 annually. The additional cost of the system was paid off in only four years, but the new system also greatly improved the efficiency of loss control. For example, more than 1,000 electrical monitors throughout the plant were installed. All air-conditioning units, boilers, and hot water heaters were monitored. Any temperature change in the building or in these units was automatically corrected and/or fire departments were called. Electrical monitors were installed on all doors and windows. If an alarm system on any window or door was turned off, or if a door was opened, lights in the central control room indicated it and the guard could take appropriate action.[11]

Sometimes loss control efforts are made in response to savings in insurance premiums. For example, in most cases the installation of sprinkler systems in buildings are reported to pay for themselves in four to five years in reduced fire insurance premiums. The fire insurance rating structure in use for commercial buildings contains rate credits for factors such as good housekeeping, absence of exposure to nearby structures, and similar factors. Substantial rate credits are also given for use of fire-resistant building materials in the original construction. The fire insurance rate for entire cities can be reduced substantially for providing better fire departments, water supplies, and other safety measures. In the field of automobile insurance, rate credits are given for such features as collapsible bumper systems, taking of safe driving courses,

[11] "Electronics Maker 'Bugs' His Plant," *Factory*, June 1971, pp. 34–35.

and on cars driven fewer than ten miles to work. Some life insurers give special rates to nonsmokers.

An example of loss control rationale which combines both economic and noneconomic motives is in the area of building safety. Inadequate protection in older high-rise buildings has resulted in frequent loss of life. To reduce the hazard, several new skyscrapers in the United States are being constructed with elaborate fire prevention measures due to the difficulty in using conventional fire-fighting methods effectively once fire breaks out. For example, the new Sears Tower in Chicago is fully sprinklered and equipped with smoke detection devices. The building is constructed in three zones so as to create natural smoke barriers. In each zone two elevators are designed to be used by the fire department in case of fire, and may be operated on emergency power supplies. The building has two-way communication and a central control center permitting continuous monitoring of the building. The additional cost for such protection is estimated at about $2.00 per square foot.[12]

Another illustration is that of a large chemical manufacturer which launched a special company-wide effort to reduce the accidental loss due to use of the company's products in the hands of customers. In one case a new paint product was developed for finishing the bottom of ships. The paint contained an arsenic chemical which would slowly bleed out and retard the growth of barnacles and other organisms. However, it was discovered that over a long period the paint may produce serious environmental damage, and the new product was abandoned. For another

product, an agricultural chemical, it was found that when transported in bulk it was sensitive to shock; the company decided to ship the chemical in cylinders at greater expense, but with greater safety. In another case a fire-retardant material designed for fabrics was used instead on furniture after research indicated it might be injurious if it came into contact repeatedly with human skin.[13] These efforts reflect a consideration of both humanitarian as well as economic considerations.

A final example of economic and noneconomic rationale in loss control lies in the coal industry. A study by the U.S. Bureau of Mines revealed that injuries per million man hours varied from 2.72 to 72.13 among ten major coal mining firms. Fatalities ranged from .28 to 1.52 per million man hours worked. The large differences in injury rates were attributed to greater emphasis on safety by some of the firms. The selling price of coal during the period of study was nearly identical for all firms in the industry.[14] Thus, some firms were apparently willing to absorb the costs of mine safety for considerations other than purely economic.

LOSS CONTROL AND INSURANCE

As noted above, insurance organizations are very active in attempting to promote loss control work. Not only is this effort accomplished through support of specialized organizations such as Underwriters Laboratories, The National Safety Council, and the National Fire

[12] *Architectural Forum*, March 1972, p. 55.

[13] "Dow's Big Push for Product Safety," *Business Week*, April 23, 1973, p. 82.

[14] *Wall Street Journal*, January 18, 1973, p. 1.

Protection Association, but other methods are employed as well. Perhaps the chief ways in which insurers work toward loss prevention other than specialized organizations are (1) policy provisions requiring loss prevention effort on the part of the insured, and (2) the rating structure for insurance.

Policy Provisions

Most property and liability insurance contracts require the insured to pay attention to preventing his own loss, or once an accident has occurred, to minimize the severity of loss. For example, the basic conditions of all fire insurance contracts suspend coverage (a) while the hazard is increased by any means within the control or knowledge of the insured, or (b) while the building is vacant or unoccupied beyond sixty consecutive days. If a loss occurs, the insured is required to protect the property from further damage. Similar provisions are found in other contracts of property and liability insurance. In marine insurance the insured is required to go further than just to protect property from further loss. Under the sue and labor clause, the insured must incur expenses (reimbursable by the insurer) to minimize loss once an accident has occurred. Thus, the insured may be required to hire tugboats to pull a ship free from a grounding.

Most types of insurance commonly exclude payments where the injury or accident is caused deliberately by or at the direction of the insured. The intent of such provisions, of course, is to remove the insurance contract from among those incentives which might bring about deliberate destruction of life or property for the insurance proceeds. Thus, in life insurance loss prevention is encouraged through the use of a suicide clause, which exempts the insurer from payment under a policy if the insured commits suicide within two years of the date he takes out a policy. Furthermore, the murderer-beneficiary cannot collect life insurance proceeds.

Rating Structures

Loss control is encouraged in many lines of insurance through granting of rate credits to the insured for loss prevention effort. A prominent example of this is in the field of fire insurance. The rating system in fire insurance is based on four major factors: type of construction, exposure to loss, type of occupancy, and the rating class of the city in which the building is located. Lower rates are assigned to concrete and brick construction than to frame construction, to properties containing inflammables than to properties containing flammables, and to buildings contained in safe cities than to buildings in an area without fire department protection. The fire insurance rating structure contains an elaborate system of charges for such factors as flammable shingles, nonstandard stairways or heating systems, poor housekeeping, and the like. Credits are given for loss prevention devices such as sprinkler systems, alarm systems, properly located fire walls, etc. In this way the insured is given positive incentives for installing loss prevention measures and is penalized through higher insurance rates for ignoring features which reduce either the frequency or severity of loss.

In the field of automobile insurance, rates are adjusted to such loss prevention measures as installation of seat belts, shock-absorbing bumpers, and the taking of safe driving courses. Penalties are imposed on insureds with bad driving or accident records or records of breaking traffic laws.

In some types of insurance, loss prevention measures are an integral part of the rating system itself. For example, factory mutual insurers insist that insureds undertake or cooperate in given loss control measures as a condition of getting coverage at all. In such situations, the insured may be required to employ guards at night, to maintain certain housekeeping routines such as keeping explosives duly segregated from other property, and to inspect boilers periodically. Another example is in the field of boiler and machinery insurance, in which the cost of inspection services by the insurer is built in as part of the insurance premium.

LOSS CONTROL AND THE GOVERNMENT — OSHA

As noted earlier, the federal government has taken a major step to control the rising trend of industrial injuries and accidents through authority granted in the Occupational Safety and Health Act of 1970 (OSHA). OSHA, which became effective in April 28, 1971, requires all employers in interstate commerce (except mining and railway employers, who are covered by other laws) to provide a work place free from recognized hazards that can cause death or physical harm to employees. Employees are also required to comply with the safety provisions of the act, but employers are responsible for seeing to it that their employees conform.

OSHA, which brought under one central administration the activities authorized under five other statutes[15]

[15] The Walsh-Healy Public Contracts Act, Service Contract Act, National Foundation on Arts and Humanities Act, Longshoreman's and Harbor Workers' Compensation Act, and the Construction Safety Act.

affecting safety in given industries, was passed in response to several conditions including the following: (1) Occupational injury rates increased from 11.4 injuries per million man hours in 1958, to 14.8 injuries in 1969. Injury frequency rates are much higher than these levels in certain industries, such as dock work, iron and steel manufacturing, and lumbering. (2) Individual state laws have not been sufficiently effective in influencing industrial safety and health. Employers had been apparently unable or unwilling to give the matter of safety and health sufficient attention. (3) Labor organizations were increasingly concerned over inadequate safety conditions and the occurrence of injuries and exposures to loss which could be prevented.

OSHA is administered by the U.S. Labor Department. Although it is the intention of the department to seek voluntary compliance with the provisions of the act, during the first nine months of its enforcement over 22,800 inspections were made, resulting in 63,000 violations, 16,300 citations, and nearly $1,500,000 in fines. In 1975 the annual rate of inspections had climbed to 88,800 showing the serious intent to enforce the law. There were reportedly an average of 3.7 violations per inspection and citations were issued in about 70 percent of the inspections. During December 1975, penalties averaged $34.82 per violation and $147.82 per inspection.[16] Under the act fines may run from $1,000 to $20,000 and one year in jail. For example, if an employer fails to correct a cited violation he may be fined $1,000 per day. He may be fined $20,000 and one year in jail for a second willful violation in which an industrial death had resulted. Curiously enough, the law

[16] Newsletter, *Excess Express*, July 1976, (Santa Monica, Calif., Merritt Co., 1976), p. 6.

provides a fine of $10,000 and up to 10 years in jail for assaulting an inspector with a deadly weapon.[17]

The inspections made by compliance officers may be unannounced. Visits may be made at the request of employees if they believe that an alleged violation of safety exists which threatens physical harm. Employee representatives have the right to accompany an inspector during his physical examination of the plant. If a violation is found, a citation must be issued in writing and this citation must be prominently posted by the employer near the place of the violation. Employers are given 15 working days to notify OSHA administrators of their intent to contest the citation — otherwise the citation is considered to be a final order and is not subject to judicial review. However, variations from a standard may be allowed for employers for one-year periods (up to a maximum of three years) if they can show inability to meet a standard due to unavailability of personnel or equipment or time to construct or alter facilities.

Employers are required to maintain certain records and make them available upon request to OSHA authorities. First, accurate data must be kept on all work-related deaths, injuries, and illnesses other than minor injuries requiring only first aid treatment, loss of consciousness, restriction of work or motion, or transfer to another job. Second, the employer must maintain records of employee exposure to potentially toxic materials or harmful physical agents. OSHA provides forms for this record keeping: Form 100, a log of occupational injuries and illnesses; Form 101, a supplementary record of

occupational injuries and illnesses; and Form 102, a summary of occupational injuries and illnesses.

Specific standards for occupational safety and health are issued under the act.[18] The standards may be grouped under the headings: (1) industrial hygiene, (2) machine operations, (3) material handling, (4) medical facilities, (5) personal protection, and (6) plant design and maintenance. Examples of standards in each case are:

(1) Under industrial hygiene, the standards set maximum levels of radiation, noise, temperatures, and pressure. Thus, the worker may not be subjected to more than 90 decibels of noise in each eight-hour day.[19]

(2) Standards covering machine operations specify among other things that dull saw blades must be immediately removed, that bearings shall be kept free from lost motion and be well lubricated, and that saws shall be sharpened and tensioned by qualified persons.

(3) Material-handling specifications require, for example, that industrial-powered trucks must be appropriate in size and power for the job they are expected to do, in accordance with detailed specifications under eleven different classes of trucks. Appropriate safety guards, fuel handling and storage, lighting, control of noxious gases, are specified. Drivers must receive acceptable training before operating

---

[17] *Meeting Occupational Safety and Health Act Regulations* (New York, Atlanta Companies, 1972).

[18] Employers and others may study details of these standards as they are issued in the general industrial standards of the U.S. Federal Register, available from the U.S. Government Printing Office.

[19] *Occupational Noise Exposure*, Regulation 1910.95. U.S. Department of Labor, Bulletin 334, *Guidelines to the Department of Labor's Occupational Noise Standards*, interprets the permissible noise exposures and outlines what controls must be taken by employers to limit the employees' exposure to noise.

powered vehicles and fifteen driving rules are spelled out.

(4) Medical facilities specifications require that workers receive prompt care for injuries, either from personnel in a company-maintained infirmary, or from others who have been trained for this purpose if an infirmary is not provided. Where the eyes or body of a worker are exposed to injury from corrosive materials, suitable facilities for quick drenching or flushing of eyes or body must be provided within the work area for immediate emergency use. Preemployment physical examinations are required under some conditions to see if workers are qualified physically for their jobs.

(5) Specifications for personal protection include standards for protective devices for workers' eyes and face, respiratory tract, head, feet, hands, and ears. For example, the regulations state that cotton stuffed in the ears will not be acceptable, but fine glass wool, ear muff, wax-impregnated cotton, or ear plugs may be acceptable. Insulating gloves against electrical shock must meet given standards. For medium exposure to foot damage, shoes must be required which give one-half inch clearance after 50 foot-pounds impact and 1,750 pounds compression.

(6) Where hazardous materials are involved, specifications also regulate plant design and maintenance as it affects stairways, ladders, scaffolding, stands, towers, signs, and various working surfaces. For example, rungs in ladders must be at least 16 inches long. Accident prevention signs and tags must be color-coded so that red will be used to mark fire protection equipment and cans of inflammable liquids. Orange is to be used on equipment which may cut, crush, or shock the worker. Other colors are specified for different uses.

OSHA and Risk Management

It should be clear from the above discussion that the requirements of OSHA are far ranging upon the operations of most employers. The risk manager will often be directly involved in its implementation. Plant design and acquisition of materials and equipment should not be undertaken without consideration of the specifications required under OSHA. The risk manager should be aware that compliance inspections can be made at any time without advance notice. He should be prepared for such inspections by seeing to it that safe operating conditions are being continuously monitored. The employer must also be prepared to submit records to the inspectors at any time. In extreme cases the employer should recognize that his entire plant may be shut down immediately until serious violations observed in the course of an inspection are corrected. In order to comply effectively with the act, most risk managers should establish a definite safety and training program in which an initial task would be to familiarize both management and workers of the details of the OSHA and its requirements as they apply to the employer's particular industry.

A 1973 survey revealed that major industries in the United States were planning large safety expenditures to obtain compliance with OSHA. For example the iron and steel industries used about 12 percent of their total capital-spending budget in 1972 for this purpose, and expected to employ about 17 percent of the capital-spending budget by 1976 for safety. A major cost in the program of the steel industry was for improvements in coke ovens which violated the standard of .2 milligrams per cubic meter for coal tar pitch volatile emissions by 4 or 5 times. Union studies revealed that workers in coke oven plants tend to get lung cancer at a rate 10 times and bladder cancer 7.5 times that of other steel workers. Respirators now used are inadequate to protect against coal tar fumes.[20] Costs of compliance with OSHA are said to be largest in iron and steel, textiles, mining, stone, clay and glass, communications, and aerospace.[21]

EXAMPLES OF LOSS CONTROL ACTIVITIES

In what types of activity are risk managers engaged in handling the loss control function? Although no comprehensive answer to this question will be attempted here, a few examples will illustrate the value of loss control:

1. A multinational men's wear manufacturer acquired a shirt-manufacturing division from another firm. The previous owner had carried insurance which had been surcharged $21,300 annually because of substandard conditions in the plant. The new owners ordered an analysis by a loss prevention engineering firm which made recommendations to correct the substandard conditions. The recommendations, which included suggested improvements to the sprinkler system, were carried out at a cost of $18,000. Within six months the additional insurance charges of $21,300 were removed.[22]

2. An engineering study of a large retail firm resulted in improvements to the property and in water supply facilities. Previous to the study HPR (highly

protected risk) standards were not met, but after the recommendations of the engineering firm had been carried out, the special rates for HPR standards were applicable, causing a reduction of $95,000 in insurance premiums which previously had been $200,000 annually.[23]

3. Through a program of systematic surveillance, risk managers have corrected conditions which resulted in increased hazards illustrated by the following cases: (1) a furniture store introduced a line of glassware with packing materials of greater combustibility than those customarily used, (2) a distributor of seeds and feeds was required to carry over a large quantity of seed from one season to the next, with a considerable increase in the danger of spontaneous ignition of the seed, (3) in one firm it was the custom to employ night watchmen without any training in the detection of spontaneous heating, explosive substances in the air, or in the explosibility of substances on the premises.[24] In each of these cases the surveillance system alerted the risk manager to the increased hazards.

4. One risk manager developed a program to discourage embezzlement among employees. The program involved transferring employees without notice, warning employees that management might inject errors into invoices, cash register tapes, and other records as a check on employee dishonesty, and warning employees that management might employ undercover observers to work permanently among employees in all categories.[25]

5. In one case management deter-

[20] *Business Week*, May 26, 1973, p. 27.

[21] *Ibid.*

[22] Leonard R. Friedman, "Using Independent Property Loss Prevention Engineering Services," *Risk Management*, May 1974, p. 45.

[23] *Ibid.*

[24] Donald L. MacDonald, *Corporate Risk Control* (New York, Ronald Press, 1966), p. 186.

[25] *Ibid.*, p. 269.

mined that thieves could remove merchandise from a store within 20 minutes during the lunch period. A program was started to stagger lunch hours so that no fewer than eight employees would be on the premises at any one time.[26]

6. In another case a procedure was started to deposit all checks by mail rather than by daily bank delivery by messenger. In this way, if a robbery occurred, checks would not be destroyed by thieves, as was usually the case.[27]

[26] *Ibid.*, p. 279.

[27] *Ibid.*, p. 280.

SUMMARY AND CONCLUSIONS

1. Loss control, aimed at reducing both the frequency and severity of losses, is a major management responsibility of increasing significance. Important concepts in loss prevention are hazard control, the chain of loss concept, system safety, the human vs. engineering approach, and the energy transfer approach.

2. Loss control effort within the firm should be coordinated with loss control and prevention carried on at other levels in society, the levels of state and federal government, private associations, insurance companies, other firms, and individuals.

3. The efficiency of loss control may be judged by both economic and noneconomic measures. The value of this activity extends much further than mere reduction in insurance premiums; properly conducted, loss control can be a major factor in increasing general levels of efficiency and profit. In many cases, however, the cost of loss control is more than offset by savings in insurance costs alone.

4. Insurance is a major impetus in loss control effort, which is encouraged by the insurance rating structure, and required by insurance policy terms and provisions.

5. The Occupational Safety and Health Act of 1970 (OSHA) is an example of major effort at the level of federal government to encourage and require most loss control activity in industry. Under OSHA safety standards in six major areas of industrial operations are specified in considerable detail. OSHA provisions are likely to have a considerable impact on manufacturing operations, plant design, material procurement, and plant supervision.

QUESTIONS FOR DISCUSSION

1. Under the provisions of OSHA an employer may obtain a 20 percent reduction in penalty for violation of the act by showing awareness of the act and demonstration of a desire to comply with the act. How might an employer make such a demonstration?

2. What is the employer's responsibility under OSHA? What specific activities would you suggest that the risk manager undertake in order to comply with OSHA?

3. In one case a firm had provided safety equipment, but the employee was not using it, and an accident resulted. Is the employer likely to be found in violation of OSHA?

4. A study showed that the cost of an accident resulting in $100 in direct costs would require the following output to recover: for an auto manufacturer, ⅔ of a low-priced sedan; for an office furniture manufacturer, 85 typist chairs; for a publisher, 17,500 newspapers. Of what value is such a comparison?

5. It was reported that a large soup maker, through a comprehensive safety program, reduced its injury frequency rate 80 percent in five years, although its man-hour exposure increased 30 percent. The overall effect of this program produced an 11 percent decrease in property-liability insurance premiums per dollar of company assets. Is the saving in insurance premium the main value of a safety program? Discuss.

6. One of the persistent problems of highway safety is the existence of a class of drivers which has been described as that of habitual offenders. Apparently no amount of fines, no length of jail sentences, and no number of suspensions or revocations of his driver's license will keep this driver off the road. In one study of this problem by the Insurance Information Institute, 33 drivers were studied who had a total of 556 convictions for traffic law violations, more than half of which were for speeding, drunk, or reckless driving. They had been involved in 76 accidents, in spite of the fact that upon 73 occasions their driver's licenses were suspended or revoked. The longest continuous record was that of a Utah man, who over a 32-year span, had been arrested 73 times, 29 times for speeding, and had 10 reported accidents. In another case a 54-year old man had over a 27-year period, spent six years in jail and paid $3,298 in fines, mostly for drunken driving without a license. What solutions would you suggest for such a problem?

7. A fire insurance underwriter stated, "Fire protection grading for a city is based upon a 10,000 point system that measures the fire department, water supply, police protection, and weather . . . Future grading will continue to emphasize the capability of the fire department to control big fires . . . The proficiency of the first firemen on the scene determines whether you have a $500 loss or a $5,000 loss." Suggest qualities that should be looked for in judging the adequacy of fire department training.

8. Among the factors tending to work against loss control, the following were cited: There is an increased tendency to use flammable materials in home construction (*e.g.,* plastic bricks, plastic furniture). This has encouraged people to buy furniture for short-term use rather than long-term use. Coupled with greater mobility of the population, greater numbers of mobile homes, and use of insurance coverage on a replacement-cost basis, the fire underwriting hazard has increased. Why would the factors cited require increased vigilance by the fire underwriter?

9. In what way, if any, does subrogation aid in the cause of loss control?

10. Professor Kenneth Herrick reported that in Great Britain after passage of the Road Safety Act of 1967, fatal accidents dropped 15 percent during the first 12 months. By 1972, in spite of increasing road traffic, auto deaths and injuries remained below the 1967 level. The greatest decrease occurred during the "drinking hours" (10 P.M. to 4 A.M.). Under the act, three times as many drivers are now prosecuted for drinking-driving as pre-1967. Second offenders are relatively rare. The success of the program was attributed to strict enforcement of the provisions requiring breath tests of drivers suspected of drinking, automatic loss of driving licenses for one year, and substantial fines and possible imprisonment. Do you believe a similar law should be passed in the United States? Discuss.

11. The Insurance Company of North America reported in 1972 that auto accidents in the firm declined by 64 percent, and fleet damage costs declined by 16 percent after a safety program was started in 1968. A company spokesman stated, "Management motivates employee participation in proper accident investigation, effective facility inspections, and off-the-job programs for employees and their families. Performance is evaluated and scored numerically." Why is the role of management so significant in implementing programs of employee safety?

12. An important loss control service provided by insurers is that of periodic inspection of boilers by specially trained insurance company engineers. The cost of this service constitutes an important segment of the rate charged for boiler and machinery insurance. What link in the chain concept of loss prevention is illustrated by this activity?

13. Discuss the relationship between the systems safety concept of loss prevention and the human approach of W. W. Heinrich.

14. At which level in society can loss control effort be most effectively conducted? Discuss.

15. Two 1973 cases involving enforcement of OSHA were reported as follows: (1) In Skil-Craft Builders, Inc., the Secretary of Labor held that permitting employees to work on a scaffold not equipped with standard rail, including midrail, toe boards, and end protection, thereby exposing them to a possible fall of 16 to 18 feet, constituted a serious violation of 29 CFR 1926.451 (a)(4). The penalty was reduced from $500 to $250 because the level of gravity of the offense was only moderate. (2) In Morrison Knudsen

Company and Associates, the Review Commission held that employer's failure to enforce the use of ear plugs constituted a serious violation of 29 CFR 1926.52, and a $600 penalty was affirmed. The noise level was between 100–112 decibels. This noise level lasted from one-half hour to two hours. (Reported in Occupational Health and Safety Reporter, Vol. 3, No. 6 [July 12, 1973], published by the Bureau of National Affairs, Inc.,) What aspects of OSHA regulations do these cases illustrate?

16. Apply or illustrate the ten strategies of Haddon's energy transfer approach to loss control in the field of automobile accidents. Are *all* of the 10 strategies appropriate for handling this problem in all firms? Discuss.

6

Risk Retention

Risk retention may be defined as a financial plan within the firm to meet fortuitous losses. Risk retention is a general term which includes different forms of self-insurance, and assumption of risk (noninsurance). The method of self-insurance may be distinguished from the method of simple assumption of risk in that the latter (in contrast to self-insurance) usually does not involve a formal plan, a special loss reserve, or a loss fund. Firms accomplish risk retention in several ways: deciding to bear all losses from a given source, deciding to bear only those losses up to some amount and purchasing commercial insurance on the excess, deciding to establish loss funds either before or after the occurrence of the loss, establishing a captive insurer, and using retrospective rating.

If a risk manager has a sufficient number of exposure units under his control, and losses roughly fall in accordance with some assumed mathematical distribution such as the binomial, Poisson, or normal distributions, formulas may be derived to assess the degree of accuracy with which he may predict losses. If this degree of accuracy is high enough, and if other conditions are met, the risk manager may profitably employ self-insurance as a method of handling pure risk. The decision to self-insure, however, should not be taken lightly. Careful consideration should be given to many conditions necessary for successful programs. These factors are discussed under the following headings:

1. Assumption vs. self-insurance

2. Partial self-insurance

3. Objectives of self-insurance

4. Factors favoring self-insurance

5. Economics of self-insurance

6. Self-insurance savings in workers' compensation

7. Limitations of self-insurance

8. Survey of self-insurance plans

9. Captive insurers

10. Future trends

ASSUMPTION VS. SELF-INSURANCE

Assumption of risk takes two forms: (1) an intentional plan to handle risk and (2) unintentional assumption of risk (obviously) without any organized plan. Intentional assumption of risk typically means deliberate acceptance of exposures to loss which are inconsequential to the firm when it is felt that no financial embarrassment or other negative consequences will result. Examples include theft or collision losses to low-valued vehicles, losses from normal bad debts, and wear and tear on buildings and equipment. These normal expenses, usually met from working capital, are often not fortuitous in nature and may be planned for as an inevitable consequence and cost of doing business. Usually it would not be financially wise to employ commercial insurance as a device to handle such small or predictable losses, which really may not properly be termed risks at all since they are not in the nature of uncertainties. If insurance were used, the insurer would have to charge the insured a premium which would probably be considered excessive since it would have to be large enough to cover not only the expected loss but a margin for the cost of doing business. The total premium would thus be in excess of the almost certain losses which would be incurred. For example, the insured might be paying $1.50 to meet $1.00 of normal expenses.

Sometimes assumption of risk is unintentional and, of course, unplanned. Needless to say, this type of assumption may endanger financial stability. Ignoring risk is seldom a satisfactory method of dealing with it.

Self-insurance, in contrast to assumption, normally involves a definite company directed plan to meet losses which are uncertain in size and frequency in any one year and which, if they occur without financial planning, are large enough to cause financial embarrassment or even insolvency. The contingencies subject to self-insurance are the same contingencies, in most cases, for which commercial insurance may also be used. These risks require some definite degree of financial planning, such as setting aside a reserve fund, earmarking of surplus for contingencies, arrangement of bank credit in advance of the need, planning for backup financing from other agencies, such as parent companies, suppliers or customers, or some combination of these methods. If no financial planning for such losses exists, the firm is actually using the method of conscious or unconscious assumption of risk discussed above. However, it is not uncommon to hear of risk managers referring to the use of self-insurance when they actually mean assumption of risk.

PARTIAL SELF-INSURANCE

It should not be assumed that the method of self-insurance, as outlined above, should be considered an exclusive way of handling risk. It is the rule, rather than the exception, that more than one method of handling risk will be used simultaneously. For example, the firm may assume the risk of collision or theft loss to vehicles up to some deductible amount, such as $500, and commercially insure the physical loss to vehicles above this amount. The firm may use self-insurance on all physical loss to vehicles and use commercial insurance on all liability claims due to negligent operation of the vehicles. In some cases the firm may retain all liability claims up to some amount, say $100,000, and obtain excess liability insurance for losses above this amount. For large firms it is not uncommon to have large deductibles of $1 million or more in areas such as fire loss exposures.

In some cases these large deductibles are accompanied by a loss fund to facilitate the handling of losses up to the deductible amount.

Another example of partial self-insurance is found in a type of rating plan known as *retrospective rating*. Under retrospective rating the business firm bears a portion of the total loss, sharing it with the commercial insurer according to a formula which allocates the total cost of coverage in accordance with the insured's incurred loss ratio. There is a basic or minimum premium and a maximum premium; the actual premium is not known until the end of the accounting period when the insured's losses are known. The word retrospective implies "looking back" over the accounting period just past. The higher the incurred loss ratio in the past period, the higher the premium charged, and vice versa. Like the straight deductible, retrospective rating gives the business purchaser a reduced premium rate for assuming part of the loss burden. In retrospective rating, however, the amount of the saving depends upon how effective the insured's loss control measures have been. A full discussion of retrospective rating is beyond the scope of this book.[1]

OBJECTIVES OF SELF-INSURANCE

There are many objectives for using self-insurance. Perhaps the most common objective is financial, to reduce the cost of handling risk and to reduce the amount of capital tied up in reserves.

[1] For more details see basic texts on insurance; J. H. Magee and O. N. Serbein, *Property and Liability Insurance* (Homewood, Ill., R. D. Irwin, 1967), pp. 770–71. Greene, *Risk and Insurance*, Chapter 26. David Bickelhaupt, *General Insurance* (Homewood, Ill., R. D. Irwin, 1974), pp. 641–43.

This assumes that the firm can handle the functions normally carried out by a commercial insurer more efficiently and effectively through its own organization than through the insurer. This assumption will be analyzed below.

Another reason for self-insurance is to obtain greater flexibility in handling risk. Commercial insurers often have more or less rigid underwriting rules which restrict the firm's freedom of action in various ways. An example would be the insurer's acceptance of one type of risk, say physical loss of property, but denial of another, say liability from specific operations. An insurer may find the life insurance exposure acceptable but may deny coverage of long-term disability exposure. A self-insurance plan may enable the firm to handle all types of risks simultaneously.

A third objective of self-insurance is to improve loss control. This may come about because the firm has greater incentive to reduce losses since an outside party, such as a commercial insurer, will not be standing the losses from lax attention to loss prevention activities. (See above discussion for retrospective rating.)

A fourth objective is the improvement of claims handling. The firm with its own fund, for example, can settle claims of foreign subsidiaries without the delays which are often involved when an outside party such as a commercial insurer is involved in making independent investigations of the loss. In the field of workers' compensation, a firm may decide that prompter claims settlement will improve employee relations. Doubtful claims may be resisted more effectively than if an outside insurer were involved. If an employer is self-insuring the workers' compensation risk, it may also be self-insuring other related plans such as long-term nonoccupational disability. In this case, the firm may be in a better position to coordinate all sources of payment to disabled employees (including unemployment benefits) so as to reduce morale hazards. For example, if an employee is receiving more pay in a disabled condition than if he were working, a morale hazard is easily recognized.

A fifth objective is to improve the quality of services which would otherwise be provided by the insurer. In many kinds of situations the charges of insurers for services such as loss prevention, replacement of property, and loss adjustments are substantial, but the quality of these services may be uncertain. The individual firm may decide that it can provide such services more effectively and at less cost.

Finally, self-insurance may be the only alternative to a firm who finds it impossible to use commercial insurance because of high costs or simple unavailability of adequate markets.

FACTORS FAVORING SELF-INSURANCE

In view of the evident appeal of self-insurance, as may be inferred from the description of common motives listed above, one may wonder how commercial insurers can exist at all and why all firms do not employ self-insurance. For example, consider the following report:

A study of the insurance of 46 fire-resistive school buildings located in seven different Colorado cities shows that over a 16-year period, $71,122 was paid out in premiums. During the same 16 years a total of $42 was collected as damage to these 46 buildings. The loss-cost ratio on these figures is somewhere near .005, or so low that it reaches an absurdity. Perhaps it is not even

worthy of being classified as insurance but rather as a $74,000 donation to insurance companies.[2]

It is not surprising that such a report may produce considerable interest among cost-conscious school boards. In fact, self-insurance programs have been established in several states to handle risks on state-owned property, with apparent success in many cases.[3] However, consider a subsequent answer to the first report in a later article by an insurance company executive.

. . . the actuarial office for the principal fire insurance companies disclosed that for the five years ending in 1951, the premiums of *all* insured fire-resistive school buildings in that state totalled $95,000 with $68,000 in claims paid. And with the low rates applicable to risks of this type, the companies over this period were furnishing protection of over $30 million to fire-resistive school property.[4]

The author went on to cite several cases in which state-run self-insurance funds had large claims which either exhausted or exceeded the self-insurance funds set up for their payment.

It is clear that conditions favoring self-insurance plans should be reviewed carefully before the decision is made by a noninsurance firm to enter the insurance business. Among these requirements are:

[2] G. D. Morrison and W. E. Scoville, "Why Not Save Millions of Dollars Through State-Wide Self-Insurance," *American School Board Journal* (August, 1953).

[3] *Ibid.* For example, successful operation of such plans were reported for Alabama, North Dakota, South Carolina, North Carolina, and Wisconsin.

[4] Walter G. Dithmer, "Is 'Self-Insurance' Insurance?," *American School Board Journal* (November, 1953).

(1) The risk of loss should involve a sufficiently large homogeneous set of objects, so situated that average losses become predictable within reasonably narrow limits. Records permitting a prior estimate of probable loss should be available. Property should be dispersed geographically so that it is not subject to simultaneous destruction by a single peril. If the firm has 1,000 buildings properly dispersed geographically, but two of these buildings are worth $1 million each, and the remainder $10,000 each, it is clear that the insured group is not homogeneous. If the loss should occur to the buildings worth $1 million, the financial results would be very adverse to a total self-insurance plan. Furthermore, as indicated in the above accounts by the self-insurance program in Colorado, when the *entire* exposure of similar property in the state is taken into account, the loss ratio may be much higher than when only a selected segment of the exposure is considered. Hence, the 46 buildings in the first case might not be large enough in number nor sufficiently homogeneous in nature to permit sufficiently accurate loss prediction, even over a relatively long period of years.

(2) The firm should have sufficient financial strength to either set aside self-insurance funds to meet expected losses, or to meet these losses from working capital without financial embarrassment. This suggests that the type of exposure to be self-insured will involve objects of relatively low financial value, so situated that catastrophic losses to a large segment of such objects are not possible. For example, one firm was analyzed and discovered to have a fleet of several thousand vehicles operating over a large territory, thousands of service stations all worth less than $20,000 each, over 1,000 tank cars averaging $2,000 in value each, several thousand

meter and regulating stations averaging $2,000 each, and many other low value plants and inventories with wide geographic spread.[5] Such a firm obviously is in a good position to meet the basic requirements for predictability and for meeting average losses without undue financial strain.

(3) The firm must be willing to undertake the administrative requirements of a self-insurance plan. These include investing self-insurance funds, keeping of adequate records, administration of claims, loss prevention work, and analysis of loss exposures. In a sense, the administration of a self-insurance plan is similar to the administration which would be done by the commercial insurer, and the firm undertaking it should recognize the technical problems which this entails. For example, specialized types of personnel may be required, such as safety inspectors, fire prevention engineers, and medical specialists. These problems are so significant that many self insurers employ independent outside organizations to perform them, *e.g.*, claims service firms.[6] Sometimes commercial insurers establish subsidiaries to handle self-insurance administration in given lines, such as workers' compensation.[7]

---

[5] W. A. D. Hare, "Self-Funding Insurance Programs — Are They Practical?," *Credit and Financial Management* (October 1969), p. 17.

[6] Paul K. Clayton, "Providing Claims Service for the Self-Insured," *Independent Agent* (March 1971), pp. 60–65.

[7] For example, the Employers Self-Insurance Service Company of Los Angeles was established in 1956 as a subsidiary of the Insurance Company of North America. This company advertises that it "provides complete self-insurance claims handling, plans and administers safety and accident prevention activities, furnishes reports required by state regulation, and services claims throughout the U.S. through a network of 160 claims offices."

THE ECONOMICS OF SELF-INSURANCE

Most self-insurance programs are started for economic reasons. In general, the objective is not only to save on insurance costs, but also to reduce capital outlays for risk reduction. Cost savings are effected in a number of ways. These include (1) reduction of expenses of risk handling, (2) reduction of losses within the corporation, (3) increasing the in-terest income which would otherwise be lost on those funds allocated for insurance, (4) deductibles, and (5) reduction of taxes. Each of these is treated below.

Expenses

Commercial insurers' expenses may range up to 45 percent or more of gross premiums, depending upon the line of insurance, type of insurer, and territory of operation. Table 6–1 gives

TABLE 6–1
Expenses of Insurers Operating in New York State,
1974, in Selected Lines

Type of Insurer	Total	Type of Expense (as a percent of premiums earned)				
		Loss Adjustment	Commis-sions & Brokerage	Other Acqui-sition	General	Taxes and Fees
FIRE						
Stock	39.7	3.7	20.0	3.5	9.2	3.3
Mutual	40.6	3.5	15.5	8.5	9.9	3.2
Factory Mutual	39.4	2.5	2.2	15.2	16.6	2.9
COMMERCIAL MULTIPLE PERIL						
Stock	42.0	7.0	17.9	4.3	9.6	3.2
Mutual	44.9	7.2	14.3	9.1	10.8	3.5
GROUP ACCIDENT AND HEALTH						
Stock (nonlife)	19.3	2.9	4.5	5.8	3.7	2.4
Mutual (nonlife)	14.9	3.2	.8	5.1	3.0	2.8
WORKERS' COMPENSATION						
Stock	29.7	8.7	8.1	2.5	6.4	4.0
Mutual	25.2	8.9	2.0	4.4	6.0	3.9
State Fund	26.6	10.2	.0	.7	7.6	8.1
AUTOMOBILE COLLISION						
Finance Companies	39.4	12.2	11.5	9.4	3.1	3.2
Stock	37.5	8.9	14.7	4.8	6.1	3.0
Mutual	33.1	10.2	6.0	9.6	4.4	2.9

SOURCE: 1974 *Loss and Expense Ratios* (Albany, N.Y.: New York State Insurance Depart-ment, 1974).

examples of these expenses. Data shown are for nationwide experience of all insurers operating in New York State in 1974. Ratios for individual insurers vary rather widely, but the averages shown are fairly typical. Mutual company expenses are generally lower than other types, but initial premiums may also be higher and underwriting standards stricter. It should not be concluded that mutuals are necessarily cheaper than stocks.

In reviewing Table 6–1, it may be observed that a self-insurer would not have to pay expenses such as taxes and fees, commissions and brokerage, and other acquisition costs. For stock companies these expenses totalled 26.8 percent of gross premiums for fire, 25.4 percent for commercial multiple peril, 12.7 percent for group accident and health, 14.6 percent for workers' compensation, and 24.1 percent for automobile collision. It is obvious that expense savings from these sources alone might encourage many firms to set up self-insurance programs.

It should be recognized that self-insurers would almost certainly experience loss adjustment and general administrative expenses in amounts equalling, or perhaps exceeding, those of a commercial insurer. The amount saved on expenses, however, might be significant if not outweighed by other factors in the self-insurance decision.

Losses

As noted previously, loss reduction may be effected more efficiently under self-insurance programs than under commercial insurance arrangements. Incentives for loss control may be greater than under commercial insurance because the self-insurer is rewarded immediately for loss reduction and does not have to wait for the com-

mercial insurer to recognize loss reduction in lower rates, higher dividends, greater services, or some combination of these. Better loss control may have indirect rewards through better employee relations, improved morale, and greater production efficiency.

To illustrate improved loss control, consider the case of Westinghouse Electric Corporation, which established a self-insurance program for the auto fleet of a car-leasing subsidiary. The company is now dealing with accident records on a day-to-day basis. As the subsidiary's president stated:

In a conventional insurance program where the big company turns over the problem of accident claims to an insurance company for the cost of premiums, basic information about the company's casualty rate gets tucked away in the insurance department, where it escapes the scrutiny of management (information such as instances of slack handling, poor driver training, and employee morale problems).[8]

The president believes that the new system increases the firm's alertness to indirect costs of an accident, such as missed service calls and the costs of shifting personnel to fill in for the injured employee. The system also results in faster claims settlement than that offered by conventional insurance plans.

Interest Income

As discussed previously, many firms will feel obligated to set up self-insurance reserve funds to meet losses rather than expect to pay losses out of working capital. However, this involves the disadvantage of setting aside funds in savings type accounts or in liquid

[8] "Self-Insured Auto Fleets Bring Savings," *Industry Week* (January 17, 1972), pp. 24–25.

securities, the return on which may not be comparable to the earnings otherwise possible if the funds were reinvested in the firm's own enterprise. Thus there is an opportunity cost of funds employed in self-insurance reserve funds that should be taken into account in the self-insurance decision.

The amount of reserves that should be set aside in self-insurance funds may often be less than the reserves required by a commercial insurer. Some insurers have been accused of over-reserving and building in to the premium structure an amount considered excessive to the potential self-insurer. Depending on the attitudes toward risk of the self-insured firm's management, the reserves set aside within the firm might be safely set at a much lower level than that which would be required by the commercial insurer.

One model, which has been used to analyze this question of proper reserve size and the opportunity cost of money, suggested by David Houston, employs the decision rule:

Buy insurance if the expected financial position of the firm at the end of the year is better than would be the case if insurance is not purchased; otherwise, do not buy insurance.[9]

The financial result at the end of the year if one buys insurance may be expressed as the existing net worth minus the insurance premium plus investment return earned on the difference. The financial result at the end of the year, if one does *not* buy insurance, depends upon the size of the reserve which the firm feels must be set aside to meet

[9] David B. Houston, "Risk, Insurance, and Sampling," *Journal of Risk and Insurance* (December 1964), p. 530. This model ignores the effect of federal income taxes on the decision to insure or not to insure.

losses and upon the amount of interest return lost because this reserve is invested at a relatively low (safe) rate of return available in liquid investments such as savings deposits or short term securities. In formula, the decision rule may be expressed:

Buy insurance if $FP_b > FP_{nb}$ at the end of the year, where FP_b is the financial position if one buys insurance, and FP_{nb} is the financial position if one does not buy insurance. The quantities FP_b and FP_{nb} may be expressed:

$$(1) \quad FP_b = NW - P + r(NW - P)$$

where FP_b = financial position or net worth if one buys insurance

NW = initial net worth invested in the business

P = premium paid for insurance

r = percentage return available to the firm on funds invested in the business or in nonliquid securities

and $$(2) \quad FP_{nb} = NW - P/2 + r(NW - P/2 - F) + iF$$

where FP_{nb} = financial position if one does not buy insurance;

$P/2$ = average insured loss per year

F = reserve fund which must be set aside for losses because one does not buy insurance

i = interest earned on the reserve fund earned in savings accounts or liquid securities

Other terms in equation (2) remain the same as in equation (1). In words, equation (2) says that the financial position at the end of the year if one does not purchase insurance is arrived at by first subtracting from the initial capital (NW) the average expected loss ($P/2$).

To this result we add amounts expressed in the third and fourth terms. The third term expresses the amount earned in the business after removing funds employed for paying losses and for use in the reserve fund. The fourth term expresses the amount of interest received on the reserve fund. In both equations it is assumed that the average loss equals one-half the premium paid, which is not entirely unrealistic. The insurance manager will purchase insurance if FP_b is greater than FP_{nb}. The difference between these two amounts may be viewed as the economic value of insurance to the firm.

To illustrate, assume that a firm with an initial net worth of $1 million has a piece of heavy equipment valued at $100,000, and that without insurance a $100,000 reserve fund is necessary since there is only one piece of equipment and no possibility of predicting average losses through the use of the law of large numbers. Assume further that the reserve fund earns interest at the rate of .04 in savings accounts and .10 if invested in the business. Assume further that insurance is available for 2 percent, or $2,000 annually. The financial position of the firm at the end of the year if insurance is purchased under these assumptions will be:

(1) $FP_b = \$1,000,000 - \$2,000 +$
       $.10(\$1,000,000 - \$2,000)$
       $= \$998,000 + \$99,800$
       $= \$1,097,800$

If insurance is not purchased and a $100,000 reserve fund is necessary, the net worth at the end of the year will be:

(2) $FP_{nb} = \$1,000,000 - \$2,000/2 +$
       $.10(\$1,000,000 - \$2,000/2 -$
       $\$100,000) + .04(\$100,000)$

       $= \$999,000 + \$89,900 + \$4,000$
       $= \$1,092,900$

Since the financial position of the firm is improved by $4,900 by purchasing insurance $[(1) - (2) = \$4,900]$, the insurance manager is advised to do so. The value of insurance is $4,900 to this firm under these assumptions.

The value of insurance can be determined more easily by a formula which is derived from (1) and (2) above. This value may be expressed:[10]

(3) $V = F(r - i) - P(1/2 + 1/2r)$

where V = value of insurance. The other terms are the same as in (1) and (2) above. In the above case, we may substitute in equation (3) the same values used before, obtaining $4,900 which is the same economic value as making the subtraction $(1) - (2)$:

$V = \$100,000(.10 - .04) - \$2,000[1/2 +$
    $1/2(.10)]$
  $= \$6,000 - \$2,000(.55)$
  $= \$6,000 - \$1,100$
  $= \$4,900$

It is worth noting that equation (3) is especially sensitive to the required size of the reserve fund, F, since F is usually large and P is usually small relative to F.

It should be noted that the Houston model is useful in analyzing the question of lost financial return by having a reserve fund and is not an answer to the entire self-insurance decision. For example, if the conditions for self-insurance do not exist, such as lack of geographical and other diversification of exposure units, one large loss may wipe out the reserve fund, leaving the firm unprotected for future losses.

[10] The formula given here differs slightly from Houston's original formula.

Deductibles

The problem of setting deductible levels is a significant one in any self-insurance plan because the corporation must bear the loss up to the amount of any deductible employed where the peril is insured commercially. The total loss to be borne equals the amount of the deductible times the number of losses in a given year in which the deductible must be applied. For example if the deductible is $100 per occurrence and the average number of occurrences per year is 10, the total deductible to be borne by the firm would be $1,000. In essence the deductible level chosen reflects the basic amount of exposure which the firm is willing to accept in its plan to meet given losses internally.

The problem of setting deductible levels may be attacked in several ways. Three techniques for this problem were analyzed in Chapter 3, the paired comparison, the expected utility, and the worry factor methods. Two other approaches to this problem are treated below: (a) Houston's model as described above, and (b) the least cost rule.

The Houston model may be helpful in determining the optimum size of deductible to employ if commercial insurance is to be used in the firm for excess losses. The amount of the deductible is, in effect, the amount for which the firm is utilizing self-insurance in a given case. In the above example, suppose the firm had decided to self-insure the first $15,000 of loss and to accept commercial insurance with a $15,000 deductible, for which it receives a lower premium, say $500. Will the insurance still have economic value to the firm? The answer depends upon the size of the reserve fund which would now be required. Assume that since the management required a full reserve previ-

ously, it will continue to require a full reserve; in this case the new reserve is reduced to $15,000, the amount of the deductible. Substituting the new values of F and P in equation (3), the insurance manager may determine that the value of insurance is $625 ($15,000 (.10 − .04) − $500 (.55) = $625). Since the value of insurance is still a positive amount, the new arrangement is still profitable.

It may be determined that commercial insurance should still be purchased if the deductible (and the reserve fund) is reduced as low as $4,583, other factors remaining the same. This is done in the above case by setting the value of insurance equal to zero in the equation (3) and solving for F.

The deductible may also be useful in analyzing the self-insurance decision when interest rates change in relation to the estimated rates of return available on funds invested within the business. In the above example, the spread between these two amounts was quite large, 6 percent. If the spread were reduced to 3 percent because interest rates rise or because profit rates decline, the financial incentive to self-insure increases. For example, in the above case, if the value of r declines from .10 to .07, the spread has narrowed to .03. The value of insurance is reduced to $182.50 ($15,000 (.07 − .04) − $500 (.50 + .035) = $182.50). By setting the value of insurance equal to zero and solving for r, it may be determined that if r falls below .0576 the value of insurance becomes negative. The firm is making so little on funds within the business that the opportunity cost of money has declined to the point that even modest amounts invested in commercial insurance are not justified (always assuming that other conditions for self-insurance are met).

The above analysis would lead to the conclusion that self-insurance plans are not likely to be profitable under the following conditions: (a) rates of return within the business firm are relatively high, (b) interest rates available on liquid securities, such as certificates of deposit or on savings accounts, are relatively low, (c) commercial insurance premiums are relatively low, (d) the perceived need for full reserves is high — *i.e.*, management is averse to risk. Self-insurance plans are likely to be profitable under opposite conditions. The Houston method may be employed to analyze individual situations.

The *least cost rule*, suggested by Professors A. E. Hofflander and L. L. Schkade,[11] is a rule for selection of automobile collision deductible which has the least total cost to the insured. The rule is applicable when the risk manager is able to develop reliable estimates of the average annual number of collisions. Although these authors confined their analysis to automobile insurance problems, the rule would appear to be quite general in its application. The rule is based on the proposition that the cost of pure risk is equal to the premium payable plus the loss to be borne by the insured under the deductible. Of course, this latter amount need not be paid if there is no loss. The possible loss up to the amount of the deductible, therefore, needs to be estimated in order to learn the total cost.

The rule, simply stated, is to select the deductible which yields to the least total expected cost, (TEC) where the term TEC equals the premium payable plus the expected unindemnified loss; *i.e.*, the loss up to the amount of the deductible. In symbols,

$$TEC = P + qD, \text{ where}$$

[11] Alfred E. Hofflander and Lawrence L. Schkade, "A Rule for Least Cost Selection of Collision Deductibles," *Annals of the Society of Property and Liability Underwriters* (March 1967), pp. 5–17.

P is the amount of the premium quoted for a given level of deductible, q is the expected number of perils occurring in a given year, and D is the amount of the deductible.

To illustrate this rule in auto collision insurance, assume that an insurer provides certain data given on premiums and deductibles (given below), and that the risk manager estimates the expected number of collisions as 20 percent of the average number of vehicles used. The above formula would be solved as follows:

$$P + (D \times q) = TEC$$

$$\$23.00 + (\$ 50 \times .20) = \$ 33.00$$
$$12.00 + (100 \times .20) = 32.00$$
$$8.00 + (250 \times .20) = 58.00$$
$$5.40 + (500 \times .20) = 105.40$$

Since TEC is lowest for a deductible of $100, this is the deductible which should be chosen, using the least cost rule.

The rule may result in the selection of other deductible amounts if the above assumptions are changed. The risk manager can test the formula for different values of *q* to see what difference the rule makes in the deductible selection. For example, if the collision frequency in this firm is .40 instead of .20, it would pay the risk manager to select the $50 deductible, which would provide the least total cost.

The above rule makes an implicit assumption that if a loss occurs, it would equal at least the amount of the deductible. Thus, it is a conservative rule since this assumption raises the total expected cost of losses above what they might be if not all losses (particularly in case of large deductibles) will come up to the full amount of the deductible. The risk manager may make an adjustment for this likelihood by multiplying the second term in the equation, qD, by some fraction, say .75, under the assumption that on the average only 75 percent of the loss under the deductible will be incurred. This would mean, for example, that in case of a $500 deductible, the expected unindemnified loss would be (5.40 + ($500 × .20 × .75)) $80.40 instead of $105.40. Such an assumption does not change the decision in the above example.[12]

Taxes

Certain tax implications of self-insurance programs should be explored to analyze the economic impact of self-insurance in any given case. As may be seen in Table 6–1, commercial insurers normally pay about 3 percent of gross premiums in state premium and other taxes. In self-insurance programs these taxes would normally represent a net savings in insurance costs.[13]

On the other hand, amounts set aside in loss reserves or in self-insurance funds are not tax deductible for federal corporate income tax purposes. This does not mean that the self-insurer loses currently the tax deduction on the entire commercial insurance premium — rather only on that portion of the premium representing pure loss which is expected. For example, if a firm is paying $10,000 annually in fire insurance and $6,000 of this amount represents

expected losses, and $4,000 in expenses and profit to the insurer, the self-insurer would lose the tax deduction currently on only $6,000. Presumably the self-insurer could incur up to $4,000 of expenses itself in operating a self-insurance program. (It may be able to save on expenses, by virtue of operating this program more efficiently than the commercial insurer.) The expenses of the self-insurer are tax deductible currently.

Losses suffered by the self-insurer are also tax deductible when they are incurred. Since it is improbable that such losses would be incurred in equal amounts on an annual basis, in some years the self-insurer would have no tax offsets for loss reserves, and in other years it would have large offsets. This would have the effect of creating some instability in after-tax profits that might not otherwise exist. It is possible that a large fire loss would create a net corporate tax loss for the year in which the disaster occurred. In such cases, however, federal tax regulations permit a corporation to carry forward and backward losses against income earned in future or prior years, respectively. Thus, if a firm suffered no fire losses for three years and then suffered a $50,000 loss in the fourth year, and this produced a net corporate loss of $30,000 for the fourth year, it would be able to carry backward the $30,000 loss against any profits earned in prior years and obtain tax refunds.

Another tax implication in self-insurance is the matter of replacing destroyed property. The firm is completely unrestricted in the decision of whether or not to rebuild a destroyed building if it has its own self-insurance fund. Under commercial insurance programs, if a firm receives funds to replace lost property, tax regulations require that the property destroyed be rebuilt within a reasonable time or the insurance funds

[12] For a more complex application of the least cost deductible rule, see Tom C. Allen and Richard M. Duvall, *A Theoretical and Practical Approach to Risk Management* (New York: American Society of Insurance Management, 1971) p. 19.

[13] Some state courts have attempted to hold self-insurers liable for premium taxes on amounts which would have otherwise been paid to commercial insurers. See Monsanto Chemical Corporation case discussion page 13 (7).

received will be treated as an involuntary sale to the insurer.[14] In such a case a capital gain may have to be paid if the cost basis of the property is below the amount received by the insured. For example, if an insured taxpayer owns a building with a cost basis of $50,000, recovers $75,000 insurance proceeds after the building is destroyed by fire, and does not replace the structure, a $25,000 capital gain must be reported. If the taxpayer rebuilds, paying $70,000 for the replacement structure, a capital gain of $5,000 must be reported, etc. It would appear that in some cases federal income taxes may reduce the value of commercial insurance to the taxpayer in those cases where the taxpayer would not normally replace a particular building that was destroyed. On the other hand, if the building is replaced, the maximum amount deductible to the self-insurer is the cost basis of the property, *i.e.*, $50,000. The self-insurer receives no tax deduction for the extra $20,000 it takes to replace the structure.

In the field of pensions and group insurance, self-insurance plans have enjoyed some tax advantages that are not available in commercially insured plans. For example, under Section 501 (c) (9) of the U.S. Internal Revenue Code, a self-insurer may set aside funds for certain contingencies in a trusteed plan which meets specific conditions and enjoy the following tax advantages: (a) exemption from state premium taxes and (b) exemption from income taxes on the earnings on funds in the trust.[15]

The net effect of federal income taxes on the self-insurance decision *in*

the long run is probably minimal. In the short run the effect may be to create some degree of instability in taxable profits in the years in which relatively large losses occur. Possible offsets to such short run instability are (a) the savings on state premium taxes, (b) the net savings on other expenses which the corporation may effect through self-insurance programs, and (c) the savings of extra taxes that may be due if property is not replaced when commercial insurance proceeds are received.

SELF-INSURANCE SAVINGS IN WORKERS' COMPENSATION

An example of the economies of self-insurance may be seen in a study of one particular type of coverage — workers' compensation. One writer estimated that savings of between 20 and 25 percent of the premiums due a commercial insurer would be possible with a self-insured plan.[16] His estimates are based on the following reasoning: In California, commercial insurers' expense allowances amount to 38.35 percent of gross premiums. Of this sum, acquisition expense is 16 percent, and 3.05 percent is taxes, licenses and fees of insurers, both of which are eliminated in a self-insurance program. In addition the time value of money is substantial, because insurers do not pay out all workers' compensation losses in the first year. Rather, losses are paid out roughly as follows: 30 percent during the first year, 30 percent during the second year, 18 percent the third year, 12 percent the fourth year, and 10 percent in the fifth year.

A self-insurer will have the use of

[14] *Internal Revenue Code of 1954* (Englewood Cliffs, N.J.: Prentice-Hall, Inc., 1971), p. 25, 338.33.

[15] An example of such a plan was described by John Franco, "Technicalities of Adopting the 501 (c) (9) Trust," *Risk Management* (October 1972), pp. 12+.

[16] David Warren, "Self-Insurance of Workmen's Compensation: A New Tool for Management," *Business Insurance* (June 8, 1970), p. 37.

funds earmarked for losses until they are needed, and can earn interest returns or can employ them within the business firm as investment capital. For example, assume that money is worth 10 percent to the employer and that the net workers' compensation premium payable to a commercial insurer would amount to $100,000 annually. Assume further that the self-insurer will have overhead expenses of 25.75 percent of net premiums, all paid out in the first year with none in subsequent years; these consist of the costs of administering claims, excess loss insurance, legal costs of disputed claims, safety engineering, and surety bond to guarantee future payments to workers. Assume that losses will equal those of the insurer, 61.65 percent of premiums. The self-insured firm's outlay on *first year* claims will be as shown in Table 6–2.

The present value of future claims under self-insurance may be compared to the present value of the $100,000 of premiums due a commercial insurer of $95,454 (.954 × $100,000). The present value of the self-insurer's first year's cost is 20 percent lower than that of the commercial insurer in this example. Furthermore, the self-insurer has an expense allowance of $25,750 annually to

meet the costs of loss control and claims handling.

LIMITATIONS OF SELF-INSURANCE

From the above analysis of self-insurance it may be seen that there are several potential limitations which should be considered in planning self-insurance plans. Experience shows that many self-insurance plans are not carefully evaluated either before or after they are set up.

(1) Many firms will not meet the required conditions for a successful plan. For example, there may be too few homogeneous exposed objects to meet the requirements of predictability of losses, inadequate financial resources to set up a self-insurance fund, and inability or unwillingness to provide the necessary personnel to administer the plan satisfactorily.

(2) The efficiency in administration of self-insurance plans may not equal or exceed that of the commercial insurer. This is particularly likely to occur if the firm is too small to spread the fixed costs of an insurance plan over a sufficiently large operating base.

TABLE 6–2

		10 Percent Present Value Factor	Present Value of Outlay
Year 1 Claims:	.30 × $61,650 = $18,495		
Expenses:	1.00 × $25,750 = 25,750		
	44,245	.95454	$42,234
Year 2 Claims:	.30 × $61,650 = 18,495	.86777	16,049
Year 3 Claims:	.18 × $61,650 = 11,097	.78888	8,754
Year 4 Claims:	.12 × $61,650 = 7,398	.71716	5,306
Year 5 Claims:	.10 × $61,650 = 6,165	.65196	4,019
	Present Value of Future Claims		$76,362

(3) The earnings available on funds otherwise used for premiums to commercial insurers may not be sufficient to justify the expense involved in setting up self-insurance plans. This is likely to be the case if the rate of return on net worth within the firm is relatively high, if interest earned on reserve funds is relatively low, if commercial insurance premiums are not excessive, and if management is relatively risk averse.

(4) Since tax laws and rulings change constantly, tax conditions may be such that self-insurance plans are disadvantageous, or any tax advantage is too small to offset the possibility of instability in reportable profits.

(5) The firm may lose catastrophic risk protection at acceptable premiums under self-insurance plans because of lack of experience, skill, and economic power in dealing with reinsurers.

(6) The firm may not wish to lose certain services offered by commercial insurers, such as safety inspections, investigation services in connection with fidelity bonds, and third party influence in dealing with employee claimants under workers' compensation.

(7) The firm may face certain legal problems because of self-insurance plans. For example, in one case the courts have held that a self-insurance plan operated by Monsanto Chemical Corporation was illegal, because it deprived the state of taxes on monies that otherwise would have been paid in to commercial insurers. This case is under appeal to higher courts, but it illustrates the problems that may arise.[17]

(8) When self-insurance is applied to group life and health plans, administrative work may be complicated under self-insurance plans due to the necessity

[17] Tom Walsh, "St. Louis Circuit Court Ruling Says Self-Insurance is Illegal," *Business Insurance* (January 15, 1973), p. 1.

of maintaining payments to sick or injured employees over a period of years, and to uncertainties as to the proper size of reserves for losses.

SURVEY OF SELF-INSURANCE PLANS

Professor Robert C. Goshay made a formal investigation of 76 self-insurance and risk retention plans in the United States and discovered several limitations of these schemes.[18] One goal of Goshay's investigation was to determine if firms evaluate the expenses and savings of the risk retention programs. The types of programs involved included fire, liability, and workers' compensation risks. He concluded that evaluating the self-insurance savings is not a common practice. Only half of the respondents made any type of evaluation, and even when this was accomplished, it was done mainly in the area of workers' compensation plans. Although respondents were asked to evaluate the amount of savings made through self-insurance, the data received were rather unsatisfactory. Nevertheless, Goshay estimated that the savings for the majority were quite small, under 15 percent of the premiums, where it was possible to obtain any estimates at all.[19]

In the field of fire insurance, it was discovered that only 17 of 43 respondents had property in more than 100 locations. About one-third of the respondents had relatively high concentrations of property, suggesting that not enough individual firms using self-insurance for the fire risk meet the basic

[18] Robert C. Goshay, *Corporate Self-Insurance and Risk Retention Plans*, Homewood, Ill.: Richard D. Irwin, Inc., 1964. See especially Chapter 7.

[19] *Ibid.*, p. 132.

requirements for sufficient spread of risk to allow adequate predictability. Data were not available on how many of these firms were also utilizing excess loss protection through commercial insurers.[20]

Nevertheless, the self-insurance plans studied showed reasonable financial stability. Average total losses amounted to less than 1 percent of net working capital. In only one case did the average losses go as high as 8 percent of working capital. Expressed as a percentage of annual revenues, the average annual losses from pure risk were less than .2 percent. One firm suffered loss equal to 1.86 percent of revenues. Those firms carried excess loss insurance with commercial carriers. Goshay concluded that the financial impact of risk retention is relatively small on the firms studied and is well within their financial capacity.[21] Most firms have apparently set a level of loss retention well within their working capital capabilities.

However, Goshay did find that the loss stability experienced by these self-insured groups varied considerably depending on the type of coverage. Loss stability was greatest in the field of workers' compensation, and the lowest in the field of fire and liability. Yet, even with the considerable degree of instability noted, the maximum losses were still not outside the bounds of financial resources of the effective firms.

CAPTIVE INSURERS

A captive insurer may be defined as an insurance company owned and operated by a noninsurance corporation, usually for the purpose of obtaining cost (mainly tax) savings and greater un-

derwriting flexibility in risk management. In many cases the captive insurer is formed as a vehicle to implement a self-insurance program. It is also commonly used to handle risks of property owned abroad. Over the period 1966–71, it is estimated that about 300 captive insurers have been formed, most of which are chartered in Bermuda.[22] Other countries often used for chartering captive insurers include the Bahamas, Antigua, Panama, and Switzerland. Colorado was the first state in the United States to pass a law deliberately designed to encourage the formation of captives in that state by providing certain exemptions from taxation and certain other regulations.[23]

Captive insurers may serve three general purposes:

1. Captives may be designed as *flow through* companies to accept reinsurance from other direct insurers. These risks are passed on to other reinsurers under various treaties. This type ·of captive is often employed when the parent corporation operates in a foreign country and wishes to facilitate the placement of standard insurance coverage of property it owns in that country. The insurance may be placed by local insurers and then reinsured through the captive.

2. Captives may be designated as a *fronting company* to secure direct access to reinsurance markets by the parent corporation without going through primary commercial insurers. In this way the acquisition and other expenses associated with the primary insurer are avoided and yet the parent corporation is able to

[20] Ibid., p. 142.
[21] Ibid., p. 162.
[22] Charles H. Groves, "The Colorado Captive Insurance Company Act Revisited," Risk Management (November 1972), pp. 48–50.
[23] Ibid.

transfer given risks to others. In many cases the captive can obtain coverage not available in the primary commercial market, such as flood, earthquake, excess liability, and other coverages at the least possible net cost.

3. Captives are often formed with the main function to avoid income taxes and premium taxes on funds otherwise directed to commercial insurers or used in self-insurance programs, and to accumulate funds under *tax shelter*. Such captives are usually set up in tax havens, *i.e.*, countries with low or nonexistent taxation.

Some captive insurers are little more than file drawer companies designed to secure some of the advantages listed above, while others are full-fledged operations which have advanced to the point that they are serving not only the insurance needs of the parent corporation, but are also selling to outside firms.

Advantages

Advantages claimed for captive insurers include:

1. Greater underwriting flexibility, and freedom from burdensome state regulation. For example, fronting companies dealing directly with reinsurers are not subject to state rating law regulation or underwriting requirements. Policy forms may be written specially for the parent corporation's requirements and need not receive advance approval by the insurance commissioner. Broader coverages are often available than would be the case if regular commercial insurers had to be employed.

2. Cost savings. As in the case of self-insurance, analyzed above, use of captive insurers frees the parent corporation from payment of many types of expenses required in the use of regular commerical insurers. These include state premium taxes, contributions to rating organizations, and acquisition expenses which are paid by regular insurers.

3. Tax shelter. An important motivation for setting up captive insurers, particularly those set up in tax havens, such as Bermuda, is to obtain certain tax advantages. First, premiums paid to captives qualify as tax deductions for federal income tax if the plan qualifies as a true insurance arrangement (such as sharing of risk and an irrevocable payment of funds to an outside party). Second, the earning on capital and reserve funds within the captive can be accumulated under tax shelter under specified conditions. For example, Bermuda does not levy income taxes on earnings in that country. U.S. law provides that if the captive qualifies as a controlled foreign corporation, its underwriting earnings from foreign insurance business are tax deferred until repatriated to the U.S. It is also exempt from underwriting earnings from insuring property located in the U.S. as long as these earnings do not exceed 5 percent of the total of all premiums earned.

Many authorities have cautioned against setting up captive insurers mainly for the purpose of avoiding U.S. taxes. Tax regulations are changing constantly and unless extreme care is taken, the parent corporation may go to the expense and trouble of setting up a captive, only to find that the tax savings it envisioned in so doing have vanished. For example, Section 482 of the U.S. Internal Revenue Code provides that the Internal Revenue Service may reallocate expenses and income between a parent corporation and its captive if it finds that there has been an arbitrary or unreasonable shift of these items to avoid U.S. taxes. Tax authorities have recently disallowed the deduction of the full premium paid by a parent corporation to its subsidiary under this section.[24] Of course, if the books of the parent corporation and the captive are consolidated and the captive is not a controlled foreign corporation, any underwriting earnings of the captive would be fully reflected in the combined statements and hence would be taxable. Perhaps the chief tax advantage of using a domestic captive would be tax deferment of earnings on loss reserves for the payment of long-term claims, such as workers' compensation claims. Such reserves, when reasonable in amount, would be allowed as a tax deduction to the captive when they are set up, but would not be similarly allowed if the parent corporation itself set up the reserves.

4. Loss control. A parent corporation may be more conscious of the advantages of loss prevention if this responsibility is delegated to a captive company with specialized personnel having appropriate skill and authority to handle this function for the particular company.

Conclusion

Captive insurers can bring several economic advantages to a firm if they are carefully set up and operated. Special

[24] Sidney R. Pine, "Tax Factors of Foreign Captive Insurance Companies," *Risk Management* (January 1972), p. 37.

care should be taken in investigating tax consequences. In general, it appears that at the present time tax advantages apply especially to offshore captives set up to insure mainly foreign properties. Domestic captives may be advantageous for insuring domestic properties. Colorado is the first state to set up laws designed to attract domestic captive insurers. Other states may be expected to follow this lead.

Other considerations in establishing captive insurers are (a) the need for special underwriting flexibility, (b) the availability of competitively priced commercial insurance, (c) political factors

TABLE 6–3

Technique	Used for Past 3 Years	Expected to be Used Within Next 5 Years
	(Percent of Respondents)	
Property risks		
Larger deductibles	75.8	88.5
Increased self-insurance	46.6	69.7
More retrospective rating	26.3	40.0
Captive insurers	12.1	44.7
Pre/post loss funding	14.0	26.8
Liability risks		
Larger deductibles	36.7	57.3
Increased self-insurance	34.6	59.2
More retrospective rating	58.5	68.5
Captive insurers	7.9	37.9
Pre/post loss funding	11.4	23.3
Employee benefit risks		
Large deductibles	12.7	21.2
Increased self-insurance	35.9	61.7
More retrospective rating	25.6	35.1
Captive insurers	5.6	26.9
Pre/post loss funding	9.9	17.0

affecting the insured's business, and (d) the size of operation and expected economies, if any, in establishing such subsidiaries.

FUTURE TRENDS

A survey of corporate risk managers in 1974 revealed that in general the use of self-insurance techniques is on the increase.[25] "Self-insurance," as defined in that study, takes several forms: loss funding, rising levels of deductibles, greater use of captive insurers, and retrospective rating plans.

[25] *Time* survey, pp. 1–3.

Based on a response of about 500 corporations throughout the United States, the survey revealed the opinions shown in Table 6–3 as to the expected use of different techniques to accomplish greater savings in risk management.

The respondents indicated that on the average the percentage of total insurable risk retained internally will increase to more than 10 percent for all three of the major types of insurance: property, casualty, and employee benefits. The respondents represented large companies, with annual sales revenue averaging $250 million for those companies with full-time risk or insurance managers.

SUMMARY AND CONCLUSIONS

1. If the conditions for self-insurance are met, the risk manager may profitably employ self-insurance as a method of handling a pure risk. By self-insurance is meant a definite plan for handling risk within the firm. The use of captive insurers is included as a concept of self-insurance.

2. A distinguishing characteristic of self-insurance as contasted to the method of assumption is that definite financial planning for meeting the costs of losses is made. This financial planning can include reserve funds, earmarking surplus for contingencies, arrangement of bank credit in advance of the need, planning for back-up financing from other agencies, or some combination of these methods.

3. Self-insurance is seldom used as an exclusive way of handling risk; rather, it is combined with other methods such as transfer, assumption, avoidance, commercial insurance, and loss prevention.

4. The major objectives of self-insurance include the following: (1) to reduce the costs of handling risk, (2) to reduce the amount of capital kept in contingency loss reserves, (3) to obtain greater flexibility in handling risk, (4) to improve loss control, (5) to improve the handling of claims, and (6) to handle risks not commercially insurable at acceptable rates.

5. Three major conditions favoring the use of self-insurance of the pure risk include: (1) The firm will have a sufficiently large group of homogeneous objects, so situated that the average losses become predictable within acceptable limits. The objects will be suitably dispersed to prevent catastrophic loss. (2) The firm should have sufficient financial strength to meet anticipated losses. Self-insurance is generally not feasible for firms which are weak financially. (3) The firm must be willing to undertake the administrative requirements of a self-insurance plan, such as record keeping, administration of claims, and investment of funds.

6. Major economies in self-insurance are being achieved mainly through reduction of expenses otherwise charged by a commercial insurer, better loss control, and by earning interest income on funds otherwise employed by the insurer in reserves. To some extent the economies achieved through self-insurance are reduced by the loss of certain tax advantages available with commercial insurance.

7. Mathematical decision rules are available to assist the risk manager in evaluating the economic effect of self-insurance and large deductibles.

8. Limitations of self-insurance include the following: (1) The firm may have too few homogeneous exposed objects for predictability. (2) Internal efficiency in operating self-insurance schemes may be low. (3) The opportunity costs for funds used in self-insurance may be high. (4) Tax considerations may sometimes make it disadvantageous. (5) Difficulties in obtaining reinsurance may exist. (6) The firm may not be able to replace services needed from commercial insurers. (7) Legal difficulties may exist. (8) Internal administrative problems in settling long-term claims may exist.

9. Under some conditions, a captive insurer may be formed advantageously and may serve essentially as a vehicle through which self-insurance is achieved. Captive insurers are especially advantageous if the firm is operating in foreign countries.

QUESTIONS FOR DISCUSSION

1. Boling Company purchases insurance for its employees as follows:

	Premium	Loss Ratio Previous Year
Weekly indemnity A & H	$ 24,000	45%
Basic hospital, medical, surgical	79,000	77%
Major medical	32,000	80%
Life insurance (group)	89,000	56%
Total	$224,000	

Its commercial insurer charges 11 percent of gross premiums to administer these plans and has $45,000 of reserves set up, which would be returned to the firm upon cancellation of coverage less any current claims that are not satisfied. The firm is considering setting up a self-insurance program and determines that it can obtain a stop-loss reinsurance agreement to cover 90 percent of any losses in excess of a 105 percent loss ratio up to $200,000 a year. The reinsurer will charge 3 percent of the gross premium now paid for administration. Analyze the cost savings and possible problems of the proposed self-insurance plan. (Make any assumptions that you think are reasonable concerning the firm's internal costs of self-insurance.)

2. A writer stated that in his company, which had a self-insurance program in the field of workers' compensation, all loss reserves are treated as expenses and deducted in the year in which reserves are created. The rationale for such a procedure is that although a federal income tax audit may occur, it would take two or three years. By the time the tax audit is made, many of the claims which made up the deduction would be closed. A tax penalty would be levied upon the taxes due on reserves not yet closed. The returns on the money invested in such reserves might amount to more than the 6 percent tax penalty which would be levied. Comment. Is such a procedure to be recommended? Explain.

3. A writer stated, "It has been my experience that a self-insured employer could save 20 to 25 percent per year under a self-insurance program . . . An employer who sustains losses of about $100,000 a year should anticipate premiums of approximately $160,000 per year in the field of workers' compensation. Based on studies of the major workers' compensation carriers' annual statements we have been able to determine that the pay-out of losses flows at the rate of approximately 34 percent of the incurred losses in the first year, 31 percent in the second year, 13 percent in the third year, 6 percent in the fourth, 4 percent in the fifth, 3 percent in the next two years, and 2 percent in the last three years, totalling 100 percent pay-out in ten years. We would anticipate that an employer of this size would have administrative expenses for claims service, etc., of $35,000. Thus, if the pay-out of losses in the first year were only $34,000, the total expenses and losses would be $69,000, as opposed to a premium of $160,000 payable to a commercial insurer. The difference may be invested to produce investment income. In the second year the employer would be expected to pay out $31,000 of losses on the first year claims, plus another $34,000 of claims in the second year, for a total loss payment of $65,000 in the second year. Adding this $65,000 to the expenses of $35,000, we have $100,000 of losses and expenses in the second year, with a savings of $60,000 when compared to the second year premium of $160,000 which would have been entailed by commercial insurance. Thus, the first two years' savings would be $151,000. By carrying out similar calculations for the subsequent years, it could be shown that the employer's total cost savings over commercial insurance would amount to $422,000, or about 25 percent of the ten-year premium figure of $1,600,000." (a) What reasoning underlies the statement that losses of $100,000 a year mean premiums of about $160,000 a year? Explain.

(b) Evaluate the cost savings in the workers' compensation self-insurance program outlined by this above writer.

4. A writer stated, "Some corporations have approached group life and hospitalization programs on a self-insured basis. The average rate for group life insurance for 500 lives runs about $.60 per $1,000 of coverage per month. Assume each of the 500 lives is insured for $5,000. You are then dealing with $2,500,000 × .60, or $1,500 per month premium dollars. This provides $18,000 a year for the payment of claims or death reserve expectancy of 3½ lives per year. On a group of 500 people, the actuarial odds are in your favor, plus you have an investment income." Analyze the above statement. Do you think 500 lives are enough for self-insurance of a group life plan?

5. An article stated that the risk manager of a large airline decided to increase the deductible on his policy covering airplane crashes, because he felt that "the most" loss that they would incur in any one year was one 707 aircraft. In the next year and a half after this decision was made, three aircraft were lost. The deductible was reduced to a level below where it had been formerly. In your opinion is it likely that any one airline would have enough airplanes to meet the requirement of predictability in the self-insurance decision? Explain.

6. A newspaper report in 1966 stated that Georgia's new self-insurance program, inaugurated May 1, 1965, had saved the state nearly $400,000 in its first year of operation. This amount stemmed from losses being 30 percent less than expected and from lower premiums paid to commercial insurers than would have otherwise been the case (the state continued to purchase excess coverage from commercial carriers). There were 55 losses during the year, the largest of which was $10,963.95 for a fire at the Milledgeville State Hospital feed mill. Under the plan the state pays the first $25,000 of loss, plus 10 percent of the excess over $25,000. The financial results showed premiums of $542,051, including $45,890.65 interest earnings on a self-insurance fund of $1,000,000 appropriated by the state legislature. Various state agencies submitted "premiums" to the state fund instead of paying these premiums for commercial coverage. Expenses and losses totalled $239,404, including $29,339 in administrative costs. The value of buildings insured under the program increased from $116 million to $364 million during the year. It was estimated that a reserve fund of $5 million would be necessary for complete self-insurance.

(a) Assess the validity of the first sentence of the above account.
(b) Assess the validity of the last sentence of the above account.
(c) Do you believe that the state should eventually abandon the excess coverage? Why or why not?

7. An author stated, "Self-insurance and self-assumption have become almost a fetish with some so-called experts, to the extent that deductibles and self-insurance are recommended to everyone and in any situation. In one recent case a $100,000 deductible was recommended where the basic premium was only in the low thousands for complete coverage."

(a) What difference do you think the author has in mind between *self-insurance* and *self-assumption?*
(b) Why was the large deductible considered unwise? Explain.

8. An author stated, "Chemical companies fit nicely into the optimum pattern for using captives. The captive is used for normal or expected risks (*e.g.*, plant equipment, stock) to the extent, say, of $50,000 per loss. Catastrophe insurance to cover the possible destruction of single plants is carried with conventional reinsurance firms. The parent company pays premiums to the captive as it would to a conventional insurer . . . An offshore captive can insure exposures not readily insurable in domestic markets: flood, loss of contract, and confiscation of property by a foreign government." Point out some of the possible weaknesses in the author's argument.

9. The Arvin Company is considering a self-insurance program for its workers' compensation claims. Presently it is paying $1 million annually to a commercial insurer, whose administrative costs are 40 percent, or $400,000. Claims are $600,000, payable as follows:

1st year	40 percent
2nd year	30 percent
3rd year	20 percent
4th year	10 percent

(a) Assuming that Arvin will have the same administrative costs as the commercial insurer, calculate the annual savings to Arvin from the cash flow effect, if cost of capital to it is 10 percent.
(b) Do you believe Arvin may make additional savings through self-insurance?

II

Transfer to Insurers:
Property and Liability Risks

7

Insurance of Property and Liability Risks

Earlier chapters have treated transfer as one of the methods of meeting risk. The transfer techniques that were identified include hedging, guarantees and warranties, hold harmless agreements, insurance and suretyship.[1] This chapter is the first of two in which the transfer of property and liability risks to insurers will be considered in some detail. The discussion will be mainly concerned with the type of risks and insurance contracts involved and some of the general characteristics of the insurance mechanism. Specific topics include:

1. Characteristics of the insurance process

2. The field of property and liability insurance
   a. Fire and allied lines
   b. Ocean marine
   c. Inland marine
   d. Automobile
   e. Aviation
   f. Burglary and theft
   g. Liability
   h. Boiler and machinery
   i. Workers' compensation
   j. Suretyship

---

[1] Some of these techniques, for example hedging, will be discussed in more detail in subsequent chapters. See Chapter 14.

k. Title
l. Multiple-peril

Of the various ways of treating pure risk, transfer to insurance companies is the most widely used. They are virtually the only professional risk takers in the economy. Their presence in the economic structure permits others to undertake business ventures that they might otherwise not consider, because the possibility of loss of property, for example, from fire and other perils might well constitute more risk than businesses, in general, could comfortably bear.

CHARACTERISTICS OF THE INSURANCE PROCESS

In its most basic form the insurance mechanism is simply a process wherein a group of people agree to share the losses that may occur to various members of the group. In practice, money (premium) is typically collected from members of the group in advance and the fund so created, augmented by interest, is used for the purpose of paying losses and expenses. Further, the conditions surrounding the transfer or risks from individuals to the group are carefully set forth in great detail in a formal contractual agreement. The organization that brings the group together and manages its affairs is called an insurer, and it is typically a stock or mutual corporation.

Although insurers as risk takers perform an extremely important function in the business world, they by no means are able to accept all risks that a business or an individual might wish to transfer to them.[2] This constitutes a limitation on insurance as a way of meeting risk. Another limitation is that only risks on which a dollar value can be placed are accepted for transfer by the insurer.[3] Further, when loss occurs, the typical property and liability insurance contract will pay only the actual cash value of the loss (replacement new less depreciation) at the time of loss with the face of the contract serving as an upper limit to settlement.[4] A third limitation on insurance as a way of meeting risk is that the insured is often

asked to meet various requirements that in effect constitute direct controls. For example, an insured may be required to pass a physical examination before he will be accepted for life insurance. In some types of insurance the insured must agree to adopt certain preventive measures such as installation of fire extinguishers and related means of lessening the probability of the occurrence of fire and of controlling its intensity. Although deductibles and coinsurance features constitute limits on the amount of recovery that the insured receives in the event of loss, they also may be viewed as controls, especially when large deductibles and/or coinsurance features may be required of business firms before the insurer will issue a contract.

There are a variety of reasons why an insurer cannot, as a practical matter, accept all risks that others may wish to transfer to them. As Arrow has observed, perhaps the most important reason is the existence of moral hazard (the possibility that the insured will deliberately bring about loss). Insurance has the peculiarity that the existence of a contract may in itself "change incentives and therefore the probabilities on which the insurer has relied."[5] The possibility that the existence of insurance contracts may reduce the incentive to succeed, whether the incentive be to operate a business with intelligence and care or to recover rapidly from an illness, stands as major deterrent to the unlimited use of insurance as a way of meeting risk and may bring about the need to share losses with the insured

[2] It is sometimes argued that an insurer could accept all risks if the prospective insured were willing to pay a large enough premium. If the premium charged became so large as to constitute trading dollars with the insurer, the advantages of the insurance system would be lost to say nothing of the added expense to the insured of sharing in the expenses of the insurer.

Limitations on insurance as a transfer mechanism were introduced briefly in Chapter 2. The discussion here serves to amplify the remarks made there and to relate them to property and liability insurance.

[3] An exception to this is life insurance where the question of the intrinsic value of the life insured does not arise. In the event of death, the face of the contract is paid.

[4] Marine insurance contracts that are written on a valued basis (value is agreed upon in advance and forms the basis of the settlement) are an exception to this statement. Replacement cost insurance is available for loss from fire and related perils, but is not the basis for settlement in most property and liability insurance contracts.

[5] For a further discussion of this point and the limitations on insurance see Kenneth Arrow, *Essays in the Theory of Risk Bearing*, (Chicago: Markham Publishing Co., 1971), pp. 134–143.

Historically, an objection to replacement cost insurance was that it might increase the moral hazard.

through various coinsurance arrangements.

Apart from the existence of moral hazard there may be other aspects of a risk that will make its transfer to an insurer open to question. In Chapter 2, four requirements that a risk must meet to be eligible for transfer were identified: (1) there must be the possibility of bringing together a large number of homogeneous risks of a particular type; (2) the risk must be such that any losses that occur must be due to chance; neither the insured nor the insurer must be able to control the happening or non-happening of an event made possible by the risk; (3) events that occur as a result of a particular risk must be definite in time and place; (4) the risk must be of a type that would not lead to loss of a catastrophic type.

The reason for the first requirement is that the pricing of insurance contracts depends on an assessment of past experience in terms of loss frequency and severity. Since premiums are charged and paid in advance, they represent an estimate of the amount that will be necessary for the insurer to collect from each insured in order to pay claims and expenses. Thus, if the insurer is to operate in a financially sound manner, it is essential that probability estimates based on past experience be fairly close to the true probability that a loss will occur. The law of large numbers offers a theoretical basis for believing that the two probabilities (true and estimated) will be close provided the number of risks brought together is very large and that any losses that occur represent independent, chance events.[6]

The homogeneity requirement is needed for purposes of equity in rating. Only those persons facing the same degree of risk should be charged the same rate. Any risks transferred to the insurance company should be in themselves homogeneous or capable of being classified into large, homogeneous groups.

The requirement that any losses that occur be due to chance relates to the assumptions underlying the law of large numbers, which are that the events that occur be fortuitous and independent. The reason for requiring definiteness in time and place is that if losses are to be paid fairly and accurately, and if appropriate loss data are to be maintained, it is essential that each loss be capable of complete identification. Insurers wish to avoid risks with a catastrophic potential because such losses might well deplete surplus or even lead to insolvency.

A number of risks now transferred to insurers do not meet the requirements of an insurable risk in their entirety. Through careful underwriting it is often possible to mitigate some of the adverse effects that might occur from failure to observe some of the requirements. Some requirements, such as homogeneity, do not lend themselves to perfect attainment. Nevertheless, the requirements do serve as a limiting factor in insurer operation, and serve to deter the transfer of a number of pure as well as speculative risks.

Even though risks may be capable of transfer to a professional risk taker, it does not follow that such risks should be transferred. One way of classifying risks is by frequency and severity. There are four possibilities:

[6] One statement of the law of large numbers is:

$$\Pr_{n \to \infty} \{|p'-p|<\varepsilon\} \to 1$$

where p' is an estimated probability, p is the true probability that an event will occur, and ε is an arbitrary positive constant. A nontechnical statement of this law was given in Chapter 2.

1. Low frequency, high severity.

2. Low frequency, low severity.

3. High frequency, high severity.

4. High frequency, low severity.

Of the four categories only those risks falling in category (1) should be seriously considered for transfer. Risks falling in categories (2), (3), and (4) probably should be retained, since they may be budgeted for, or if not budgeted, the financial impact should be arranged for in other ways.

THE FIELD OF PROPERTY AND LIABILITY INSURANCE

The business of insurance as it is practiced in the United States consists of insurers that sell life and health and related types of insurance and insurers that write property and liability insurance. In general, life insurers may not write property and liability insurance and vice versa. However, through the use of subsidiaries, property and liability insurers can and do write life insurance and life insurers are now beginning to establish property and liability subsidiaries. Health insurance is sold by both types of insurer and in a number of instances by firms specializing in this field. In this chapter only property and liability insurance will be discussed.

Broadly speaking, property and liability insurance as a field encompasses all forms of non-life insurance. The contracts that are sold cover losses to property both real and personal that are caused by such elements as fire, windstorm, robbery, liability, and many other perils. No one contract will necessarily cover all situations, but it is possible to purchase contracts that will cover a wide variety of risks.[7]

The principal lines of insurance that constitute the field of property and liability insurance are: fire and allied lines, ocean marine and inland marine, crime, liability, automobile, aviation, boiler and machinery, workers' compensation, surety, and title. In each line there are a number of contracts available to cover a variety of related risks, as well as contracts that combine lines of insurance (multiple-line insurance contracts).[8]

Fire and Allied Lines

The fire and allied lines branch of property and liability insurance is designed to provide protection against the uncertainties that result from the possibility of loss caused by such perils as fire, windstorm, and hail that represent destruction from the forces of nature.[9] The principal contracts that are offered in this line of insurance are the standard fire insurance contract plus various forms and endorsements,[10] sprinkler

---

[7] The difference between a mono-line and multiple-line contract will be discussed later in this chapter, see p. 146. In general a multi-line contract includes the liability risk along with the physical damage to property risk.

[8] Three lines not discussed in this chapter are crop-hail, glass, and credit. For an indication of their premium volume see Table 15–1.

[9] In this book the word *peril* will be used when cause of loss is meant. The word *hazard* is sometimes used as a synonym for "peril," but strictly speaking, a hazard is some force that increases the probability that loss will occur from a particular peril. See Chapter 2.

[10] Some of the specific perils covered by this contract and some of the other contracts

leakage insurance, tenants' improvements and betterments, deferred payment insurance, yard improvements insurance, builder's risk, standing timber insurance, profits insurance, errors and omissions, replacement cost insurance, rain insurance, earthquake, and flood insurance. With a few exceptions, it is now possible to cover all major risks of physical damage from forces of nature that face the owners of both real and personal property whether used for business or nonbusiness situations.

Ocean Marine

Ocean marine, a branch of the general field of transportation insurance, is the oldest of the various types of insurance including life. Designed to protect against the risks facing ocean-going and inland ships, including cargo being transported by them, this field of insurance has long been of great importance to the world of commerce. The principal types of contract available are hull, cargo, protection and indemnity (essentially liability insurance for the owner of the vessel), freight (charges for carrying cargo), builders' risk, officers' protective, and longshoremen's and harbor workers' compensation. Marine insurance contracts are generally written on an all-risk basis, which means they offer comprehensive coverage to the property in question with few exclusions, limitations, or exceptions. The hull contract is an example of a multiple-line policy.

Inland Marine

Inland marine insurance as it is now understood, has been developed in comparatively recent times and extends the notion of ocean marine insurance to transportation of goods over land.[11] It is sometimes called "dry marine" to distinguish it from "wet" or ocean marine. This distinction, however, is not entirely accurate. Some inland marine contracts cover risks associated with transportation over water such as coastal waters, rivers, canals, and lakes. For example, although yachts are written under an ocean marine contract, outboard boats and motors are typically written under an inland marine form. Also, ocean marine contracts have a warehouse-to-warehouse clause that covers goods shipped by vessel from the time they leave the warehouse of the shipper until they reach the warehouse of the consignee and, thus, cover a type of overland risks. Inland marine insurance is not limited to transportation risks. Instrumentalities of transportation such as bridges and tunnels are regarded as falling within the classification of inland marine insurance. Floater policies and block policies, designed to protect various types of personal property while in transit, are inland marine coverages, although many of them protect property while in a fixed location and are not exclusively transportation contracts. Since inland marine insurance during the course of its development extended over a broad field, it was inevitable that it

---

will be discussed in Chapter 8. No effort will be made in this or subsequent sections to define or describe all of the risks and/or insurance contracts mentioned. Detailed descriptions may be found in publications such as *The Fire, Casualty, and Surety Bulletins* (see bibliography).

[11] Inland marine insurance was an outgrowth of ocean marine insurance and was responsive to needs created by the rise of new methods of transportation, which needs were largely not met by existing ocean marine forms. However, it is possible to find examples of inland marine type contracts that were in existence hundreds of years ago.

would overlap with older lines of insurance. The resulting confusion and concern has largely been alleviated by the development of a nationwide marine definition sponsored by the National Association of Insurance Commissioners first in 1933 and revised in 1953. Some minor changes have been made since that time. Both versions were adopted by most states.[12]

Some of the more important contracts that are classified as inland marine are: inland transit contract; trip transit contracts; postal insurance contracts; registered mail contracts; first-class mail insurance contract; armored-car and messenger insurance contracts; processors' floater contract; garment contractors' insurance contracts; truckmen's legal liability interest; bailees' customers contracts; blanket motor cargo insurance contract; contracts covering bridges, tunnels, and instrumentalities of transportation and communication; personal property floater contract; musical instrument floater; cameras, projection machines, and equipment floater; furs and jewelry floater; outboard motors and motorboats floater; sportsmen's floater; fine arts floater; silverware floater; wedding presents floater; physicians' and surgeons' equipment floater; contractors' equipment floater; salesmen's floater contracts; radium floater contract; stamp collection floater; theatrical floater contract; jewelers' block contract; and farm equipment and animal floaters.

Although inland marine insurance contracts are seemingly diverse, there is a unifying principle. All of them contemplate insuring property in motion, even though in some instances the insurance is extended to cover the property while in a fixed location. This fact is in contrast to fire and allied lines insurance where it is generally assumed, with some exceptions,[13] that the property insured will not be moved from the described premises.

Automobile Insurance

Automobile insurance is a part of the broad field of transportation insurance and is properly a marine line. Traditionally it has not been classified that way. Automobile insurance contracts, as now written, have the distinction of being among the earliest multiple-line contracts and provide in one policy protection against virtually all of the risks associated with the ownership and operation of the automobile. Automobile insurance is generally not available as a part of other insurance contracts, although there are a few exceptions. For example, some commercial general liability contracts contain coverage for the automobile liability risk and there is a possibility that insurance for the automobile will become a part of the homeowners contract.

There are many types of automobile contracts available to the public. They can be classified as contracts developed by the national rating bureaus and those that are independent or nonbureau. Examples of bureau forms are the Family Automobile Policy, the Special Autombile Policy, and the Basic

---

[12] See Robert I. Mehr and Emerson Cammack, *Principles of Insurance*, Sixth ed., (Richard D. Irwin, Inc., 1976), pp. 302–303 and pp. 309–317.

[13] For example, traditional homeowners contracts provide coverage for personal property in transit but have a limitation of 10 percent of the amount of insurance applicable to contents under the contract. This is an additional amount of insurance and some contracts indicate that the amount of coverage in any event shall not be less than $1,000. Homeowners '76 does not place a percentage limit on personal property in transit but covers personal property "owned or used by any insured while it is anywhere in the world."

Automobile Policy. The first two of these forms are only available for insuring private passenger automobiles, farm automobiles, or utility automobiles. Such vehicles must be owned by an individual or a husband and wife. The basic contract is not as broad in terms of coverage as the other two but is available for a variety of uses. Some persons for various reasons cannot qualify for the family or special policies but may be insured under the basic contract. The basic form is also available to insure a wide variety of vehicles such as trucks, buses, and motorcycles. Independent contracts may differ in various ways from the bureau forms but they are becoming increasingly similar.

Automobile insurance in terms of written premiums is the most widely sold type of property and liability insurance. Anyone or any business owning an automobile is in need of protection against economic loss arising out of automobile accidents. Thus, in individual or business planning for risk, serious consideration must be given to the ownership of vehicles and the resultant exposure to risk, particularly the risk associated with legal liability.

Aviation Insurance

Like automobile insurance, aviation insurance is logically a part of the broad field of marine or transportation insurance. But, also, like automobile insurance, it has been treated separately. Some of the language used in aviation insurance is similar to that used in the marine field but, in general, it follows the automobile pattern. Aircraft Hull and Aircraft Liability insurance are written mainly through insurer pools; however, a few insurers will write such insurance on their own forms.

Aircraft insurance contracts are nonstandard. The principal types are Aircraft Hull Insurance, Aircraft Liability Insurance, Hangar Keepers Legal Liability, Nonownership Liability, Airport Liability Insurance, and Crop-dusting Liability Insurance. Hangar Keepers Legal Liability is ordinarily written as an endorsement to Airport Liability Insurance. Nonownership liability may be written as an endorsement or as a separate contract. Aircraft insurance is new but of increasing importance, especially to business firms, since many firms now operate aircraft for business purposes.

Crime Insurance

The insurance contracts thus far considered have in almost every instance contemplated that any accidental losses that occurred would result from noncriminal activities. Since losses from criminal activities such as robbery, burglary, or larceny involve millions of dollars every year, it is not surprising that insurance contracts were developed to protect against the financial impact of these losses. Historically, theft insurance has been divided into two parts. Theft caused by employees was regarded as falling in the field of corporate suretyship, and fidelity bonds were regarded as the appropriate way for dealing with the risk of employee dishonesty. Theft of various types by outsiders was provided for by contracts sold by property and liability insurers. Today many multiple-line insurers include fidelity and surety bonds among the contracts they sell. Also, there are a number of combination contracts that include theft of all kinds, including in some cases, employee dishonesty, among the perils insured against.

There are many contract forms available in the field of crime insurance. Among them are a variety of personal theft insurance contracts and such commercial contracts as the Mercantile Open

Stock Policy, Mercantile Safe-Burglary, Mercantile Robbery, Paymaster Robbery, Money and Securities Contract — Broad Form, Storekeepers Burglary and Robbery, Blanket Crime, Bank Burglary and Robbery, Safe Deposit Boxes, Depositors Forgery, Bankers Limited Forgery, and Forged Securities.

Liability

Liability insurance is generally regarded as a part of the field of property insurance even though it might seem on first consideration not to involve the destruction of property. Nevertheless, the possibility of liability being imposed may bring about the loss of assets by depleting cash or necessitating the conversion of other property into cash.

All individuals and business firms face the risk that they may be *legally* required to pay damages. These damages may arise as a result of negligence which may be their own or the negligence of someone for whose actions they have responsibility. Damages may also arise as a result of a breach of contract or from the assumption of the liability of others often through a hold-harmless agreement or through a hold-harmless clause in an existing contract.

Since the possibilities for the imposition of liability are numerous, the number (and variety) of liability insurance contracts is very large. Since the liability arising from the ownership and operation of automobiles and aircraft is typically treated separately (see above), the concern here will be other types of liability for which specific contracts exist. Among these other types are: Contractual liability; business firms public liability; hospital liability; physicians, surgeons, dentists, and other individual practitioners liability; lawyers liability; druggists liability; elevator li-

ability (although in the majority of jurisdictions it is no longer regarded as a separate general liability insurance line); fiduciary liability; personal liability; farmers personal liability; personal injury (libel, slander, false arrest, detention, malicious prosecution, invasion of privacy, etc.) liability; product-completed operations liability; storekeepers liability; fire legal liability personal umbrella liability; employers liability; directors and officers liability and the liability of insurance agents, accountants, and similar professionals.

Although the list of situations involving liability is extensive, it should be kept in mind that it is possible to combine a number of liability coverages in one contract (Comprehensive General Liability, for example), or to include liability with various property coverages (Homeowners and Special Multiple-Peril Contracts, for examples.) Whatever the subject matter, as it relates to liability, virtually all liability contracts contain very similar insuring agreements. It is typical for the insuring agreement to contain wording to the effect that the insurer "will pay on behalf of the insured all sums which the insured shall become legally obligated to pay as damages because of . . ." In most instances the agreement to pay covers property damage as well as bodily injury. In addition, the typical contract agrees that the insurer will pay as an additional benefit the costs of defending the insured against a damage suit even if it is groundless, false, or fraudulent.

The spirit of all liability contracts is that the insurer will respond only if the insured is *legally* obligated to pay. Nevertheless, most liability contracts contain benefits that do not depend on legal responsibility. For example, many such contracts agree to pay medical benefits to injured parties other than the insured (except for some contracts such as automobile, which include the insured, even though the insured may not have been at fault.) This benefit is sometimes referred to as insurance of the moral obligation of the insured in the event of bodily injury. Likewise, there is often a provision to pay for damage to property of others, up to a fairly small maximum, even though fault of the insured has not been assessed. The reason for such a coverage is the moral obligation of the insured to pay for property damage of modest amounts occurring within his purview.

Liability insurance is probably one of the most important of all of the property-liability coverages in that the possible impact of loss of assets may well be the greatest in this area. The problem is complicated by the fact that the amount of possible loss is not determinable in advance, since such a determination is often dependent on the decision of a jury. This fact is in contrast to most property situations where the maximum amount of loss depends on the value of a piece of property, which, within limits, can be determined in advance. To cope with the problem of an unknown amount of possible loss, liability insurance is typically written with high limits. These limits may be expressed as a single sum or in terms of a maximum amount per person and a maximum amount per accident or occurrence. The limitations and exclusions in liability insurance are typically not severe and the coverage is effective in protecting against losses of considerable magnitude.

Workers' Compensation

Workers' compensation laws make employers responsible (without regard to fault) for the financial consequences of injuries to employees that arise out of and in the course of employment. Insurance contracts are available in which the insurer agrees to pay the damages specified by the particular workers' compensation law to which the employer is subject. Since workers' compensation may also be regarded as an employee benefit, a discussion of it will be given in Chapter 11.

Boiler and Machinery

Boiler and machinery or, perhaps, more aptly, power plant insurance came into being as a branch of property and liability insurance primarily because the peril of loss from explosion or accidently tearing asunder of steam boilers and related objects was excluded from the standard fire insurance contract. With the rise of manufacturing and the widespread use of steam boilers the need for protection from the consequences of the explosion of boilers became clear.

The insuring agreement of the basic boiler and machinery policy covers the insured against loss from an accident to an object.[14] The loss that is covered includes damage to the object itself; expediting expenses; property damage liability; bodily injury liability; defense, settlement, and supplementary payments; and automatic coverage of newly acquired vessels. Contracts and endorsements providing coverage in addition to that provided in the basic policy are available. Among these are: consequential damage insurance, furnace explosion insurance, outage insurance, power interruption insurance, residence boilers and vessels, auxiliary piping, and boiler and machinery use and occupancy. Like many other forms

[14] The *object* is specifically described in the schedule attached to the contract. Further discussion of boiler and machinery insurance is given in Chapter 8.

of property insurance, boiler and machinery coverage may be included, by appropriate endorsements, in commercial package policies.

Suretyship

Strictly speaking the field of bonding is a separate (albeit transfer) method for dealing with risk. Since bonds are sold by property and liability insurers, often through subsidiaries, they will be considered here. The risk involved in suretyship (or surety bonding) is failure to perform and the financial loss that might ensue as a result of that failure. Surety bonds are of two main types, those that guarantee performance in such activities as construction or court appearances and those that guarantee honesty (fidelity) of employees who, for example, have access to cash or other financial instruments.

Perhaps the main difference between suretyship and insurance is that in the former no loss is expected by the insurer, while in the latter the reverse is true. In suretyship the premium is a fee for service (the surety investigates the contracter, say, and is practically certain he can meet his obligations before entering into the contract); in insurance the premium contains an amount that is intended for the payment of loss. Further, if loss does occur under a surety bond, the surety expects to recover from the principal. There is no such contemplation in insurance. Other differences are: (1) a surety bond is always a three-party contract — surety (risk taker), principal or obligor (person who is required to perform), and obligee (beneficiary of the performance), while an insurance contract typically involves only two parties — insurer (risk taker) and the insured (person or corporation that transfers the risk); (2) the surety bond is purchased by the principal for the benefit of the obligee, while in property and liability insurance the purchaser of the contract is typically the beneficiary; (3) under a surety bond a principal may cause loss intentionally, while this type of loss is rare in insurance.

There are many kinds of bonds, although they may be roughly classified as fidelity bonds, blanket bonds, financial guarantee or surety bonds and forgery bonds. Strictly speaking all bonds are surety bonds and classification mainly helps in identifying the nature of the performance to be guaranteed. The names of some of the bonds (without regard to classification) are: Excess Bankers' Blanket Bonds; Credit Union Blanket Bond; Small Loan Companies Blanket Bond; Blanket Bond for Building and Loan and Savings and Loan Associations; Bankers Blanket Bond; Charge Card issuers Bond; Bankers Liability Indemnity Bond; Finance Companies Blanket Bond; Stockbrokers Blanket Bond, Fiduciary Bonds; Plaintiffs and Defendants Bond such as Attachment, Release Attachment, Replevin, Counter-Replevin, Dissolve Injunction, Appeal, Stay of Execution, Admiralty Bonds, and Bail Bonds; Bid, Performance, and Payment Bonds; Fidelity Bonds such as Name Schedule Bonds, Position Schedule Bonds, Commercial Blanket Bond, and Blanket Position Bond.

Many of the bonds mentioned in the preceding paragraph are pure bonds in that they have the characteristics discussed for bonds as opposed to insurance. Others, such as the Bankers Blanket Bond, which may additionally protect against perils other than those typically found in bonds, are more insurance-like in their structure, while retaining many of the characteristics of typical bonds. Bonds extend protection to risk areas that are of financial significance but have traditionally not been

Title

covered by the usual insurance contracts.

Title

The risk insured against in title insurance is that defects in the title of real property that existed before the date of the contract may come to light and bring about future loss to the person to whom the title has been transferred.

On first consideration it might seem that defects in title would be so rare as not to require any particular protection against their financial consequences. The facts are that many sources for defective title exist, and although prevention of defects through careful search reduces the possibilities of loss to a minimum, there is still a chance that some defect will go undetected. Some of the sources of defects in title are: outstanding mortgages, mechanics liens, secret marriages, and missing heirs.[15]

There are a number of ways that some assurance as to the soundness of the title may be given to buyer of real property without introducing the notion of title insurance. There has long been a system of the public recording in the United States that requires that deeds and other documents affecting the transfer of real property be recorded in a public place, typically the recorder's office in the county seat of the county in which the property is located. Since these records are public documents, the prospective buyer of real property may "search" the title if he wishes; in fact the law assumes that the buyer is familiar with such public information.[16]

It is somewhat unrealistic to expect the typical buyer to have sufficient sophistication to do an adequate job of investigating the title of property and over the years this task has been relegated to professionals. One of the older ways of providing an opinion on the soundness of a title is the conveyancer system which is widely used in "New England, along the Atlantic Seaboard, and in the South."[17] The system operates by having a lawyer who is an expert in land titles conduct a search and present an opinion about the soundness of the title. Another system for examining a title grew out of the conveyancer system and involves the use of laymen as abstractors. In the Middle West, in particular, abstract companies were organized and abstractors accumulated information on titles of land within their particular area of operation. It is then possible for an abstractor to offer an opinion on a title. Often, especially today, such an opinion is used in connection with a title examination by an experienced attorney. Still another way of providing some assurance about title quality is the Torrens System, which was developed in Western Australia. This system involves the use of courts in the registration of title. After application has been made to the court, a public hearing is held, and subsequently a certificate is issued that becomes the basis for title. Mortgage liens and judgments must be registered to be valid. There is also a statute of limitations. An indemnity fund is set up to provide redress for those persons who may have valid claims not known at the time of registration. Although Torrens Statutes were enacted in some 20 states,[18] the system has never been especially popular.

[15] For longer list see *Title Insurance Companies*, (Stamford, Conn.: Philo Smith, Landstreet & Company, Ins., 1969) p. 1.

[16] The presumption is somewhat impractical. See *Ibid*.

[17] *Ibid*.

[18] California subsequently repealed its Torrens law.

The main problem that arises with most systems for providing an opinion on the quality of a property title is that no guarantee emerges which states that the title is without defect. Should a title prove defective, the buyer must institute a suit to try and recover damages for any loss that he might sustain. This is true in the Torrens System, for example, even though an indemnity fund has been established.

Title insurance, although it, too, does not guarantee the title, serves as a way to overcome most of the objections raised against noninsurance ways of meeting the title risk. It is a means of combining "the functions of the abstracter and the attorney . . . with that of the insurer."[19] Although the word *insurance* is used in describing the field of indemnification of losses arising from defective titles, the fact is that title insurance differs in many ways from most forms of insurance. As in bonding, the insurer does not expect loss or at worst a minimal loss. The premium is for the service rendered by the title company in searching the title. Further, title insurers do not insure against fortuitous future contingencies, as is the case with the usual types of insurer. As opposed to risk assumption and distribution, title companies emphasize risk avoidance and elimination. Also, in contrast to most insurance the premium for the coverage is paid only once. Most title insurance is written by specialty companies set up for that purpose and operating independently, but some are subsidiaries of property and liability insurers.

Multiple-Line

The discussion of the scope of property and liability insurance has

thus far dwelled on the individual risk categories for which separate property and liability insurance contracts are available. Historically, property and liability insurance was written on a mono-line basis and anyone wanting to insure a number of risks typically acquired a large number of contracts.[20] In the 1950s state insurance laws were changed to permit multiple-line underwriting and multiple-line contracts, with the result that many perils can be insured against through the use of one contract. A variation on the theme is to bring a number of individual contracts together in a single package.[21]

Some early examples of multiple-line contracts in property and liability insurance are the hull contract in ocean marine insurance, the boiler and machinery contract, and various automobile contracts. Some inland marine insurance contracts (such as block contracts and floaters), although they do not involve liability, are essentially multiple-line in that some casualty coverages are included as a part of the contract. After the legislation of the 1950s a number of new contracts were developed that emphasized the multiple-line approach. Among them are the Manufacturers Output Contract, the Special Multi-Peril Contract, and the Farmworkers Contract, which were designed for business use. On the personal side the best examples of multiple-line contracts are the various forms of the Homeowners policy.

---

[19] *Title Insurance Companies*, p. 5.

[20] The way insurance statutes were then written insurers were licensed on a mono-line basis and insurance contracts reflected this form of organization.

[21] Some types of insurance are typically not found in multiple–line or package policies. Examples are automobile, workers' compensation, and surety bonds.

SUMMARY AND CONCLUSIONS

1. Insurance as a way of meeting risk is widely used by business firms, and insurers are virtually the only professional risk takers in our society.

2. In its most basic form insurance is a process wherein a group of persons agree to share the losses that may occur to various members of the group.

3. Insurers are not able to accept all of the risks that others may wish to transfer to them.

4. Risks may be classified by frequency and severity. One such classification is low frequency, high severity; low frequency, low severity; high frequency, high severity; and high frequency, low severity. Those risks falling in the first classification are best suited for transfer.

5. Property and liability insurance as a field encompasses all forms of nonlife insurance.

6. The principal lines of insurance that constitute the field of property and liability insurance are: fire and allied lines, ocean marine and inland marine, theft, liability, automobile, workers' compensation, aviation, boiler and machinery, surety bonds, and title.

7. Multiple-line insurers, multiple-line underwriting, and multiple-line insurance contracts are now widespread in property and liability insurance. They serve to unify the field and often result in a more efficient solution to insurance problems.

QUESTIONS FOR DISCUSSION

1. Discuss the limitations of insurance as a way of treating property and liability risks. To what extent is it possible to overcome these limitations?

2. Consider the risk of financial loss resulting from the damage to property of fire, flood, earthquake, theft, windstorm, and collision of automobiles. To what extent do these risks meet the requirements of an insurable risk?

3. Risks may be classified according to frequency and severity. Analyze the following risks and decide whether you would expect them to occur frequently or infrequently and the degree of the severity of the resulting loss: fire, windstorm, hail, explosion, theft, riot, smoke, falling objects, weight of snow, accidental discharge of water from plumbing fixtures, breakage of glass, bodily injury liability, and automobile accidents. In performing the analysis consider consequential loss and other types of loss that may be pertinent. Indicate the extent to which your response might depend on specific situations.

4. Discuss the extent to which the risks mentioned in (3) might be candidates for retention rather than transfer. Give reasons for your response.

5. What is meant by a "line of insurance?" List the lines of insurance that constitute the field of property and liability insurance.

6. Workers' compensation laws impose liability for work injuries that arise out of and in the course of employment on the employer without regard to fault. What are the specific benefits provided by these laws? In what ways do they vary among the states? To what extent is the federal government involved in workers' compensation?

7. Liability suits for injuries caused by products have increased considerably over the last ten years. Define the product liability risk. Why do you believe it has increased in importance? To what extent is the product's risk accepted by insurers?

8. Another area in which liability suits have increased in recent times is malpractice. Define the malpractice risk. To what extent is insurance available to afford protection against the financial consequences of legal action?

9. Distinguish between inland marine risks and ocean marine risks. Why was it necessary historically to adopt a fairly extensive definition of inland marine insurance?

10. There are those who believe that title insurance, strictly speaking, is not insurance. Cite reasons in support of this point of view.

11. The word "insurance" like the word "risk" may be defined in a variety of ways. How would you define insurance? What are the characteristics of an insurable risk?

12. Prepare a risk analysis for the Calwood Lumber Company. See Chapter 20, Case F.

8

Structure of Property and Liability Insurance Contracts

In this chapter the structure and contents of some of the property and liability insurance contracts used by risk managers in their treatment of property and liability risks will be discussed. In particular consideration will be given to:

1. The form of property and liability insurance contracts

2. Clauses common to property and liability insurance contracts

3. Some legal principles

4. Special multi-peril contract

5. Loss of income — business interruption insurance

6. Liability contracts including workers' compensation

7. Transportation contracts

THE FORM OF PROPERTY AND LIABILITY INSURANCE CONTRACTS

The vehicle used for transferring risk from an individual or business firm to the insurer is the insurance contract. This contract, plus riders and endorsements, constitutes the agreement between the insured and the insurer and details the conditions under which the transfer takes place. Basically, all insurance contracts may be divided into four parts: declarations, insuring agreement, exclusions and limitations, and conditions.[1]

Declarations

This section of the contract appears first and contains information designed to identify the insured, the property, and the type or types of coverage, together with the term of the contract, the face amount of insurance, and the premium. Other types of information may be added depending on the type of contract and the circumstances surrounding the transfer. In property and liability insurance, declarations are usually fairly brief, often given orally by the insured, and even though they appear as a part of the contract are typically unsigned by the insured. The declarations supply the basic but not necessarily the sole information needed by the insurer in deciding whether to issue the contract and at what price.

[1] Some contracts, such as the standard fire insurance contract, are obviously not in this form, but it is possible to rearrange the various clauses to put them in the four-part form, if desired. The same is true of life insurance contracts.

149

Insuring Agreement

The insuring ageement, a formal statement detailing what the insurer promises to do in return for the premium paid, and in reliance on statements made by the insured, ordinarily follows the declarations. This statement may be fairly lengthy and complicated, as in the case of the liability insurance contract, or it may be fairly brief as in fire insurance. The perils insured against and services promised are stated and defined (and where appropriate, other definitions are given), although instead of naming the perils insured against, the insuring agreement may be of the all-risk type in which all risks of loss or damage are covered except for specific exclusions. If there are limitations on the amount of recovery in addition to the face of the contract, these may be stated in the agreement. The insuring agreement is the most important section of the contract, since it contains the basic information about the nature of the risk transfer and what may be recovered in the event of loss.

Exclusions and Limitations

Insurance contracts (see above) are written either on an all-risk basis or on a named-peril basis. In the former case the contract insures against all risks except those specifically excluded in the contract, while in the latter only losses resulting from named perils are covered. An all-risk contract is typically preferred since it offers the broader coverage. However, whichever way the contract is written, it is clear that no insurer undertakes to insure against all risks of loss or damage, and even perils which are covered are normally subject to limitations and/or exclusions. These exclusions, in general, are of two types.

Certain kinds of property are excluded or certain perils are excluded or both things may occur. Sometimes excluded property may be added by endorsement and the same is true of perils.[2] Whatever the situation, it is important that the insured understand the exceptions surrounding the transfer and be aware of any residual risk to which he may be exposed that is not covered by the usual insurance contract.

Conditions

The clauses in the contract that may be classified as conditions state the things the insured must do to enforce his rights under the contract. One type of condition enables the insurer to deny liability for loss if the probability of that loss has been increased. Most of the conditions refer to the type of information that must be supplied by the insured in the event of loss or define certain rights of the insured if dispute arises in regard to the loss. It is essential for the insured to know what his duties are. Otherwise, he might fail to recover a loss that was payable except for the fact that he did not comply with all of the terms of the contract.

Binders

Often in property and liability insurance an agreement may be reached that a particular contract is to be consummated, and some written evidence of the agreement is needed before the policy can be prepared. To take care of this contingency a memorandum called a *binder* is issued, which is a temporary

[2] Additionally, it will be recalled that only property that can be valued in a dollar sense is the subject matter of property and liability insurance. Thus, property having sentimental value only is not insurable.

insurance contract. The binder contains the essential facts about the transaction such as date, amount, name of insured, and risk to be covered. In the event of loss, the binder serves in lieu of the policy and has the same force as if the policy had been issued.

CLAUSES COMMON TO PROPERTY AND LIABILITY INSURANCE CONTRACTS

Very few property and liability insurance contracts are standard in that precisely the same contract in a given field is sold by all insurers.[3] Nevertheless, most property and liability insurance contracts have provisions in common that are applicable regardless of the subject matter of the contract, even though the wording may not be exactly the same from contract to contract. The principal common elements are assignment, cancellation, coinsurance, mortgage rights, notice of loss, proof of loss, other insurance, and valuation.

Assignment

Property and liability contracts, with the exception of marine insurance contracts, are not freely assignable and may be assigned in the sense of substituting one insured for another, only with the consent of the insurer. This practice is consistent with the notion that insurance contracts are personal contracts and that the characteristics of the insured are given consideration when the contract is formed.

[3] The principal standard contract is the basic fire insurance policy. The New York Standard Contract is a statutory contract in 43 jurisdictions. Although other fire contracts are not precisely like the New York contract, they differ very little.

Cancellation

With the exception of some marine insurance contracts, all property and liability insurance contracts may be cancelled during the term of the contract by either the insurer or the insured. If the insurer cancels, it must give sufficient notice to allow the insured to obtain other insurance (usually five to ten days), and return the premium on a pro rata basis. The insured may cancel at any time, but, if he does, the premium is returned on a short-rate basis, meaning that he will receive something less than the pro rata return. The reasons for treating the insured differently, depending on which party initiates the cancellation, are that the insured should not be penalized for an action of the insurer taken for its convenience, and that the insured should be willing to pay the premium that would have been charged if he had sought insurance for less than the term specified in the contract in the first place.[4]

Coinsurance

Coinsurance clauses do not appear in every property and liability insurance contract, but are fairly common in fire insurance contracts covering commercial property. By coinsurance, as far as property insurance is concerned, is usually meant the sharing of losses by the insured based on the relationship between the face amount of the contract and the value of the property insured or some specified percentage thereof.

The coinsurance clause in a fairly typical property insurance contract reads as follows:

[4] Lower rates per day as the term lengthens has long been recognized in insurance. Thus, the rate for a three-year contract is typically less than three times the annual rate.

The Company shall not be liable for a greater proportion of any loss to the property covered hereunder than the limit of liability under this policy for such property bears to the amount produced by multiplying the coinsurance percentage applicable (specified in this policy) by the actual cash value of such property at the time of the loss.

As an illustration of the operation of this clause, consider the following facts: A fire insurance contract has been entered into for face amount, $30,000. A loss of $5,000 occurs. The actual cash value of the property insured is $50,000 at the time of loss. The coinsurance percentage is 80 percent.[5] The amount that the insured would recover is determined as follows:

$$\frac{\$30,000}{(.8)(50,000)} \cdot \$5000 = \frac{3}{4} \cdot \$5000 = \$3750$$

The insured, as a result of the coinsurance clause, coinsures to the extent of $1,250 of the loss. The clause becomes meaningless if the loss is equal to or exceeds the required percentage of actual cash value, since in no event is more than the face of the contract paid.

The main reason for the coinsurance[6] requirement is that most property losses are partial losses and that the probability of loss is higher for partial losses than for total losses. Since fire insurance rates, for example, are quoted on a flat rate per $100 of face amount of insurance, an inequity is created between those who insure for less than the

value of the property and those who insure for full value. Ideally, those in the latter category should be charged a lower rate per $100 of value and those in the first category a higher rate. For reasons of practicality, a graded rating system has not been set up, and coinsurance is relied upon as a way of inserting equity into the rating system.

Mortgagee Rights

Property insurance contracts, particularly those covering buildings of various types, typically have clauses designed to protect the interest of persons having liens on the property. The principal type of lien is the mortgage. The basic fire insurance contract, for example, provides space in the declarations section for the naming of the mortgagee and lines 68 to 85 give a statement of rights of the mortgagee. In addition, the form attached to the contract contains the Mortgagee Clause. In general this clause gives full protection to the mortgagee even in situations where the mortgagor may have violated the contract.[7]

Notice of Loss

Virtually all insurance contracts contain a clause in the conditions section of the contract stating when and how an insured must give notice of loss. The standard fire insurance contract, to cite an example, requires that the insured "give immediate written notice to the Company. . . ." Although wording similar to this is found in most property and liability insurance contracts, as a

---

[5] Any percentage is possible, but 80 percent is typical.

[6] Coinsurance is limited by law in some states and in others it is specifically permitted. The typical situation is that coinsurance may be used or may not be depending on the wish of the insurer.

[7] For an example of a settlement under the mortgagee clause see Albert Mowbray, Ralph H. Blanchard, and C. Arthur Williams, Jr., *Insurance*, 6th ed. (New York: McGraw-Hill Book Co., 1969), p. 171.

practical matter, most insurers will accept oral notice to an agent. How immediate the notice must be may depend on circumstances and the practices of a particular insurer. Regardless of what practices may be, the prudent insured will read the contract carefully and observe the instructions therein given.

Proof of Loss

It is common in property and liability insurance for the conditions section of the contract to contain information about what the insured must do to establish his claim that loss has occurred. The fire insurance contract, for example, indicates that proof of loss must be filed within sixty days of the notification of loss. The requirement for proof of loss is part of a larger section in the contract that details the responsibility of the insured in the event of loss. The proof of loss must contain a statement about

. . . the time and origin of the loss, the interest of the insured and all of others in the property, the actual cash value of each item thereof and the amount of loss thereto, all encumbrances thereon, all other contracts of insurance, whether valid or not, covering any of said property, any changes in the title, use, occupation, location, possession or exposures of said property since the issuing of this policy, by whom and for what purpose any building herein described and the several parts thereof were occupied at the time of loss and whether or not it then stood on leased ground. . . .[8]

The proof of loss part of the fire insurance contract is more detailed than in most contracts, but the typical loss sections of property and liability contracts

[8] New York 1943 Standard Fire Insurance Contract, lines 100–110.

are fairly specific about the insured's obligations.

Closely related to the instructions regarding filing of proof of loss is the section of property and liability insurance contracts regarding the right of insureds to sue for recovery of a claim. Typically, such suits are not sustainable unless the insured has complied with the requirements of the contract and then only if suit is filed within a year after the loss.

Other Insurance

One of the problems that arises in property and liability insurance contracts because of their indemnity nature is the amount of the settlement in the event there are other contracts covering the same property for the same perils in whole or in part. In some contracts other insurance is prohibited, while in others specific permission is given.

Many property and liability contracts provide for a pro rata sharing of the loss which preserves the principle of the common law sharing rule. The pro rata clause states that no insurer shall be "liable for a greater proportion of any loss than the amount hereby insured shall bear to the whole insurance covering the property against the peril involved. . . ." In the fire insurance contract "whether collectible or not" is added but this phrase does not appear in statements of the pro rata rule in some other contracts.

In some property and liability insurance contracts, other insurance is treated on an excess basis. If all of the contracts involved have the excess clause, however, the settlement is usually on a pro rata basis. In some situations, the contract written first responds first and other contracts respond as excess in the order in which they were written.

Valuation

Since property and liability insurance contracts are contracts of indemnity the insurer usually promises to pay only the cash value of the loss at the time of loss, which is interpreted to mean replacement cost less depreciation. Thus, an insurance settlement is not based on market value nor on the book value. The face value of the contract simply serves as an upper limit to recovery. Since questions of the value of a piece of property at the time of loss can lead to controversy, property and liability insurance contracts ordinarily provide, in addition to a statement of the basis of settlement, provision for appraisal.

Some property and liability insurance contracts agree to loss settlement on a replacement cost basis. Such a provision appears in Homeowners contracts, provided the face amount of the contract is at least 80 percent of replacement cost new at the time of loss. It is possible for replacement cost endorsements to be placed on fire insurance contracts, although such endorsements are not common. As was indicated in Chapter 7, some insurance contracts particularly in the field of marine insurance are written on a valued basis. In such contracts the insurer agrees to settle, in the event of loss, on the basis of the value of the property that was agreed upon at the time the contract was made.[9]

[9] The concept of agreeing on value at the time of entering into the contract and using that value as a basis for settlement in the event of total loss arises in nonmarine property and liability insurance in the form of valued policy laws, which exist in some states. These laws are often limited to total losses of real property and typically only apply to losses from certain perils.

Subrogation

In property insurance contracts where the principle of indemnity applies, a subrogation clause is included which states that the insurer is subrogated to any rights the insured may have to proceed against a third party because of the party's negligence. The insurer may recover only to the extent that it has paid the insured. If the amount that the insured receives from a third party is less than the amount of the loss, the insurer's claim comes after that of the insured. Thus if an insured had a $15,000 loss, received $10,000 from the insurer, and $12,000 from a third party, the insurer would be entitled to $7,000 of the latter amount, since the insured may receive full indemnity for his loss. The result of subrogation is that the insured has not received more than he has lost. Further, the use of the subrogation clause keeps insurance rates lower than they would be if subrogation did not exist. Another reason for subrogation is that it tends to place the burden of loss on the person responsible.

SOME LEGAL PRINCIPLES

The insurance contract is a legal document containing a set of promises and, in general, it must meet the same requirements that any contract must meet in order to be enforceable. Thus, there must be an offer and acceptance, capacity to contract, a valuable consideration, and the contract must be for a legal purpose. Insurance contracts differ from the usual type of commercial contracts in a number of ways. Commercial contracts are typically commutative (there is a fairly even exchange of values) whereas insurance contracts, along with gambling contracts are aleatory. An aleatory contract is one in which there is an uneven exchange of values, and one party (the insurer) agrees to perform only if certain events occur. The conditions form a part of the agreement and the insured may receive a large sum in comparison to a relatively small premium. Insurance contracts are also, typically, unilateral, that is, the act of paying a premium is exchanged for the promise of the insurer. If credit is extended for the premium, the contract becomes bilateral because a promise is exchanged for a promise. Another feature of insurance contracts is that they are personal contracts. Even if the subject matter of the contract is property, the characteristics of the person owning the property is an important item for the insurer in determining whether it wants to accept the risk. Finally, insurance contracts are contracts of utmost good faith (*uberrimae fidei*) and the insurer places great reliance on the honesty of the insured and his willingness to reveal accurately the characteristics of the risk he wishes to transfer.[10]

In addition to these basic contract essentials, insurance contracts are surrounded by other legal doctrines that reflect the nature of the insurance transaction. The most important of these doctrines are indemnity, insurable interest, concealment representation and warranty, and waiver and estoppel.

Indemnity

It is generally agreed in insurance that insurance contracts are contracts

[10] In this and succeeding sections, the emphasis will be on the property and liability aspects of the legal principles surrounding insurance contracts. The major differences between property and liability insurance and life and health insurance will be considered in Chapter 17.

of indemnity. That is, in the event of loss, the insured should recover no more than the cash value of the loss. Although there are exceptions to this principle in property and liability insurance, as well as in life insurance (See Chapter 9), the doctrine holds for most nonlife insurance contracts. The implication of the doctrine is that no one should gain from an insurance transaction but should receive only the value in financial terms of what was lost. Thus, the insured should be no better or worse off financially than he was before the loss. If the possibility of gain did exist, there is danger that the moral hazard would be increased with resultant difficulties for the efficient conduct of a property and liability insurance business.

Insurable Interest

The doctrine of insurable interest requires that no one be insured unless he stands to suffer financially in the event a loss occurs. In property and liability insurance, the insurable interest need attach from a legal point of view, and except for one or two states, only at the time loss occurs, although in most insurance transactions the insurable interest will exist at the time the contract is entered into as well. The reasons for requiring an insurable interest are to prevent wagering, lessen the moral hazard, and to have a basis for measuring the extent of the loss. Various types of ownership convey an insurable interest in property. The main requirement is that a prospective insured have a legal hold on the property. A mortgagee may, for example, insure property to the extent of his interest. Other types of property interests (to the extent of the interest involved) may convey an insurable interest are liens, leaseholds, stockholders interests, security interests, and contract rights.[11]

Concealment

Concealment means failure on the part of the insured to disclose (voluntarily) information to the insurer. In the United States in nonmarine forms of insurance, concealment involves knowledge of a fact on the part of an insured and lack of knowledge of the fact on the part of the insurer. In addition the fact must be material. Also, there must be an intent to deceive the insurer in the mind of the insured. In brief, in nonmarine insurance the concealment must be fraudulent. In marine insurance law a concealment of a material fact will void the contract even if the insured was unaware that the fact was material. There are some exceptions to the concealment doctrine. An applicant is not required to voluntarily reveal self-disgracing facts and he will not be charged with concealment if the fact is one that the insurer might be presumed to know or could easily have inquired about.[12]

In general, in most commercial transactions, there is no duty to reveal facts voluntarily by one party to the contract to the other party even though the first party knows that the second party does not know some particular fact and that it may be material.[13] The insurance rule about concealment appears to be fairly unique. Historically the reasons for making an exception for insurance were: (1) the insurance contract is aleatory and the possibility exists that a large sum will be payable by the insurer even though the insured has paid comparatively very little. If the prospective insured has knowledge and the insurer does not that a particular event insured against is very likely to happen or has already occurred, the insured has an unfair advantage. In situations where chance is presumed to govern the outcome, failure to reveal such knowledge is morally reprehensible; (2) the prospective insured has superior knowledge in respect to his own risk and unless he reveals this knowledge he has an inherently unfair advantage; and (3) insurers rely heavily upon full disclosure by the applicant in making decisions about acceptance or rejection. Although, theoretically, by diligent search the insurer might be able to discover most material facts, such a search is expensive, and over the years there has been a belief on the part of insurers that the costs of insurance are lower if the applicant's honesty is relied upon.

Representation and Warranty

"A representation is a statement made by the applicant for insurance, or by someone acting for him and by his authority, to the prospective insurer, before the making of the contract of insurance and not embodied as a term of the contract."[14] A misrepresentation made by the insured by falsely answer-

[11] See Edwin W. Patterson, *Essentials of Insurance Law*, 2nd ed. (New York: McGraw-Hill Book Co., 1957), pp. 111–16. The legal facts presented in this and subsequent paragraphs are based on this reference.

[12] This discussion of concealment has been limited to the American common law. In English law an innocent material concealment is grounds for avoidance in all lines of insurance. Further, in the United States, in one state the common law has been modified by statute to make concealment grounds for voiding the contract whether or not it was intentional. See *ibid.*

[13] There are some exceptions to this statement. See *ibid.*, p. 447.

[14] *Ibid.*, p. 378.

ing a question asked of him may enable the insurer to rescind or void a contract. Although oral answers to questions may be considered as well as written ones, difficulties in establishing precisely what was said in oral responses has meant that, for the most part, cases involving misrepresentation have been limited to situations where a written application for insurance has been required. In life insurance by statutes enacted in many states only statements made in a written application and attached to the contract can be used by an insurer in the event it wishes to rescind a contract on the basis of misrepresentation. A misrepresentation of a fact must be shown to be material (*i.e.*, it made some difference in the acceptance or rejection of the risk and/or the terms on which the risk was accepted), if it is to be used to void the contract. In general the misrepresentation of an objective fact is sufficient ground for the voidance of the contract.[15] Representations that are made a part of the contract become warranties.[16]

The word *warranty* has several meanings in the commercial world. As the word is used in connection with insurance contracts, its meaning is generally that expressed in the New York insurance statutes:

150. The term "warranty" as used in this section, means any provision of an insurance contract which has the effect of

[15] *Ibid.*, p. 442. For an extended discussion of representation see *ibid.*, Ch. 9. Note the misrepresentation must be of a material fact. Honest statements of opinion even though incorrect do not serve to void the contract.

[16] Life insurance generally forms an exception to this statement, since statutes in many states prevent the conversion of representations made on an application into warranties.

requiring, as a condition precedent of the insurer's liability thereunder, the existence of a fact which tends to diminish, or the nonexistence of a fact which tends to increase, the risk of the occurrence of any loss, damage, or injury within the coverage of the contract. . . .

Warranties are used in relation to causes of insured events and seek to eliminate potential causes of such an event. An affirmative warranty is one that need exist only when the contract is made. A promissory warranty is one wherein an insured agrees that a condition, fact, or circumstance will persist during the life of the contract. Warranties may be express or implied. An express warranty is a term of the contract, which is either written or printed and is made a permanent part of the contract. An express warranty may also be made a part of the contract by reference. An implied warranty is one that is not written and does not appear in the insurance contract. Implied warranties are used only in marine insurance and are three in number: the ship must be seaworthy at the beginning of the voyage, must proceed with dispatch and not deviate from its usual course between named points, and must not be engaged in an illegal venture.

The effect of a breach of warranty is to make the insurance contract unenforceable for losses that happen after the breach occurs. In most states the breach does not have to be material.[17]

Waiver and Estoppel

Waiver and estoppel are doctrines that may prevent an insurer from asserting a defense such as breach of war-

[17] This discussion is necessarily brief. For an extended treatment see *ibid.*, Chapters 7 and 8.

ranty, misrepresentation, concealment, or lack of coverage under the contract because additional facts may show that such a defense has been waived by statement or action of the insurer or possibly his agents and is not available as a means of denying a claim. A waiver may be defined as a voluntary relinquishment of a known right. Estoppel prevents a person from asserting a right which by his own action he had previously relinquished. Estoppel can operate even though a right has not been voluntarily given up. An insurer may be estopped from denying liability under a contract that was issued by an agent even though the agent knew some part of the contract had been breached at the time of issue.

The doctrines of waiver and estoppel most often arise, as a practical matter, in connection with the acts of insurance agents in their work with insureds. Possible waivers may occur during negotiations for the contract, during the term of the contract, or in the process of setting a loss. Insurers attempt to protect themselves from possible actions of an agent that may result in waiver by inserting in the contract a statement to the effect that no waiver is valid unless contained in the contract or reduced to writing and added to the contract. Although such statements may be effective in many instances, there is no guarantee that the insured is aware of such a statement before the contract is issued and before he has had a chance to read it. Further, if it is possible for provisions of contracts to be waived, there would seem to be a possibility that the waiver clause could also be waived. There appears to be support for the position that the waiver clause at best serves as a warning to the insured about the limited authority of agents.[18]

[18] Legal doctrines surrounding the power of agents will be discussed in Chapter 15.

PROPERTY AND LIABILITY INSURANCE CONTRACTS

In the preceding sections of this chapter the emphasis has been on those aspects of property and liability insurance contracts that have general applicability regardless of the specific risk being considered. As a practical matter the content of the insuring agreement and the limitations and exclusions surrounding it, as well as some other parts of the contract, will depend on the risk or risks being insured. Since there are many different property and liability risks and many different contracts covering them, it is impractical in a single chapter to construct a catalogue of all property and liability insurance contracts now offered in the United States, together with a statement about their specific contents.[19] In a specific case the contracts required by a particular business firm to meet its needs will depend on the risk analysis prepared by the risk manager and by his judgment, given a firm's policy statement, about how the risks are to be treated. No general prescription can be given that will apply without modification to all business situations. Nevertheless, there are certain contracts that have wide applicability and, with some modifications, are used by a wide range of businesses. Contracts that many firms find essential are fire covering real property, perhaps in more than one location, contents of buildings, and property in transit; liability coverages including such items as

[19] For additional information about a wide variety of property and liability contracts, see J. H. Magee and O. N. Serbein, *Property and Liability Insurance*, 4th ed., (Homewood, Ill.: Richard D. Irwin, Inc., 1967); *Fire, Casualty, and Surety Bulletins* (Cincinnati, Ohio: National Underwriter Company, 1976); R. C. McCormick, *Coverages Applicable* (Indianapolis: The Rough Notes Company, 1970).

public liability, directors and officers liability, product liability and contractual liability; business interruption; crime, including defalcation by employees, and burglary and robbery by outsiders; boiler and machinery and workers' compensation.

In this section the Special Multi-Peril contract will be taken as an example of a multi-line contract that covers fire, liability, crime, and boiler and machinery and is often used, where it applies, in place of a collection of monoline contracts covering the same perils. Workers' compensation and employers' liability are treated separately, since such contracts are not included in the special multi-peril contract. Similarly, liability other than public liability, business interruption, and certain transportation contracts will be treated apart from special multi-peril.

Special Multi-Peril

The special multi-peril contract is a multiple-line contract providing basic property and liability coverages; it is adaptable to the needs of a wide variety of businesses. It is divided into four sections: (1) property coverage; (2) liability coverage; (3) crime coverage; and (4) boiler and machinery coverage. Coverages 3 and 4 are optional and are not necessarily needed by all businesses.

Section I. Property Coverages

The special multi-peril general property form is a named-peril form and insures against all direct loss to the property covered under the contract caused by fire, lightning, windstorm and hail, explosion, sudden and accidental damage from smoke, vehicles or aircraft, riot, and riot attending strike and civil commotion. By explosion is meant "direct loss resulting from the explosion of accumulated gases or unconsumed fuel within the firebox (or combustion chamber) of any fired vessel or within the flues or passages which conduct the gases of combustion therefrom."[20] Losses caused by vehicles or aircraft mean direct loss "resulting from actual physical contact of an aircraft — or a vehicle with the property covered hereunder or with the buildings containing the property covered hereunder, except that loss by aircraft includes direct loss by objects falling therefrom."[21] The other perils are fairly self-explanatory, although some of them are subject to limitations.

The limitations and exclusions surrounding the perils are found in the contract as a part of the statement of perils and partly in a separate section of the contract labelled *Exclusions*. In relation to windstorm and hail, the insurer does not accept liability for losses caused "directly or indirectly by frost or cold weather or ice (other than hail), snow or sleet, whether driven by wind or not."[22] Similarly, the insurer does not accept responsibility for damage to the interior of buildings or the property covered therein if it is caused "by rain, snow, sand, or dust, whether driven by wind or not,"[23] although if the wind or hail causes direct damage to the roof or walls of a building causing openings the insurer will respond to interior damage by these perils. Likewise, the insurer is

---

[20] *Study Kit for Students of Insurance* (Chicago: American Mutual Alliance, 1976), p. 214. The discussion of the multi-peril contract is intended to be illustrative and not exhaustive. The emphasis is on property and perils covered. For complete information on deductibles, coinsurance, conditions, and exclusions, the reader should consult the contract.

[21] *Ibid.*

[22] *Ibid.*, p. 213.

[23] *Ibid.*

not liable for water damage from sprinklers or other piping unless they have been directly damaged by windstorm or hail.

In regard to explosion the insurer is not liable for loss of steam boilers, steam pipes, steam turbines or steam engines by explosion, "if owned by, leased by, or operated under the control of the insured." Also, "shock waves caused by aircraft, generally known as 'sonic boom'; electric arcing, rupture or bursting of rotating or moving parts of machinery caused by centrifugal force or mechanical breakdown; water hammer; and rupture or bursting of water pipes are not explosions for purposes of this section."[24] Under the peril of smoke, coverage does not exist for agricultural smudging or industrial operations. In providing coverage for losses from vehicles or aircraft the insurer does not accept responsibility for losses caused by any vehicle "owned or operated by the insured or by any occupant of the described premises or to any aircraft or vehicle, including contents thereof, other than stocks of aircraft or vehicles in the process of manufacture or for sale."[25] Under the peril of riot, riot attending a strike, and civil commotion, the insurer does not accept liability for "loss resulting from damage to or destruction of the described property owing to change in temperature or humidity or interruption of operations whether or not such loss is covered by this policy as to other perils."[26]

Certain causes of loss are specifically excluded in the contract. Among these are loss caused by "(1) earth movement, including but not limited to earthquakes, landslide, mudflow, earth sinking, earth rising or shifting; (2)

flood, surface water, waves, tidal water or tidal wave, overflow of streams or other bodies of water, or spray from any of the foregoing, all whether driven by wind or not; (3) water which backs up through sewers or drains; (4) water below the surface of the ground including that which exerts pressure on or flows, seeps, or leaks through sidewalks, driveways, foundations, walls, basement or other floors, or through doors, windows or any other openings in such sidewalks, driveways, foundations, walls, or floors."[27] If fire or explosion ensues from any of these losses, the contract will respond, but only for the loss caused by fire or explosion. There is also a war and governmental action exclusion, as well as a nuclear exclusion. Other exclusions are: (1) the insurer is not responsible for loss arising out of "enforcement of any local or state ordinance or law regulating the construction, repair, or demolition of buildings or structures unless such liability is otherwise specifically assumed by endorsement";[28] (2) there is no insurance under the contract for losses caused by "electrical currents artificially generated unless loss by fire or explosion as insured against hereunder ensues"[29] and then only for the ensuing loss; (3) the insurer is not liable for "loss caused by or resulting from power, heating or cooling failure, unless such failure results from physical damage to power, heating or cooling equipment situated on premises where the property covered is located caused by a peril insured against. . . ."[30]

Basically two types of property are covered under the general property form of the special multi-peril contract.

24 Ibid., p. 214.

25 Ibid.

26 Ibid.

27 Ibid., p. 215.

28 Ibid.

29 Ibid.

30 Ibid.

They are buildings (Coverage A) and personal property (Coverage B) in fixed location, although these coverages are extended to include newly acquired property, property off-premises, personal effects, valuable papers and records, trees, shrubs, and plants, extra expense, and replacement cost.

Coverage for buildings at the described location includes not only the building(s) itself (themselves) but all additions and extensions attached to it (them.) Additionally the following types of property associated with buildings are covered:

1. All fixtures, machinery, and equipment constituting a permanent part of and pertaining to the service of the building.

2. Materials and supplies intended for use in construction, alteration or repair of buildings.

3. Yard fixtures.

4. Personal property of the insured as landlord used for the "maintenance or service of the described buildings, and including fire extinguishing apparatus, floor coverings, refrigerating, ventilating, cooking, dishwashing and laundering equipment, shades and outdoor furniture (but not including other personal property in apartments or rooms furnished by the insured as landlord)."[31]

5. Debris removal.

Business personal property is covered if owned by the insured and usual to the occupancy of the insured and "while in, or on the described building, or in the open (including vehicles) on the described premises or within a hundred feet thereof"[32] including:

[31] *Ibid.*, p. 213.
[32] *Ibid.*

"Bullion, manuscripts, furniture, fixtures, equipment and supplies not otherwise covered under this policy, and shall also cover the insured's interest in personal property owned by others to the extent of the value of labor and materials expended thereon by the insured."[33] Other situations included under the general heading of personal property that are insured include:

1. Tenant's improvements and betterments.

2. Personal property of others is covered at each location to the extent of 2 percent of the limit of liability for personal property (Coverage B) subject to a maximum of $2,000. The property must be on the described premises or within 100 feet thereof and must be in the care, custody or control of the insured. Any coinsurance clauses in the contract do not apply to this particular coverage.

3. Debris removal.

Additional types of property covered have been mentioned briefly. The insured may apply up to 10 percent, subject to a maximum of $25,000 of the limit of liability for buildings (Coverage A), to cover "new additions, new buildings and new structures when constructed on the described premises and intended for similar occupancy."[34] The coverage also applies to buildings acquired by the insured "at any location, elsewhere than at the described premises, within the territorial limits of this policy and used by him for similar

[33] *Ibid.*
[34] *Ibid.*, p. 214. There is a time limit imposed. Coverage does not go beyond 30 days from the start of construction but may be less than that if the contract expires sooner or if the values of new construction are reported before that time.

occupancies or warehouse purposes."[35] Newly acquired personal property is covered to the extent of 10 percent of the limit stated for personal property (Coverage B), subject to a $10,000 maximum, for direct loss by a "peril insured against to such property at any location (except fairs and exhibitions) . . . elsewhere than at the described premises, within the territorial limits of the policy."[36] The insurance on newly acquired property ceases 30 days from the date of such aquisition or on the date values of the buildings, new construction, or personal property "are reported to the Company, or on the expiration date of the policy whichever occurs first." An additional premium must be paid for the reported values from "the date construction begins or the property is acquired."[37]

Property normally at a fixed location is insured while off-premises for purposes of "cleaning, repairing, reconstruction, or restoration." This extension does not apply to merchandise or stock nor does it apply to property in transit, "nor to property on any premises owned, leased, operated, or controlled by the insured." The dollar amount of the coverage is 2 percent of the sum of the limits of liability for Coverage A (buildings) and Coverage B (personal property) subject to a $5,000 maximum.[38]

Personal effects belonging to the insured, officers, partners, or employees "while located on the described premises" are insured subject to a number of limitations. The maximum amount of insurance is $500 of the limit applicable to Coverage B (personal property) but no more than $100 is applicable to any one individual. The extension does not apply "if the loss is covered by any other insurance, whether collectible or not, or which would have been covered by such other insurance in the absence of this policy."

Valuable papers and records are insured under an extension of coverage up to $500 of the limit of liability of Coverage B (personal property) against direct loss in any one occurrence provided the loss is caused by a peril insured against under Coverage B. The type of papers and records contemplated are: "books of account, manuscripts, abstracts, drawings, card index systems, film, tape, disc, drum, cell and other magnetic recording or storage media for elecronic data processing, and other records," all belonging to the insured and located as described in the declarations. The dollar limit specified is the total amount that can be collected even though more than one location is involved. Further, only the "cost of research and other expense necessarily incurred by the insured to reproduce, replace, or restore such valuable papers and records" is covered.

Trees, shrubs, and plants are not insured under either Coverage A or Coverage B but are included, with limitations, in the extensions of coverage. The limiting amount of insurance is up to $1,000 of "the sum of the limits of liability specified for Coverage A and Coverage B" for direct loss at the described location for any one occurrence. The insurer limits its liability for any one tree, plant, or shrub to $250 "including expense incurred in removing debris thereof." The perils insured against are fire, lightning, explosion, riot, civil commotion, or aircraft but only to the extent that these perils are included in the special multi-peril contract.

[35] *Ibid.*

[36] *Ibid.*

[37] *Ibid.*

[38] The quotation in this paragraph and the next six paragraphs are *Ibid.*, pp. 214–15.

In many instances after loss occurs, the insured may be able to conduct the business by making extra expenditures for the temporary use of property. Extra expense in this context means "the excess of the total cost incurred during the period of restoration chargeable to the operation of the insured's business over and above the total cost that would normally have been incurred to conduct the business during the same period had no loss occurred." The salvage value of property used temporarily will be taken into account when adjusting loss. Extra expense of the type here contemplated is insured in the extensions of coverage section of the special multi-peril contract subject to the following limitations: (1) the insured must use "due diligence and dispatch to repair, rebuild or replace such part of said buildings or personal property thereof as have been damaged"; (2) the insurer is not liable for loss of income to the insured or any other consequential or remote loss; (3) the insurer is not responsible for "the cost of repairing or replacing any of the described property or the cost of research or other expense necessary to replace or restore books of account . . . except cost in excess of the normal cost of such repair, replacement or restoration necessarily incurred for the purpose of reducing the total amount of extra expense. In no event shall such excess cost exceed the amount by which the total extra expense otherwise payable under this extension of coverage is reduced."

The last property item listed under extensions of coverage is replacement cost. The coverage is limited to those situations where the "full cost of repair or replacement is less than $1,000." In such situations the insurer will pay the replacement cost without deduction for depreciation. "Coverage shall be applicable only to a building structure . . .

but excluding carpeting, cloth awnings, airconditioners, domestic appliances and outdoor equipment, all whether permanently attached to the building structure or not." The insurer is not responsible for payment under this section "unless and until the damaged property is actually repaired or replaced on the same premises with due diligence and dispatch, and in no event, unless repair or replacement is completed within a reasonable time after such loss." The insurer also is not liable unless the amount of insurance covering the building structure equals or exceeds the result obtained by multiplying the actual cash value of the property at the time of loss.

Certain types of property are not covered in the special multi-peril contract. The specific property exclusions are:

1. Animals and pets; aircraft, watercraft, including motors, equipment and accessories (except rowboats and canoes, while out of water and on the described premises); automobiles, trailers, semi-trailers or any self-propelled vehicles or machines, except motorized equipment not licensed for use on public thoroughfares and operated principally on the premises of the insured. This exclusion does not apply to animals and pets, motorcycles and motor scooters, trailers designed for use with private passenger vehicles for general utility purposes or carrying boats, and watercraft, including motors, equipment and accessories, while not afloat when held for sale or sold but not delivered and specifically covered by endorsement.

2. Outdoor swimming pools; fences; piers, wharves and docks; beach or diving platforms or appurtenances; retaining walls not constituting a part of building; walks, roadways

and other paved surfaces; unless such items are specifically covered by endorsement.

3. The cost of excavations, grading or filling; foundations of buildings, machinery, boilers or engines which foundations are below the undersurface of the lowest basement floor, or where there is no basement, below the surface of the ground; pilings, piers, pipes, flues and drains which are underground; pilings which are below the low water mark.

4. Outdoor signs, whether or not attached to a building unless specifically covered by endorsement.

5. Household and personal effects contained in living quarters occupied by the insured, any officer, director, stockholder, or partner of the insured or relatives of any of the foregoing, except as provided in the extensions of coverage or unless specifically covered by endorsement.

6. Growing crops and lawns.

7. Trees, shrubs, and plants, except when held for sale or sold but not delivered, or to the extent provided in the extension of coverage.

8. Property which is more specifically covered in whole or in part under this or any other contract of insurance.

There are also some property exclusions relating directly to the perils of windstorm and hail that have not been mentioned previously. Unless the contract has been endorsed to the contrary, the insurer will not be responsible for windstorm or hail damage to "(1) grain, hay, straw, or other crops outside of buildings; (2) windmills, windpumps, or other towers; (3) crop silos or their contents; (4) metal smokestacks or, when outside of buildings, awnings or can-

opies (fabric or slat) including their supports; (5) outdoor radio or television antennas including their lead-in wiring, masts or towers; (6) trees, shrubs, and plants."

Section II. Liability Coverage

Section II of the special multi-peril contract provides protection against the risk of being required legally to pay damages because of negligently injuring other persons or their property. The first coverage listed under Section II is Coverage C (bodily injury and property damage liability), which reads as follows:

The Company will pay on behalf of the insured all sums which the insured shall become legally obligated to pay as damages because of bodily injury or property damage to which this insurance applies, caused by an occurrence and arising out of the ownership, maintenance, or use of the insured premises and all operations necessary or incidental to the business of the named insured conducted at or from the insured premises and the Company shall have the right and duty to defend any suit against the insured seeking damages on account of such bodily injury or property damage, even if any of the allegations of the suit are groundless, false, or fraudulent, and may make such investigation and settlement of any claim or suit it deems expedient, but the Company shall not be obligated to pay any claim or judgment or to defend any suit after the applicable limit of the Company's liability has been exhausted by payment of judgments or settlements.[39]

In addition to paying damages the insurer agrees, and in addition to the applicable limit of liability, to pay the

[39] The quotations in Section II are from *Ibid.*, pp. 217–19.

costs of defending a suit including "all costs taxed against the insured in any suit defended by the company and all interest on the entire amount of any judgment therein which accrues after entry of the judgment and before the Company has paid or tendered or deposited in court that part of the judgment which does not exceed the Company's liability thereon."

The insurer also agrees to pay, as an additional amount of insurance, premiums on appeal bonds, bonds to release attachments (but not in an amount in excess of the applicable limit of liability of the contract), and bail bonds required "because of accident or traffic law violation arising out of the use of any vehicle to which this policy applies." The insurer places a limit of $250 on what it will pay per bail bond and does not agree to apply for or furnish any of the above-mentioned bonds. The insurer accepts the responsibility for paying the expenses "incurred by the insured for first aid to others at the time of an accident for bodily injury to which the policy applies," and the "reasonable expenses incurred by the insured at the Company's request in assisting the Company in the investigation or defense of any claim or suit, including actual loss of earnings not to exceed $25 per day." These expense items are also in addition to the limits of liability for Coverage C.

The final major item of coverage in Section II is for premises medical payments (Coverage D). Under this provision:

The Company will pay to or for each person who sustains bodily injury caused by accident all reasonable medical expense incurred within one year from the date of the accident on account of such bodily injury, provided such bodily injury arises out of (a) a condition in the insured premises or (b) operations with respect to which the named insured is afforded coverage for bodily injury liability under this policy.

As is evident from the way the coverage is worded, there is no requirement that the insured be legally obligated to make medical payments before the insurer will respond. Immediate medical care may well mitigate the seriousness of the injury and lessen the extent of the obligation under Coverage C.

A number of exclusions surround the liability and medical coverages. Under medical payments there are four categories of exclusion. The first category relates to the ownership of certain types of property. There is no medical insurance under this policy for bodily injury arising out of "operations on or from premises — owned by, rented to, or controlled by the named insured" other than insured premises. Also, the insurance does not apply to bodily injuries "arising out of the ownership, maintenance, operation, use, loading or unloading of any automobile, aircraft, or watercraft owned or operated by or rented or loaned to any insured," nor is there any insurance for any other automobile, aircraft, or watercraft "operated by any person in the course of his employment by any insured." The exclusions in regard to watercraft do not apply if the craft is on shore on the insured premises. The automobile exclusion does not apply to the "parking of an automobile on the insured premises, if such automobile is not owned by or rented or loaned to any insured." There are also restrictions relating to the ownership, maintenance, operation, use, loading or unloading, or transportation of mobile equipment.[40]

The second category of exclusions relates to certain types of operations

[40] See the contract for the specific nature of these restrictions.

that may be carried on by an insured. Thus, there is no medical payments coverage for bodily injury "included within the completed operations hazard or the products hazard," or "arising out of operations performed for the named insured by independent contractors" (with some exceptions). Medical coverage is not provided for bodily injury resulting from the selling, serving, or giving any alcoholic beverage in certain situations, such as violation of statute or serving or selling liquor to a minor, if the named insured is a person or organization engaged in the business of manufacturing, distributing, selling or serving alcoholic beverages . . ." The rule is modified slightly if the insured is not in the liquor business but is an owner or lessor of premises used for such purposes. There is no medical coverage for bodily injury "arising out of demolition operations performed by or on behalf of insureds."

The third group of exclusions relates to limitations on who may receive medical payments. Medical payments for bodily injury are not available to the "named insured, any partner therein, any tenant or other person regularly residing on the insured premises or any employee of the foregoing if the bodily injury arises out of and in the course of employment therewith. Other exclusions relate to any person: "(a) while engaged in maintenance and repair of the insured premises or alteration, demolition, or new construction at such premises; (b) if any benefits for such bodily injury are payable or required to be provided under any workers' compensation, unemployment, or disability benefits law, or under any similar laws; (c) practicing, instructing, or participating in any physical training, sport, athletic event, or contest."

The fourth group of exclusions, which in reality is one exclusion, relates "to any medical expense for services by the named insured, any employee thereof, or any person or organization under contract to the named insured to provide such services."

The liability coverage (Coverage C) has seventeen exclusions, ten of which apply primarily to the bodily injury part of the coverage and seven to property damage. The bodily injury exclusions are similar to those for medical payments and encompass restrictions relating to ownership and operation of automobiles, aircraft, or watercraft, mobile equipment, workers' compensation[41] situations, and other items mentioned in the preceding paragraph. In addition insurance under Coverage C does not apply "to liability assumed by the insured under any contract or agreement except an incidental contract; but this exclusion does not apply to a warranty of fitness or quality of the named insured's products or a warranty that work performed by or on behalf of the named insured will be done in a workmanlike manner." Further, the insurance under Coverage C does not apply "to bodily inury or property damage arising out of the discharge, dispersal, release or escape of smoke, vapors, soot, fumes, acids, alkalis, toxic chemicals, liquid or gases, waste materials, or other irritants, contaminants, or pollutants into or upon land, the atmosphere, or any water course or body of water; but this exclusion does not apply if such discharge, dispersal, release, or escape is sudden and accidental."

[41] Exclusions of this type are to be expected since liability in relation to use of such items as automobiles, aircraft, and watercraft is normally insured under separate contracts. The workers' compensation risk is also separately insured. The same comments apply to the medical payments coverage.

The exclusions that relate primarily to property damage seek to prevent recovery under Coverage C for damage to property that belongs to the insured or that is in his care, custody, or control. They also seek to place limits on property damage situations involving the insured's products. For example, the insurance provided under Section II does not apply to property damage to "(1) property owned by or occupied by or rented to the insured, (2) property used by the insured, or (3) property in the care, custody, or control of the insured or as to which the insured is for any purpose exercising physical control; but parts (2) and (3) of this exclusion do not apply with respect to liability under a written sidetrack agreement and part (3) of this exclusion does not apply with respect to property damage (other than to elevators) arising out of the use of an elevator at premises owned by, rented to, or controlled by the named insured." One of the exclusions relating to products reads, "to damages claimed for the withdrawal, inspection, repair, replacement, or loss of use of the named insured's products or work completed by or for the named insured or of any property of which such products or work forms a part, if such products, work or property are withdrawn from the market or from use because of any known or suspected defect or deficiency therein." There is an exclusion for bodily injury or property damage "arising out of demolition operations performed by or on behalf of the insured" and also an exclusion for "property damage to premises alienated by the named insured arising out of such premises or any part thereof."[42]

---

[42] The exclusions mentioned here are by way of illustration. For a complete statement of exclusions relating to property damage and bodily injury the reader should consult the special multi-peril contract.

Section III. Crime

The part of the special multi-peril contract that relates to property does not insure against the peril of crime. It is possible for the business firm to include this coverage as a part of the package by the addition of Section III to the contract. The form that constitutes Section III may be Form MLB-300 (comprehensive form) or MLB-301 (blanket crime form). The emphasis in this discussion will be on the comprehensive form.

The insuring agreement specifies five coverages: I, Employee Dishonesty; II, Loss Inside the Premises; III, Loss Outside the Premises; IV, Money Orders and Counterfeit Paper Currency; and V, Depositor's Forgery. Employee dishonesty relates to fraudulent or dishonest acts that involve employees. Limits on liability may be stated on a per employee basis or on a total basis regardless of the number of employees. Loss inside the premises covers situations where money and securities are lost from "actual destruction, disappearance, or wrongful abstraction within the premises or from within banking premises or similar recognized places of safe deposit."[43] Property other than money and securities is covered, if loss or damage results from safe burglary and premises robbery. Insurance against the loss of other property includes "loss or damage to a locked cash drawer, cash box, or cash register by felonious entry into or abstraction of the container. Damage to premises is covered if it stems from safe burglary, robbery, or felonious abstraction or from burglarious entry into the premises and the insured owns the

---

[43] *Fire, Casualty, and Surety Bulletins*, (Misc. Casualty, and Surety Bulletins), (Misc. Casualty CM-2).

building or is liable for the damage."[44] Loss outside the premises refers to the loss of (1) money and securities and (2) other property. In the case of money and securities the protection is against actual destruction, disappearance, and wrongful abstraction "while being conveyed by a messenger or an armored car company or while in the living quarters of the home of a messenger, with no requirement that the money and securities be in the course of conveyance."[45] Coverage for other property is limited to robbery "from an armored car company or messenger who is conveying it and against theft from the living quarters in the home of a messenger."[46] Money orders and counterfeit paper currency coverage provides against loss that may come about as a result of the insured's acceptance of a money order issued by a post office or express company or through the acceptance of "counterfeit paper currency of the United States or Canada."[47] The depositor's forgery cover applies "to loss caused by forgery or alteration of a check, draft, promissory note, or similar written promise."[48] Assuming the insurer agrees to the defense, legal expenses arising out of refusal to pay forged checks are a part of the coverage. Further, "the interest of the bank in which the insured maintains a checking or savings account may be included in the insured's proof of loss."[49]

There are a number of exclusions that apply to the crime form. Among them are war and nuclear reaction, applicable to insuring agreements II and III, and under these agreements there is

[44] Ibid.

[45] Ibid., Misc. Casualty, CM 3.

[46] Ibid.

[47] Ibid.

[48] Ibid.

[49] Ibid.

no coverage for accounting or arithmetical errors or omissions, such as giving a customer too much change. A significant exclusion that applies to insuring agreement II is loss by fire to property other than money and securities. Fire loss is covered by other parts of the special multi-peril contract. Under insuring agreements II and III, there is an exclusion for "loss due to any fraudulent, dishonest, or criminal act by an employee, director, trustee, or authorized representative of any insured, while working or otherwise and whether acting alone or in collusion with others; . . . this exclusion does not apply to safe burglary or robbery or attempt there at." Also under insuring agreement II, there is no coverage for "loss of money contained in coin-operated amusement devices or vending machines, unless the amount of money deposited within the device or machine is recorded by a continuous recording instrument therein."[50]

Section IV. Boiler and Machinery

Although Sections I and II of the special multi-peril contract are mandatory, Section IV, like Section III is an optional coverage. The general property form of Section I excludes explosions of steam boilers, steam pipes, steam turbines or steam engines and for businesses with this type of exposure, Section IV is an appropriate coverage. In general terms, this section of the contract insures against loss arising from an accident to an object. Both of these words require definition. By an *accident* is meant:

A sudden and accidental breakdown of an object, or a part thereof, which mani-

[50] Ibid.

fests itself at the time of its occurrence by physical damage to the object that necessitates repair or replacement of the object or part thereof, but accident shall not mean: (a) depletion, deterioration, corrosion, or erosion of material; (b) wear and tear; (c) leakage of any valve, fitting, shaft seal, gland packing, joint, or connection; (d) the breakdown of any vacuum tube, gas tube, or brush; (e) the breakdown of any electronic computer or electronic data processing equipment; (f) the breakdown of any structure or foundation supporting the object or any part thereof; (g) the explosion of gas or unconsumed fuel within the furnace of any object or within the passages from the furnace of said object to the atmosphere; or (h) the functioning of any safety device or protective device.[51]

The definition of object identifies three groups of objects, and if the insured has objects of the type defined coverage is mandatory for all of them. The definition of object in Section IV is:

Group 1. Any steam boiler, electric steam generator, hot water boiler, fired water heater, or fired pressure vessel, including as part thereof (1) any condensate return tank used with any such vessel, which is a hot water heating boiler, (4) any indirect water heater used for hot water supply service which is directly in the water circulating system of such vessel and which does not form a part of a water storage tank, and (5) any piping on premises of the insured, or between parts of said premises, with valves, fittings, traps, and separators thereon, which contains steam or condensate thereof, generated in whole or in part in such vessel, and any feed water piping between such vessel and in feed pump or injector.

Group 2. Any metal unfired pressure vessel as folows: hot water storage tank with or without internal heating coils, coil water heater, electric water heater, tank for the storage of compressed air, and hydropneumatic tank.

Group 3. Metal piping with valves, fittings, traps or separators thereon containing steam or condensate thereof, on or between parts of the premises of the insured supplied by boilers or vessels not owned, operated or controlled by the insured and compressed air piping on the premises.[52]

The insuring agreement of Section IV provides four coverages. Coverage I insures against loss on property of the insured. This property includes that defined as an insured object, as well as all other real or personal property if the loss has been caused directly by an insured accident. Coverage II provides for expediting expenses such as cost of temporary repairs, overtime, and expediting costs of permanent repairs. Coverage III provides property damage liability. This coverage in effect supplements Section II in that it extends coverage to property of others without the care, custody, or control exclusion if the loss has been caused by an insured accident. Coverage IV provides payments for defense, settlement, and supplementary payments. This coverage is similar to that provided under Section II of the special multi-peril contract.

There are some exclusions and limitations that apply to the boiler and machinery coverages. Under loss of property of the insured there is no coverage for loss from "fire, water, or other means to extinguish fire, combustion explosion outside the object, flood, delay, or interruption of business or from each of power, light, heat, or other indirect result."[53] Coverage II is available "only if the limit of loss has not been exhausted in paying claims on the in-

[51] *Fire, Casualty, and Surety Bulletins,* (Power Plant S$_{mp-1}$).

[52] *Ibid.,* (Power Plant S$_{mp-2}$).
[53] *Ibid.,* (Power Plant, S$_{mp-4}$).

sured's property."[54] Similarly, Coverage III is applicable "only to the extent of any remaining amount of the limit of loss after losses on property of the insured and expediting expenses have been made."[55]

Also Coverage III is regarded as excess over other valid or collectible insurance[56] that the insured may have covering the risk. Bodily injury liability insurance is not necessary for Section IV, since Section II of the special multiperil contract is mandatory and one of its coverages is bodily injury liability. There is also no specific automatic coverage for newly acquired objects, although the condition referring to premium adjustment "provides that a premium charge be made for objects added during the policy year. This, in effect, provides the same coverage for newly acquired objects as is already protecting similar property."[57]

There are, of course, the usual war and nuclear hazard exclusions.

Although the special multi-peril contract as analyzed here is applicable to a wide variety of business situations, its flexibility may be enhanced by the addition of endorsements and optional forms. For example, instead of the general property form, the special property form may be used, which provides all-risk property coverage rather than named peril. Also, for certain types of property, such as industrial, there are a number of endorsements, particularly under boiler and machinery coverage that may be useful in adapting multiple-line coverages to the needs of manufacturing organizations.

[54] Ibid.

[55] Ibid.

[56] Other valid and collectible insurance is defined as "including any deductible or self-insured retention to which such insurance may be subject."

[57] Ibid., (Power Plant, S_{mp-5}).

LOSS OF INCOME — BUSINESS INTERRUPTION INSURANCE

One of the limitations on recovery of loss that appears in the insuring clause of the standard fire insurance contract (which forms a part of the special multi-peril contract) is that the insured may not receive "compensation for loss resulting from interruption of business or manufacture."[58] This exclusion may be nullified by adding a business interruption insurance form to the special multi-peril contract.

Business interruption insurance is designed to protect against the loss of "prospective earnings because of the interruption of business by fire or other hazards insured against, to the extent of the net profits prevented, plus such fixed charges and expenses as necessarily continue during the interruption, but only to the extent that such fixed charges and expenses would have been earned had no interruption due to an insured peril occurred."[59] It may be thought of as business disability insurance. Since business interruption insurance protects against the loss of business income, it is an important coverage and one that deserves serious consideration in risk planning.

[58] The insuring agreement also contains a statement that the liability of the insurer shall not be more than "the amount that it would cost to repair or replace the property with material of like kind and quality. . . ." This statement prevents claims for profits on finished goods since it limits loss to replacement cost and not selling price. Loss of profits on finished goods may be insured by attaching an appropriate endorsement to the special multi-peril contract. This type of insurance will not be discussed here although like business interruption, it is a consequential loss. Unlike business interruption, however, it does not involve the element of time.

[59] John H. Magee and Oscar N. Serbein, *Property and Liability Insurance*, 4th ed., (Homewood, Ill.: Richard D. Irwin, Inc., 1967), p. 228.

A business interruption insurance form that is often used is the gross earnings form for mercantile or non-manufacturing risks.[60] The insuring agreement in this form:

(1) Covers against loss resulting directly from necessary interruption of business caused by damage to or destruction of real or personal property by the peril(s) insured against, during the terms of this policy, on premises occupied by the insured and situated as herein described; (2) in the event of such damage or destruction this Company shall be liable for the actual loss sustained by the insured resulting directly from such interruption of business, but not exceeding the reduction in gross earnings less charges and expenses which do not necessarily continue during the interruption of business, for only such length of time as would be required with the exercise of due diligence and dispatch to rebuild, repair, or replace such part of the property herein described as has been damaged or destroyed, commencing with the date of such damage or destruction and not limited by the date of expiration of this policy. Due consideration shall be given to the continuation of normal charges and expenses, including payroll expense, to the extent necessary to resume operations of the insured with the same quality of service which existed immediately preceding the loss.[61]

If it is possible for the insured to reduce the loss from business interruption by resumption of operations (complete or partial) or by making use of merchandise or other property, such reduction will be taken into account in determining the loss. The contract also covers "such expenses as are necessarily incurred for the purpose of reducing loss under this policy (except expense incurred to extinguish a fire), but in no event shall the aggregate of such expenses exceed the amount by which the loss otherwise payable under this policy is thereby reduced."[62] A coinsurance clause is a part of the form, although it does not apply to expenses related to reducing loss.

Gross earnings are defined as the sum of (a) "total net sales and (b) other earnings derived from the operation of the business less the cost of (c) merchandise sold, including packaging material therefore; (d) materials and supplies consumed directly in supplying the service(s) sold by the insured; and (e) service(s) purchased from outsiders (not employees of the insured) for resale which do not continue under contract." There is also a statement in the form to the effect that in "determining gross earnings due consideration shall be given to the experience of the business before the date of damage or destruction and the probable experience thereafter had no loss occurred."[63]

There are not many limitations or exclusions. A limitation is placed on the length of time for which the insurer will be liable in situations involving media for electronic data processing. The insurer will not be liable for more than (a) "30 consecutive calendar days or (b) the length of time that would be required to rebuild, repair, or replace such other property herein described as has been damaged or destroyed whichever is the

[60] Pierpont identifies three types of business interruption insurance: gross earnings, gross earnings with extension of period of operation, and extra expense. The second type provides for situations where sales may be less after restoration of the business than before because some customers have gone elsewhere. See Joseph R. Pierpont, "Business Interruption — What It Covers," *Risk Management*, XXIII, (December 1976), pp. 34–37.

[61] *Study Kit for Students of Insurance*, p. 9.

[62] *Ibid.*

[63] *Ibid.*

greater length of time."[64] A special exclusion declares that the insurer will not be liable for any increase in loss resulting from: "(a) enforcement of any local or state ordinance or law regulating the construction, repair, or demolition of buildings or structures; or (b) interference at the described premises, by strikers or other persons, with rebuilding, repairing, or replacing the property, or with the resumption or continuation of business; or (c) the suspension, lapse or cancellation of any lease, license, contract, or order unless such suspension, lapse, or cancellation results directly from the interruption of business, and then this Company shall be liable for only such loss as affects the insured's earnings during, and limited to, the period of indemnity covered under this policy nor shall this Company be liable for any other consequential or remote loss."[65]

OTHER LIABILITY CONTRACTS

The special multi-peril contract provides adequate liability coverage for many businesses, although it is limited as was emphasized earlier, to occurrences arising out of the "ownership, maintenance, or use of the insured premises. . . ."[66] Thus, the liability coverage is not comprehensive in the sense of applying to liability situations occurring away from the premises and by specific exclusion does not cover most contractual liability. Also, in general, liability arising out of the operation or use of vehicles, such as automobiles, is not covered, and liability for work-connected injuries to employees is excluded.

[64] Ibid.

[65] Ibid.

[66] Ibid., p. 217.

Further, there is no coverage for the employer's responsibility under workers' compensation laws. Product liability is not covered. All of these situations may. be provided for under contracts available from property and liability insurers. Comprehensive liability contracts may be purchased that will cover off-premise liability and contractual liability. Some of these contracts will cover automobile liability as well. Separate contracts covering automobiles, aircraft, and watercraft are available. These are typically multiple-line contracts and provide physical damage as well as liability coverage.[67]

The problem of work injuries and the liability of the employer, therefore, is handled separately. As was noted in Chapter 7 every state has a workers' compensation law which imposes liability on the employer for injuries to employees that arise out of and in the course of employment. The law specifies the compensation to be paid. Workers' compensation laws vary from state to state and because of various limitations do not necessarily apply to all employers. Most of the laws are now compulsory, but a few are elective. While workers' compensation laws typically do not require transfer of the employer's risk to insurers, insurance contracts are widely used as a way of meeting the obligation imposed on employers, or that may be imposed by a law suit if the workers' compensation law is not ap-

[67] These contracts are not too unlike the special multi-peril except they cover a single type of property such as an automobile, aircraft, and ships and contain provisions that are specifically tailored to the risk presented by vehicles travelling on highways, waterways, and in the air and may be carrying passengers and/or cargo. Considerations of the details of these contracts would be fairly repetitious and the reader is referred to references given earlier for additional information.

plicable to a particular employer. The specific contract used to cover the risk is the Workmen's Compensation and Employers' Liability Policy. The insuring agreement of this contract specifies two coverages — Coverage A (workers' compensation) and Coverage B (employer's liability). The insuring agreement for Coverage A states that the insurer agrees "to pay promptly when due all compensation and other benefits required of the insured by the workers' compensation law."[68] Coverage B is liability coverage and the insurer agrees to pay all sums that the insured becomes legally liable to pay because of bodily injury to employees. Coverage B does not apply, of course, if benefits are available under workers' compensation, occupational disease, or similar laws. One of the important features of the contract under Coverage A is that the insurer is directly liable to the person entitled to benefits (employee) and must pay that person even though the insured may become bankrupt or insolvent or in default.[69]

Liability insurance has increased in importance over the years, partly because of the increased awareness of the public about their legal rights and partly because of many large awards that have been made by juries. Areas in which some fairly serious problems have arisen in recent times are product liability and malpractice. The frequency of suits alleging injury to the public from faulty products caused by negligence has increased substantially causing many business firms to analyze carefully their needs of product liability insurance. Similarly, malpractice suits have increased with the result that

many professions, especially physicians, have been faced with reluctance on the part of some insurers to provide coverage. Risk managers are also increasingly aware of the need their firms may have for directors and officers liability insurance (D and O), brought about by the needs these persons may have for protection against suits alleging negligence in the performance of their duties. Brockmeier reported that in a survey conducted in 1976 of 1,730 companies of various types, 71 percent carried D and O insurance.[70]

TRANSPORTATION CONTRACTS

The special multi-peril contract offers only very limited protection for business personal property while away from the premises. For businesses that ship products or otherwise have property off the premises, contracts falling under the headings of marine or inland marine insurance may be necessary. These contracts may be especially important if the shipper retains title to goods until they have reached their destination or has responsibility under an installment contract or some other type of agreement. The precise types of contract needed will depend on circumstances. Some businesses may need postal insurance beyond that available from the postal department. Others may need ocean-going cargo contracts. Since space does not permit an analysis of all contracts available in the transportation area, the discussion here will concentrate on the manufacturers output policy, which has fairly wide applicability. The contract is all risk and "insures against all risks

---

[68] *Ibid.*, p. 111.

[69] Workers' compensation as a legal remedy and an employee benefit is considered in Chapter 11.

[70] Warren G. Brockmeier, "Status of D and O Liability Coverage," *Risk Management*, XXIV (January 1977), p. 20.

of direct physical loss to the property covered from any external cause (including general average and salvage charges on shipments covered while waterborne) except as hereinafter excluded."[71]

The interests covered by the M.O.P. (except as excluded) are:

a. The interest of the insured in all personal property owned by the insured;

b. The insured's use interest in improvements and betterments to buildings not owned by the insured;

c. The interest of the insured in, and legal liability for personal property of others in the actual or constructive custody of the insured;

d. Personal property of others

    (1) sold by the insured which the insured has agreed prior to loss to insure for the account of the purchaser during course of delivery;

    (2) In the custody of the insured which the insured has agreed prior to loss to insure;

    (3) Sold by the insured under an installation agreement whereby the insured's responsibility continues until the installation is accepted by the purchaser.[72]

The contract does not insure the following types of interests and property:

a. Currency, money, notes, or securities, precious metals or their alloys;

b. Property while covered under import or export ocean marine policies;

c. Aircraft or watercraft;

d. Animals, growing crops, or standing timber;

e. Property sold by the insured under conditional sale, trust agreement, installment payment, or other deferred payment plan;

f. Loss resulting from interruption of business or other consequential loss;

g. Machinery used for the service of the buildings containing property insured hereunder, nor permanent fittings and fixtures attached to and constituting a part thereof; this exclusion does not apply to improvements and betterments to buildings not owned by the insured.

h. Property located in or forming part of any underground mine or of any mining or well-drilling operation.[73]

There are sixteen exclusions relating to perils. In addition there are territorial exclusions. Among the exclusions are war; nuclear reaction, radiation, or radioactive contamination, although direct loss by fire resulting from these items is covered; criminal, fraudulent, or dishonest activity on the part of such persons as the insured, officer, director, or employee; earthquake, with some exceptions; flood, with some exceptions; "by explosion or rupture of steam pipes, steam turbines, steam engines, steam boilers, gas turbines, or other pressure vessels, which are operated under the actual control of the insured;" mechanical breakdown of machinery or equipment; "automobiles, automotive trucks, and trailers which are being operated under their own power or towed (whether or not in motion at time of loss) caused by or resulting from collision and overturn;"

[71] *Study Kit for Students of Insurance,* p. 66.

[72] *Ibid.*

[73] *Ibid.*

"caused by or resulting from delay, loss of market, loss of use;" mysterious disappearance including shortages disclosed on taking inventory; "rain, snow, sleet, or dust to personal property in the open (other than property in the custody of carriers for hire);" and loss by wear and tear.[74]

[74] *Ibid.* A few excluded items are not listed here. The reader should consult the contract for details.

SUMMARY AND CONCLUSIONS

1. The contents of insurance contracts may be placed in four categories: declarations, insuring agreements, exclusions and limitations, and conditions.

2. Common elements of property and liability insurance contracts include assignment, cancellation, coinsurance, mortgage rights, notice of loss, proof of loss, other insurance, subrogation.

3. The basic legal principles surrounding property and liability insurance contracts include such concepts as indemnity, insurable interest, concealment, representation and warranty, and waiver and estoppel.

4. The special multi-peril contract is a multiple-line contract that provides basic property and liability insurance contracts for a wide variety of businesses. As a minimum it has sections providing property and liability benefits, and it may have sections covering crime and boiler and machinery insurance.

5. Business interruption insurance protects against the loss of prospective earnings because of the interruption of business by fire or other risks insured against to the extent of the net profits prevented. Also included are fixed charges and expenses that would have been earned had there been no business interruption.

6. The special multi-peril contract provides liability insurance mainly for occurrences arising out of the ownership, maintenance, and use of premises. Other liability situations must be provided for through separate contracts. Examples are contractual liability, workers' compensation and employers' liability, and liability associated with the operation of vehicles such as automobiles, aircraft, and watercraft.

7. The special multi-peril policy offers only limited protection for business personal property away from the premises. Types of transportation policies that may be necessary are: postal insurance, ocean marine, and inland marine.

8. The manufacturers output policy has fairly wide applicability and insurers against all risks of direct physical loss to the property covered from any external cause, including general average and salvage charges on shipments covered while waterborne. This agreement is subject to some exclusions.

QUESTIONS FOR DISCUSSION

1. State briefly what is meant by the following terms as they relate to property and liability insurance contracts: cancellation, coinsurance, and subrogation.

2. Discuss the provisions in a typical property and liability insurance contract in regard to other insurance. Why do statements about other insurance appear in these contracts?

3. When a loss occurs in property and liability insurance, a question of valuation of the loss normally arises. Discuss bases for valuation in loss settlements.

4. How are mortgagee rights in property typically provided for in property insurance contracts?

5. Interpret the apportionment clause of the special multi-peril contract.

6. State the meaning of the following concepts: indemnity; insurable interest; concealment; representation and warranty; and waiver and estoppel.

7. J. R. Jones, Inc. carries a special multi-peril policy to cover a mercantile establishment consisting of a single multi-storied building. Under Section I of the contract the building is insured in the amount of $500,000 with a 80 percent coinsurance clause. Several months after the contract was entered into a fire occurs damaging the building in the amount of $50,000. At the time the loss occurred, it was determined that the actual cash value of the building was $800,000. How much would Jones, Inc. recover from the insurer?

8. Jones, Inc., under Section II of the special multi-peril policy, carries bodily injury and property damage liability insurance with aggregate limits of $1,500,000. The firm receives a letter in which a claim is made by a customer stating he was injured on the insured's premises as a result of falling when his right foot went through the floor because of a defective piece of flooring. A clerk in the office of the president of the firm files the letter in a correspondence file. Later the firm is served with a notice of suit brought by the customer, which it immediately forwards to the insurer. What are the obligations of the insurer?

9. S.S. Smith, Inc. is insured under a workers' compensation and employers' liability insurance contract. An employee is injured and makes claim for compensation. Although the insurer acknowledges that compensation should be paid, it does not honor the claim because Smith, Inc. had violated the contract by refusing to allow the insurer's inspectors to examine its plant. If the insurer's view is upheld, what are the employee's rights? Why?

10. Prepare an essay on the changes that have occurred in property and liability insurance contracts in the last ten years.

11. Distinguish between multiple lines insurance and all lines insurance.

12. Recommend an insurance program for Calwood Lumber Company (See Chapter 20, Case F).

III

Transfer to Insurers: Personnel Risks

9

Life and Health Insurance in Risk Management

Historically, risk managers were mainly responsible for treating property and liability risks faced by the business firm. In comparatively recent times recognition has been given to the fact that the loss of human assets through the death of key employees or through disability can be, in many instances, as serious as the loss of buildings and other types of inanimate property. Thus, a complete program in risk management should give consideration to the assessment of personnel risks and their possible consequences. The branch of insurance treating of these risks is life and health insurance, and the involvement of the risk manager will depend to a considerable extent on the scope of his function. If he is responsible for the employee benefit planning of the firm, virtually all forms of group life, group health, and group annuities are of interest to him, as well as key management insurance and the funding of business continuation plans. In this chapter primary attention will be given to the nongroup aspects of life and health insurance. Group arrangements will be discussed in the chapters on employee benefits.

The major topics to be considered in this chapter are:

1. The field of life and health insurance

2. Types of life insurance contracts

3. Types of annuity contracts

4. Types of health insurance contracts

5. Bases for issuing life and health insurance contracts

6. Differences between life and health insurance and property and liability insurance

7. The life insurance contract

8. Basic structure of individual health insurance contracts

9. Underwriting of health insurance

10. Business uses of life insurance

THE FIELD OF LIFE AND HEALTH INSURANCE

Contracts protecting against the financial consequences of the uncertainties surrounding the continuation of life and health are sold by life insurers.[1] Specifically the risks insured against are death,

[1] Health insurance was first sold by casualty companies and was historically a casualty line. Although property and liability insurers still write health insurance, the field is now dominated by life insurers and specialty health insurers such as Blue Cross and Blue Shield.

181

superannuation, and disability including medical care.

Types of Life Insurance Contracts

Life insurance contracts may be classified as term, whole life, endowment, and combinations thereof.

Term insurance contracts, as the appellation suggests, provide coverage for a fixed time period which may vary from a month or two to a term beyond age 65. Perhaps the most usual terms are 1 year, 5 years, 10 years, 20 years, and term to age 65. Although term contracts typically carry a face amount that remains constant throughout the term, both increasing and decreasing term contracts are available. The basic benefit provided by term contracts is that the beneficiary under the contract receives the face of the contract in the event the insured dies within the specified term. There are two features of term contracts that are often of value to the prospective purchaser. One of these is a provision for renewability and the other for convertibility. The renewable provision permits the insured at his option to renew the contract for another term on expiration of the old term without evidence of insurability. The premium paid will be the one applicable to the attained age. The conversion privilege enables the insured to convert the contract before the expiration of the term to a contract which has a cash value.

Whole life insurance contracts do not have a fixed term — they provide protection for the insured throughout

his life span.[2] The insurer agrees to pay the beneficiary the face of the contract whenever the insured dies. Normally premiums are paid annually for the whole of life. A variation on this procedure is the limited payment life contract wherein the contract continues until the end of life, but the premiums are payable for a specified period such as 20 or 30 years. If death occurs before the end of the premium payment period, premiums are payable, of course, only until the time of death. If the insured lives beyond the payment period, no further premiums are payable, although the contract continues in force.

Endowment insurance contracts are in reality combination contracts and could be classified under that heading. Traditionally, however, the endowment has been treated as a separate kind of contract and will be considered that way here. The insuring agreement of the endowment contract contains two promises. The first promise is that the insurer will pay the beneficiary the face of the contract if the insured dies within the endowment period, which might be, say, 10, 15, 20, 25, or 30 years or until age 65. The second promise is that the insurer will pay the insured the face of the contract if he survives the endowment period.[3] Another way of viewing the endowment contract is that it is a combination of a term insurance contract and a pure endowment.[4] A pure endowment contract is one where the insured will receive the face of the contract if he survives the endowment

[2] Whole life contracts do not extend beyond the maximum age listed in the mortality table. Since the face of the contract is paid to the insured if he lives to the maximum age, the contract in effect becomes an endowment at that age.

[3] An important feature of life insurance contracts is that they are typically written for the benefit of a third party called a beneficiary, who is not a party to the contract.

[4] The endowment contract offers the possibility that the insured will receive the face of the contract. An example of another life contract where this is possible is described in footnote 2.

period. If he does not survive, nothing is payable to anyone.

There are many ways in which basic life insurance contracts such as term and whole life can be combined to form new types of contracts. Among the better known of these combination contracts are the family income policy, the family maintenance policy, the family protection policy, and modified whole life. The family income policy combines a decreasing term life insurance with whole life. The purpose of the decreasing term contract is to provide income during a specified period, while the whole life contract provides a lump sum payment. The family maintenance policy is similar to the family income contract except that it agrees to pay an income from the date of death for a specified period while the family income policy will pay only to the end of · a period that begins with the inception of the contract. This fact means that the term contract involved in the maintenance policy must be level in amount. The family protection policy is designed to provide a means for insuring each member of the family with the amounts of insurance for wife and children bearing a predetermined relationship to the amount of insurance on the life of the husband. The insurance coverage for the husband is ordinarily whole life insurance, while the insurance issued to the wife and children is on a term basis. Another type of combination plan is modified whole life, which is essentially a term insurance contract with a relatively short term that is automatically convertible to whole life insurance. The result is a comparatively low premium for, say, five years and then a higher premium for as long as the contract is in force. The net effect of the combination is to produce at the end of the reduced premium period a whole life contract

with a premium somewhat higher than it would have been at the age of issue and somewhat lower than it would have been if issued new at the attained age.

Types of Annuity Contracts

Life insurance contracts serve as a possible solution to the problem that the income stream to the family may be shut off by the premature death of the breadwinner. Superannuation is the problem that the breadwinner will live beyond the time he can produce income through employment, although his need for income persists. Annuity contracts of various types have been devised to meet the need for income for those persons who live beyond the employment years. An annuity is basically a series of payments. The word "annuity" suggests an annual payment, although in practice any series of payments made more often or less often than annually constitutes an annuity. Annuity contracts sold by life insurance companies are typically life annuities, meaning that the continuance of the series of payments depends on the continued survival of the life insured. Basically the insurer promises to pay the insured, in return for an appropriate premium or cash payment from the insured, an income, payable periodically, for life.

Life annuities are not especially easy to classify, since they may involve single lives or multiple lives, may be paid for by a single premium or an installment premium, may have refund provisions or no refund provisions, and may start shortly after the contract is entered into or may be deferred for a period of years. For purposes of this discussion life annuities will be classified as (1) basic forms and (2) modifications and extension of the basic types.

Basic Forms

The basic forms of life annuities are life annuities due, immediate life annuities, deferred life annuities, and joint life annuities.

A life annuity due is one where the first annuity payment is made at the beginning of the payment interval. Since no deferment period is assumed, this means the first payment is made on the inception of the contract. Life annuities due may be for the whole of life or they may be temporary in the sense of continuing for a specified number of years. An immediate life annuity is one in which the first annuity payment is made at the end of the payment interval. Thus, if an annuity were to be paid annually, the first payment would be one year after the inception of the contract. As was the case for annuities due, immediate life annuities may continue for life or for a specified period of years. Either immediate life annuities or life annuities due may be issued on a deferred basis. This fact means that the first annuity payment does not take place until after a number of years have elapsed. Although immediate life annuities and life annuities due are typically paid for with a single premium, a deferred life annuity is usually purchased with installment premiums paid during the period of deferment. Joint-life annuities, as the words suggest, refer to annuities covering two or more lives. A fairly popular form is the joint-and-survivor annuity issued on two lives. A single annuity is payable while the two lives survive and on the death of one of them will continue during the life of the survivor.

Modifications and Extensions

Annuities sold by life insurers are basically for the purpose of providing retirement income. The contracts may essentially follow the format of the basic annuity forms or they may combine some of these forms along with life insurance. Some of the better known retirement income contracts are the retirement annuity, the retirement income policy, and the variable annuity.

The retirement annuity policy is a deferred life annuity that is paid for by installment premiums during the lifetime of the insured. The annuity commences at retirement age, say 65, and continues as long as the annuitant lives. Although life insurance is not included as a part of the contract, there is a death benefit payable if the insured dies before entering upon the annuity. This benefit consists of the accumulated gross premiums without interest or the cash value, depending on which is larger. The cash value consists of the part of the gross premiums accumulated at interest that are not needed for the expenses of the insurer. A variation on the retirement annuity is the retirement income policy, which is a combination of a deferred annuity and decreasing term insurance. One of its special features is that it provides life insurance in the amount of $1,000 per $10 of monthly annuity benefit. Thus, if the insured dies before reaching retirement age, his beneficiary will receive at least the face of the contract.[5]

The variable annuity, which was first introduced in the early 1950s was in response to the criticism that traditional annuities had fixed dollar benefits and that these dollars were subject to serious purchasing power erosion during periods of inflation. Under the variable annuity the amount of the annuity

---

[5] The insurer agrees to pay either the face amount of the contract or the cash value, whichever is larger. A substantial number of years must elapse before the cash value exceeds the face amount.

benefit varies depending on the behavior of a common stock fund. A typical procedure is to use a substantial portion of the premium paid each month or year to purchase units in a stock fund. At retirement these units are converted into an annuity. The value of the annuity units will depend on the performance of the fund and will typically vary from year to year. The success of an annuity of this type in correcting erosion caused by inflation will depend on how well the stock market parallels cost of living changes.[6]

Types of Health Insurance Contracts

Health insurance contracts may be classified as (1) disability insurance contracts and (2) medical expense insurance contracts. Disability contracts are designed to replace income or some part of it that may be lost through the inability to work as a result of accident or sickness. These contracts may be written on a short-term basis where the maximum benefit period does not exceed two years or on a long-term basis where the maximum benefit period exceeds two years, and in some instances, such as in the case of accident, may continue for life.

Medical expense insurance consists of hospital expense, surgical expense, regular medical expense, major medical expense, and dental expense insurance. Medical expense insurance of these types may be written using contracts covering only certain aspects of medical expense, such as hospital costs, or contracts may be issued covering all of the types of medical expense. In some contracts disability expense may also be added. With the exception of major medical expense insurance, medical insurance contracts are written on a "first

dollar basis," that is, they are written without deductibles or coinsurance arrangements, although they normally contain dollar limits on the amount that will be paid, say, per day for hospital expenses or for surgical operations of various types. Major medical expense insurance is written with a high overall expense maximum (maxima considerably in excess of $25,000 are not uncommon) and is subject to both a deductible and coinsurance provision. Thus, if the contract is written with a $100 deductible and an 80 percent coinsurance provision and a maximum of $25,000, the first $100 of medical expense would be borne by the insured, with the insurer paying 80 percent of the expense in excess of $100 up to the $25,000 maximum.

BASES FOR ISSUING LIFE AND HEALTH INSURANCE CONTRACTS

In marketing their product[7] insurers proceed in a variety of ways. Contracts may be issued on a group basis or an individual basis; some types of contract are described as ordinary and others are industrial; and in some cases benefits may be fixed or variable.

All life, health, and annuity contracts may be issued on an individual basis, meaning that an individual is the insured, is a party to the contract, and is the unit of selection or the underwriting unit. Life, health, and annuity contracts may also be issued on a group basis. When this occurs, the group is the unit of selection and individual underwriting typically does not take place. A master contract is issued between the insurer and the employer, if an em-

---

[6] Further discussion of annuity contracts will be found in Chapter 13.

[7] The product of the insurer is here taken to be the contracts sold by the insurer, as described in the preceding section.

ployer-employee group, or with the appropriate entity in other types of group. (Examples of nonemployer-employee groups are members of a labor union or members of a professional association.) Certificates are given to employees, which describe the benefits provided by the master contract but do not in themselves constitute a contract with the employer. There are rules concerning minimum size of group and these may vary depending on whether the contract is for life insurance, health insurance, or an annuity. Also size is a function of the type of group. There are also rules about participation of eligible employees, which in turn are related to whether the employee contributes a part of the premium or whether the employer pays all of it. Where there is employee contribution, it is generally required that seventy-five percent of the employees participate in the plan. If the employer pays the entire premium, all of the employees must be included in the insurance plan.

There are a number of variations on the group theme. In health insurance groups are sometimes insured on a franchise basis. In such cases individual contracts are issued to the employees, although certain aspects of group coverage are preserved, such as payroll deduction for the premium and possible employer participation in administration. One reason for writing insurance on a franchise plan is that it may be used with fairly small groups in situations where the usual type of group insurance would not be permitted. In life insurance franchise plans are typically called wholesale insurance.

In addition to having a group division, large life insurance companies have ordinary divisions and a number of them have industrial divisions. The ordinary division is typically responsible for whole life, endowment, and

term insurance contracts issued on an individual basis in face amounts of $1,000 or more. Also in ordinary life insurance, premiums are payable no oftener than monthly. Industrial life insurance, by way of contrast, is issued in face amounts of less than $1,000. It is normally paid for on a weekly basis, and the premiums are collected by agents who go to the homes of the insured.

Life insurance and annuity contracts may be issued on a fixed or variable basis. The concept of a variable annuity was described in a preceding section. Variable life insurance, where the amount of insurance paid to the beneficiary varies with the performance of a mutual fund, has been sold in Canada and Europe in recent years, but is in its infancy in the United States and further development awaits resolution of regulatory questions. To the extent that variable life insurance has been sold in the United States, it has been largely of the type where the benefits have been linked to a cost-of-living index. The extra insurance needed to reflect increases in cost of living was provided by term insurance, which was automatically issued each year.

DIFFERENCES BETWEEN LIFE AND HEALTH INSURANCE AND PROPERTY AND LIABILITY INSURANCE

Before considering some of the basic concepts of life and health insurance, it is useful to review some of the characteristics of life insurance that set it apart somewhat from the traditional forms of insurance that may be labelled "property and liability."[8] The risk in-

[8] The contrast here will be between life insurance and property and liability insurance. Health insurance is a casualty line, although

sured against is the uncertainty surrounding the continuance of life. The primary purpose of life insurance is to provide financial protection to survivors in the event of the death of an individual on whom the survivors had looked for financial support. The uncertainty surrounding death has some unique characteristics that do not apply to the risks dealt with in property and liability insurance. For one thing death is certain to occur sometime, and the probability that it will occur increases as the individual gets older. Partial losses are not possible, and in the event of total loss no effort is made to place a value on the life of the deceased. Also, in contrast to property and liability insurance, life insurance (endowment insurance is a partial exception) is usually written for the benefit of a third party, called the beneficiary, who is not a party to the contract and whose personal characteristics presumably do not affect the risk.[9] Further, in property and liability insurance the subject matter of the contract is an asset on which a fairly accurate monetary value can be placed and which, presumably, remains an asset throughout the life of the contract. In

life insurance a life that may be an asset at the inception of the contract, in the earning power sense, can become over time dependent on others for care and maintenance.[10]

The unique characteristics of life insurance are reflected in the practices of life insurers and in the contracts that they issue. Since the life insurance contract is mainly for the benefit of the beneficiary, certain contract provisions, such as the incontestable clause and settlement options are primarily in support of the beneficiary's interest. Likewise, the creditor-proof nature of the contract, although not a contractual provision serves as an additional protection to the beneficiary. Inasmuch as questions of indemnity, value, and partial loss do not arise in life insurance, the face of the contract is payable upon the death of the insured and the contract is in effect a cash payment contract that does not require an elaborate claims procedure. To accomplish their purposes life insurance contracts typically extend over long periods of time including the life of the insured. Since the risk is an increasing one, a system of level premiums has been devised to counteract the undesirable aspects of an increasing premium. This, in turn, brings about certain by-products of the system that are reflected in the contract. Some examples are loan provisions and nonforfeiture provisions.[11]

---

it is widely sold by life insurance companies. Some of its characteristics are related to property and liability insurance and some to life insurance. Where appropriate these dual characteristics will be briefly discussed.

[9] The generalization that property and liability insurance contracts are mainly written for the benefit of the named insured is valid, although workers' compensation contracts are an exception. Also, in liability insurance contracts the word "insured" may include persons other than the named insured, and some property insurance contracts may cover property belonging to others. It may be argued that even though the named insured is the direct beneficiary others, such as families, indirectly benefit. Life insurance contracts also provide certain "living benefits," such as, in some instances dividends and cash values, but these are not the primary purpose of the contract.

[10] It should be emphasized that the issue of value does not really arise in life insurance. Some effort may be made at the inception of the contract to relate the face of the contract to the present value of the future earning power of the prospective insured. Even so, these computations do not represent the value of a human life, and may even be fairly inaccurate as estimates of the present value of an unknown amount of future income.

[11] The content of these provisions will be discussed in the next section. The level premium system is workable because in the

Although health insurance like life insurance relates to losses affecting human life rather than property, the health risk can be, and to a considerable extent is, treated in a fashion similar to property and liability insurance. In sickness (including accident) and the resulting disability, an actual cash value can be placed on the loss, since medical expenses and lost income can be determined with some accuracy. The result is that health insurance contracts can be written in an indemnity fashion, although the internal limits of these contracts (such as daily hospital benefit and amounts allowed for surgery) are often well below the amounts charged and the contract becomes essentially a cash payment contract.

The similarity of health insurance to property and liability insurance is further emphasized in that the contract is for the benefit of the named insured. Typically it also covers other family members (children beyond certain ages are excluded), which is a feature of some property and liability insurance contracts as well. On the financial side, including premium computations, health insurance is also similar to property and liability insurance. In at least two areas of health insurance contractual provisions are closer to life insurance practices than to property insurance. Health insurance contracts may be issued on a noncancellable basis and other insurance provisions often are absent from the contract. Further, claims procedures, while more involved

than in life insurance, are less elaborate than is typically the case in property and liability insurance.

THE LIFE INSURANCE CONTRACT

Many of the basic concepts and characteristics of life insurance, and particularly those most relevant to the use of life insurance in risk management problems, are acquired through the study of the life insurance contract. Although there are a variety of life insurance contracts available in the market, they differ principally in the content of the various insuring agreements. The other provisions of the contract are remarkably similar. The discussion that follows will be based on the content of the whole life contract.

The whole life insurance contract may be divided into four parts: (1) basic information, (2) general provisions, (3) special provisions, and (4) riders and endorsements.

Basic Information

Basic information about the life insurance contract is found on the first and second pages of the contract. Typical of this information is the insuring agreement, which in a whole life policy will say that the insurer will "pay the face amount . . . to the beneficiary, upon surrender of this policy and upon receipt at its home office of due proof of death of the insured."[12] There will also be data on the name and age of the insured, the type of plan, the sum insured (face amount), the amount of the premium, a list of riders and endorsements, the name of the owner of the contract,

---

early years of the contract the insured pays more after policyholder dividends, if the contract is participating, than is needed to pay his share of current claims and expenses. This excess is retained by the insurer and accumulated at interest, since it will be needed to help provide the face amount that is payable on death. In effect, there is a decreasing amount of risk as time goes on. The excess is a liability from the standpoint of the insurer.

[12] *Study Kit for Students of Insurance*, p. 277.

and the names of primary and secondary beneficiaries.

General Provisions

There are twelve general provisions in the typical whole life insurance contract. These are: the entire contract, incontestability, suicide, reinstatement, premiums, grace period, death benefit, rights of owner, change of owner or beneficiary, assignment, misstatement of age or sex, and alteration of the policy.

Entire Contract

The statement in the policy labelled "entire contract" makes it clear that the policy and the application "constitute the entire contract between the parties." There is a further provision to the effect that "all statements made in the application shall, in the absence of fraud, be deemed representations and not warranties."[13] This statement about the contract serves to clarify the fact that only statements in the application may be used in defense of a claim and oral or other agreements are not applicable. The further statement that responses contained in the application are representations is important, since normally statements by the insured that are made a part of the contract are regarded as warranties.

Incontestability

A feature of the life insurance contract that is of considerable importance to the insured is that the contract is incontestable after two years. This fact means, in effect, that the contract is noncancellable on the part of the in-

13 *Ibid.*, p. 283.

surer, although the insured may always cancel the contract by not paying premiums.

Suicide

The willingness of the life insurer to accept the suicide risk after two years is an exception to the rule that only events that occur by chance are the proper subject matter of insurance. If suicide occurs before two years have elapsed, the only benefit is a return of premiums, normally paid in a lump sum.

Reinstatement

If the insured does not pay the premium under the contract, and the grace period has expired, the life insurance contract is in default, and the only benefits available are those provided by the nonforfeiture provisions of the contract. If the insured does not surrender the contract for cash, he may reinstate the contract during his lifetime subject to certain conditions. First, reinstatement must take place within a certain time period, which in most contracts is 5 years, subject to submission of evidence of insurability satisfactory to the insurer. Often there is also a provision that permits reinstatement within 31 days after the premium is in default without evidence of insurability. Second, overdue premiums must be paid with interest, usually 5 percent, compounded annually. The insured must also pay or reinstate indebtedness with interest the same as for overdue premiums.

Premiums

The length of the statement about premiums varies somewhat with the insurer. Normally there is a statement that premiums are payable in advance. Also, there is usually provision for paying premiums oftener than annually, such as semiannually, quarterly, or monthly.

Grace Period

After the first premium is paid, subsequent premiums are subject to a grace period of 31 days, which means the insured has 31 days in which to pay the premium after the due date.

Death Benefit

The statement about the death benefit clarifies the amount to be paid to the beneficiary. The death benefit is the face amount. However, in certain instances the benefit may be more or less than this figure. If there is indebtedness on the contract, it is deducted before payment is made to the beneficiary. Similarly, if death occurs during the grace period, "the unpaid premium on the premium basis then in effect will be deducted from the amount otherwise payable to the beneficiary."[14] On the other hand, if there are dividend credits held by the insurer, these will be added to the face amount.

Rights of the Owner

The owner of the life insurance contract may be the insured but is not necessarily so. Whoever is owner of the policy may exercise the rights granted to him by the contract or by the insurer. For example, the owner may change the beneficiary under the policy and the succession of ownership. His rights are subject to any written assignment received by the insurer.

[14] Ibid., p. 278.

Change of Owner or Beneficiary

A feature of the life insurance contract that adds considerably to its flexibility is that the beneficiary, unless there has been an irrevocable designation, may be changed by the owner without the consent of the beneficiary. The owner may likewise be changed. The changes may not occur until a request has been made to the insurer. In some instances the policy must be sent to the home office of the insurer for an endorsement reflecting the change. Typically, anyone the owner wishes may be designated as a beneficiary.

Assignment

Life insurance contracts are generally freely assignable, but the assignment is not binding on the insurer until such time as it has been notified and has received a true copy of the written assignment. The interest of the beneficiary is subject to the assignment, and the assignment is subject to any indebtedness that may exist under the contract.

Misstatement of Age or Sex

If age or sex has been misstated, the payment to the beneficiary will be the amount that would have appeared on the face of the contract for the specified premium at the correct age or sex.

Alteration of the Policy

In general, in insurance contracts, provisions in the contract may not be waived unless approved by an officer of the insurer who has authority to do so. A typical provision in the life insurance contract is: "Only the president, a vice president, the secretary, or an assistant secretary of the company has power on behalf of the company to change, modify, or waive the provisions of this policy and then only in writing."[15]

Special Provisions

The special provisions in the contract[16] are dividends, guaranteed loan privileges, conversion privileges, nonforfeiture benefits, and optional methods of settlement. Certain of these provisions — dividends, loan values, and nonforfeiture benefits — arise because of the way the contract is issued. For example, life insurance contracts are issued on a participating or nonparticipating basis. If issued on the latter basis a section in the contract about dividends is not necessary. Similarly, life contracts are typically issued on a level premium basis. This basis gives rise to individual policy reserves on contracts written for the whole of life or for a long term because of the substantial prepaying of costs by the insured in the early years of the contract. One of the by-products of this system is the legal requirement of nonforfeiture values.

Dividends

If a life insurance contract is issued on a participating basis, estimates of mortality, interest, and expenses that enter into the premium computation are typically conservatively made in contrast to premiums on a nonparticipating basis which are as accurate as possible. More may be charged on a participating basis than is needed to pay claims, expenses, and to set up appropriate reserves. Any surplus arising from re-

dundant estimates is paid to the policyholder in the form of a dividend.[17] Dividends to the policyholder must be paid on an annual basis, and the dividends section of the contract lists at least five ways in which dividends may be used. They may be used to reduce the premium with the policyholder paying the difference between the premium and the dividend, or they may be used to purchase additional paid-up additions to the contract. They may be paid in cash or left with the insurer to accumulate with interest payable at a rate determined by the insurer but at no less than a relatively small guaranteed amount. Dividends may also be used to help pay-up the policy. If no option is selected by the policyholder, some contracts state that the insurer will apply the dividend to purchase paid-up additions.

Loans

After the first year, loans are available in an amount based on the cash value of the contract including the value of paid-up additions. There are advantages to borrowing on a life insurance contract. No reason need be given for seeking the loan. The rate of interest payable is guaranteed by the contract and is 5 percent in many contracts now outstanding. The loan need not be paid back, but if it is not, it will be deducted from the face of the contract on the death of the insured. If interest is paid regularly, there is no problem about keeping the policy in force. There is a possibility, if interest accrues, that the policy will become void. A typical policy provision states: "If and when total indebtedness, including in-

---

[15] *Ibid.*, p. 282.

[16] The provisions discussed in this section are not labelled "special provisions" in the contract. They are given that label here as a way of classifying the provisions of the contract.

[17] This dividend is viewed as a return of premium and should not be confused with a dividend to stockholders which comes as a result of the profit-making activities of an insurer organized as a stock company.

terest due or accrued, equals or exceeds the then value of this policy plus the value of any paid-up additions and any dividend accumulations, and if at least thirty-one days prior notice shall have been mailed by the company to the last known address of the owner and of the assignee of record, if any, this policy shall terminate and become void."

A valuable aspect of the loan provision of a life insurance contract is the automatic premium loan. This type of loan will keep the policy from lapsing, if the premium remains unpaid after the expiration of the grace period.

Conversion Privileges

Life insurance contracts contain a conversion privilege that enables the insured to change from the contract the insured has to another one of different type and/or amount. Thus, a whole life insurance contract could be converted, for example, to a limited-payment life, endowment, or retirement income policy. The change must be acceptable to the insurer, and the insured is required to pay any additional costs that may arise from higher premiums and reserves of the new contract.

Nonforfeiture Benefits

Life insurance contracts that produce reserves are required to have nonforfeiture provisions. These contracts contain, in addition to a statement about nonforfeiture, a table of guaranteed benefits. The nonforfeiture benefits offered by the contract are the cash value, extended term insurance, and paid-up whole life insurance. In the case of the cash value the insurer has the right to defer payment for a period of six months. If the contract, in the event of forfeiture, is continued as extended term insurance, the amount of the in-

surance will be the face amount of the contract in default plus paid-up additions and dividend accumulation less indebtedness under the contract. The length of the term will depend on the size of the cash value, since it will be used as a net single premium at the attained age of the insured to purchase the extended benefits. The paid-up whole life insurance option results in a reduced-level face amount, but the contract will continue at that amount for as long as the insured lives. The amount of the reduction will depend on the size of the cash value, since the latter will be used as a net single premium at the attained age of the insured to purchase a contract with a reduced face amount.

Optional Methods of Settlement

All life insurance contracts provide for the settlement of the proceeds of the contract, in the event of the death of the insured, in a variety of ways. Typical of the options are settlement in a lump sum, various annuity arrangements, and accrual of proceeds at interest. The annuity options include payments of a specified amount payable until the proceeds are exhausted; payments for a specified period with the amount depending on the time period selected in years; and monthly payments for life. The life payments may be with or without payments certain. Some contracts also provide joint and survivor monthly life income payments, and joint and survivor life income payments with two-thirds payable to the survivor. Survivor options may be elected by the owner or by the beneficiary in the event no option has been selected.

Riders and Endorsements

Life insurance contracts, like other insurance contracts, may be endorsed in various ways. There are three endorsements or agreements that are often attached to life insurance contracts. These agreements are (1) waiver of premium in the event of disability, (2) double indemnity (accidental death benefit agreement), and (3) guaranteed insurability. A separate premium is charged for each of these agreements and they are subject to maximum age limitations. Thus, waiver of premium in the event of disability normally does not extend to disabilities that commence after age 65, the accidental death benefit does not extend beyond age 70, and insurability protection beyond age 40.

Waiver of Premium

The benefit provided under the waiver of premium agreement is that the insurer will waive payment of the premium under the contract during the continuance of the total disability of the insured if the total disability commences, say, before age 65. The waiver of premium does not reduce the amount payable under the contract in the event of death, nor are nonforfeiture values or dividends affected. The insurer does not accept the risk of total disability if the disease or injury occurred before the issuance of the policy unless declared in the application, nor does the agreement apply to disability arising out of deliberately self-inflicted injuries. Disability arising from "any act of war, declared or undeclared, or from military, naval, or air service for any country at war, declared or undeclared"[18] is also excluded.

The benefit is not paid unless the disability has continued without interruption for six months.[19] Further, the

[18] Study Kit for Students of Insurance, p. 274.

[19] Although this period gives a presumption of permanent disability, this presumption

disability must come under the definition of total disability stated in the contract. A definition frequently used is that total disability exists if the insured is continuously unable "to perform substantially all the work pertaining to his occupation or business" because of illness or accident. Usually this definition of disability is used only for the first 24 months of total disability. After that the definition changes and total disability means "continuous inability of the insured, resulting from disease or injury to engage in any occupation or business for which the insured is or has become fitted by education, training, or experience. . . ." Certain injuries are regarded, apart from the definition of liability, as conferring total disability as long as the condition persists. Examples are the entire loss of sight of both eyes or the loss of use of both hands.

Proof of the continuance of total disability is required and such proof may involve submission by the insured to a physical examination by a physician. If the insured does not comply with the requirements for proof, benefits under the agreement cease.

Accidental Death

The benefit promised under the accidental death agreement is normally that twice the face amount of insurance provided by the contract to which the agreement is attached will be paid if death is a "direct result of accidental bodily injury occurring independently of all other causes." The agreement also states that death must occur within a stated period after such accidental injury, usually 90 or in some contracts, 180 days.

Although the basic life insurance contract is virtually free of limitations

is only for the purpose of determining when liability begins.

and exclusions surrounding the cause of death, the accidental death agreement contains a number of exceptions. One such statement of exceptions reads as follows:

No benefit is payable under this agreement if the death of the insured results directly or indirectly from: suicide, whether the insured be sane or insane; war, declared or undeclared, or any act incident thereto; service in the military, naval, or air forces of any country at war, declared or undeclared, or any civilian noncombatant unit serving with such forces ('any country' includes any international organization or combination of countries); travel or flight in, or descent from or with, any kind of aircraft aboard which the insured is a pilot or member of the crew or is a student or instructor of aeronautics or is giving or receiving any kind of training or instruction or has any duty incident to the operation of said aircraft or is testing equipment or personnel; bodily or mental illness, disease, or infirmity of any kind, or medical or surgical treatment therefore; the administration, injection or taking of any drug or hypnotic or narcotic, accidentally or otherwise; injury received while committing or attempting to commit a felony.

The accidental death benefit has limited use for planning, particularly in those situations where the chief purpose of the insurance is to replace income lost by the death of the breadwinner. There would seem to be no reason why survivors would only need the face amount of the contract in the event death occurred from sickness but twice the amount if death occurred by accident.

Protection of Insurability

The benefit provided by the protection of insurability agreement is that the insured may purchase a new life insurance contract (or endowment or retirement income policy) on certain option dates specified in the contract without evidence of insurability. The right to purchase new insurance is surrounded by certain rules. The amount of new insurance may not exceed the amount stated on the schedule page of the contract and the application for new insurance must be received not later than an option date. Further, the number of option-date ages decreases as the age at issue of the contract to which the agreement has been attached increases. If, for example, the original contract is issued between ages 0 and 23, there are five option-date ages, but if issued between ages 36 and 37, there is only one option date age, namely, 40. An option date is the anniversary of the policy on which the insured's age at nearest birthday is equal to one of the ages specified in the policy as an option-date age. Some contracts permit a substitute option date which is related to date of marriage or birth or legal adoption of a child. Waiver of premium in the event of disability provisions and an accidental death agreement may be added to the new contract subject to certain conditions. For example, an accidental death agreement normally requires evidence of insurability satisfactory to the insurer.

HEALTH INSURANCE CONTRACTS

The role health insurance plays in risk management may not be entirely obvious. Group health insurance is an important employee benefit and the risk manager may be involved in the administration of such benefits. Individual health insurance is useful in estate planning, since erosion of estate assets by accident and sickness may be protected against by appropriate contracts. A similar argument may be made for key men in large organizations.

Health insurance contracts are not standard and it is not possible to select one contract as being representative of all such contracts.[20] In the discussion that follows some of the principal provisions of various types of health insurance contracts will be reviewed as a way of providing insight to some of the basic principles of health insurance.

Basic Structure of Individual Health Insurance Contracts

The content of a health insurance policy will depend on the specific type of contract being considered. However, all health insurance contracts can, in general, be placed in a framework consisting of a face page and schedule page, benefit pages, general provisions, and attachments.

Face Page and Schedule Page

The face and schedule pages contain certain basic policy data such as name and address of the insured, type of contract, insuring agreement, consideration clause, form number, and a statement about renewal. Of these various items the renewal provisions require additional comment.

Since health insurance began as a part of casualty insurance, its early practices in regard to cancellation and renewal followed the traditions of property and liability insurance, which, in general, were that contracts could be can-

---

[20] Life insurance contracts are not standard either, but the difference from contract to contract are not as great as in health insurance, and it is possible to talk about a typical life insurance contract in a way that is not possible in the field of health.

celled within term at the option of either the insured or insurer, and at the end of the contract term could be renewed only with the insurer's consent. The tradition in life insurance was that life contracts could not be cancelled by the insurer after the incontestable period had expired and during the incontestable period only if the insured had specific grounds for doing so, such as misrepresentation. Renewability was not a question in whole life insurance as long as the insured paid premiums. Term life contracts with a renewability provision could be renewed at the end of the term at the option of the insured until a specified age.

As health insurance evolved a variety of practices were followed in regard to cancellation and renewal, some of which followed the property and liability tradition, others the life insurance tradition, and still others that seemed to be a combination of the two. There are now four basic patterns: (1) contracts that are renewable at the option of the insurer and cancellable within term by the insurer and those that are noncancellable within term but which are renewable at the option of the insurer; (2) contracts that give the insurer a restricted right of nonrenewal in that they limit the situations in which renewal can be refused; (3) contracts that guarantee renewal but which permit the insurer to raise rates on a class basis (individuals cannot be singled out for rate increases); (4) contracts that are noncancellable and guaranteed renewable at a guaranteed premium. The latter type of provision is generally found only in disability income and accidental death and dismemberment contracts.

Benefit Pages

This part of the contract will be discussed below in a separate section.

General Provisions

The general provisions consist, in addition to some administrative provisions, of the uniform policy provisions that are required by state law to be placed in individual health insurance contracts.

The uniform policy provisions are of two types, those that must be placed in the contract (required) and those that may be placed there if the insurer wishes (optional). There are twelve required provisions. The first provision is a statement that "this policy, including the copy of the application, the endorsements, and the other attached papers, if any, constitutes the entire contract of insurance." There is a further statement that any changes in the policy must be approved by an executive officer of the insurer and must be endorsed on the contract. An agent has no authority to change the contract or to waive any of its provisions. The second provision places a time limit on certain defenses and is similar to the incontestable clause in the life insurance policy. The provision is in two parts. Part A provides that after two years from the issue date of the policy "no misstatements, except fraudulent misstatements, made by the applicant in the application for such policy shall be used to void the policy or to deny a claim for loss incurred or disability (as defined in the policy) commencing after the expiration of such two-year period." Part B provides that loss incurred, commencing after two years, may not be reduced or denied "on the grounds that a disease or physical condition, not excluded from coverage by name or specific description effective on the date of loss, had existed prior to the effective date of coverage." The third provision provides that a grace period must be granted for the payment of the premium. The fourth provision relates to reinstatement and provides that a policy that has lapsed for nonpayment of premium can be reinstated by the acceptance of the insurer of an overdue premium. A reinstatement application may be required and only accidents and sicknesses occurring after the reinstatement date are covered. For sickness there is a provision that only sicknesses occurring 10 days after the reinstatement date are covered. The fifth provision states that the insured is required "to furnish the company with a notice of claim within 20 days, or as soon as reasonably possible." Provision six requires that the insurer once notified must furnish claim forms within 15 days. If claim forms are not furnished, the claimant "shall be deemed to have completed the requirements of this policy as to proof of loss . . ." Provision seven states the time limits imposed for filing proofs of loss. In general, proof must be filed "within 90 days after the termination of the period for which the company is liable." Provision 8 and 9 state the rules surrounding payment of claims. Generally, claims are payable as soon as proof of loss has been received by the insurer to the insured or designated beneficiary. In the case of loss of life, if there is no designated beneficiary of the insured, in some cases, as an optional provision, payment is made to a hospital or physician. Provisions 10, 11, and 12 contain statements about physical examination and autopsy, legal actions, and change of beneficiary. The insurer has the right at its expense to conduct physical examinations when necessary in connection with claims and in death situations to perform an autopsy unless the latter is forbidden by law. Legal action may not be taken for 60 days after proof of loss has been filed and not after 3 years have elapsed. The insured may assign the contract and change the beneficiary as he wishes unless he has for some reason given up the right to do so.

There are eleven optional uniform provisions as follows: (1) change of occupation, (2) misstatement of age, (3) other insurance in this insurer, (4) insurance with other insurer I, (5) insurance with other insurer II, (6) relation of earnings to insurance, (7) unpaid premium, (8) cancellation, (9) conformity with state statutes, (10) illegal occupation, and (11) intoxicants and narcotics. Of these provisions 4, 5, 7, 8, 10, and 11 are not often used. The others are fairly common, although competition tends to restrict the use of 6. Option 9, although generally optional, is required by some states. Provision 1 recognizes the importance in some forms of health insurance of occupation in the rating structure. The provision requires that, if a change occurs from a nonhazardous occupation to a hazardous one, benefits will be reduced to correspond to what the premium already set would buy for the more hazardous occupation. If the change is to a less hazardous occupation, there will be a return of any overpayment of premium to the insured if he requests it. Provision 2, which relates to misstatement of age, is much like the corresponding life insurance provision. A misstatement does not void the contract, but the benefit is adjusted. Provision 3 allows the insurer to control the amount of health insurance that it will write on any one life. Provisions 4 and 5 relate to the troublesome problem of insurance with other insurers. The first of these provisions permits pro rata settlement of medical expense claims, if other insurance is in force and the insurer has not been notified of its existence. The second of the two provisions (provision 5) permits a pro rata settlement of disability claims. Provision 6 is applicable only to noncancellable and guaranteed renewable disability policies and is designed to control situations where the benefits payable exceed the usual income of the insured. Overinsurance of this type is not permitted. Provision 7 allows the deduction of any unpaid premium that may exist at the time of claim from the benefit that is payable. Cancellation is permitted under provision 8. Provision 10 allows the insurer to deny liability if the claim arises as a result of a felony or illegal occupation. Provision 11 allows the insurer to refuse to pay benefits if the loss came about while the insured was under the influence of liquor or narcotics.

Attachments

It is customary in health insurance contracts to attach the application to the policy. Other endorsements or riders may also be added.

Benefits

The benefits provided by health insurance contracts may be classified as disability, business expense disability, accidental death and dismemberment, and medical.

Disability Benefits

Disability insurance contracts provide an income benefit payable weekly or monthly for a specified time during the persistence of total disability. The amount of the benefit is related to and is usually less than the salary or wages of the insured. This type of insurance is sometimes called loss of time insurance or income protection insurance. The disability may be caused by either accident or sickness.

The length of time for which benefits are paid will depend on the elimination period and the maximum benefit period. The elimination period is the time after disability starts in which benefits are not paid.[21] The length of the elimination period normally will depend on whether the disability had been caused by accident or sickness. In the case of accident the elimination period is normally zero days. For sickness it may vary from 7 to 90 days. The maximum benefit period places a limit on the length of time benefits are payable regardless of how long the disability lasts. As in the case of the elimination period, the maximum benefit period is usually different for accidental injuries than for disability from sickness. In the case of accident, benefits may be payable for life assuming the disability continues that long. Sickness benefits are often payable for no longer than 2 years. The difference in treatment of the two causes of disability is largely related to the fact that accident disability costs less to insure. Accident disability permits a more objective determination than is the case with sickness and occurs with less frequency for most ages and for nonhazardous occupations.

Whether a given injury is regarded as resulting in total disability, depends on how total disability is defined. All disability contracts contain appropriate definitions. Historically, total disability was defined as the "inability of the insured to engage in any gainful occupation." Over time this definition has been liberalized so that it is typical now for total disability to be defined as "inability of the insured to engage in his oc-

cupation" for, say, a period of 2 years, and if, after that, the disability persists, the definition changes to inability to "engage in any gainful occupation for which he is reasonably fitted by education, training, and experience." Disability contracts contain waiver of premium clauses which waive the premium under the contract in the event of total disability. The insurer also agrees not to cancel or to refuse renewal during the period of disability.

Partial disability benefits are fairly common, especially if the disability was caused by accident. Sickness partial benefits, however, are available. The usual provision for partial disability benefits is that they are payable only when they immediately follow a period of total disability.

Some special situations may arise in connection with occupational disabilities and recurrent disabilities in situations where disability may not immediately follow an accident or sickness.

Disability policies usually pay the benefits described in the contract regardless of whether the source of the injury was occupational or nonoccupational. However, some insurers offer contracts that exclude disability that may be regarded as arising out of or in the course of employment.

Sometimes a period of temporary recovery will separate two periods of total disability. A question sometimes arises about whether the second disability is a continuation of the first or a new disability. The general rule is that the second disability is regarded as a continuation unless the individual involved has been back to work for at least 6 months. The problem has some significance, since if the disability is regarded as a continuation, benefits will not be paid for as long as they would be if the second disability were regarded as a new one.

---

[21] The elimination period as described here is sometimes referred to as a waiting period. In this text the expression "waiting period" will be reserved for situations where certain conditions or sicknesses would not be covered until a certain amount of time had elapsed. The elimination period is comparable to a deductible in other types of contracts, and it has some of the same advantages that other deductibles have.

On occasion disability does not set in immediately after an accident or sickness, and a problem may arise in trying to link the injury and the disability. To meet this problem there is a provision in the contract that the disability must occur within 90 days.

Disability contracts sometimes have guaranteed insurability provisions that permit (on certain anniversaries) the purchase of additional amounts of monthly income. Typically disability contracts will have provisions to the effect that disability insurance will terminate at a specified age, which may be 65 or somewhat lower for women. It is sometimes possible to extend the age, if the insurer is willing to agree.

The disability policy has a number of exceptions or limitations although these provisions are not terribly restrictive. The principle exclusions are: (1) war, whether declared or not; (2) participation in the armed forces, although there may be a right to reestablish coverage after discharge; (3) pregnancy, childbirth, and any complications; (4) intentionally self-inflicted injuries including attempted suicide; (5) air travel unless the insured is a fare-paying passenger; (6) residence abroad, if for an extended period, since coverage may be limited to 12 months.

Business Expense Disability Benefits

For some types of business, such as medical practice, disability of the proprietor may result in serious business problems regarding income, and the results are similar to those encountered when business income is disrupted, as a result of fire or related perils. Business expense disability benefits will cover such expenses as rent, light, heat, employee salaries, property taxes, and telephone.[22] Some expenses are not covered, such as the salary of the proprietor.

Accidental Death and Dismemberment Benefits

Accidental death and dismemberment contracts provide for a payment called the principal sum that is made in the event of accidental death. Additionally there are lump-sum benefits payable for certain types of accidental dismemberment such as loss of hands, feet, eyes, or fingers. The dismemberment benefits are related to the principal sum. For example, the principal sum might be payable for the loss of two feet or one-half the principal sum might be available for the loss of one eye. Contracts of this type are subject to the same kind of reservations that exist for the double indemnity provision of the life insurance contract.

Medical Expense Benefits

As was explained earlier in the chapter, medical expense benefits include hospital expense benefits, surgical expense benefits, doctors' expense benefits (sometimes referred to as medical expense), and such specialty benefits as nurses' expense, dental care, and convalescent or nursing home care. Most or all of these benefits may be provided by one contract, for example, the major medical expense contract, or it may be necessary, depending on the type of coverage desired, to have more than one contract with each contract being somewhat specialized in terms of the benefit covered.

Hospital expense benefits are provided mainly by specialty insurers such

[22] For a complete list consult the contract.

as Blue Cross or by commercial insurers (life and casualty) or by those group practice plans operating on a prepayment basis that are associated with hospitals. The principal benefit offered is hospital room and board, which typically carries a limit on the amount that will be paid. The insurer pays cash to the insured who, in turn, may use the money to pay the hospital. Blue Cross is an exception to this statement, since it enters into contracts with hospitals, and pays them directly, rather than through the insured. Similarly, group practice plans associated with hospitals provide service rather than cash benefits. In addition to room and board, hospital contracts pay for certain miscellaneous benefits like use of operating room, diagnostic services (*e.g.,* laboratory and X-ray), anesthetics, drugs, medical equipment, and supplies. These benefits typically are supplied up to some specified cash limit. Blue Cross and group practice plans, again, form an exception. Coverage for outpatient charges are typically limited to an emergency accident benefit.

Surgical expense benefits are provided by the same types of insurer that supply hospital benefits.[23] The benefits are designed to reimburse the insured for the charges surgeons make for operations (and in some instances charges o f anesthesiologists). The amount of the benefit is normally limited to a schedule of charges that appears in the contract.

The doctors' expense benefit, sometimes called the medical expense benefit,[24] may be offered as a part of

---

[23] Not all Blue Cross plans provide surgical benefits. However, these may be provided by Blue Shield plans which may operate from an administrative viewpoint in association with Blue Cross.

[24] Medical expense in this text refers to the entire range of services performed by physicians and surgeons.

the contract providing for hospital expense or it may accompany the surgical contract. In some instances it may appear as a separate rider or occasionally as a separate contract. The benefits provided are physician home and office calls.

Benefits such as private duty nursing, convalescent or nursing home care, and dental care often do not appear as a part of the usual medical care insurance contracts. Contracts like major medical cover private duty nursing and group contracts increasingly provide dental benefits. Nursing home care is still not extensively provided, although some contracts provided some coverage for limited periods.

Medical care insurance contracts contain a number of exclusions. Among the most important are: (1) accident or sickness benefits if they are provided under workers' compensation or similar laws; (2) care in a government facility unless a charge is made; (3) rest cure; (4) mental or emotional illness unless there is specific coverage in the contract; (5) pregnancy, although limited benefits are provided in some contracts; (6) war, whether declared or undeclared; (7) cosmetic surgery, unless needed as a result of injury; (8) eye refractions, glasses, or hearing aids; (9) dental care except for injuries resulting from accident.

Underwriting of Health Insurance

Space does not permit a detailed account of individual health insurance underwriting. Two aspects of underwriting, however, deserve brief consideration. One of these aspects relates to waiting periods and the other to preexisting conditions. Waiting periods relate to initial periods following the original effective date of the contract when the coverage under the contract is not yet in effect. Waiting periods usually fall into one or the other of two categories or types. One type is a waiting period of 14 to 30 days, which is applicable to sickness generally but not to accidents. The latter are ordinarily covered immediately. A second type is a fairly long waiting period that is applied to specific situations. An example would be a 10-month waiting period before pregnancy benefits would be available or a 6-month period for such conditions as appendicitis, tonsillitis, or hernia.

Waiting periods as described above are related to the problem that surrounds preexisting conditions in health insurance. The assumption is generally made that sickness covered under the policy and the loss therefrom is contracted and commences during the time the contract is in force. Thus, preexisting conditions are not covered until after the time during which the insurer can challenge the contract on the grounds of a preexisting condition has expired. The rule applies, regardless of what the insured has stated on the application or what the insurer may know about the underwriting history of the case at time of issue. One way the insurer can treat preexisting conditions of which it has knowledge and which it prefers not to insure is to place a rider in the contract that excludes a particular condition from coverage.[25]

BUSINESS USES OF LIFE INSURANCE

The business uses of life insurance may be classified as group life insurance, key man insurance, split dollar insurance,

[25] Edwin L. Bartleson, *et. al., Health Insurance,* 2nd ed., Chicago: Society of Actuaries, 1968, p. 41.

deferred compensation, and the funding of business continuation plans. Some or all of these uses may be helpful to the risk manager as he advises the business firm about risk problems relating to the protection of human assets.

Group Life Insurance

Many individual life insurance contracts may be written on a group basis. The practices surrounding group insurance differ in many ways from those that are found in individual insurance. From a business point of view the chief use of group insurance is the provision of various employee benefits. A discussion of group insurance, therefore, will be deferred to the chapters on fringe benefits for employees.

Key Man Insurance

The successful operation of many businesses depends heavily on the skill of the owner or on the skills of a relatively few employees. The main purpose of key man insurance is to protect the firm against monetary loss brought about by the early death of a key employee. The attributes of the key man are typically that he possesses skill and knowledge that would take some time after his death to replace or he may through his personal contacts be a source of business or he may be an important factor in the ability of the firm to obtain credit. Not only would the proceeds from a life insurance contract provide the funds needed to conduct a search for a replacement, a permanent form of life insurance would provide accumulating cash values during the life of the key man that might be utilized in the event of an emergency.

The type of life insurance contract used for key man insurance will depend on the circumstance surrounding the case. Either whole life or term insurance is often used.

Split Dollar Insurance

Split dollar life insurance is a way in which two parties may share in the cost of providing insurance on the life of one of them. It is now most often used as an employee benefit, although perhaps its first use was for the purpose of having a father help a son with the latter's insurance needs. The basic idea of split dollar insurance arises out of the fact that in permanent forms of insurance the face amount may be viewed as a combination of the reserve on the contract and the net amount at risk. As time passes the net amount at risk decreases and the reserve increases. In an arrangement between an employer and an employee, the employee is the insured. In terms of paying the premium the employer would pay the portion of the premium representing the increase in cash value and the employee would pay the balance. The plan permits a fairly substantial, though decreasing, amount of insurance at comparatively low cost. On the death of the employee, the employer would have a right to the cash value of the contract and the employee's beneficiary would receive the balance.[26]

[26] For further information see William B. Lynch, "Split-Dollar Plans" in Davis W. Gregg and Vane B. Lucas, *Life and Health Insurance Handbook*, 3rd ed., pp. 676–689.

Deferred Compensation

Deferred compensation agreements are arrangements between employers and employees wherein the former agrees to defer some compensation for present services until some time in the future usually until after retirement. This type of agreement is usually designed to defer some of the compensation of highly paid employees to a time when total income of the employee will be lower, as will the applicable income tax rate.

Although the contents of deferred compensation contracts may vary, there is a need to fund the agreement and this may be done through the accumulation of cash, by use of securities, by use of annuities or through life insurance. Life insurance has many advantages for this purpose. A contract that is often useful is the whole life paid-up-at-65 policy. The cash value at 65 could be used to pay the benefits under the deferred compensation agreement.

Business Continuation Plans

In the next chapter the use of life insurance for funding business continuation agreements will be discussed as an important aspect of estate planning. One of the advantages of insurance as a funding medium is that the purchaser of the business interest will have funds available immediately to discharge his financial obligation.

SUMMARY AND CONCLUSIONS

1. A basic knowledge of life and health insurance is essential to the risk manager, since the treatment of personnel risks often involves the use of life and health insurance contracts.

2. The basic types of life insurance contracts are term, whole life, endowment, and their combinations.

3. The basic forms of life annuities are life annuities due, immediate life annuities, deferred life annuities, and joint life annuities.

4. Health insurance contracts are designed to protect against the loss of income caused by accidents and sickness and to pay for medical expenses.

5. Life, health, and annuity contracts may be issued on a group or individual basis and they may also, in the case of life insurance and annuities, offer fixed or variable benefits.

6. The general provisions in a typical whole life insurance contract include items having the following titles: entire contract, incontestability, suicide, reinstatement, premiums, grace period, death benefit, rights of owner, change of owner or beneficiary, assignment, misstatement of age or sex, and alteration of the policy.

7. Special provisions of a whole life insurance contract are: dividends, guaranteed loan privileges, conversion privileges, nonforfeiture benefits, and optional modes of settlement.

8. There are three endorsements that are often attached to life insurance contracts: 1) waiver of premium in the event of disability, 2) double indemnity (accidental death benefit agreement), and 3) guaranteed insurability.

9. Health insurance contracts include those issued by commerical insurers and by specialty insurers such as Blue Cross and Blue Shield, and by independent medical groups.

10. Life insurance contracts may be used in business to provide group life insurance, key man insurance, and split dollar insurance, and they may be used to fund deferred compensation agreements and business continuation plans.

QUESTIONS FOR DISCUSSION

1. It is sometimes stated that annuities are not life insurance. Do you agree?

2. Develop a classification of annuity contracts. In your classification give consideration to such items as time when payments begin, responsibility of the insurer upon the death of the annuitant, and the number of lives involved.

3. A split dollar life insurance plan is arranged between an employee age 35 and his employer. To provide the benefits a nonparticipating whole life insurance contract in the amount of $200,000 is purchased. The annual premium is $3,800. Construct a table showing the death benefit available to the employer and the employee's family at the end of each of the first 20 years the contract is in force. What are the total premiums that would be paid by the employer at the end of 20 years? What is the total that would be paid by the employee? Assume the following cash values under the contract for the first 20 years:

Policy Year	Cash Value	Policy Year	Cash Value	Policy Year	Cash Value	Policy Year	Cash Value
1	$ —	6	$13,800	11	$32,200	16	$52,200
2	600	7	17,400	12	36,200	17	56,200
3	3,800	8	21,000	13	40,200	18	60,200
4	7,000	9	24,600	14	44,200	19	64,200
5	10,400	10	28,200	15	48,200	20	68,200

4. A whole life insurance policy of face amount $100,000 that had been in force for 25 years lapsed because of nonpayment of premiums. By reference to a copy of a whole life contract what would the cash value of the contract be? Suppose the insured did not wish to surrender the contract for cash, but preferred extended term insurance. How long could the contract be kept in force on that basis? What would the face amount be?

5. Assume the same facts as question 4 except that the contract was to be continued as paid-up insurance. What would the face amount of insurance be?

6. Summarize the loan provisions of life insurance contracts. The fact that interest is charged for loans is sometimes misunderstood by insureds. How would you explain this provision in the contract to someone not particularly familiar with life insurance?

7. An insured owned a whole life insurance contract with face amount of $300,000. On his death his widow, age 70, who was his beneficiary, elected to receive the face of the contract as a life annuity with payments certain for 10 years. By consulting a whole life insurance policy determine the amount of monthly income the widow would receive.

8. Given the same facts as question 7, suppose the widow wanted the proceeds paid at the rate of $2000.00 monthly. How long would the payments continue?

9. Given the same facts as question 7, suppose the widow wanted the proceeds settled in equal monthly installments over 10 years. What would the size of the monthly payment be?

10. X has a major medical expense insurance contract with a $200 deductible and a 80 percent coinsurance clause. The contract maximum is $50,000. As a result of a serious illness involving surgery, X amassed hospital and medical bills of $20,000. He notified his insurer and submitted appropriate information. How much would the insurer pay?

11. Assume James R. Brown, age 30, is interested in planning for the security of his family through life insurance. His wife is age 28 and they have one child, age 2. His income is $17,000 per year and he has not yet purchased a home. His assets, other than his earning power, consist of home furnishings and $6000 in a savings bank. Assume that he is fully and currently insured and that his average annual earnings for social security purposes are $9,000. Brown has no life insurance at present, and he estimates his family's needs in event of his death as follows:

1. Last expenses (To be provided by his savings account)

2. Money needed during readjustment — $10,000

3. Income needed while child is dependent — $1000/month

4. Money for child's education — $20,000 (To be available when child reaches age 18).

5. Life income for wife — $800/month.

What advice would you give him about the amounts and types of life insurance he should buy?

12. Explain the significance to the insured of the following provisions of the life insurance contract: incontestable clause, policy and application constitute the entire contract, misstatement of age.

10

Estate Planning

One of the applications of life insurance to the affairs of individuals or businesses is its use in protecting an estate from certain types of shrinkage caused by inadequate planning on the part of business owners or individuals who have accumulated assets and who wish their estates to be preserved, even though death may bring an end to their ability to manage the property they have accumulated. In a general sense, estate planning encompasses the entire process of estate accumulation and distribution, and all types of insurance are designed to protect against the financial consequences of estate loss. In a narrower sense, and in the sense often meant, estate planning is a process related to the distribution of assets after death. In this chapter the discussion of estate planning will be largely limited to problems of estate conservation for the purpose of obtaining maximum support for the family after the death of the creator of the estate.[1] The assumption is made that an estate has been or will be adequately maintained during the life of the person who was responsible for the accumulation.

The following topics will be treated:

1. Principles and purposes of estate planning

2. Estate analysis
   a. Personal and family data
   b. Financial objectives
   c. Assets and liabilities
   d. Income and expense data
   e. Life and health insurance
   f. Laws governing estate distribution

3. Management of the estate
   a. Problems of estate accumulation
   b. Occupational sources
   c. Savings and investment opportunities
   d. Factors that serve to reduce the size of the estate

4. Creating an estate plan
   a. Wills
   b. Trusts
   c. Gifts
   d. Business interests in estate planning

5. Titling of property

6. Testing and monitoring the plan

[1] See Robert Brosterman, *The Complete Estate Planning Guide* (New York: New American Library, 1970). Brosterman's definition of estate planning is "The creation, conservation, and utilization of family resources to obtain the maximum support and security for the family during the lifetime and after the death of the planner." This definition has been modified for purposes of this chapter since problems of estate accumulations are beyond the scope of this text.

206

PRINCIPLES AND PURPOSES OF ESTATE PLANNING

Estate planning as such is not a new concept. The need for the accumulation of an estate and provision for its distribution after death has long existed, and legal codes providing the rules for estate transfer have been in existence for many years with some of them dating as far back as the early Egyptians.[2] However, it has been only in comparatively recent times that a systematic study has been made of the principles and processes surrounding estate planning and its use in managing the uncertainties that arise about the loss of assets that may result in the distributive process after death.

One of the broad purposes of estate planning is to assist the person who creates an estate in his efforts to accumulate and preserve assets both during his lifetime and after death. The processes involved are applicable to small as well as large estates, and everyone with an interest in estate conservation should be encouraged to review his estate from a planning point of view. Estate planning is not solely tax planning, although in any estate plan the impact of taxes is considered in relation to their role as an estate erosion factor, as well as the need for liquidity in order to pay them. Although tax minimization may be a goal in many estate plans, it is seldom the only or the most important objective of the planning process.

Ideally estate planning is best approached as a team effort. The fields of law, accounting, investments, and life underwriting are involved in all estate plans. Historically and currently the life

[2] See Lawrence J. Ackerman, "Estate Planning Principles" in Davis W. Gregg and Vane B. Lucas, *Life and Health Insurance Handbook*, p. 845, 3rd ed. (Homewood, Ill.: *Life and Health Insurance Handbook*, 1973.)

underwriter has usually been the person responsible for initiating the process. His interest normally arises out of his responsibilities in life insurance programming for individuals who wish to add to their life insurance portfolio. Since the proper programming of life insurance necessitates the acquisition of considerable knowledge about a client's financial affairs, it is appropriate for the life underwriter to make suggestions about how an estate might be planned to accomplish a stated set of objectives. The implementation of any plan will typically involve the drawing of wills, preparation of trusts, and other legal matters, requiring the work of an attorney. So too, tax considerations will enter into the preparation of an optimal plan, and the accountant can often be of help in this phase of the work. One of the basic principles of estate planning is that it is a cooperative effort, and the assistance of insurance men, attorneys, bankers, accountants, and investment experts should be sought at the beginning of any estate planning process.

Although estate planning is often thought to be largely personal in character as opposed to commercial, it is often true that for many estates the principal asset is a business interest of some type and much of the work of planning centers around the disposition of such interests after death.

ESTATE ANALYSIS

The first step in setting forth an estate plan is to gather information about the content of the estate. This task may be accomplished in a variety of ways, but it is generally advisable to use a questionnaire or schedule in order to assure a systematic accumulation of facts and to avoid omitting items of importance. A number of schedules are in use by life insurance salesmen for this purpose. Although they are not necessarily uniform, all such schedules should contain information of the following types: personal and family data; financial objectives, a statement of assets and liabilities; income and expense data; types of insurance protection; and current estate distribution plans.

Personal and Family Data

The amount of personal and family data obtained will depend somewhat on the planner but should, as a minimum, include name and residence of the client, age, and place of birth. It should also include occupation and title as well as the client's social security number. Also, the business address should be included and the name of the employer. On the family side the spouse's name, birth date, and age should be obtained, as well as occupation and title, business address, social security number, and the name of the employer. Names of children should be recorded along with birth dates and, possibly, estimated educational costs. It might also be appropriate to include the names of the client's attorney, accountant, stockbroker, insurance agent, and banker.

It is desirable for the estate planner to obtain information about any existing estate plans. In particular the existence of nonexistence of a will should be determined, as well as facts about trusts and related documents that are relevant to planning.

Financial Objectives

Financial information of various types is essential to estate planning and a first consideration is a clear statement of financial objectives and goals. Such a statement might include retirement plans. As a minimum it should offer guidance as to the relative importance of various types of assets and attitudes toward growth vs. income in relationship to investment.

Assets and Liabilities

A statement of assets would include such items as preferred and common stocks, mutual funds, real estate, personal property, bonds, trust funds, cash in banks, and other assets of a miscellaneous sort. Although aggregate amounts might be all that would be necessary in some instances, for planning purposes it is usually helpful to record the type of assets in some detail. For example, in connection with stocks a detailed listing by company, number of shares, date acquired, initial cost, present market value, and rate of return would be helpful. Likewise, cash in bank should be recorded in such a way as to indicate whether the money is in a checking account, savings account (other than savings and loan), savings and loan, and certificates of deposit. Similarly, bonds should be listed by type and face amount along with data on market value, and appropriate information on rate of return. Liabilities may be of various types and might well include charge accounts, bank notes, other notes, and installment obligations.

Income and Expense Data

In many estate planning situations, supplying an adequate income to survivors is often an important objective. As a starting point in the determination of the income needed, a review of the current income status of the family is necessary. This review would include a statement about earned income as well as dividends, interest, rents, and other sources of income that may accrue to the family. Some effort to estimate future income is helpful, since an estimate of the need of survivors will depend to a considerable extent upon the evaluation of living standards over time. Expense data should include a detailed statement of living expenses involved in maintaining the home, the family, and such items as taxes, insurance, and loans. Further, an estimate of the widow's or widower's expenses should be made, since these expenses are of prime importance to the estate planner.

Life and Health Insurance

Inasmuch as life and health insurance serve to protect the estate from certain types of erosion, a record of existing contracts is a necessary part of estate analysis. The necessary type of information would include, in the case of life insurance, data on the face amount of insurance, primary beneficiary, cash value, and type of contract. Health insurance contracts should be analyzed in terms of type of contract and benefits provided. There may be contracts other than individual ones that provide coverage. Group insurance contracts of various types including annuities, officers and directors liability, life insurance used to fund buy and sell agreements, and key man insurance may be relevant. Any annuities issued on an individual basis should also be analyzed. Every effort should be made to discover all insurance agreements that have a bearing on the analysis, including personal and business property and liability contracts, since these documents have a bearing on the protection of assets such as homes, other buildings, and personal property.

Laws Governing Estate Distribution

Laws governing estate distribution are state laws and vary across the country. In the event there is no will, the law describes how the estate will be distributed among heirs. If there is a will, procedures are provided for proving the will and for making certain the provisions of the will are honored. Laws regarding the taxation of the estate are federal and state. Of particular importance for federal estate tax purposes is the determination of the size of the decedent's estate. In the community property states of Arizona, California, Idaho, Louisiana, New Mexico, Nevada, Texas, and Washington the husband owns one-half and the wife one-half of all property that either or both earned or accumulated during their marriage. In the event of the death of the husband or wife, estate taxes are levied on only one-half of the community property. In other states a result similar to this may be obtained through the use of the marital deduction which permits the husband to give up to one-half of his adjusted gross estate to his wife free of estate tax. The wife, in a similar manner may give up to one-half of her adjusted gross estate to her husband.[3] It is essential that the estate planner, while he is analyzing the estate, determine the laws that apply in a particular case and the effect these laws will have on the size of the estate that will ultimately be distributed to beneficiaries.

MANAGEMENT OF THE ESTATE

Since estate planning depends on the existence of an estate or at least a plan to

[3] In the Tax Reform Act of 1976 the estate tax marital deduction is $250,000 or one-half the gross estate, whichever is larger.

create one, some consideration should be given to the problems of the accumulation and deterioration of estates.

Problems of Estate Accumulation

There are three major sources of estate assets: (1) investment opportunities that may be associated with an individual's occupation; (2) savings and investment opportunities that are available to individuals regardless of occupation; and (3) life insurance.[4]

Occupational Sources

Large as well as some small corporations typically provide extensive employee benefit packages in addition to salary. All employees may be given the opportunity to participate in pension plans, group life insurance, group health insurance (including disability), and often savings and profit-sharing plans are made available. For employees classified as executives, opportunities for providing financial security may go well beyond the basic benefits provided to everyone. Key man life insurance, cash or stock bonuses, stock options, deferred compensation, split-dollar life insurance, and similar plans may be available as a means of accumulating assets that will ultimately become part of an estate to be distributed to heirs.

Self-employed persons also have opportunities to accumulate assets for estate purposes. For owners of small or large businesses, the business itself may provide the principal asset of the estate and may be relied upon as a means of support of the owner's family in the event of his death. Ownership may take

several forms such as close corporations, partnerships, or sole proprietorships. In addition to owners of businesses the self-employed also include independent professional persons such as physicians, dentists, engineers, lawyers, writers, and actors, as well as other persons with professional skills who are not employed by organizations of various types. Although historically self-employed professionals did not enjoy the same opportunity for employee benefits as those persons employed by business and similar firms, comparatively recent legal changes have made it possible for professionals to create benefits of the employee type particularly in the area of retirement. By forming unincorporated associations or by incorporating professionals may create for themselves a number of corporate benefits. For those professionals who do not wish to incorporate or form an association, the Keogh Act is available as a way of providing for retirement.[5]

Savings and Investment Opportunities

All individuals regardless of the nature of their occupations have the opportunity to invest in various savings and related institutions, as well as in real estate, stocks, bonds, and other financial instruments. Accumulations resulting from such investments may well constitute the bulk of many estates.

Insurance

Life insurance may be used as a way of creating an estate or it may be used as a way of protecting an estate by

---

[4] For an extended discussion of these and other items of estate accumulation see Brosterman, *The Complete Estate Planning Guide*, pp. 40–132.

[5] Professionals may also have the opportunity to invest in businesses in lieu of accepting a fee in cash, or they may work part time for institutions and thus have some of the tax advantages that are possible for employees.

providing funds for estate taxes, probate costs, and other cash demands that arise at the time of death. Various forms of life insurance such as term, whole life, and family income plans may be used depending on the specific estate or programming problem.[6]

A particular advantage of life insurance is its flexibility. A number of its clauses enable it to be used in a variety of ways in the process of estate planning and settlement. In particular the various settlement options may be of help in providing income for beneficiaries or in helping to provide a stated amount of income required in an estate plan.

Health insurance, although not contributing directly to estate accumulation, plays an important role in protecting the estate from the heavy inroads of medical expenses and loss of income that come about through accident and sickness. A large number of contracts are available for this purpose.

As in the case of health insurance, property and liability insurance serves to protect the estate. Property of various types may be destroyed or lost through fire, windstorm, theft, liability suits, and many other risks. An estate planner should review a client's property and liability program carefully and recommend adequate protection if it does not exist.

Factors That Serve to Reduce the Size of the Estate

During the time that an estate is being accumulated and at the time it is being distributed events may happen that will serve to reduce its size.[7] The forces of deterioration or impairment occurring at time of death may be classified as follows: (1) taxes, (2) debts, (3) death costs, (4) administrative and related costs, (5) improperly drawn and or outdated legal instruments, (6) economic conditions, (7) ineffective management, and (8) inadequate insurance.

Taxes

Income and property taxes left unpaid at the time of death are a claim on the assets of the estate and must be paid. Further, from a planning point of view, the effect of income taxes on heirs who may be left the income from certain assets might well be considered especially in situations where the heirs have substantial incomes.

The tax that has the greatest effect on estate distribution is the federal estate tax which is levied on the right of the decedent to transfer property to heirs. Estate taxation has had a long history both in the United States and Great Britain. The first death tax in the United States levied by the federal government was in 1797. This tax was a tax levied on such items as letters of probate and administration and was repealed in 1802. At the time of the Civil War another effort was made to establish an estate tax and a law was passed in 1862 which was repealed shortly after the war. The first federal estate tax law of the type now in existence was passed in 1916. This law has been modified over the years and has become more severe but has remained as a part of the federal tax structure. The most recent change was in 1976 when methods of

---

[6] See Chapter 9 for discussion of the major types of life insurance.

[7] Although the emphasis in this section is on factors leading to estate reduction after death, many of the same forces operate while the estate is being accumulated. Examples are inappropriate use of debt, adverse economic conditions, faulty investment judgment, ineffective management, and inadequate insurance. See Davis W. Gregg and Vane B. Lucas, *Life and Health Insurance Handbook*, pp. 845–6.

levying estate and gift taxes were modified by the Tax Reform Act of 1976.

In arriving at the amount of estate tax to be paid, it is necessary to begin with the concept of the gross estate, which consists of the total value of all of the property owned by the decedent including any property in which he had an interest. Determination of the gross estate can be complicated since it involves not only such property as cash, stocks, bonds, and real estate but also such items as transfers in contemplation of death, property previously transferred but in which some ownership rights or rights to alter have been retained, property over which the decedent may have had power of appointment, property held in joint tenancy, annuities, and life insurance on the life of the decedent payable to the estate or payable to other beneficiaries, if the decedent had incidents of ownership in the policy at the time he died. Death benefits from social security or workers' compensation are not included as a part of the gross estate nor is real property situated outside the U.S. Some of these latter types of property are surrounded by rules and exceptions, and the estate planner should seek the advice of a tax accountant or lawyer in determining the amount to be included in the gross estate.

The next step in determining the amount of federal estate tax owed is the computation of the adjusted gross estate, which is equal to the gross estate less the sum of such items as funeral expenses, administration expenses, claims against the estate, unpaid mortgages and liens if the full value of the property is included in determining the gross estate, state death taxes on charitable transfers, and losses from casualties of various kinds during estate administration. In community property states where only one-half of the community property is regarded as the decedent's estate, if the various deductible expenses were incurred for the benefit to the community, only one-half of each allowed deduction would be subtracted from the decedent's estate. It is possible for some expenses to apply entirely to the decedent's estate in which case the entire amount would be deducted. If the decedent's estate consists only of community property or noncommunity property, the computation of the adjusted gross estate is not especially complicated. However, both types of property may exist in some estates, in which case the computation is more complex. Once the adjusted gross estate has been determined the marital deduction may be taken, if the requirements surrounding such a deduction have been met. The taxable estate is the adjusted gross estate less the marital deduction.[8]

Once the taxable estate has been determined, estate taxes may be computed. One of the consequences of the Tax Reform Act of 1976 was the development of a unified rate schedule for estate and gift tax (See Appendix C), thus eliminating the more favorable gift tax rates that existed under prior law. The amount of the estate tax is now determined by taking the difference between the sum of the tax on all taxable gift and estate transfers after December 31, 1976, and the gift tax paid on gifts after that date. The tax so determined may be reduced by the unified estate tax credit. This credit in 1981 and thereafter will be $47,000. Between 1977 and 1980 the credit will be $30,000 in 1977,

---

[8] No effort is made in this chapter to describe the federal estate tax law in detail or to make the reader proficient in various estate tax computations. The rules and computational details may be learned by consulting various estate tax manuals. Note that under the tax Reform Act of 1976, the concept of an exemption was eliminated. Thus, the $60,000 specific exemption is no longer available.

$34,000 in 1978, $38,000 in 1979, and $42,000 in 1980. The credit may be reduced by 20 percent of $30,000 (the gift tax lifetime exemption under the old law) if the gift tax exemption was used after September 8, 1976, and before January 1, 1977. Although specific exemptions are no longer used, a tax credit of $47,000 corresponds to an "equivalent" exemption of $175,625.

Another type of death duty is the inheritance tax, which is levied by the states and is a tax on the right of heirs to receive property. Inheritance taxes are less severe than the federal estate tax, and the amount to be paid will vary depending on the state. The rates and rules may be determined by consulting the relevant state law.

Debts

Debts, if not disposed of before death, may be a fairly serious source of estate impairment. These obligations may range from unpaid bills to longer range debts such as mortgages. One of the duties of an administrator or executor of an estate is to determine the extent and nature of outstanding debts and to arrange for their settlement before transferring property to heirs.

Death Costs

Death costs include medical expenses incurred during the last illness, general expenses, and other costs such as help for the family home which may have been incurred. The amount of these costs will vary depending on the length and severity of the last illness and the type of funeral desired.

Administrative and Related Costs

The settlement of estates and the distribution of property to heirs takes place under the laws of the state of domicile that govern these matters, and under the supervision of an appropriate court. If an executor has been named in a will, he is responsible for identifying the assets of the estate, settling the claims against the estate and for distributing the remainder in accordance with the will. In the event no executor is named, the court will appoint an administrator whose functions are similar to those of an executor. If there is no will, the laws of the state governing distribution in the event of intestacy will apply. There are expenses connected with the settlement process which include court costs, executor fees, attorney fees, and various miscellaneous charges. The total of these charges will vary with the size of the estate with the larger estates paying larger fees. On a percentage basis, however, if may well be that for smaller estates, a larger percentage of the total gross estate goes for administrative expense than is the case for the larger estates. For estates in excess of $100,000 the impact of administrative fees is likely to be considerably less than the impact of taxes of various types. For many estates, administrative expenses may well amount to less than 10 percent of the gross estate.

Improperly Drawn or Outdated Legal Instruments

Legal instruments that are improperly drawn or outdated may result in difficulty for heirs. A will that has not been reviewed or revised over many years may or may not be suitable at the time of estate settlement. A number of problems may arise. Any specific bequests that may have been made may well be inappropriate after a number of years. Further, since specific bequests are settled first, the size of the estate may have changed to the point that specific bequests would deplete the estate leaving nothing for other heirs. It is also possible that the family situation has changed and bequests that may have been appropriate at one time are no longer so.

A fairly common problem with wills is an inappropriate designation of the executor. In many instances a family member is made an executor which may result in an inefficient distribution of an estate, or grief over loss may lead to inability to carry out the functions assigned to such a person. Probably in most instances, it is desirable to name a bank or similar institution as the executor or possibly some person not family connected who has special skill and training in estate matters.

There are, of course, other legal instruments besides wills that are used in estate planning. Trusts of various types, business continuation agreements, and possibly other documents, like wills, may suffer from being out of date because of changing circumstances. There is always the possibility that errors have been committed and if these go undetected, difficulties may arise. To avoid deterioration to the estate from improperly drawn documents, periodic reviews of all legal instruments should be made to assure that they are currently accurate and relevant.

Economic Conditions

During the accumulation of an estate and also at the time of distribution, economic conditions affect the size of the estate, and especially at the time assets are distributed may result in serious shrinkage. Such shrinkage may be exacerbated if the estate turns out to have liquidity problems. In accumulating an estate, emphasis is often placed on capital growth and on investment in real estate and securities that may not be readily convertible into cash. Forced sale of assets to meet liquidity requirements at the time of death may lead to serious losses, if such sales occur during periods of depressed prices. Another factor to be considered is the fact that if a sale is forced it may lead to lower selling prices than would otherwise be the case.

Ineffective Management

Failure to manage the assets of the estate effectively during the accumulation phase and at the time of distribution may seriously impair the amount of funds available to heirs. The consequences of inadequate management may lead to serious difficulties for surviving family members who may be dependent on the estate for financial maintenance, particularly if employment opportunities are not available. Perhaps the best way to avoid deterioration of the type described here is to seek competent investment advice from experts and to select experienced persons as executors of wills and trustees of living or testamentary trusts.

Inadequate Insurance

One of the virtues of insurance of all types and from the standpoint of estate planning, life and health insurance in particular, is that it may serve to protect the assets of the estate from losses caused by chance events. Uninsured serious illnesses may make inroads on assets, and inadequate life insurance may result in liquidity problems at the time an estate is settled. Uninsured losses of property may also reduce the size of an estate. Even though some insurance may exist, if it is inadequate in amount or the type of contract is inappropriate, the net result may be inadequate protection of estate assets.

CREATING AN ESTATE PLAN

Any estate plan must begin with a statement of objectives. There are people who, as a matter of personal philosophy, do not wish to accumulate an estate nor are they concerned about leaving an estate to others. In such cases, there is no particular reason to create an estate plan. In situations where an estate plan is appropriate, there may be a variety of objectives depending on the person or persons involved and these objectives may vary from one person to another.

Examples of possible objectives in the event of estate distribution are: (1) providing for a handicapped child; (2) providing an income for widow and children without depleting the assets of the estate; (3) providing for the transfer of assets in such a way that only the income from the assets may be used except in the case of dire emergencies; (4) providing for the education of children; (5) to relieve a widow from the responsibility of managing a business or working with the husband's former business associates; (6) to provide for elderly parents or other dependents; (7) to pass on an estate as intact as possible as a matter of family obligation or responsibility; and (8) equal distribution of the estate to heirs. Some or all of these objectives may be applicable in a particular case or there may be additional objectives or unusual situations to be taken into account.

Once a set of objectives or goals has been formulated, the task of the estate planner is to decide what steps should be taken to produce a plan that will accomplish the objectives as far as possible. Use of gifts, wills, trusts, business continuation agreements, life and health insurance, and possibly other instruments, or some combination of these, may be necessary to effect a suitable plan. In relatively uncomplicated cases the plan may be fairly easy to create and carry out. In complex situations this may not be the case, but in any event the resulting plan should be understandable and workable and an improvement over no planning at all. Since any plan will of necessity depend on a specific set of objectives, it is not possible to arrive at an ideal plan that will fit all situations. Therefore, in what follows, the common tools or instruments of planning will be discussed. Which tools or combinations thereof should be selected will repend in a particular case on the planner's ingenuity and skill.

Wills

A "will is a legally enforceable declaration of a person's instructions as to matters to be attended to after his death and is inoperative until his death."[9] In many instances a will may be the only estate plan that an individual has, since wills ordinarily give instructions as to how property is to be distributed and to whom. Even if the estate plan involves documents in addition to a will, the will may well be the starting point in estate planning. In common law countries, the state permits the individual citizen to dispose of his property in the event of his death by will. The power thus given the individual to dispose of his property at death according to his wishes is quite broad, although there are a few, fairly minor restrictions. One example of such a limitation is that a will to be effective must meet the requirements of a valid will. Also, in most states a husband cannot disinherit his wife.

Wills may be classified as (1) attested, (2) holographic, and (3) nuncu-

[9] G. S. Stephenson and N. A. Wiggins, *Estates and Trusts*, 5th ed. (Englewood Cliffs, N.J.: Prentice-Hall, Inc., 1973), p. 36.

pative. An attested will is one that has been prepared by the use of a typewriter or it may be handwritten or some combination of the two. It cannot be oral. It must be dated, signed, and witnessed typically by two people, at the time the will is prepared. A holographic will is one prepared by the individual whose property is involved (testator) in his handwriting, and is not witnessed. Holographic wills are valid in less than one-half of the states. A nuncupative will, which is seldom used, except in emergency situations, is oral and made before witnesses who have been assembled for that purpose. It is used typically during a last illness by a person who cannot make an attested or holographic will. Such wills are then reduced to writing. Although it is possible to make a will that has not been attested, such wills are fairly uncommon even where they are permitted. The usual practice is to prepare attested wills usually with the advice of an attorney.[10]

Although wills are commonplace, it should not be assumed that the absence of a will means that no plan for estate disposition or distribution exists. All states have laws governing the distribution of estates in the event an individual dies intestate (without a will). These laws vary and are impersonal, but are designed to take into account such matters as the rights of relatives, the problems surrounding guardianship of children, and the need for estate management. Since the laws are designed to provide a general solution to widely varying individual problems, the will that the state provides rarely coincides with individual preferences and can lead to difficult situations. For example, in a number of states, if a husband dies without a will, the surviving widow is entitled to one-third to one-half of the es-

tate with the balance of the estate going to the children in equal shares. In the event there are no surviving children, the widow may have to share the estate with her husband's relatives. Further, since in cases of intestacy, the law selects the guardian for minor children and the administrator of the estate, unpleasant problems can arise particularly if there is a quarrel about who the guardian or administrator should be. Expenses of settling the estate may be increased. One example would be the fact that administrators must be bonded and the costs typically are charged to the estate.

The problems cited here and many others can be obviated through a properly drawn and executed will.[11] Within the limitations mentioned earlier in the chapter, the maker of a will may choose his beneficiaries, decide how he wants property left to minors, select the executor, and in general arrange estate distribution in accordance with his wishes.

Trusts

A trust is "an arrangement whereby one person has the legal title to property which he holds for the benefit of someone else who has the equitable title to the property."[12] Stephenson and Wiggins indicate that there are five characteristics found in all trusts.[13] First, there must be a creator (alternative expressions are grantor, trustor, donor, or settlor), who is the person or organization who transfers assets to the trust. He also designates the trustee, names the beneficiary, and determines the terms of the trust. If the trust is testamentary (created under a will), the

[10] For a more complete discussion of the technical aspects of wills see *Ibid.*, pp. 36–54.

[11] See Brosterman, *Estate Planning Guide*, pp. 197–209, and also Stephenson and Wiggins, *Estates and Trusts*, pp. 18–54.

[12] Stephenson and Wiggins, *Ibid.*, p. 63.

[13] *Ibid.*, p. 64.

creator of the trust must be a natural person. Living trusts (inter vivos trusts) may be created by one individual or by an entity (such as a corporation or association), if that entity can hold legal title to property. Second, there is a trustee. Although trusts can be created without naming a trustee, they do not become operative until such time as a trustee is designated. A trustee may be an individual or corporation or some other organization, as long as he or it is permitted to own property. It is possible for a cotrustee to exist. The trustee is the entity that assumes legal title to the assets being transferred to the trust. Third, since trusts are created for the benefit of some person or organization of persons, there must be a beneficiary. The beneficiary may be the grantor of the trust or some other person or group of persons or corporation. Minors may be beneficiaries as well as persons regarded as incapable of looking after themselves. Fourth, the trust must consist of property. The property may be personal or real or both as long as it is capable of being owned. Fifth, there must be a trust agreement. This is a legal document signed by the grantor. If the trustee has been appointed, he signs an acceptance statement, and the entire document is notarized. The agreement contains, among other things, a statement about the property that is to be a part of the trust and also describes the powers of the trustee. Additional powers may be available to the trustee through statutes applicable to the state where the trust is being administered.

The position of trustee is one that requires a high sense of responsibility, and the trustee may be subject to legal action for failure to discharge his responsibilities in a faithful manner. His duties are numerous and include in addition to generally administering the trust with reasonable care and skill such items as furnishing of financial information to beneficiaries, keeping appropriate accounts, taking title to property transferred to the trust, enforcing claims, investing assets wisely, and paying income to beneficiaries.[14]

Trust agreements generally contain a statement about who the successor trustee is to be in the event a trustee dies or resigns.

Trusts may be classified in various ways but basically, as noted above, they are one of two types: Created by will (testamentary) or created between living persons (inter vivos). Under the heading of living trusts there may be, for example, insurance trusts, employee trusts, and corporate trusts. In this chapter, the discussion will be limited to personal trusts as opposed to those created primarily for business purposes.

Living Trusts

Living trusts have the properties that are common to all trusts and in addition have characteristics that distinguish them from testamentary trusts. Although it is possible for an individual creating a living trust to be the trustee, if the trust is for the benefit of someone else, or to be a cotrustee, if the trust is for his benefit, the typical arrangement is for an individual to create a trust by entering into an agreement whereby he agrees to transfer property to another person or to a business entity (say a bank), who in turn agrees to hold the property in trust and to manage it for the benefit of the grantor or other beneficiaries provided for in the trust agreement.

Because of the nature of a living trust, the grantor may take some part in the administration of the trust. He may

[14] This list contains the main duties but is not complete. For additional information see *Ibid.*, pp. 66–71.

serve as an adviser to the trustee, for example, on investment problems or he may help with problems involving beneficiaries. Living trusts may be revocable or irrevocable and there may be provisions for amending the trusts. If the grantor reserves the right to revoke the trust, he may, upon proper notification to the trustee, end the trust and take his property back. If a trust is made irrevocable, it cannot be revoked or terminated. The power to amend the trust may be very important particularly if the trust is irrevocable. The grantor may well, for example, want to change beneficiaries or the terms surrounding the distribution of benefits.

Living trusts are often useful in estate planning. Some of the principal uses are: (1) reduction or perhaps avoidance of probate costs; (2) management of personal financial affairs; (3) management of estate matters for those persons no longer able to do so themselves; (4) testing of plans for a person's estate; and, (5) reduction of taxes of various types. Some of these uses are applicable mainly to revocable living trusts and some to both revocable and irrevocable trusts. Item five is applicable only to irrevocable trusts.

The revocable living trust is an extremely useful and flexible instrument for lifetime planning. On the death of the grantor or settlor the assets of the trust may be distributed free from probate. All of the provisions that might be placed in a will can be placed in a revocable living trust and with greater flexibility, since the requirements for change of provisions is less cumbersome for the trust. In general, in order for a revocable living trust to avoid probate it must be funded during the grantor's lifetime or funded at his death from sources outside his will.[15]

Since wills are public documents, a trust may be used to minimize contests of wills or to minimize publicity in case a child, say, is disinherited.

Perhaps the most valid reason for creating a revocable living trust is to provide management of property.[16] The possibilities for this use are various. An extremely busy executive or professional person may not have time to oversee his own investments and may wish to use the revocable living trust as a way of insuring careful and professional management of his assets. An older person who realizes that he is no longer able to manage skillfully his own affairs may create a revocable living trust as a way of avoiding serious losses that might occur from his mismanagement or oversight.

In some cases a revocable living trust may be used to get a preview of how an estate plan might work out. An individual could create a revocable living trust and observe how the trustee manages the assets of the trust. This might well give some clue as to how his estate would be managed after death.

A revocable living trust has no tax advantages, since assets are not being removed from the estate. No gift tax is involved since the grantor is not giving anything away, and the principal of the trust is taxable in the estate of the grantor.

The irrevocable living trust, on the other hand, may have tax advantages. The grantor of an irrevocable trust will not have to pay income taxes on the income from the trust provided the trust

---

[15] A funded trust is one wherein assets have been revocably transferred to the trust by the grantor during his lifetime. An unfunded trust is a revocable trust created by the grantor during his lifetime to which only token assets have been transferred. See discussion on life insurance trusts.

[16] See Paul A. Ormand, "The Use of Living Trusts in Tax Planning," (unpublished paper, 1973).

meets certain requirements, one of which is that the grantor does not receive any income from the trust and does not retain any incidents of ownership.[17] Estate and inheritance taxes may be lowered through an irrevocable trust, inasmuch as such a trust results in the removing of assets from the estate. Gift taxes may be payable. Although irrevocable trusts are usually thought of in terms of their help in tax planning, they have other, nontax advantages, that should be considered. Older persons facing senility may create revocable living trusts, but it is possible that the irrevocable trust would be preferable, particularly if there was some possibility that in their confusion they might revoke a trust unwisely. Younger persons who want the benefits of management may also find that irrevocable trusts would protect them from errors of judgment that might lead them to revoke a trust for the wrong reasons. Irrevocable trusts may also be used for the purpose of providing for the education of beneficiaries or their children. As in the case of revocable trusts, irrevocable ones can serve to consolidate the family assets or benefit in the diversification of trust investments.

If the grantor of an irrevocable trust wishes to introduce flexibility into the trust, he may do so through the use of the power of appointment. The use of this device assumes that the grantor is not especially concerned with the direction of ultimate distribution of the trust and is willing to give an appropriate person the power, say, to change beneficiaries or to alter other interests. There are no adverse estate tax consequences as long as the person holding the power does not use it for his own benefit or for the benefit of his estate.

Another use of an irrevocable trust is the short-term trust. Although revocable trusts may be short-term, if the trust is made irrevocable for ten years or more, the incidence of the tax on the income changes. In revocable trusts the income is taxed to the grantor. In the irrevocable trust with term of ten years or more, the income during the term of the trust will belong to the beneficiary. The income may be currently distributed to the beneficiary in which case it is taxed to him or it may be accumulated in which case it is taxed to the trust. Accumulated income must be distributed to the beneficiary no later than the termination date of the trust. The beneficiary must pay taxes on the income as if it had been distributed to him as earned. He receives credit for taxes paid by the trust. One of the uses of a trust of this type is to temporarily shift income from a taxpayer in a high income tax bracket to a person in a lower bracket. This procedure is most effective when the assets transferred to the trust are income producing. A gift tax is involved in this kind of transfer to the extent of the value of the income interest.[18]

Although short-term trusts have a number of uses, whether they are used may depend on some external considerations. The grantor may not be able to give up his capital or some part of it during the term of the trust. A financial emergency might require more capital than he had outside of the trust. Further, income tax savings might be out-

---

[17] For other requirements, see Brosterman, p. 173.

[18] There are specialized living trusts that for space considerations cannot be treated in detail here. Multiple trusts may be useful for shifting income by distributing it over a number of trusts and thus splitting income with the result that taxes will be levied at lower rates. Trusts may be used for gift and lease-back arrangements with some possible savings in taxes. The interested reader should consult O.B. Fiore, "New Possibilities and Old Pitfalls in Irrevocable Living Trusts," *Trusts and Estates,* January 1972, pp. 8–11.

weighed by other factors including the costs of setting up the trust such as attorney fees, trustee fees, and similar items.

Life Insurance Trusts

An important use of living trusts is the life insurance trust. These trusts, as is the case with other living trusts, may be revocable or irrevocable. One of their chief characteristics is that life insurance policies, typically on the life of the grantor, are owned by a trustee or a trustee is the beneficiary. The trust property may consist wholly or partly of these contracts.

Most life insurance trusts are revocable. Although this type of trust does not have tax advantages, it is flexible and can be changed by the grantor if the need should arise. In the absence of a trust, life insurance policies may be made payable to named beneficiaries or to the estate. If the latter designation is used, the proceeds go through probate and are subject to claims of creditors. In either case there is no assurance that the proceeds will be used wisely or in accordance with the wishes of the decedent, although a careful selection of settlement options may help to prevent dissipation of proceeds. A frequent use for revocable life insurance trusts is as a transfer instrument after death occurs. The procedure is carried out by making a will to provide that the probate assets of the decedent be transferred (poured over) into an already existing life insurance trust. The goals of estate transfer are then accomplished by the trust.[19] Life insurance that forms the assets (or part of them) of a trust enjoys the advantages of life insurance paid to a

[19] The living trust used for this purpose need not be a life insurance trust but the procedure described is most often associated with this type of trust.

named beneficiary and in addition the grantor has all of the advantages ascribed to a revocable living trust.

The irrevocable life insurance trust enjoys the same advantages as irrevocable living trusts generally, although the income tax advantage will not exist unless the trust is funded and unless the insurance is on the life of someone other than the grantor.[20]

Testamentary Trusts

Testamentary trusts are trusts created by a will. The trust does not take effect until after the death of the creator. Since testamentary trusts are associated with wills, it is important in considering the question of testamentary trusts to consider what the property is that is to be passed on and what the various alternative procedures are for accomplishing dispositive goals. The first step in making a will is to consider what the property to be distributed is. It is well to consider that some types of property, although forming a part of the entire estate and subject to estate taxation, do not form a part of the probate estate and do not pass to beneficiaries via a will. Examples of property of this type are: jointly owned

[20] An unfunded life insurance trust is one wherein the trustee does not have the duty of paying premiums, since the grantor of the trust assumes this responsibility. In a funded trust the trustee is provided with funds out of which he can pay premiums. Typically this is done by transferring securities or other property to the trust and the trustee is instructed to pay premiums out of income from the property or possibly out of principal. It is possible to set up an installment trust wherein the trustee has the duty to pay premiums but the trust does not have sufficient property to provide for all of the premium or premiums out of income. In this case, it would be necessary to add money each year to the trust principal so the trustee could pay the premium.

property with the right of survivorship; living trusts (with exceptions related to powers of appointment and short-term beneficiaries); and contracts for the purchase or sale of business interests.

Once the property that is to be bequeathed has been determined, the basic decision that must be made is whether the estate is to be left outright or in trust. If property is left outright, the person receiving it may do as he wishes with his inheritance. In some instances this may be the preferred procedure and the maker of the will need determine only who the beneficiaries are to be and what proportion of the estate they are going to inherit.[21]

There are a number of reasons for considering and adopting the idea of leaving property in trust: The person making the will may wish (1) to protect minors and incompetent or irresponsible beneficiaries from wasting their inheritances through poor management on their part or lack of knowledge; (2) to keep a particular asset within the family; (3) to provide professional management of the estate for the benefit of beneficiaries; or (4) to minimize the impact of certain types of taxes. Once the decision to adopt the trust as a part of the estate plan has been made, much that has been said earlier in this chapter about living trusts is applicable to testamentary trusts. How income is to be paid to beneficiaries, provisions for invading the trust in emergency situations, and other arrangements are similar to those of living trusts. The form of the testamentary trust is somewhat different and certain items such as revocability and irrevocability do not apply.

The first three uses of testamentary trusts mentioned above are self-evident. The fourth use, that of mini-

mizing taxes, needs some elaboration. If a husband leaves property to his wife in trust with the stipulation that she receive the income from it and after her death the trust be distributed to other beneficiaries named by her husband (or continued in trust for them), the trust will not be included in the widow's estate for estate and inheritance tax purposes. Thus, the trust is not taxed twice. Had the property been left outright to the widow and had she retained it, it would have been a part of her estate and on her death would have been taxed. Since the husband's estate was taxed on his death, this portion of her estate would be taxed twice.[22]

It is sometimes useful to create two testamentary trusts. Recognizing that if the marital deduction is to be utilized, the widow must control one-half of the estate, the husband's estate could be divided into two equal parts. One part could be designated as the marital deduction trust and could be constructed in such a way as to qualify for the deduction. The other part could be formed into a trust and the widow could be given the right to income from it, but at no time would she control the corpus. On her death, the second trust would pass to beneficiaries named by the husband. Assuming that the husband wanted his widow to have a certain income and assuming that one-half of the estate would not provide this income, the marital deduction trust could be set up as a wasting trust. The arrangement might well be that the widow would use principal and interest from the marital deduction trust to provide the specified income until that trust was exhausted. This would mean that as

[21] There are some limits on the freedom of disposition. See Brosterman, *Estate Planning Guide*, pp. 235–37.

[22] The Tax Reform Act of 1976 generally requires taxation of generation skipping trusts. Thus, a trust set up for great-grandchildren with grandchildren receiving income during their lives would be taxed in the grandchildren's estate. For details of the rule see the Act.

principal was used, the income from the trust would go down. Income taxes would also go down, since the part of her income represented by principal would not be taxed. While the first trust was being used, income could be accumulated in the second trust and later distributed to the widow. Although she would have to pay income taxes as though it had been distributed to her in the year it was accumulated, she would have a credit for the tax the trust paid. An averaging method is also available for determining the amount of income to be taxed. The net result might well be a saving in income taxes. On the widow's death, the second trust would not form a part of her estate and would not be taxed. If the widow died before the marital deduction trust was exhausted, whatever remained in that trust would be taxable in her estate.

Additional Comments on Trusts

In the preceding discussion, trusts were classified in various ways. An additional classification is simple vs. complex. In a simple trust it is required that all income must be distributed currently with income being taxed to the beneficiary whether or not it is distributed. A complex trust is one in which accumulation of income is permitted and the beneficiary is taxed only on the amount distributed and the trust is taxed on the rest.

Although trusts may be quite useful for many purposes, any decision to utilize them in estate planning must take account of costs. The principal costs are for attorneys and trustees whose fees normally are stated as a percentage of the corpus or a percentage of income. The percentages vary somewhat and the grantor should determine these costs as a part of the planning process.

In setting up a trust, a question usually arises about who should be the trustee. Sometimes a member of the family is willing to serve and may do so without charging a fee. Such a solution in many instances may be satisfactory but problems can arise. A member of the family may or may not have the management and investment skills required and there may be difficulties with other members of the family. Consideration should always be given to naming a trustee with professional skills and interests. Corporate trustees are often advisable and a bank with a trust department or some other corporate trustee will normally have the skills required, since they are accustomed to managing estates. Further, they can provide continuity of management which may be important for trusts that extend over many years.

Problems that may arise in connection with beneficiaries should be carefully considered. At the time a trust is set up the income from the corpus might be adequate for the beneficiary or beneficiaries. Over time emergencies could occur that would require heavy expenditures. Consideration should be given to placing a provision in the trust that would allow the trustee to invade the trust at his discretion in the event such invasion seemed appropriate. Where there is more than one beneficiary the needs of the various beneficiaries may change. This contingency can be provided for through the use of a sprinkling trust. In such a trust the trustee has the power to sprinkle income to the group of beneficiaries, and he can respond to situations where one beneficiary has a greater legitimate need than another. Further, it may be that the grantor knows that a beneficiary has considerable difficulty managing money and the possibility of squandering income is a real one. In this situation, a "spendthrift" trust may be appropriate.

In this type of trust, for example, it is possible to prevent the beneficiary from selling his interest in the trust. Also, the trustee may be given the power to pay for items like rent and other necessities, and to participate actively in conserving money for the beneficiary.

Gifts

Depending on specific objectives and estate needs, gifts can be an important aspect of estate planning. Since gifts result in removing assets from the estate, they should be used in situations where the owner of the estate will not be ultimately left in need or find himself in straightened circumstances as a result of not having sufficient funds in the event of an emergency. Gifts may take various forms. They may be transfers of cash from one person to another or transfers of real property. There may be gifts in trust, gifts to set up charitable foundations, gifts of life insurance, or arrangements whereby the donar receives an annuity in exchange for a gift. For any of these situations to result in true gifts the donor must relinquish his rights in the assets that are given.

There are several reasons why lifetime giving may be advantageous. It may provide a way for giving family members an opportunity to own property and to gain experience in managing securities and other types of investment. Further, from the standpoint of estate planning, gifts can be helpful in mitigating the erosive effects of estate and inheritance taxes as well as administrative expenses.[23] Giving does not need to be restricted to a donor's lifetime. Charitable bequests, to be distrib-

uted after death, will also limit the impact of estate and inheritance taxes. The main reason that tax advantages arise from gifts is that gifts reduce the size of the estate. It is also possible after consideration of exclusions and exemptions, as well as the marital deduction provided by the federal gift tax law, that the donor will not pay a gift tax at all, if the size of the gift does not go beyond the amount of exclusions and exemptions.

Federal Gift Tax

The idea of taxing gifts dates from 1864 where gifts of land were treated as successions for tax purposes. This tax was discontinued in 1870. Other attempts to impose gift taxes occurred in 1894 (as a part of the income tax law of that year) and in 1924 as a separate tax. It was not until 1932 that the gift tax became a continuing part of the federal tax structure. This tax is a transfer tax and is applied to the value of the property transferred. The most recent change in the gift tax occurred in 1976 with the passage of the tax reform act of that year.

Certain features of the federal gift tax law alluded to above are particularly important to the estate planner. First, there is an annual exclusion. An individual may give $3,000 each per year to as many persons as he pleases without paying a gift tax. Since the exclusion is available to both husband and wife, they can give together as much as $6,000 per year to any person. Second, there is no longer a lifetime exemption of $30,000. However, a gift tax credit is available that can be applied to the tax that might be due on gifts. The credits allowed are the same as for the federal estate tax except that for gifts made after December 31, 1976, and before July 1, 1977, the maximum credit is

---

[23] Gifts during life may also result in a saving in income and capital gains taxes, particularly if the property involved is appreciating in value and is income producing. The income tax aspects will not be treated here.

$6,000. Third, there is a marital deduction for gifts that one spouse may make to another. The 1976 tax law increased the deduction that was previously available. Under the new law the marital deduction is unlimited for the first $100,000 of lifetime transfers. There is no marital deduction to a spouse if the gift is between $100,000 and $200,000. If a gift is made in excess of $200,000, the marital deduction is 50 percent of the gift. Fourth, gifts in contemplation of death are not permitted. If a gift occurs within three years of death, it will be taxed as part of the estate, unless it can be shown that the motive for the gift was not impending death. Fifth, deductions can be taken for charitable, public, and similar gifts.[24]

Business Interests in Estate
Planning

In many instances one of the chief assets (or perhaps the chief asset) in an estate is a business upon which the owner relies for income in order to support his family. It is often the owner's hope that on his death the business will continue to supply income for the surviving family. With careful planning the hope may become an actuality. Without it, problems may arise that will ultimately cause the surviving family to be in need.

The types of business most often involved in estate planning are sole proprietorships, partnerships, and close corporations. Death of a sole proprietor, a partner, or a major or minor stockholder obviously affects the businesses with which these persons were associated. In the case of the sole proprietor,

[24] For additional information see Edwin H. White, *Fundamentals of Federal Income Estate and Gift Taxes* (Indianapolis, Ind.: The Resource Review Service of America, Inc.)

the business is terminated and the assets and liabilities of the business become the assets and liabilities of the estate. The administrator or executor of the estate must take charge, and depending on a variety of circumstances, it may be necessary to sell the business in order to carry out the terms of the will and to pay debts and expenses. (The executor may become personally liable if he continues the business without authorization from the will to do so.) If the sale is forced, it may be difficult to get a fair price for the asset. There may be other economic consequences resulting from the termination of a proprietorship such as loss of jobs by employees or cessation of income to the surviving family. As in the case of the sole proprietorship, a partnership is dissolved on the death of one of the partners. The economic and legal effects of dissolution are much the same as for a sole proprietorship. In addition the surviving partner (or partners) may have lost a considerable amount of his (their) investment(s), his (their) job(s), and plans for the future. The death of a majority or minority stockholder in a close corporation does not bring about the dissolution of the business. Nevertheless, problems for the survivors can and do arise. If a majority stockholder dies, his interest ultimately passes to his legatees, which may cause difficult problems for minority stockholders. Further, the new majority interest may not be able to provide the same kind of management expertise and leadership that was provided by the deceased majority stockholder, assuming that he was active in the business and responsible for much of its operation. Although the death of a minority stockholder will not upset the control of the business, new minority interests can create problems for management including the possibility of harassment for the majority.[25] Another difficulty is that shares in a close corporation typically do not have an active market, and even if survivors wished to sell their stock, they might find it difficult to do so, except at an unfair price.

In view of the difficulties that may arise in the absence of careful planning for the disposition of business interests after death, it is well for the estate planner to consider ways in which these interests may be conserved without causing undue difficulty for survivors. In general it is desirable to have a plan that would avoid erosion of the business asset through forced sale, that would not involve surviving family members in the operation of the business in the event they did not possess the interest, compatibility, and skills to do so, and that would assure the continuation of the business as a healthy entity in the economy. Although business interests may be passed by will, this procedure does not guarantee that the above objectives will be met. Attempting to continue a sole proprietorship for example, after the death of the proprietor can lead to legal as well as economic problems. Even if the business does ultimately pass to family heirs, they may not be able to operate the business at a profit and their inheritance may be finally lost. A method of providing business continuation that has proved effective and that does accomplish the goals set forth, is the use of a buy and sell agreement.

If the business to be continued is a sole proprietorship, there may be a key man who would be willing to continue the business after the death of the proprietor and enter into a buy and sell agreement while the proprietor was still living wherein on the death of the proprietor the key man would buy the business at an agreed upon price determined by an arm's length negotiation. The effectiveness of such an agreement will depend on suitable funding. One way of being certain that funds will be available for the purchase is for the key man to insure the life of the sole proprietor for the amount of the sale. This solution will enable the estate to be settled more rapidly than might otherwise have been the case. A fair price for the business will be received in cash, and the executors will be relieved of difficulties that might otherwise have arisen.[26] There are additional benefits. The problems of family participation are resolved and the proprietor's widow is relieved of business worries. Further, the proprietor is able to accomplish his objectives of business continuation and the employee is able to acquire an attractive asset.

In the event the form of business organization is a partnership, a solution similar to that for a sole proprietorship may be worked out.[27] In this case a buy and sell agreement is entered into be-

---

[25] For a detailed discussion of these matters see Edwin H. White and Herbert Chasman, *Business Insurance*, 4th ed. (Englewood Cliffs, N.J.: Prentice-Hall, Inc., 1974).

[26] Life insurance is not the only method of funding a buy and sell agreement. The employee might try to save the money or to pay in installments or borrow money. There is no assurance that these methods will work out. However, if the sole proprietor is uninsurable, one or more of these alternatives may of necessity be used.

[27] The assumption here, as in the case of the sole proprietorship, is that an alternative to liquidation is being sought. The usual alternatives such as, continuation of the business without an agreement, establishing a new partnership with heirs, and purchase of the surviving partner's interest by the heirs, which might occur after the death of the partner, very often present legal as well as financial problems. The same can be said for most of the alternatives that are available before death with the exception of the buy and sell agreement between partners. For an extended discussion of these points see White and Chasman, *Business Insurance*, 4th ed.

tween two or more partners wherein the partners agree that on the death of one of them the survivors will pay his widow or legal representative an agreed-upon price for the deceased partner's interest and the survivors will be the sole owners of the business. One way of funding an agreement of this type is for each partner to hold life insurance on the lives of the other partners in the amount of his share of the purchase price in the event the other partners die first. The partnership, as such, is not involved in the agreement. Instead of a buy and sell agreement of the type just described, it is possible for the partnership to enter into an "entity" type agreement which may be especially useful if there are a number of partners. The partnership as an entity becomes a party to the contract, which provides for continuation of the partnership in the event of the death of a partner. The payment to the estate is from partnership funds. If life insurance is used for funding the agreement, the insurance will be on the lives of all of the partners. The partnership will own the policies and pay the premiums. It will also be the beneficiary. The benefits accruing to the interested parties from either a buy and sell agreement or an entity agreement are much the same *mutatis mutandis* as for the sole proprietorship.

Although survival of the business as such is not involved in close corporations, changes in stock ownership, as was described earlier, can create problems for surviving stockholders and for the management of the corporation. As in the case of the sole proprietorship and the partnership, these problems often can be resolved by a buy and sell agreement funded with life insurance.[28] The agreement is among all stock-

holders where, in the event of the death of one, the survivors promise to purchase the stock of the deceased at an agreed-upon price. If funding is by life insurance, an insurance policy is taken on the life of each stockholder. The amount of each contract is the amount of the stockholder's interest. If the agreement requires the corporation to buy the deceased's shares the corporation should be designated as beneficiary of the insurance proceeds. Other arrangements are possible. The buy and sell plan may be administered by a trustee in which case the trustee should be named as beneficiary, or in the absence of a trusteed arrangement the surviving stockholders may be designated as beneficiaries. This would seem especially suitable if the agreement calls for the surviving stockholders to purchase the deceased's stock.

A fairly common problem for estates is lack of liquidity, and this problem can be especially severe where a business interest is the chief asset of the estate. Life insurance provides one way of providing liquidity. However, in the case of a business, it may be preferable to take cash from the business to pay administrative expenses and estate taxes. One way to obtain money for estate taxes is through a Section 303 redemption, which permits, in certain circumstances, a tax-free redemption of the decedent's stock if the amount redeemed does not exceed the total of taxes, funeral, and administration expenses.[29] Another way to handle pay-

---

[28] There are alternative ways of financing similar to those discussed for the sole proprietorship.

[29] In order to utilize this method the value of the deceased's stock must exceed 50 percent of his net taxable estate or 35 percent of the value of his gross taxable estate. If the conditions for redemption are met the amount received will not be treated as a dividend and not taxed as such. Because the estate tax value of the stock and the redemption price are typically the same, the capital gains tax will not be a problem.

ment of estate taxes is to utilize installment payments. This method is available for the portion of the federal taxes that can be ascribed to the closely held business and may be used by the sole proprietorship and partnership as well as the close corporation. The value of the business must bear the same relationship to the value of the estate as is the case for stock redemption. Also there are requirements relating to the deceased's capital interest. There are drawbacks to this procedure particularly if the estate's assets decline in value over time and there is insufficient money to pay the installments. This could lead to personal liability on the part of the executor.

In estate planning involving business interests, it is necessary at some point to place a value on the business. For one thing such an evaluation is necessary in computing estate taxes. For another, if a business interest is given away during the lifetime of the owner, the value of the gift must be known in order to determine if a gift tax is payable. Unfortunately determining the value of a sole proprietorship, a partnership, or a close corporation is not always an easy matter. If a buy and sell agreement exists, the price stated in the agreement will normally be taken as an adequate determination of value.[30] In the absence of such an agreement other methods must be used, and no generally accepted procedure or formula exists for arriving at a determination of value. Various factors may be taken into account, such as: the history of the business and an assessment of trends; book

value, although this is rarely actual value; earning capacity and dividend-paying capacity of the firm; economic climate and the prospects for the particular firm being evaluated; and possibly goodwill.

Life and Health Insurance

As has been indicated previously in this chapter, life insurance may be used to provide funds for payment of taxes, administrative and funeral expenses, to fund buy and sell agreements, and to protect a firm against certain losses caused by the death of a key man. Health insurance may be used to protect against losses to the estate from economically catastrophic illness. Additionally, life insurance may be used as a way of building an estate and is virtually the only way of creating an estate immediately. One of the virtues of the life insurance contract from a planning point of view is its flexibility. It may be assigned as collateral for a loan. If the contract is one of the permanent forms, it may be used as the source of a loan. A variety of settlement options may be used to meet income requirements of beneficiaries.[31]

The usefulness of life insurance in meeting the financial needs of families brought about by the death of a person on whom the family has been dependent has resulted in formal procedures known as life insurance programming. In some instances this programming relates to life insurance only; in other situations it may be part of estate planning generally, where the total financial resources of the family are taken into account and tax considerations are a part of the plan.

[30] For a more extended statement and a discussion of the requirements that must be met see, Walter Cummings, "The Extent to Which the I.R.S. Will Respect 'Pegged' Valuations Contained Within Stock Purchase Agreements: The State of the Art," (Unpublished paper, 1973).

[31] For a discussion of these options, see Chapter 9. Since the various uses of life insurance were considered there, they will not be repeated in detail here.

When life insurance is used in estate planning, it becomes one of a number of tools available to meet the goals of an estate plan. It may be particularly helpful in meeting such needs as payment of administrative expenses and funeral costs, payment of debts, providing an educational fund for children, and providing income for the widow. The type and amount of life insurance would normally be determined after the availability of other assets to meet specified needs has been considered. In this connection, social security benefits must be taken into account, since survivorship benefits for the widow and dependent children will provide a floor on which to build additional income needs. A lump-sum death benefit is also a part of the social security package.

TITLING OF PROPERTY

Real property may be titled in a variety of ways. Apart from the common situation in which a title or right to real property is held by one person are situations in which property is held by an individual with one or more other individuals. In this category are tenancies in common, joint tenancies, tenancies by the entirety, and community property. In the case of a tenancy in common, the tenant's interest in the property goes to his heirs and not the surviving co-owners. In the case of joint tenancies, the tenant's interest on death passes to the surviving co-owners and not to his heirs. (Although one of his co-owners, say his wife, may also be one of his heirs.) Tenancy by the entirety is not recognized by all states. Where it is recognized, it applies only to husband and wife, and they are neither joint tenants nor tenants in common. The tenancy cannot be terminated unless both parties consent (which is not the case with a joint tenancy.) On death of one of the tenants, the property passes to the survivor or survivors.[32]

The significance of titling for the estate planner is that how property is titled will determine how it passes to heirs. For example, property titled on a joint and survivorship basis does not pass through probate. In the case of community property the husband or wife can will only one-half of such property, although the husband may control and dispose of community property as long as the marriage continues.[33] In community property states some types of property, such as inheritances or purchases with separate funds (whether before or after the marriage) and property acquired before the marriage by husband or wife, are treated as separate property and may be willed by the husband or wife depending on which one owns the property. It may also be disposed of during marriage by the owner without the consent of the other. Another factor that the estate planner must keep in mind is that funds in jointly titled bank accounts and papers in jointly titled safety deposit boxes will not be immediately available after the death of one of the tenants, since such accounts and boxes must be frozen until tax authorities have had an opportunity to determine their value.

In some instances in estate planning it may be necessary to retitle property in order to accomplish an appropriate plan. In any event it is well to consider whether property is properly titled and whether changes should be made for the benefit of the estate.

[32] The basic rules relating to community property were discussed earlier in this chapter.

[33] See Stephenson and Wiggins, *Estates and Trusts*, pp. 7–8 for further details.

TESTING AND MONITORING THE PLAN

Once an estate plan has been constructed, it is appropriate to test the plan to see how it would work out in the event of death. A hypothetical probate could be run and checks could be made to see if any flaws develop. Even though the trial run works out well, it should not be assumed that a plan once constructed never needs change. Any estate plan should be reviewed periodically to determine whether it is still viable. Changes can and do occur in peoples lives and this fact should be recognized by making appropriate changes in the existing plan.

SUMMARY AND CONCLUSIONS

1. Life insurance may be used to protect an estate from shrinkage that may be caused by taxes, the business cycle, debts, and similar items.

2. Estate planning encompasses the entire process of estate accumulation and distribution, but in this chapter only the distributive process is considered.

3. A broad purpose of estate planning is to help a person who creates an estate to preserve assets accumulated during his lifetime and after death.

4. Estate analysis involves collecting information about personal and family characteristics, financial objectives, assets and liabilities, income and expenses, types of insurance protection, and current estate distribution plans.

5. Estate management includes a consideration of problems of estate accumulation and estate deterioration.

6. Possible objectives in estate distribution may include providing for a handicapped child, providing an income for widow and children without depleting the assets of the estate, providing for transfer of assets so only the income from the assets may be used except in dire emergencies, providing for the education of children, relieving a widow from the responsibility of managing a business, providing for elderly parents or other dependents, passing on an estate as intact as possible as a matter of family responsibility, and equal distribution of an estate to heirs.

7. An estate plan may involve the use of gifts, wills, trusts, business continuation agreements, life and health insurance, and possibly other financial and legal instruments.

8. Titling of property is an important consideration for the estate planner, since how property is titled will determine how it passes to heirs.

9. The final step in the estate planning process is testing and monitoring the plan. Since changes occur in peoples' lives, a plan for periodic review is necessary if the plan is to accomplish its objectives.

QUESTIONS FOR DISCUSSION

1. On February 1, 1977, X gives Y $100,000. Earlier (on November 1, 1976), X had given Y $250,000. Assume the $3000 annual exclusion had been used separately for Y and that X had used his $30,000 lifetime exclusion before giving Y the $250,000. How much gift tax would X pay?

2. James Smith dies on February 24, 1977, and leaves a taxable estate of $450,000. He had made no taxable gifts before 1977 or after 1976. How much estate tax would be payable?

3. What is meant by gross estate, adjusted gross estate, and taxable estate?

4. Discuss the factors to be considered in designing an estate plan.

5. List the factors to be considered in estate analysis. Discuss each briefly and state its significance in the estate planning process. What steps might you take to be certain that no estate items had been overlooked?

6. What are the major sources of estate assets? What role does life insurance play in estate accumulation? How might it be used in designing an estate plan?

7. Discuss the estate and gift tax provisions of the Tax Reform Act of 1976. What were some of the reasons for the changes that occurred in the estate tax?

8. Describe the probate process. What is its purpose? There are some types of property transfer that pass outside probate. Give three examples. Are there any advantages to having property exempt from probate?

9. Wills may be classified as attested, holographic, and nuncupative. What are the distinguishing characteristics of each?

10. What are the uses of health insurance in estate planning? What types of health insurance contracts should be considered in designing an estate plan?

11. Prepare a solution to the E. M. Cory case which follows.

12. Prepare a solution to the Charles Milton, Sr. case. (See Chapter 20, p. 530.)

An Insurance Plan
for E. M. Cory

Through a referral of a satisfied client, Mr. Roy Brown, a General Insurance Company agent, had approached Mrs. Emily Cory to see if his estate planning service might be of value to her. After an initial meeting, Mrs. Cory agreed to allow Mr. Brown to analyze her estate. At a second meeting, Mr. Brown picked up all necessary data for his estate analysis.

Mrs. Cory, aged 63, had taken over her husband's welding shop after his recent death. She became the owner of the business, but her married son, Paul, aged 41, actually ran the business operation. Mrs. Cory handled all paper work and front office duties.

Another son, Joe, aged 35, is crippled and confined to a wheelchair, but does perform limited desk duties at the shop.

A third child, her daughter, Ann, aged 33, is married to a fireman and has seven children. She is not involved in the business, nor is her husband.

In talking with Mrs. Cory, Mr. Brown discovered that all her property was in her name alone, and therefore titled as separate property. Mrs. Cory's estate was composed of the following assets:

Asset	Value
Residence	$ 30,000
Business Real Estate & Building	70,000
Common Stocks	8,000
Personal Effects	1,000
Cash in Bank	35,000
Interest in Business	35,000
Permanent Insurance	1,000
TOTAL NET ESTATE	$180,000

In calculating the final estate settlement costs on the above estate, Mr. Brown found that the following unavoidable charges would have to be paid by the executor at the time of Mrs. Cory's death. These charges are based on federal and California statutory law:

Administration and Expenses	$13,500
Federal Estate Tax	22,750
California Inheritance Tax	3,750
Total Estate Costs	$40,000

Reprinted from *Stanford Business Cases 1965* with the permission of the publishers, Stanford University Graduate School of Business, © 1965 by the Board of Trustees of the Leland Stanford Junior University.

At the time Mr. Brown picked up all the necessary data for his analysis, he also asked Mrs. Cory for her objectives concerning the distribution of her estate at the time of her death. Their discussion brought forth the following objectives:

(1) Assure distribution of her estate in order that her three children will be treated equally so that future misunderstandings will be avoided.

(2) Preserve the business intact to make sure it continues after her decease.

(3) Keep death costs to an absolute minimum.

(4) Provide sufficient cash for death costs to eliminate forced sale of good property.

In analyzing Mrs. Cory's present will, Mr. Brown found it to be a simple will whereby each child would get one-third of her net estate at her death. Also the will appoints all three children as executors of their mother's estate and does not distinguish between business assets and personal assets.

ASSIGNMENT

(1) What problems are involved in settling a family estate?

(2) Why is liquidity important at the time of a person's death? Is Mrs. Cory's estate sufficiently liquid?

(3) Of what value is insurance in estate planning? Would you recommend additional insurance in this case? How much, if any? Who should own the policy? For what purpose should it be used?

(4) How can the type of will affect estate settlement costs? Does Mrs. Cory's present will fulfill her objectives concerning the estate's distribution among the children?

Is it likely that the business will be preserved under the present will?

11

Employee Benefits

The responsibility that the risk manager may have for employee benefits was outlined in Chapter 1. In some instances he might have the full responsibility for planning and implementation, while in others his function might be purely advisory. In any event, his knowledge of risk and ways of meeting it should be of considerable value in implementing and managing employee benefit programs.

Space does not permit a detailed consideration of all possible employee benefit plans. Topics considered in this chapter are:

1. The field of employee benefits

2. Reasons for employee benefit plans

3. Group life insurance

4. Group health insurance

5. Other health plans

6. Legal expense insurance

7. Statutory benefit plans

8. Administration of employee benefit plans

9. Group property and liability insurance

Pension and related plans will be treated in Chapter 13.

THE FIELD OF EMPLOYEE BENEFITS

Broadly speaking an employee benefit may be defined as any help of a pecuniary kind (or nonpecuniary but which might conceivably be valued in dollar terms) provided by an employer for an employee in addition to salary or wages paid for work performed.[1] Given this broad view of employee benefits, the list of such benefits is fairly long. The United States Chamber of Commerce definition may be taken as an example of a detailed statement of the scope of employee benefits.[2] The Chamber places these benefits into five categories: (1) Legally required payments for employee security. This group includes such items as workers' compensation; federal and survivors' insurance and disability and health insurance; and various insurance benefits for railroad workers. (2) Pensions and other agreed-upon payments. Included in this category in addition to pensions, are various benefits that often

[1] This definition omits psychic and similar benefits that may be derived from work. Although such benefits are, in a sense, employee benefits, they wll not be so treated in this chapter.

[2] Employee Benefits 1975, Washington, D.C.: Chamber of Commerce of the United States, 1976, p. 8.

are provided by group insurance such as group life, group accident and health, travel accident, and group accidental death and dismemberment. Other agreed-upon payments often include sick leave; private unemployment benefits; allowances paid at termination of employment or, as in workers' compensation, in excess of legal requirements; purchasing discounts for employees, free meals, payments to employees who may be in special need; tuition refunds; and stock purchase plans. (3) Payments for non-productive time while on the job. Items falling in this category are rest periods, lunch periods, wash-up time, travel time, time for changing clothes, and possibly other situations where the worker is not producing goods and services. (4) Payments for time in which the worker is not at work. In this category are such things as vacations for which pay is provided, bonuses in lieu of vacation, paid holidays, paid sick leave, jury duty, death in the family, and payments for state or national guard duty. (5) Other payments not categorized above. It is difficult to give an exhaustive list of possible employee benefits, since some benefits may be fairly unique to some institutions. Among the fairly common benefits not previously mentioned are profit sharing plans. Christmas bonuses, periodic medical examinations, recreational facilities, deferred compensation, split-dollar life insurance, group property and liability insurance plans, and prepaid legal benefits.

REASONS FOR EMPLOYEE BENEFIT PLANS

It is not uncommon today for employers to provide employee benefits valued at 30 percent or more of the employee's salary. Thus, the total compensation paid to an employee is the basic salary plus 30 percent of that salary. It is sometimes argued that the employer should give the employee the amount spent for employee benefits as additional salary and let the employee provide for his own security. Although such a plan might be defensible, the tradition in American business has been to separate salary from other types of payment. The reasons for this attitude deserve careful consideration.

1. Problems of employee financial security. Before employee benefit packages became widespread, few employees were able or had sufficient self-discipline to provide financial security for themselves and their families. Even if the desire to make independent provision was strong, long periods of uncompensated unemployment or illness often made it impossible to carry out a financial plan. Employers and fellow employees often felt a responsibility to help, but such help was often sporadic and inadequate. A systematic way of discharging employer responsibility was adopted by many employers in the form of group life insurance, group accident and health insurance, and group pensions. Programs of this type provided a nondiscriminatory way of providing assistance in time of need. It also helped to improve the morale and productivity of employees. They may also be low cost, since expenses of underwriting and administration are low compared to individual plans.

2. Competitive considerations. Once employee benefits became widespread among business firms, any business not providing them was at a competitive disadvantage. Thus, substantial nonsalary benefits became an important factor in attracting and retaining capable employees.

3. Tax benefits. In general employer contributions to group life insur-

ance plans, group accident and health plans, and qualified pension plans are income tax deductible by the employer as business expense. In the case of pensions, the cost to the employer is deductible whether the cost is in the form of an insurance premium or in the form of a payment to a noninsured plan subject to certain maximum limits. (See Chapter 13.) Similarly, in health insurance the employer may deduct the cost of the plans whether insurance is the funding medium or whether benefits are paid to the employee on a direct basis. Whether the employer may deduct premiums is also governed by a general rule that provides that insurance premiums (or benefit payments) plus other employee compensation must be reasonable when viewed against the services provided by the employee.

It is generally true that employer contributions do not have to be reported by the employee as income for tax purposes. An exception to this statement is that if group life insurance coverage exceeds $50,000, the employee must declare whatever the employer paid for the coverage that exceeded $50,000. This may be offset in whole or in part if the employee is paying part of the premium. Benefits received by employees from group life insurance, accident and health, and pensions are subject to favorable income tax treatment. The proceeds (face amount) of group life insurance contracts is not taxed as income (but is subject to estate and possibly inheritance taxes). Benefits paid to an employee by an insurance company or directly by the employer to pay for medical care do not have to be reported as income by the employee assuming the amount received does not exceed the amount paid for the care. Although the IRS does permit the deduction of medical expenses, if they exceed a certain percentage of income, these expenses

may not be deducted if they have been reimbursed by the employer or the insurer.

The taxation of disability benefits paid for by the employer was modified by the Tax Reform Act of 1976. A maximum annual exclusion of $100 weekly ($5200 per year) has been established for persons under age 65, who are permanently and totally disabled. The exclusion is subject to reduction for those persons whose annual adjusted gross income is in excess of $15,000. The amount of the reduction depends on the amount the adjusted gross income exceeds $15,000. If the excess is $3,000, say, then the annual exclusion is reduced by that amount and becomes $2200. The definition of permanent total disability established by the Act is inability "to engage in any substantial gainful activity by reason of any medically determinable physical or mental impairment which can be expected to result in death or which has lasted or can be expected to last for a continuous period of not less than 12 months."

4. Advantages to the employee. Apart from tax considerations, employee benefit plans often are advantageous to the employee in other ways. In the case of group insurance plans, individual underwriting is typically not done, and the uninsurable employee may be able to acquire protection through group insurance that would not otherwise be available. In group health insurance preexisting conditions are often disregarded, which is typically not true for health insurance written on an individual basis. Thus, differences in underwriting rules as between individual insurance and group insurance may redound to the employee's benefit. If the employee is required to contribute to a particular plan, the contribution is usually made through payroll deduction, a practice that is convenient for the em-

ployee and tends to insure continuity of coverage. Another advantage for the employees is that his out-of-pocket cost for protection may be quite low. In some plans the employer pays the entire cost. In others the employee may contribute a part of the cost or in some instances the whole cost, but because of the cost advantages of group insurance the amount paid by the employee will usually be quite a bit lower than similar protection under individual plans.

5. Legislative and related actions. The substantial increase that took place in employee benefits during and immediately following World War II was caused to a considerable extent by the wage freeze that occurred during World War II and the Korean War, since employee benefits were not subject to the freeze thus giving the employer the opportunity to increase compensation through increased nonsalary benefits. Another major factor was the decision in 1948 by the National Labor Relations Board and the courts that employee benefits were an appropriate subject for collective bargaining. This decision brought about increased interest on the part of unions in employee benefits, and union pressure and interest continues to be an important factor. Although direct legal activity affecting employee benefits has been important to their growth, other types of legal action have also had a significant impact on the steadily enlarging pattern of benefits. Examples of such activity are the many extensions that have occurred in social security in the last thirty years and the many liberalizations that have occurred in the definitions of a group in the field of insurance.

6. Social and economic factors. Widespread interest in employee benefits is also partly due to changes that have occurred in social organization

and economic forces. The fact that many persons now live in urban areas has brought about changes in attitudes toward security. It is no longer feasible for families to provide security through communal living arrangements as was once possible in a predominantly agricultural economy. It is increasingly necessary for each person to have adequate programs to provide income during old age and/or disability. Formal programs have also been made necessary because inflationary forces have rendered saving more and more difficult. Thus, it is unlikely that an individual could, apart from an employer-sponsored benefit program, provide adequately for his own security. Another factor that has brought about increased awareness on the part of the public of the need for financial security is the vast federal social security system, which has called attention to the need for planning for contingencies that may bring about an interruption of earned income.

GROUP LIFE INSURANCE

The decision to install a group life insurance program is ordinarily not made by the risk manager alone. Committees representing employees and management may make recommendations, or where unions are involved new programs or changes in old ones may come about through the collective bargaining process. Whatever the genesis of the decision process, the risk manager will normally have the responsibility for advising on the details of installing the program, and, in firms where the personnel department does not administer the program, may have responsibility for day-to-day administration. The chief responsibility of the risk manager is likely to center around problems associated with the design of the program, and where insurers are involved, preparing the specifications of the program to be considered by insurers when submitting proposals. The chief elements to be considered in design are eligibility, benefits, and financing. These elements are present in any employee benefit program, but will be discussed in this part of the chapter in relation to group life insurance.

Eligibility

By eligibility is meant the determination of who is to be covered under the program. On first consideration one might assume that all employees of the employer would be covered. In practice the decision is not that easy. Not all persons who may be regarded as employees have the same attachment to the firm that employed them. Thus, employees may be categorized in terms of their employment status. In general, employees may be classified as active or retired. Active employees may in turn be categorized as salaried or employees working for wages based on an hourly or weekly rate. Similarly, employees can be classified as managerial or nonmanagerial. In some businesses professional or nonprofessional is a suitable classification. Within these categories employees may be on leave or temporarily laid off. In nonmanagerial positions, they may be seasonal, temporary, transient, or part-time.

Historically, in planning benefit programs, such as group life insurance, retired employees were excluded from coverage. Although it is now more common to include the retired, such coverage is normally limited in amount. Among active employees it is usual not to cover temporary, transient, part-time, or seasonal employees. The reasons for

not doing so usually center around the problems of increased costs of administration and the fact that employer responsibility is limited for employees whose attachment to the employment is somewhat tenuous. Employees who have been temporarily laid off or are on leave normally are able to retain coverage at least for a limited period of time. Although dependents of employees are not employees, in some types of employee benefits coverage of dependents is common. In group life insurance such coverage is rare. Even though certain classifications of employees may be excluded from coverage, it does not follow necessarily that all remaining employees are covered. If the program is contributory, and if group insurance is involved, underwriting rules normally required 75 percent of the eligible employees to agree to the coverage. Working wives, bachelors, and others may not feel the need for life insurance and may not join the plan. In order to install a plan it may be necessary to limit coverage to subsets of employees where there is a sufficient number of employees who desire to participate in the program. Another consideration is that the group be large enough to meet legal requirements about size.

Once questions about the types of employee to be covered have been settled, a further question arises about when the coverage is to attach. Where insurance is involved, underwriting rules require that employees be actively at work in order to be covered. Employees not in that category would not be in the program until they return to work. Further, it is usual to require new employees to satisfy a waiting period before coverage becomes effective. This period may be a month, three months, or longer depending on the nature of the program. The primary reason for such a requirement is to eliminate administrative problems associated with employee turnover.

Another type of eligibility question that arises is whether dependents are eligible for coverage. In group life insurance it is typical not to insure the lives of dependents, although dependents are normally the beneficiaries of the employees' coverage. The reasons for the fairly slow growth of dependent life insurance are to some extent statutory, since some states forbid its issuance and, even if not forbidden, some states limit the amount that may be covered to modest levels. Further, unions do not appear to be interested in including dependents as insured, and, hence it does not appear very often in collective bargaining agreements. As an underwriting matter only large groups are eligible for coverage and typically only dependents who are already insured with group life coverage would be eligible.

Benefits

The basic benefit offered by life insurance contracts is that the face of the contract will be paid to the beneficiary upon death of the insured. This benefit is typically modified by stating the time period in which death must occur. Thus, contracts are for a term of years or the whole of life or some variation on this theme. The basic reason for offering the benefit is that it will replace (wholly or partly) the income lost to dependents through death of the insured. Theoretically almost any life insurance contract issued on an individual basis may be offered on a group basis, although as the business has developed the offerings on a group basis are usually limited to group term life insurance, group ordinary life insurance, and group paid-up life. In addition, group accidental death

and dismemberment insurance may be a type of life insurance offered.[3]

Group Term Life Insurance

Group one-year renewable term life insurance is the most common plan for providing life insurance to employees. This type of coverage is experience-rated and the premium paid each year depends in part on the experience of the group. The premium also depends on a recalculation of the premium which is based on the attained age distribution of the group.

Among the more important aspects of group life insurance contracts are the provisions for continuing protection in the event the employee is no longer a member of the group. First, there is a conversion privilege that permits the employee to convert his group coverage to individual coverage without showing evidence of insurability. If the reason that the employee loses his coverage is that the master contract has been terminated, the conversion privilege is more restricted than if the employee leaves the group but the master contract continues in force. In this case usually the employee must demonstrate that he has had group coverage for, say, five years. The amount of the new contract is typically limited to a fairly small amount such as $2000 and may be less if a new group policy is installed. Second, there is a continuation of coverage for 31 days after the employee leaves employment which gives him time to carry out the conversion process. Third, group life insurance may be continued during periods of lay-off and leave of absence if these periods are simply interruptions of full-time and

[3] This coverage is sometimes classified as a part of health insurance. Its benefits encompass both life and health insurance.

continuous employment. Fourth, there is a waiver of premium provision. Usually this provision subject to certain rules simply provides that the insurance continues in force and that premiums do not have to be paid during the total disability of an employee. There are alternative forms. One alternative provides for the payment of the face amount of the insurance to an employee in a lump sum or typically in monthly installments. The employee must become totally and permanently disabled before a specified age, which is often 60. Another alternative is an agreement to pay death claims that may occur during the year immediately following termination of employment. The employee must be continuously and totally disabled after leaving employment, and death must take place before a specified age, say, 65.

Other contractual matters of particular interest to the employee relate to beneficiary designations, settlement options, and assignment. The employee may name anyone he prefers (other than his employer) as beneficiary. Settlement options are not as liberal as in individual life insurance but installment options are usually available. Assignment may or may not be allowed depending on the provision in the contract and the law of a particular state. Some states and some policies prohibit assignment.

Although group term life insurance has many advantages, there are also limitations. There is no requirement that an employer must keep a group life master contract in force, and the employee faces the possibility that the contract will be discontinued. Group life insurance cannot be transferred from one employer to another, and, although convertibility exists, relatively few people exercise the options. Further, conversion may be quite expensive, particularly if the insured is in an older age range. Group term life insurance does not develop cash values and the employee does not have access to policy loans.

Group Ordinary Life Insurance

As has already been noted, group term life insurance does not have cash values, and it is an expensive coverage for the employer to provide for retired employees. One way these difficulties may be overcome is through the use of group ordinary life insurance. This form of life insurance is the same as whole life insurance that was described in Chapter 9 except, of course, it is written in accordance with the rules and traditions of group insurance. It is normally provided as a rider to a group term life insurance contract. This rider allows an employee to allocate all or some of his group term insurance to a variety of forms of group ordinary insurance. Among the forms typically offered are whole life, paid-up whole life (*e.g.*, paid-up at 65), and retirement income. The overall amount of insurance usually does not change, but the relative proportion of term and permanent insurance will shift as the employee exercises his option.

A variation on group paid-up ordinary life insurance mentioned in the last paragraph is to combine group term life insurance with increasing accumulations of paid-up whole life insurance. The paid-up insurance is obtained by purchasing single-premium whole life insurance. Since the overall amount of insurance remains the same, the net result is an increasing amount of paid-up insurance and a decreasing amount of term insurance. One advantage of this process is that by the time of retirement a substantial amount of paid-up life insurance is available to the employee.

One of the problems for group

permanent insurance is the position taken by the Internal Revenue Service in 1950 that employer contributions (in contrast to group term life insurance) are taxable to the employee as income if nonforfeitable rights in the insurance have been retained by the employee. Subsequent revisions in the Internal Revenue Code permitted employer contributions for group permanent life insurance, without such contributions being taxable to the employee, if the plan adhered to certain stipulations, the most important of which were that the part of the premium attributable to term insurance had to be clearly stated and the employer's contribution had to be limited to that amount. Also all employees eligible for the insurance plan had to be given an opportunity to acquire the permanent insurance.

Except for the permanency of the benefits, group whole life insurance is not greatly different from group term insurance in terms of contractual provisions. There is the opportunity for continued protection in the event of the severing of the group relationship similar to those found in group term insurance. Also, cash values which accumulate on a regular basis normally are not available except at time of termination, and there is usually the option of continuing the permanent part of the insurance in force, particularly if employment has lasted for five or more years.

Group Survivor Income Benefit Insurance

Group survivor income benefit insurance provides a way of supplementing social security, group term life insurance, and other sources of income that may be available to survivors but may be inadequate for their needs. Although a form of life insurance, it differs from group life in that the benefit is only paid in equal monthly installments and is paid only to a person who qualifies as a survivor (typically a spouse and/or dependent children). Also, benefits are payable only as long as a survivor is in existence. The benefit amount is normally related to earnings. One possibility is for the surviving spouse to receive 25 percent of the deceased employee's monthly earnings, while the surviving children may receive 15 percent subject to a maximum for the family of 40 percent.[4] Benefit payments are not made ad infinitum. The spouse's benefit usually ceases at age 62 and children's benefits stop when there are no living unmarried children under age 19. Except for the nature of the benefit, the other contractural provisions for group survivor income insurance, such as continuing protection, are much like other types of group life insurance. Since group survivor insurance is somewhat complex, administration is somewhat more difficult.

Group Accidental Death and Dismemberment Insurance

Many life insurance contracts issued on an individual basis contain a rider that provides for payment of twice the face amount of the contract in event death occurs accidentally. Group life insurance contracts do not have a double indemnity feature. If an employer desires this type of insurance for his employees on a group basis, he may purchase group accidental death and dismemberment insurance. As the name of the coverage suggests, benefits are payable under the contract only in event of an accident. Generally these benefits

[4] Other possible ways of handling the benefit are (1) to provide a specified amount independent of salary size and applicable to all employees, and (2) to base the benefit on job classification.

are of two types: (1) a death benefit (called the principal sum) equal to the amount provided by group life insurance and (2) a lump-sum disability benefit payable for certain situations specified in the contract. Examples are loss of a foot, a hand, or an eye or possible multiple losses of these types. The benefit is based on the principal sum. If one foot is lost, one-half the principal sum is payable. If both feet are lost, the whole principal sum will be paid. Similar rules apply for the loss of both eyes or both hands.

Unlike other forms of group life insurance there is no conversion privilege, the coverage is typically not assignable, and does not continue beyond retirement age. However, it may be kept in force during leaves, layoffs, and strikes. Also, unlike other forms of group life insurance benefits are payable only in the event of accident and there are some specific exclusions. Among the latter are war, suicide at any time, disease, aircraft flight other than as a passenger, and poisoning. The same type of arguments that can be leveled against double indemnity riders in individual life insurance contracts can be offered in opposition to accidental death and dismemberment. In planning for the financial security of a family there would seem to be no reason why more money should be available in the event death is by accident than if it occurs from natural causes.

Since group accidental death and dismemberment insurance is fairly inexpensive compared to other forms of group life insurance, employers often offer it on a voluntary, employee-pay-all basis. The offering of coverage on this basis is facilitated by a fairly liberal attitude (where state law permits) on the part of insurers in regard to the proportion of employees insured (in some cases it may be as low as 30 percent)

and in allowing the employee to select the amount of insurance subject to a minimum and maximum.[5]

Level of Benefits

One of the basic principles of group insurance is that the employee should not determine the amount of insurance carried on his/her life. To do this might well lead to selection against the insurer, since lives in a group are typically not medically selected. In order to arrive at equitable benefit amounts some rule or formula is developed. A fairly common rule is that the level of the benefit should be equal to the annual salary of the employee or some multiple thereof. A variation on this theme is that the size of the benefit should be related to position or rank with the larger amounts of insurance going to persons of executive rank. Still another rule is that the benefit amount should be related to age. If the amount decreases with age, the larger amounts of insurance would go to the younger lives on the theory that more protection is needed by employees with young families. When this principle is adopted, the amount of insurance at retirement age is not zero but is comparatively small. Coverage may or may not continue into retirement. Other possible benefit formulas are (1) all employees should receive the same amount and (2 the benefit should be related to length of service.

The problem of benefit determination can become quite complicated, especially if two or more rules of determination are combined. It would be possi-

[5] For additional discussion of the fundamental principles of group insurance and types of group life insurance, see Davis Gregg and Vane B. Lucas, *Life and Health Insurance Handbook*, 3rd ed. (Homewood, Ill.: Richard D. Irwin, Inc., 1973), pp. 351–91.

ble, for example, to set up a two-dimensional rule that would take both salary and age into account. Normally, extensive combinations are not used, since simplicity of administration is normally a desirable goal.

Financing

Financing questions center around two considerations: (1) how are the benefits to be funded and (2) who will make the contributions necessary for the payment of benefits. The funding question in group life insurance is normally resolved through the purchase of a master contract with a life insurer. Although self insurance is a possibility, it is typically not used with group life insurance. Assuming that funding with an insurer has been decided, an important problem for the employer is deciding which insurer to select. This matter will be considered in Chapter 15.

The basic financing decision in group life insurance is whether the plan should be contributory or noncontributory. By a contributory plan is meant one in which the employee pays part or all of the premium. A noncontributory plan is one in which the employer pays the entire premium. There are arguments for and against each plan. Among the arguments for a noncontributory arrangement are that (1) all employees are covered, maximum participation is achieved, and adverse selection is minimized; (2) there is a tax advantage for the employee;[6] (3) the employer has better control of the benefit program; (4) installation of the program is made easier inasmuch as enrollment problems are simplified; (5) administration of the program is easier, since there are no payroll deductions.

[6] See page 235.

The arguments for a contributory plan are: (1) employee interest is at a higher level because of increased employee participation in the plan and employees have more control; (2) to the extent the employer contributes he makes more effective use of his money in that temporary employees and others feeling they do not need the insurance will not participate; (3) employee contributions serve to increase the amount of money available for benefits and thus a better and more effective benefit program can be installed.

These arguments are not readily resolved in the abstract. What is best in any particular situation will depend on the circumstances surrounding the decision. Employer-pay-all plans seem to be increasing in favor.

Data to Be Obtained from the Insurer

Assuming the decision has been made to insure the group life insurance benefits, the risk manager has the task of seeking proposals from insurers. This involves supplying design data of the type just discussed as well as an age distribution of employees. It is also necessary for the risk manager to obtain information from the insurers that will be useful in deciding which insurer to select. Factors pertinent to the decision process are: rates, retentions, reserves, and service and administration.

Rates. It is useful in seeking information on rates to prepare a questionnaire designed to cover the questions that normally arise. As a minimum, data would be needed on the gross monthly premium rate per $1,000 for the type of coverage(s) specified, including a statement about the actuarial basis used. It is also appropriate to ask about possible discounts and the length of time for which rates can be guaranteed. If discounts are available the insurer should be asked to show both gross and net rates. The policy of the insurer in regard to experience rating should also be determined.

Retention. Retention refers to the amount retained by the insurer for expenses, premium taxes, and profits. This is the part of the premium not ultimately returned to the policyholder in the form of claims or dividends. It varies among insurers, and other things being equal, low retention is a favorable factor in comparing insurers. It is also of interest to determine if retention is guaranteed for a period of years. Insurers operating in the state of New York, for example, are not permitted to issue such a guarantee. Premium taxes vary among the states, and some of them treat insurers domiciled in the state differently from those domiciled outside. Clearly this fact, can have an important bearing on the retention figures.

Reserves. Insurers compute reserves ar the end of the policy year for incurred but unpaid claims. This computation is done before dividends are paid. Since the size of the dividend is related to the level of the reserves, the employer has an interest in knowing how the reserve is calculated. The policy of the insurer in regard to the disposition of redundant reserves in the event the policy is cancelled is another factor to be considered by the employer. Some insurers will return the excess reserves regardless of when the contract is cancelled. Others will not.

Service and administration. It is possible in group insurance for the employer to undertake a number of administrative tasks in relation to the coverage. The employer will also want to know what services the insurer provides. Among the items the employer may wish to inquire about are: (1) insurer policy on payment of claims including information about the office from which claims will be paid and whether the employer could write checks on the insurers account for a relatively small part of the claim for the use of the beneficiary; the employer might also wish to know if a local bank could be used as a depository for premiums; (2) insurer policy on information booklets, enrollment cards, and certificates including the cost of these items; an employer might want to use his own enrollment cards or print his own booklet, if a rate reduction could be obtained as a consequence; (3) insurer policy on use of its own personnel to talk to employees and explain the coverage to them. In addition to covering the items just mentioned, the employer might also want a specimen copy of the master contract and a copy of the insurer's latest financial statement.[7]

GROUP HEALTH INSURANCE

Group life insurance is designed to help with the financial problems that arise as a result of the premature death of a person upon whom a family is dependent. The problem is two-fold. Income for the family is lost, and large expenses arise in the form of estate settlement costs and taxes, as well as the costs of burial. Another area in which a similar two-fold financial problem arises is that of accident and sickness. Here there is loss of income because a person cannot continue working, and heavy expenses come about because of hospital and physicians' bills and possibly the need for extra help for the home. The field of

[7] For a more complete discussion see William M. Howard, *Cases on Risk Management* (New York: McGraw-Hill Book Co., 1967), pp. 90–116.

insurance designed to help with this problem is health insurance, in particular, in this chapter, group health insurance. The loss of income problem is met through disability insurance contracts and the extra-expense problem by medical care contracts. There is no contract that undertakes to pay for extra help for the home.

The design of group health insurance plans involves the same elements as for group life insurance. Eligibility rules are similar. One fairly important difference is that, although in group life insurance dependent coverage is rare, such coverage is common in medical care insurance.

Benefits

Benefits will be discussed under the general headings of group disability insurance and group medical care insurance.

Group Disability Insurance

Group disability insurance is similar to that issued on an individual basis, except, as in other forms of group insurance, the unit of selection is the group and members of the group are insured via a master contract issued to the employer or to the ownership entity of some other type of group. Certificates not having the force of a contract are issued to employees. The importance of this type of insurance is illustrated by the fact that the probability of a disabling illness or accident during a person's working lifetime is higher than the probability of death during the same span.

Short-Term Disability

Insurance contracts providing for maximum benefit periods of 2 years or less are classified as short-term disability contracts. Typical benefit periods for contracts of this type, which usually cover only nonoccupational disability, are 10, 13, or 26 weeks, or 1 or 2 years. Benefits normally begin immediately when the cause of the disability is an accident, but are subject to a 7-day or possibly longer waiting period for sickness. The imposition of a waiting period reflects the less definite nature of sickness as compared to accident, as well as the greater frequency of sickness. Further, waiting periods like deductibles, serve to reduce the cost of insurance and to eliminate claims for disabilities of an essentially inconsequential nature. Benefits may be limited by an annual maximum determined on a cumulative basis. A problem that sometimes arises in disability situations is how to treat recurrent periods of disability especially if they occur shortly after an earlier illness or accident from which there was an apparent recovery. It is not always easy to determine whether the subsequent disability is essentially a continuation of the earlier disability or whether it is due to a separate and unrelated cause. One solution to the problem that is fairly typical is to regard the subsequent disability as a part of the first if less than two weeks of active employment separate the two disabilities, except in situations where it can be demonstrated that the second disability arose from an unrelated cause. The decision about whether a second disability is or is not a part of the first can be of some importance to the insured. For example, if the subsequent disability is a continuation, the number of days of benefits will be less than if it were determined to be a new disability.

The amount of the benefit is typically determined as a percentage of wages and typically varies between 50 percent and 66⅔ percent.

Long-Term Disability

Long-term disability plans are typically designed to provide benefits after payments on short-term plans cease or after sick-leave benefits or salary continuation benefits are exhausted. In short-term contracts the cause of the disability is typically limited to nonoccupational situations, whereas in long-term contracts coverage is usually provided for occupational as well as nonoccupational accidents or sickness.

Since benefits to be paid under the contract are designed to replace lost wages because of total disability, it is necessary to define what is meant by these terms. Total disability may be defined in at least three ways. However, a typical definition is that during the first two years of total disability an employee will be regarded as totally disabled, if he is unable "to perform any and every duty pertaining to his occupation and is not engaged in any occupation or employment for wage or profit." After two years if total disability continues, it will be defined as the inability of an employee "to engage in any and every duty pertaining to any occupation or employment for wage or profit for which the employee is or becomes reasonably qualified by training, education, or experience." As is readily apparent, the definition becomes less liberal the longer disability continues. By salary or wage is usually meant monthly salary exclusive of bonus, overtime, or any other extra income. Further, the amount of the salary is the salary amount existing on the first day of the calendar month immediately preceding inability to work because of disability.

In the insuring agreement of the contract the insurer agrees to pay a benefit defined in the contract if an employee becomes totally disabled from accidental bodily injury or sickness. The promise is subject to certain qualifications. First, due proof must be submitted to the insurer. Further, the claim must be made before age 65 and the employee must have been totally disabled for a period of 90 days.[8] In some types of contract there must be a certification on the part of both the employer and employee about other benefits that may be available to the employee, and there must be evidence that these benefits have been applied for. Once the qualifications have been met the benefit paid is typically two-thirds of salary subject to a maximum amount. There is no benefit payable for the 90-day qualifying period, and a deduction is made for other benefits payable. It is also typical to waive payment of premium during the disability period. There are some specific exclusions. Among them are (1) refusal to pay benefits if the employee has not been treated by a duly qualified physician; (2) disabilities arising from pregnancy, childbirth, or miscarriage; (3) disabilities that may come about through illegal activities; (4) disabilities caused by war whether declared or not; (5) serving in the Armed Forces for any nation or international authority; (6) disabilities that are self-inflicted. If there are successive periods of disability, there must be 6 consecutive months of continuous active work before a new period of disability is declared. An exception is made when the new disability is entirely unrelated to the previous disability.[9]

Disability contracts contain a number of other provisions. These relate to such items as notice and proof of

---

[8] The qualifying period may vary among insurers. Similarly, the age 65 limitation may vary. Also distinction may be made between accidents and sickness.

[9] The contractual provisions cited here are those found in many contracts. Variations exist and any particular contract may differ to some degree.

claim, proofs of loss, payment of claims, change of beneficiary, and assignment.

Group Medical Expense Benefits

Group medical expense benefits are similar to those provided on an individual basis. Business firms and other institutions typically provide group insurance covering hospital and medical expenses as well as coverage for major medical expense.[10] There are some differences in the underwriting and administration of group plans as opposed to individual ones. In the underwriting of group plans the group is taken as the unit of selection and normally there are no limitations about preexisting conditions or general state of health. While it is fairly unusual in individual plans for other health insurance to be taken into account in a settlement under a particular contract, in group insurance other existing insurance is normally taken into account in claim settlements. Another significant aspect of group contracts is the conversion period that permits employees to convert to a group contract on leaving employment.

One type of benefit that is more typical under group plans than individual ones is the dental benefit. For many years dental insurance benefits except for certain surgical procedures were not available on either an individual or group basis and constituted a major exception in most health insurance contracts.

Group dental insurance plans began in the mid 1940s and developed fairly slowly in the 1950s and 1960s. It is estimated that less than two million persons were covered by 1968. By 1975 this number had grown to about 22

million, and it is expected that more than 50 million persons will be covered by 1980.[11] Although group dental insurance is more widespread than ever before, it is still comparatively rare in that probably only 1 out of 5 large firms include it in their employee benefit programs.[12]

Dental insurance plans are typically comprehensive and cover all the areas of dental service: diagnostic, preventive, restorative, as well as such specialties as endodontics, oral surgery, orthodontics, periodontics, and prosthodontics. Services such as drugs, emergency care, general anesthesia, and special consultations are also often a part of the plans. The amount of reimbursement tends to vary with the type of service with diagnostic and preventive services often fully reimbursed while such services as periodontics might be only partially paid for, say 50 percent, and no benefit or a substantially reduced benefit, might be available for orthodontics. There may also be deductible requirements especially where services involving dental specialties are supplied.[13]

Dental insurance plans may be offered as a part of a general health care benefit or as a separate plan. Also benefits may be on a reasonable and customary basis or on a scheduled basis. Separate plans are often preferred, although more expensive, because of their better benefits. Similarly benefits issued on a reasonable and customary basis are preferable to scheduled plans because, among other reasons, they are more re-

---

[10] Specific benefits will not be detailed here, since they are similar to those provided under individual contracts. See Chapter 9.

[11] *Benefit Plan Bulletin* (Johnson and Higgins, June 1975) p. 1.

[12] *Ibid.*

[13] Details vary among plans. Some plans pay 80 percent of the maximum allowed by a schedule without regard to type of service. Similarly some plans have a general calendar year deductible except for the employee's children.

sponsive to inflation.[14] Schedules tend to be fairly detailed. Some are divided between general services and prosthetics. Among the general services are the usual dental specialties plus separate sections for items like visits and examinations, roentgenology and pathology, extractions, and cysts and neoplasms.

Dental insurance plans like other insurance plans are subject to limitations and exclusions. When provided as a part of a general medical expense contract, they will generally be subject to the limitations and exclusions applying to all health benefits in addition to those applying only to dental care. Among the specific dental exclusions might be loss caused by war; services provided by a nonlicensed physician or dentist except for dental prophylaxis if the latter is supplied by a licensed dental hygienist under the supervision of a dentist; treatment that is mainly cosmetic; and charges for the replacement of dentures, under certain circumstances, and subject to certain limitations.

Funding

The benefits under health care plans are funded through self-insurance (disability plans in particular); contracts with commercial insurers; contracts with specialty insurers such as Blue Cross and Blue Shield; and through independent, group practice organizations.

OTHER HEALTH PLANS

Not all plans available to employees are sponsored by employers. Unions often supply extensive health benefits to their members, sometimes through group insurance arrangements and sometimes by supplying health service through the maintenance of hospitals and other health facilities. It is also true that employers sometimes supply health services directly by retaining physicians and in-house medical departments. Of particular interest in relatively recent times has been the independent group practice plan that supplies service on a prepayment basis. Some of these plans are now Health Maintenance Organizations and recent legislation is of particular interest to employers.

Health Maintenance Organization Act of 1973

The Health Maintenance Organization Act of 1973 is of considerable interest to employers and risk managers primarily because of a requirement of the Act that an employer "must offer to employees the option of having their medical benefits provided through a qualified Health Maintenance Organization, or through the conventional delivery system."[15] In particular the law states that "Each employer which is required during any calendar quarter to pay its employees the minimum wage specified by section 6 of the Fair Labor Standards Act of 1938 (or would be required to pay his employees such wage but for section 13a of such Act), and which during such calendar quarter employed an average number of employees of not less than 25, shall, in accordance with regulations which the secretary shall prescribe, include in any health benefits plan offered to its employees in the calendar year, beginning after such calendar quarter, the option of membership in qualified health maintenance organizations which are engaged in the provision of basic supplemental health services in the areas in which such em-

---

[14] For additional information see *Ibid.*, pp. 2–3.

[15] Public Law 93-222, Section 1310.

ployees reside."[16] The law recognizes that H.M.O.s may be organized on a group practice basis or may offer services through an individual practice association (or associations). If more than one H.M.O. operates in an area, and if at least one operates on a group practice basis and at least one as an individual practice association, then the employee must be given a choice between one or the other bases of operation or the choice of opting for conventional medical benefits and delivery. Although there are legal barriers to the setting-up of H.M.O.s in about 20 states, the new law provides that H.M.O.s established under its aegis will not be affected by limiting state laws. It is not contemplated that the requirements of the new law will increase the costs of the employer. The law states: "No employer shall be required to pay more for health benefits as a result of the application of this section than would otherwise be required by any prevailing collective bargaining agreement or other legally enforceable contract for the provision of health benefits between the employer and its employees. . . ."[17]

The Health Maintenance Act of 1973 defines a health maintenance organization as a legal entity "which (1) provides basic and supplemental health services to its members in the manner prescribed by subsection (b), and (2) is organized and operated in the manner prescribed by subsection (c)."[18] Subsection (b) provides some general guidelines as to method of payment for services rendered, as well as the way in which medical services are to be supplied. The basic health services provided by the plan are to be paid for on a periodic basis "without regard to the dates health services (within the basic health services) are provided."[19] Further, the payment must be determined "without regard to the frequency, extent, or kind of health service (within the basic health services) actually furnished."[20] Another requirement is that the rate be determined under a community rating system. There is a provision that the periodic payment "may be supplemental by additional nominal payments which may be required for the provision of specific services (within the basic health services). . . ."[21] However, such payments may not be required if they serve as a "barrier to the delivery of health services."[22] Any payments made for supplementary health services must also be on a prepayment basis and determined under a community rating system. In terms of the delivery of health services the Act requires that basic health services be provided "through health professionals who are members of the staff of the health maintenance organization or through a medical group (or groups) or individual practice association (or associations).[23] Exceptions are recognized in cases of unusual or infrequently used services and in situations where a health service must of necessity be provided to a member of a H.M.O. before it could be supplied by the group. A health professional is defined as a physician, dentist, nurse, podiatrist, optometrist, or such other individual "engaged in the delivery of health services as the Secretary may by regulation designate."[24]

16 Public Law 93–222, 93rd Congress, S.14, (December 29, 1973), Section 1310(a).

17 Ibid., Section 1310(c).

18 Ibid., Section 1301(a).

19 Ibid., Section 1301(b).

20 Ibid.

21 Ibid.

22 Ibid.

23 Ibid.

24 Ibid.

The Act also contains rules about such matters as the accessibility of health services, the financial soundness of the H.M.O., enrollment, organization of the policy-making body, and health education.

The expression "basic health service" is defined as:

1. physician services (including consultant and referral services by a physician;

2. inpatient and outpatient hospital services;

3. medically necessary emergency health services;

4. short-term (not to exceed 20 visits), outpatient, evaluative, and crisis-intervention mental health services;

5. medical treatment and referral services (including referral services to appropriate ancillary services) for the abuse of or addiction to alcohol and drugs;

6. diagnostic laboratory and diagnostic and therapeutic radiologic services;

7. home health services, and

8. preventive health services including voluntary family planning services, infertility services, preventive dental care for children, and children's eye examinations conducted to determine the need for vision correction.[25]

By supplemental health services is meant:

1. services of facilities for intermediate and long-term care;

2. dental care not included as a basic health service . . .

25 *Ibid.*, Section 1302.

3. mental health services not included as a basic health service . . .

4. vision care not included as a basic health service . . .

5. long-term physical medicine and rehabilitative services (including physical therapy), and

6. the provision of prescription drugs prescribed in the course of the provision by the health maintenance organization of a basic health service . . .[26]

An important aspect of the Health Maintenance Organization Act of 1973 is the encouragement it gives to the establishment and expansion of health maintenance organizations. This encouragement takes the form of possible grants for feasibility surveys; grants for "planning projects for the establishment of health maintenance organizations or for the significant expansion of the membership of, or areas served by, health maintenance organizations";[27] loan guarantees for loans for planning projects; and loans and loan guarantees for initial operating costs.

Final regulations concerning the compliance of employers became effective November 28, 1975. The Federal Register will from time to time contain lists of organizations qualifying as H.M.O.s. The regulations provide guidance on many administrative matters including responsibility for qualification and payroll deduction.[28]

26 *Ibid.*

27 *Ibid.*, Section 1304.

28 Amendments to the Health Maintenance Organization Act of 1973 have been passed by the House and Senate and at this writing (July 1976) are in conference. They may affect such areas as definition of basic and supplemental services, minimum number of employees required, community rating, and certain enrollment requirements.

GROUP PROPERTY AND LIABILITY INSURANCE

With the exception of one state (Michigan) property and liability insurance for employees or members of other groups cannot be written on a true group basis.[29] Many states, however, permit the mass merchandising of property and liability insurance. Mass merchandising is similar to group insurance in that contracts are marketed to a group, such as the employees of an employer, and the employer negotiates the plan and deducts the premium from payroll. It differs principally in that individual contracts are issued to employees and both underwriting and rating are on an individual basis. It is similar to franchise merchandising in other types of insurance.

Property and liability insurance as an employee benefit has generally been limited to automobile and homeowners insurance contracts, although sometimes one encounters other coverages such as personal excess liability. Mass merchandised plans are not particularly widespread. Bickelhaupt has estimated that only about 8 percent of property and liability premiums come from plans that have been sold on a mass merchandising basis mainly to large firms.[30] There are advantages and disadvantages to an employee in purchasing insurance through a group process. Among the advantages are payroll deduction and benefits that may accrue from the employer's negotiating ability and fewer underwriting restrictions. Costs often are lower for the employee, although not necessarily so. Among the disadvantages for the employee may be the lack of direct contact with an agent selected by the employee, and often less direction when placing insurance, since employers may give less advice and counsel than would be the case for the more traditional group life and health coverages.

There are those who believe that property and liability insurance as an employee benefit will become more widespread in the future particularly if state regulatory statutes become more favorable, and if some of the cost advantages (for example, employer contribution to the cost) of true group insurance can be realized. Greater acceptance from independent agents would also be helpful. In the meantime, unions may more and more demand property and liability insurance as an employee benefit.

LEGAL EXPENSE INSURANCE

Although at present group insurance arrangements in the United States to provide for legal expense are essentially in the experimental stage, group arrangements (not involving insurance) are well known, and there has been interest on the part of unions and others in the idea of legal expense insurance as an employee benefit.

It has been estimated that between 1,400 and 3,000 group legal service plans have been established in the United States.[31] A group legal service plan is one wherein a group (such as a group of employees) has access to legal services supplied by a panel of lawyers. Typically the panel is closed, meaning

---

[29] A true group basis would be one in which a master contract would be issued to an employer and the group would be selected as a unit.

[30] Bickelhaupt, David L., *General Insurance*, 9th ed. (Homewood, Ill.: Richard D. Irwin, Inc., 1974), p. 133.

[31] Werner Pfenningstorf, *Legal Expense Insurance* (Chicago: American Bar Foundation, 1975), p. 4.

that services are supplied by a specified group of lawyers who have agreed to participate in the plan. Although each employee pays for legal services without recourse to an insurance arrangement, costs are typically lower than would be the case if the employee sought out his or her own lawyer. The cost reduction comes about through the efficiencies of the group arrangement.

Prepaid legal service plans, which are insurance arrangements, are not widespread, but it is estimated that at least six insurers offer these plans. Early in the 1970s the American Bar Association became interested in legal insurance and sponsored a pilot program in Shreveport, Louisiana. The plan covered members of a labor union in Shreveport. It operated on an open panel system which permitted free choice of lawyers. The losses and expenses of the plan were covered by dues or premiums charged each member. Four major benefits were provided by the plan: "(1) $100 worth of advice and consultation, not to exceed $25 per visit; (2) $250 worth of office work and negotiation ($10 deductible); (3) $325 worth of services for judicial and administrative proceedings, plus $40 for court costs and witness fees, plus $150 for out-of-pocket expenses ($25 deductible if client is moving party); and (4) a major legal expense benefit of 80 percent of the next $1,000 in expenses incurred over benefits payable under (3) above if client is the defendant or responding party."[32] These benefits were subject to certain exclusions, among them being litigation involving business matters, fines, class actions, shopping for other opinions, and preparation of income tax returns.

There are a number of arguments that favor the establishment of legal plans. For one thing, there appears to be a considerable need that is generally not clearly understood and legal plans could and do serve an educative function. Further, it is often possible to effect savings by utilizing the efficiency of a closed panel of attorneys, and, also, to obtain better rates because of the bargaining power of groups. Another advantage is that high costs that may be associated with legal problems arising by chance may be spread through the insurance mechanism over the entire group. Despite the advantages that may be cited, prepaid legal plans have not been widely established. Marketing difficulties have arisen including the problem of persuading members of groups to participate. Terminology associated with the plans as well as the details have not been well understood. Also, questions about supervision by insurance authorities have arisen and have often not been completely resolved.

STATUTORY BENEFIT PLANS

The benefit plans considered thus far in the chapter may be described as voluntary, since whether they are established depends on the employer's willingness to do so.[33] There are a number of employee benefit plans in the United States that are mandatory in that they have been established by statute and employer compliance is required. Chief among these plans are workers' compensation; unemployment insurance; old age, survivors, health, and disability insurance; and various state nonoccupational disability plans.

[32] Mark Martin, "Prepaid Legal Expense Forecast for Future," *For the Defense*, XIII (October 1972), p. 88.

[33] Plans that are set up as a result of union demands to some extent form an exception to this statement.

Workers' Compensation

Workers' compensation is the oldest of the social security programs in the United States. With the exception of the Longshoremen's and Harbor Workers' Compensation Act and the federal law covering civil employees, all workers' compensation laws are state laws and exist in all states, the District of Columbia, and Puerto Rico. The purpose of this legislation is to compensate employees for the financial loss sustained as a result of injuries due to accidents and sicknesses that arise out of and in the course of employment. The employer is required to pay damages according to statutory provision regardless of who is at fault. The employer may meet this responsibility through buying insurance or in most states by self-insuring.

The laws of the different jurisdictions vary considerably. Most of the laws are compulsory meaning that every employer subject to the Act must comply with its provisions. Employees are required to participate, also, except in Arizona and New Hampshire. The remaining laws are elective, which means the employer may decide whether to accept or reject the Act and the employee may also choose.[34] In general, public as well as private employment comes under the law. Not every type of employment is covered. Those most often excluded are farmwork, domestic service, and casual employment. A substantial number of states make no exemptions based on the number of employees in a firm. Other states have exemptions which vary from firms having fewer than 2 employees to

those with fewer than 15. Most injuries and diseases are covered, although occupational diseases have more limitations than accidents.

The benefits provided by workers' compensation laws are medical, temporary total disability, permanent partial disability, permanent total disability, death benefits (including burial expenses), allowances for children and other dependents, and rehabilitation benefits. Some of the benefits, *e.g.*, rehabilitation, are not universal. The amount of the benefit is typically stated as a percentage of weekly wage subject to a maximum and to a term of payment. Waiting periods are usually imposed during which no benefits are paid, although most laws permit retroactive payments to the date of injury if the disability continues beyond a certain time period.[35]

Unemployment Insurance

Title III of the Social Security Act provides for grants-in-aid to the states for the administrative expenses associated with state unemployment insurance laws. Each state is free to develop its own unemployment insurance program with the result that variation exists among the various jurisdictions. Coverage is determined by considering size of firm, the nature of the employment relationship, and where the employee works. Although the minimum number of employees the employer must have before the firm comes under the law varies, the minimum is typically low and one is not uncommon. In general, states require evidence of an employer-

[34] In practice employees rarely elect out. Further, if the employer elects out, he loses the common law defenses of assumption of risk, negligence of fellow employees, and contributory negligence.

[35] Benefit amounts and maxima vary considerably among the states. The reader should consult the laws of the various states or a summary such as *State Workmen's Compensation Laws*, United States Department of Labor.

employee relationship in order for an employee to be eligible for benefits. Since some employees may work in more than one state, the laws contain provisions for covering multistate workers. Usually they are covered in the state in which they will seek employment. Some employments are specifically excluded and these vary from state to state. Examples of fairly typical exclusions are agricultural labor, domestic service in private homes, and service for relatives.

The benefits provided by the various state laws vary considerably and a fair amount of complexity exists in the matter of determining workers' benefit rights. However, virtually all of the laws have the concepts of a qualifying period, a benefit year, a weekly benefit amount, and duration of benefits. Many states also impose a waiting period. In unemployment insurance it is important that the person desiring benefits demonstrate that he/she has had a satisfactory attachment to the labor force. To determine benefit rights the worker must demonstrate that he/she was in covered employment during a qualifying or base period. The rights thus established remain fixed for a time period called a benefit year. In the vast majority of states the base period depends on when the employee first files for benefits or begins to draw benefits (beginning of benefit year). In many states there is a lag between the end of the base period and the start of the benefit year. The base period in all states is four quarters in length. It is a requirement in all states that during the base period, the employee must have earned the amount of wages specified in the law and must have worked for a certain time period. The benefit year is typically 52 weeks in length.

The amount of the weekly benefit typically depends on average weekly earnings in the quarter of the base period in which they were highest. The amount is only a percentage of the average and is subject to maxima and minima. There is also a limitation on duration of benefits with twenty-six weeks tending to be a maximum. In some states there may be allowances for dependents. In all states a worker must in addition to base period requirements establish eligibility to receive benefits. In general he/she must be able to work, available, and the unemployment must be caused by lack of work. There are also actions such as discharge for misconduct that will disqualify an employee.

Unemployment benefits are paid for by employers who are charged a payroll tax. The federal tax is 3.2 percent, although the employer may credit up to 90 percent of the federal tax any contributions required by the state if the latter has an approved state law. The employer may also credit savings that may arise in the state tax because of an approved experience rating plan.

Old Age, Survivors, Health, and Disability Insurance

The Social Security Act in addition to its concern for unemployment establishes old age and survivors benefits, disability benefits, and medical care insurance benefits for persons aged 65 and over.

Old Age and Survivors Insurance

Old age and survivors insurance was established in 1935 and has been modified over the years until today it covers 9 out of 10 workers in the United States. The program is generally mandatory, and both the employer and the employee must contribute to its cost.

Retirement benefits are payable to retired workers as early as age 62, if they have met the eligibility requirements established in the Social Security Act. Wives or husbands of retired workers also receive benefits (one-half the amount received by the retired workers), and in some instances unmarried children (depending usually on age) may be eligible. The amount of the benefit received depends on average earnings during the years an employee was covered under Social Security. The benefits are indexed and are automatically increased if the cost of living increases 3 percent or more. Examples of the amount of benefit payable are given in Table 11–1.

Survivors benefits (deceased worker's survivors) are payable to the following categories of persons:

Unmarried children under 18 (or 22 if full-time students).

Unmarried son or daughter 18 or over who was severely disabled before 22 and who continues to be disabled.

Widow or dependent widower 60 or older.

Widow, widowed father, or surviving divorced mother if caring for worker's child under 18 (or disabled) who is getting a benefit based on the earnings of the deceased worker.

Widow or dependent widower 50 or older who becomes disabled not later than 7 years after worker's death, or in case of a widow, within 7 years after she stops getting checks as a widow caring for worker's children.

Dependent parents 62 or older.[36]

[36] *Your Social Security* (Washington, D.C.: U.S. Department of Health, Education, and Welfare, Publication No. (SSA) 75-10035, May 1975), p. 8.

In some situations payments may be made to divorced wives.

The benefits described above (OASI) are financed through contributions of the employer and employee. Through 1977 the contribution rate is 4.375 percent each for employer and employee. Only earnings up to $16,500 per annum (in 1977) are counted in figuring the amount of tax to be paid. Self-employed persons are also covered. Their contribution rate was 6.185 percent in 1977. It is estimated that both the contribution rate and the wage base will increase, probably fairly regularly, in the future.

Health Insurance

Disability insurance was provided as a part of Social Security in 1954, followed by Medicare (medical benefits for persons 65 and over) in 1965. Since 1973 some medical benefits for persons under age 65 have become available. Benefits for persons with severe kidney disease are covered under Medicare even though these persons are under 65. Similarly, persons who have been paid disability benefits for 2 or more consecutive years are eligible for medical benefits.

Disability benefits are available to persons severely disabled before age 65. A person is eligible if the disability prevents him or her from working and if it is expected to last for at least 12 months or if death is expected. Benefits continue for as long as the person is disabled. Benefit amounts are treated in a fashion similar to retirement.

Medicare benefits are in two parts: (1) hospital insurance and (2) medical insurance (physicians' services). Persons eligible for Social Security checks or railroad retirement checks are automatically included in hospital insurance. Medical insurance must be applied for and a separate premium paid. Hospital

TABLE 11-1
Examples of Social Security Payments (Effective June 1977)
Average yearly earnings after 1950 covered by social security

Benefits can be paid to a:	$923 or less	$3,000	$4,000	$5,000	$6,000	$8,000*	$10,000*
Retired worker at 65	114.30	236.40	278.10	322.50	364.50	453.10	502.00
Worker under 65 and disabled	114.30	236.40	278.10	322.50	364.50	453.10	502.00
Retired worker at 52	91.50	189.20	222.50	258.00	291.60	362.50	401.60
Wife or husband at 65	57.20	118.20	139.10	161.30	182.30	226.60	251.00
Wife or husband at 62	42.90	88.70	104.40	121.00	136.80	170.00	188.30
Wife under 65 and one child in her care	57.20	125.00	197.20	272.60	304.20	339.80	376.60
Widow or widower at 65 if worker never received reduced benefits	114.30	236.40	278.10	322.50	364.50	453.10	502.00
Widow or widower at 60 if sole survivor	81.80	169.10	198.90	230.60	260.70	324.00	359.00
Widow or widower at 50 and disabled if sole survivor	57.30	118.30	139.20	161.30	182.40	226.60	251.10
Widow or widower with one child in care	171.50	354.60	417.20	483.80	546.80	679.80	753.00
Maximum family payment	171.50	361.40	475.30	595.10	668.60	792.90	878.50

* Maximum earnings covered by social security were lower in past years and must be included in figuring your average earnings. This average determines your payment amount. Because of this, amounts shown in the last two columns generally won't be payable until future years. The maximum retirement benefit generally payable to a worker who is 65 in 1977 is $437.10.

SOURCE: *Your Social Security* (Washington, D.C., Department of Health, Education and Welfare) Publication No. (SSA) 77-10035.

insurance, although subject to a deductible, is quite comprehensive and includes limited benefits for treatment in an extended care facility. Medical benefits are subject to deductibles and coinsurance, and some types of treatment are not covered. However, in general, the benefits are substantial.

Hospital and disability insurance are paid for by the employer and the employee at the same time they pay for old age and survivors insurance. Currently, 1.475 percent is added to the contribution rate for OASI. Thus, the total rate charged for retirement, disability, and medicare was 5.85 percent in 1977 for the employee and the same amount for the employer. The self-employed contributed a total of 7.9 percent. For persons over 65 who wish to purchase medical benefits, $7.20 (as of July, 1977) is deducted from their Social Security checks.

State Non-Occupational Disability Plans

Six jurisdictions — California, Hawaii, New Jersey, New York, Puerto Rico, and Rhode Island have nonoccupational disability funds. These funds are intended primarily to provide short-term disability benefits for eligible workers. In California, New Jersey, and Rhode Island the laws are a part of the unemployment compensation statutes and are supported by a tax on wages. In Rhode Island and California the tax is paid by employees only, but in New Jersey the employer is also taxed. In New York the law is a part of the workers' compensation statute.

In California, New Jersey, and Puerto Rico it is possible for benefits to be provided through a state fund, but private plans are also possible. For a private plan to be established in California it must be demonstrated that the private plan is more liberal in some respect than the state fund. It must be "acceptable to a majority of the employees and not result in a substantial selection of risks adverse to the fund."[37]

ADMINISTRATION OF EMPLOYEE BENEFIT PLANS

The widespread use of employee benefit plans in compensation practices of employers has resulted in an increasing amount of attention being given to the administration of these plans. Administrative problems are, in general, of two types: (1) internal concerns surrounding the installation and maintenance of plans and (2) external considerations that arise from, among other things, increasing regulation and the changes that occur in statutory benefits.

Internal Considerations

In most large firms the person directly in charge of employee benefits is either the officer in charge of personnel or the risk manager. Depending somewhat on the size of the firm, these officers may have a number of assistants who are responsible for various aspects of the plans under the guidance of a benefit manager. In general, the administrative aspects of benefit work can be divided into the areas of design and installation of plans, administration of claims, recording of plan experience, cost control, and information dissemination.

Design and Installation of Plans

The design of benefit plans typically involves decisions about types of

[37] Davis W. Gregg and Vane B. Lucas (eds.), *Life and Health Insurance Handbook*, 3rd ed. (Homewood, Ill.: Richard D. Irwin, Inc., 1973), p. 408.

benefit, financing of plans, and funding media. These problems have been discussed, and the nature of the decisions involved in the preceding pages of this chapter.[38] The installation of plans, once the design decisions have been made, involve enrolling of employees, arranging for payroll deductions, and establishing appropriate files and other records.

Administration of Claims

The extent of the involvement of the employee benefit department in the administration of claims will depend on whether the benefit plans are self-insured or funded through insurers or other intermediaries. If the benefits are self-insured, the employer (through the employee benefit department) has full responsibility for settling claims with employees. This fact means that procedures must be developed for claim notification, filing, processing, and payment, as well as for discussing with the employee any limitations that may surround recovery under the claim. When payment of a claim is the responsibility of an insurer or other third party, the employers' role may be limited to receiving and transmitting notification of loss and in assisting in filling out of forms. In some instances, insurers grant authority to the employer to settle claims in the name of the insurer subject to some dollar maximum. In such situations the employers' role is considerably enlarged. Regardless of the source of the employer's authority in claim settlement, it is usually necessary to set up procedures for handling complaints from employees who may feel that they have not been dealt with fairly. In some instances it is desirable to establish a

grievance committee to which employees can submit their complaints and receive a hearing.

Records

The keeping of adequate records is necessary not only for financial purposes but for statistical purposes as well. Some employee benefit plans such as group life insurance and workers' compensation are experience rated and accurate records are necessary to establish claim experience. It is also useful to have records that will establish a profile of plan participants and changes that occur over time. Another type of record that is helpful is an on-going study of trends in employee benefits and changes that may be occurring in the benefit plans of competitors. Such information can be helpful in revising benefit offerings and in responding to demands for change.

Cost Control

The efficient operation of employee benefit plans requires careful attention to the control of costs. Of considerable help in this regard is the development of programs designed to prevent or reduce loss. Such programs can be direct, such as safety devices on machines which are designed to prevent injury; or indirect, such as limitations on the amount of recovery in disability plans in order to discourage malingering. Since the risk manager of the firm is normally responsible for programs designed to prevent loss and promote safety as a way of dealing with risk, prevention programs for improving the loss experience under benefit plans should be coordinated with him even though he might not be responsible for benefit plans in general.

[38] The design of pension plans will be considered in Chapter 13.

Cost control programs as they relate to employee benefits may be classified as follows: (1) programs designed to reduce the number of claims made; (2) programs designed to reduce the impact of loss; and (3) programs designed to limit or reduce the dollar amount of the claim. An example of the first category of programs would be occupational health and safety programs that undertake to prevent accidents and sickness. In the second category of programs would be found such things as rehabilitation activities that tend to reduce the length of time an employee might be disabled or benefit design standards that tend to make continued disability unattractive or that discourage adverse selection. In the third category above would be placed such items as deductibles and coinsurance provisions in insurance contracts and realistic determination of, for example, medical care costs.

Information Processing

Although employee benefits constitute a substantial proportion of the total compensation of many employees, they tend to be less well understood by the employee than other aspects of the remuneration. Thus, communicating with employees about the value and extent of benefit programs constitutes a significant part of the work of the employee benefits manager. Communication typically takes a variety of forms. Some firms prepare fairly elaborate brochures that list the benefits available and explain the pertinent details of each. Often the employee benefits section of the firm will have an individual or individuals available to counsel with employees about their benefits. Another method of communicating is through open meetings where employees listen to presentations that may use movies, slides, and other visual aids to help explain the value of the various benefit programs. Even though an employer may not have an elaborate information program, it is necessary, as a minimum, to communicate through memoranda changes in existing programs and the installation of new ones. In advising employees the employer undertakes the risk that information given will turn out to be wrong and that an employee will suffer substantial financial loss. Such a contingency may give rise to a legal suit alleging malpractice on the part of the employer. This is one of the many risks the risk manager must assess as he or she plans for the overall treatment of a firm's risks.

External Considerations

Employee benefits, like other aspects of the operation of a business firm, are often affected by forces outside the control of the firm. Of particular importance to benefit managers are the activities of unions and the actions of legislatures at the state and federal levels.

Unions

As was explained earlier in this chapter, employers are required to negotiate with unions about employee benefits. Although the risk manager does not typically participate in the bargaining process with the union, he will often be called upon to furnish information and negotiate with insurers. Thus he should be familiar with the union demands, be aware of new developments, and have knowledge of the strengths and weaknesses of current benefit plans.[39]

[39] Mehr, R. I. and Hedges, R. A., *Risk Management — Concepts and Applications*, pp. 329–30.

Legislative Action

Legislative actions of interest to benefit managers are either essentially regulatory in nature or actions that mandate certain benefits. Legislation that is essentially of a regulatory type has become increasingly important particularly at the federal level. Examples are the Health Maintenance Organization Act discussed earlier in this chapter and the Employee Retirement Income Security Act (ERISA), which will be discussed in Chapter 13. These laws require that the employer meet certain standards in the areas of health benefits and pensions. Examples of legislation that mandate benefits are the workers' compensation laws of the various states, the federal Social Security Act, and the nonoccupational disability laws that exist in six states. Since there is a tendency for these laws to be frequently revised, the benefit manager must spend a considerable amount of time keeping up-to-date on changes as they occur. He must also be aware of new legislation such as National Health Insurance that may be under consideration. In many instances he will need to confer with the legal department on the interpretation of often complex legislation.

SUMMARY AND CONCLUSIONS

1. An employee benefit is any help of a pecuniary kind (or nonpecuniary but which might conceivably be valued in dollar terms) provided by an employer for an employee in addition to salary or wages paid for work performed.

2. The Chamber of Commerce of the United States places employee benefits into five categories: legally required payments, pensions and other agreed-upon payments, payments for nonproductive time while on the job, payments for time in which the worker is not at work, and other payments such as medical examinations or recreational facilities.

3. There are a number of reasons for employee benefits including employee financial security, competitive considerations, tax benefits, legislative requirements, and social and economic factors.

4. Group life insurance is provided for employees through a master contract issued to the employer. The principal forms of group life insurance are group term, group ordinary, group survivor income, group accidental death and dismemberment.

5. Group health insurance includes disability payments as well as payments for medical expenses such as surgical procedures, hospital room and board, and home and office calls.

6. Group dental insurance plans are now more common, and it has been estimated that one out of five large firms include them in their employee benefit programs.

7. Group health insurance contracts are typically provided by commercial insurers or Blue Cross or Blue Shield. However, other organizations, such as group practice plans, also offer programs for employees. An example would be Kaiser Plans or the Health Insurance Plan of Greater New York.

8. The Health Maintenance Organization Act of 1973 requires employers to offer employees the option of having medical benefits provided through a qualified Health Maintenance Organization or by the conventional type of medical care delivery system.

9. It is estimated that between 1,400 and 3,000 group legal service plans exist in the United States. These plans typically give employees access to legal services supplied by a panel of lawyers.

10. Statutory benefit plans exist for employees. Examples are workers' compensation, unemployment insurance, OASHDI (old age, survivors, health, and disability insurance), and state nonoccupational disability plans.

11. The administration of employee benefit plans involves internal as well as external concerns. Among the former are the installation and maintenance of plans, and among the latter are problems of regulation and changes that occur in statutory plans.

QUESTIONS FOR DISCUSSION

1. Define the following words or phrases: employee benefit, total compensation, group insurance, short-term disability, long-term disability, total disability, health insurance, and statutory benefit plans.

2. Discuss the scope of employee benefit plans. Do you believe the scope of such plans has widened in recent years? Why or why not?

3. What are the chief design elements in employee benefit plans? Discuss briefly what is meant by each.

4. It is not unusual for an employer planning to install a benefit plan to ask a number of insurers to submit proposals. In requesting a proposal for, say, group life insurance, what type of information would an employer normally seek from an insurer? What sort of data would an insurer require an employer to submit?

5. Typically, what type of life insurance is used in group life insurance plans? What other types are possible? How do you account for their infrequent use?

6. Describe the benefits offered by a typical group medical expense plan. What are some typical exclusions?

7. Discuss dental insurance plans from the standpoint of history, benefits, exclusions and funding.

8. What is the purpose of the Health Maintenance Organization Act of 1973? Why is it of special interest to employers?

9. Assess the present status of mass merchandised property and liability insurance plans. What are the advantages and disadvantages of such plans?

10. Discuss group legal expense insurance plans from the standpoint of extent, benefits, and future prospects.

11. List the primary statutory benefit plans. Describe each briefly. In your description discuss the origin of these plans and their present status.

12. What is meant by internal considerations in the design of employee benefit plans? Briefly explain the nature of these considerations.

12

Preretirement Counseling
and Early Retirement

As noted earlier, an increasingly important part of the risk manager's functions is that of working with employee benefits. One of the most important employee benefits is the company pension or retirement program. In response to the retirement problem more and more employers have established private pension programs and are undertaking what has been termed preretirement counseling. Preretirement counseling (PRC) programs, very often run by risk and insurance managers, have been instituted in industry with two main objectives: to ease the transition of the employee from active work into retirement, and to maintain the productivity and morale of the employee who is approaching retirement. Significant among the decisions affecting both the employee and the employer in achieving these objectives is that of early retirement, *i.e.*, developing sound policies dealing with the question of retiring workers prior to some norm of retirement age, such as age 65. This chapter deals with the main problems of retirement, early retirement, and PRC. The material is organized as follows:

1. The retirement problem

2. Productivity and the older employee

3. Productivity and resistance to retirement

4. Adjustment to retirement

5. Problems and trends in early retirement

6. Preretirement counseling programs

THE RETIREMENT PROBLEM

Retirement presents many challenges to modern society in general and to employers in particular. In important respects the retirement phenomenon presents both economic and psychological problems. Economic problems arise because more and more retired persons in society must be maintained by the working population. The number of retired persons, now about 10 percent of the U.S. population, is growing, and the proportion of working population is declining. In general this phenomenon is caused by increased longevity, early retirement, and delayed entry into the labor force by young persons who have been remaining in school for longer periods than formerly. Among the problems faced by employers concerning the retirement problem are rising costs of pension programs, scarcity of skilled labor to replace early retirees, and productivity and morale of both young and aging employees. Younger employees tend to favor early retirement policies since it increases promotion opportunities, but the cost of this policy can be great.

The income status of the aged is not an encouraging one. About 30 percent of those individuals over 65 live in poverty, compared to 10 percent of persons younger than age 65. An important cause of this is unemployment among the aged, who are faced with declining opportunities for work. After retirement many older workers' savings are soon exhausted and their main asset, the home, becomes more and more costly to maintain. Social Security and private pension incomes are not rising fast enough to offset the indicated adverse trends.[1]

Thus the older worker may be expected to resist retirement unless pensions are adequate.

An important problem of retirement also lies in the difference in life expectancies between men and women. In 1968 in the United States there were 6 aged women for each 4 aged men and the discrepancy was widening. By 1990 it is expected that there will be 170 aged women for each 100 aged men. At birth the life expectancy for men and women in the United States is 67 and 74, respectively.[2] Since fewer women are protected under private pension programs than men, and since women who are protected generally earn less than men, their economic status during retirement is generally much poorer than for men. Women who are dependent upon their husband's social security or private pension also usually receive smaller than adequate pensions.

Psychological problems of retirement have been evident, although they are not so well documented as economic problems. For example, there are a number of indications that people do not always adjust well in retirement. The suicide rate is much higher for white males over 65 than for those under age 65.[3] It is commonly observed that many people have heart attacks, psychological breakdowns, and other physical disorders shortly after retirement; a condition related not so much to age as it is to unemployment. Such evidence appears to be associated with the fact that retired individuals often experience loss of self-esteem, because of loss of social status, lack of responsibility, and absence of daily routine which was associated with active work.

Employers' Response

Employers have recognized many of the implications of the retirement problem, both in their capacity as corporate citizens as well as members of a free enterprise system. Most employers have now established corporate pension programs. Many have established PRC programs to ease the adjustment of loyal workers once they have left active work. About half of all employers in one study had established programs for voluntary early retirement to accommodate those wishing to leave the work force before normal retirement age, generally age 65.[4] However, many employ-

---

[1] U.S. Senate Special Committee on Aging, *Economics of Aging: Toward a Full Share in Abundance*, Hearings, 91st Congress, 1st session, Part I — Survey Hearings (Washington: U.S. Government Printing Office, 1969), pp. 158–228.

[2] Herman B. Brotman, "Who Are the Aged: A Demographic View," address presented at the 21st Annual University of Michigan Conference on Aging, Ann Arbor, Michigan, August 5, 1968.

[3] James E. Birren, *The Psychology of Aging* (Englewood Cliffs, N.J.: Prentice-Hall, Inc., 1964).

[4] Mark R. Greene, H. Charles Pyron, U. Vincent Manion, and Howard Winklevoss, *Early Retirement: A Survey of Company Policies and Retirees' Experience* (Eugene, Ore.: University of Oregon, 1969), p. 20.

ers have viewed preparation for retirement as an individual responsibility and have taken no action, or only token action, to help prepare the worker for retirement.

As a way to reduce personnel costs some employers have compounded the problem of retirement by adopting employment policies prohibiting or discouraging the hiring of older workers, or of terminating workers prior to the time that pensions are vested in the worker. Such policies have made it difficult for workers who have lost their jobs to obtain new jobs; or, if they do so, to earn at the same wage level as previously. Not only do such workers suffer reduced incomes, but their accumulation of pension rights may be seriously impaired as well. For example, in one study of 115 male unemployed middle-aged managers and engineers from California, who had obtained new jobs after being unemployed for longer than 6 months, the average income dropped 15 percent. About 37 percent had to accept jobs in small businesses, compared to only 7 percent so employed previously. Significant changes in type of industry of employment occurred, although very few shifted geographical locations to find a job.[5]

In a 1970 study of unemployed engineers, prompted by the Institute of Electrical and Electronics Engineers, Inc., it was reported, regarding pension plans, ". . . they have a subtle influence on whether mid-age and older workers are retained in times of cutbacks. . . . Whether or not an employee is vested in his company's plan may play a large part in determining if he is terminated. The pension plan aspect also bears heavily on decisions concerning the hiring of mid-age and older

workers, because pension premium costs for them can be higher. Many corporations also include life insurance as a fringe benefit, and these premiums also go up with age."[6]

Some of employer response to the retirement problem has been taken in the belief that productivity declines with age. Some employers have considered ways to overcome resistance to retirement in order to "ease out" the older worker as gracefully as possible. These two factors are considered below.

PRODUCTIVITY AND THE OLDER EMPLOYEE

It has commonly been believed that productivity, morale, and general effectiveness of employees tends to decline with age. A presumption is made, directly or indirectly, that younger employees, almost by definition, are more desirable workers than older persons. Acceptance of this belief has created a major interest in early retirement as a means of getting rid of the older workers.

One considerable restraint to early retirement, however, is the high cost of providing pensions. Not only is there less time to accumulate funds for early retirement, but the funds that are accumulated will have to be spread over a larger number of retirement years. The net effect of these two factors is to reduce sharply the amount of the pension benefit payable for each year prior to normal retirement date. If the employer makes up the difference in retirement benefit by making special contributions to early retirees, the cost is considerable and may often be accompanied by re-

[5] Lee D. Dyer, "Implications of Job Displacement at Mid-Career," Industrial Gerontology (Spring 1973), pp. 38–46.

[6] John M. Kinn, "Unemployment and Mid-Career Change: A Blueprint for Today and Tomorrow," Industrial Gerontology (Spring 1973), p. 51.

ductions in wage increases or in other types of employee benefits whose value must be weighed against the values of early retirement.

In view of these problems it is advisable to examine carefully the validity of the presumption that older workers actually do, in fact, become less productive or generally less satisfactory than younger workers. Most of the scientific studies of aging refute the proposition that the aging worker necessarily becomes less productive than the young worker. Most students of the subject believe that some persons decline in ability more than others and that age ought to be studied not only chronologically but also functionally. For example, in one study it was reported that the best performing group was the older aged group who were allowed to work at a slower pace in a task in which new material was being learned. In this study older women showed more improvement than younger women if the speed of presentation of material was held down.[7]

In a review of major findings on this subject, Laufer and Fowler came to the following conclusions:[8]

1. Although strength declines with age, a worker who has been performing his job will be able to continue, barring some pathological condition.

2. Speed of reaction slows down with age, especially after age 60, but frequently performed tasks are less subject to aging effects than infrequently performed tasks.

3. Speed of performance slows down with age more than strength. Between age 20 and 60 speed tends to reduce about 50 percent, while strength is reduced only about 25 percent. If older workers are placed on a job in which he can move at his own pace he will likely be satisfactory.

4. Vision and hearing decline with age, but "in most jobs today in the United States the physical demands are well below the capacities of most normal aging workers."[9]

5. Older workers are different, but not as different as many think.

An important reason for the generally negative views taken of older workers stems from a type of sociological research in problems of the aging known as age structure analysis. In age structure analysis a cross sectional view is taken of all persons at different ages and comparisons are made. Thus, it has been found that older people are generally less well educated than younger people. This is due to rising educational standards over time, and a lag in the educational level of old behind young persons may exist for many years. Such a fact, of course, should not imply that as a person gets older he tends to decline in educational status, or in his intelligence (recognizing that education and intelligence are highly correlated). Yet such conclusions are commonly drawn and important policies are formulated based on them.

In describing this problem Reilly states,

These striking age differences in education have widespread ramifications throughout the society. Since comparatively few older people are well educated, few of them pos-

[7] Ross Stagner, "An Industrial Psychologist Looks at Industrial Gerontology," *Aging and Human Development*, Vol. 2 (February 1971), pp. 29–37.

[8] A. C. Laufer and W. M. Fowler, Jr., "Work Potential of the Aging," *Personnel Administration*, Vol. 34 (March 1971), pp. 20–25.

[9] *Ibid.*, p. 24.

sess those characteristics, typically valued in our culture, that are associated with high education. Thus, the less educated majority of older people are less likely than the few who are well educated to remain active; they are more likely to retire and less likely to belong to voluntary associations or to read or to want to learn more. They have lower incomes. They are distinctly less happy and less optimistic about the future; but at the same time they are less introspective and less ready to doubt their own adequacy as spouses or parents. They are more negative in their view of death and think about it more, although fewer of them are disposed to plan for it.[10]

It is not surprising that a negative view is sometimes taken of the aging worker. However, it should be recognized that the inherent ability of an older worker to adjust, to learn, and to create is not necessarily impaired by the findings, in age structure analysis, that older workers as a group, when compared with younger workers, do not measure up well. As Reilly stated,

The older worker's productivity shows no consistent decline. Scholarship is maintained at a fairly high level into old age. There is little evidence that aging brings sexual impotence. The typical older person seems to have a strong sense of his own worth, to minimize his self-doubts, and not even to regard himself as old . . .[11]

There is a fallacy in concluding that differences among age categories in society are *due* to the aging process. To take another example, it is often reasoned that because income of older workers is lower than that of younger workers, income tends to fall off after about age 45. Such is not the case. A

[10] M. R. Reilly, *Aging and Society* (New York: Russell Sage Foundation, 1968), p. 4.

[11] *Ibid.*, p. 7.

typical individual's income tends to rise throughout his career up until retirement. At the same time this person's income may fall below that of a younger person because the latter individual started at a higher beginning level. In still another area,

. . . studies appeared to show that achievement in various scientific and artistic fields reached a peak in the early years of life, although a more appropriate analysis showed peaks for most fields at age 40 to 49, or even later, with continuing performance thereafter. Here the fallacy arose through the use of published biographies of individuals of differing longevity. This method can give spurious weight to the productivity of the earlier years by excluding those potentially productive men who did not live long enough to fulfill their promise.[12]

Undoubtedly additional research into the aging process is desirable before any final conclusions can be drawn. The research method of "life cycle analysis" under which study is made of the changes that occur in human beings as they proceed from one stage in the life cycle to another, is sorely needed. It seems evident, however, that management's decisions about the aging employee should not be based on common stereotypes about the older worker's waning powers. Rather, consideration should be given to the characteristics of aging workers employed, the needs of the job, and other specific conditions within the firm, before policies on PRC, early retirement, and retirement programs are adopted. For example, the personnel needs of a coal mining firm and an electronic manufacturer are entirely different and appropriate policies about retirement should also be entirely different. In making retirement deci-

[12] *Ibid.*, p. 8.

sions the employer should recognize that older persons should be viewed as individuals and not solely as members of particular groups from which they derive certain attitudes, values, beliefs, customs, and modes of behavior. Older persons should not be viewed as undistinguishable members of a single homogeneous age group.

PRODUCTIVITY AND RESISTANCE TO RETIREMENT

Regardless of the particular preconceptions of the aging worker held by management, there is a general desire by management to avoid negative impacts upon worker productivity that might be traced to old age or to the worker's resistance to retirement. Resistance to retirement may not only be associated with poor productivity and efficiency of the aging worker himself, but also it may affect the productivity of other workers. For example, younger workers may leave the firm if older workers are allowed to remain on the job indefinitely, absorbing higher paid and more skilled jobs, preventing promotion of the younger worker.

Resistance to retirement may be associated with a number of factors. In a study in which one of the authors participated 230 active older employees in California, age 60 to 65, were interviewed. It was found that about 28 percent disliked the idea of retirement and tended to be in agreement with common negative stereotypes about retirement (low income, poor health, lack of status, etc.).[13] It was found that those workers who tended to have a negative attitude

toward their work, however, tended to be among those most highly resisting retirement. For example, nearly 54 percent of the workers expressing a low degree of satisfaction with their supervisor also resisted the idea of retirement. Only about 30 percent of this negative attitude group accepted or welcomed the idea of retirement.[14] It is possible that those who resist retirement, and who have all the fears associated with that resistance, tend also to have low morale, negative attitudes toward supervision, and hostile attitudes toward the employer.

It was found in the study that high resistance to retirement appeared to be most closely related to feelings among workers that they would experience poor health, low income, low living standards, and poor enjoyment of personal activities following retirement. Resistance to retirement was not associated with *current* incomes of the aging worker. It was somewhat surprising to discover in this study that workers in fair or poor health currently, and who perceived that they would not have good health in retirement either, resisted retirement, apparently not welcoming retirement as a chance to rest and recover.

The implications of the findings on resistance to retirement to the employer is, in general, that the employer should attempt to minimize resistance to retirement, whatever its causes. The best estimate is that about one-third of all aging workers apparently resist retirement, and are also heavily represented in a group with negative attitudes toward their employer and their job. (It is not known whether resistance to retirement causes negative attitudes, or whether negative attitudes causes resistance to retirement.) One way to attack this problem is through PRC, a practice

[13] Mark R. Greene, H. Charles Pyron, U. Vincent Manion, and Howard Winklevoss, *Pre-retirement Counseling, Retirement Adjustment and the Older Employee.* (Eugene, Ore.: University of Oregon, 1969), p. 77.

[14] *Ibid.,* p. 89.

which is being followed by a growing number of employers.

ADJUSTMENT TO RETIREMENT

In the 1968–69 study referred to previously, interviews were held with 416 retired and 232 active older workers in California. The main factors affecting adjustment to retirement were found to be retirement income, attitude toward health, belief in the stereotypes about retirement, number of retirement activities, attitude toward the company, and enjoyment of activities. These appear to be the crucial variables in predicting retirement adjustment.

The findings of this study appear to support the following conclusions: Better productivity and morale of the older active worker and subsequent improvement in retirement adjustment can be achieved if the worker (a) is not disenchanted with the idea of retirement, (b) has received accurate information about retirement and the income he may expect to receive, (c) has good physical and mental health, and (d) is encouraged to make plans, to expand the number of his interests, and to participate in various activities both before and after retirement. When these conditions are not present, the worker is likely to have a negative attitude toward his employer. The implications of this conclusion for the establishment of effective PRC programs is obvious.

PROBLEMS AND TRENDS IN EARLY RETIREMENT

An important trend in U.S. industry is the movement toward early retirement.[15] Labor union settlements in recent years have consistently provided for earlier retirement of union members. For example, as of 1967 over 70 percent of the members of the "big three" automobile worker unions retired before 65, up from 11 percent in 1957.[16] In the transportation industry the teamster unions have lowered the retirement age to 57 with no actuarial reduction. The Social Security System in the United States (OASDHI) has reduced the age at which covered persons may retire. For example, before 1956, age 65 was the earliest age at which workers could retire under OASDHI. In 1956 the retirement age for women was reduced to 62 (and in 1961 it was reduced to 62 for men) at an actuarial reduction in benefits of $\frac{5}{9}$ percent per month before age 65 (20 percent reduction for a full three-year early retirement). Widows of deceased workers may retire at age 60, with actuarial reduction in benefits. By 1964, 28 percent of the men in the United States between age 62 and 64 were receiving OASDHI benefits.[17]

As noted previously, early retirement may be costly, both for the employee and the employer. The employee is likely to receive a sharply reduced retirement income, a factor which will complicate his satisfactory adjustment in retirement. The employer may discover that he not only loses valuable skilled and experienced workers, but he may be subjective to pressures to supplement the retirement income of the early retiree. In the United States about 10 percent of the population is over 65.

[15] "Drift to Early Retirement," *Fortune* (May 1965), pp. 112–15.

[16] Willard E. Solenberger, International Union, UAW, address before the Fourth Annual Institute of Pension Planning Administration and Regulations, March 1968, from data prepared by the UAW Social Security Department, Februaary 1968.

[17] Lowell E. Galloway, *The Retirement Decision* (U.S. Department of Health, Education, and Welfare, Research Report No. 9, June 1965).

By the year 2050 this percentage is expected to be 16.[18] If it became universal, early retirement would mean that society would have to support a much larger group of dependent individuals than is now the case. Recognizing some of these problems, in 1977 the U.S. Congress was seriously studying measures which would lead to eliminating mandatory retirement ages. Several states have also considered such laws. In spite of this, early retirement in industry generally is denitely increasing as discussed below.

A mail survey of 1,072 male randomly selected early retirees from 73 companies in different industries throughout the United States was taken in 1969.[19] Information about early retirement practices was obtained from 186 firms. Early retirements was defined as retirement at or before age 62. Tests of retirement adjustment were given to all early retirees. Major findings of this study were:

1. In 1968, 48 percent of the salaried and 46 percent of the hourly paid workers retired at or before age 62. About 50,000 workers were retired that year from the responding companies.

2. In the previous 10 years 58 percent of the respondent firms reported an increase in early retirements, compared to 2 percent reporting a decrease and only 33 percent reporting no change.

3. Early retirement was at age 55 in 68 percent of the companies, at age 60 in 21 percent, at age 62 in 5 percent,

[18] George E. Rejda and Richard J. Shepler, "The Impact of Zero Population Growth on the OASDHI Program," *Journal of Risk and Insurance*, Vol. XL, No. 3 (September 1973), p. 315.

[19] Greene *et al.*, *Early Retirement*, pp. 14–21.

and at age 50 in 5 percent of the companies. Early retirement was permitted much more frequently in large firms (employing 10,000 or more) than in smaller concerns.

4. Nearly 20 percent of the companies encouraged, 76 percent neither encouraged or discouraged, and only 10 percent discouraged early retirement among their employees.

5. About 50 percent of the companies offered some type of financial incentive for early retirement. The most common method was to offer some sort of supplemental pension payment until a person is eligible for Social Security, reducing the pension payment thereafter. In about 25 percent of the cases the firms offered the same pension as if the worker had retired at normal retirement age. Nearly 85 percent of all responding employees indicated they had some income in adition to their employer pensions. Nearly 80 percent of the workers reported that their total retirement income was either "just enough" or "more than enough."

Several commonly held beliefs about early retirement are challenged by the above survey. Early retirement is far more extensive than previously believed, with age 55 being the most widely accepted minimum age for those workers electing early retirement. It seems clear that without financial assistance early retirement would not be as popular as it is. However, most retirees in this study reported that they had sufficient retirement income. Furthermore, most early retirees apparently are not seeking work although their health would permit it. Most early retirees are not forced out, by their employers, but rather, retire voluntarily (albeit with some financial encouragement to do so).

Finally, retirees have generally made a satisfactory adjustment in their new roles and the traditional stereotyped image of the aged person with low income, poor health, and with a bleak outlook does not apply to them. Those who had made plans before retiring were especially likely to have a good adjustment.

The implications of these findings in supporting PRC are important. Since advance retirement planning is apparently one of the important keys to satisfactory retirement, and since PRC definitely encourages such planning, it is clear that PRC programs should be offered if the personnel objectives discussed in this chapter are to be achieved. PRC programs should attempt to encourage planning and should try to create favorable attitudes toward retirement. In such programs companies should attempt to overcome negative stereotypes about the status of the aged, so that fear and apprehension about retirement will be reduced. PRC programs for those who will retire early are perhaps more important than for those who retire at the normal retirement age. This is true because more of the early retirees are in good health, are able to work, and are therefore more in need of meaningful activities to occupy their time than regular retirees. Furthermore, their retirement incomes may have a tendency to be lower than regular retirees for reasons mentioned earlier. Having an adequate income in retirement is perhaps the *sine qua non* of successful retirement adjustment.

PRERETIREMENT COUNSELING PROGRAMS

Previous comments have implied that the need for PRC programs is becoming increasingly recognized. A review of the literature reveals, however, that existing programs are relatively new and tend to be somewhat limited in nature. In general these programs began to appear in the United States only after World War II. For example, Inland Steel Corporation started PRC in 1950. In this program a letter was sent to the worker at age 55, an interview was carried out at age 60, and another interview at age 64 to review the worker's pension with him.[20] The University of Michigan and the University of Chicago began offering leadership training in PRC in 1950. The United Auto Workers (AFL–CIO) labor organization also developed a course in PRC.[21]

A study by the National Industrial Conference Board in 1964 revealed that of 974 companies surveyed, 65 percent had some type of PRC, but no attempt was made to define what was actually meant by "counseling."[22] A study by Wermel and Beideman determined that only about one-third of the 415 firms surveyed had comprehensive counseling, as opposed to a very limited variety of counseling confined largely to informing the employee about his pension rights.[23] Eastern firms had developed more comprehensive programs than western firms. Over half of the firms

---

[20] Don C. Charles, "Effect of Participation in a Pre-retirement Program," *The Gerontologist* (Spring 1971, Part I), p. 24.

[21] A description of these programs and a brief 10-year history of their operations is given by W. W. Hunter, "Pre-retirement Education," *Geriatrics*, Vol. 17 (1960), pp. 793–800.

[22] National Industrial Conference Board, *Study in Personnel Policy: Retirement of Employees*, No. 143 (New York: National Industrial Conference Board, 1966).

[23] Michael T. Wermel and G. M. Beideman, *Retirement Preparation Programs: A Study of Company Responsibilities* (Pasadena: California Institute of Technology, 1961).

had established them for less than five years.

Another study of the programs in 58 firms, undertaken in 1968, yields useful insights into the question of typical topics in PRC covered and the length of time devoted to them.[24] PRC programs from the 58 firms were from 9 basic industries. These firms employed approximately 600,000 workers. It was discovered that small firms (with less than 1,000 employees) generally do not have PRC programs. On the other hand about three-fourths of the large firms (over 5,000 employees) and one-third of the medium firms (1,000–5,000 employees) offered PRC to their employees. About half (48 percent) of the responding companies had limited PRC programs, counseling employees mainly about financial matters relating to the company pension plan. Of the remaining companies, only 12 offered intensive counseling covering more extensive topics. These 12 programs, each had been established at least 5 years, were in firms with mandatory retirement policies, generally were conducted on company time, involved at least 6 hours of counseling, commenced at age 60 or earlier, and were in firms maintaining personnel counseling records. These 12 programs were selected for more intensive review.

Topics covered in comprehensive PRC programs included pension and Social Security benefits, personal financial planning, health after retirement, housing and living accommodations, leisure time activities, retired-work activities, and legal aspects of retirement. Ten of the 13 companies employed full- or part-time counselors. A few reported that they carried on post-retirement programs, as well as PRC. Most indi-

cated the existence of special policies for older workers such as job redesign, extended sick leave, medical examinations, and options to work less than 40 hours a week.

Objectives for PRC programs were stated as to ease the employees into retirement with the least amount of discord, and in the most equitable way possible, and to acquaint employees with the values of retirement and how to use and retain these values. The most frequently mentioned benefits of the program were to encourage planning by the employee, better morale, and to make information available to the employee.

Most of the 12 programs start when the employee is age 55. Four provided a combination of group and individual counseling. Attendance was voluntary and estimates of attendance ranged from 30 to 100 percent. Half of the companies invited spouses, and between one-third and one-half of the spouses attended. The majority of firms provided between 6 and 15 hours of counseling, although in some the time extended to more than 20 hours. In only one case did the union participate in conducting the program.

G. G. Fillenbaum conducted a study of 6,000 nonteaching personnel at a large university. In this group no PRC existed at the time of the survey, which was taken to learn the extent of interest in such a program. The university had compulsory retirement at age 65.[25] Fillenbaum discovered that (a) age 45 appears to be the age at which the most individuals began to be receptive to PRC, (b) interest in PRC increases as educational level and occupational

[24] Greene et al., Preretirement Counseling, Ch. 4.

[25] G. G. Fillenbaum, "Retirement Planning Programs — At What Age and for Whom?" The Gerontologist (Spring 1971, Part I), pp. 33–36.

status decreases, (c) although almost all respondents agreed that preretirement planning was a good thing, only 66 percent reported thinking about retirement, and only 28 percent have actually made any plans. Most planning that has been done is carried out by those with higher educational levels. Planning is not related to age, sex, or race. Those with lower occupational and educational status and with long service records worry the most, but do the least planning, about retirement.

It may be concluded that PRC as it currently exists in U.S. industry is not usually comprehensive in nature, dealing as it does primarily in financial matters. Neither does the typical firm start PRC as early as they should for maximum impact. Most companies do not begin PRC until age 55, although strong interest is evident among employees as early as age 45. There is no evidence that PRC is aimed particularly at lower occupational levels in the firm, although it is this group that appears to need PRC the most and is most interested. Small firms tend to ignore PRC almost entirely. Nevertheless, interest in PRC seems to be growing, and with increasing proportions of aged persons in the population, it will likely continue this growth.

Effectiveness of PRC

A number of studies have shown that PRC programs can be effective in achieving their objectives of reducing anxiety, creating positive effects on personal adjustment before and after retirement, encouraging planning and conveying information.[26] Charles proved that a course in preretirement subjects had definite effects in increasing a

worker's concern about retirement, and his involvement in organizations conducting various activities serving retirement.[27] The course was given in 1967 to 5 groups of workers in different industries with an average age of 57. The course consisted of seven 2-hour lecture, film, and discussion sessions. It covered legal and financial planning, insurance, health and welfare, psychological aspects of retirement, use of leisure time, and continuing education. Individual counseling was available but infrequently requested. Tests were administered before and after the course was given in order to evaluate its effect. Personal attitudes showed a definite change, with participants having a more positive attitude toward their own competency, self-worth, and financial acumen. Interestingly enough, Charles found that no evidence emerged to suggest the necessity of differentiating the group by occupational or educational levels, by marital status, by sex, or by other criteria.[28]

In the 1968 California study the attitudes of older workers and retirees in 8 organizations, 4 with PRC programs and 4 without such programs, were analyzed.[29] The 8 organizations contained 4 medium- (1,000–5,000 employees) and 4 large- (over 5,000 employees) sized groups. Two were in insurance, 2 in aviation and aerospace, and 4 in communication. Employees and retirees were selected at random from different skill levels and were interviewed personally. The final sample was composed of 232 older employees, 214 regular retirees, and 202 early retirees.

---

[26] Hunter, "Pre-retirement Education," p. 798.

[27] Charles, "Effect of Participation," p. 24.

[28] Ibid., pp. 27–28.

[29] Greene et al., Pre-retirement Counseling, Ch. 2.

By comparing the answers of persons who had had PRC with those who had not, it could be determined whether significant differences occurred between the 2 groups and by inference, whether or not PRC accounted for the differences.

Among the major findings of this study were: (1) there were few significant differences in the replies when these replies were compared solely on the basis of whether the organization had a PRC program. This apparently stemmed from the fact that only about 57 percent of the employees in companies with PRC programs actually attended. It is clear that there is no spillover effect to nonattendees from PRC programs.

(2) For those retired individuals who had taken PRC, compared to those who had not, significant differences (at the 5 percent level of significance or greater) occurred in the following:[30]

a. adjustment in retirement as measured by a test of inner happiness and contentment

b. length of time required for retirement adjustment

c. extent of plans made for retirement

d. holding of negative stereotypes about retirement

e. discrepancies appearing in the expected levels of retirement income

f. perceived adequacy of retirement income

g. number of retirement activities undertaken

All of the above differences showed positive effects of PRC. Thus, those with PRC had better adjustment, required less time for adjustment, made more plans, held fewer negative stereotypes about retirement, had more accurate perceptions about their future retirement income, were more satisfied with their retirement income, and were involved in more retirement activities than those without PRC. In addition there was some evidence, but not conclusive evidence, that PRC tended to have a favorable effect on 4 of 7 variables tested relating to employee morale. An employee who had participated in PRC had a tendency to be more favorably inclined toward his company, toward his job, toward his supervisor, and toward the concept of mandatory retirement, than those who had not had PRC.

In the study, comparisons were made between (a) retirees who had taken PRC and found it helpful, and (b) retirees who had taken PRC and reported that it was not very helpful. There was little significant difference between these 2 groups in their replies to 19 indices of retirement adjustment. In other words, most of the differences found were between those who had taken PRC and those who had not.[31] Thus, exposure to PRC, whether or not the participant said he found it helpful, was proved to be better than no exposure at all.

From Table 12–1 it may be observed that in general PRC participants found the topics presented either helpful or very helpful. After a person is retired he tends to report that certain topics, such as pension and social security benefits, are more helpful than is reported by older active workers approaching retirement. The older worker, on the other hand, is more concerned

---

[30] Ibid., pp. 137–56.

[31] Ibid., p. 178.

TABLE 12–1
Attitudes of Employees and Retirees
on PRC Topics

PRC Topic	Percentage of Those Finding It Helpful or Very Helpful	
	Employees	Retirees
Pension benefits	86.5	94.3
Social Security benefits	88.8	94.1
Other financial planning	88.6	94.2
Health maintenance	94.8	97.2
Housing and living accommodations	86.7	81.6
Retired work activities	91.4	84.3
Legal aspects of retirement	97.2	89.2
Mental health	95.5	88.4

SOURCE: Greene *et al.*, *Pre-retirement Counseling*, pp. 268–70.

with housing, retirement activities, legal aspects, and mental health than the retiree.

When asked about the age at which PRC should commence, about half of both employees and retirees in this study favored 1 to 5 years prior to retirement. However, there is a tendency for more retirees to favor PRC at an earlier age, such as 11 years or more before retirement, than is true of employees. Apparently after one has retired he perceives the need for a longer period of PRC, perhaps so he can do a more thorough job of planning than would otherwise be possible. This finding tends to agree with the participants' responses in the study by Fillenbaum, reported above, where respondents favored age 45 as a time for beginning PRC.

SUMMARY AND CONCLUSIONS

1. Increasingly, the risk and insurance manager may be asked to deal with problems and policies relating to retirement, pensions, and preretirement counseling (PRC). Not only are the number and proportion of older persons in society increasing, but private industry appears to be taking more responsibility for preparing older workers for retirement so as to increase the productivity and morale of the work force.

2. There is a definite trend toward early retirement in the U.S. Studies indicate that about half of the labor force is now retiring before age 65. In various ways early retirement is costly. These costs can be reduced through better planning, both by the employee and the employer. Available evidence suggests that declining productivity of the aged worker may not be the significant factor in justifying early retirement that it is commonly thought to be. Productivity of the worker does not necessarily decline with age, but may actually increase.

3. Some evidence exists that PRC may tend to reduce resistance to retirement. Strong evidence exists to indicate that PRC is associated with successful adjustment to retirement. Those who resist retirement tend to make a poor adjustment during retirement later on. Resistance to retirement is associated with employees who have morale problems and negative attitudes toward the employer. Employers who are successful in reducing resistance to retirement are more likely than others to experience better morale and higher productivity among their workers.

4. Major factors associated with successful retirement adjustment are satisfactory retirement income, good health, participation in retirement activities, holding an interesting job prior to retirement, and having a favorable attitude toward the job and the supervisor. PRC tends to develop positive attitudes about retirement and to overcome negative stereotypes commonly held by workers concerning their image of the status of retirement. Strong evidence exists to support the conclusion that adequate retirement planning is associated with successful retirement adjustment.

5. More and more industrial firms, especially large companies, are establishing PRC programs. More often than not these programs are not comprehensive in nature but are confined to pension and other financial matters. The best evidence suggests that to be most effective, PRC should be comprehensive in nature, and should commence at least 10 years prior to retirement. PRC seems to hold the greatest interest for those with lower educational levels. In field studies it was found that PRC sessions are attended by only about half of those eligible.

6. PRC programs tend to produce significant results, when compared to those who are not exposed to it, in the following: increased amount of retirement planning, satisfactory adjustment in retirement, reduced length of time required for adjustment, absence of negative sterotypes about retirement, perceived adequacy of retirement income, and number and enjoyment of retirement activities. In addition, PRC programs appear to have some positive influence on the morale of older workers.

7. Major topics covered in PRC programs include pension and Social Security benefits, financial planning, health maintenance, housing and living accommodations, retired work activities, legal aspects of retirement, and mental health.

8. There are many unanswered questions about PRC, early retirement, and retirement adjustment which need further research. For example, more study needs to be made as to the cost of early retirement and the extent to which PRC may reduce this cost by reducing retirement resistance. How can PRC be made more effective? Should the trend toward early retirement be slowed? How can employee benefit programs be altered so as to facilitate and improve retirement adjustment?

QUESTIONS FOR DISCUSSION

1. The retirement problem has both economic and psychological dimensions. Give illustrations of each.

2. Why does age structure analysis tend to encourage the belief that older persons are inadequate in various ways? What type of analysis is needed for adequate explanations of the aging process?

3. An author stated, "Stereotypes often held about the aged are not valid. Older people are *not* cranky, do *not* have a hostile attitude, are *not* constantly complaining about how they are treated, etc. Age should not be a crucial variable in judging performance." Do you agree? If not, how should the performance of a worker be judged?

4. Do you think it is true that some employers tend to discharge workers just prior to the time that their pension rights become vested, as has sometimes been charged? Why might an employer be tempted to do this? Explain.

5. Give some examples of how the U.S. Government may be encouraging early retirement; delayed retirement. Explain.

6. It is stated that the early retirement decision is evidence of risk aversion in the individual. Do you agree? Why, or why not?

7. Is one likely to find that discontented workers are most likely to be looking forward to retirement as a way of escaping an unsatisfactory situation? Why, or why not?

8. Various studies of retired persons have revealed the typical retiree to have a satisfactory income, to be in reasonably good health, to be active and relatively happy. This conflicts with the "disengagement theory" of retirement under which a retiree is said to gradually withdraw from active life. Analyze a retired person you know and indicate which, if any, of the above two classes he falls.

9. Discuss possible reasons for the finding that planning for retirement tends to be associated with good retirement adjustment.

10. Should the risk manager become involved in PRC? Why, or why not?

11. How common is early retirement? In your opinion what factors are operating to encourage early retirement? discourage it?

12. What topics should be covered in a comprehensive PRC program as opposed to the typical program now offered in industry?

13. A medical doctor was quoted as follows: "You can expect a happy productive old age for 80 percent of the population if they prepare themselves in their 40s and 50s . . . Preparing is a matter of not getting fat, regular exercise, moderate use of alcohol and no smoking." Comment. In what way is the doctor's comment too limited?

14. In 1973 an article stated, in part, "Arthur Reed, age 112, of Oakland, California, still rides a bicycle. Until he was 98 he rode his bike 150 miles each year to Fresno where he farmed cotton. Charlie Smith, 130, thought to be the oldest living American, retired at 113 when people thought he was too old to climb trees picking a citrus grove. He sells soft drinks outside his little house in Bartow, Florida. Larry Lewis, 106, runs 6.7 miles a day in San Francisco's Golden Gate Park. Pablo Picasso turned out as much high-priced art up to his recent death at 91 as ever, just as Titian did at 99. Pablo Casals remains the world's outstanding cellist at 96. Dr. Paul Dudley White, the heart specialist, practiced his heart specialty and rode his bike in Boston at 86. Retired Supreme Court Justice Tom C. Clark, at 86, sat as a federal district judge, a new job for him." What do these men apparently have in common? What lessons for analysis of problems of the aging does their experience suggest?

13

Formal Retirement Plans

Pensions and related plans constitute a major employee benefit, and require expertise on the part of the risk manager or other executive who may have responsibility for them. A principal objective of this chapter is to present some of the basic theory relating to pensions in a form that is relevant to the work of the risk manager. The following specific topics will be considered:

1. Pension design
   a. Eligibility
   b. Retirement age
   c. Benefits
   d. Finance

2. Costs

3. Tax considerations

4. Employee Retirement Income Security Act of 1974

5. Profit-sharing plans

6. Employee stock ownership trusts

7. Self-employed and related plans

8. Tax-sheltered annuities

9. Other types of deferred compensation

10. Administrative considerations

11. Multiemployer plans

Inability to work because of the aging process is a problem that faces all members of the labor force whether they are employed by another or self-employed. Much uncertainty surrounds the determination of when work will become severely limited or impossible because of age. This fact is true even though a firm or organization may have a well-defined retirement age, since many persons may wish to continue working beyond that time and will seek work where age is not a limiting factor. For the self-employed the time of retirement is largely self-determined, although in many instances it may depend on chance events.

Even greater uncertainty surrounds the adequacy of income that may be available from social insurance or other sources during times when work may be impossible, unavailable, or undesirable for a variety of reasons. During periods of strong inflation the uncertainty is greatly exacerbated and planning for adequate income becomes particularly difficult. Another factor contributing to the need for retirement income is the fact of increased longevity. Over a period of 60 years life expectancy at birth has increased approximately 25 years, and it is estimated that by 1980, 10 percent of the population will be over 65.

The fact of increasing need might not in itself present difficulty if the resources to meet it were readily available. Unfortunately, this is often not the case. Studies of the assets owned by persons over age 65 reveal that few families are able to accumulate assets of substantial magnitude over their working lifetimes. There are a number of reaons why such accumulation is difficult. For some, long periods of disability may have prevented the establishment of a savings program. For virtually everyone an increasing tax burden, along with participation in a society calling for fairly high levels of consumption, has resulted in difficulty in planning adequately for old age.

That most individuals and families do not provide adequately for income during old age has been increasingly recognized. The response to the need has been largely through the establishment of formal pension plans. Although plans of various types have existed in the United States for approximately 100 years, starting with the American Express Company plan in 1875, the major development of these plans has occurred since World War II.[1] A principal reason for the postwar development was the freezing of wages and the resulting emphasis on employee benefits and the bargaining requirement placed on employers.[2] The rapidity of development between 1950 and 1973 is demonstrated in Tables 13–1 and 13–2. Private plans have shown the greatest increase in terms of persons covered, although governmental programs, except for railroad retirement (see Table 13–1) have

[1] Only nongovernmental plans are considered in this chapter. On the governmental side, old age and survivors insurance (OASI) represents a substantial public retirement plan. This plan also has disability and medical benefits (OASDHI).

[2] See Chapter 11, p. 236.

shown substantial increases also. Table 13–2 provides a somewhat more detailed picture of private pensions and deferred profit-sharing plans. The number of plan beneficiaries has increased by 1,262 percent, while the amount of benefit payments has shown an even more substantial increase.

PENSION DESIGN

Retirement benefits in the private sector may be provided in a number of ways and under various auspices. For the self-employed persons individual retirement plans may be established. For most employed persons group provision is normal and the groups may be, for example, employees of a common employer, members of unions, employees of more than one employer (multiemployer groups), or employees of nonprofit organizations. Whatever the nature of the group, any plan designed to be of benefit to the members of the group upon their retirement must be carefully designed. The principal design elements are similar to those for other employee benefit plans and are: (1) eligibility, (2) retirement age, (3) benefits, and (4) finance.

Eligibility

Not all employees actively at work when a pension plan is installed are automatically enrolled in the plan. The process of determining who may be enrolled and the qualifications they must possess is the process of determination of eligibility. The reasons for establishing eligibility rules are mainly to lower the administrative costs of the plan by eliminating employees who may be subject to high turnover or whose attachment to employment may be somewhat tenuous. Thus, hourly workers, part-

TABLE 13–1
Number of Persons Covered by Major Pension and Retirement Programs
in the United States (000 Omitted)

	Private Plans		Government-Administered Plans			
Year	With Life Insurance Companies	Other Private Plans	Railroad Retirement	Federal Civilian Employees†	State and Local Employees	OASDI‡
1930	100	2,700	1,400	432	800	—
1935	285	2,525	950	483	1,000	—
1940	695	3,565	1,349	745	1,552	27,622
1945	1,470	5,240	1,846	2,928	2,008	40,488
1950	2,755	7,500	1,881	1,873	2,894	44,477
1955	4,105	12,290	1,876	2,333	3,927	64,161
1960	5,475	17,540	1,654	2,707	5,160	73,845
1961	5,635	18,440	1,662	2,855	5,309	76,295
1962	5,770	19,370	1,643	2,943	5,654	78,953
1963	6,060	19,990	1,664	2,985	5,940	81,035
1964	6,710	20,350	1,650	3,069	6,330	83,400
1965	7,040	21,060	1,661	3,114	6,780	87,267
1966	7,835	21,640	1,666	3,322	7,210	91,768
1967	8,700	22,280	1,641	3,499	7,594	93,607
1968	9,155	22,860	1,625	3,565	8,012	95,862
1969	9,920	23,410	1,620	3,627	8,303	98,012
1970	10,580	23,900	1,633	3,625	8,591	98,935
1971	10,880	N.A.	1,578	3,596	9,079	100,392
1972	11,545	N.A.	1,575	3,737	9,563	103,976
1973	12,485	N.A.	1,582	4,030	10,050	108,268
1974	13,335	N.A.	1,592*	4,057*	10,845	108,854

Note: These data represent various dates during the year, since the fiscal year of the plans are not necessarily the same. Trends from year to year are not affected. The number of persons covered include survivors or dependents of deceased workers or beneficiaries as well as retired workers. Retirement arrangements for members of the armed forces, and provisions for veterans pensions, are not included in these data. The number of persons included in each category includes some duplication due to persons being covered by more than one plan, such as being currently covered in their place of employment, but also having vested benefits from previous employment, as well as Social Security in most instances. A survey sponsored by several government agencies indicated that the unduplicated number of persons not yet retired and covered by private plans was 27,500,000 at year-end 1972. Duplication cannot be removed from the figures for private plans with life insurance companies, but is estimated to be as much as 10%.

N.A. — Not Available.

* Estimates.

† Includes members of the U.S. Civil Service Retirement System, the Tennessee Valley Retirement System, the Foreign Service Retirement System, and the Retirement System of the Federal Reserve Banks, which includes the Bank Plan and the Board of Governors' Plan.

‡ Includes persons employed with coverage in effect at year-end including the self-employed, workers retired for age or disability, dependents of retired workers and survivors of deceased workers, who are receiving periodic benefits.

SOURCE: *Compiled by the Institute of Life Insurance.* Reproduced from *Life Insurance Fact Book*, New York: American Council of Life Insurance, 1976, p. 36.

time employees, and employees near retirement may be excluded. The formal eligibility rules designed to accomplish the above objectives may involve statements about (1) minimum age, (2) maximum age, (3) years of service, (4) earnings requirement, and (5) employment classification.

Pension plans that have been established through collective bargaining usually do not include a statement about minimum age. In other plans where such a statement may be found the age specified must be below age 30, if the plan is to meet the requirements of the internal Revenue Service.[3] ERISA limits the use of a maximum age as a part of eligibility requirements. In the case of defined contribution plans, no maximum age may be used. For defined benefit plans, a maximum age can be employed, but, in any event cannot be less than age 60 if age 65 is assumed to be the normal retirement date. One reason for having such a requirement is that it is quite expensive to establish pension benefits for persons within a few years of retirement. Earning requirements are not particularly common in pension plans, although in some cases it may be required, for example, that earnings exceed the amount subject to Social Security tax in which case plan benefits must be integrated with Social Security. Employment classifications were once common in pension plans with a typical provision being that only salaried employees could participate. Such classifications are less often used now because of Internal Revenue Service requirements.

[3] The requirements of ERISA about minimum age have been incorporated into the Internal Revenue Code. ERISA will not permit a minimum service requirement beyond one year or age 25 whichever comes later. There is an exception to the rule for institutions with immediate vesting. See Appendix B, pp. 600–601.

As was indicated above, if pension plans are to enjoy certain tax advantages, they must be qualified with the Internal Revenue Service. Requirements of particular interest to eligibility apart from those already mentioned are:

1. It (plan) must cover 70 percent or more of all employees or if the plan requires employee contribution, and if 70 percent or more of all employees are eligible to participate in the plan, at least 80 percent of those eligible must elect to participate.

2. It (plan) will benefit such employees as qualify under a classification set up by the employer and found by the Internal Revenue Service not to be discriminatory in favor of officers, stockholders, or highly compensated employees.[4]

Either of the above two requirements must be met if the plan is to qualify.[5]

Retirement Age

Although the question of retirement age may arise in certain ways in many employee benefit programs, it has particular relevance in retirement plans. Of relevance are such concepts as normal retirement age, early retirement age, and late retirement age. Decisions about these matters are important to both the employer and the employee. For the former the amount and pattern of cost will be affected and for the latter the amount of the benefit.

The concept of a normal retirement age is generally accepted in business, although not universally. Sixty-

[4] Everett T. Allen, Jr., Joseph J. Melone, Jerry S. Rosenbloom, *Pension Planning*, Third ed. (Homewood, Ill.: Richard D. Irwin, Inc., 1976), pp. 102–103.
[5] *Ibid.*, p. 102.

TABLE 13–2
Private Pension Plans with Life Insurance Companies in the United States

Type of Plan	Number of Plans	In Force at Year End			Payments into Plans in Year (000,000 Omitted)	Pension Payments During Year	
		Number of Persons Covered	Total Reserves (000,000 Omitted)	Separate Account Reserves (000,000 Omitted)		Number of Persons Receiving Payments	Pension Payments (000,000 Omitted)
1972							
Deferred Annuity Group Annuities	13,540	1,835,000	$13,025	N.A.	$ 910	560,000	$ 610
Deposit Administration Group Annuities*	20,290	7,535,000	29,275	N.A.	2,860	640,000	920
Individual Policy Pension Trusts	123,970	1,325,000	3,725	N.A.	660	75,000	95
Group Permanent Life Insurance	6,560	270,000	800	N.A.	85	25,000	25
HR 10 (Keogh) Plans	135,480	270,000	650	N.A.	145	3,000	5
Tax-sheltered Annuities	74,210	580,000	1,575	N.A.	380	12,000	10
Other Plans	27,790	620,000	3,250	N.A.	465	45,000	50
Total	401,840	12,435,000	$52,300	$ 9,800	$ 5,505	1,360,000	$1,715
1973							
Group Annuities*	38,420	10,210,000	$43,750	$ 8,700	$ 4,265	1,285,000	$1,670
Terminal Funded Group Plans	1,640	95,000	1,225	50	295	50,000	60
Individual Policy Pension Trusts**	145,420	1,685,000	4,750	200	845	90,000	125
HR 10 (Keogh) Plans	N.A.	295,000	750	50	145	5,000	5
Tax-sheltered Annuities	N.A.	675,000	1,925	450	425	15,000	10
Other Plans	N.A.	645,000	3,650	100	470	50,000	55
Total	—	13,605,000	$56,050	$ 9,550	$ 6,445	1,495,000	$1,925

1974

Type of Plan							
Group Annuities*	42,920	10,555,000	$46,825	$ 7,950	$ 5,200	1,330,000	$1,915
Terminal Funded Group Plans	2,310	110,000	1,450	50	240	50,000	75
Individual Policy Pension Trusts**	160,810	1,810,000	5,200	200	970	110,000	140
HR 10 (Keogh) Plans	N.A.	345,000	925	100	200	5,000	5
Tax-sheltered Annuities	N.A.	770,000	2,250	450	570	20,000	35
Other Plans	N.A.	680,000	4,125	100	540	55,000	60
Total	—	14,270,000	$60,775	$ 8,850	$ 7,720	1,570,000	$2,230

1975

Type of Plan							
Group Annuities*	54,090	10,325,000	$54,500	$10,900	$ 6,735	1,440,000	$2,160
Terminal Funded Group Plans	3,250	145,000	1,950	60	340	85,000	110
Individual Policy Pension Trusts**	176,410	1,960,000	5,675	440	1,075	100,000	140
HR 10 (Keogh) Plans	N.A.	450,000	1,300	150	345	10,000	10
Tax-sheltered Annuities	N.A.	935,000	3,150	790	750	20,000	35
Individual Retirement Accounts	N.A.	440,000	375	40	355	—	—
Other Plans	N.A.	720,000	4,750	140	650	60,000	65
Total	—	14,975,000	$71,700	$12,520	$10,250	1,715,000	$2,520

Note: Data are revised.
N.A. — Not Available.
* Includes Immediate Participation Guarantee and Deposit Administration Plans.
** Includes Group Permanent Plans.
SOURCE: *Life Insurance Fact Book*, New York: American Council of Life Insurance, 1976, p. 39.

five is a common retirement age, but may be modified by being stated as a right given to the employee to retire at that age but that mandatory retirement will not take place until, say, age 68.[6] Most pension plans now permit retirement at ages younger than the normal retirement age (early retirement), but rarely younger than 55. If the employee chooses early retirement the size of the pension will be reduced, since the full benefit will not have accrued until the normal retirement age and for the additional reason that the benefit will be paid over a longer time. The concept of early retirement has elicited considerable interest in recent years, and some employers seeking to encourage employees who desire to do so to retire early have set up pension plans that pay a larger amount for early retirement than would be the case if the full actuarial reduction had been applied. Late retirement after the normal retirement age is also possible in many plans, although typically the employer must give his consent. One reason for permitting late retirement is to give the employer some flexibility in planning his staffing needs. The benefit amount may not in some cases be any different from what would have been paid at the normal retirement date, while in some plans the amount is increased in accordance with actuarial calculations. Sometimes employees are permitted to accrue additional credits.

Benefits

The primary purpose of pension plans is to provide income to employees who are no longer working for a particular firm or institution because of ad-

vanced age. Various reasons are given for making such a provision on the part of an employer. It may be argued that employers have a moral obligation to provide for employees who have given faithful service over a number of years, but who, because of age, are no longer able to work efficiently. Another rationale is that pensions represent deferred wages and that part of the total compensation paid to employees while actively at work consists of payments made by the employer toward a pension to be made available at retirement age.

The amount of the income benefit is determined by the application of a formula. Benefit formulas may be classified as (1) defined contribution or (2) defined benefit. A defined contribution formula is one that requires a definite contribution, typically expressed as a percentage of wage or salary. The amount of the benefit ultimately paid to the retired employee is not known in advance but will depend on the size of benefit purchased by the various contributions that have been made. A feature of this type of formula is that earlier years of service weigh more heavily than later years. A defined benefit formula is one in which the size of the benefit is determined, and the amount of the contribution varies depending on how the benefit is defined. Defined benefit plans often have formulas expressed in terms of both earnings and service. Thus, one possibility might be that the benefit would be a percentage of annual earnings multiplied by the number of years of service. It is possible for the formula to relate to earnings only with no mention of service. Such a formula might provide for compensation based on earnings at retirement or on an average of earnings during the last 5 years before retirement. Some formulas do not relate to earnings but base the benefit on service by stating that X

---

[6] Sixty-five or ten years of participation, whichever occurs last, is defined by ERISA as normal retirement age. See *Ibid.*, p. 27. Recent action (fall 1977) by Congress may result in age 70 as the normal retirement age.

dollars per year will be paid at the retirement date for each year of service. A maximum number of years is usually stated. Still another possibility is to not relate the benefit in any specific way to either earnings or service. The formula might provide a flat benefit to employees who on retirement have served a specified number of years. As an additional feature these formulas may integrate or make allowance for benefits available under Title II of the Social Security Act. (Old Age and Survivors Insurance.)

In addition to income benefits, pension plans may provide death and/or disability benefits. In certain individual plans, such as those funded with retirement income policies, life insurance is an important feature. In plans involving retirement annuities life insurance is not an integral part of the plan, but a death benefit in the form of a return of accumulated premiums is available. Once an annuity has been entered upon, some plans provide death benefits through a refund provision or through a guarantee of a specified number of payments. Group plans and trust fund plans do not often provide death benefits, although postretirement death benefits in the form of survivor options are becoming more common. One possibility is for the employee to select a joint and survivor annuity with the survivor receiving a somewhat smaller payment than when both parties were alive.

In some instances disability benefits are offered as a part of a pension plan, although the more typical treatment of disability is to treat it in a separate contract. When disability benefits are a part of the retirement plan, the treatment of them is fairly variable. The usual objective is to provide income during disability and to protect pension rights.

Finance

The financing of pension plans involves answering three questions: (1) Who is to pay for the plan? (2) When are the payments to be made? and (3) Who agrees to husband (manage) the funds and pay benefits?

Who Pays for the Plan?

Pension plans are paid for through contributions made by employers or employees or both. The amount of the contribution is determined by the benefit formula adopted in defined benefit plans and by the percentage of wage selected in defined contribution plans. These amounts in turn reflect managerial decisions about the suitability and adequacy of whatever plan has been adopted. Although employees may contribute to pension plans, the trend over the years has been toward larger and larger employer contributions with a number of plans on an employer-pay-all basis. In 1950 employers contributed approximately 85 percent of the funds and by 1973 this figure had increased to approximately 92 percent. The amount of money contributed to the plans has increased considerably over the years, reflecting the larger number of persons now covered by pension plans. The pros and cons of employer vs. employee contributions were discussed in Chapter 11 in relation to employee benefits other than pensions. In the pension field, to the extent that retirement income is to be regarded as deferred compensation, it would seem appropriate for the employer to make the entire contribution.

When are the Payments to be Made?

The timing of contributions depends on the method selected by the employer for the funding of the benefits. Three funding methods are possible: (1) terminal funding, (2) split funding, and (3) advance funding. Terminal funding is a procedure whereby the employer sets aside the amount of money necessary to provide pension benefits to the employee at the time he (the employee) retires. The funds thus contributed may be used as a single premium to purchase an annuity for the employee from an insurer. The principal advantage of this method of funding is that it gives the retired employee considerable benefit security. Among the disadvantages are the fact that the total amount of the contribution is larger than would be required under advance funding and the pattern of contributions will be variable and the impact on the firm might be substantial in any one year depending on the number of persons retiring. Further, terminal funding is possible only with noncontributory plans and it does not give active employees very much benefit security.[7]

Split funding occurs when two different agencies are involved in the administration of pension assets. An example of this type of funding arises when a trustee is used to administer pension contributions for active employees, and an insurer is used to pay benefits to retired employees through an annuity purchased by a transfer of funds from the trustee to the insurer.

Advance funding is the method most often used by private pension plans to accumulate the funds needed for financing the plan. This method is one in which the employer (and in contributory plans the employee) makes periodic payments to a pension fund or plan well in advance of the retirement of an employee. Thus, contributions

[7] With the passage of ERISA, terminal funding is no longer possible with qualified plans.

may be made, say, monthly on behalf of an active employee from the time he is eligible under a pension plan until his retirement date. Advance funding has a number of advantages. Of particular significance is the fact that the contributions required for each employee are smaller than for any other type of funding. A further advantage is that these contributions are spread evenly over the lifetime of a plan, and that the method easily accommodates the possibility of employee contributions. Also, advance funding plans are typically qualified with the Internal Revenue Service, and the tax advantages thus gained are advantageous to the employer. There are not many disadvantages to advance funding. For some firms contributions to a pension fund may well represent an opportunity cost, and they may be reluctant to commit assets that might earn more if employed differently. An additional, but perhaps minor, disadvantage is that qualifying a plan with the Internal Revenue Service involves inconvenience and expense.

Who Manages the Funds and Pays Benefits?

Broadly speaking funds accumulated for pension purposes are either managed by a trustee (trusteed plans), deposited with an insurer (insured plans), or are managed by a combination of the two. Tables 13–1 and 13–2 show that noninsured plans are far more common in the United States than insured ones. Life insurers, corporate fiduciaries, and individuals serving as trustees are known as funding agencies. These agencies carry out their responsibilities to provide pension benefits through the use of funding instruments. In trusteed plans the funding instrument is the trust agreement. In insured plans the funding instruments are insurance and annuity contracts of various types. Combination plans typically involve placing some of the contributions in a trust fund and placing the balance with an insurer in payment of premiums for life insurance or annuity contracts.

Trusteed Plans

The use of trust agreements as the basic instrument for funding private pension plans is the oldest of the various methods that have been used to provide pension benefits. Basically a trusteed plan is a plan where a trustee under the terms of a trust agreement has the responsibility for receiving, investing, and administering funds designed to provide benefits under a pension plan. In addition to his investment and managerial duties the trustee is typically responsible for "the direct payment of benefits to eligible participants under the plan."[8] Further, for a plan to be categorized as trusteed all or a high percentage of the plan assets must be under the control of the trustee.

One of the chief advantages of a trusteed plan is its flexibility. Funds are not allocated to particular employees, which permits the use of any type of benefit formula.[9] In contrast to insured plans, trusteed plans make no guarantees about mortality and interest. The trustee's responsibility is mainly to manage the assets under his care in a reasonable and prudent way. He is not responsible for the adequacy of the fund in terms of whether enough money is available to provide the benefits specified in the pension plan. The problem of adequacy falls to the employer.

[8] Allen, Melone, and Rosenbloom, *Pension Planning*, p. 211.

[9] Although any type of formula may be used, defined contribution formulas are fairly rare and definite benefit formulas are typical.

Insured Plans

Insured plans can be conveniently grouped into (1) individual policy plans, and (2) group plans. The relative importance of these plans in terms of number of plans, number of persons covered, number of persons receiving payments, and similar items is shown in Table 13–2. Individual policy plans are more frequent than group plans, but the number of persons covered is greater under the group plans.

Individual policy plans are most often used by small firms. It has been estimated that approximately "65 percent of all insured corporate plans currently in force use individual contracts at least in part, to fund benefits."[10] The insurance contracts typically used in individual plans are ordinary life, life paid-up at 65, endowment at 65, retirement income, and retirement annuity. The benefits provided in these contracts were discussed in Chapter 9. The most popular of these contracts for individual policy plans that are fully insured is the retirement income contract. This contract requires evidence of insurability and may be difficult to use in cases where insurability is a problem, although recent, more liberal underwriting rules have reduced the difficulties considerably. Since the retirement annuity does not require evidence of insurability, it is often used for funding purposes. If individual policy plans are to be fully qualified by the Internal Revenue Service, it is necessary for the employer to create a trust and transfer to a trustee the responsibility for holding the individual insurance policies. This requirement has given rise to the term "pension trust" as a way of describing individual policy plans that fall in this category. Under fully qualified

[10] Allen, Melone, and Rosenbloom, *Pension Planning*, p. 135.

plans ordinary life, paid-up at 65, and endowment at 65 contracts are not used, since the face amount of such contracts might have to be as much as 100 times the monthly pension benefit. Contracts of this type are usually used in conjunction with a conversion fund. The cash value of an ordinary life contract might, on the average, produce 35 percent of the amount needed as a single premium to produce the pension benefit. The balance of the benefit would come from the conversion fund.

Group insured pension plans include such funding instruments as group permanent insurance, group deferred annuities, group deposit administration plans, immediate participation guarantees, group single premium annuity contracts, individual account contracts, and contracts wherein the insurer provides investment services only. Group permanent life insurance contracts involve a master contract with the employer but the benefits are similar to those provided by individual ordinary life contracts and may be used with a conversion fund. Group deferred annuities have the advantage of not being heavily regulated and not subject to excessive underwriting controls, but their relative inflexibility compared to deposit administration plans has caused them to decline in popularity over the years. The benefits provided are similar to those available under individual deferred annuities.

Group deposit administration plans were developed by insurers as a means of competing with the flexibility inherent in trusteed plans. Under a deposit administration arrangement an employee does not have an annuity purchased for him until retirement actually takes place. There is no limitation on the type of benefit formula that may be used. Contributions sent to the insurer were typically mingled with the insurer's general investments, although now separate accounts are fairly widely used. A separate account offers the advantage of more flexibility in investments and the opportunity to decide about the appropriate mix of fixed income and equity securities. Although deposit administration plans carry some guarantees such as guaranteed annuity purchase rates and guaranteed interest rates for a specified time period, the number of guarantees is not great in recognition of the greater flexibility offered. This is illustrated by the fact that since the employer largely controls the amount and timing of contributions, there is a limit to the kind of guarantees that insurer can give about the adequacy of the fund for the provision of benefits.

Competitive demands have led to a number of variations on the deposit administration theme. Most of the changes are in the direction of even greater flexibility with insurer guarantees virtually eliminated. An example is the group immediate participation guarantee contract in which there are no guarantees about annuity purchase and interest rates, and where pension payments may be charged against the fund in place of the actual purchase of an annuity. An investment facility contract is another example of a desire for maximum flexibility. In these contracts the insurer is not obliged to purchase annuities and benefits are not guaranteed under contract.

Variable Annuities

Historically, and to a considerable extent today, annuity payments (benefits), once begun, did not change in amount. With the advent of strong inflation, annuities of a fixed amount have become increasingly inadequate as a way of providing retirement income. As a way of coping with inflation the concept of a variable annuity has been introduced. In this type of annuity the amount of the benefit will depend on the behavior of a segregated fund invested in equity securities. Variable annuity contracts may be classified as (1) immediate variable annuities purchased with a single premium; (2) deferred variable annuities purchased with a single premium; and (3) periodic payment variable annuities. The meaning of these expressions is similar to that for nonvariable annuities.

The procedure for determining the ultimate benefit received under a variable annuity involves two steps. First, the premium paid or purchase price of the annuity is converted into annuity units, by determining at the time the premium is paid the monthly benefit purchased in dollars. If, for example, the monthly annuity purchased is $750 and the value of 1 annuity unit as determined by the equity fund is $15, the premium paid has purchased a monthly benefit of 50 annuity units. This number of units remains fixed, but the value over time will change depending on the value of the fund. The second step, then, is to determine each time the annuity is paid its value in dollars, which in turn depends on the value of an annuity unit at that particular time.

Employers who make use of variable annuities for pension planning, often combine fixed amount annuities with variable annuities. A fairly common procedure is to allow the employee to determine the percentage of the total contribution (employee's as well as employer's) that is to go toward each type of annuity. The final pension will then be the sum of the benefits provided by the nonvariable and variable portions.

Although variable annuities offer the possibility of protection against inflation, they are not a perfect vehicle for this purpose. Stock prices and dividends do not necessarily parallel increases in living costs and may go in the opposite direction. Employee dissatisfaction may arise for this reason. The uncertainties inherent in variable annuities from the employee point of view have tended to damper acceptance of them. Other factors impeding growth have been the general feeling on the part of labor unions that they prefer annuities indexed to the cost of living, and the disadvantage to the employer of not being able to reap the benefit of investment gains.[11]

COSTS

Of particular importance to the employer are the costs associated with a pension plan. These costs cannot be known in advance and of necessity are only estimates. The true or ultimate cost of a pension plan "cannot be determined until the last retired worker dies and all benefit payments under the plan are thereby terminated."[12] Put in slightly different terms, the ultimate cost of a pension plan is equal to the sum of actual benefits paid and actual administrative expenses less actual investment earnings.[13] Estimates of cost depend on estimates of these factors.

The issues and problems surrounding the costs of pensions, as they impact the employer and the employee are perhaps best understood by distinguishing between costs associated with annuities that may be purchased from an insurer as a way of funding and providing a benefit, and costs that arise during the accumulation phase of pensions in trusteed noninsured arrangements using defined benefit plans.

[11] *Ibid.*, p. 207.
[12] *Ibid.*, p. 71.
[13] *Ibid.*, p. 217.

Annuity Costs

Annuities may be purchased for purposes of providing retirement income on either a group or individual basis. Since recent tax legislation has provided income tax deductions for individual retirement savings plans, considerable interest has developed in individual tax-deferred annuities. In this discussion no effort will be made to cover all aspects of annuity costs but rather individual annuities of the type that might be used for tax-sheltered plans will be taken as an example of the cost considerations that arise.

The monthly amount of an annuity received while life persists (annuity rent) depends on the annuity rate (price per $1,000 of proceeds) charged by the insurer and on the amount of money available to be used as the purchase price (investment accumulation or cost of the annuity assuming no refunds).[14] The annuity rate varies among insurers on both a guaranteed and current basis, as does the amount of investment accumulation. An individual wishing to maximize the amount of the annuity he will receive must give consideration to both the rate and the accumulation.

In a recent study of 42 insurers (15 mutual and 27 stock),[15] the variability of annuity rents and rates was studied in some detail. On the assumption that the investment accumulation was obtained by depositing with an in-

surer $100 per month for 20 years, it was found that annuity rents varied in a manner illustrated by Table 13–3. Of interest, also, is the variation exhibited in annuity rates. On a guaranteed basis rates varied from $6.11 per $1,000 of proceeds to $7.67 per $1,000 and on a current basis from $7.81 to $9.91. Investment accumulations also showed considerable variability. The highest accumulation on a guaranteed basis was $37,734 and the lowest $27,343. Comparable figures on a current basis were $54,403 and $36,743. Insurers offering the best rates on a current basis did not necessarily offer the best guarantees and vice versa. Also large insurers often performed less well than smaller ones.

The nature of the variability led Greene et al to conclude that it paid the consumer to shop around when purchasing annuities. It also appears because there is not a very strong correlation between annuity rates and investment accumulations that the consumer should consider accumulating funds with an insurer that displays superior investment performance and then transferring the accumulation to an insurer with superior guarantees for annuity rates.

Funding Methods for Trusteed Noninsured Plans

Assets out of which pensions will ultimately be provided are generated by costs that have been determined by actuarial computations and have been translated into contributions by an employer[16] to a fund managed by a fiduciary. By a funding method (or actuarial

[14] Typically the purchase price is made up of the accumulations resulting from contributions to a defined contribution plan.

[15] Mark R. Greene, John Neter, and Lester I. Tenney, "Annuity Rents and Rates — Guaranteed vs. Current," A paper presented before the Annual Meeting of the American Risk and Insurance Association, Boston, Mass., August 1976. The 42 insurers represented about 51 percent of the total assets of all U.S. life insurers in 1974.

[16] Employees may contribute too, although most industrial plans are noncontributory. However, it can be argued that the employee's contribution has in effect been contributed by the employer, since the source of the employee contribution is wages that come from employment.

TABLE 13–3
Annuity Rents

	Guaranteed	Current	Current ÷ Guaranteed
Top-ranking insurer on guaranteed rent (No. 37)	$289.42	$422.26	1.46
Lowest-ranking insurer on guaranteed and current rent (No. 22)	177.73	314.47	1.77
Top-ranking insurer on current rent (No. 43)	234.10	512.48	2.19
Average Rent	222.46	416.96	1.87

SOURCE: Mark R. Greene, John Neter, and Lester Tenney, "Annuity Rents and Rates — Guaranteed vs. Current," A paper presented before the Annual Meeting of the American Risk and Insurance Association, Boston, Massachusetts, August 1976, p. 9.

cost method) is meant a way of developing pension plan costs so an appropriate accumulation (required reserve) will be available at the normal retirement age.[17] Among the reasons for adopting appropriate funding methods are the need to provide better benefit security through a reasonable estimate of the assets needed at retirement to provide the pension specified by the benefit formula designated in the pension plan, and by the requirement of the tax laws that tax deductions be supported by a recognized funding method.

The employer's liability for a pension for an employee at a normal retirement of age 65 may be represented by the formula

Pension liability = (annual benefit) $\ddot{a}_{65}^{(12)}$

where $\ddot{a}_{65}^{(12)}$ is the present value of a life annuity due of $1 per annum payable monthly. Establishment of funding methods to accomplish the goal represented by this liability is complicated by the fact that when a pension plan is in-

[17] Barnet N. Berin, *The Fundamentals of Pension Mathematics* (Chicago, Society of Actuaries, 1972), p. 6. The formulas used in the following paragraphs are based on this source.

stalled many employees will have been employed for a number of years and a past service liability will be present. This liability must be taken into account in establishing procedures for developing cost formulas.

There are five funding methods that are in fairly common use by actuaries. They are: (1) unit credit; (2) individual entry age normal; (3) entry age normal, frozen initial liability; (4) attained age normal, frozen initial liability; and (5) aggregate cost. The first two of these methods will be discussed briefly. A discussion of the other methods may be found in books on pension mathematics.[18]

Unit Credit

The unit credit method is perhaps best used in situations where a definite benefit can be specified for each year. It is not unusual in pension plans for a benefit to be defined as a percentage of each year's salary or a flat dollar amount may be named. In determining costs under the unit credit method, it is necessary to compute the future service

[18] *Ibid.*

cost and the accrued liability. The appropriate formulas are:

$$(FSC) = (FSB)\,\frac{N_{65}^{12}}{D_x}$$

and

$$(AL) = (AB)\,\frac{N_{65}^{(12)}}{D_x}$$

where

FSC = future service cost

FSB = future service benefit arising from service in current year.

AL = accrued liability

AB = accrued benefit

$\dfrac{N_{65}^{(12)}}{D_x}$ = present value of a life annuity due of $1 per annum for a person aged x payable monthly with the first payment at age 65. The N and D are commutation symbols.[19]

The total liability is obtained by adding the results of the above formulas for all active and retired participants.

For many pension plans the accrued liability is not funded immediately but over a number of years. Therefore, assets in the fund will not necessarily cover the accrual. The unfunded liability is defined as the difference between the assets and the accrued liability. Since actuarial estimates of the unfunded liability may not be precisely realized, actuarial gains (or losses) may occur. Actuarial gain is defined as the difference between the expected unfunded liability and the actual unfunded liability.

Individual Entry Age Normal

For pension plans that have benefit formulas based on final pay the in-

dividual entry age normal procedure may be the costing method of choice. It involves the concept of normal cost or the level annual (or possibly monthly) premium that is needed to fund the pension benefit over the working lifetime of the employee.[20] Normal cost, then, may be viewed as a life annuity due payable annually or possibly monthly to the trust fund, from the time an employee enters employment until he reaches age 65. Making use of commutation symbols the formula for normal cost may be written as[21]

$$(NC) = (PB)_{65}\,\frac{N_{65}^{(12)}}{N_{EA} - N_{65}}$$

where NC = normal cost

(PB)$_{65}$ = pension benefit at age 65.

N = commutation symbol. See Appendix F. EA = entry age.

Although the normal cost is computed as the amount that it would be necessary for an employer to contribute on behalf of the employee from the time he entered employment until retirement, it is clear that no pension plan may have existed at the time some of the employees began their employment. Thus, at the time a plan is installed there will be an accrued liability. This liability may be viewed as the difference between the present value of the projected benefit at the attained age of the employee and the present value of future normal cost payments. In formula terms

$$(AL) = (PB)_{65}\,\frac{N_{65}^{(12)}}{D_{AA}} - (NC)\,\frac{N_{AA} - N_{65}}{D_{AA}}$$

where AA = attained age

[19] For further explanation see Appendix F, page 619.

[20] *Ibid.*, p. 9.

[21] The formula is the one given in *Ibid.*, p. 9.

All of the symbols in this equation have been defined previously or may be found in Appendix F, page 619.

In making estimates of cost actuaries must make some assumptions about the magnitude of the factors that enter into cost determination. These factors are (1) number employees retiring, which in turn is affected by mortality rates among active employees, rate and duration of disability, turnover rates, and rate of retirement; (2) mortality rates among retired lives; (3) expenses; and (4) interest. The choice of assumptions can have an important affect on the incidence of costs.[22]

Not everyone who participates in a pension plan while actively at work will receive benefits at the normal retirement age. Some will die before reaching their retirement years, some will leave employment, others may become disabled, and still others may retire earlier or later than normal. Mortality estimates are taken from tables that have been prepared for the purpose and usually the same table is used for active and retired lives. The most recent annuity table is the 1971 Group Annuity Table, which is now used by a number of actuarial firms. Previous tables that were widely used were the 1937 Standard Annuity Table and the 1951 Group Annuity Table. Turnover rates pose a difficult problem for actuaries, although some assistance is available from published tables. Factors affecting turnover are age composition of the group, length of service, economic conditions, personnel policies, and working conditions.

Although benefits constitute the principal cost of a pension plan, the expenses of administering the plan must also be taken into account in an assessment of total cost. If individual plans or group contracts are adopted, a loading

[22] Allen, Melone, and Rosenbloom, *Pension Planning*, p. 81.

for administrative and other expenses is a part of the premium. In trusteed plans the employer must be prepared to pay, in addition to administrative expenses, such items as actuarial fees, legal expenses, and investment costs.

Other things being equal, the higher the rate of interest assumed in the present value calculations involved in the funding methods previously discussed, the smaller the contributions required of the employer will be and the larger the role of investment earnings in the paying of benefits. Thus, the actuary has the task of selecting an interest rate that will accomplish employer objectives and at the same time be consistent with the actual level of interest rates over a long period of time. In addition, selection of the rate should involve consideration of the size of the fund, the investment policy of fund trustees, and other factors that may be related to investment earnings.

TAX CONSIDERATIONS

A strong incentive for the establishment of pension plans is the favorable income tax treatment available to qualified plans. For the employee the tax advantages are: (1) contributions made by the employer on behalf of the employee are not taxable to the employee as income until benefits are received upon retirement; (2) a death benefit paid on the death of an employee and received by a named personal beneficiary does not need to be included as a part of the deceased's estate, to the extent it represents employer contributions, when listing the assets for federal estate tax purposes; (3) a lump-sum distribution that comes about because an employee leaves his job or that is made after the employee reached age 59½ will receive favorable tax treatment. For the employer the advantages are: (1) contributions made to the pension plan are deductible as a business expense; and (2) income derived from investing the contributions is not taxed until benefits are paid.[23]

Space does not permit a detailed consideration of all the requirements that must be met before the Internal Revenue Service will qualify a plan.[24] In general the coverage requirements specified by the Internal Revenue Code must be met, as well as certain contribution and benefit requirements. As an ex-

[23] For a detailed discussion, see *Ibid.*, 101.

The value of a tax shelter in long-term savings programs is illustrated by the following example:

Assumption (1): Saver is in 34% marginal income tax bracket. Annual interest return of 7.5% is available. After-tax return of 5% is earned.

	Without Tax Shelter	With Tax Shelter
Annual amount saved, payments made in advance	$ 100	$ 100
Taxes due currently	34	0
Available for savings	$ 66	$ 100
Value of annual savings in 20 years		
at 5%	$2291	
at 7½%		$4655
Percent advantage by using tax shelter		
$(\frac{4655}{2291} \times 100)$	103%	

Assumption (2): Funds are removed in a lump sum and saver is in same tax bracket as before (34%).

Funds removed from savings	$2291	$4655
Taxes due (34%)	0	1583
Spendable balance	$2291	$3072
Percent advantage by using tax shelter		
$\frac{3072}{2291}$ (× 100)	34%	

[24] See *Ibid.*, p. 102–17 for a summary of the requirements.

ample of the latter, the plan must not discriminate in favor of officers, stockholders, or highly compensated employees (prohibited group). Other requirements are that the plan must be in writing and must be communicated to employees. With minor exceptions contributions may not be diverted by the employer until all plan liabilities have been satisfied. The plan must be permanent and the benefits definitely determinable. Also, the plan must meet other requirements such as vesting set forth by ERISA (Employee Retirement Income Security Act of 1974).

Once benefits under a pension plan have been distributed to the employee, various tax requirements apply. Two general principles may be stated as they relate to the federal income tax: (1) the usual monthly pension distributions upon retirement are taxed in accordance with the annuity rules set forth in the Internal Revenue Code; (2) lump-sum distributions, *e.g.*, once paid as a result of severance of employment, may be partly treated as a long-term capital gain with the remainder subject, assuming certain rules have been met, to a special income-averaging device. The precise tax treatment in any particular situation should be related to the contingency that brings about the distribution and any variations from the general rules should be noted. Some specific situations that may arise in addition to those previously mentioned are income taxation of death benefits, taxation of disability benefits, and taxation of plan termination benefits.[25]

EMPLOYEE RETIREMENT INCOME SECURITY ACT OF 1974

The Employee Retirement Income Security Act has been referred to a

[25] See *Ibid.*, pp. 119–33.

number of times in this and preceding chapters. Since its impact on employee benefit plans has been substantial, it is appropriate to consider it in more detail.

Although formal pension plans have been in existence for a number of years, their effectiveness has, in many instances, been disappointing. In the past many plans were inadequately funded with the result that promised benefits could not be paid. The widespread lack of adequate vesting often meant that it was difficult for an employee who changed jobs to accumulate an adequate pension.[26] Even for employees who did not shift from one employer to another, loss of a job shortly before retirement could result in a loss of a pension. Recognition of these and other problems led Congress to study the problem of retirement income security. The result of the study was Public Law 93–406, better known as the Employee Retirement Income Security Act of 1974 (ERISA). In discussing its reasons for believing the law was necessary, Congress cited the following facts:

1. Benefit plans have grown rapidly and substantially in recent years in terms of size, scope, and numbers of employees.

2. The economic impact of these plans and their operational scope has become increasingly interstate.

3. A large number of employees and their dependents rely heavily on benefit plans for continued well-being and security.

4. Benefit plans can be regarded as being affected with national public interest.

5. Benefit plans are important factors in employment stability and successful industrial relations.

6. They are also important in commerce because of the interstate character of many of the activities that surround them such as actions of interstate employers and employee organizations.

7. Benefit plans often make use of the mails and other instrumentalities of interstate commerce in carrying out their activities.

8. Since adequate safeguards for the protection of employees and their beneficiaries did not exist, it was desirable to create such safeguards in order to promote the general welfare and free flow of commerce.[27]

The Act consists of four titles: I. Protection of Employee Benefit Rights, II. Amendments to the Internal Revenue Code Relating to Retirement Plans, III. Jurisdiction, Administration, Enforcement; Joint Pension Task Force, etc.; and IV. Plan Termination Insurance. The contents of these titles are summarized in Appendix B (page 597 to 607) with particular reference to Titles I and II.

PROFIT-SHARING PLANS

For a number of years profit-sharing plans have been available in a number of industries as a part of the employee benefits program. Broadly speaking any

---

[26] By vesting is meant the transfer of ownership to the pension plan participant of the employer's contributions to a retirement income plan, if the employee ceases to be employed by a particular employer before qualifying for retirement benefits. ERISA offers three alternative vesting procedures. Each qualified plan is required to select one of them. See Appendix B.

[27] Public Law 93-406, 93rd Congress, H.R.2 (September 2, 1974), p. 4–5.

plan where contributions are based on business profits may be described as a profit-sharing plan. Benefits may be paid currently in cash or stock or they may be deferred or they may be paid on a partly cash and partly deferred basis. In this chapter interest will center on those plans that provide deferred benefits and are established as alternatives to formal pension plans or as supplements to them.

As in the case of pensions, profit-sharing plans, if they are to possess certain tax advantages, must be qualified by the Internal Revenue Service, which defines profit-sharing plans as follows:

A profit-sharing plan is a plan established and maintained by an employer to provide for the participation of his profits by his employees or their beneficiaries. The plan must provide a definite predetermined formula for allocating the contributions made to the plan among the participants and for distributing the funds accumulated under the plan after a fixed number of years, the attainment of a stated age, or upon prior occurrence of some event such as layoff, illness, disability, retirement, death, or severance of employment.[28]

The requirement set forth by the Internal Revenue Service for qualification are similar to those discussed for pension plans.[29] Of particular interest are the rules surrounding contribution requirements and the distribution of benefits.[30]

It is not essential for a profit-sharing plan to have a definite contribution formula that has been determined

in advance. Nevertheless, since a plan to qualify, must be thought of as permanent, the employer is required to make substantial and recurring contributions. A consequence of this type of flexibility is that contributions can be adjusted to the current financial position of the firm and its capital needs.[31] Even when a discretionary formula is used it is not unusual for minima or maxima to be stated. One reason for imposing a maximum rate of contribution from profits might be to protect stockholders from too heavy an inroad on the rate of return on capital.[32] The Internal Revenue Service places a limit on the amount of contributions from profis that may be deducted on an employer's income tax return. The basic limit is 15 percent of the annual compensation of employees participating in the plan, although this is subject to carry-over provisions. Thus, it is possible for deductions to be higher or lower in a given year than the basic 15 percent. However, this variation is subject to an overall annual limitation of 25 percent of payroll currently covered.

When distribution of benefits is deferred under a profit-sharing plan, the vesting rules of the Employee Retirement Income Security Act apply. The disposition of nonvested employer credits presents a somewhat different problem for profit-sharing plans than for pensions. In the latter case nonvested funds serve to reduce employer contributions. This rule does not apply to profit-sharing plans so a possibility exists that discrimination will occur in favor of higher salaried employees, since funds remaining in the plan would increase benefits for those that remain. Presumably Congress believes that this does not present a serious problem under existing ERISA

---

[28] Reg 1.40–1(b) (1) (ii).

[29] For a discussion of details see Allen, Melone, and Rosenbloom, *Pension Planning*, pp. 287–310.

[30] Only the employer's contribution will be considered here. Employee contributions are rare in profit-sharing plans.

[31] Allen, Melone, and Rosenbloom, *Pension Planning*, p. 290.

[32] *Ibid.*, p. 291.

rules. In general profit-sharing plans have allocation formulas that determine how forfeited benefits are to be distributed among the remaining participants. After a specified number of years some plans will permit withdrawal of a portion of vested benefits and some plans have loan provisions. Another aspect of fund distribution that may have advantages for many participants is that a trustee of a profit-sharing plan may be empowered under the trust agreement to purchase life and health insurance contracts and annuities.

Since profit-sharing plans may be used in lieu of formal pension plans, some interest attaches to the relative merits of the two approaches to retirement income. Among the advantages to the employer of profit-sharing plans are: (1) the close connection between improved productivity and sharing in increased profits; (2) the possibility of substantial benefits to participants over the long run; (3) flexibility of contributions and lack of a necessity to fund a definite benefit; (4) relative ease with which a wide variety of benefits such as life insurance, loans, and withdrawals may be provided. An employer may prefer a formal pension plan if (1) he believes a definite retirement benefit is more effective in promoting employee morale; (2) he wishes to provide a reasonably substantial benefit for employees who begin their employment at a relatively advanced age; (3) he wishes to integrate pension benefits with those provided under Social Security; (4) he wishes to provide a substantial death benefit.[33]

The principal disadvantage of a profit-sharing plan from an employer's

viewpoint appears to be the possibility of higher cost because of more rapid vesting and because the employees share in favorable investment experience. Some of the possible disadvantages of a pension plan are the relative inflexibility of contribution and benefit (for defined benefit plans) formulas and the fact that pension adequacy is not directly linked to employee performance.

EMPLOYEE STOCK OWNERSHIP TRUSTS (E.S.O.T.)

Closely related to profit-sharing plans are Employee Stock Ownership Trusts. These trusts may be used to provide retirement income in a manner similar to profit sharing and other pension plans and can be qualified under the relevant provisions of the Internal Revenue Code. Employee stock ownership trusts have been defined as "deferred compensation trusts created by corporations for the exclusive benefit of employees."[34] The corporation may make tax deductible contributions to the trust for the benefit of employees to the extent of 15 percent of payroll that relates to those employees.

A distinctive feature of E.S.O.T.'s is that the trust is created to invest its assets in employer stock or employer real property. It must also make its distributions to employees in employer stock. Further, an employee stock ownership trust is permitted to borrow money to acquire stock or other assets.[35] Many of these features are in direct contrast to profit-sharing plans where stock invest

---

[33] In profit-sharing plans "the premium for life insurance must be less than 50 percent of the total accumulations credited to a participant's account." This may be a disadvantage to older employees in that a lower level of death benefit will be produced, see *Ibid.*, p. 305.

[34] Robert A. Frisch, *The Magic of E.S.O.T.: The Fabulous New Instrument of Corporate Finance*, (Rockville Centre, N.Y.: Farnsworth Publishing Company, Inc., 1975) p. 7.

[35] *Ibid.*, p. 8.

ments in employer stock are limited to 10 percent of the assets of the profit-sharing trust. Further, distributions of profit-sharing plans are usually in cash, and contributions can be made only out of profits. Also profit-sharing plans cannot borrow money to purchase stock or other assets.

Among the advantages to the corporation of an employee stock ownership trust are that cash flow, working capital, and net worth may be improved through the sale of stock to the trust and that a market is provided for the stock. A possible advantage to the participant is the possibility of having the trust buy stock from the participant in lieu of a 303 redemption. Among the disadvantages of an E.S.O.T. are possible stock dilution, poor performance of the employer's stock, and shift in the control of the plan.

If an E.S.O.T. is qualified by the IRS, it must meet requirements about eligibility, vesting, funding, and similar matters. Shares in an E.S.O.T. are typically allocated by formula, which may be based on length of service and compensation or both, or the allocation may be based on the relationship between the employee's salary and total covered payroll. At retirement the employee receives stock. It may be possible for the employee to sell it to the trust, the corporation, or to other stockholders. The stock received is only taxed when the retired employee sells the stock at a price above the E.S.O.T. cost basis and then only as a capital gain.[36]

SELF-EMPLOYED AND RELATED PLANS

Prior to 1962 self-employed persons (predominantly sole proprietors and partners), although able to provide pen-

[36] For further details see *Ibid*.

sions for themselves, could not enjoy the tax advantages available to employed corporate stockholders. In 1962 with the passage of HR10 (Keogh Plan) certain tax advantages were extended to the self-employed and these advantages were further increased with the passage of ERISA,[37] which also provided tax advantages to employees whose employers did not provide a formal pension plan.

Self-employed

A self-employed person may deduct from his income for tax purposes 15 percent of his earned income, but in no event more than $7,500, as a contribution to a pension plan for himself, if he has also established a qualified pension plan for his full-time employees. Generally the same funding techniques used in corporate plans are available to plans established under HR10.[38]

Individual Retirement Savings

As was previously noted, income tax deductions are available to individuals. ERISA provides as a deduction "amounts paid in cash during the taxable year by or on behalf of such individual for his benefit: (1) to an individual retirement account . . . ; (2) for an individual retirement annuity . . . ; (3) for a retirement bond."

By an individual retirement account is meant "a trust created or organized in the United States for the exclusive benefit of an individual or his beneficiaries," but only if the trust meets certain requirements. Space does

[37] See discussion on page 606. Note that for the self-employed, lump-sum distributions do not qualify for long-term capital gains treatment. Further, death benefits are included as a part of the gross estate.

[38] Public Law 93-406, 93rd Congress, H.R.2 (September 2, 1974) p. 132.

not permit detailing all of the requirements here. Among them are that "no part of the trust funds will be invested in life insurance contracts, the interest of an individual in the balance of his account is nonforfeitable, and the assets of the trust will not be commingled with other property except in a common trust fund or common investment fund."[39]

By an individual retirement annuity is meant "an annuity contract, or an endowment contract (as determined under regulations prescribed by the Secretary or his delegate) issued by an insurance company."[40] As in the case of the individual retirement account, certain requirements must be met. Three of the 5 requirements listed are: "(1) the contract is not transferrable by the owner; (2) the entire interest of the owner is nonforfeitable; (3) the entire interest of the owner will be distributed to him not later than the close of his taxable year in which he attains age 70½, or will be distributed in accordance with regulations prescribed by the Secretary or his delegate, over (A) the life of such owner or the lives of such owner and his spouse, or (B) a period not extending beyond the life expectancy of such owner or the life expectancy of such owner and his spouse."[41]

A retirement bond "is a bond issued under the Second Liberty Bond Act, as amended, which by its terms or by regulations prescribed by the Secretary or his delegate under such Act" meets 5 requirements specified in the law. Examples of the requirements are that the bond be nontransferable, that it provides for payment of interest or investment yield only on redemption, and that it provides that no interest or investment yield is payable if the bond is redeemed within 12 months after the date of its issuance."[42]

The amount allowable for a deduction for retirement savings "to an individual for any taxable year may not exceed an amount equal to 15 percent of the compensation includible in his gross income for such taxable year, or $1,500 whichever is less."[43] Some other limitations such as deductions are not permitted after age 70½, and no deductions are allowed if the individual was a participant in certain other plans such as qualified pension and related plans.

TAX-SHELTERED ANNUITIES

For employees of qualified charitable organizations or of public school systems tax deferred annuities are available as a way of sheltering certain amounts of income from current taxation, although taxes must be paid after the annuity is entered upon. An advantage of annuities of this type is that they serve to shift part of the income tax burden to a period in life (retirement) when presumably income and hence the income tax to be paid will be lower. Another advantage is that they may be used to supplement basic retirement plans in which the employee may be participating.

Certain requirements must be met before the tax shelter becomes available. The institution involved must be of the type contemplated by the law (*e.g.*, charitable organization or public school system). The prospective annuitant must be an employee and not an independent contractor. The employer is required to purchase the annuity and the annuitant's rights must be nonforfeitable unless he/she fails to pay future

[39] *Ibid.*, p. 131.

[40] *Ibid.*, p. 132.

[41] *Ibid.*, p. 132.

[42] *Ibid.*, pp. 136–137.

[43] *Ibid.*, p. 130.

premiums. The premium paid must not exceed the exclusion allowance. If it does, the excess will be taxed.[44]

Since the amount of income sheltered cannot exceed the exclusion allowance, it is essential to understand how the allowance is defined. The definition given in the Internal Revenue Code is "an amount equal to the excess, if any, of (A) the amount determined by multiplying (i) 20 percent of the includable compensation, by (ii) the number of years of service over (B) the aggregate of the amounts contributed by the employer for annuity contracts and excludable from the gross income of the employee for any prior taxable year."[45] There are situations in which the full 20 percent is not available. For example, the 20 percent will be reduced by "contributions of the employer to any other tax deferred annuity; qualified pension, profit-sharing, or annuity plan; qualified bond-purchase plan; etc."[46] It is possible under varying assumptions to state formulas for the maximum level premium that may be paid. Some of these formulas can become rather complicated depending on the facts in the case.[47]

Historically, it was the position of the Internal Revenue Service that tax liability would not be deferred if the premiums paid were in place of salary or salary increases even if the employee so requested. This position was changed in 1958 and it is now possible for an employee to request a salary reduction, or not to take an increase, in the amount of the allowable premium, and this amount would not be regarded as taxable income to the employee. If an employee wishes to shelter some of his income in the manner just described, he must enter into an agreement with the employer to take a reduction in salary or not to take an increase in the amount of the premium. The employee must earn the amounts involved after the agreement has been entered into. Another factor to be considered is that the formula previously stated will be modified since the salary involved will be reduced by the amount of the reduction.

OTHER TYPES OF DEFERRED COMPENSATION

Although qualified retirement plans of various types are the most widely used vehicles for providing deferred compensation for employees, they have, primarily because of their nondiscriminatory requirements, certain disadvantages when the objective is to provide deferred compensation for a selected group of highly paid executives. A major reason for wanting to defer income for high income employees is the high income tax rates that prevail and that tend to dampen the effectiveness of salary increases. By deferring income until retirement the tax burden may be mitigated.

When deferred income is decided upon the usual procedure is for the employer to enter into a contract with the employee in which the employer agrees, at the time the employee retires, to pay

---

[44] Based on Allen, Melone, and Rosenbloom, *Pension Planning*, pp. 370–71.

[45] Internal Revenue Code, 403 (b) (2). Tax deferred annuities were also considered in ERISA and the provisions of that law should be reviewed in considering contribution limits.

[46] Allen, Melone, and Rosenbloom, *Pension Planning*, p. 374. The exclusion allowance formula is fairly technical. The maximum deductible amount, in general, is 16⅔ percent of gross salary but the actual permissible exclusion allowance in any individual case should be determined in consultation with one's tax adviser.

[47] *Ibid.*, p. 375 and pp. 382–85.

him a specified sum for a period of years or for life. There may be benefits for the widow in the event of the death of the retired employee and there may be other provisions providing for certain contingencies. For example, there may be prohibitions on competitive activity and it may be required that the employee remain with the employer until retirement.

Although deferred compensation agreements may be appropriate as a way of providing some of the compensation of executives, they may not accomplish their intentions if money is not available to meet the promised payments. Therefore, it is desirable for these agreements to be funded. The funding may take the form of setting amounts aside in cash or securities for the employee in a fund beyond the employer's control; or the funding may be in the form of life insurance or annuities. If life insurance is used a straight life policy may be appropriate or possibly a more flexible arrangement would be life paid-up-at-65.

If a deferred compensation agreement is not funded, it appears that the employee will not be taxed on the income until it is received. If the agreement is funded, the tax situation will depend on the forfeitability or nonforfeitability of the employees' rights to the fund. Since some uncertainty exists about what constitutes a substantial forfeiture, many deferred compensation contracts are not technically funded.

ADMINISTRATIVE CONSIDERATIONS

Although the administration of pension and other deferred compensation plans has always been an important aspect of employee benefit management generally, in recent times, with the passage of the Employee Retirement Income Security Act, it has taken on an increased significance.

The task of administration may be divided into two parts: (1) administrative duties associated with plan development and installation, and (2) duties associated with the routine management of the plan.

Plan Development and Installation

The decision to establish a retirement income plan is normally made at the top administrative level of the firm after the officer in charge of employee benefits has offered advice and counsel, including the preparation of staff reports of various types. Once the decision to install a plan has been made, it is necessary to prepare legal documents of various types. Depending on the type of plan, there may be documents associated with the plan itself, and a separate trust agreement for the purpose of creating a trust into which the assets of the plan will be placed. The fiduciary of the plan will need to consider the powers to be given to the trustee especially in regard to investment policy. Tax considerations must be taken into account at the time installation and information is supplied to the Internal Revenue Service in order to qualify the plan. Enrollment forms must be prepared and distributed to employees, along with forms requesting authorization of withholding in the event the plan is contributory. Consideration should be given to how the plan is to be announced to employees and the type of document to be distributed to employees as evidence of their participation. It will also be necessary to install appropriate record-keeping procedures.

On-going Management of the Plan

Once a plan has been installed and is in operation, routine administrative procedures are required for the plan as a whole and for the individual participants in the plan.

Plan as a Whole

Administrative duties for the plan as a whole will involve appropriate accounting records, actuarial determinations, records other than accounting and actuarial, personnel decisions, and communications to top management and to employees.

As was discussed earlier in this chapter, the Employee Retirement Income Security Act imposes rather elaborate disclosure and reporting requirements. The plan is the reporting unit and the participant is regarded as the one who primarily uses financial statements. Thus, the statements should provide the participant with a basis for judging whether the plan will have the resources to pay benefits when they become due. A secondary use of the financial statement is to give some information about the performance of the fiduciaries and administrators. A number of questions arise about certain accounting procedures. For example, should accrual basis accounting or cash basis accounting be adopted? How should the assets be measured? (Historical cost, current value, or other.) "Should some measure of the obligation for pension benefits be presented (a) as a liability or equity interest in the financial statements, (b) as

a footnote or other disclosure, or (c) not at all? How should the financial activities of the pension plan be reported? What disclosures should be required in pension plan financial statements?"[48] Resolutions to these questions will be necessary as the plan administrator seeks to comply with federal reporting requirements.

The Employee Retirement Income Act also requires reports prepared by actuaries. In many plans an actuarial determination of the employer's liability for benefits will be necessary. Actuaries should discuss with the plan fiduciaries the various actuarial cost methods available, the pros and cons of each, and a determination should be made as to the best method for the type of plan contemplated. Likewise the appropriateness of various actuarial assumptions about such items as interest, mortality, and turnover should be discusssed and the effects of changes in these items explained.

Records other than those relating to accounting and actuarial matters must be maintained. Items relating to the plan as a whole such as names, addresses, and telephone numbers of trustees, committee members, life insurance agents, consultants, attorneys, and accountants must be maintained. Similarly statistical records of plan experience should be kept.

Selection and training of personnel to help with plan administration are important. Persons with knowledge of pension plan operation are needed to help with the counseling of employees

[48] These issues are discussed at length in *FASB Discussion Memorandum (an Analysis of the Issues related to Accounting on Reporting for Employee Benefit Plans* (Stamford, Conn.: Financial Accounting Standards Board, October 1975), pp. 21–143.

both at the time of entering the plan, during membership, and at the time of retirement. Continued education of plan employees is needed to keep them abreast of the many changes that occur legislatively as well as in types of plans. Knowledge of trends in the field and innovations that may occur elsewhere should be a part of the employers' responsibility.

Regular communication with the employees of the firm and with top management is another responsibility of the plan's administrators. In some firms this takes the form of a regular newsletter or bulletin in addition to whatever special reports may be necessary and customary. A regular bulletin provides the opportunity to announce plan changes, to record legal matters that may affect the plan participants, and to keep participants informed generally about the progress of the plan.

Individuals

Although retirement income plans generally are for the benefit of individual participants, there are some administrative matters that relate to specific individuals. For example, when an employee retires it is necessary to discuss the benefits available including choices and options and to arrange for the payment of benefits. In the case of termination before retirement, it is also necessary to arrange for any benefits that may have accrued. It may be appropriate to offer information on tax requirements to employees or to help them locate appropriate counsel. Further, it is essential to have specific data about each employee such as social security number, date of birth, effective date of participation in the plan, normal retirement date, and a current beneficiary designation.

MULTI-EMPLOYER PENSION PLANS

Although multi-employer pension plans do not involve the formal merger of two business firms, they do require cooperation outside the confines of a particular firm, and it is logical to consider them as involving for pensions, at least, a type of merger or association with other firms.

A multi-employer pension plan may be defined as a plan where the employees of a number of employers are covered under one pension plan that typically has been set up as a result of union negotiation. These plans are most common in industries where multi-employer collective bargaining agreements are common. Members of the Teamsters, Laborers, and Clothing Workers are substantially represented. Under multi-employer arrangements employees may move among plans and thus accumulate credited services from more than one employer. These plans are managed by a joint board of trustees, and the various employers contribute a specified amount to a fund.

The growth of multi-employer pension plans has been substantial over the last 25 years. Some 7,522,906 employees were covered in 1973. The comparable figure for 1950 was approximately one million. Also in 1973 approximately two and one-half million workers were covered in plans having 100,000 or more employees. Over one-half of the plans involved 10,000 or fewer employees. The largest number of plans was found in situations involving between 1000 and 5000 employees. As might be expected there was a tendency for the number of plans to increase as the size of the plan decreased. Only 0.5 percent of the plans were of size 100,000 employees or more.

The amount of the monthly retirement benefit exclusive of social security under multi-employer pension plans varied from less than $30 to $400 and over. The arithmetic mean benefit weighted by workers covered was $158.21. The largest number of participants, accounting for 22.4 percent of the total fell in the benefit category $70 to $80. These benefits were not large compared to the needs that are likely to occur in an inflationary economy. Looking at benefits in terms of plans, it is seen that there were more plans that provided benefits over $100 per month than there were providing less than that figure.

As was explained earlier in this chapter, benefit formulas differed among single-employer plans. Similar variation is found in multi-employer arrangements. Most of the participants in multi-employer plans either had benefits based on service or the benefit was of a uniform amount. Approximately 65 percent of the participants had a benefit based on service. In terms of the funding medium most of the participants were in self insured plans with approximately 61 percent covered in plans with service benefit formulas. For employees in insured plans this type of formula accounted for 91 percent of the participants.[49]

[49] The data in this and the preceding paragraphs of this section are from Harry Davis, "Multi-employer Plan Provisions in 1973," *Monthly Labor Review*, Vol. XCVII (October 1974), pp. 11–14.

MULTI-EMPLOYER PLANS AND ERISA

In general ERISA treats multi-employer plans in a manner similar to single employer plans. Under Title II (Amendments to the Internal Revenue Code Relating to Retirement Plans) a section relating to collectively bargained plans states the rules applicable to multi-employer plans in such matters as participation, vesting, funding, and similar items. Quotations from the provisions of the law will serve to illustrate the treatment given to these plans.

"Participation — Section 410 shall be applied as if all employees of each of the employers who are parties to the collective-bargaining agreement and who are subject to the same benefit computation formula under the plan were employed by a single employer.

"Vesting — Section 411 (other than subsection (d) (3) shall be applied as if all employers who have been parties to the collective bargaining agreement constituted a single employer, except that the application of any rules with respect to breaks in service shall be made under regulations prescribed by the Secretary of Labor.

"Funding — The minimum funding standard provided by Section 412 shall be determined as if all participants in the plan were employed by a single employee."

SUMMARY AND CONCLUSIONS

1. Studies of assets owned by persons over age 65 show that few families are able to accumulate assets of substantial magnitude over their working lifetime.

2. The principal pension design elements are eligibility, retirement age, benefits, and finance.

3. Financing questions that arise in pension plan design include: 1) Who is to pay for the plan? 2) When are the payments to be made? 3) Who agrees to manage the funds and pay benefits?

4. Pension plans may be financed solely by the employer, by the employee, or by contributions by both the employee and the employer.

5. The timing of contributions depends on the method selected by the employer for the funding of benefits. With the passage of ERISA advance funding is required.

6. Funds accumulated for pension purposes are typically managed by a trustee or are deposited with an insurer. Management of the funds may involve both the insurer and the trustee.

7. Costs of a pension plan can only be estimated, and actual costs are determined only after the last retired worker has died and benefit payments under the plan have ceased.

8. There are five actuarial cost methods that are in fairly common use: 1) unit credit; 2) individual entry age normal; 3) entry age normal, frozen initial liability; 4) attained age normal, frozen initial liability; and 5) aggregate cost.

9. Pension plans qualified by the Internal Revenue Service receive favorable tax treatment. Among the advantages for the employee are: 1) employer contributions are not taxed to the employee as income until benefits are received in retirement; 2) a death benefit paid to a named personal beneficiary does not need to be included as a part of the deceased's estate for purposes of the federal estate tax to the extent it represents employer contributions. Employer advantages include: 1) contributions to the pension plan are deductible as a business expense; 2) income from investing the contributions is not taxed until benefits are paid.

10. The Employee Retirement Income Security Act (ERISA) of 1974 governs the operation of pension plans and consists of four titles: I. Protection of employee benefit rights. II. Amendments to the Internal Revenue Code relating to retirement plans. III. Jurisdiction, administration, enforcement; joint pension task force, etc. IV. Plan termination insurance.

11. Profit-sharing plans are programs where contributions are based on business profits, and benefits may be paid currently in cash or stock or they may be deferred.

12. Employee stock ownership trusts are deferred compensation trusts established by corporations for the exclusive benefit of their employees. The trust is created to invest in employer stock or real property.

13. Plans are available for self-employed persons and for individuals who may be employees of firms without pension plans. Self-employed plans are known as Keogh Plans and employee plans as IRA's (Individual Retirement Account).

14. Employees of qualified charitable organizations, or of public school systems, may invest in tax-deferred annuities and shelter certain amounts of income from current taxation.

15. A multi-employer pension plan may be defined as a plan where the employees of a number of employers are covered under one pension plan. Typically the plan has been developed as a result of union negotiation.

QUESTIONS FOR DISCUSSION

1. What are the principal design elements to be considered in the establishment of pension plans? Discuss each briefly.

2. A variety of key concepts have been introduced in this chapter. Test your understanding of some of these concepts by defining the following words or phrases: advance funding, split-funding, trusteed plans, insured plans, variable annuities, actuarial cost methods, unit credit, individual entry age normal, profit sharing plans, E.S.O.T., Keogh plans, I.R.A., tax sheltered annuities, deferred compensation, and qualified plan.

3. What is the significance of the Employee Retirement Income Security Act of 1974? (ERISA) How many titles does it contain and what are they?

4. Define vesting. What are the minimum funding standards established by ERISA?

5. ERISA requires that employee benefit plans, including pension plans, name a fiduciary. Who might be named a fiduciary and what responsibilities would the fiduciary assume?

6. What is the purpose of plan termination insurance?

7. Distinguish between a pension plan and a profit sharing plan. List the advantages of each.

8. In fairly recent times Employee Stock Ownership Trusts (E.S.O.T.) have been advanced as a way of providing retirement income. Define an E.S.O.T. What are its distinctive features?

9. In what circumstances are Keogh Plans (H.R.10) useful for providing retirement income. How do they differ from individual retirement accounts? (I.R.A.'s)

10. What are the advantages of tax-sheltered annuities? To whom do these advantages accrue? What is meant by the "exclusion allowance"?

11. Prepare a solution to Case H, pages 536–546. Southern Saw Service, Chapter 20.

IV

Special Problems
in Risk Management

14

Handling Speculative Risk

Some risk managers apparently believe that they should deal only with pure, not speculative, risks. These analysts do not believe that the subject of speculative risk is of major interest to the risk manager. Yet, there are many important ways in which this position is not justified. Many problems in speculative risk are of concern to the risk manager in one way or the other. The ways in which this is the case are explored in this chapter.

In contrast to pure risk, which deals only with loss-producing events, speculative risk deals with uncertainty surrounding the occurrence of events that may produce either a profit or a loss. A general management decision to manufacture a new line of products, for example, involves speculative risk since either a profit or a loss can result from this decision. Typically, the risk manager does not make such decisions, which are in the domain of other executives. Yet, these decisions should involve the work of the risk manager because they may also assume pure risks, the cost of which might be so high as to make the whole project uneconomical.

This subject is discussed under the following headings:

1. The risk manager and speculative risk

2. Insurance methods of handling speculative risk
   a. Type A plans
   b. Type B plans

3. Noninsurance methods of handling speculative risk

THE RISK MANAGER AND SPECULATIVE RISK

There are two possible relationships between the risk manager and general management concerning speculative risks. First, the risk manager may take the narrow view as to decisions on speculative risks — that these are outside his domain with the exception of analzying ways in which these risks also involve pure risks which must be managed. Second, the risk manager may take a broad view — he may see himself involved directly in developing ways of managing speculative risks themselves, including the use of insurance techniques, as well as other techniques.

Pure Risk Management

If a risk manager takes the first view of his functions, he must establish internal procedures by which he may become aware of. new speculative risks assumed by the firm as promptly as possible, so that pure risk aspects can be analyzed and managed expeditiously. Thus, if the firm is planning a new manufacturing facility in a given location, many insurance problems, loss control problems, safety management problems, and others should be considered in the decision. For example, will there be adequate water supplies at the new location for property fire prevention? Is the plant being designed so as to minimize fire insurance costs? Should sprinkler systems be installed? These and other problems can be analyzed by the risk manager so as to enable general management to plan the new investment more efficiently than would otherwise be the case.

Other examples of ways in which the risk manager has an interest in speculative risks assumed by the enterprise include new product development, new sales territories opened, new manufacturing processes, mergers with other enterprises, and similar management decisions. Such decisions often have important implications for risk management. In merger decisions, for example, the value of a firm to be acquired is importantly affected by liabilities for pension payments which may be unfunded by the firm to be acquired. Such a liability may be overlooked by those not particularly aware of pension problems. Similar risk management areas include potential liabilities from manufacture of hazardous products, pending suits, obligations under leases requiring certain insurance, and transportation risks.

The risk manager will need to know if new sales territories are being opened up because workers' compensation insurance must be arranged for employees operating in new states or countries. If potential new manufacturing processes or new products involve particular hazards requiring special insur-

ance or loss control measures, the risk manager needs to know in as far advance as possible, so that the costs may be analyzed before the final decision is made. Numerous other similar questions involving the risk manager need to be answered in connection with general management decisions regarding to speculative risks.

Speculative Risk Management

If the risk manager takes a broad view of his role in the enterprise, he may become more directly involved in the decision processes involving speculative risks. This does not mean that the risk manager will attempt to take over the functions of other executives charged with line responsibilities over decisions involving speculative risks. Rather, the risk manager will attempt to advise other executives in various ways in which different risk-reducing devices may have value in the management of speculative risks. There are two general headings under which this topic is explored in this chapter: (1) methods involving insurance, and (2) methods not using insurance.

INSURANCE METHODS OF HANDLING SPECULATIVE RISK

Speculative risk typically has been considered uninsurable by commercial insurers. The reasons accounting for this include the following:

1. Speculative risks are not considered to be subject to sufficiently precise prediction by commercial insurers.

2. Such risks are often subject to the catastrophic hazard — losses may occur simultaneously to an unaccept-

ably large proportion of the exposure units.

3. It is difficult to obtain a sufficient spread of risk so that losses in one area can be offset by gains in another in any one time period.

4. To insure speculative risk would require that the insurer become a business partner with the insured in many cases, a condition not usually considered feasible.

5. Losses are not really fortuitous, being within the control of the insured at least to some extent. In effect this means that the insured can bring about his own loss, having in many cases a financial incentive to do so.

To illustrate, consider the risk of price fluctuations of a retailer's inventory. Suppose a retailer sought insurance against the contingency that he would be unable to sell his stock at a given average price, or that he would be unable to realize a stated gross profit margin on his operations. It is easy to see that if the insurer offered such a guarantee, an important part of the entrepreneurial risk of a retail enterprise would be transferred from the merchant to the insurer. If the insurer took a large number of similar risks in a given territory and a business depression occurred in that area, catastrophic losses might result. If the premium charged were high enough to support such losses, the merchants would probably find it unattractive because the premium would equal or exceed the expected profit margin. Furthermore, since the merchant would have little risk himself, he would have inadequate incentive to exercise skill and care in the selection of his merchandise, in the promotion of his merchandise, in selection of sales personnel and in performing many other tasks to make his operation a success. If such a contract were issued, suitable controls would have to be installed to avoid such a situation. For example, the contract might require the merchant to bear a proportion of any loss and to give up a proportion of any gain to the insurer. It is not hard to imagine why commercial insurers have tended to avoid speculative risks.

Yet, specific speculative risks are insured commercially in some cases and differing degrees of speculative risk exists in most instances even where it is intended to insure only the pure risk. The risk manager must often find ways and means of handling the speculative risk, even if a commercial insurer cannot be found to take it.

Insurance plans may be classified as Type A, those involving both pure and speculative risk, and Type B, those involving only speculative risk.

Type A Insurance Plans

Examples of private insurance arrangements which involve both pure and speculative risks include the following:

1. Domestic and export credit insurance

2. Surety and fidelity bonds

3. Replacement cost coverage on certain types of property insurance

4. Variable life insurance

Credit Insurance

Domestic Credit Insurance

Domestic credit insurance is perhaps one of the oldest types of commercial insurance contracts in which elements of both pure and speculative risk are present.[1] Under these plans a business firm which suffers a credit loss because a debtor fails to pay his account may be reimbursed, subject to certain limits. The contract specifies certain events which will be accepted as *prima facie* evidence that the debtor cannot or will not pay (such as death or absconsion of a sole debtor, filing of bankruptcy, etc.). However, the mere fact that the debtor does not pay, for whatever reason, is sufficient to create a claim under the policy.

The pure risk element in credit insurance rests in the fact that at least some of the reasons for bad debts lie in the occurrence of accidental events, such as fire, explosion, windstorm, or other similar fortuitous circumstances which interrupt or destroy the operations of the customer, preventing him from meeting his obligations. These causes are generally a minor cause of insolvencies, most of which stem from managerial inexperience or incompetence.

The speculative risk in credit insurance stems from the fact that the purchaser of this contract may have a tendency to accept doubtful credit risks if he knows that through insurance, credit loss may be transferred to the insurer. If successful, he expands his sales and profits. If not, the insurer bears most of the loss. As a matter of fact, one of the sales arguments for credit insurance is the use of this contract judiciously to expand sales to accounts which might otherwise be rejected for fear of credit loss.

Thus, credit insurance tends to

contain a large element of adverse selection against the insurer and the insurer is asked to accept risks that do not meet many of the requirements of insurable perils mentioned above. For example, (a) the loss is partially within the control of the insured (by accepting poor credit risks); (b) the loss is subject to the catastrophic hazard (business depression may cause wholesale reneging on credit due to poor sales); (c) the loss is difficult to predict usually because both business conditions generally, and business difficulties individually, are hard to anticipate without special and usually unavailable information. (The files of credit insurers are full of cases in which bankruptcy of an account occurred in spite of favorable Dun and Bradstreet ratings just prior to the loss).[2]

Credit insurers control the speculative risk in many ways and continue to operate in this field successfully, although their total business volume is relatively small.[3] Major ways of controlling losses and minimizing risks include:

(1) Amounts of coverage granted are closely geared to credit ratings, so that the insured is prevented from granting large amounts of credit to firms with poor ratings, as judged by the largest independent credit evaluation service in the United States, Dun and Bradstreet.

(2) The credit insurance contract contains provisions that provide an incentive for the insured to report any

[1] Coverage was written in the United States as early as 1890. Many insurers have operated in this field over the years, but presently only two major companies write this insurance — The American Credit Indemnity Company and The London Guarantee Company.

[2] See Mark R. Greene, "An Analysis of Credit Insurance," (Doctoral dissertation, Ohio State University, 1955).

[3] Total volume of credit insurance premiums collected in the United States in 1970 is only about $20 million, compared to $22 billion for all lines of property and liability insurance sold that year by stock insurers and $9 billion by mutual insurers. *Best's Aggregates and Averages* (Morristown, N.J.: A. M. Best Company, 1971).

delinquent credit account promptly, so that immediate and vigorous efforts can be made by the credit insurer to collect the account before it ages beyond the point of redemption. In this way loss prevention activity is built into the contract from its inception. Prompt collection activity by the insurer is often successful.

(3) Credit insurers usually write most of their policies on a general coverage form, which requires the insured to cover all of his accounts, both good and bad. In this way a spread of risk is obtained and the insured cannot select out for coverage only specific customers, whose credit worthiness may be in doubt.

(4) Two types of deductibles are required, a flat dollar amount (the primary loss) designed to eliminate from the coverage the normal bad debt losses of the typical firm in the insured's industry, and a percentage, usually 10 or 20 percent, designed to require the insured to bear a proportion of any bad debt loss. This gives the insured an incentive to select relatively safe accounts for credit, and reduces the chance that he will make a profit by selling the account to the insurance company. This assumes that the insured's profit on a sale will normally be less than the percentage deductible that he is required to bear.

(5) Agents in the field are not permitted to grant binding coverage on the spot. All applications for credit insurance must first pass the scrutiny of the home office underwriter. This arrangement enlarges the insured's control over the risks it assumes over what would be the case if relatively untrained personnel were allowed to bind coverage in the field.

(6) Credit insurance is not sold to retailers because the credit risk of the final consumer is not judged to be sufficiently measurable, nor the general quality of retail credit management sufficiently high, to permit the insurer to control losses adequately.

(7) Credit insurers attempt to diversify their exposures geographically and among different industries, so as to minimize the catastrophic risk.

It may be seen from the above that insurance on a speculative risk is possible and profitable for both parties (the insured and the insurer) providing proper safeguards are employed. The insured has protection that values represented by goods sold on open account will not be lost due to conditions outside his general control. This is particularly applicable if most of his sales are made to a relatively few customers, failure of any one of which would cause the insured financial embarrassment or insolvency. The insured may be able to expand his sales beyond what would otherwise be possible because of the superior credit knowledge and collection organization of the credit insurer. The existence of the insurance may reduce his fear of bad debt losses so that he will not unduly restrict credit terms to *all* customers, because of the failure of one or two important accounts. The credit insurance contract also gives the insured an incentive for better internal credit management and control, thus helping him reduce normal bad debt losses, and to make more careful credit investigations of new accounts. This may permit more liberal credit policies than might otherwise be possible. In short, credit insurance, together with better loss prevention and credit management, may so reduce the insured's degree of subjective risk in granting credit that more profitable operations are made possible.

It should be observed that without the controls mentioned above, the insurer could not afford to assume the speculative risk and credit insurance would not be possible. The conclusion is that the secret of insuring speculative risk (as well as pure risk) lies in the underwriting controls and systems that are employed.

Export Credit Insurance

Much of what has been said about the speculative risk aspects of domestic credit insurance applies also to export credit insurance (See also the discussion of export credit insurance in Chapter 18). In the latter field, however, additional risks exist which private insurers are not generally willing to accept. In general, private insurers do not accept the risks relating to political events which can cause bad debt losses from open account sales made to overseas customers. The political risk is insured by an agency of the United States government, the Export-Import Bank. Political risks stem from such sources as war, revolution, blocked or delayed transfer of currency, changes in the rate of exchange, blockage in the conversion of money from local to contract currency, and withdrawal or cancellation of import licenses.

The commercial risk (risk of ordinary insolvency) is also greater abroad than in domestic markets. Sources of increased hazards include language barriers; difficulties in interpreting foreign financial statements; inexperienced, incompetent, dishonest credit personnel or business owners; greater difficulties in obtaining reliable credit information; frequent demands for elongated credit terms; and increased costs of credit collection, including the high costs of bringing court action in foreign nations.

In spite of these difficulties, export credit insurance has been made available by a consortium of about 50 insurers in the United States known as the Foreign Credit Insurance Association (FCIA). Commercial banks also participate in this coverage directly and indirectly. Short-term (180 days credit terms or less) and medium-term (180 days to five years) policies are written. Export credit insurance has been encouraged by the United States government as a means of expanding United States exports and thus helping to correct an adverse balance of trade which has existed between the United States and its foreign customers in recent years.

Methods similar to those used in domestic credit insurance have been employed to control the speculative risk in export credit insurance. These include: (1) careful credit investigation of foreign customers through networks of international credit agencies, including banks; (2) exclusion of coverage for certain countries or certain customers deemed to have an excessive probability of loss; (Some countries seem to have a chronic adverse balance of payments or may be characterized by political upsets and may be excluded for these reasons, *e.g.*, Chile.); (3) use of a rating structure based on terms of payments, the general credit evaluation of the country of destination, and the exporter's own credit loss record; (4) use of coinsurance deductibles, usually 10 percent; (5) requirement that the foreign buyer pay down at least 10 percent of the invoice value of the goods in advance of shipment; and (6) transfer to the U.S. Government certain portions of the risk (*e.g.*, the political risk). These methods illustrate that each type of speculative risk requires individual thought and effort before suitable means are found to make the insurance mechanism feasible.

Surety and Fidelity Bonds

A substantial volume of business is written by insurers in the area of fidelity and surety bonding, which is characterized by substantial speculative risk. Sureties issuing fidelity bonds guarantee to the purchaser (obligee) that losses due to dishonesty of employees (obligors) will be reimbursed. Under surety bonds, the obligee is reimbursed for losses due to failure of third parties (usually contractors) to perform faithfully an obligation under a contract or other agreement. In both cases the speculative risk exists because the obligee enters into a contract or hires employees for the purpose of making a profit, which depends on either, or both, the honesty and/or business capacity of a third party to perform his assigned task. Furthermore, the loss is partially within the control of the insured obligee. For example, inadequate salary scales, poor employee screening methods, and poor internal accounting controls may encourage employee stealing.

In building contract bonding, awards for the construction of a building project are generally awarded to the lowest bidder, but a bond is required to assure faithful performance of the contract. In effect the surety is asked to assume the risk that if the contractor is unable to perform, for any reason, the owner will be reimbursed for any extra costs (including anticipated profit) that are involved in obtaining another contractor to complete the project. An element of adverse selection against the surety exists because building owners are encouraged (partially because of the protection against loss given to them by the bond) to accept the lowest bid, regardless of the financial capacity, honesty, or business ability of the con-

tractor. In effect the bonding company, or surety, must make an investigation of the contractor, assure itself of the ability and capacity of the obligee, and in other ways act as a business partner to the owner.

Insurers protect themselves against loss and attempt to reduce risk in issuing surety and fidelity bonds by several means:

1. Extensive networks are maintained for investigating the honesty, business ability, and financial capacity of individuals or firms to be bonded. Bonds will be denied to individuals with known criminal records, histories of poor past performance, or inadequate financial resources or credit.

2. If losses should occur, the bond provides a recourse by the surety against the defaulting obligor and salvage of the loss is often substantial.

3. The surety may exercise various degrees of financial controls as the construction work proceeds. For example, payments by banks to the contractor during the course of construction will be made only as work proceeds and certain portions of the work are completed and subcontractors are paid.

Using these and other ways to minimize risk and reduce hazards, speculative risk is made insurable.

Replacement Cost Insurance

Another example of risks involving both pure and speculative risks is in the field of replacement cost insurance. Endorsements are available on most commercial residential buildings and upon some types of personal property to cover the full replacement cost of the property if it is destroyed by given perils, usually fire, lightning, explosion, windstorm, and the like. Under replacement cost coverage the insured recovers any loss without the usual deduction for depreciation, which generally applies to physical damage contracts. The speculative risk exists because if one of the insured perils causes loss, the insured may actually make a profit from the occurrence of the perils. For example, if a building has originally cost $100,000, has been depreciated on the insured's books to $50,000, and requires $150,000 to replace with new materials, the replacement cost endorsement will not only provide for payment of the insured's book value, but will create what is in effect a capital gain by reimbursing the insured the full $150,000. The insured may lack the incentive not only to prevent the loss from occurring in the first place but in addition to avoid actions to reduce the size and scope of the damage once it has occurred.

Of course the fire insurance contract requires the insured to do everything he can to save and preserve the property at the time of loss, but in practice, it is easy to see that there are varying degrees of diligence with which the insured can carry out this contractual requirement. It is possible, furthermore, that the availability of replacement cost coverage creates a moral or morale hazard by giving the insured an incentive to purchase the coverage initially with the thought of causing his own loss in order to make money off the insurer, or to sell his building to the insurer at a profit.

Variable Life Insurance

Variable life insurance is a relatively new form of coverage in which the face amount of protection is ar-ranged to reflect changes in the cost of living. Two basic types are discussed here. In the first type the insurer assumes speculative risk, as well as pure risk. In the second type, the insurer assumes only pure risk. In the first type of plan, the amount of protection varies according to a cost-of-living index (in the United States, the Bureau of Labor Statistics Consumer Price Index); and in the second type, the face amount varies according to changes in the value of the stocks in which the premiums are invested after the policy is in force. In both types the risk of death of the insured, a pure risk, exists.

In the first type, where the cost-of-living index determines the face amount of protection, the insurer assumes the inflation peril, and hence the contract can be said to cover a speculative risk. This plan has been offered by a stock company, the Life Insurance Company of Georgia, in the United States since 1963. Under its provisions, the premium is level throughout its existence, and the maximum amount by which the face amount can rise is twice its original value, thus limiting the insurer's risk in case of runaway inflation. The insurer's risk is also reduced in that premiums and cash values under the policy are set relatively high (about 65 percent above ordinary life). The insurer thus earns interest income higher than that of other whole life policies and has a greater cushion of income out of which to absorb any unusual fluctuations in the rate of growth in inflation. The insured has guarantees of minimum cash values. Any excess earnings due to appreciation of investments accrues to the benefit of the insurer.

Until 1972 the second type of variable life insurance contract, where face value is linked to stock market performance, has only been offered in the United States under group contracts.

Prior to 1973 it had not actually been offered to the public as an individual policy. Individual contracts have been offered to the public by insurers in The Netherlands for a number of years. Under their provisions, the amount of life insurance protection and cash values rise if the stock market rises, and falls if the market falls. There is the assumption that inflation or deflation is linked to changes in the stock market. However, it is the insured, not the insurer, who assumes the speculative risk (inflation), because the cash values and face amount of the contract are not guaranteed by the insurer. If the value of the underlying securities in which the premiums are invested rises, it is the insured, not the insurer, who reaps the advantage (or disadvantage, if the value declines). However, the face amount of these contracts is arranged so that it never declines below the original face amount; this is accomplished by building into the premium the cost of a term life insurance policy. Thus, the insurer takes the pure risk of mortality, and the insured takes the speculative risk.

Type B Insurance Plans

Examples of insurance arrangements which involve mainly speculative risk include

1. Mutual fund insurance

2. Strike insurance

3. Mortgage loan guarantee insurance

Mutual Fund Insurance

For several years mutual fund insurance has been offered under contracts reimbursing the insured for loss if the value of a portfolio of securities falls below its initial offering price after a stated period of years, usually ten

years. An example is the plan offered in 1971 by National Securities and Research Corporation, manager of several mutual funds. This plan, issued on the Fairfield Mutual Fund, is underwritten by Harleysville Mutual Insurance Company of Harleysville, Pennsylvania. The purchaser of a mutual fund receives guarantees that if the value of his investment, plus insurance premiums, sales commissions, and administrative charges, falls below the amount of originally invested within varying periods (10, 12½, or 15 years), he will be reimbursed the difference. The investor must agree to reinvest all dividends. If he withdraws before the end of the term of years agreed upon, he loses his insurance coverage. Amounts ranging from a minimum of $3,000 to a maximum of $180,000 are accepted. For this guarantee, the investor pays an insurance premium which totals 6 percent of the initial investment, usually payable monthly. For example, the premium for the ten-year plan would be ½0 of 1 percent per month for the coverage.[4]

It seems likely that the risk of loss undertaken by the insurer under these circumstances is quite modest. In one study of 168 funds, over the period 1961–70, only one would have caused a loss to the insurer because of relatively poor market performance.[5] Over a very long period, investment returns in the stock market have averaged between 8 and 9 percent.[6] In a ten-year period if this rate of return is demonstrated, one may expect the value of a typical diversified mutual fund to rest at a level about twice its initial level. Only a very

[4] *Wall Street Journal* (May 14, 1971), p. 8.

[5] *Ibid.*

[6] Lawrence Fisher and James H. Lorie, *Rates of Return on Investments in Common Stocks* (Chicago: The Center for Research in Security Prices, 1963).

major depression similar to the period 1929–32 in the United States, or extremely inept management performance could be expected to cause the ending value of the fund to be less than its initial value. The risk is reduced considerably by (1) the requirement of reinvestment of dividends and (2) the loss of coverage if the investor withdraws. For example, if half of the initial participants withdraw from the plan, not an unreasonable assumption, the effective insurance premium is considerably higher than 6 percent since the premiums paid by those who withdraw are kept by the insurer. This increases the insurer's margin of safety. The reinvestment of dividends also increases the insurer's safety margin. This follows because if the mutual fund is invested to yield only a modest return of 4 percent, it will increase by almost 50 percent in value from reinvested dividends alone. (In ten years, $1,000 will grow to $1,480 at 4 percent compound interest.)

For periods shorter than ten years, it would appear that mutual fund insurance might be considerably more risky because of the sharp fluctuations in stock market prices which occur. Even in this case, however, the idea of stock market insurance may not be entirely impossible. Professor James A. Collier conducted a classroom experiment[7] in which individual students were given a sum of play money to invest in the stock market with the option of purchasing insurance against loss, due to market fluctuations subject to a 10 percent deductible. Three periods were selected for the experiment, one in a falling market, one in a transitional market, and one in a rising market. In the experiment the students were re-

quired to state what insurance premium they would be willing to pay as a percentage of the amount invested. (The premiums were 2.3 percent, 2.0 percent, and 1.0 percent, respectively.) These amounts were sufficiently low that the insurer would have lost money in both the declining and the transitional market, but would have had gains in the rising market. These problems might easily have been solved for a real life insurer by appropriate adjustments in the size of the deductible and/or increases in the premium. An interesting finding in the experiment was that the students did not tend to select extremely speculative securities, thus transferring heavy risks to the insurer. This minimized the adverse selection that might have been expected in such a situation.

Strike Insurance

Loss due to work stoppages from strike assumes important dimensions as a cost of doing business. It is estimated that over the years 1969–71, an average of 757 working days per 1,000 employees was lost due to strikes and lockouts in the United States, which had the second highest strike rate in the industrialized world. (Italy is first with 1,794 working days lost per 1,000 employees.)[8]

Strike insurance has been developed in the United States mainly in the agriculture, airlines, railroad, general contractors, and newspaper industries. Industries particularly vulnerable to union pressures and to strikes tend to have certain characteristics, including:

1. If there are several unions which operate in a given industry, there may be a tendency for strikes to occur because of interunion rivalry.

[7] James A. Collier, "The Insurability of Speculative Risk" (from a paper delivered to the Risk Theory Seminar of the American Risk and Insurance Association, April 1972.)

[8] *Experiodica* (Zurich, Switzerland: The Swiss Reinsurance Company, December 1972), p. 6.

2. In industries producing goods or services which can be consumed only at a given time or be lost entirely (*e.g.*, transportation service) union power is enhanced.

3. If the industry cannot stockpile its product before a strike or recapture revenue lost from a strike (*e.g.*, newspapers), its bargaining position is weakened.

4. Industries with shortages of skilled workers are vulnerable to union pressures.

5. Industries with high fixed costs, whose products are perishable or have no close substitutes, or whose sales are relatively insensitive to price changes (inelastic demand) also have insecure bargaining positions. In these industries the losses which would occur in the event of strike may be expected to outweigh the increased costs of labor due to union demands.

6. Industries characterized by oligopoly, *i.e.*, relatively few sellers each of whom can supply a needed product or service if one industry member is struck, are vulnerable to union pressure.

The strike peril is considered to produce a speculative risk uninsurable by commercial insurers for several reasons. First, the loss is at least partially within the control of the insured. For example, an employer might cause a strike to come about either because he refuses to pay reasonable wages or employee benefits, because he refuses to bargain, or because he antagonizes workers in other ways, such as by having poor working conditions. If the employer's behavior is successful and no strike for higher wages occurs, he may profit from it by saving on labor and

other costs that might otherwise be incurred. Second, the strike peril is subject to the catastrophic hazard to some extent, because a strike against one employer often produces similar shutdowns among other employers through picketing, material shortages, or cancelled orders. Third, it is felt that the very existence of insurance might bring on strikes because employers might be more likely to resist union demands. Finally, the legality of strike insurance has been contested, and insurers usually wish to avoid legal battles.[9]

Although commercial insurers have avoided strike insurance, associations of employers have nevertheless employed the insurance mechanism to spread the risks among members of their industries. In these plans most of the elements of an insurable plan exist. Various problems have been overcome, so the insurance device can operate successfully. Examples of strike insurance are:

The Railroad Plan. One well known strike insurance plan was developed by the railroad industry in 1959. The Association of American Railroads sponsored a "Service Interruption Agreement" and employed the Imperial Insurance Company, Ltd., of the Bahamas, to administer it. The railroad industry possessed many of the characteristics listed above, making it susceptible to union pressure, including multiunionism within the industry (over 40 craft unions), high fixed costs, irrecoverable loss of revenue in the event of shutdown, and in many cases permanent loss of business to competing lines. Furthermore, striking workers received unemployment insurance benefits under a plan to which the railroads were the only contributor; thus, the railroads

9 J. S. Hirsch, Jr., "Strike Insurance and Collective Bargaining," *Industrial and Labor Relations* (April 1969), p. 401.

were in effect helping to finance strikes against themselves.[10] Finally, a relatively low profit rate in railroading reduced the lines' ability to withstand strikes.[11]

The railroad plan protected individual railroads under specified conditions, paying a struck railroad up to $600,000 per day for specified fixed costs up to 365 days. Benefits are withheld if the government should seize control of the line, or if more than 50 percent of the industry is struck simultaneously. Strikes are covered only if they resulted from union demands contrary to the provisions of the Railway Labor Act, or are contrary to recommendations of a presidential emergency board. The minimum annual premium under the plan is $150,000. The actual premium due, however, is subject to the decision of an industry administrative board which determines whether the struck line is entitled to payments and then levies an assessment against the unstruck lines. The maximum premium cannot exceed 20 times the insured's daily indemnity for fixed costs. Significantly, the plan covers only specified fixed costs, not profits or losses from permanent reductions in traffic due to the strike. The actual premium charged is equal to that proportion of total daily indemnities of all members which the daily indemnities of each railroad bears to the total. Thus, if a given railroad's daily indemnity is equal to 10 percent of the total daily indemnities of all members, it must pay 10 percent of the costs paid to the struck line. It should be observed that under this arrangement each railroad must bear a portion of its own loss, if it is the one struck. This pro-

vides an incentive for loss prevention on the part of each line.

The railroad strike plan appears to be working satisfactorily. As of 1969, benefits had been paid in several brief strikes against small railroads and in three strikes against larger lines. There was a 25-day strike in 1960 against the Long Island Railroad, a 12-day strike in 1960 against the Pennsylvania Railroad, and a 30-day strike in 1962 against the Chicago and North Western Railroad. There was no indication that strike insurance affected the settlement of these disputes or contributed to the length of the strike.[12] Courts held the strike plan to be legal.[13]

Building Contractors. Strike insurance among building contractors, administered by the Associated General Contractors of America, was started in 1970, because of the tendency for unions to strike a small contractor and then attempt to force the settlement terms on other contractors, each of whom tend to be small and relatively weak. The building industry has been termed a splintered industry especially susceptible to strikes against individual members. Furthermore, because of the shortage of skilled labor, a worker for one contractor can strike against his employer. The major elements of the insurance arrangements followed the general lines of the agreement developed in the railroad industry. The plan provides indemnity up to $360,000 per day, up to a limit of 60 days per year, starting after the eleventh day of the strike. Members agree to remain in the plan for five years. The deductible principle is employed here to eliminate small claims.

Airlines. Strike insurance among about ten major airlines in the United

[10] "New Focus on Strike Insurance," *Business Week* (September 24, 1960), p. 29.

[11] Vernon M. Briggs, Jr., "The Strike Insurance Plan of the Railroad Industry," *Industrial Relations* (February 1967), p. 205.

[12] *Ibid.*, p. 210.

[13] 375 U.S. 830 (1963). See also *W. P. Kennedy* v. *Long Island Railroad*, 211 F. Supp. 480, 487–90 (S.D.N.Y., 1962).

States was begun in 1958. At first the plan provided benefits equal to a maximum of 25 percent of the normal air transport operating expenses. After some experience with the formula, this was later increased to 50 percent for the first two weeks of the strike, 45 percent for the third week, 40 percent for the fourth week, and 35 for each succeeding week. The payments are made by operating airlines and are limited to 1 percent of its operating revenues for the preceding year.[14] The payments are designed to divert what would otherwise be windfall (strike-related) revenues earned by unstruck airlines and to restore these revenues to those carriers shut down by the strike.[15] A somewhat complex formula attempts to separate revenue lost due to strike to a member airline from revenues lost to nonmembers.[16]

Newspapers. Strike insurance plans in the newspaper industry are said to date back to the 1930's.[17] At present a plan sponsored by the American Newspaper Publishers Association (ANPA) covers about 430 newspapers in the United States. The plan pays a struck newspaper up to $11,000 a day, starting with the eighth day of the strike (with double indemnity on Sunday) up to a maximum of about $550,000 a year. An aggregate maximum indemnity of $2,250,000 exists for all papers in one city or under one labor contract. Publishers pay about $135 a year for each $100 of daily indemnity for 25 days' coverage, or $225 for 100

days, plus 10 percent additional for the double indemnity coverage on Sundays.[18] In a strike against eight New York newspapers in 1962, newspapers were reported to recover between 30 and 50 percent of their fixed costs under the plan.[19] Among the provisions of the plan are (1) payments limit losses to loss of only fixed costs and profits in the event the paper continues to publish and (2) publishers must offer to arbitrate the dispute.

It will be observed that the newspaper strike insurance plan contains many familiar insurance provisions, such as deductibles, double indemnity, requirements that the insured cooperate to reduce or limit losses, and loss limitations. Although the plan is administered by the Mutual Insurance Company, Ltd., of Bermuda, the real risk is taken by the members of ANPA jointly.

Agriculture. A strike insurance plan exists among farmers in California against out-of-pocket expenses involved in producing a specific crop, with benefits limited to 75 percent of any loss. Premiums vary according to the value of a particular crop to be insured. In case of widespread strike bringing about catastrophic losses, farmers can be assessed up to one additional premium for the payment of losses. A similar strike insurance plan exists in Hawaii to cover the sugar production. Because sugar cane is grown for two years before harvesting, strikes may not interfere with immediate loss of sales, but they can disrupt planting and harvesting schedules. Accordingly, the plan is set up to reimburse the farmer for production losses up to six years after the actual strike has occurred. Indemnities are based on the differences between normal production, and actual

[14] *Wall Street Journal* (September 18, 1969), p. 16, and (November 6, 1969), p. 7.

[15] George Rejda, "Strike Insurance," *Best's Insurance News* (January 1964), p. 2.

[16] Harold D. Watkins, "Aid Past Will Fail to Meet Strike Loss," *Aviation Week and Space Technology* (August 22, 1966), p. 24.

[17] *Business Week* (December 22, 1962), p. 19.

[18] *Ibid.*

[19] *Ibid.*

production which later falls below normal due to the strike.[20]

It can be noted that the farmer must suffer 25 percent of his actual strike loss, and is subjected to assessments. He thus is given a financial incentive to prevent or reduce strike loss.

Evaluation. Even though strike insurance plans have not been offered by commercial insurers, it is seen from the above discussion of the different plans that basic insurance principles have been developed to provide mutual aid among affected policyholders. Strike insurance plans involve most of the basic methods of insurance. For example,

1. Specialized ways have been developed to control costs and encourage loss prevention (*e.g.*, the airline plan limits premiums and allows only partial recovery of losses, diminishing as the strike progresses).

2. There is a transfer of funds from those not suffering losses to those who do.

3. The contingency (strike) is clearly defined and limited.

4. The amount of losses payable is limited and ways have been found to measure covered losses due (*e.g.*, in the railroad plan, the listing of specific items of fixed expenses).

5. The catastrophic hazard is controlled by shutting off indemnities if a majority of the members in the industry is shut down by strike.

6. The deductible principle is used to eliminate small claims (*e.g.*, the 11-day waiting period in the building contractors plan).

7. So far these controls and limitations have apparently prevented the encouragement of strikes by increasing

[20] Rejda, "Strike Insurance," p. 23.

the employer's incentives to bargain in good faith.

Although it is too early to make a final evaluation of the total success of strike insurance plans, initial results indicate that these plans have employed insurance principles intelligently to meet a problem which is probably solvable by no other means short of government intervention. Although these plans involve a large element of speculative risk, the insurance device has been made sufficiently adaptable to handle them.

Mortgage Loan Guaranty Insurance

The risk of default of real estate loans has been deemed sufficiently serious to warrant cooperative effort to reduce it through insurance. Risk transfer increases the availability of loans because it makes it easier for lending groups to sell existing insured mortgages in the secondary mortgage market, thus replenishing their supply of lendable funds. Because of reduced risk, interest rates charged to borrowers are probably lower than they would otherwise be. However, the default risk is speculative, since default is at least partially within the control of the lender, as well as the borrower. If the lender does not fear default, he may reduce credit standards. The risk is subject to catastrophic loss, since default is often brought on by general unemployment which may affect a substantial portion of the borrowers in a given area.

Mortgage loan guarantee insurance has been offered privately in the United States as early as 1855 in New York. Title insurance firms originally handled the coverage.[21] After World

[21] James Graaskamp, "Development and Structure of Mortgage Loan Guaranty Insurance," *The Journal of Risk and Insurance*, Vol. 34, No. 1 (March 1967).

War I the business grew rapidly until, by 1930, fifty New York insurers were offering this coverage. However, due to several unsound practices and other factors, the private mortgage loan business collapsed in the depression of 1929–32 when widespread foreclosures on real estate occurred. Among these factors were: (1) Insurance was issued on loans that were not amortized over the life of the loan and had balloon payments due, which could not be met by the borrower without an extension of credit. (2) Insurance covered 100 percent of the loan. (3) Requirements of the insurer to maintain realistic loss reserves were absent and adequate capitalization was lacking. (4) Payments by insurers of dividends were made from unearned surplus. (5) Insurers issued mortgages on unimproved real estate. (6) There was inadequate regulation of insurance practices.[22] Accordingly, the U.S. Congress took action to offer coverage to fill the void.

Mortgage loan guarantee insurance has been offered by the United States Federal Housing Administration (FHA), a governmental agency, since 1934. This program has grown so that by 1970, the FHA insured about one-third of all new homes started. The foreclosure rate on insured home loans has been low; in 1969 only 6.14 mortgages per 1,000 were foreclosed.[23] From these data it would appear that the credit risk on home loans since 1934 has been modest. The FHA has operated profitably with its present premium

charge, which is one-half percent annually of the insured loan balance.

It was not until 1956 that private mortgage loan guarantee insurance first reappeared with the establishment of the Mortgage Loan Guarantee Insurance Corporation (MGIC) of Wisconsin. Since that time about eight other companies have been established. MGIC, however, continues to dominate the industry. With about 70 percent of the total insurance in force, MGIC operates in 49 states.

Several weaknesses which formerly characterized the industry have been corrected, and it is believed that the industry now operates on a sound basis in competition with the FHA. For example, under the provisions of private mortgage loan guarantee insurance, (a) the insured investigates individual applications for coverage made by the borrower and can make its own credit investigation before granting insurance. (b) Only the top 20 percent of the loan, not in excess of 90 percent of the appraised value of the property, is insured. (c) No single loan guarantee in excess of 10 percent of the insurer's capital and surplus is made. (d) Insurance is not given on speculatively built property, nor on property larger than a four-family residence. (e) Loss prevention efforts are made in cooperation with lenders to prevent delinquencies. (f) Regulation has been strengthened so that adequate loss reserves are set up; only amortized loans are insured and total loan exposure cannot exceed 25 times the insurer's capital surplus and unearned premium reserves. (g) Dividends can be paid only from earned surplus.

Premium charges have been set at levels somewhat below those of FHA, reflecting in part the reduced risk involved in the present insurance system.

It may be concluded that the risk

[22] Based on a report of hearings conducted by G. W. Alger, Insurance Commissioner of the State of New York, dated October 5, 1934, to determine the reason for the collapse of mortgage loan insurance companies, and reported by Mr. Bruce Thomas, President, Continental Mortgage Insurance Company, in a speech delivered June 25, 1971.

[23] *1969 HUD Statistical Yearbook.* p. 28.

element in offering mortgage loan guarantee insurance has been greatly reduced over what it was before the 1930s. Private insurers thus again have discovered ways to control speculative risk and to make it insurable at a profit.

NONINSURANCE METHODS OF HANDLING SPECULATIVE RISK

Although they are often not recognized as such, methods have been developed in many areas of business management in which the main effect and rationale is the reduction of speculative and pure risk. Examples of these methods are discussed below under two major headings: (a) marketing and manufacturing, and (b) finance and investment.

Marketing and Manufacturing

Many practices in marketing and manufacturing can be examined in the light of their risk-reducing characteristics. Examples of these practices are hedging, promotion techniques, employee compensation techniques, quality control, and patents.

Hedging

Hedging is a procedure designed to neutralize price risks that would otherwise have to be assumed by merchants and manufacturers under certain conditions. Hedging permits a merchant to transfer the risk of price fluctuations in commodities (and sometimes in currencies) to speculators. The need for hedging may be seen simply by posing a problem facing a merchant contracting to sell goods for future delivery at a price to be fixed currently. If the merchant does not already own the goods, he faces the possibility that their price

may rise by the time he must make delivery and he will suffer a loss or earn a profit lower than would otherwise be the case. If the merchant already owns the goods and the price rises by the time of future delivery, he loses the opportunity of selling them at a price higher than he has previously agreed to sell them. Through hedging, these problems may be avoided and the merchant's regular operating margin preserved. Hedging also requires that the merchant give up the opportunity of gains that would have been made if the price of goods *falls* before he must fulfill his contract.

To illustrate hedging let us take a common example of the buying hedge. Assume that a manufacturer, Jones, is building electrical products requiring the purchase of 25,000 pounds of copper, which is selling for $.50 per pound. He enters into a contract on March 1 to deliver these products in September, based on the current copper price (spot price) of $.50 per pound. Jones has three alternatives: (1) he may buy the copper now and pay storage, insurance, and other costs until the copper is needed; (2) he may wait until the copper is needed before buying and run the risk that the price may rise; and, (3) if he rejects the first two alternatives as undesirable he may hedge.

If he hedges, he enters into an equal and opposite transaction in the futures market for copper by buying copper futures. Buying copper futures is making a contract to buy 25,000 pounds of copper in the future, in this case September, at a price (determined currently), which, let us say, is $.55 per pound. This contract is the opposite to the one he has already made — that of selling products requiring the use of copper based on the current price. Assume that the price of copper rises $.05 per pound between March and September. In this case Jones would be required to buy copper at $.55 in order to complete his manufacturing contract. He thus loses $.05 per pound on his actual copper purchases; however, the value of the futures contract would normally also have risen by $.05 to $.60 per pound, and this contract can now be sold at a profit of $.05 per pound, thus canceling out his loss. In this way, Jones breaks even on the total transaction, which is the purpose of his hedge.

These transactions may be summarized as shown in Table 14–1. The futures prices normally exceed current market prices by a fairly stable margin (called the spread) based on average costs of storage, insurance, and interest. Uncertain world supply and demand factors cause daily price fluctuations, as well as longer term price movements in commodity prices.

The need for and success of a hedge depends on several basic factors:

1. To provide liquidity there must be an active futures market for the commodity in question. Such markets exist in the United States in graded, standardized, and homogeneous commodities such as copper, wheat, corn, oats, sugar, silver, wood, cocoa, cotton, plywood, broiler chickens, soybeans, hogs, and potatoes.

2. The goods in question are susceptible to substantial price fluctuations over relatively short periods.

3. The goods may be stored for relatively long periods.

4. The spread between the current price of the commodity and the futures price must be reasonably steady. For example, if the spread in the above illustration had narrowed from $.05 to $.04, Jones would have lost $.01 per pound on the total transaction instead of breaking even.

5. The hedger must be satisfied to break even on his hedge.

Advantages of hedging include:

1. The merchant or manufacturer is able to concentrate on the main enterprise in which he is engaging and is freed from speculating in raw materials. He, thus, can maintain his normal operating margin with more assurance.

2. Through hedging bank credit is often more easily available and interest costs lower than would be the case otherwise.

3. The futures market permits the seller to more safely set his prices in ad-

TABLE 14–1

	Current Market Transaction		Futures Market Transaction	
Stage 1	*March.* Sell 25,000 pounds of copper at $.50 per pound (by agreeing to sell manufactured copper products)	$.50	*March.* Buy 25,000 pounds of September copper futures at $.55 per pound	$.55
Stage 2	*September.* Buy copper on open market to fulfill manufacturing contract	$.55	*September.* Sell futures market contract at $.60 per pound	$.60
	Net Loss	($.05)	Net Gain	$.05

vance with less fear of loss due to price fluctuations. In such a case, his competitive position may be enhanced, because he can shave his operating margins below those of competitors who do not hedge and who must therefore ask a higher margin to offset risk.

4. The firm may use the futures market to assure delivery of a raw material in the future at a predetermined price without incurring the cost of financing, insurance, and storage of the goods until they are needed.

If the size of the firm is too small to warrant hedging, the firm may rely on middlemen whose operations are larger, and in this way gain the advantages of hedging. For example, in copper and cotton, a few large dealers tend to control most of the raw material supply, and these dealers protect themselves against price fluctuations in the futures market through hedging.[24]

Promotion Techniques

Many basic techniques in promoting the sale of products rest on the basis of risk reduction in the minds of the potential customer. Examples of these techniques are branding, product warranties, testimonials, and advertising.

Until a product has established a reputation for satisfactory quality, perceived risk may be a powerful deterrent to sales. Well-known products can often command a price premium over less well known products because of this factor, even though the inherent quality of the products may be equivalent. This results from the fact that consumers tend

to avoid risk, if possible, and are willing to pay for this privilege.

Branding

Brands have the main purpose of identifying a product or service in the minds of a consumer to encourage repeat purchases and to facilitate the buying process. A major advantage of establishing a well-known brand is to reduce the degree of perceived risk in the minds of the consumer so as to reduce fear of the unknown, establish confidence, and reduce anxiety over whether or not the product will be satisfactory. Once the consumer has tried a given brand and likes it, he is much more likely to purchase this particular brand again than he is to purchase an unknown brand, unless the price of the unknown brand is sufficiently below that of the well-known brand. The price differential might be considered as an insurance premium the consumer is willing to pay for risk reduction. For example, in one study of perceived risk and consumer decision making, it was found that consumers were much more likely to purchase goods by telephone if they perceived a low degree of risk by so doing.[25] Merchants take advantage of this by training telephone sales personnel how to overcome buyer uncertainty through better product knowledge, assurances of consumer satisfaction, and the like.

Product Warranties

A promotional product warranty is another established technique for reducing the degree of perceived risk in

[24] G. J. Zenz, *Futures Trading and the Purchasing Executive* (New York: National Association of Purchasing Agents, 1971), p. 30.

[25] Donald F. Cox and S. U. Rich, "Perceived Risk and Consumer Decision-making — The Case of Telephone Shopping," *Journal of Marketing Research* (November 1964), pp. 32–39.

the minds of consumers so as to remove hindrances to buying.[26] If the consumer realizes that the goods are guaranteed, or that he can return them if they are not satisfactory, he is much more likely to buy than if such a guarantee did not exist. Very large retailing empires have been built on this slogan, typified by the "satisfaction or your money back" guarantee made famous by Sears, Roebuck, and Company in the United States. Warranties on automobiles for varying periods or numbers of miles driven are also basic to the marketing strategy of most auto manufacturers. Product warranties have been especially successful in products with relatively high prices, long lives, and which are relatively complex in nature.[27]

Testimonials

Testimonials are another method by which consumer anxiety and buying resistance may be overcome. As such, the testimonial is a risk reduction technique which enjoys wide acceptance in marketing promotional strategies. Employing famous individuals to endorse products is an example of such a strategy. Testimonials are also widely used in insurance and other intangible services where the consumer often needs reassurance that the service will be satisfactory before he makes a purchase. Interestingly enough, even after a purchase is made consumers will often seek reassurance from others that their decision has been correct. Leon Festinger has demonstrated that people attempt to reduce the degree of perceived risk *after* a decision has been

made, as well as before.[28] For example, consumers are found more likely to notice product advertising after they have purchased the company's product than before. Smokers are less likely than nonsmokers to believe that cigarets cause cancer. Insurance salespersons usually have no difficulty in persuading the purchasing customer to refer him to other prospects and to permit using his name as a reference. The purchasing customer finds reassurance in his own decision by persuading others to buy as well.

Advertising and Market Research

One of the central purposes of advertising is to present product ideas, advantages, and uses, and to establish a favorable reputation for a company and its product lines in the minds of consumers. Marketing research aimed at discovering consumer characteristics is basic to successful advertising. Except for direct mail, most advertising effort is designed to lay the groundwork for actual sales through retail or wholesale outlets. As such, advertising has an important role to play in reducing the degree of risk perception among consumers regarding the company and its products in promoting brands and in pushing product warranties. Consumers are more likely to deal with well-known companies and use their products than to deal with unknown companies. Another way in which advertising reduces risk is to permit the seller to appeal to given market segments whose buying characteristics are quite well known. Advertising is thus more efficiently conducted and has a greater probability of

[26] Jon G. Udell and Evan E. Anderson, "The Product Warranty as an Element of Competitive Strategy," *Journal of Marketing* (October 1968), pp. 1–8.

[27] *Ibid.*

[28] Leon Festinger, *The Theory of Cognitive Dissonance* (Stanford, Ca.: Stanford University Press, 1958).

creating an effective marketing program so that the cost of unsold inventories and related costs can be better avoided.

An important way in which consumers are singled out for attention, *i.e.*, segmented, is on the basis of the way in which they perceive risk. For example, Russell I. Haley has shown that one important class of consumers are those who basically are worriers.[29] Advertising to such individuals can stress the risk-reducing characteristics of the product and can be so designed that the consumer will be especially attracted to this particular product. Lipstein has also shown that different brands can be successfully ranked according to the degree of anxiety the consumer associates with them. An important need exists for additional research in the area of determining which aspects of products or services most worry the consumer.[30]

Employee Compensation Techniques

As in the case of marketing, management has developed several risk reduction techniques in personnel management, particularly those relating to employee compensation. Most compensation systems are designed to provide incentive for efficiency and to maximize output. Hiring workers involves substantial financial commitments which are often fixed in nature. In many cases, heavy training and break-in costs are involved. As a result, there is a desire to reduce employee turnover and to maintain morale. Among the techniques used are (1) employee benefit programs (non-salary compensation) and (2) salary incentive programs such as bonuses, commissions, and profit sharing.

1) As was discussed in Chapter 11, employee benefits include employer contributions to such programs as pensions, group life and health insurance, various social insurance plans, vacation allowances, sick leave, and other subsidies. A basic purpose of such plans is to attract and retain a better class of employees than would be possible without them. To some extent these programs may substitute for higher pay that would otherwise be paid. Studies have confirmed that employers with more extensive programs of employee benefits tend to be characterized by lower labor turnover.[31]

Employee benefits reduce the risk and the costs of employee turnover in two important ways. First, these benefits create an atmosphere of security in the working environment. An employee realizes that if he becomes ill or disabled, or dies, he and his family will have a given measure of financial assistance at the time of need. Second, if an employee leaves his position, he may sacrifice some of his benefits that he has accumulated. For example, the new employer may not have as good a program as the old, even though he may offer a higher salary. Since the value of employee benefits is generally not taxable income to the employee, it takes a substantial increase in salary to offset loss of these benefits. As another example, if an employee leaves before his pension program becomes vested, he will lose

[29] Russell I. Haley, "Benefit Segmentation: A Decision Oriented Tool," *Journal of Marketing* (July 1968), pp. 30–35.

[30] Benjamin Lipstein, "Anxiety, Risk, and Uncertainty in Advertising Effectiveness Measurements," in Lee Adler and Irving Crespi (eds.), *Attitude Research on the Rocks* (Chicago: American Marketing Association, 1968), p. 20.

[31] Mark R. Greene, *The Role of Employee Benefit Structures in Manufacturing Industry* (Eugene, Oregon: University of Oregon, 1964).

the benefit of an accumulation of employer contributions to this pension program. Most employer pension plans do not become vested in the employee until five or ten years, or longer. If the employee leaves before this period, he loses any right to a pension which he ultimately would receive at retirement. As another example, an employee's vacation allowance is usually geared to length of service. If an employee changes positions he often will receive a shorter vacation with the new employer, until he has earned greater seniority in the new position.

2) Salary incentive programs have several risk dimensions that may not always be recognized as devices to shift risk from the employer to the employee. Commissions, bonuses, and profit-sharing plans, for example, gear part of the employee's compensation directly or indirectly to job performance either of him individually, or of the employee group. For example, if a salesman is working on commission, but fails to sell, he receives reduced compensation, even though he may have spent his time and often paid travel costs from his own pocket. If an employee group is poorly organized, or if a strike occurs and factory output suffers, bonuses or profit-sharing payments will suffer. Thus, the employee must bear some of the risk of loss, either individually or collectively. This may occur even if the basic cause of the loss is outside the control of either the employee or the employer.

In some cases employee benefit plans and salary incentive plans may work at cross purposes. The former attempts to increase job security, while the effect of the latter may be to decrease it. For example, if a pension program is funded through a profit-sharing plan, as it is in many cases, the contributions to the pension plan may vary

according to the profits of the enterprise. In his attempt to shift operational risk to the employee through a profit-sharing plan, the employer may defeat the potential security-creating value of the pension plan. If this were more widely recognized, steps could be taken to prevent it. For example, pension plans could be made entirely independent of direct employee compensation. Bonus and commission plans could be coupled with fixed salary components to give the employee a basic salary security without destroying his incentive to produce.

Quality Control

Most manufacturing systems are characterized by some attempts at quality control. This is accomplished through inspection of production line output to assure that minimum standards are being met. Quality control is essentially a loss prevention device, and reduces the risk of loss due to customer rejection of the merchandise, lawsuits for damages due to the operation or use of defective products, costs of recall of defective products, damage to the firm's reputation for quality products, and the like.

Patents

A patent is a device to reduce the risk due to loss of investment in developing new products, only to have them copied by others. The imitators can usually sell such products at a reduced price, made possible by the fact that they have not had to incur heavy developmental costs. The importance of patents to encourage new inventions has long been recognized in the laws of most countries and without this important protection, the incentive to develop new products would be greatly lessened. Thus, the importance of risk reduction has been recognized by governments.

Finance and Investments

A significant amount of management activity in investment portfolio analysis and finance is aimed at risk reduction and risk control.

Investment Portfolio Analysis

In the field of investment analysis, formal treatment of the risk element, as well as expected profits from the management of an investment portfolio, is now accepted practice, with the goal being to maximize profits *given* some risk level which is acceptable to management. Techniques to obtain specific measures of risk have been developed, and sophisticated portfolio managers in mutual funds, insurance companies, and banks are no longer satisfied to specify investment objectives in terms of generalities such as "risky" or "safe." For example, the risk in a portfolio may be expressed in terms of the standard deviation of returns in that portfolio.

In the selection of an investment security, consideration of the "beta coefficient" is common. The beta coefficient measures the sensitivity of the price of a stock to overall market fluctuations and is thus a measure of investment risk. A beta coefficient may be derived from a least squares regression analysis between weekly or monthly percentage changes in the price of a given security and the corresponding changes in the price of some general stock market index over the same period, say, five years. If the beta coefficient of a stock or a portfolio of securities is 1.7, the price of this stock or the portfolio will be expected to rise or fall 1.7 percent if the general market for all

stocks rises or falls 1.0 percent, indicating more than average sensitivity, and hence more risk for this stock or portfolio when compared to market averages. If the stock or portfolio rises more than or drops less than expected, based on the beta coefficient, the difference may be measured and used as an evaluation of the performance of the portfolio manager.

Analysis of the risk element in portfolio management can also be used to determine the optimum number of securities in which to invest. In one study, for example, it was shown that risk in the portfolio was not reduced significantly after more than ten different securities were represented in the portfolio.[32]

Financial Analysis and Planning

Financial strategy involves many considerations in which techniques of controlling risk are very helpful. Examples include (a) mergers and business expansion in diversified areas, (b) forms of business organization, (c) bankruptcy procedures, (d) leverage, (e) capital budgeting, (f) techniques in credit management, and (g) analysis of environmental risk.

Mergers

Business mergers often are undertaken to reduce risk as well as to gain enlarged profit opportunities. The merger movement in world business has been in progress at an accelerating pace since World War II. Mergers have been both the horizontal and vertical types. Horizontal mergers occur at the same level in the channel of distribution and

[32] John L. Evans and Stephen H. Archer, "Diversification and the Reduction of Dispersion: An Empirical Analysis," *The Journal of Finance*, vol. 23 (December 1968), pp. 761–67.

serve to broaden sales outlets or manufacturing operations over a wider geographical and population area. This has the effect of smoothing out fluctuations in sales and profits that would otherwise occur because of regional recessions, caused by such factors as population and industrial shifts, or changing consumer tastes. Vertical mergers tend to stabilize a firm through assuring both sources of supply and company controlled outlets at the wholesale or retail level. In this way speculative marketing risk is reduced.

Mergers of both types stabilize operations in many ways. For example, firms in one industry may obtain greater stability by acquiring firms in other industries whose products are complementary, *e.g.*, ice and fuel, heating and air conditioning, railroads and trucking, and life insurance and mutual funds. So-called conglomerate mergers have been popular in recent years, in which firms from entirely different industries sometimes merge for mutual benefit. For example, a firm leasing computer equipment merged with a much larger property-liability insurer for financial reasons. The insurer was able to supply capital needs for the computer firm.

Business Organization Forms

One of the most commonplace ways of limiting risk is to use the corporate form of business organization. Through incorporation, the owners of the business are able to limit any business losses to the amount of capital paid in. Partnerships and sole proprietorships have the disadvantage of exposing all of the personal assets of the owners to claims of business creditors, which could lead to bankruptcy. Furthermore, through the corporation much larger amounts of capital may be accumulated than through other business forms. This

leads to large-scale business enterprise, which is itself a way to reduce risk through permitting greater diversification of production and marketing than could otherwise take place.

Bankruptcy

Laws permitting bankruptcy are also risk-limiting devices. Through bankruptcy, under specified conditions, debts may be discharged by the courts, and the bankrupt firm or individual may be allowed a new start without burdensome debt. The laws transfer business risk to creditors. On the other hand, they also reduce the risk of creditors by establishing definite priorities in dividing up the assets of the bankrupt firm, assuring reasonable fairness and prevention of fraud. Because of these statutes it is possible for business firms and individuals to start new enterprises with separate corporations on an experimental basis. The amount of capital to be committed to the enterprise can be limited, and if the enterprise fails, the losses are also limited. In this way, part of the risk is shifted to creditors.

Leverage

Leverage is the utilization of debt as a method of raising capital so as to maximize the returns on equity capital supplied by the organizers. Since debt securities like bonds or mortgages, as well as bank loans, usually carry a fixed return and have a definite repayment schedule, most types of debt increase the risk to the owners, as well as to offer larger returns on equity if the business is successful. However, debt securities or loans can also be arranged to limit risk. For example, payback periods can be lengthened, and even fixed interest payments can be made contingent upon the success of the enterprise and can be subject to delay in repayment.

To illustrate, suppose that a firm is organized with $1,000,000 of assets, for which creditors put up $700,000 and the owners invested the remaining $300,000. Assume that the creditors demand 7 percent interest, and that the total return on assets is 10 percent before interest or debt repayment. The following financial information is available:

Net return, before interest ($1,000,000 × .10)	$100,000
Less interest (.07 × $700,000).	49,000
Net return to stockholders	$ 51,000
Ratio of return to creditors	.07
Ratio of return to stockholders' equity ($51,000/$300,000)	.17

Through leverage, the stockholders obtain a return of 17 percent on the $300,000 of capital they have contributed, which is considerably greater than the return on total assets. This follows because of the limited return to creditors. However, through the leverage the stockholders also assume certain risk. If total return on assets before interest falls to 5 percent, the following results appear:

Net return, before interest ($1,000,000 × .05)	$50,000
Less interest (.07 × $700,000)	49,000
Net return to stockholders	$ 1,000
Ratio of return on owners' equity	.003

In this case the stockholders barely were able to cover interest obligations, let alone service any debt repayment. A fluctuation in earnings, in this case a reduction of 50 percent, reduced the stockholders' return by nearly 100 per-

cent. Any further reduction in earnings would mean losses and perhaps ultimate bankruptcy.

To limit the risk illustrated above, stockholders can limit the amount of debt to a relatively small portion of the total capitalization. Another method of limiting risk is to provide advance arrangements for delaying or suspending debt repayments, or by making interest obligations contingent upon being earned (income bonds, for example). In some cases creditors are given equity rights in the enterprise as a condition of making loans initially and thus have incentives for seeing the business succeed. Such arrangements may facilitate the granting of additional credit, if needed.

Of course, stockholders can also avoid debt obligations and thus avoid the risk introduced by these securities altogether. This is done by financing the enterprise entirely through common stock which requires no interest or repayment obligations. A disadvantage of this procedure is to forego the possible advantages of leverage. Furthermore, sometimes it is difficult or impossible to raise funds through equity financing.

Capital Budgeting

Capital budgeting is a process under which opportunities for investment by a business firm are subjected to careful analysis according to rate of return and risk, and ranked in the order of desirability before investment decisions are made. To illustrate let us consider two examples: (1) a case in which the investment decision is made first by calculating the expected value of different opportunities and the risk element is considered informally, and (2) secondly by considering the expected value of decisions and analyzing the risk element formally.

1) In the first case, assume that a manager is to consider only two alternative investments, project X and project Y. The possible returns on the investment in the first year, with corresponding probabilities, are:

Project X		
Possible Return	Probability	Expected Value
−20%	.50	−.10
+40%	.50	+.20
		+.10

Project Y		
Possible Return	Probability	Expected Value
−10%	.50	−.05
+30%	.50	+.15
		+.10

The probability assignments of possible outcomes are made by management on a subjective basis from past experience. Although the expected value of the return to management in the two projects is the same, i.e., 10 percent, it is obvious that more risk characterizes project X than project Y, because the range of possible returns is greater. It seems equally obvious that if other factors affecting the decision are the same, a risk-averting management will choose project Y over X because Y offers lower risk at no sacrifice of expected return. On the other hand, a risk-loving management might prefer project X, because it offers a higher possible chance of gain, i.e., 40 percent, even though the possible loss is also higher, i.e., 20 percent.

2) The risk element in capital budgeting can be analyzed more formally by calculating the numerical values for risk and comparing several alternative combinations of expected returns and risk. In the above example, risk may be easily expressed numerically using the following ratio:

$$\text{Risk} = \frac{\text{expected return} - \text{least possible gain}}{\text{expected return}}$$

The risk in project X would be $\frac{.10 - (-.20)}{.10} = 3$, and that of project Y is $\frac{.10 - (-.10)}{.10} = 2$. We conclude that the risk of X is 50 percent greater than Y. The highest possible return is 33⅓ percent greater in project X than in Y. Management must decide if the possibility of 33⅓ percent more gain is worth a 50 percent increase in risk. Expressed in these terms, the decision process may be somewhat more rational than would be the case with the informal approach where no calculations for the value of risk are made.

The analysis and influence of the cost of risk management devices should be introduced into the capital-budgeting decision. Although a full development of this topic is beyond the scope of this text, a simple illustration will demonstrate the point. Assume that management is considering an investment in a new plant, and that the minimum after-tax cash flow required on all new investments is 10 percent. The new plant (estimated to last 20 years) is found to cost $100,000. Applicable depreciation is 5 percent annually, expected net cash revenues, other than charges for handling pure risk, are $20,000, and income tax rates are 50 percent. The present value of the net cash flow, after taxes is:

Gross revenues	$ 20,000
Less: Depreciation	− 5,000
(.05 × 100,000)	
Taxable income	$ 15,000
Less: Taxes (50%)	− 7,500
After-tax income	$ 7,500
Plus: Depreciation	+ 5,000
NCF (Net Cash Flow)	$ 12,500
Present value of $1 per year for 20 years, at 10 percent[33]	× 8.514
PV of NCF, after taxes	$106,425

Gross revenues	$20,000
Less: cost of pure risk	3,000
Gross cash flow	17,000
Less: depreciation	5,000
Taxable income	12,000
Less: income taxes (50%)	6,000
After-tax income	6,000
Plus: depreciation	5,000
Net cash flow, after taxes	$11,000
Present value factor	× 8.514
Present value of cash flow	$93,654

Before the cost of pure risk is introduced into the calculation, it is seen that the present value of the cash income flow makes the investment worth it under criteria in use, since this present value ($106,425) exceeds the initial outlay for the investment, $100,000. Now suppose that the risk manager makes the following estimates of the cost of pure risk:

Type of Loss	Average Annual Expected Cost (As a percent of the initial investment)
Physical perils of fire, windstorm, explosion, etc.	1.5
Liability risk	.75
Sprinkler system and other types of loss prevention	.75
Total	3.0
Annual cost in dollars (.03 × $100,000)	$3,000

When the costs of managing pure risk are introduced, the present value calculation is as follows:

[33] From a table of present values. Calculation assumes that $1 is to be received at the end of each year.

With the costs of pure risk considered, the present value of the cash flow is $6,346 ($100,000 − $93,654) less than present worth of the initial investment ($100,000), and so the investment would not meet the current criteria employed by management. By reference to tables of present value it can be determined that the interest equivalent necessary to produce a present value of $100,000 of the estimated $11,000 annual cash flow is only 9%. Thus, when the cost of pure risk is added to the capital budgeting decision, management is obtaining only 9%, not 10%, on the investment. In the above calculation, it may be noted that the present value of the after-tax cost of handling pure risk, $1,500 ($3,000 × .50) is $12,771 ($1,500 × 8.514). This amounts to 12.7% of the original investment, a substantial sum.

Simulation

Another formal way of handling risk in financial planning is by simulating financial results by computer methods. A full development of this subject is beyond the scope of this text. One such simulation is the Monte Carlo method, under which random numbers are drawn and assigned to different values selected by management for simulation. For example, probabilistic estimates by management can be applied to several different values in a profit and loss statement, and a cumulative probability distribution drawn up for each range of values. The computer can be programmed to select at random each value in the income statement and compute a number for net income based on these random selections. As many iterations as desired may be made, say 1,000 iterations. A probability distribution of these iterations for final net income can then be presented. Management can interpret such a distribution, for example, as a probability of between 40 and 50 percent that final net income from a given project will range between $500,000 and $600,000, and that there is a 5 percent probability that profits will be as low as $100,000.[34] In this way complex problems involving risk can be handled which would not be practical without electronic data processing.

Credit Risk

An important risk facing management is the possibility that creditors will fail to pay debts, thus causing financial embarrassment or outright insolvency. Adverse credit repayment experience can also produce overly rigid credit standards and cause sales to be lost. The insurance method of handling the credit risk was discussed earlier in this chapter. Noninsurance methods may also be employed. For example, risk may be reduced through appropriate diversification of customers by geographical area, by credit ratings, by products purchased, or other ways. The risk may be transferred to others by selling the accounts to bank factors, or to the government, as is done for the perils of political risks.

The avoidance method may be employed by requiring cash in advance for certain types of customers. Collection machinery can be installed to follow up immediately on delinquent accounts, thus illustrating the loss prevention method. A method of evaluating the risk present in an entire set of accounts has been suggested by Cyert and Thompson, using the method of "Markov chains."[35] Under this procedure management places each customer in a given risk category, based on such factors as his past paying record, financial status, and the like. Probabilities are assigned to the likelihood of each customer becoming past due in his account, by 30, 60, 90 days and over, i.e., moving from one state to another. The model calculates the expected value and variance of the discounted net revenue of each class of customer. The coefficient of variation of the discounted net expected revenues is the basic measure of risk in the portfolio of accounts. This coefficient is calculated each day by computer and the results distributed as a guide to credit managers as to the status of the firm's credit risk. Sales and credit policies can be adjusted to correspond to the degree of risk present. For example, new customers can be selected on the basis of their expected

[34] For a good review of major types of simulations used in statistical decision making, see William A. Spurr and Charles P. Bonini, *Statistical Analysis for Business Decisions* (Homewood, Ill.: Richard D. Irwin, 1967), Chapter 17. See also J. W. Schmidt and R. E. Taylor, *Simulation and Analysis of Industrial Systems* (Homewood, Ill.: Richard D. Irwin, 1970), pp. 258–324. An application of these methods is found in T. F. Anthony and H. J. Watson, "Probabilistic Financial Planning," *Journal of Systems Management* (September 1972), pp. 38–41.

[35] R. M. Cyert and G. L. Thompson, "Selecting a Portfolio of Credit Risks by Markov Chains," *Journal of Business*, vol. 41 (January 1968), pp. 39–46.

contribution to profits rather than on some simplified category of credit worthiness.

Option Writing

Many types of business firms hold assets in the form of marketable securities such as common stocks and bonds. One method of reducing risk inherent in this type of operation is the use of option writing to hedge against short-term price fluctuations (generally up to nine months) in stocks in the open market. Writing options is similar to the process of commodity hedging described above. In effect, the process is one in which the firm enters into equal and opposite transactions in a futures market for certain listed securities, usually securities which the firm holds as investments. In 1973, a market for trading in options to buy and sell in the stocks in the future was established by the Chicago Board Options Exchange (CBOE).

To illustrate how use of option trading may reduce investment risk, assume that the Y Insurance Company has bought as an asset 1,000 shares of a stock in which options are traded on the CBOE. Currently (say in March), the price of the stock is $75 and Y writes (sells) an option to sell this stock (a call option) at $70 (called the striking price) at any time before July for a price of $9. Y receives $9 per share, reducing its true investment in the stock to $66. (For the sake of simplicity, the illustration ignores the effect of sales commissions.) Now the stock could fall as low as $66 before Y could lose on this particular investment. Y thus receives down-side protection of 12 percent ($9/75 = .12$) by writing the call option.

If the price of the stock rises sufficiently above the striking price before its expiration in July, Y could be required to sell its investment at the striking price of $70. It would become profitable for the owner of the option to exercise his option to buy once the price equals or exceeds $79. For example, if the price rises to $80, the option owner could require Y to sell the stock at $70. The option owner, whose total investment is now $79 ($70 plus the $9 paid for the option), would gain $1 per share. If this occurs, Y has still netted a profit of $4 per share,[36] calculated as follows:

Original purchase price	$75
Selling price	− 70
Loss on stock	− 5
Income from writing option	9
Net gain on total transaction	+$ 4

If Y had not written an option, its total profit would have been $5 per share instead of $4 ($80 − $75). Thus, Y has given up some chance of gain return for limiting its potential loss. If the price rises above $79, Y would have gained more by not writing the option, but would not have enjoyed the downside protection.

In the above illustration, note that if the stock never rises above $79 before July, the option will expire and probably will not be exercised. In this case, Y holds stock which has a net basis of $66 and registers up to a potential gain of $13 a share, or 19.7 percent ($79/$66 = 1.197$), before running any risk that the option will be exercised. As shown above, if the option is exercised, Y's net gain is only $4, or 6.1 percent ($4/$66 = .061$), and Y must forego

---

[36] In practice Y would probably not sell the stock, but would eliminate its obligation to sell by repurchasing an equivalent option contract, whose price would have risen to $10. Y thus would lose $1 on the options transaction, but would gain $5 on the stock itself, netting $4.

additional potential gain if the stock rises above $79. For this reason, option writing serves best as a device to limit investment risk when the option writer is investing in stocks which are not expected to fluctuate greatly in short periods.

In one study of 32 stocks in which options were traded on the CBOE over a period of 129 weeks in 1973–76, it was shown that a strategy of writing options on securities held as investments produced superior returns to a buy-hold investment strategy and with less risk.[37] It should be noted that not all states permit institutional investors to engage in the option markets.

Environmental risk

Uncertainties in the environment in which business and society operate can produce losses which stem from what may be termed environmental risk. Examples include losses from poverty, family disintegration, overpopulation, unemployment, juvenile delinquency, and other social and governmental ills. Business losses may take many forms: destruction of property from large-scale riot and looting, loss of sales revenue, labor turnover, excessive costs to conform to auto pollution regulations, absenteeism, loss of production efficiency, political confiscation of property, currency debasement, and others. In many cases the basic cause of loss may not be recognized. For example, overcrowding may increase mental imbalance and crime. The smog problem in major cities in the world may stem from overpopula-

tion in relatively small geographic areas. The automobile exhaust fumes from millions of workers' automobiles in Los Angeles, Tokyo, London, and other large cities have produced such pollution in the air that major illness, absenteeism, and poor morale present industry with major detriments to efficiency.[38]

The environmental risk for firms operating in unfamiliar territories abroad is generally larger than that characterizing domestic operations because of lack of thorough knowledge of the foreign environment. The risk can be measured by inference from social and economic data. For example, one writer studied 15 factors contributing to overseas environmental risk, developed a ranking of various countries throughout the world, and devised a method of adjusting the expected average return on investment in each country for the risk element.[39] To illustrate, if a firm expected a return of 14 percent on an investment domestically, and the risk rating of a foreign country was .50, the adjusted expected return on investment required for making an investment in this country would be 28 percent. Factors judged to contribute most to reducing the environmental risk in this study were political stability, cultural compatibility, economic growth, attitudes of nations toward foreign investment and incentives offered for foreign investments, and ease of conversion of currency to foreign exchange.

[37] Gary L. Trennepohl, "Covered Options for Insurance Company Investment Departments," *The Journal of Insurance Issues and Practices*, vol. 1, no. 1 (March 1977), pp. 42–51.

[38] Mark R. Greene, "Research Problems for Marketing Insurance in the 1970s," *Annals of the Society of Chartered Property and Casualty Underwriters* (December 1970), pp. 293–312.

[39] F. T. Haner, "Environmental Risk Index of Business International, Inc.," (1967, mimeographed).

SUMMARY AND CONCLUSIONS

1. Speculative risk is defined as uncertainty which surrounds the occurrence of events which can produce either a profit or a loss. Although speculative risk is generally considered uninsurable by private insurers, there are several examples illustrating that commercial insurance is actually written to cover speculative risk. Furthermore, many so-called pure risks, risks in which only a loss can occur, actually involve a speculative element.

2. Examples of commercial insurance involving both pure and speculative risks are domestic and export credit insurance, surety and fidelity bonds, replacement cost, coverage on property, and variable life insurance.

3. Examples of commercial insurance involving mainly speculative risk are mutual fund insurance, strike insurance, and mortgage loan guarantee insurance.

4. Noninsurance methods of handling speculative risk are numerous. In the area of marketing and manufacturing they include the practice of hedging; promotion methods such as branding, product warranties, testimonials, and advertising; employee compensation techniques; quality control; and patent protection. In the area of finance and investments, methods, such as measuring portfolio risks, use of mergers, use of the corporate form of business organization, bankruptcy, leverage, option writing, capital budgeting techniques, techniques in credit management, and analysis of environmental risk, are all important in modern business management.

QUESTIONS FOR DISCUSSION

1. A news story stated, "negotiations were at a standstill in the week-old baker's strike that has idled 12,000 bakery workers in five western states." In your opinion, is strike insurance a plan that might be needed and is it feasible for bakeries? Why or why not?

2. Under a plan in the United Kingdom a society of 25,000 builders, duly certified by lenders, have instituted a home warranty plan under which a buyer has a 10-year guarantee on the home he purchases from any member of the society. Under the plan, when a builder plans to begin work on a house he must notify the National House Builders Registration Council, an independent nonprofit body whose goal is to maintain and improve standards. This Council conducts spot-checks as work progresses. If the builder cannot provide a registration certificate, which is ultimately issued by the Council, he finds it difficult to sell the home at prevailing prices, because mortgages on unregistered houses are hard to obtain and credit for future operations is jeopardized. In what sense is this an insurance plan against speculative risk? If so, how are losses kept within bounds and who pays the premium?

3. In a full-page advertisement in the *Wall Street Journal*, a large brokerage house stated, "We've come up with a new way to measure investment risk. It can tell you how volatile your portfolio is, compared with the S & P 500. For example we might find that your portfolio has a volatility of 1.5. Meaning that it has tended to jump 50 percent higher than the S & P in bull markets and drop 50 percent lower in bear markets . . . the difference between expected return and the actual return represents your manager's contribution. For example, suppose the S & P drops 20 percent over a year's time. If your portfolio drops 25 percent, you might think your manager has done a bad job because your portfolio is down 5 percent more than the market. But if you knew your volatility was pegged at 1.5, you'd think differently." (a) Why does the ad above imply that one should praise the investment management when the portfolio value dropped 5 percent more than the market? Explain. (b) Evaluate the risk measurement plan as a gauge of management performance.

4. An announcement stated, "Insurance companies will now be permitted to write investment guarantee insurance in California under two bills signed into law by Governor Ronald Reagan. The new kind of insurance made possible by the measures will assure investors in mutual funds and other types of securities that they at least will be able to collect the money they put in their investments, either upon their death or at the end of the policy period. Under the new California law, carriers that wish to offer the new coverage must have minimum capitalization of $2 million, as well as a special contingency fund of not less than $1 million to provide for loss to policyholders purchasing other types of insurance from the same insurer should such losses result under the investment return policies."

(a) Is such a contingency as described above insurable? Why? Which requirements of insurability are met and which are not met?

(b) Should the new coverage be written on policies such as 5-year or 10-year term? Why or why not? What other conditions would you attach to the policy for sound underwriting? Why?

(c) In your opinion is the contingency fund sufficient? Why or why not?

5. In your opinion is the risk of loss in a mutual fund sufficient to attract sufficient sales of insurance against price decline to make the plan feasible? Why or why not?

6. An article stated, ". . . Insurers are no longer content merely to lend money for construction of apartments, shopping centers, and other structures and collect a fixed-interest return. They demand a share in the ownership and management and a large slice of the profits . . . to investors who have been accustomed to getting only an interest return on loans . . . an exposure to equities is like the taste of blood to a young lion." How does this viewpoint square with the traditional concept that insurers are concerned only with pure risk? Discuss.

7. A writer studying environmental risk indicated that the lowest risk element for foreign investors existed in countries such as Canada, Australia, West Germany, Switzerland, Belgium, The Netherlands, Sweden, and the United Kingdom, all of which had ratings of 80 or higher on a scale in which the high score means low risk. The highest risk countries were the Belgian Congo, United Arab Republic, Indonesia, Nigeria, Sudan, India, Kenya, and Chile. For example, on this scale, Chile had twice as much environmental risk as Canada. What factors do you think are the most important in producing these large differences in environmental risk? Why? Discuss.

8. Differentiate hedging from insurance as a way of handling risk.

9. A flour miller agrees to manufacture and deliver within six months a certain quantity of flour which will require 50,000 bushels of grain. The price of the flour is based on the current price of grain of $2.50 a bushel. The miller's normal operating margin is $.10 per bushel, and he fears that by the time he must buy and process the grain the price may have risen enough to offset this margin. Explain and illustrate how hedging can help solve his problem.

10. Obtain some copies of advertisements for products in which the message appears to appeal to the subjective risk perception of the intended buyer. Assess the power and impact of the message. Do you believe that messages designed to increase the degree of perceived risk are more or less effective than messages designed to reduce perceived risk? Discuss.

11. Do you believe that generous programs of employee benefits succeed in helping employers to reduce labor turnover and improve efficiency? Why?

12. A writer stated, "There should be concern about the long-range implications of full acceptance by professional investment managers of the proposition that higher returns are assured by taking greater risks. The reasons for this concern are as follows: (1) the risk-reward theory is not supported by actual experience, (2) the definition of risk . . . is highly arbitrary and misleading, and (3) the theory is self-contradictory." The writer argued that a growth company, typically considered risky by traditional measures, is actually the least risky in the long run because of its long-run expected increase in profits and prices. He also argued that if risk is always accompanied by high rewards, investors buying at the top of the market when risks were greatest would, on the average, do better than those who bought securities evenly over both ups and downs of the market cycle. Evaluate the writer's arguments. Do you agree or disagree?

13. You are given the following facts to assist you in a capital-budgeting decision. A firm is considering making an investment to produce a new style dress. There is a 75 percent probability that total industry sales of the new style will be $10 million, and a 25 percent chance that it will be $20 million. It is estimated that this firm has a 75 percent chance of obtaining at least 5 percent of total industry sales. The expected profit margin on the sales is expected to be 10 percent with a 75 percent probability, and 15 percent with a

25 percent probability. Find (a) the most likely profit, (b) the least likely profit, and (c) the best possible profit. How is risk recognized in this problem?

14. A risk manager learns that his firm is considering a new investment which will create certain problems and costs on the handling of pure risk. Specifically, he calculates that the average annual expected costs of multiple-peril coverage will be $10,000. Furthermore, in order to obtain coverage even at this price, it will be necessary to transport water supplies by special pipeline at an additional average annual cost of $5,000. His management believes that unless the firm can earn at least 10 percent on a new investment it is not worthwhile. Management has calculated that after-tax net cash flow of the new investment to be $105,000 a year. The initial investment required for the expansion is $900,000. When the risk manager informs general management that handling pure risk will add at least $15,000 to the gross costs he is informed that this appears to be a relatively modest amount, especially since it is deductible for income taxes, and will not influence the final decision.

(a) Without considering the cost of handling pure risk, does the proposed investment meet general management's required return of 10 percent? (The present value of $1 a year for 25 years at 10% is $9.077.) Show calculations.

(b) Answer (a) above if the cost of handling pure risk is considered. Assume that the cost of handling pure risk is fully deductible for income taxes, which are at the rate of 50 percent.

(c) Should the costs of handling pure risk enter into the capital-budgeting decision?

15

Selection of Insurers and Agents

Once the decision to transfer risk to an insurer has been made, the risk manager must make a number of additional decisions. These decisions center around the availability of a market for the type of insurance contract or contracts sought, the selection of the best insurer for a particular risk situation, and the determination of which intermediary (agent or broker) would be most helpful in assisting with the details of the transfer.[1]

Major topics treated in this chapter are:

1. Size of insurance markets
2. Ownership types
3. Selection factors (insurers)
4. Selection of agents and brokers

INSURANCE MARKETS

Ample insurance markets are normally maintained for the usual types of personal and business coverages such as fire and extended coverage, homeowners, workers' compensation, and

similar lines. A large number of insurers offer these coverages, and they are typically available with few if any underwriting problems. There are, however, a fairly large number of risk situations for which insurance coverages may not be available or, if available, may be written only by a small number of insurers, often with restrictions of varying degrees of seriousness. Much of the market that is maintained for the transfer of unusual risks is provided by insurers and organizations that are willing to write excess and surplus lines.

The excess and surplus lines field may be divided into four parts:

1. Regular or standard lines which find their way into the excess and surplus lines field because of their size (capacity problems) or their hazardous features (nonstandard risks).

2. Specialty, unusual or off-beat lines, many of which were for many years handled almost entirely through London Lloyds or other nonadmitted outlets.

3. Malpractice insurance—whether professional liability coverage aimed at bodily injury claims or errors and omissions protection against liability for property losses — for a wide

---

[1] It is not intended to suggest that intermediaries are necessary in all contacts with an insurer. In some situations it may be desirable to approach the insurer directly.

range of businesses, professions, and institutions.

4. Coverages of greater scope and depth than most standard contracts.[2]

Examples of standard situations which might present difficulty are fire insurance for a restaurant where fire risk may be severe and automobile insurance for an individual who has had repeated accidents. Specialty lines would include animal accident insurance, damage to pianists' hands, or contact lens insurance. Malpractice insurance, particularly in recent times and especially for physicians, has been available in an increasingly limited way. Insurers found such coverage difficult to write because of high losses and the difficulty in maintaining adequate premium income. Coverages whose scope and depth might go well beyond the usual extent of protection afforded by insurance contracts are illustrated by flood, building collapse, and liability insurance covering very high limits.[3]

In addition to the supply problems that may arise because of the characteristics of a particular risk are the effects on supply that are brought about by economic, social, and political conditions that may be inimical to the maintenance of broad insurance markets. The dismal profit picture of property and liability insurers in 1974 and 1975 is an example of an economic factor that tends to dampen any extension of markets into unusual risk situations and which leads to higher insurance prices and selective underwriting. In the middle and late 1960s at the height of rioting in the inner cities and on college campuses, many insurers withdrew

from writing many forms of property insurance on buildings in threatened areas or would write the coverage only if the insured would accept very high deductibles. The advent of Medicare led many insurers to abandon the field of health insurance for persons over 65 or to write such insurane only as a supplement to the insurance provided under the Social Security Act. Over a period of time the extent of the supply of insurance varies and the risk manager must keep abreast of developments in the marketplace, if transfer to professional risk takers is to be a viable means of meeting risk.

In general, surplus and excess lines insurance markets are provided by individual insurers (including reinsurers), insurance pools, or by captive insurers.

Individual Insurers

The Agent's and Buyer's Guide has a substantial section which lists individual insurers willing to consider types of insurance (coverages) that may not be available in the standard markets. Some 500 different coverages are included. Among them are abstractors liability, acupuncturists professional liability, aircraft, animals, collection agencies (errors and omissions), employment counselors, dance studios, directors and officers liability, employee benefit programs liability, foreign credit insurance, foreign operations, franchise chain stores, growing crops, houseboats, legal insurance, livestock, manufacturers output, motion pictures cast insurance, oil insurance, pension consultants, sporting events, taverns, television broadcasters, and producers liability, saw mills, theaters, trustees and fiduciaries liability, travel agents, tree surgeons, warehousemen's liability, water damage, weather hazards, and wrap-up plans.

[2] *Agent's and Buyer's Guide* — 75 (Cincinnati: The National Underwriter Company, 1975), p. 13.

[3] *Ibid.,* p. 14.

Nonstandard situations in life and health insurance may also be of concern to risk managers. Help in locating markets is proved by *Who Writes What*.[4] This publication covers such items as benefit limits, renewal and conversion features, distribution of proceeds, unusual insureds, modified or discount premium plans, multiple-line coverage, multiple lives, special markets, values and dividends, riders, rating and restriction removal or modification; miscellaneous provisions and coverages, and in the case of health insurance, specific treatment and expense plans.

In the section dealing with benefit limits, names of insurers are listed who are willing to write benefit limits in excess of those normally provided by most contracts. Under renewal and conversion features, it is possible to obtain, for example, a contract permitting automatic conversion from term to whole life, as well as automatic conversion for substandard lives. It is also possible to obtain term insurance for unusual durations; another possibility is to obtain term contracts of a nonrenewable or nonconvertible type for low face amounts. Variations in terms of how proceeds are to be distributed are possible including, for example, lump sum withdrawals before retirement in the case of annuities, or income advances to a beneficiary.

Unusual insureds include such categories as alcoholics, amputees, aviators, forest fire fighters, test pilots, antique airplanes, eye disorders, habitual offenders in automobile accidents, bartenders, bookmakers, deep sea divers, missiles and rockets, sky divers, and tunnel, subway, and shaft construction. A number of modified premium plans are available in the excess and surplus lines market. Examples are de-

posit terms, flexible premium retirement annuities, modified premium plans of a nonusual type, nonsmokers plans and discounts, and nondrinkers life insurance. Some life insurers issue package contracts through the use of affiliates that combine life, health, property, and liability insurance. Other coverages of an essentially multiple-line nature are life agents errors and omissions, team disaster coverage for athletes, business travel, and voluntary workers compensation.

Many of the problems that arise in life insurance are also present in health insurance. One point of difference arises in specific treatment and expense plans. Some situations that may require special treatment are abortion, alcohol and drug addiction, allergies, dental expense, services of Christian Science practitioners, pre-existing conditions, paramedic treatment, prescription drugs, preventive medicine, and vision care. A few companies offer health maintenance organization coverage. In some instances this is done through the insurer's own facility and sometimes through existing facilities.[5]

Underwriting Groups

There are a number of risks that are not easily assumed by individual insurers but that lend themselves to cooperative treatment through pools or syndicates. Among the better known of these groups are: American Accident Reinsurance Group, American International Underwriters Corporation, American Hull Insurance Syndicate, Associated Aviation Underwriters, Cotton Fire and Marine Underwriters, Factory Insurance Association, Foreign Credit In-

---

[4] *Who Writes What* (Cincinnati: The National Underwriter Company, 1976).

[5] For additional information on nonadmitted markets see Samuel H. Weese, *Non-Admitted Insurance in the United States* (Homewood, Ill.: Richard D. Irwin, Inc., 1971).

surance Association, General Cover Underwriters Association, Mutual Atomic Energy Liability Underwriters, Mutual Inland Marine Underwriters of New England, Nuclear Energy Liability Property Insurance Association, Oil Insurance Association, Rain and Hail Insurance Bureau, the Selected Insurance Risks Plan, and the United States Aircraft Insurance Group.

These pools maintain offices and staffs and vary considerably in size in terms of the number of member companies involved. Perhaps the largest of these is the Nuclear Energy Liability Property Insurance Association with 120 member companies. This group undertakes to provide "all-risk property insurance and nuclear liability insurance coverage for risks which are engaged in activities presenting nuclear hazards of such magnitude that conventional insurance facilities normally available through individual companies are inadequate to provide necessary coverage."[6] Underwriting capacity is large. In the case of property insurance it amounts to $130 million per risk and for liability, $110 million. Among the smaller groups is the New York Mutual Underwriters with three member companies, which "writes fire insurance, extended coverage, and package policies on most properties, including forms, in New York State."[7] A feature of all of these groups is that profits and losses are divided among the members, and operating methods are developed that seek to make each group profitable.

Captive Insurers

A captive insurer is one that is wholly owned by a noninsurance corporation and which usually insures only

[6] *Agent's and Buyer's Guide*, p. 466.

[7] *Ibid.*, p. 465.

the risks of that corporation. (See previous discussion in Chapter 6.) Although in many ways this is a form of self-insurance, technically it is a transfer technique, since the insurers involved are separate corporations. One advantage of this method of operation is that the captive has access to reinsurance markets. Another advantage is cost reduction by elimination of certain expenses such as commissions. Many captives also take the risks of others after they have met the insurance needs of their owners. During the last ten years captive insurers have been used increasingly by multi-national corporations. It has been estimated that approximately 500 captives are domiciled in Bermuda.[8] Bermuda is a preferred location because of unoppressive regulatory conditions, favorable tax treatment, freely convertible currency, and low costs.[9]

SIZE OF INSURANCE MARKETS

As of 1977 there were approximately 4,700 insurers domiciled in the United

[8] Bernard J. Daenzer, "Effective Use of World Insurance Markets Can Ease Current Crunch," *Risk Management*, vol. 23, (February 1976), p. 10.

[9] "Captives Revisited," *Risk Management Reports* (Report No. 1, 1975), Chicago: *Business Insurance*, pp. 16–40. In an appendix to this report there are listed 360 firms that have captive insurers. Of the captives listed sixty-four were domiciled outside Bermuda. The authors of the report classify captive insurers three ways. The first classification is the "pure" captive (the definition of the captive insurer as given in the text), the second is the "association" captive, "which is formed by a trade association or group of organizations to solve a specific problem" (p. 14), and the third a "senior" captive or "profit center insurance subsidiary." See, also, "Captive Insurance Companies — 1976." This report suggests that the captive insurance companies constitute a "movement."

States, approximately 2,900 of which were in the property and liability field and 1,800 in life and health. These organizations involved around 1,620,000 persons (of these 700,000 were in property and liability insurance), approximately half of whom were agents and brokers. The remaining half were employed in insurance offices. Total assets of the insurance business as a whole as of 1975 amounted to about $383 billion. Three-fourths of these assets (approximately $289 billion) were accounted for by the life and health insurance field, reflecting the extent to which life insurers accumulate funds and their importance in the capital markets.

The scope of the insurance business may be illustrated by reviewing the premium income of the principal types of insurance offered to the public.[10] Table 15–1 shows the distribution of premiums for various types of property and liability insurance. Automobile insurance clearly dominates the property and liability insurance field, accounting for almost 40 percent of the premium volume. Next in importance in terms of premium volume is workers' compensation followed by fire insurance and such multiple-line contracts as homeowners and commercial multi-peril. The property and liability field is fairly evenly divided, from the point of view of premiums, between commercial coverages (contracts written to protect business

[10] In the United States because of the licensing laws of the various states no single business entity may write all lines of insurance. Basically, insurers are licensed either as property and liability insurers or life and health insurers, although health insurance may be written by either type. Further, it is possible through the use of subsidiaries for a property and liability company to offer life insurance and a life insurance company to offer property and liability insurance.

property) and individual or personal coverages (e.g., homes, private passenger automobiles, and similar contracts). However, in automobile insurance somewhat over 80 percent of the premium volume is derived from personal automobile insurance. The large and steady growth of total property and liability insurance premiums that has occurred since 1950 is demonstrated by Table 15–2. Premiums received in accident and health insurance written by property and liability insurers have, in general, declined in recent years, particularly in 1971.

Total life insurance in force in the United States (ordinary, group, industrial, and credit) in 1975 amounted to almost $2.1 trillion. This figure represents an 11 percent increase over 1973. Table 15–3 shows the total premiums received by United States life insurers to be somewhat over $58 billion with almost $29 billion attributable to life insurance and $19 billion to health insurance. Approximately 15 percent of the total is for the purpose of annuity considerations.

TYPES OF INSURERS BY DOMICILE

Thus far in the discussion insurers have been broadly classified by the type of insurance written, but they may be classified in other ways, too. One possibility is to classify by state of domicile. Insurers with a home office in a particular state are said to be domiciled in that state and are domestic companies. Insurers selling insurance in a particular state but whose home office is outside the state, but still in the United States, are said to be foreign insurers. An insurer with a home office outside the United States is an alien in-

TABLE 15–1
Property and Liability Insurance
Total Net Premiums Written,* 1973–75

	1973	1974	1975
Auto Liability, Pvt. Passenger	$ 8,513,997,000	$ 8,666,843,000	$ 9,600,000,000
Auto Liability, Commercial	2,242,774,000	2,270,063,000	2,500,000,000
Total Auto Liability	$10,756,771,000	$10,936,906,000	$12,100,000,000
Auto Physical Damage, Pvt. Passenger	5,341,633,000	5,324,724,000	5,700,000,000
Auto Physical Damage, Commercial	1,077,357,000	1,136,249,000	1,200,000,000
Total Auto, Physical Damage	$ 6,418,989,000	$ 6,460,973,000	$ 6,900,000,000
Total, All Automobile	$17,175,760,000	$17,397,879,000	$19,000,000,000
Medical Malpractice**	N.A.	N.A.	700,000,000
Other Liability	N.A.	N.A.	3,000,000,000
Total Liability (other than auto)	$ 2,701,318,000	$ 2,935,993,000	$ 3,700,000,000
Fire Insurance and Allied Lines	3,417,120,000	3,455,766,000	3,500,000,000
Homeowners Multiple Peril	3,630,242,000	3,991,811,000	4,500,000,000
Farmowners Multiple Peril	182,987,000	223,397,000	270,000,000
Commercial Multiple Peril	2,508,832,000	2,846,900,000	3,200,000,000
Workers' Compensation	4,761,174,000	5,413,436,000	6,100,000,000
Inland Marine	1,057,583,000	1,127,272,000	1,250,000,000
Ocean Marine	650,406,000	760,505,000	800,000,000
Surety and Fidelity	700,379,000	747,662,000	780,000,000
Burglary and Theft	129,376,000	128,185,000	120,000,000
Crop-Hail	192,354,000	259,800,000	312,439,000
Boiler and Machinery	136,626,000	140,960,000	155,000,000
Glass	36,105,000	33,372,000	31,000,000
Credit	84,887,000	69,033,000	50,000,000
Aircraft	160,134,000	163,143,000	175,000,000

* Net premiums written represent premium income retained by insurance companies, direct or through reinsurance, less payments made for business reinsured.

** Not reported separately prior to 1975.

Source: Best's Aggregates & Averages; National Crop Insurance Association (1975 figures are preliminary estimates), as reported in *Insurance Facts*, 1976 ed. (New York: Insurance Information Institute), p. 11.

surer. In general, because of regulatory procedures an insurer wishing to do business in a particular state must be licensed in that state and meet the requirements set forth by the insurance statutes. Thus, in a particular state many more insurers may be licensed to sell insurance there than have home offices in the state. Some insurers do operate outside their state of domicile on an unadmitted or unauthorized basis. An example would be insurers selling through the mail. Generally, agents licensed in a particular state may not place business with an unadmitted insurer unless it can be demonstrated that duly licensed insurers cannot supply a market. Independently of an agent, con-

TABLE 15–2
Total Net Premiums Written for All Lines of Property
and Liability Insurance, 1951–75
(000 omitted)

	Accident and Health	All Other	Total		Health and Accident	All Other	Total
1951	$ 494,137	$ 7,280,595	$ 7,774,732	1964	$1,520,603	$16,796,029	$18,316,632
1952	549,880	8,220,090	8,769,970	1965	1,643,648	18,419,820	20,063,468
1953	650,556	9,021,980	9,672,536	1966	1,659,145	20,430,912	22,090,057
1954	705,365	9,202,407	9,907,772	1967	1,690,329	22,138,588	23,828,917
1955	803,947	9,735,379	10,539,326	1968	1,778,903	24,247,133	26,026,036
1956	915,624	10,214,448	11,130,072	1969	1,980,032	27,244,869	29,224,901
1957	1,038,140	11,058,160	12,096,300	1970	1,908,841	30,958,185	32,867,026
1958	1,115,586	11,712,680	12,828,266	1971	1,010,331	34,704,563	35,714,894
1959	1,244,673	12,839,687	14,084,360	1972	1,255,525	38,061,998	39,317,523
1960	1,357,600	13,615,031	14,972,631	1973	1,518,687	40,961,085	42,479,772
1961	1,484,526	13,989,146	15,473,672	1974	1,718,787	43,433,572	45,152,359
1962	1,628,825	14,405,364	16,034,189	1975	1,750,000	48,250,000	50,000,000
1963	1,362,764	15,811,924	17,174,688				

SOURCE: Best's Aggregates & Averages (1975 figures are preliminary estimates), as reported in *Insurance Facts*, 1976 ed., p. 12.

sumers may purchase insurance from an unadmitted insurer but take some risks in doing so, such as the difficulty that may be encountered in settling claims and/or in bringing suit.

OWNERSHIP TYPES

One of the basic and fairly important ways of classifying insurers is by

TABLE 15–3
Income of U.S. Life Insurers, 1975

Life Insurance Premiums	$29,336,000,000
Annuity Considerations	10,165,000,000
Health Insurance Premiums	19,074,000,000
Total	$58,575,000,000

SOURCE: *Life Insurance Fact Book,* 1976 (New York: Institute of Life Insurance, 1976), p. 55.

type of ownership. Broadly speaking, insurers in the private sector are structured from an ownership point of view as organizations designed to make a profit for individuals or groups who have supplied capital (and may or may not be insureds), or as organizations owned by policyholders (insureds) and for whom no profit is intended in the sense of a payment for the risk of capital, apart from premiums (or possibly assessments) contributed to the business. Insurers that may be listed in the first category are private individuals or partnerships, Lloyd's associations, and stock insurance corporations. In the second category are mutual corporations, reciprocals, and fraternal orders. Public sector insurers are governmentally owned and the capital of private individuals is not at risk beyond the premiums paid.

In the United States well over 90

percent of all insurance is sold by either stock corporations or mutual corporations. Stock corporations are owned by their stockholders and are operated with the intention of earning a return on the investment represented by the capital stock. Mutual corporations are owned by their policyholders and are nonprofit organizations. Although large mutuals operate on an advance premium basis,[11] smaller property and liability mutuals, particularly in agricultural areas, may operate as assessment mutuals and seek contributions from their policyholders after a loss has occurred. The mutual form is often used for insurers designed to sell to particular classes of insureds such as factories, mills, grain elevators, hardware stores, and drug stores.

Both mutuals and stock companies are used in life and health insurance and property and liability insurance. In the former category the largest insurers and those doing a substantial part of the business are mutual corporations, although the majority of life and health insurers are organized as stock companies. The reverse is true in property and liability insurance where the largest insurers, with a few exceptions, are owned by stockholders, even though the dominant form of organization in terms of number of insurers is mutual.

Fraternals

Apart from mutuals of various types there are three other forms of cooperative or nonprofit organizations that are used as insurers. Two of these, fraternal societies and Blue Cross–Blue Shield organizations, are found in life

and health insurance, and one of them, reciprocal exchanges, in property and liability insurance. Fraternal societies are groups formed for social and benevolent purposes and often feature insurance benefits as a part of the organization. In some instances the societies have both social and beneficial members with only the latter participating in the insurance benefits. Historically these societies typically operated on an assessment basis with fairly restrictive contracts. Today, most fraternal insurers operate in a fashion similar to commercial life insurers.[12]

Blue Cross–Blue Shield

Blue Cross–Blue Shield organizations are specialty insurers operating in the field of health insurance. Founded circa 1929 Blue Cross organizations supply hospital insurance benefits — typically room and board plus hospital extras — to subscribers who may be members of a group or who may be seeking insurance as individuals. The contracts offered are written on a service basis meaning in practical terms that the Blue Cross plan pays the hospital directly rather than through the insured. The accommodations for which full reimbursement is offered are generally semiprivate.[13] Blue Shield plans are the physician provider counterpart of the hospital plans. The contracts offered provide a schedule of the benefits provided by physicians who agree to accept the terms of reimbursement provided by Blue Shield organizations. Al-

[11] Advance premium mutuals may issue assessable and nonassessable contracts, although assessment liability is typically limited. Larger advance premium mutuals operate on a nonassessment basis, since they have met the surplus requirements set by the various states for nonassessment operation.

[12] See S. S. Huebner and Kenneth Black, Jr., *Life Insurance*, 9th ed. (Englewood Cliffs, N.J.: Prentice-Hall, Inc., 1976), pp. 473–479.

[13] This statement should not be taken to mean that the insured always receives hospital service with no direct payment on his/her part. Blue Cross contracts have exclusions and limitations, and some types of service, such as private duty nursing, are not reimbursed.

though Blue Cross and Blue Shield are generally separate organizations, they often provide certain administrative services on a joint basis and some Blue Cross plans provide physician benefits in addition to the typical hospital ones.

Reciprocals

Reciprocal exchanges are found among the insurers in property and liability insurance, although they represent a small proportion of the number of insurers in that field. A reciprocal exchange is an unincorporated association of insureds managed by an attorney-in-fact. Each insured (or subscriber) is in effect a part owner of the enterprise, and assumes a definitely established underwriting liability, but his liability is several and not joint. Reciprocal exchanges are frequently used as a way of providing market capacity in areas where adequate markets may not exist. For example, in recent times, reciprocals have been formed to provide malpractice insurance for physicians. They also play a substantial role in automobile insurance.

Lloyd's

A proprietary-type ownership organization not previously considered at length is that of individuals serving as insurers. This form of ownership is not used in the United States except in a minor way. (See discussion of American Lloyd's below.) However, one of the best-known insurers in the world, Lloyd's of London, is organized on the basis of individuals (underwriters at Lloyd's) accepting responsibility as insurers or risk bearers. There are in the neighborhood of 3,000 underwriters at Lloyd's separated into syndicates varying in size from a few members to pos-

sibly 100. The business of each syndicate is conducted by an underwriting agent. The insurance contract is ultimately effected by brokers who represent insureds circulating among underwriting agents. The liability assumed by the underwriters at Lloyd's is several and not joint. Lloyd's operates in all parts of the world and is particularly well known in marine insurance and as a specialty insurer. Risk managers find that Lloyd's often provides a principal market for unusual risks. American Lloyd's operate on the same general principals as Lloyd's of London, although there are important differences. Features of American Lloyd's that differ from Lloyd's of London are: (1) American Lloyd's are managed by an attorney-in-fact; (2) they are not numerous (about thirty in the United States) and mainly do business in Texas; (3) liability of individual insurers may be limited; (4) many of the risks are reinsured.

Governmental Agencies

The role of the government as an insurer has increased in recent years and today in the neighborhood of 50 percent of the premiums collected for insurances of various kinds are paid to the government. Both the state and federal governments act as insurers with the federal government being more heavily involved. Among the major federal programs are urban property insurance, flood insurance, federal deposit insurance (banks), and certain Social Security programs (old age and survivors insurance, disability insurance, Medicare). An example of state involvement in insurance is unemployment insurance. (There is a federal grant-in-aid program for administrative costs for states that meet certain requirements.) And there are various workers' compensation funds, six of which are compulsory and eleven competitive. In some instances the risk manager will have no choice but to insure with the state, as for example, those few states that have compulsory funds for workers' compensation and do not permit self-insurance. In other instances the risk manager may find the government serving as an insurer of last resort in cases where the private sector does not provide coverage. On the employee benefit side, the risk manager may well be required by company policy to integrate possible Social Security benefits with employee benefits provided on a group basis through private insurers.

Dividend Participation

The principal product of the insurer is the contract. With a few exceptions insurance contracts are not standard and once the decision to transfer has been made, the risk manager has the task of not only selecting the insurer but also the appropriate contract. One aspect of contracts that has implications for the incidence of cost is that some contracts are issued on a participating basis and some are nonparticipating. By a participating contract is meant one in which a return of part of the premium that has been paid in advance will be returned in the form of a dividend in the event the experience of the insurer is better than expected. A nonparticipating contract is one in which there is no return of part of the premium. From the standpoint of cost, participating contracts carry higher premiums than nonparticipating ones. The ultimate cost to the insured of a participating contract is the premium paid less the dividend. Under competitive conditions this difference should be comparable to the price charged for the nonparticipating contract.

SELECTION FACTORS

As the preceding discussion has indicated, insurers vary in terms of their ownership characteristics and often in their practices, and the risk manager has the problem of deciding which insurer is best for a particular risk transfer situation. In some instances, such as limited markets, the decision may involve a small number of insurers, but in many situations a large number of insurers may be possibilities.

A decision rule that is often adopted is to select the insurer that offers the lowest price for the coverage desired, but is at least equal to the other insurers being considered in terms of solvency and service.[14]

Solvency

Of considerable importance to any insured is the ability of the insurer to pay claims in a timely fashion. One of the primary purposes of insurance regulatory statutes is to check on the financial soundness of insurers and to protect the public from possible loss. Since comparatively few established insurers have failed over the last fifty years, solvency has not been a great issue for the insured. However, the rather well-publicized difficulties of a few insurers in recent times, and the underwriting problems of property and

[14] The criteria listed above are the principal ones. However, in a brochure entitled *How to Select the Right Insurance Company*, Bankers Life Company suggested the following items to consider in selecting a life insurance company: Stock or mutual ownership organizations, size of company, length of time the company has been in existence, state in which the company is licensed, completeness of the line of insurance products, and type of local representation. See *How to Select the Right Life Insurance Company* (Des Moines, Iowa: Bankers Life Company, 1971), pp. 17–26.

liability insurers in general has once more focused the attention of the public on the problem of financial soundness.

There is perhaps no way that the risk manager can be absolutely sure that a prospective insurer will not encounter financial difficulty in the future. Nevertheless, it is possible for him to make some determination about financial integrity and capacity to accept risk through the review of balance sheet and other items that are indicators of financial soundness. Since many of the factors that are used in assessing solvency are also considered in the determination of insurance capacity, the discussion of such items as financial ratios, asset quality, liabilities, underwriting standards, and reinsurance practices has been placed in Chapter 16. Accordingly these items will not be treated here.

Sources of Financial Information

There are a number of publications that provide financial information about insurers that are helpful to the risk manager. Perhaps the most extensive sources are the books published by Alfred M. Best and Company. Two volumes, *Best's Insurance Reports Property and Liability* and *Best's Insurance Reports Life and Health,* contain balance sheet data, history of the insurer, information on the management of the firm, including a list of officers and directors, and certain statistical information relating to various aspects of the firm's operation. A volume that is of value in obtaining data on underwriting losses is *Best's Fire and Casualty Aggregates and Averages.* There are sections on underwriting expenses of stock and mutual companies and also on the underwriting experience of these companies according to line of insurance. A

large number of companies are reported on and much detailed information is given.

For risk managers who would like assistance in selecting insurers, a volume, *Best's Key Rating Guide Property and Liability,* is available. This volume "supplies for quick reference Key Ratings and comprehensive statistics showing the financial condition, general standing, and transactions of (1) stock property-casualty insurance companies licensed anywhere in the United States, whether domestic or foreign, including those which write reinsurance exclusively; (2) about three hundred and thirty-five prominent American mutual property-casualty insurance companies; (3) reciprocal insurance exchanges, whether writing property-casualty or any other kind of insurance; (4) American Lloyds' associations."[15] There is also contained in the publication a list of all mutual insurance companies in the United States of which Best and Company has addresses.

The Key Ratings are of considerable interest and are divided into two parts: general policyholders' ratings and financial ratings. The first rating system consists of the following designations: A+ and A (Excellent), B+ (Very Good), B (Good), C+ (Fairly Good), and C (Fair). The second rating system (financial) uses Roman numerals and is based on a determination of the combined magnitude of financial safety factors such as policyholders' surplus and equities in unearned premium and loss reserves. Deductions are made for indicated shortages in reserves. The rating system is shown in Table 15–4.

In preparing its ratings Best and Company makes a thorough study of

---

[15] *Best's Key Rating Guide Property-Liability* (Morristown, N.J.: A.M. Best Company, 1976), p. xxxi.

TABLE 15–4

Best's Financial Ratings

	Safety Factor
Class I	$250,000 or less
Class II	250,000 to 500,000
Class III	500,000 to 750,000
Class IV	750,000 to 1,000,000
Class V	1,000,000 to 1,500,000
Class VI	1,500,000 to 2,500,000
Class VII	2,500,000 to 3,750,000
Class VIII	3,750,000 to 5,000,000
Class IX	5,000,000 to 7,500,000
Class X	7,500,000 to 12,500,000
Class XI	12,500,000 to 25,000,000
Class XII	25,000,000 to 50,000,000
Class XIII	50,000,000 to 75,000,000
Class XIV	75,000,000 to 100,000,000
Class XV	100,000,000 or more

SOURCE: *Best's Key Rating Guide Property-Liability*, 1976, p. xxxvii.

the firms on which it reports. It takes into account underwriting, economy of management, adequacy of reserves, resources available to absorb unusual shocks, and the soundness of the investments.

Historically Bests did not rate life insurers in the same fashion as property and liability insurers. However, starting in 1976, they issued policyholder and financial ratings similar to those that had been available in the property and liability field for a number of years. The rating categories are the same as those just described for property and liability insurance. Life insurers are rated on such factors as competency in underwriting, cost control, efficient management, adequate reserves, and soundness of investment.[16]

[16] Prior to 1976 Bests published a list of Recommended Life Insurance Companies; however, alphabetical and numerical designations were not used.

Quality of Service

In addition to providing protection against the financial consequences of chance losses, insurers offer a variety of services, and the quality of these services may be an important consideration in selecting one insurer over another. Among the most important of the services are: (1) consultation and advice through the agent about the risk to be transferred and the insurance contracts available; (2) help with loss prevention and reduction; (3) promptness and fairness in the settlement of claims; (4) advice about risk identification and analysis, and (5) service benefits.

Many insurers offer advice about insuring risks. For most consumers much of this advice comes via agents and brokers, although insurers may provide a service through an extensive product line and a willingness to modify contracts to take into account customers' needs. It is not uncommon for risk managers to seek the advice of intermediaries, such as agents or brokers, as they carry out their responsibilities in risk identification and analysis. Many large brokerage firms, for example, will offer advice on the design of pension and other employee benefit plans, as well as advice on other aspects of the risk management program.

Prevention and consequent loss reduction is important to the insured, as well as the insurer, since it assists in the lowering of costs to both. The insurer can be of considerable help to the insured in suggesting methods of loss prevention and by offering lower rates if, say, sprinklers are installed or if smoking is prohibited in buildings. In some cases insurers may provide inspectors, as in boiler and machinery insurance, who will make periodic visits to plants for the purpose of detecting poor maintenance or other situations that could lead to loss. Although insurers rarely promise inspections as a contractual matter, the fact that they nevertheless render such service is often a motivation for buying the contract in the first place.

Once loss has occurred the insured is often in need of considerable help in carrying out the conditions in the contract relating to loss notification, proof of loss, value of the loss, and other details that surround a loss settlement. Agents or brokers may render a substantial service by assisting with details and by expediting various parts of the settlement process. In addition to whatever the agent or broker ·may do, the insurer contributes by sending out high-quality adjusters and by offering to settle fairly and promptly.

Although the service provided by an insurer is often thought of as something apart from the contract, in some types of contract the insurer may agree to provide a service benefit. An example of this type of service is a Blue Cross contract that provides a hospital benefit that is not paid directly to the insured. The latter is provided with hospital care and the insurer (Blue Cross) pays the hospital according to an agreed-upon rate. Another example of a service benefit, also from the health field, is the benefits offered by Health Maintenance Organizations where a variety of medical services are provided in connection with a prepayment plan.

Service is an important aspect of the evaluation of an insurer, but is often difficult to determine. There are no publications that rate the services provided by insurers. Further, service varies considerably from one insurer to another. The risk manager must often rely on knowledge of the reputation of various insurers as to service, and on the knowledge others may be willing to offer based on their experience.

Cost

Assuming the insurers under consideration are equal in terms of financial soundness and service, the one selected would normally be the one offering the lowest cost for the contract or contracts to be purchased. One of the difficulties the consumer has in trying to determine cost at the time of purchase of an insurance contract is that the price paid for the contract (premium) is only an estimate of what the ultimate cost may be to the insurer and in many instances is only an estimate for the insured.

In property and liability insurance, if the contract purchased offers no possibility of dividends or other rate adjustments (such as might be provided through retrospective rating, for example), then the initial premium paid represents the cost to the insured, and the problem of seeking the lowest cost becomes one of comparing prices quoted by insurers, assuming the benefits provided by the contracts being compared are identical. Since insurance contracts are generally nonstandard, some uncertainty surrounds the process of price comparison. Further complications arise from the fact that published information on the prices charged for various property and liability insurance contracts by insurers is not generally available to the insured.

If the property and liability contract is written on a participating basis so that dividends are a possibility or other types of rate adjustment are available, the cost to the insured is the initial premium less dividends or adjustments. Cost in this case can only be estimated, since dividends are not guaranteed and rate adjustments are made at the end of the year and depend on the experience under the contract.

In seeking price information the risk manager should be aware that prices will vary among insurers of a given type as well as among types of insurers. Methods of acquiring business, underwriting standards, loss settlement procedures, and other aspects of conducting an insurance business affect cost to the insurer and thus price to the insured. Of the various expenses encountered by the insured, acquisition cost is probably the most important in terms of its effect on price. Although generalizations about types of insurer and pricing are difficult, there is evidence to suggest that the typical advance premium mutual operating in the field of property and liability insurance sets a lower initial premium than its counterpart among stock insurers. Another possibility is that the mutual will set the same premium as the stock but will pay a dividend. It should be kept in mind that in the property and liability field mutual contracts may be assessable. Among other types of insurer assessment mutuals, reciprocals, American Lloyd's Associations, and governmental insurers tend to be low cost.[17]

Determination of cost in life insurance involves many of the same problems encountered in property and liability insurance, as well as some problems peculiar to the life field. Life insurance contracts may be written on a participating or nonparticipating basis and premiums quoted are estimates of future costs. Since mutual insurers in life insurance write only participating contracts, these contracts tend to dominate. Thus, in price comparisons the premium

quoted for a nonparticipating contract is judged against the price quoted for a participating contract less dividends. Inasmuch as dividends are not guaranteed and can only be estimated, such comparisons involve some uncertainty. Further uncertainty is introduced by the fact that life insurance contracts are nonstandard.

For life insurance contracts that are kept in force throughout their term (including the whole of life), the cost to the insured per annum is the premium charged less any dividends or other adjustments that may be payable. However, in the life insurance field, considerable interest has always surrounded the net cost to the insured (of contracts that generate cash values) in the event the contract is terminated and the cash value is received. Two methods for determining this net cost have received considerable attention. The first method (and the older one) may be described as traditional net cost and the second (newer) method is called the interest adjusted net cost method.

The traditional method of determining cost after the contract has been in force, say 20 years, is to add the annual premiums paid over the 20 years, subtract the total dividends paid and from that difference subtract the 20-year cash value. This result may then be divided by 20 to get the average cost per year. In a number of instances the cost may turn out to be negative.

A major criticism of the method just outlined is that it does not take interest into account. To overcome this difficulty the interest-adjusted method was developed. This method proceeds by accumulating the premiums paid over, say, a 20-year period at an appropriate rate of interest and subtracting from that amount the accumulated value of the dividends paid assuming

[17] See C. Arthur Williams, Jr. and Richard M. Heins, *Risk Management and Insurance*, 3rd ed. (New York: McGraw-Hill Book Co., 1976), pp. 479–80.

the same interest rate. The difference represents the net amount paid as premiums. The next step in the procedure involves subtracting the 20-year cash value from the results of the first subtraction. This gives the insurance cost, which can be converted into the interest-adjusted cost per year by dividing by. the amount to which $1 deposited annually will accumulate at the same interest rate as assumed in the preceding computations. The cost index can be computed by dividing the interest-adjusted cost per year by the number of thousands of dollars in the face amount of insurance. Interest-adjusted costs for a large number of insurers have been computed and are available in a book published by the National Underwriter Company.[18]

In contrast to property and liability insurance, there is a great deal of information available to the risk manager and the public about life insurance rates. Among these publications are *Best's Flitcraft Compend*, (Oldwick, N.J.: A.M. Best Company, published annually, and *Life Rates and Data* (Cincinnati: The National Underwriter Company), 1977.

Practical Aspects of Selecting an Insurer

Since risk management plans, particularly in larger firms, may be fairly complex the risk manager may seek the help of a single agency (or brokerage firm) or group of cooperating agencies (or brokerages) and place the details of the transfer program in their hands. It should be kept in mind that large corporate insurance buyers with large insurance staffs may deal directly with in-

surers. Thus, it does not follow that the risk manager will necessarily work through agents or brokers. Or he may divide the program into parts and place each part with a different agency (or brokerage). In making his selection either of producers or insurers, the risk manager may make use of some type of competitive bidding or he may undertake individual negotiations. In any event he will exercise considerable care in his selection.

SELECTION OF AGENTS AND BROKERS

Insurers differ from many other businesses in that they ordinarily do not contact the public directly. The product they have for sale — the insurance contract — is typically offered through intermediaries (agents or brokers).[19] This method of marketing (use of agents or brokers) does not imply lack of interest on the part of insurers in sales. There is typically a vice-president of marketing or an agency vice-president in the home office, and his department is involved in training agents, advertising, and in other ways assisting in the sale of the product.

Insurers making use of the agency concept generally, in organizing their field forces, operate on a general agency system, a branch office system, or direct reporting system. The general agency system is one wherein the United States is divided into geographical areas and a general agent is placed in charge of the area and has the responsibility for developing business for the insurer in that area. The general agent is compensated on a commission basis, and operates as an independent businessman.

---

[18] Price Gaines, Jr., Editor, *Interest Adjusted Index* (Life Insurance Payment and Cost Comparisons) (Cincinnati: The National Underwriter Company, 1975).

[19] The reader will recall that some insurers are direct writers in that their contracts are sold by employees or are offered by mail.

His relationship to the insurer is defined by a contract. He ordinarily maintains a staff of subagents who report to him. The system is more often used in life insurance than in property and liability. The branch office system is essentially an extension of the home office to various geographical areas. The branch office in itself is not an agency, although its employees may work with agents and brokers. Persons working in the branch office, including the manager, are on salary and carry out the policies established by the home office. The direct reporting system, which is the system under which many agents work, particularly in property and liability insurance, is a system wherein local agents are appointed in various communities by insurers. They report to the home office and are responsible to it.[20]

Local agents may represent more than one insurer (Independent Agency System) and such multiple representation tends to be typical of property and liability insurance. In some instances agents represent only one insurer (Exclusive Agency System); although such representation is sometimes used in property and liability insurance, it is more common in life insurance. Whether representation is multiple or exclusive, the agent is independent, although the degree of independence may be somewhat less for exclusive agents.

Many insurers, particularly in property and liability insurance, will accept business placed by brokers. Since brokers do not represent insurers, they have extensive access to insurance markets. Many large brokerage firms offer a wide variety of services that are of help to the risk manager in the discharge of his reponsibilities, in addition to assisting in the obtaining of adequate insurance coverage.

There are insurance representatives who have special or sometimes limited duties or functions. For example, in addition to defining agents and brokers the Model Uniform Agents and Brokers Licensing Act defines Surplus Lines Insurance Broker, Limited Insurance Representative, and Consultant. A surplus lines insurance broker, as defined in the Act, is one who "solicits, negotiates, or procures a policy of insurance in an insurance company not licensed to transact business in this state which cannot be procured from insurers licensed to do business in this state." A limited insurance representative is one "authorized by the Commissioner to solicit or negotiate contracts for a particular line of insurance which the commissioner may by regulation deem essential for the transaction of business in this state and which does not require the professional competency demanded for an insurance agent's or insurance broker's license." Limited representatives might be travel agents, airline personnel, bank personnel, and similar persons who might need to sell insurance in connection with their regular business activity. Insurance consultants do not sell insurance but may offer advice about an insurance policy including an opinion about its advantages or disadvantages.

---

[20] The words "agent" and "broker" have been used so far without formal definition. An insurance agent may be defined as "an individual, partnership, or corporation appointed by an insurer to solicit applications for a policy of insurance or to negotiate a policy of insurance on its behalf." An insurance broker "is any individual, partnership or corporation who, for compensation, not being a licensed agent for the company in which a policy of insurance is placed, acts or aids in any manner in negotiating contracts for insurance or placing risks or effecting insurance for a party other than himself or itself." — Model Uniform Agents and Brokers Licensing Act (Washington, D.C.: National Association of Insurance Commissioners, June 8, 1973).

Responsibility of the Agent or Broker to the Insured

Although technically the broker represents the insured and the agent the insurer, both place business for the insured and owe him certain duties. The legal consequences "do not rest on whether the operative is called a 'broker' or 'agent' (or 'general agent'). These are merely identifying terms for a general economic function and for recognition in the industry's system of sales. The important facets are the actual relationship, what the parties say and do, their relative access to information, the reasonableness of reliance and the reasonable expectations which flow from their connection."[21]

Legally an agent or broker is held to high standards of professional conduct. For example, the insured has a right to expect that the agent or broker will exercise due diligence in obtaining appropriate insurance on the best terms available and that he or she will know the various insurers and their requirements. Among other specific duties identified by Harnett are (1) duty to provide coverage after agreeing to do so; (2) duty to advise the insured promptly if coverage has been denied or is not available or cannot be placed; (3) duty to place insurance with authorized and financially solvent insurer; (4) duty to notify the insured in the event of cancellation; and (5) duty to exercise any expertise that the agent or broker leads the insured to believe that he or she has. Failure to exercise these duties may lead to legal action against the agent or broker.[22] Although the agent or broker owes certain duties to the insured, it is also true that the insured has certain responsibilities. The insured has an obligation to read the insurance contract and the application that may accompany it. It is also true that he has no right to act or rely on advice which he may know to be improper or which is obviously wrong or inappropriate. However, since insurance contracts are complicated, the lack of sophistication on the part of the insured may be taken into account by the court.[23]

Responsibility of the Agent or Broker to the Insurer

Since the agent or broker serves as an intermediary between the insured and the insurer, he owes duties to both parties. His responsibility to the insured has already been discussed. Agents generally (whether insurance or otherwise) must exercise due care in representing their principals and must not exceed the scope of their authority. Insurance agents (or brokers) in particular must not, for example, (1) fail to cancel an insurance contract promptly and properly if requested to do so by the insurer; or (2) fail to supply appropriate information to the insurer. In addition he must not give unauthorized instructions or interpretations to insureds, sell to imprudent risks, or delay in supplying underwriting information to the insurer. The sales person must conduct himself in a completely honest manner and disclose material facts, represent medical data correctly, and in general not hurt or defraud the principal.[24]

Licensing of Agents and Brokers

All states require agents and brokers to be licensed. With the exception of Michigan and Texas, most states where a substantial insurance business

21 Bertram Harnett, *Responsibilities of Agents and Brokers* (New York: Matthew Bender, 1975), pp. 2–15.

22 *Ibid.*, pp. 1–32.

23 *Ibid.*, p. 32.

24 *Ibid.*, pp. 1–14.

is conducted license them separately.[25] Two states, New York and California, do not license life insurance (including annuities) brokers, although brokers in those states may write any other line of insurance for a commission. Also, in these states the requirements for brokers, including examinations, are more stringent than for agents, presumably because the broker is clearly independent and is not linked to any insurer.

The general practice in licensing agents is to issue a separate license to the agent for each insurer he is to represent and to specify on the license the types of insurance he may sell. Clearly he cannot sell any lines not marketed by the insurer to whom he is licensed. It is possible for an agent to be licensed to more than one insurer, and it has been estimated that on the average each agent holds six licenses.[26] A variation on this procedure of licensing is illustrated by California, where each agent receives a basic license on which appointing insurers may be listed. Lines of insurance are not licensed separately; however, the agent is limited to whatever lines are sold by the insurers he represents. Also, in some states certain lines of insurance such as life or marine may have special licensing requirements.

The qualifications and requirements that must be met by an applicant for an agent's or broker's license vary among the states. Typically there is an age requirement, such as the attainment of age 18 or 21. Many states require the passing of a written examination that is given by the insurance department, and may also require the accomplishment of a certain number of classroom hours in

an insurance course approved by the Commissioner. In Texas only life and accident and health agents must take a written examination, while in Michigan the examination requirement is at the discretion of the Commissioner. Other variations exist, but even in those states with comparatively stringent requirements, a minimal kind of emphasis seems to be placed on educational attainment. Licenses are generally renewed annually and fairly automatically. Special licenses may be required by certain types of sales personnel such as surplus line agents, consultants, and solicitors. A solicitor in this context is a person who usually works for an agent or broker and who assists in the sale by finding a customer, but who does not complete the sales transaction. Such personnel are licensed, for example, in California, Michigan, Illinois, and New Jersey. An examination may or may not be required depending on the state.[27]

Some effort is made in insurance statutes to specify standards of conduct for sales personnel. Rebating by agents is generally prohibited. Surplus line laws regulate the type of insurer (admitted or nonadmitted) with which agents may place business. There are often regulations relating to advertising and sales representations. In some states there are provisions in the statutes prohibiting twisting or the practice of trying to persuade an insured to drop one policy and buy another. Normally the agent is charged with twisting only if it is clear the policy he wishes to sell is less good for the insured than the one the insured already has. If an agent or broker is convicted "of any felony or misdemeanor violation of the insurance code or of moral turpitude" he may automatically face revocation or suspension of

[25] Dual licensing is possible.

[26] Bertram Harnett, *Responsibilities of Agents and Brokers*, p. 24.

[27] *Ibid.*, p. 33.

his license, or renewal may be refused or a license denied.[28] In other situations involving a breach of duty, similar sanctions are possible but not necessarily on an automatic basis.

Selection of Agents and Brokers

The selection of agents and brokers does not pose some of the same questions that arise in the selection of insurers. Solvency is not a basic issue in relation to agents and brokers, since it is the solvency of the insurer that is of primary concern to the risk manager. Similarly price and the related issue of cost are factors in selecting an insurer rather than agent, since it is the insurer who determines price and not the agent. The chief considerations in selecting an agent or broker appear to be service, knowledge, and integrity.

Service

As in the case of selecting an insurer, there are no published guides that rate agents and brokers on the basis of service rendered to their clients. Yet differences in this regard do exist. Among the services an agent or broker might provide the risk manager are help in shopping for coverages, advice on risk identification and analysis, property appraisals, and assistance in loss settlement. Given time the risk manager will acquire experience in judging the service potential of agencies and brokerages, as well as their interest. He will also have the benefit of the experience others have had.

Knowledge

One of the principal reasons the state has for licensing agents and bro-

[28] *Ibid.*

kers is to certify to the public that these persons are competent to perform the duties of their vocation. Yet, to date, the various states have not gone any great distance in demanding more than a minimal kind of insurance knowledge. Even the model bill prepared by the National Association of Insurance Commissioners does not specify educational preparation much beyond that currently required. Nevertheless, many agents and brokers have acquired knowledge beyond that required for licensing by pursuing studies leading to the C.L.U. or C.P.C.U. designation. The C.L.U. (Chartered Life Underwriter) is a life insurance designation awarded by the American College of Life Underwriters after the candidate has completed a series of written examinations that are set and graded on a national basis. The C.P.C.U. (Chartered Property and Casualty Underwriter) is a designation similar to the C.L.U. for property and liability insurance. Further, many agents and brokers have completed college and university courses in insurance and other business subjects and are professionally qualified as business managers. It is not a difficult matter for the risk manager to determine the educational background, achievement, and experience of the agents or brokers he is considering. Careful review of these factors should be an important part of the selection process.

Integrity

Members of the public, as well as risk managers, to the extent that they work through agents and brokers, normally, of necessity, must place a great deal of confidence in the notion that the agent or broker will represent their interests honestly, fairly, and competently. As in the cases of service and competence, there are no published guides that will provide guidance about the integrity of an agent or broker. The risk manager must rely on the reputa-

tion of various firms and his own investigation of the performance of insurance salespersons.

SUMMARY AND CONCLUSIONS

1. Although insurance markets are normally available for such business and personal coverages as fire and extended coverage, homeowners, workers' compensation, and similar lines, there are situations where insurance is available only on a limited basis and with a variety of restrictions.

2. Economic, political, and social conditions often affect the maintenance of broad insurance markets.

3. Surplus and excess lines insurance markets are provided by individual insurers, insurance pools, and captive insurers.

4. Examples of underwriting pools are: American Accident Reinsurance Group, American International Underwriters Corporation, American Hull Insurance Syndicate, Associated Aviation Underwriters, Cotton Fire and Marine Underwriters, Factory Insurance Association, Foreign Credit Insurance Association, General Cover Underwriters Association, Mutual Atomic Energy Liability Underwriters, Mutual Inland Marine Underwriters of New England, Nuclear Energy Liability Property Insurance Association, Oil Insurance Association, Rain and Hail Insurance Bureau, the Selected Insurance Risks Plan, and the United States Aircraft Insurance Group.

5. A captive insurer is one that is wholly owned by a company that is not an insurer and only insures the risks of that company.

6. In 1974 there were some 4,700 insurers domiciled in the United States. About 2,900 of these firms were property and liability insurers and 1,800 were in life and health.

7. As of 1974 the total assets of the insurance business amounted to about $347 billion.

8. In the United States over 90 percent of all insurance is sold by either stock corporations or mutual corporations. Other forms of ownership are fraternal societies, Blue Cross-Blue Shield organizations, reciprocal exchanges, and Lloyd's associations.

9. Factors to be considered in selecting an insurer are: solvency as judged by quality of the assets, financial ratios, accuracy of the amounts carried as liabilities, underwriting policy and reinsurance practices, cost, and service.

10. Possible sources of financial information are: *Best's Insurance Reports Property and Liability, Best's Insurance Reports Life and Health, Best's Fire and Casualty Aggregates and Averages, Best's Key Rating Guide Property and Liability.*

11. In selecting agents and brokers, consideration must be given to service, competence, and integrity.

QUESTIONS FOR DISCUSSION

1. What is meant by an insurance market? What problems may arise in maintaining these markets?

2. Excess and surplus lines may be divided into four parts. What are these parts? Give examples of contracts that may fall in each of the identified categories.

3. What are the chief sources of surplus and excess lines insurance? What are some of the characteristics of these sources?

4. Compare life and health insurers with property and liability insurers with respect to total premiums written and total assets. How do you account for the fact that total assets differ considerably while premiums written are fairly comparable?

5. Over fifty percent of the total net premiums in property and liability insurance are accounted for by three lines of insurance. What are these lines?

6. Certain liabilities carried on insurance company balance sheets are estimates rather than exact figures. Identify these liabilities. What affect may errors in them have on the financial position of the insurer?

7. Select three property and liability insurers. By use of appropriate reference material determine their underwriting experience over the last three years. Also determine Best's financial ratings for these firms.

8. Select a life insurer. Write a brief report summarizing its financial experience during the last five years. What comments would you have about service offered by this insurer and about the cost of its contracts in relation to other insurers?

9. A whole life insurance policy was issued to a male age 30 in the amount of $10,000. The premium paid was $211.20 per year. The annual dividends were $50.30 and the cash surrender value by the end on the twentieth year was $3260. Determine the cost of insurance by the interest-adjusted method (assume 4% interest) and by the traditional method. Comment on the difference in the results. Which method do you prefer? Why?

10. Describe the system now used by insurers for marketing insurance contracts. In what ways may agents and brokers assist in the risk management function?

11. What are the factors to be considered in selecting agents and brokers? Suggest ways in which these factors can be assessed.

12. Present a solution to the case which follows:

In 1976 Scientific Atlanta has just adopted a new philosophy concerning insurance buying. Formerly, the company used to operate directly through two insurance companies — the Employers' Mutual of Wassau for workers' compensation and general liability coverage, and Protection Mutual for property insurance. Scientific Atlanta has now enlisted the services of an insurance broker, Johnson & Higgins.

BACKGROUND

Scientific Atlanta, an Atlanta-based organization, employing over 1,300 people, is engaged in the development, manufacturing, and sale of communications equipment. Formed in 1954 by six graduates of the Georgia Institute of Technology, the company has sales in excess of $40 million.

The company's production is divided into three main groups: communications, instrumentation, and mechanical products. The communications group accounted for approximately 40 percent of the company's net sales in 1975, and includes such products as satellite earth-station equipment, cable television equipment, and security products.

Since 1971, Scientific Atlanta had furnished the wireless communication equipment used by the Rollins Protective Service, Inc. for its home security systems.

The instrumentation group devel-

ops products for use in telemetry, microwave systems, and antenna installations. The company spends a significant portion of its research budget on instrumentation development.

The mechanical products group develops and manufactures cabinets and enclosures for electronic equipment. The company has a wholly owned subsidiary in Scotland that manufactures most of their enclosures.

Operations are not seasonal, but the equipment does have a limited life due to obsolescence and improved product development.

Scientific Atlanta has four main manufacturing plants in the Atlanta area, one in Scotland, one in Anniston, Alabama, and one in New Jersey. There are also two foreign sales offices in London and Paris.

THE NEW INSURANCE ORGANIZATION

Scientific Atlanta changed to a broker (Johnson & Higgins) for several reasons. In one instance, the company was installing an antenna structure in Italy and the general liability insurance company (Wassau) quoted a $13,000 premium cost for insuring various liability exposures. Scientific Atlanta officials regarded this figure as being high; instead of requesting immediate coverage they questioned the validity of the quoted amount. The insurer then discovered that it had neglected to convert from lira to dollars, and as a result the cost of coverage should have been $1,000 instead of $13,000.

In another case, Scientific Atlanta also had contracted to install a cable TV system for the island of Nantucket and needed insurance coverage for that particular job. As it turned out, the company had been required by state law in Massachusetts to have auto liability coverage on all its vehicles above certain required limits. The first knowledge of this requirement came not from Wassau, but through being informed of a fine for not having appropriate coverage.

Scientific Atlanta has two employees who oversee their insurance programs — Mr. Grant Allen, Chief Engineer & Safety Engineer; and Ms. Ann Ford, Assistant Corporate Secretary. Neither performed all of the functions of a risk manager. For example, Ms. Ford was expected to keep track of the insurance policies, to be familiar with the coverages, and to act as a liaison between Scientific Atlanta and the insurance markets. Ms. Ford has no expertise in the insurance field other than having taken a basic insurance course at Georgia State University.

INSURANCE AND RISK HANDLING

The company operates a fleet of trucks, and it self-insures the collision peril, but uses commercial insurers for the liability risk. There is a $5,000 deductible on all property insurance. The plant in Scotland acquires insurance coverage locally.

Scientific Atlanta assumes the risk of errors and omissions. The company has experienced very few losses in this area. A loss that did occur four years ago came about when Scientific Atlanta

installed a cable TV antenna tower for a rural community. Due to a mistake in the antenna's design, the antenna began to fall after it had been operational for almost three months. The insurance coverage would reimburse Scientific Atlanta if the antenna were to fall and cause bodily injury, but all the costs of re-engineering the labor were directly absorbed by Scientific Atlanta. The company spent approximately $750,000 to

TABLE 15–5

Liability Coverage	Annual Premium
Workers' compensation $100,000/employee	$ 68,000
General liability & auto liability $1,000,000 bodily injury; $100,000 property	52,000
Umbrella policy coverage $20,000,000	
Foreign products liability $1,000,000 bodily injury; $100,000 property	1,000
Director & officers' liability $1,000,000 total; $5,000/person	4,500
Pension trust liability policy $2,000,000 coverage; $1,000 deductible	$ 2,000
Fidelity $1,000,000 coverage; $5,000 deductible	1,000
Travel accident liability policy $50,000 coverage	1,500
Nonowned aircraft; $1,000,000 coverage	300
Property Coverages	
Fire; $16,470,000 coverage	
Business interruption; $18,000,000 coverage	
Difference in condition policy (D.I.C.) $11,500,000 coverage	35,000
	$165,300

put the antenna system in working order again.

This was one of the few losses experienced due to errors and omissions. Mr. Allen had stated that ". . . as a whole, the company is more worried about its exposure to loss than actual losses incurred," but still the risk is assumed. Mr. Allen believed that Scientific Atlanta was very lucky so far in this area.

Insurance policies and their annual premiums are shown in Table 15–5.

QUESTIONS

1. Did Scientific Atlanta have sufficient reasons for appointing a broker? What other developments or conditions suggest the need for a broker?

2. What specific understandings should be made with the new broker? Explain.

3. Evaluate Scientific Atlanta's current risk management program.

APPENDIX A

	000's Omitted			
SUMMARY OF OPERATIONS	1975	1974	1973	1972
Net Sales				
Cost of Sales	$35,734	$26,351	$20,214	$16,209
Research & Development	1,204	829	972	396
Marketing & Admin.	5,072	4,263	3,553	3,046
Interest	556	435	255	251
Other Income	(592)	(300)	(105)	(96)
Earnings Before Taxes on Income	2,398	1,798	1,290	536
Taxes on Income	1,151	863	610	260
Net Earnings	$ 1,247	$ 935	$ 680	$ 276
SUMMARY FINANCIAL POSITION				
Working Capital	$ 7,820	$ 9,589	$ 7,548	$ 5,783
Net Property, Plant, & Equipment	5,367	4,077	3,786	3,617
Other Assets	585	424	446	632
Long-term Debt	3,179	5,183	4,003	3,065
Deferred Taxes on Income	1,001	633	441	369
Stockholder's Equity	9,592	8,274	7,336	6,598

16

Insurance Capacity

An important problem facing the risk manager is that of obtaining commercial property and liability insurance on acceptable terms and prices. Periodically it becomes much more difficult to obtain coverage than at other times. The willingness and ability of insurers to offer coverage depends upon their capacity to underwrite risk. Capacity, in turn, is dependent upon both financial and psychological factors. The risk manager should understand the capacity problem in insurance in order to deal effectively with pure risk in his own firm.

Major factors affecting the willingness and ability of insurers to cover risk are:

1. The profit and policyholders' surplus position of the insurer

2. Subjective attitudes toward risk of the underwriter

3. Underwriting knowledge and skill

4. The underwriting cycle in profits

5. Opportunity costs of funds

6. The growth rate of insurers

7. Homogeneity of risks

8. Reinsurance facilities

9. Regulation

Many of the above factors, to be discussed below, are interrelated and must be considered simultaneously by the underwriter in reaching insurance decisions.

THE PROFIT AND POLICYHOLDERS' SURPLUS POSITION

A basic understanding of the capacity problem starts with an appreciation of the financial ability of insurers to underwrite. If an insurer has inadequate profit levels, its surplus, or cushion for losses, is also likely to be inadequate, and its ability to accept new risk may be impaired. To understand the financial position of the insurer it is useful first to review five basic financial statement ratios. To illustrate, consider the hypothetical financial information for the Unlimited Insurance Company, a property and liability insurance underwriter, in Table 16–1.

From Table 16–1 the five balance and income sheet ratios may be calculated, showing the financial position of Unlimited (Table 16–2).

Ratio No. 1, net worth to debt, is a solvency measure. Net worth is the sum of the common stock and surplus, also

TABLE 16–1
Financial Information of Unlimited Insurance Company
December 30, 19——

Assets		Liabilities	
Cash, marketable stocks and bonds	$10,000,000	Loss reserves	$ 2,000,000
		Unearned premium reserves	3,000,000
		Common stock**	1,000,000
		Surplus**	4,000,000
	$10,000,000		$10,000,000

Latest year operating data:
Premium volume

Fire and allied lines	$ 5,000,000
Liability, including auto	5,000,000
Premiums written	$10,000,000
Losses incurred	$ 5,000,000
Expenses	4,500,000
Underwriting gain*	500,000
Investment profit	500,000

* Premiums — losses and expenses.

** The sum of common stock and surplus, the net worth, is also termed "policyholders'" surplus.

called the policyholders' surplus. The ratio reveals the ability of Unlimited to absorb reductions in assets which may be brought about either by operating losses or declines in asset values on the stock market. Net worth is a cushion for losses. A ratio of 1/1 means that total assets could decline in value by one-half, before the solvency of the company would be threatened by assets falling below total debt.

Ratio No. 2, premiums to net worth, is another solvency measure re-

vealing potential losses in relation to net worth. This ratio is also a measure of financial leverage. Premiums written represent new business and concomitant exposure to loss. The higher ratio No. 2 is, the greater financial risk the insurer accepts. In the case of Unlimited this ration is 2/1. This means that if a loss of 5 percent of premiums occurs, the reduction in policyholders' surplus would be 10 percent. This may be verified by noting that a loss of 5 percent equals $500,000, and that $500,000 is

TABLE 16–2

	(000's omitted)
1. Net worth to debt	$ 5,000/$ 5,000 = 1
2. Premiums written to net worth	$10,000/$ 5,000 = 2
3. Loss and expenses to premiums written (the combined ratio)	$ 9,500/$10,000 = .95
4. Total underwriting and investment profit to premium written	$ 1,000/$10,000 = .10
5. Total gain (profit) to net worth	$ 1,000/$ 5,000 = .20

10 percent of the capital and surplus of $5 million. If Unlimited doubles its premium writings to $20 million from the present level of $10 million, ratio No. 2 would also double to 4/1. Then a change in profit or loss of 5 percent of premiums would mean an increase or reduction in policyholders' surplus of 20 percent. Stated differently, if such losses continued for five years, all of Unlimited's surplus would be lost unless offset by investment gains.

Ratio No. 3, losses and expenses to premiums written, also called the combined loss and expense ratio, is a basic measure of underwriting profitability. A value of 100 for this ratio means that the insurer is about at the break-even point in its underwriting. Anything less than 100 indicates the existence of underwriting profits. In the case of Unlimited, the underwriting profit is 5 percent of premiums written.

Ratio No. 4, underwriting and investment profit to premiums written, indicates the total profitability of the insurer from both underwriting and investment operations. Ratio No. 5 expresses this profit as a percentage of net worth. Unlimited is earning 10 percent on premiums written and 20 percent on net worth, a very satisfactory earnings rate.[1]

It may be observed that investment earnings in Unlimited are equal to its underwriting gains. This situation is very common in the property-liability insurance industry. Investment earnings have been an important source of profits and have stabilized the financial position of the property and liability insurance industry over the years. In fact, for the industry as a whole, underwriting operations are typically at or near break even and the major source of earnings has been from investments, including stock market capital gains. For example, an analysis of major stock insurers in the property and liability field over the period 1961–73, showed that total underwriting gains were $.52 billion, compared to $19.08 billion in investment gains. Underwriting losses occurred in six of the 13 years, and investment gains occurred in nine of the 13 years, with only small losses in the remaining four years. The return on net worth ranged from −7.09 percent to 26.21 percent, indicating the relatively unstable nature of insurance industry profits.[2]

From the above analysis one may see that financial capacity to underwrite risk depends importantly upon profits and policyholders' surplus position of the insurer. If an insurer unduly extends its operations by accepting new business, its ratio of premiums written to policyholders' surplus will also be increased, perhaps to the point where the firm is quite vulnerable to insolvency if this new business results in even modest losses for a few years. Furthermore, underwriting losses may not always be offset by investment gains. In some years there are serious stock market losses which could adversely affect company solvency if they coincided with underwriting losses as well.

It follows that the risk manager, in judging the capacity of a given insurer to accept new risks, should start with a

---

[1] There are several other financial statement ratios that have been found to be significant in judging insurer solvency and capacity. A complete analysis of this subject is beyond the scope of this book. See J. S. Trieschmann and G. E. Pinches, "A Multivariate Model for Predicting Financially Distressed P.L. Insurers," *Journal of Risk and Insurance*, vol. 40, no. 3 (September 1973), pp. 327–28; and Roger Kenney, *Fundamentals of Fire and Casualty Insurance Strength* (Dedham, Mass.: Kenney Insurance Studies, 1957).

[2] Mark R. Greene, *Risk and Insurance* (Cincinnati: South-Western Publishing Company, 1977), p. 623.

simple analysis of the balance sheet and income statements. This analysis should be undertaken not only to judge capacity, but also to judge the likelihood of insolvency. It would be of little comfort for risk manager to place his risk with an insurer, only to discover after a loss that the insurer could not meet its obligations. Furthermore, the risk manager cannot rely solely upon the fact that insurance companies are subject to state regulation which requires that the company remain solvent at all times and charges the state insurance commissioner with the duty of enforcing this law. In spite of the vigilance of state regulatory authorities even large insurers occasionally go bankrupt.[3] The careful risk manager will make his own investigation of the financial capacity of the insurer he is considering.

The question arises as to what values should exist for the ratios discussed above. Unfortunately, there are no simple universally accepted norms for judging financial condition. More important than absolute values are the trends that may be observed in a given insurer. If ratio No. 1 is falling and ratio No. 2 is rising, obviously the financial condition of the insurer is declining. Another important consideration in judging the ratios that are observed is the consistency and reasonableness with which accounting policy is maintained. The debts on an insurer's balance sheet are in the nature of estimates. Loss reserves, for example, are set up to pay for claims whose final cost may not be known for months or years.

[3] Notable among large companies to go into receivership was the Equity Funding Life Insurance Company whose officers were discovered in a giant scandal in 1973 in which false life insurance business was recorded in order to defraud reinsurers. See also Robert E. Nelson, "Property-Liability Company Exits," *The Journal of Risk and Insurance*, vol. 38, no. 3 (September 1971).

If these reserves or estimated liabilities are overstated or understated, obviously the calculation of balance sheet ratios will be similarly distorted. Unfortunately, it is seldom practicable for the outside analyst to learn objectively about the policies used by the insurer in setting up loss reserves. However, substantial alterations in loss reserves, unaccompanied by corresponding changes in the volume of premium writings, should be viewed with suspicion, since this might indicate arbitrary accounting manipulations to improve the looks of the balance sheet.

Another factor in interpreting balance sheet ratios lies in the nature of the unearned premium reserve. This reserve reflects the insurer's obligation to policyholders for premiums paid in advance, but as yet unearned by the insurer. If the policy is cancelled, part or all of these premium reserves must be returned to the insured. It is generally considered that these reserves are redundant for two major reasons: (a) The premium contains an expense allowance which is incurred mainly in the first year of the life of the policy paid for from funds represented by company surplus. As the policy runs its course the premium is earned and the profit, including the expense allowance, is returned to surplus. Thus, that portion of the unearned premium reserve representing expenses (between 30 and 40 percent) does not actually represent a liability, but instead is really a part of the insurer's surplus. (b) A portion of the unearned premium reserve, agent's commissions, must be returned on a pro rata basis if the policy is cancelled. This portion does not represent a true liability. For this reason an insurer's liabilities may err on the side of being excessive and the ratios thus showing a less conservative picture than that which actually exists.

Some notion of normalcy for balance sheet ratios may be obtained by comparing the ratios developed for a given insurer with other similar insurers or with ratios characterizing the industry as a whole. For example, in the United States, about 2,900 insurers were operating in property and liability insurance. In 1974 these insurers had $84 billion of assets, $21 billion of policyholders' surplus, $63 billion in liabilities, and wrote $45 billion in premiums. The industry as a whole, therefore, had a ratio of net worth to debt of about .33 and a ratio of premiums to net worth of 2.1. For the industry as a whole net underwriting loss in 1974 was $2.7 billion and investment gains were $3.5 billion.[4]

If the entire insurance industry were operating as one large insurer, it seems clear that the financial capacity of the U.S. insurance industry would not currently be particularly strained. Many financially sound individual insurers operate at ratios of premiums to policyholders' surplus of 3/1 or higher. Applied to the U.S. industry as a whole, a ratio of 3/1 would indicate an ability to accept $63 billion (3 × $21) in new premiums, about 1.5 times the level actually accepted in 1974. Of course, the industry is not operating as one large insurer and the financial situation in many individual insurers will not permit doubling of the level of business accepted currently. Major reasons for this are explored below.

Returning to the example of Unlimited Insurance Company, we may gain further insight into its capacity by applying certain other ratios commonly

[4] Insurance Facts, 1975. (New York: Insurance Information Institute, 1975). See also, George E. Pinches and James S. Trieschmann, "The Efficiency of Alternative Models for Solvency Surveillance in the Insurance Industry," Journal of Risk and Insurance, December 1974, pp. 563–77.

used by state insurance regulators in judging insurer solvency. One of these ratios is that the insurer may not cover a single risk in excess of 10 percent of its policyholders' surplus, or collect more than 2 percent of its premium income from any one loss exposure. Applying these ratios, we see that Unlimited should accept no more than $500,000 of loss exposure on a single risk, nor collect more than $200,000 in premiums on a single exposure. However, it does not appear that Unlimited could accept risks implied by these guidelines. A loss of $500,000, for example, might not reduce surplus unacceptably, but if the company accepted a number of risks each of which had a maximum exposure of $500,000, it would take only ten total losses in a given year to eliminate the company's surplus. Nor would the 2 percent of premiums guideline likely be acceptable. A typical fire insurance premium rate may be 1 percent of the value of the property. In this case the guideline would indicate that Unlimited could accept a fire risk of $20 million, which is twice the amount of the assets owned by the company.

In practice, of course, Unlimited would employ reinsurance to deal off that portion of a large risk which is too large for its existing financial position. Reinsurance will be examined below. It is sufficient to note at this point that the risk manager must carefully consider the reinsurance treaties available to an insurer, and the capacity of the reinsurers themselves, in judging the total capacity available for risk transfer.

CAPACITY AND SUBJECTIVE ATTITUDES TOWARD RISK

From the above analysis it may be suspected that there are no hard and fast limits employed in applying financial ratios to determine capacity to underwrite new risks. Executive judgment is important in setting the limits. An important factor affecting this judgment is the mental attitude toward risk of the underwriter or his superiors. Presumably, a risk-averting management might set more restrictive limits than those suggested above, and a risk-loving management could easily set more liberal limits. The record of one of the largest stock insurers in the U.S., for example, shows in one year that it wrote $14 of premiums for each $1 of surplus. For such a company a 5 percent underwriting loss would mean a reduction in surplus of 90 percent. This insurer's management apparently either does not perceive excessive risk in its operations or is willing to accept relatively great underwriting risk.

Insurance management's subjective attitudes toward risk has traditionally been conservative, too conservative, in the opinion of some authorities. The aggregate data cited above for the property and liability insurance industry supports this notion. They reveal very conservative financial ratios. Thus, the rate of return on total assets for the industry in 1971 was only 3 percent, suggesting conservative investment policies, particularly so in a year of underwriting gains.

Underwriting capacity is difficult to augment by raising funds in the equity markets because the modest returns on assets in the industry has resulted in typically low stock market evaluation of insurance industry common stocks. For example, it is not uncommon to find the common stocks of leading insurers selling below book value, reflecting negative investor opinion of both conservative dividend pay outs and relatively low profit rates in the industry. As David Houston wrote some years ago:

Most likely, surplus figures for U.S. insurers are high as a result of accounting practices and an overconservative bias on the part of companies. In this context, the Kenney rule, which asserts that an insurer should have one dollar of policyholders' surplus for every two dollars of premium volume, seems very conservative . . . Viewing the policyholders' surplus as the buffer fund, the Kenney Rule may be restated as follows: the buffer fund should be equal to the pure premiums. Intuitively one would suspect that a much smaller buffer would suffice, since its only purpose is to cover losses in excess of those which are expected.[5]

Robert A. Hershbarger has developed a mathematical model simulating the operations of a property-liability insurer to test underwriting capacity under different conditions. Using this model to discover the main constraints to underwriting capacity, Hershbarger concluded that the primary underwriting restriction was psychological in nature and was derived from managements unwillingness to commit resources to the underwriting function. In the model, psychological capacity was a function of the rate of return needed in order to persuade management to commit a given percentage of the company surplus to underwriting. Interestingly enough, in Hershbarger's model neither the net worth to debt nor premiums to surplus ratios, nor statutory regulations operated as real constraints to underwriting capacity.[6]

[5] David B. Houston, "Risk Insurance and Sampling," *The Journal of Risk and Insurance*, vol. 31 (December 1964), p. 532. For further discussion of the Kenney Rule, see Kenney, *Fundamentals of Insurance Strength*, pp. 209–23.

[6] Robert A. Hershbarger, *A Simulation Model for a Multiple-Line Insurance Company* (Unpublished Doctoral Dissertation, University of Georgia, 1972).

Mental attitudes toward risk of the underwriter and of insurance executives generally affect and are affected by several interrelated factors discussed below. For example, these attitudes have an important effect on financial and investment policies. Among the more important factors affecting mental attitudes toward risk are the underwriting cycle and the knowledge, skill, and experience of insurance managers.

KNOWLEDGE AND SKILL OF THE UNDERWRITER

As we have seen previously, underwriting capacity is affected importantly by the amount of funds made available to back up the promises of the insurer. Even though the underwriter is willing and experienced in a given line of risk, he will not be able to accept risk if the company's surplus is too low. On the other hand, the inexperienced underwriter may be too timid to accept risks even if his company's surplus is sufficient.

The amount of insurance capacity is closely related to the knowledge, skill, and experience of the underwriter. The underwriter is a key executive in an insurance company. Ignorance of the particular characteristics of the insured's business will tend to increase the degree of uncertainty in the mind of the underwriter as to the true risk he is accepting. It is only logical that the uncertainty generated by ignorance will increase the underwriter's caution, and so reduce the willingness to insure. Capacity to insure is affected both by willingness and ability of the insurer to accept risk. As Arne Fougner pointed out, in listing man-made restrictions upon capacity:

Factual knowledge with respect to hard-to-place lines is frequently lacking, resulting in potential commitments being restricted or precluded just because underwriters prefer to err on the conservative side.[7]

On the other hand, evidence suggests that high levels of knowledge, skill, and experience by the underwriter, where it exists, may operate to enlarge insurance capacity. For example, it is likely that the success of specialty insurers in accepting risks rejected by others is due to the special knowledge and skill of their underwriters in given areas of business. Specialty insurers prosper in covering such risks as taxicab fleets, computer-processing equipment, properties subject to earthquake, and motorcycles — all properties often rejected by more generalized carriers. Marine insurance carriers were among the first specialty insurers. Lloyds of London still makes this coverage their specialty. In life insurance, some insurers specialize in coverages such as business insurance, or in substandard risks. Blue Cross and Blue Shield organizations have captured a large portion of the private basic medical and hospitalization coverage market using a specialized approach. The risk manager must in many cases look to specialty insurers with their specialized professional underwriters for needed capacity in given lines.

THE UNDERWRITING CYCLE

Another influence on the mental attitudes toward risk of insurance underwriters is the fluctuation in underwriting profits. Underwriting gains in profits tend to move in cycles of five or six years. By observing these cycles, the

---

[7] Arne Fougner, "The Capacity Problem," in H. Wayne Snider, *Readings in Property and Casualty Insurance* (Homewood, Ill.: Richard D. Irwin, Inc., 1959), p. 184.

risk manager may predict roughly when underwriting will tend to be loose and when it will be tight. Obviously, after suffering underwriting losses underwriters tend to be more careful as to which risks they will accept and will tend to employ more restrictive underwriting standards. The opposite occurs after a period of underwriting gains. Figure 16–1 illustrates the underwriting profits and losses and investment gains, as a percentage of premiums earned, for the period 1920–70 for U.S. stock insurers in property and liability insurance.

From Figure 16–1 it will be observed that peaks in underwriting results occurred in 1922, 1928, 1935, 1943, 1948, 1954, 1959, and 1965, roughly every six years. Investment gains, on the other hand, were fairly stable. One of the reasons for these cycles in underwriting profit is the phenomenon of rate regulation, which is characterized by time lags that prevent prompt adjustment of rates to reflect adverse underwriting experience. Adverse loss experience may be caused by catastrophes, by loose underwriting, or by absence of adequate loss reserves, in relation to the premiums collected.

In the rising phase of the cycle, when underwriting profits are improving, underwriters begin to realize that they have more financial capacity than previously. For example, in 1973 an insurance executive noted that "reinsurance markets in the world are now facing over-capacity compared with the situation five years ago."[8] Competition for business tends to encourage underwriters to ease up on underwriting standards, accepting somewhat marginal risks and reducing effective rates. This phenomenon, together with factors such

[8] J. A. S. Heave, Chairman of the Reinsurance Officers Association, at the annual meeting of the association, London, 1973.

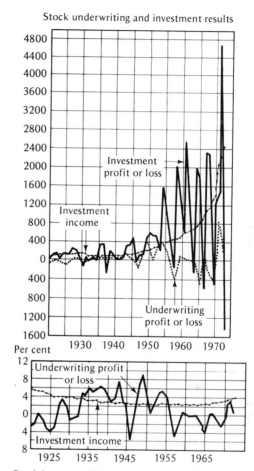

Figure 16–1

as catastrophes, tends to produce adverse loss experience and the cycle ultimately turns downward. Insurers then attempt to secure permission from regulators to charge higher rates. They also tighten underwriting standards, reject marginal risks, and take other steps to stem losses. Permission to charge higher insurance rates is often slow in arriving. One of the reasons for this is that insurers must submit loss data which will support the need for higher rates, but these loss data generally take at least two or three years to develop, as the policies run their course. In the meantime, underwriting losses begin to mount. The decline in underwriting losses is finally arrested by a combination of tightened underwriting standards and rate adjustments which are ultimately forthcoming, and the cycle begins its upward movement once again.

One underwriting cycle in insurance (1948–54) was described by Arne Fougner. In observing the "capacity problem" in the United States following World War II, Fougner noted that rapid inflation, economic expansion, resumed driving of automobiles, vastly increased civilian production, and spurting construction caused premium volume in all branches of American insurance to expand beyond the ready capacity of the insurance industry based on its limited capitalization and stringent reserve requirements. Yet "when increased rates produced improved results the capacity problem largely disappeared insofar as the run-of-the-mill business was concerned. Subsequently, repeated hurricanes in the early '50s created new problems." [9]

The risk manager wishing to take advantage of the underwriting cycle in insurance may do several things. First, he may attempt to negotiate renewals of insurance programs in the light of the current phase of the underwriting cycle which the industry appears to be experiencing. During the rising phase he can expect to negotiate more favorable terms and conditions than would be possible during the declining phase. Second, he may study the underwriting cycle of his particular insurer to learn if

[9] Fougner, "Capacity Problem," p. 183.

this insurer is experiencing a cycle different from that of the industry as a whole, and proceed accordingly. Third, he may present loss experience data of his own firm to the insurance underwriter to justify more favorable terms and conditions than might otherwise be possible. For example, if the loss ratios of his own company are declining, he may present his case more effectively in any phase of the underwriting cycle for the insurance industry generally than would be possible without such data.

OPPORTUNITY COSTS OF FUNDS

As indicated on page 373, investment gains among property and liability insurers have usually exceeded underwriting gains by a wide margin. As a result, some insurers have tended to emphasize the investment function including investments in other noninsurance services, rather than the underwriting function in their operations. This tends to cause in some cases an artificial restriction on insurance underwriting capacity, as available funds are used in noninsurance areas where risk is often less and the net return is greater. Thus, many insurers are employing funds in real estate, mutual funds, leasing of equipment, banking, and in other areas of financial services.

One evidence of this phenomenon in American insurance has been the "merger movement," during the post-World War II period. These mergers have been initiated by three major types of firms: insurance, financial, and industrial. A majority of insurance mergers have been initiated by insurers who have combined for various reasons. Noninsurance firms such as banks and industrial corporations have also been active in merging with insurers. The Insurance Information Institute estimated that over a two-year period, 1968–69, in the United States, merger actively caused about $1.5 billion of capital, amounting to about 3 percent of the total assets of property and liability insurers, to be diverted from insurance operations.[10]

It should be observed that although some mergers do indeed have the effect of removing funds from the insurance business, other mergers may have an opposite effect, resulting in enlarged capacity. For example, some mergers initiated by industrial corporations (*e.g.*, Ford Motor Company, Sears Roebuck, J. C. Penney, and Deere and Company) may actually result in infusions of new capital from the manufacturer into their wholly owned insurance subsidiaries. Furthermore, mergers between insurance companies do not necessarily restrict capacity, but may increase it through better utilization of manpower, greater stability of earnings, reduction of taxation, and better service to the consumer through more complete packaging of insurance coverages. All of these factors should result in the enlargement of earnings, and, therefore, surplus.

CAPACITY AND GROWTH RATES OF INSURERS

For reasons which will be discussed below, rapidly growing property and liability insurers tend to have greater "surplus strain" than those whose rates of growth are level or declining. It follows that the capacity of fast-growing insurers will tend to be more restricted than others. If the entire industry is in a period of rapid growth, the problem

[10] *Insurance Facts, 1971.* (New York: Insurance Information Institute, 1971), p. 27.

may be felt generally, as was the case in the United States after World War II, when premium volume approximately doubled each ten years. During the period 1947–71 annual premiums collected in the United States increased sevenfold, compared to a sixfold increase in policyholders' surplus. It is not surprising that U.S. industry has been aware of a capacity problem in the post-World War II period. The industry accepted approximately one-sixth more business for each dollar of surplus in 1971 than it took in 1947.

One basic cause of surplus strain for an insurer whose business is increasing stems from the use of cash accounting rather than accrual accounting for expenses. Accounting requirements under most state laws demand that first year expenses of writing new business be charged entirely against the first year earned premiums, even though the policy may be issued for a period longer than one year. Since most of the expenses on a new policy are incurred in the first year, this method of accounting usually produces a book loss during the first year, which is made up in subsequent years. To meet this loss, surplus must be charged, and, hence, the surplus strain referred to above comes about.

To illustrate this phenomenon, consider the following simplified hypothetical case: On January 1 the Newly Formed Insurance Company, a fire insurer, writes 100 fire policies on a three-year basis, collecting $100,000 in advance premiums. Losses are expected to be 60 percent (20 percent annually); acquisition expenses, 35 percent; and profits, 5 percent of premiums. Acquisition expenses are all incurred in the first year. Losses turn out to be exactly as predicted. On December 31, the insurer's financial statements reveal the following:

Premiums written (PW)	$100,000
Less:	
Unearned premium reserve (two-thirds of PW)	66,666
Earned premiums	$ 33,334
Less:	
Losses incurred (20 percent)	20,000
Expenses incurred (35 percent)	35,000
Statutory underwriting loss	($ 21,666)

Although operating income and outgo is exactly as planned the insurer shows a statutory underwriting loss of $21,666 which must come from surplus. As the policies run their course this loss is recovered. If no new business is written in the second or third years, the income statement for each of these years appears as follows:

Premiums written	$ 00
Less:	
Increase in unearned premium reserve	− 33,333
Premiums earned	$33,333
Less:	
Losses incurred	20,000
Expenses incurred	0
Statutory underwriting gain	$13,333

During the second and third years we discover that although the insurer wrote no new business, the run off from the first year's business produced an underwriting gain. During the second two years, statutory underwriting gains total $26,666. The first year loss of $21,666 has now been offset, leaving a $5,000 profit, as anticipated when the 5 percent profit margin was originally built into the rate.

It is worth noting that during the first year, when the company was growing and developing potentially profitable new business, its income statement

seems to appear unfavorable to the uninitiated observer. During the second two years, when its growth was halted entirely, its income statement appears very favorable. The risk manager should be aware of this phenomenon when judging the capacity of the insurers with whom he is dealing. To learn the true financial position of the firm, he must make an adjustment in the statutory earnings to reflect the degree to which the unearned premium reserve is actually overstated due to the advance payment of first year expenses from surplus. This quantity has been termed the "equity in the unearned premium reserve." To obtain the adjustment the risk manager should add back into the statutory underwriting losses that percentage of the increase in the unearned premium reserve which is equal to the first year expense allowance of the insurer. In the above example this adjustment would be as follows:

Year 1	
Statutory Underwriting Loss	$21,666
Plus: 35 percent of the increase in the unearned premium reserve (.35 × $66,666)	23,333
Adjusted underwriting gain	$ 1,667

Years 2 and 3	
Statutory Underwriting Gain	$13,333
Less: 35 percent of the increase in the unearned premium reserve (.35 × $33,333)	11,666
Adjusted underwriting gain	$ 1,667

With these adjustments the underwriting profit of the insurer is evened out at $1,667 annually (totalling $5,000) over the three-year period. The surplus strain is due to accounting requirements and not unfavorable underwriting conditions. Full realization of this phenomenon by the underwriter and the risk manager should alleviate the mental anxiety which might otherwise dampen the willingness of the insurer to accept new risks.

CAPACITY AND THE HOMOGENEITY OF RISK

The capacity of an insurer to accept new risk depends significantly upon the risk the insurer faces with a given portfolio of exposure units. Insurer risk depends upon the number, homogeneity, and nature of the exposures being insured. Intuitively, it is easy to recognize that if two insurers have equal amounts of policyholders' surplus and premiums written, but one has a portfolio of collision policies on 1 million automobiles while the second has a portfolio of policies on 100,000 trucks for large limits of physical damage and bodily injury liability loss, the total risk of the second insurer is likely to be greater than the first.

Insurer risk depends upon four main factors: (a) the number of homogeneous exposure units covered, (b) the degree to which losses are independent of one another, (c) the probability, mean, and standard deviation of losses,

and (d) the minimum degree of accuracy with which the insurer requires in predicting the total number and amount of claims it will experience with a given portfolio of risks. These factors must be considered in relation to the size and strength of the insurer. A way of summarizing insurer risk is to state that it depends upon the success with which the law of large numbers operates enabling the insurer to predict losses. If the insurer could predict losses exactly, it would face no risk as such at all, since risk is generally defined as the variation of actual losses from expected, or probable, losses. Hence, if there is no variation, there is no risk. The law of large numbers states that as the number of exposure units increases, the variation of actual from probable losses declines and approaches zero as the number of exposure units approaches infinity.

Some simple arithmetic illustrations of the law of large numbers will suffice to explain the major factors affecting the risk of the insurer. In Case 1 assume that there are two insurers, A and B, with portfolios of risks as shown. Losses are distributed in accordance with the binomial probability distribution.

CASE 1

	Insurer A	Insurer B
(1) Exposures	900 autos	3,600 autos
(2) Probability of loss	20 percent	20 percent
(3) Expected loss frequency (mean loss)	180 collisions	720 collisions
(4) Standard deviation of loss	12 collisions	24 collisions
(5) Risk, as measured by the coefficient of variation [(4) ÷ (3)]	12/180 = .667	24/720 = .334

Note that in Case 1 each insurer is faced with the same probability of loss, 20

percent. Insurer B, with 3,600 automobiles, has four times as many autos and half as much risk as A. Other things being equal, risk varies inversely with the square root of the number of exposures. As the number of cars in-creases indefinitely, the risk measured by the ratio of the standard deviation to the mean (coefficient of variation) approaches zero.

CASE 2

	Insurer C	Insurer D
(1) Exposures	900 autos	900 autos
(2) Probability of loss	10 percent	20 percent
(3) Expected loss frequency	90 collisions	180 collisions
(4) Standard deviation	9 collisions	12 collisions
(5) Risk	9/90 = .10	12/180 = .0667

In Case 2, the number of exposures is held constant, but the loss probability of Insurer D is double that of Insurer C. Note that contrary to intuitive expectations, the risk declines as probability increases if the number of exposure units is held constant. This is true because with higher probabilities the certainty of loss increases. Hence, the deviation from expected loss declines until, as probability of loss approaches 100 percent, risk vanishes. Case 2 demonstrates that Insurer D can pay out more in losses but suffers less risk than Insurer C.

Accuracy Required

Some insurers will wish much greater accuracy in their loss predictions than others. As shown above, greater accuracy (less risk) is obtainable by increasing the number of exposures covered or by accepting business with greater loss probability. The question as to the interrelation of these two factors and their relationship to acceptable errors in loss prediction is discussed in Chapter 3.

Conclusion

The effect on capacity of the four major factors affecting insurer risk may now be more fully appreciated. If an insurer has only a small number of exposures in a given field, it will usually be willing to underwrite a larger number of *similar homogeneous* exposures in order to reduce its total risk. This follows because the coefficient of variation[11] declines as the number of exposures increases, other things being equal. Thus, if the risk manager is offering the insurer an exposure unit which fits into such a portfolio of risks, the risk manager's offering actually increases insurance capacity by reducing insurer risk. On the other hand, if the offering is entirely different from the line of exposures already covered by a given insurer, the offering will reduce capacity by increasing the insurer's risk above that of the current level.

The risk-aversion or risk-taking characteristics of the insurer can be inferred from the accuracy of predictions required or from the confidence levels demanded, in a given case. Large corporations may be able to demonstrate that their exposures are large enough to en-

[11] One student of the capacity problem termed this measure the "exposure ratio," and demonstrated similar conclusions. See James M. Stone, "A Theory of Capacity and the Insurance of Catastrophic Risks (Part I)," *The Journal of Risk and Insurance*, vol. 40, no. 2 (June 1973), pp. 235–36.

able very accurate loss predictions at high levels of confidence. The risk manager can thus reduce the degree of risk perceived by the underwriter and obtain better terms or lower rates.

Clearly, if the risk manager is offering a new exposure whose potential loss is great, perhaps so great as to threaten the solvency of the insurer if a major loss occurs, the insurer is likely to reject risk, even if the expected value of the loss is low. This follows from the proposition stated above that risk varies inversely with probability. For example, suppose an insurer has a policyholders' surplus of $1 million and is offered a risk at a premium of $50,000 whose probable loss distribution is as follows:

Probability of Loss	Size of Loss	Expected Value of Loss
.98	–0–	–0–
.019	$100,000	$1,900
.001	$10,000,000	$10,000
	Total expected value	$11,900

The insurer may reject this risk even at the relatively high premium of $50,000, because of an unacceptable probability (.001) of catastrophic loss and consequent ruin of the insurer. It is certain that a $10 million loss would cause the insurer's insolvency, unless it had appropriate reinsurance (see below).

CAPACITY AND REINSURANCE FACILITIES

The nature and extent of reinsurance treaties is an important influence on underwriting capacity. Reinsurance is a method by which a primary insurer, called the ceding company, may shift part or all of its risk to another insurer called the reinsurer. If the reinsurer, in turn, shifts part of its risk to other carriers, the process is termed retrocession. A ceding insurer can also become a reinsurer through membership in a treaty under which a group of primary insurers agree to share or pool each others' risks.

It is obvious that when a primary insurer can pass on risk to others, its own capacity for handling new business is augmented at least temporarily. Unfortunately, some types of reinsurance treaties can be relatively costly to the ceding insurer, and may in the long run reduce the capacity of the ceding insurer through reducing its profit (and surplus) growth below that which would otherwise prevail. In this event, however, it is the reinsurer which earns the profit and so total underwriting capacity available in the market is not necessarily reduced by the cost of the reinsurance mechanism. Furthermore, the ceding insurer is often able to recover some of its reinsurance costs through earning profits on reinsurance accepted from others.

Perhaps the major way in which reinsurance increases total underwriting capacity at any given time is through reducing the total risk faced by all insurers who are, thereby, able to obtain a greater spread of loss than would otherwise be possible. Thus, if a $30 million loss exposure to one insurer can be divided into 60 exposures of $500,000 each to different insurers, the total risk is less; and underwriting capacity is greater than would otherwise be the case. It is through reinsurance that such a division can be made. The cost of reinsurance is rationalized by the belief that it is better to have a lower but more stable profit than a higher average profit which is somewhat unstable. The very existence of reinsurance is evidence of the risk-averting stance taken by most insurance underwriters.

In addition to reducing total risk, the reinsurance mechanism contributes to the efficiency of the insurance industry in other ways. First, a primary insurer may discover that its underwriting exposures are unbalanced. It may wish to eliminate a certain portfolio of risk exposures entirely, thus reducing a substantial exposure to loss in an area where premium volume may be too small to justify it. Through reinsurance the entire block of business may be removed from its books and the original policyholders are not inconvenienced through cancellations.

Second, a risk manager may wish to use the reinsurance market to accept business generated by a company-owned captive insurer. The regulations applicable to the operations of reinsurers permit much greater freedom and flexibility than those applicable to primary insurers. For example, reinsurance rates are not subject to close regulation, and the costs of dealing directly with a reinsurer, rather than a primary carrier, are less.

Third, reinsurance helps contribute to increased underwriting flexibility in the industry by relieving small new insurers of liability for meeting unearned premium reserve requirements on business deemed inappropriate for their current needs. As we have seen previously, a rapidly growing new insurer may be restricted in its growth by surplus strain imposed by the cash accounting methods. Through reinsurance new business can be shifted out of the company, and with it the corresponding unearned premium reserve requirement. For example, in the case of the Newly Formed Insurance Company, the management could decide on December 31 to reinsure the fire insurance business,

which carries a $66,666 unearned premium reserve requirement. The reinsurer would probably expect to pay $66,666 less expected losses ($40,000) on this block of business and less its expected profit, say, 5 percent of premiums ($3,333). Thus, Newly Formed would receive $23,333 which is just equal to the amounts taken from surplus to meet the first year expenses of the business. Through reinsurance Newly Formed would be able to recover its equity in the unearned premium reserve and could employ these funds to underwrite other business.

To illustrate how reinsurance accomplishes its purpose of distributing risk, let us examine typical reinsurance agreements. (Reinsurance is examined in more detail in another chapter.) Examples of two general types will be mentioned here: (a) pro rata treaties and (b) excess treaties. In pro rata treaties, losses and premiums are shared in some stated proportion for all members of the treaty. In excess treaties, the ceding insurer bears the first portion of all losses and any excess loss is paid by the reinsuring members.

Perhaps the most commonly employed contracts of pro rata reinsurance are called *surplus treaties*. Surplus treaties represent the transfer of risk on specific loss exposures (*i.e.*, buildings, truck liability, etc.) to other members of the treaty. The larger the amount of the risk retained (called net retention) by the ceding insurer, the greater the amount which will be accepted by the other members of the treaty. For example, under a first surplus treaty if the ceding insurer retains $20,000 on each loss exposure it may be permitted 5 lines, or $100,000 (5 × $20,000) on any one loss exposure unit. If it retains $30,000 per exposure, it may be permitted to transfer 8 lines, or $240,000 per exposure unit, etc. In such a case, the primary insurer could accept up to $270,000 on any one loss exposure of this type. In the event of loss, each member of the reinsurance pool pays in proportion to the amount of insurance it has accepted, or some other stated proportion. Sometimes members of the treaty will form second surplus or third surplus treaties to accept risks beyond the limits of the first surplus treaty.

Under the second type of treaty, the *excess of loss treaty*, the reinsurer does not pay a pro rata portion of any loss, but is obligated to pay only when aggregate losses of the ceding insurer have exceeded a given amount which is retained by the ceding insurer. Thus, if the ceding insurer retains $20,000 and cedes $80,000 of a given exposure to loss, and there is a $20,000 partial loss, the reinsurer would pay nothing; on the other hand, if the loss is $50,000, the reinsurer must pay $30,000. Since most losses are partial and will fall below the retention, the reinsurer's accounting requirements are minimized. For similar reasons, the costs of such contracts to the ceding insurer are generally smaller than under pro rata treaties.

REGULATION AND CAPACITY

Insurance is one of the most heavily regulated of all industries, particularly in the United States. In varying ways this regulation tends to reduce underwriting capacity. Chief among the types of regulation of this nature are the following: (a) minimum capital and surplus requirements, (b) rate regulation, and (c) investment regulation.

Capital and Surplus Requirements

All states in the United States specify minimum capital and surplus re-

quirements for all insurers chartered to do business within state boundaries. These requirements vary greatly and have far-reaching effects upon insurer operations. In New York the minimum capital and surplus requirement for an insurer writing all lines is $3,550,000. (Smaller amounts are specified for insurers writing only specified lines of coverage.) In other states the minimum capital requirement is as low as $70,000 (Arizona), about 2 percent of the requirements of New York. Other states' requirements fall in between these extremes. Undoubtedly, in some cases capital and surplus requirements are in excess of what they need to be, and in other cases they may be less. In any event, the capacity to underwrite business is importantly affected by these requirements since insurers not meeting the minimum requirements are excluded from participating in given lines. In other cases, insurers allowed to write with inadequate capital and surplus may end up in insolvency, thus removing part or all of what assets they controlled from the pool of capital available to insurers generally.

State laws also regulate the size of various reserves and impose deposit requirements for the protection of policyholders. For example, a common requirement is that a given percentage of premiums collected must be shown on the balance sheet as loss reserves, whether or not justified by the level of actual losses. As noted above, unearned premium reserves must be set up on a pro rata basis over the life of the policy, and may not be reduced because most of the expenses of the policy have been incurred in the first year. As Arne Fougner pointed out, many of these requirements, aside from being inconsistent from area to area, are not actually necessary for the protection of policy holders.

". . . too many restrictions exist in the form of deposits for admission to markets, guarantee funds, retention of premium and loss reserves, etc., inhibiting flow of business, and restricting the liquidity and capacity of active or potential reinsurers. Far too often such requirements are dictated more by reasons of convenience, tradition, and investment yields, than by genuine needs from a pure insurance point of view."[12]

Rate Regulation

As pointed out before, an important determinant of capacity is the level and trend of underwriting profit. Rate regulation has an important influence on profits because in most states insurers must still obtain advance approval of rate changes from insurance commissioners before they can be applied to customers. Even in states permitting insurers to adopt rate changes without prior notification of insurance regulators, these rates must still ultimately be approved. Approval is granted usually only after insurers can demonstrate, through the accumulation of past data on losses and expenses, that the rate change is justified. Since this takes time, a lag is introduced between the need and fulfillment of rate adjustments. The result is a boom and bust cycle in underwriting profits. (See discussion of the underwriting cycle above.)

An unfortunate effect of rate regulation is to encourage, in the short run, a condition of fixed rates under which insurers must operate. If the underwriter believes a given risk is superior to the average in its rating category, he will accept the risk, and if not, he will tend to avoid it. Automatically, certain risks are below standard and are avoided while others are above standard and are sought after. As Ingolf Otto stated,[13]

". . . insurers spend a vast amount of time, energy, and money in trying to attract the 'cream business' and trying to avoid the 'substandard business.' The term 'substandard risk' has no real content. At the proper rate, no risk is substandard."

Another problem introduced by rate regulation is the fact that certain types of expenses of insurers may not be recognized in justifying rate increases — for example, allowances for catastrophe reserves. Neither are such allowances usually recognized as income tax deductions in most areas. If underwriters tend to lack adequate catastrophe reserves they may be reluctant to accept risks that might be prone to catastrophic losses. Hence, insurance capacity for the jumbo risk is often lacking.

Investment Regulation

All states regulate the nature of investments permitted by insurance companies. The objective of most types of investment regulation is to ensure that funds paid in by policyholders are protected, and to ensure the continued ability of the company to pay claims when due. Funds represented by unearned premium reserve requirements and loss reserves must generally be invested conservatively in bonds, mortgages, and other fixed income-type obligations which presumably have the least risk and the greatest liquidity among available investments. In meeting financial requirements, insurers are not even permitted to count certain assets, called nonadmitted assets; such

---

[12] Arne Fougner, "Capacity Problem," p. 184.

[13] Ingolf Otto, "Capacity," *Journal of Insurance* (March 1961), p. 59.

as furniture, fixtures, office buildings, and the like, since presumably these assets are not available for liquidation in order to meet insurance claims.

It is generally true that investments carrying the least risk also offer the least rate of return to the investor. The question arises as to whether insurers really need to invest so conservatively as the law requires. In most cases, insurers will not be required to sell assets in order to pay insurance claims, since current revenues will usually be more than sufficient for this purpose. Thus, liquidity need not be an overriding investment consideration for insurers. In addition, returns from bonds and mortgages as a rule will not equal those obtainable from well-selected common stocks or real estate. For example, studies have shown that long-term investment programs in common stocks yield between 8 and 9 percent, while investments in bonds and mortgages will average close to 5 percent.[14]

It is widely recognized that state investment regulation has had a tendency to cause rather conservative investment policies by insurance companies. However, in many cases insurers have not invested their assets as liberally as permitted by state law. To the extent that this is true, insurers will tend to obtain lower investment returns than would otherwise be possible. This has an obvious effect in reducing underwriting capacity, since investment earnings are basic to the financial health and continued growth of all types of insurers.

The growth of insurance-controlled assets in the United States, for example, has not equalled the growth of other financial institutions. To some ex-

tent this is almost certainly due to the modest investment returns of the industry. In one study it was shown that over the period 1963–71, all types of insurers increased their long-term capital investments by 53.2 percent. This may be compared to a total growth of long-term capital funds in the U.S. economy of 95.2 percent.[15] A leading insurance statistical agency reported average investment returns as a percent of mean assets among stock property and liability insurers in the United States as follows:[16]

1970	3.57
1965	2.78
1960	2.55
1955	2.38
1950	2.42
1945	2.47
1940	2.93

Investment returns among life insurers in the United States were reported as follows:[17]

1970	5.34
1965	4.61
1960	4.11
1955	3.51
1950	3.13
1945	3.11
1940	3.45

It is interesting to note that life insurers obtained consistently greater returns on investments than property and liability

[14] Lawrence Fisher and James H. Lorie, *Rates of Return on Investments in Common Stocks* (Chicago: Center for Research in Security Prices, University of Chicago, 1963).

[15] Banker's Trust Company, *The Investment Outlook for 1971*, Table I. Percentages calculated.

[16] *Best's Aggregates and Averages, Property-Liability, 1971* (Morristown, N.J.: A. M. Best Company, 1971), p. 32.

[17] *Life Insurance Fact Book, 1972* (New York: Institute of Life Insurance, 1972), p. 60.

insurers over the years, although they are subjected to similar regulatory restrictions. Furthermore, life insurers have not generally experienced periodic limitations of underwriting capacity. It seems very likely that better investment performance among property-liability insurers would go a long way to relieve the periodic capacity problem which seems to plague the industry.

Capacity and Guaranty Funds

Nearly all states have enacted some type of legislation insuring the solvency of property-liability companies, up to stated limits of liability.[18] The purpose of these laws is to establish a mechanism to guarantee the payment of claims to policyholders and to assist in the detection and prevention of insurer insolvencies. The cost of protection is met through an assessment of an association of insurers operating in each state. The maximum liability limit is typically set at $300,000 with a $100 deductible, and with the maximum aggregate liability of the association limited to the obligations of the insolvent company, but not to exceed some percentage, say 1 percent, of an insurer's net premiums in the preceding year. Any obligations unpaid under these limitations are carried over to a subsequent year. In many cases, the cost of the plan is met indirectly by the state government because required assessments of insurers to the association are allowed as a credit against the premium tax in the state. In most states, only given types of insurance are covered, with life, health, and ocean marine insurance prominent among the excepted lines.

The existence of guaranty funds

[18] As of 1975, all states except Alabama, Arkansas, and Oklahoma had passed such laws.

adds to the effective capacity of private insurance in that all insurers affected could conceivably be more liberal in their underwriting or could accept a larger ratio of premiums to surplus than would otherwise be the case. The risk manager may be directly concerned with these guaranty fund provisions in the event that one of his insurers becomes insolvent. However, due care should be paid to the limitations of the funds.

Among these are: (1) Because of statutory limitations (e.g., a maximum annual claim against the association of 1 or 2 percent of net premiums written) it is possible that large losses which cause an insurer to become insolvent, may not be met promptly by the guaranty fund. (2) The existence of the funds may bring about more careless underwriting, less attention to making careful selection of insurers on the part of the risk manager, less scrutiny by state regulators of unsound practice of insurers, and greater unwillingness to grant rate increases, than would otherwise be the case. For example, if an insurer knows that its promises will be backed up by the fund there might be some tendency to relax sound insurance restrictions in order to maximize premium writings, leading to more insolvencies than would otherwise result. (3) Because the guaranty funds depend on assessments, and (except for New York) are not prefunded, there may be delays in meeting legitimate claims of policyholders. (4) Not all types of insurance are covered.

Although guaranty funds are designed mainly to insure and help prevent insolvency, they have an effect on insurance capacity in that the resources of the entire insurance industry in given states may be marshalled to meet claims of bankrupt companies, if necessary. Thus, through the combination method, resources of strong insurers not fully utilized may be made available for losses elsewhere. However, these funds are not cure-alls and the risk manager should not assume that they eliminate all capacity problems.

Utilizing Capacity Principles in Risk Management

The risk manager may obtain greater efficiency in his insurance programs if he understands and uses the principles of insurer capacity as developed above. Some of the more obvious lessons which can be inferred from these principles are listed below:

(1) Dealing with larger insurers is likely to provide the risk manager with greater insurance capacity for at least three major reasons: (a) The larger insurer is likely to perceive less risk than the smaller insurer because of the likelihood of obtaining greater spread of loss exposures. (b) The larger insurer is likely to command greater reinsurance capacity than the smaller insurer because common types of reinsurance treaties base reinsurance lines on the size of the primary insurer's retention. The larger insurer is likely to be able to retain more of the risk than a smaller insurer. (c) Larger insurers generally are stronger financially than small insurers.

(2) In spite of what has been stated in (1) above, the risk manager may often find excellent insurance markets among smaller regional or specialized insurers seeking to expand their business. If the risk manager has a risk which fits into the product line of the speciality insurer, he can often obtain insurance on better terms than would be possible in a larger multiple-line carrier.

(3) The risk manager is more likely to obtain continuing coverage on reasonable terms from insurers who are profitable and who have satisfactory ratios of net worth to debt and premiums written to policyholders' surplus. If the combined loss and expense ratio is consistently less than 100 percent, the insurer is making underwriting gains and is more likely to be able to accept risk than insurers who are experiencing underwriting losses. If the insurer is also obtaining investment, profit capacity is likely to be even greater. If losses are occurring, underwriting is very likely to be tight. An insurer writing too much business for the size of its policyholders' surplus (say, a ratio of premiums to policyholders' surplus greater than four to one) is likely to suffer more instability in its underwriting capacity than insurers writing less.

(4) If the risk manager can find an insurance underwriter with risks similar to those of the risk manager's company, he has a greater likelihood of obtaining more favorable terms and capacity than otherwise. This follows because in this case the risk manager's loss exposure very possibly will enlarge the insurance capacity of the insurer rather than diminish it, by permitting a greater spread of homogeneous risks by that insurer. As a corollary, the risk manager who needs specialized risk covers may find greater capacity among specialized underwriters than among general underwriters.

(5) The risk manager stands perhaps a better chance for long-term underwriting adequacy from an insurer that is growing modestly, as opposed to an insurer growing very rapidly. The latter type insurer is more likely to be aggressive in soliciting business, but it is likely to be less able to show consistent underwriting capacity because its rapid growth may bring on surplus strain due to the costs of expansion.

(6) The best time to seek enlarged capacities among insurers is during the rising phase of the underwriting cycle. It should be recognized that not all in-

surers will be in the same phase of the underwriting cycle at the same time. This provides the imaginative risk manager some challenge for locating those insurers best situated to accept risk.

(7) Risk managers may enlarge the capacity presented to them by assisting the underwriter to enlarge his knowledge of the risk presented. Risk managers who present records of loss histories, data on the efficacy of loss prevention efforts, and assurances of cooperation with the underwriter in inspections and loss control, will have a much greater chance for better insurance service and capacity than would otherwise be true. A corollary is that the risk manager should try to develop a continuing communication with the underwriter so as to update the underwriter's knowledge and to increase his skill in dealing with risk.

(8) The risk manager should recognize that the independent agent or broker may be very important in presenting underwriting information effectively to the insurer's home office personnel. Accordingly, he should work closely with various agency intermediaries in providing them information about the risk. He should also recognize that in many cases the agent or broker can exert considerable pressure upon underwriters to accept risks from the marginal customer in order to retain profitable business from other customers.

One of the sources of power of the independent agent is that the insurer does not have the legal right to contact final consumers (the agent's customers) with the idea of persuading good customers to remain with the insurer. In other words, the agent controls his business and can cancel customer's insurance with one carrier and place it in another. The insurer is dependent upon its agents to produce good business and if the insurer is not competitive, either in offering adequate capacity or satisfactory premium rates, the agent may decide to remove his customers from that insurer. The risk manager may increase his bargaining ability with both the agent and the insurer if he will employ only one agent or broker, and allow the agent to offer both good and bad risks of the risk manager as a package to increase the amount of leverage which can be applied to the underwriter.

SUMMARY AND CONCLUSIONS

1. Many factors affect the capacity of insurers to accept risk. In general, capacity is enlarged as increases occur in profits and surplus of the insurer. Capacity also varies directly with homogeneity of subjects exposed to loss, with knowledge and skill of the underwriter and his mental willingness to take risk.

2. Underwriting capacity usually varies inversely with rapid changes in insurer growth rates, and with market interest returns available on invested capital.

3. Favorable regulatory environments and the availability of adequate reinsurance facilities are important factors affecting the ability and willingness of insurers to accept risk.

4. Risk managers can take advantage of certain factors affecting insurance capacity in order to obtain coverage for their firms on more favorable terms than would otherwise be the case.

QUESTIONS FOR DISCUSSION

1. Operating data for the Woodland Mutual Insurance Company are given below. What factors would you cite, if any, in these data to show that underwriting capacity is (a) increasing, or (b) decreasing? Would you recommend this insurer? Why, or why not?

Year	Policy holders' Surplus	Total Assets	Direct Premiums Written	Combined Loss and Expense Ratio	Under- writing Gain	Net Invest- ment Income
1966	770	1,169	885	104.4	− 38	23
1967	1,338	2,337	1,512	109.5	−141	55
1968	1,135	2,257	1,935	115.8	−254	55
1969	1,124	2,507	2,408	98.8	− 39	57
1970	858	2,277	2,389	120.3	−369	65
Totals and averages			9,128	110.8	−841	255

(All figures are in $1,000's, except ratios.)

2. Liberty Mutual Insurance of Boston, Massachusetts, is one of the largest insurers in the United States, with total assets of about $1.5 billion in 1970. About one-third of its business is in the field of workers' compensation insurance. The next largest line is automobile insurance. The 1970 ratio of premiums to policyholders' surplus was 5/1 and the ratio of net worth to debt was .14.
(a) What is the meaning and significance of the two ratios mentioned? Are these ratios conservative or nonconservative? Discuss.
(b) What other information would you seek to help interpret the two ratios mentioned? Why?

3. Financial data for the Olympic Insurance Company, part of the Transamerica Group, of Los Angeles, California, for the five-year period 1966–70 are given below. Best's Insurance Reports commented as follows about this insurer:

"Because of certain peculiarities in production sources and expense allocations between the Olympic Insurance Company and the Countrywide Insurance Company . . . reinsurance arrangements were effected in 1967 by the two companies with Olympic taking on a substantial portion of Countrywide's business. The large block of the reinsurance assumed was retroceded by the Olympic in 1968. Net premium writings of the Olympic for 1967 and 1968 as a consequence, developed wide fluctuations. After a period of rapid growth, management in 1967 concluded that too much business was being written. During the next three years, further action was taken to substantially reduce marketing commitments. Certain classes of business were discontinued including withdrawal from the reinsurance field."

Year	Total Admitted Assets	Reported Policy-holders' Surplus	Net Premiums Written*	Combined Loss and Expense Ratio	Under-writing Gain	Invest-ment Gain
1966	$22,110	$10,998	$10,707	105.7	− $1,193	$1,988
1967	34,259	11,391	31,981	92.7	− 95	688
1968	32,649	9,966	17,520	108.1	− 1,201	4,936
1969	19,402	3,757	2,279	202.5	− 4,678	825
1970	4,706	3,410	− 2,477	—	− 3,685	366
			$60,010	117.4	−$10,852	$8,803

     * Adjusted for reinsurance ceded and accepted.

     (All figures are in $1,000's, except ratios).

On December 31, 1970, Olympic's balance sheet showed no loss reserves, compared to about $14 million the year previously. Assets were composed mainly of stocks and bonds in roughly equal proportions.

(a) Suggest possible financial reasons for the officers of Olympic coming to the conclusion that too much business was being written.

(b) What accounts for the negative premiums written and absence of loss reserves in 1970?

(c) Assess the financial and underwriting capacity position of Olympic. In what ways is reinsurance being used?

4. An insurance analyst argued that if an insurer pursues a conservative investment policy, it is also likely to be able to increase underwriting capacity. Do you agree? Why or why not?

5. Why should a risk presented to one underwriter be thought to increase the insurer's risk, and when presented to another underwriter, be thought to decrease the insurer's risk? Discuss.

6. Inflation is said to cause a serious reduction in insurance capacity. Why?

7. Commenting in 1972 on the excellent profitability of small regional insurers, an author stated, "Last year was excellent for fire and casualty insurers; underwriting profits surged and investment income maintained its steady growth. At the start of 1972, however, few expected to see the underwriting upturn continue at anywhere near the same pace. Some even predicted lower margins. But Mercury General's first quarter results, together with those of other regional insurers, indicate that 1972 profits for this group may turn out better than expected."

(a) Why might small regional insurers show better underwriting results than the industry generally?

(b) What is the implication for insurance capacity of the flourishing regional underwriters?

8. Writing in 1972, an investment analyst, Edward B. Goodnow, in recommending the stocks of Japanese nonlife insurers, stated, "One item in the group's favor is that Japanese insurance companies operate in a regulatory climate that's different from the U.S. They don't get squeezed for a year or two before they get rate increases. The Japanese government . . . wants the insurers to make an adequate return and build up their reserves. As a result . . . the Japanese insurance industry has never had an extended period of bad earnings." In the light of this comment, would you expect the underwriting cycle in Japanese insurance companies to be as pronounced as it is in the United States? (See Chart 16–1.)

9. Mr. Edward B. Goodnow in an investment analysis of Japanese nonlife insurers stated, "The final key to evaluating these companies is something called a catastrophe reserve. The Ministry of Finance permits Japanese insurance companies to put up to $6\frac{1}{2}$ percent of their annual premium income into a tax-free catastrophe reserve. There isn't any such item in the U.S. because a nonrecurring catastrophe is simply charged to general reserves and surplus. Since there is no charge against the catastrophe reserve in the normal course of things in Japan, we've added it back into earnings. It makes stocks that seem cheap to begin with look even cheaper."

(a) Are catastrophes "nonrecurring" as is implied in this quotation? What is the implication of this practice of setting up catastrophe reserves to the question of insurance capacity?

(b) In your opinion, is it conservative practice to add back into surplus the amounts in the catastrophe reserves to determine the book value of Japanese insurance stocks?

10. The text states, "The risk manager should understand the capacity problem in insurance in order to deal effectively with risk in his own firm. Do you agree? Why or why not?

11. Financial and other data for the Thurston National Insurance Co., Tulsa, Oklahoma, were reported by Best's (see below), resulting in the lowest of Best's policyholders' ratings, "C" (fair) and a financial rating of "Class III" (a net worth of between $500,000 and $750,000). Mr. B. J. Jones, vice-president, believes the "C" rating is not justified.

Balance Sheet
(000's)

	Admitted Assets			Liabilities	
		Year			Year
	Year X	X-1		Year X	X-1
Bonds	$ 935	$1,020	Loss reserve	$ 698	$ 992
Stocks	595	1,000	Unearned premium	657	1,224
Mortgages	24	65	Other	101	142
Real Estate	175	213	Total	$1,456	$2,358
Cash	33	172			
Premium balances	123	250			
Reins. recoverable	21	89	Capital	316	316
Accrued interest	17	16	Surplus	194	203
Other	43	52			
	$1,966	$2,877		$1,966	$2,877

Selected 5-Year Data

Year	Assets	Policy-holders' Surplus	NPW	Loss Ratio	Expense Ratio	Combined Ratio	Underwriting Results	Net Investment Income	Other Investment Results
X-4	$2,498	$ 701	$ 2,449	61.8	36.2	98.0	−152	45	− 63
X-3	2,907	741	2,419	71.7	33.4	105.1	−147	67	− 31
X-2	3,085	1,001	2,480	66.0	37.0	103.0	− 83	76	41
X-1	2,877	519	2,900	74.4	34.7	109.1	−279	84	− 95
X	1,966	510	1,476	68.7	42.1	110.8	18	89	−122
Totals and averages			$11,724	69.0	36.2	105.2	−643	361	−270

Management

The company was chartered 20 years previous to this report with total capital of $100,000 ($50,000 of capital and $50,000 of surplus). Recent underwriting losses were experienced mainly in automobile insurance. "Other investment results" showed losses stemming from stock sales.

In the last year the company sharply reduced its premium writings in order to restore underwriting profits. It withdrew from unprofitable agencies and lines of business.

The company has about 90 agents. It operates in multiple lines. Latest year premiums were collected as follows:

| | DPW* | NPW* | Loss Ratio ||
			Year X	Year X-1
Fire	$ 195	$ 90	28.4	37.0
E.C.	78	41	44.3	39.0
HO Multiple Peril	420	230	50.4	56.7
Comm. Multiple Peril	25	14	48.0	17.7
Workers' Compensation	15	14	25.6	75.2
Auto B.I.	461	434	59.4	71.6
Auto P.D.	239	225	65.6	70.6
Auto Phys. D.	426	408	62.9	61.6
Other	24	20	—	—
	$1,883	$1,476	57.0	64.3

* DPW-NPW = Amount reinsured.

Reinsurance is purchased more in some lines than others. Company retention limits are as follows:

Workers' Compensation	$15,000
Auto BI & PD	15,000
Auto Physical damage, 1 vehicle	15,000
Any combination of loss, 1 vehicle	15,000
Motor cargo	Quota Share
Multi-peril	Quota Share of first $15,000 + First Surplus Treaty
Catastrophe fire and auto PD	$15,000–$300,000 each occurrence

Facultative arrangements are also maintained on specific accounts. The company operates in two states, Oklahoma and Arkansas.

Representing Mr. I. M. Best, from the rating agency, defend the "C" rating given to the company in Year X. See Chapter 15 for an explanation of Best's ratings.

17

Insurance Rate Making and Underwriting

As was seen in the preceding chapter, rating methods and underwriting may have a very large effect on the ultimate cost of insurance to the insured (business firm or individual) and to the availability of insurance markets. Experience rating procedures and other aspects of insurance pricing may well provide an incentive to insure. On the other hand inadequate rates of return for the insurer can serve to dry up markets and to limit the effectiveness of the insurance method as a way of meeting risk. Similarly, stringent underwriting rules can reduce the availability of insurance except in highly limited and special situations. A basic knowledge of rating and underwriting is essential to the risk manager if he is to make the most enlightened decisions in problems involving risk transfer.

These functions are discussed under the following headings:

1. Rate making in life insurance
   a. Cost factors
   b. Computation of life insurance premiums
   c. Practical considerations in life insurance premium computation

2. Rate making in property and liability insurance
   a. Rate making in fire insurance
   b. Rate making in casualty insurance
   c. Practical considerations in property and liability insurance rate making

3. Underwriting
   a. The underwriting process
   b. Underwriting by line of insurance

RATE MAKING IN LIFE INSURANCE

In insurance a rate is the price per unit and a premium is the price paid for a particular contract. In life insurance rates are quoted per $1,000 of face amount. The procedures for computing a rate in life insurance are fairly formal and involve fairly complex mathematical formulae. Rates are computed in the actuarial departments of life insurance companies, and each insurer establishes its own premiums. A distinction is made between a net premium and a gross premium. By the former expression is meant a premium computed by taking into account only mortality and interest, while by the latter expression is meant a premium that includes an allowance for expenses of the insurer, as well as for mortality and interest.

The Cost Factors

The risk assumed by the life insurer is that the death of the insured will occur in a particular time interval.

Thus, in order to compute an appropriate premium it is necessary for the insurer to estimate, as one of the costs that it must meet, the losses (in life insurance the face amount of the contract) that will have to be paid in the future. The estimates are made by using a mortality table, which is an instrument that provides estimates of the probability that death will occur at various age intervals (annual) starting at age 0 and ending (typically, in tables of insured lives) at age 100. Mortality tables also provide a statement (based on an arbitrary radix) of the number of persons alive at various ages and the number dying from one age to the next.

A factor of considerable importance from a cost point of view is the substantial improvement that has occurred in mortality since the middle of the nineteenth century. The improvement that has occurred at all age levels is evident, although the gains have been most dramatic at ages under 50. Recent gains in mortality at all ages have been less marked than was true in the decades immediately following the turn of the century. The significance of decreasing mortality on the cost of insurance is discussed by Guertin in his paper on the computation of life insurance premiums. He estimates that the use of up-to-date mortality experience results in "a decrease in rates of about 15 percent on the average with the biggest percentage drop at the higher ages but the percentage drop is reasonably uniform throughout the age pattern."[1]

Since insurance premiums including those in life insurance are collected in advance, interest earned on funds not needed immediately may be used to help pay claims. Thus, interest is one of the cost factors that is taken into account in calculating life insurance premiums. The selection of an interest rate will depend on a number of factors including whether the contract in question is participating or nonparticipating. One guide to selection is the interest paid on fully taxable United States government bonds. This rate has varied from approximately 2.37 percent in 1945 to approximately 6 percent in 1974. By way of comparison the net (after investment expenses) rate of investment income of United States life insurance companies (before income taxes) has varied from 3.11 percent in 1945 (A minimum of 2.88 percent was reached in 1947.) to 6.25 percent in 1974, if separate accounts are included, and 6.31 percent if separate accounts are excluded.[2] The general effect of an increasing interest rate, other things being equal, is to decrease the premium charged for life insurance. Guertin states that "a change in interest rates of ½ percent makes a difference in rates of 5 percent on the average with the highest percentage drop at the lower ages."[3] The combination of decreasing mortality and increasing interest rates has in general led to decreasing life insurance premiums since 1945.

The third cost factor to be considered in life insurance computations is that of the expenses involved in the production of life insurance contracts and in carrying out the promises of the insurer. These expenses may be classified as follows: "(1) investment income; (2) buying and selling securities; (3) procuring new business, underwriting, and issuing policies; (4) maintaining and servicing existing policies; and (5) pay-

[1] Alfred N. Guertin, "Life Insurance Premiums," The Journal of Risk and Insurance, XXXII (March 1965), p. 36.

[2] See Life Insurance Fact Book, 1975, (New York: Institute of Life Insurance, 1975), p. 56.

[3] Guertin, "Life Insurance Premiums," p. 36.

ing claims."[4] The expenses associated with the production of investment income and in buying and selling securities do not enter directly into premium calculations. The reason for this is that expenses associated with such activities, as in maintaining an investment department and in administering loans, are deducted from the investment income. Similarly, costs of buying and selling securities are handled by adjustments to their cost or selling price. The other categories of expense mentioned above are directly considered in premium computations. With the exception of claim expenses and costs of paying surrender values, expenses associated with the maintenance of an insurance business are divided, using cost-accounting principles in three categories: "(1) expenses allocable as a percentage of premium income, (2) expenses allocable on a per policy basis, and (3) expenses per $1,000 of insurance."[5] Costs of paying surrender values and expenses associated with claims are treated as additional benefits. During periods of strong inflation the increase in the expenses of operating an insurance company will tend to reduce the savings that occur through improved mortality and higher interest rates.

Computation of Life Insurance Premiums

Basically all insurance premiums are made up of two elements. One part consists of the insured's share of loss costs and the other his (her) share of expenses. In life insurance the part of the premium representing loss costs (the net premium) is computed first, and the result of that computation is increased by the amount needed for expenses to obtain the gross premium

[4] *Ibid.*, p. 38.

[5] *Ibid.*

(selling price). The basic principle followed in the computation of loss costs is that the present value of the benefits offered by the contract is equal to the net single premium or that premium paid once and invested at the rate of interest assumed in the computation that would be sufficient to pay the insureds' share of future losses. In determining the present value of the benefits it is generally assumed that premiums are paid in advance and that claims (losses) are paid at the end of the year.[6]

As an illustration of the technique used in premium computations in life insurance, consider a contract wherein the insurer agrees to pay $1,000 to a beneficiary in the event the insured dies within five years. Assume, further, that the insured is 25 years of age at the time he enters into the contract and that the insurer uses the 1958 Commissioners' Standard Ordinary Table (see Appendix D) for mortality estimates and assumes interest at 3 percent. The net single premium for the contract would be determined as follows:

Let $A^1_{25\,\overline{5}|}$ = Net single premium for a five-year term insurance contract issued at age 25.

The present value of the benefits offered by the contract must equal the net single premium and are computed by finding the discounted expected value of the losses in each of the five years.

[6] The assumption that premiums are paid in advance is a realistic one, since insurance premiums are universally charged in advance. The assumption that claims are paid at the end of the year is not realistic, since claims are paid promptly when loss occurs and are typically not deferred. The assumption about claims is not necessary if one wishes to introduce somewhat more complicated mathematics. Generally in practice, such refinements are not introduced, since the error involved in not doing so is not great.

The discounted expected value of the loss in the first year can be found by multiplying the face of the contract (the amount that could be lost) by the probability that a person aged 25 will die during the first year and by multiplying that product by $(1.03)^{-1}$. Thus, for the first year

$$(\$1,000) \cdot \frac{18481}{9,575,636} \cdot (1.03)^{-1} =$$
$$(\$1,000)(.00193)(.97087379) =$$
$$(\$1,000)(.0018738) = \$1.874 \quad (1)$$

The probability factor was obtained by dividing the number of persons age 25 dying between ages 25 and 26 (according to the 1958 C.S.O. Table; see Appendix D, pages 610–11) by the number of persons alive at age 25. The discount factor or the present value of $1 due one year from the present was obtained from a book of interest tables.

In determining expected values for the remaining four years expressions similar to (1) must be obtained taking into account the fact that the probabilities involved are that a person age 25 will die in the second, third, fourth, or fifth years and that the money to pay losses will not be needed until the end of each of those years. The appropriate mathematical expressions are:

$$\$1,000 \cdot \frac{18,732}{9,575,636} \cdot (1.03)^{-2} =$$
$$(\$1000)(.0019562)(0.94259591) = \$1.843$$
$$\$1,000 \cdot \frac{18,981}{9,575,636} \cdot (1.03)^{-3} =$$
$$(\$1000)(.0019822)(0.91514166) = 1.814$$
$$\$1,000 \cdot \frac{19,324}{9,575,636} \cdot (1.03)^{-4} =$$
$$(\$1000)(.0020180)(0.88848705) = 1.793$$
$$\$1,000 \cdot \frac{19,760}{9,575,636} \cdot (1.03)^{-5} =$$
$$(\$1000)(.0020636)(0.86260878) = 1.790$$

Thus the net single premium for the term insurance contract under discussion is:

$$A^1_{25\,\overline{5|}} = \$1.874 + \$1.843 + \$1.814 + \$1.793 + \$1.780 = \$9.104 \quad (2)$$

Although it is possible for a life insurance contract extending over a number of years to be paid for by making a single payment, the usual procedure is to pay for the contract annually. The net annual premium may be obtained from the net single premium by recognizing that the annual premiums form, in the case of the term contract, a temporary life annuity due.[7] The net single premium, then, must equal the present value of the net annual premiums.

In the problem under discussion the annual premiums would be paid for five years. If $P^1_{25\,\overline{5|}}$ represents the annual premium for the contract, then

$$A^1_{25\,\overline{5|}} = P^1_{25\,\overline{5|}}\, \ddot{a}_{25\,\overline{5|}}$$

and

$$P^1_{25\,\overline{5|}} = \frac{A^1_{25\,\overline{5|}}}{\ddot{a}_{25\,\overline{5|}}} = \frac{\$9.104}{\$4.699} = \$1.94 \quad (3)$$

where

$A^1_{25\,\overline{5|}}$ = Net single premium for a 5-year term insurance contract issued at age 25

$P^1_{25\,\overline{5|}}$ = Net annual premium for a 5-year term insurance contract issued at age 25

$\ddot{a}_{25\,\overline{5|}}$ = Present value of a temporary (5-year) life annuity due of $1 per annum issued at age 25 (see Appendix F, page 619).

[7] In the case of a whole life insurance contract the annual premiums form a life annuity due.

The computations arrived at thus far have not taken expenses into account. A possible formula for this purpose is

$$P' = P(1+K) + C \qquad (4)$$

where $P' =$ gross premium (selling price) and K is the expense factor reflecting expenses that vary with size of premium and C is the expense factor that is independent of the type of contract.[8]

Once values of C and K have been determined the gross premium may be obtained by substituting into (4).

The illustration just considered has been specialized to a particular age and term, but the method used may be generalized to any age x and any finite term, say n. Further, the method used may be extended to other plans of insurance such as whole life, endowment, and combinations thereof and the procedures may be adapted to group insurance and industrial insurance. For example, the formula for whole life insurance would be the formula for term insurance extended to age 100. Also, it need not be assumed that annual premiums will be paid for the same period covered by the insurance. Limited payment plans are possible and in many instances desirable.

Practical Considerations in Life Insurance Premium Computation

Although the use of formulas of the type just discussed are basic to life insurance premium computations, they tend to create the impression that such computations involve very little, if any, judgment and that the process is comparatively easy. Actually, in practice, fairly difficult estimation problems arise in determining appropriate values for the cost factors, and the nature of the estimates and the various factors considered differ between contracts sold on a participating basis and those sold on a nonparticipating basis. Guertin in the article referred to earlier in the chapter discusses some of the basic considerations in determining gross premium rates particularly as these apply to nonparticipating contracts. He identifies six factors: "(1) a suitable mortality rate, (2) an appropriate rate of interest, (3) a rate of withdrawal or a persistency rate, (4) factors of unit expenses out of which appropriate expense margins will be defined, (5) a factor for contingencies and fluctuations in experience, and (6) a factor to produce a margin of profit."[9]

A number of considerations arise in selecting appropriate mortality rates. Since nonparticipating policies do not provide for a return of premium in the form of a dividend, it is essential that the mortality rates assumed be as accurate as possible and nonredundant. Further, it may be desirable to recognize the differences in male and female mortality and to quote separate premium rates for men and women. Similarly, questions may arise as to whether age is to be taken as nearest birthday or on a last birthday basis and whether policy size is to be taken into account and rates differentiated according to the amount of insurance purchased. Another consideration that arises is whether lapse rates are to be taken into account in premium computations. If the asset shares and the surrender

[8] Horace R. Bassford, "Premium Rates, Reserves, and Non-forfeiture Values for Participating Policies," *Transactions Actuarial Society of America*, XLIII, p. 328.

[9] Guertin, "Life Insurance Premiums," p. 24.

values provided by the contract are approximately the same, adjustment of the premium to take lapse rates into account may not be necessary. If the differences are greater than can be ignored, an adjustment of the premium to take lapse rates into account is a possibility or the surrender values may be adjusted.

The need for realistic and accurate estimates applies to interest and expenses as well as to mortality. It may also be necessary to make specific recognition of the need to plan for contingencies and to provide a margin for profit. In order to have the data needed for these computations, trends in interest rates and expenses and the profitability of the insurer must be studied carefully on a continuing basis.

When life insurance contracts are issued on a participating basis, the need is mainly for safe estimates of the cost factors, since any surplus that arises that is not needed for claims, expenses, and contingencies of the insurer will be returned to the policyholder. Dividends are not guaranteed and redundant estimates provide a margin for safety in the event the experience of the insurer is worse than expected. The cost factors identified are typically the ones used on page 393. In selecting estimates of these factors the emphasis tends to be on the side of conservatism. Thus, the mortality table selected will not necessarily reflect the most recent experience of insured lives and may be one of the published tables such as the 1958 Commissioners' Standard Ordinary Table.

The interest rate selected for premium computations in participating contracts will typically be lower than the insurer expects to earn. Considerable emphasis is placed on the long-term nature of many life insurance contracts and for the interest rate selected

to be one that is the "lowest rate which might reasonably be experienced over an extended period."[10] Estimates of expenses are also conservative, and in the case of mutual insurers specific provision for profit is not appropriate, since there are no dividends payable to stockholders.

RATE MAKING IN PROPERTY AND LIABILITY INSURANCE

The broad objectives in rate making in property and liability insurance are similar to those in life insurance, but specific methods and procedures differ markedly, and it is useful to consider some of the differences between the two subdivisions in the field of insurance.[11]

In contrast to life insurance where rating bureaus are unknown and rates are computed by each insurer, the use of bureaus is common and typical in property and liability insurance, and only comparatively recently have a few large insurers computed their own rates. Bureaus are basically associations of insurers and member companies often use bureau rates and forms, although in many jurisdictions deviations from such rates are permitted and individual filing is possible. One of the arguments for using bureaus is that the bringing together of data from a large number of insurers provides better estimates of future experience, especially for fairly small insurers. Closely associated with rate computation is the problem of rate regulation. Again, property and liability

[10] Bassford, "Premium Rates for Policies," p. 332.

[11] Rate making in health insurance is not specifically considered in this chapter. Its methods, however, are closely related to those of casualty insurance, which is a part of property and liability insurance.

insurance differs from life. With the exception of ocean marine insurance, property and liability rates are subject to regulatory statutes (See Chapter 19). This fact is in contrast with life and health insurance where rate regulation is practically nonexistent.[12]

Although actuaries have been common in life insurance since its inception, they have been fairly rare in property and liabilty insurance. It was not until the rise of automobile and workers' compensation insurance that the casualty actuarial field began to develop. Although the very large property and liability insurers now have actuaries, they are still not commonplace and do not play as dominant a role in rating and reserving procedures as their life insurance counterparts.

A first step in the insurance rating process is the classification of risks for the purpose of establishing homogeneous groups where each member of the group is subject to the same degree of risk. In life insurance the classification system is fairly simple, since persons seeking life insurance contracts are grouped mainly by age,[13] but in property and liability insurance classificatory systems are generally more complex, particularly in fields such as automobile insurance where the risks may be classified by such items as territory, place where the automobile is principally garaged, age and sex of driver, and type and use of the vehicle. Adequate classification systems are not always easy to

establish and the problem seems particularly difficult in property and liability insurance.

Perhaps the greatest contrast between life insurance and property and liability insurance in regard to rate making exists in the diversity of methods used in the latter field. Taken as a whole there is probably less formality and more judgment used in setting property and liability insurance rates than is the case in life insurance. In some fields, such as marine insurance, rating appears to be essentially on an individual basis with any particular rate depending upon bargaining between the broker and underwriter, although discussions about the past rate experience is an important factor. Fire insurance rating is somewhat more formal than in marine insurance and involves the concepts of class as well as individual rating. Buildings, such as homes, are class rated, but commercial structures are typically individually rated through the use of schedules, which depend on judgment about structural characteristics. Those lines of property and liability insurance that may be classified as casualty insurance involve fairly formal procedures in rate computations. Two types of rating, manual (class) and experience, are used and rates are based on tabulated data.[14] In certain lines of casualty insurance, such as workers' compensation, the statistical and mathematical procedures involved have been fairly highly developed and the rating process is complex.

Other differences between life insurance and property and liability insurance are of some significance in rate making. In property and liability insur-

---

[12] This is not to say that no statutes exist that affect life and health insurance. For example, New York has an expense limitation law.

[13] This remark is not intended to imply that classification does not exist for risks that are substandard health-wise or that risks may not be classified by sex. However, historically and generally age has been the main method of classification.

[14] Experience rating is not unknown in the life and health insurance fields, since group life and health insurance is often experience rated.

ance contracts are generally short term. In personal lines contracts are typically written for one year. Life insurance contracts by way of contrast are often written for the whole of life or for fairly long terms. Thus, rates can and do change frequently for insureds in property and liability insurance, whereas in life insurance, for a particular insured, the premium for the contract will remain the same for as long as the contract is in force. In life insurance interest is used as a specific cost factor and enters directly into computation formulas. This fact is not true for property and liability insurance, although investments earnings are taken into account in determining the overall profitability of the insurer. Another rate-making factor that sometimes causes confusion is that the language used in describing the rating process differs. In life insurance one speaks of the probability of death or survival and about the expected value of the loss, and probability factors enter into the rating formulas. In property and liability insurance explicit probability computations typically do not enter into rating formulas, although clearly probability concepts are inherent in any measurement of uncertainty. The concern is usually with assessing past loss experience and estimating what the future experience will be in dollar terms.

Clarification of some of the comments made above about property and liability rating is perhaps best achieved by a more detailed consideration of rating methods used in some of the major branches of property and liability insurance.

Rate Making in Fire Insurance

Fire insurance rates are of two types: (1) class (or minimum) and (2) specific (or tariff). Class rates apply to certain types of property such as dwellings, churches, and apartment buildings. Classes based on construction (frame or masonry), occupancy (mainly number of families), and class of fire protection are constructed for types of property where construction and occupancy are similar enough to make rate classes fairly homogeneous. The rate for the class is determined by using the pure premium method, which is discussed on page 402.

In situations where class rating is not appropriate, such as manufacturing properties and other commercial buildings, specific rates are computed. These rates are determined by applying schedules to individual properties. A schedule is an instrument designed to measure the fire risk of a particular building. Credits and charges are given depending on the extent to which the building differs from standard conditions surrounding construction, occupancy, protection, and exposure. The schedules most often used are the universal mercantile schedule and the analytic system.

Universal Mercantile Schedule

The universal mercantile schedule used in the past largely in the East and South was designed to rate mercantile risks, although it has found a somewhat more general use. Its starting point is a standard building in a standard city. The rate developed for such a building is called the basis rate. From this rate is developed a key rate, which is the rate for a standard building in a given city. Once the key rate for a given city is determined, the rate for a particular building in that city is determined by making flat credits and/or charges to the key rate. An example would be:

Key Rate		$ .50
Charges		
Frame	$ .60	
Roof (shingles)	.10	
Nonstandard stairway	.10	
Nonstandard heat	.10	.90
Building Rate		$1.40[15]

The rate is for $100 face amount of fire insurance.

Analytic System

The analytic system was developed by A. F. Dean in the latter part of the nineteenth century and was originally mostly used in the western part of the United States. Today it is widely used throughout the United States. Among the differences between the universal mercantile system and the analytic system are: (1) the universal system uses flat or absolute credits and charges while the analytic expresses such items as percentages; and (2) the universal system starts with a key rate developed from a basis rate while the analytic system starts with a basis rate, which is determined by taking into consideration the construction of the building,[16] the class of exterior fire protection for brick and stone buildings and buildings of frame construction and the height of the building. The basic rates under the analytic system are determined for each state or rating territory and are based on the underwriting experience of the territory. The class of

15 John H. Magee and Oscar N. Serbein, *Property and Liability Insurance*, 4th ed., (Homewood, Ill.: Richard D. Irwin, Inc., 1967), p. 745.

16 The analytic system classifies buildings into categories labelled A, B, & D. Fireproof buildings are Class A, brick and stone buildings are Class B, Class D buildings are of frame construction.

exterior fire protection is based on a grading schedule prepared by the Insurance Services Office, which places cities in the United States into ten different categories depending upon such items as water supply, fire department, fire alarm, building laws, fire prevention, and structural conditions. Baring deficiency points are assigned to each of these categories with a maximum possible total of deficiency points of 5,000. The analytic system also gives consideration to occupancy and recognizes three general classes (1) mercantile, (2) industrial, and (3) miscellaneous. Causes of fires, media by which they are spread, and the effects of fires are analyzed and appropriate tables are prepared. Exposure, or the possibility of the spread of fire, is another factor that is taken into account.

An example of the calculation of an individual building rate using the analytic system is:

Basic Rate		$ .61
	Charges	
Height	10%	
Basement	15	
Area	10	
Roof	20	
Interior Finish	20	
Open stairway	20	
Occupancy	100	
Total percentage charges	195%	
	1.95 × 0.61 =	1.19
		$1.80
Less fire extinguisher credit, 5%		.09
Individual building rate		$1.71[17]

Expressing charges and credits as percentages of the basic rate has the advantage of allowing the entire rating

17 *Ibid.*, p. 748.

structure to move proportionately as the basic rate undergoes change.

Casualty Insurance

As in life insurance and fire insurance, the starting point in calculating casualty insurance rates is the establishment of an appropriate risk class. The class rates determined for each of the classes are usually referred to as manual rates. Classification used for rates is subject to review by the official in charge of the various insurance departments.

Manual rates may be computed by using either the pure premium approach or the loss ratio approach. The loss ratio is defined as follows:

$$\text{Loss ratio} = \frac{\text{Incurred Losses and Loss Adjustment Expenses}}{\text{Premiums Earned}}$$

The complement of this ratio is the expense ratio, which may be defined as:

$$\text{Expense ratio} = \frac{\text{Expenses other than Loss Adjustment Expenses}}{\text{Premiums Earned}}$$

and the

$$\text{Loss ratio plus Expense ratio} = 1.$$

Stern cites as an example of the expenses that are taken into account in premium computations the data in Table 17–1.

In computing an appropriate premium (or selling price) for a particular classification using the pure premium approach, it is only necessary to divide the average loss and loss adjustment cost for a particular classification (pure premium) by the loss ratio for that classification or

$$P = \frac{\text{Average loss cost}}{\text{L.R.}}$$

where P = premium or selling price and LR = loss ratio.

It is assumed in the figure representing the average loss cost in formula (1) that trend factors and credibility have been taken into account. By credibility is meant an assessment of the degree to which the data can be believed and relied upon to represent the true loss experience of the insurer. In general, credibility is based on volume of experience. Table 17–2 indicates a possible assignment of credibilities for automobile insurance.

To the extent that the experience on which the rate is to be based is not credible, it is necessary to make an adjustment.[18] Since there is a time lag in the reporting of the latest experience, it is not available to be reflected in the rate computations. This fact plus the fact of inflation means that trend factors must

TABLE 17–1

Standard Loss and Expense Items Private Passenger and Commercial Cars	
Production Cost Allowance	20.0%
General Administration	5.5
Inspection and Bureau	1.0
Taxes, Licenses, and Fees	3.0
Underwriting and Profit Contingencies	5.0
Subtotal	34.5
Expected Losses and Loss Adjustment Expenses	65.5
Total	100.0

SOURCE: Philip K. Stern, "Rate Making Procedures for Automobile Liability Insurance," *Proceedings Casualty Actural Society*, LII (1965), p. 165.

[18] For an example of an adjustment method see Stern, "Rate Making Procedures," p. 166.

SPECIAL PROBLEMS IN RISK MANAGEMENT

TABLE 17–2
Assignment of Credibilities

Number of Claims	Credibility	Number of Claims	Credibility
0–10	0	390–530	.60
11–42	.10	531–693	.70
43–97	.20	694–877	.80
98–172	.30	878–1083	.90
173–270	.40	1084 and over	1.00
271–389	.50		

SOURCE: Stern, "Rate Making Procedures," p. 166.

be taken into account in estimating future loss experience. Statistical methods are used to determine appropriate trend factors.[19]

The formula for "pure premium" is:

$$\text{Pure Premium} = \frac{\text{Incurred losses and Loss Adjustment Expenses}}{\text{Number of earned exposures}} \quad (5)$$

Thus, the pure premium which is typically expressed in dollars and cents, is the average loss cost (including loss adjustment expenses) per unit of earned exposures.[20]

The loss ratio method involves the computation and comparison of actual and expected loss ratios. The previous year's rates are then adjusted by observing the difference between the two ratios. If the difference is quite small, an adjustment may not be necessary.

Merit Rating

Merit rating has been defined as the "technique for assigning different rates to insureds who fall within the same broad class of risk exposures."[21] Merit rating may be subdivided into two general categories: (1) schedule rating and (2) experience rating. Schedule rating is a process wherein a particular risk is subjectively rated by assigning credits and demerits to a particular risk depending on how it varies from an announced standard. This method of merit rating, although once used in casualty insurance, is now mostly limited to fire insurance. Experience rating is a merit-rating procedure in which numerical data are utilized in describing the experience of a particular risk and the actual past loss experience of a particular insured is utilized in determining the rate to be charged for the ensuing policy year. A modification factor to be applied to the rate is the following ratio:

$$M = \frac{A\text{-}E}{E}$$

where M = modification factor

A = previous period loss ratio.

E = expected loss ratio used in computing the manual rate.

Since credibility factors and trend factors are typically taken into account, the modification formula becomes

$$M = \frac{A\text{-}E}{E} \times C \times T \quad (6)$$

where C = credibility factor

and T = trend factor

A form of experience rating that is often used in such lines of insurance as

[19] Ibid., p. 174.

[20] The life insurance counterpart of the pure premium is the net premium.

[21] Irving Pfeffer and David R. Klock, Perspectives on Insurance, Englewood Cliffs, N.J.: Prentice-Hall, Inc., 1974, p. 336.

workers' compensation, automobile liability, general liability, automobile physical damage, burglary, and glass is retrospective rating which may be defined "as a modified cost plus approach to determining the commercial insured's final premiums."[22] The formula for the retrospective premium may be written as:

Retrospective Premium = (Basic Premium & Converted Losses) (Tax Multiplier)

where

"Basic premium = Insurer expenses, profit and contingencies but excluding loss expenses and tax expense plus a charge related to maximum premium control. . . . minus a savings related to minimum premium control. . . .

"Converted losses = incurred losses of the risk for the period of applicability of the retrospective plan multiplied by a loss conversion factor which provides loss expense."[23]

Tax Multiplier = premium tax that varies by line of insurance and state.

In retrospective rating the insured does not know until the end of the policy period what his exact premium for that period will be. Retrospective premiums are subject to minimum and maximum rates and the insured pays the minimum premium at the beginning of the policy year.

[22] John R. Stafford, *Retrospective Rating*, 3rd ed. (Palatine, Ill.: J and M Publications, 1974), p. 3.

[23] *Ibid.*, p. 4.

Practical Considerations in Property and Liability Rating

The formulas and procedures described in the preceding paragraphs provide in broad outline the methodology used in computing property and liability insurance premium rates. In practice the construction of appropriate classes, reporting data to rating bureaus, determining trend factors, and other matters involve a considerable amount of statistical work and the exercise of good judgment.

Liability insurance may be used to illustrate some of the practical problems of rate determination in the field of property and liability insurance. Liability as a line of insurance is made up of a number of sublines among which are:

1. Owners', Landlords' and Tenants' (O.L.&T.)

2. Manufacturers' and Contractors' (M&C)

3. Farmers' Comprehensive Personal Liability (FCPL)

4. Comprehensive Personal Liability (C.P.L.)

5. Elevator Liability

6. Product Liability

7. Owners' or Contractors' Protective Liability

8. Contractual Liability

9. Liquor Law Liability

10. Water Damage Liability

11. Professional Malpractice Liability

12. Workers' Compensation and Employers' Liability

13. Automobile Liability

14. Aircraft Liability

15. Nuclear Energy Liability

The sublines listed above may be further subdivided according to coverage. The typical coverages are: bodily injury, property damage, medical payments, and personal injury, all of which are independently rated. Further, the types of liability making up the sublines are not mutually exclusive. Many of them may be written as a part of the O.L.&T. contract for example, or the comprehensive general liability policy. Certain of the sublines, such as workers' compensation, aircraft liability, and nuclear energy liability are written separately and do not appear as a part of a more general liability contract. It frequently happens that liability risks do not develop premium and loss experience of sufficient magnitude to warrant experience rating. For this reason there has been an effort to try to achieve equity through a large number of manual classifications. Lange states, "The rates for these numerous classes may be varied by state, or even by city, depending on the nature of the coverage provided. For example, the class rates for Owners', Landlords' and Tenants' subline vary by rate territory, resulting in a total of over 30,000 individual manual rates."[24] Lange also points out that an underwriter will not necessarily have a single basic manual rate for a commercial building but will have to apply a number of rates in order to specify a premium. This comes about because one part of the building, say, may house a store while another part may be used for offices. The risk differs for each of these occupancies.

Another aspect of property and liability rate making that has received considerable attention over the years is that interest is not specifically taken into account in the formulas used for rate making. This fact is in contrast with life insurance where interest has always been one of the cost factors in the formulas.[25] By taking interest or investment earnings into account in setting rates is meant any procedure that undertakes to modify any one of the three basic factors — losses, expenses, and profit — that enter into rate determination in property and liability insurance. No general resolution of the problem has emerged, although the investment return issue has been raised in public hearings in a number of states.[26]

It is not possible within the constraints of a single chapter to cover all of the literature that bears on the problem of rate making and related subjects. For the reader with some mathematical background the following books will enlarge his knowledge and mastery of the field of rate making and related areas: Karl Borch, *The Mathematical Theory of Insurance* (Lexington, Massachusetts: D. C. Heath and Company, 1974); C. W. Jordon, Jr. *Life Contingencies*, 2nd ed. (Chicago, Illinois: Society of Actuaries, 1968); and Hilary L. Seal, *Stochastic Theory of a Risk Business* (New York: John Wiley & Sons, Inc., 1969).

UNDERWRITING

The actuarial department of an insurer is generally responsible for rates, while

---

[24] Jeffrey Lange, "General Liability Insurance Ratemaking," *Proceedings of the Casualty Actuarial Society*, LIII (1966), p. 29.

[25] This is not to say that interest is not taken into account in establishing the profitability of a property and liability insurer. See Chapter 16.

[26] For a substantial discussion of the investment return issue see Robert H. Cooper, *Investment Return and Property Liability Insurance Ratemaking* (Homewood, Ill.: Richard D. Irwin, Inc., 1974).

responsibility for rating structures and classifications is often jointly shared by the actuarial and underwriting departments.[27] Thus underwriting or risk selection is closely linked with the rating policy of the insurer.[28] Underwriting has a central position with most insurers and underwriting profit or loss often depends on the skill of the underwriting department.

In broad outline the principles of underwriting and the objectives are similar for life insurance and property and liability insurance. Nevertheless, since the subject matter is different and the procedures vary, it is useful to consider underwriting in the two fields separately.

Property and Liability

Historically property and liability insurers were organized on a mono-line basis. The underwriting function was organized in a similar manner and underwriters specialized in fire, marine, liability, or some other line of insurance. With the advent of multiple-line legislation in the 1950s and the introduction of multiple-line contracts, property and liability underwriting gradually shifted from line specialization to the underwriting of a multiple-line or package contracts as a whole. Some insurers undertook to organize the underwriting function on a personal lines vs. commercial lines basis. Although some specialization continued to exist within commercial lines, the emphasis was clearly on a unified approach.

[27] Robert B. Holtom, *Underwriting Principles and Practices* (Cincinnati: The National Underwriter Company, 1973), p. 26.

[28] In addition to risk selection the underwriter is responsible for classification and rating, policy forms, and decisions about reinsurance.

The Underwriting Process

Holtom has identified the following steps in risk selection: "(1) Secure information; (2) develop alternative courses of action; (3) decide on the best course and take action; (4) evaluate the selected course of action; and (5) make corrections that are indicated."[29]

There are three reasons for securing information. First, a policy cannot be issued unless some information is available such as name and address of the insured and a description of the property covered. Second, information must be available to help the underwriter guard against moral hazard or the tendency for some applicants to have a higher probability of loss than the average. Third, knowledge is needed to protect against the possibility of adverse selection or the possibility that those persons who are most willing to buy insurance may have a high probability of loss. In making decisions about which applicants should be selected and which rejected, information is sought on moral qualities such as honesty, dependability, and ethical behavior; housekeeping and living habits; physical condition of property and/or persons; financial and business factors; and past experience of the applicant including where applicable driving record or number of times contracts have been cancelled.[30]

There are a number of sources of information. A primary source is from agents and brokers or other producers. They forward, when applicable, an application and a photograph of the property as well as a producer's report and answers to specific questions. Another

[29] Holtom, *Underwriting Principles*, p. 58.

[30] *Ibid.*, p. 61.

source of information is inspection reports of various types. These reports may seek to evaluate the morality and integrity of the applicant through, for example, visits in the applicant's home and conversations with neighbors. Other inspection reports may seek information on the physical characteristics of the premises through an actual visit to the premises or they may seek financial information through a review of the books of the applicant. A third source of data consists of contacting banks, creditors, customers, competitors, neighbors, police and fire departments, court houses, and school officials. All of these persons or agencies can often supply information that bears directly on various characteristics of the applicant. Court houses, for example, can supply information on bankruptcies, deeds, license applications, and similar matters. Other information sources are bureaus, such as rating bureaus, arson and theft bureaus, and trade associations; governmental agencies, examples of which would be the census bureau and the departments of motor vehicles of the various states; other insurers; employees of the insurer such as engineers; and insurer records, since an applicant may have more than one contract with a particular insurer.[31]

The second step in the underwriting process is to evaluate the data that have been collected and to develop alternative courses of action. In organizing the information received the underwriter must distinguish between objective and subjective data and must determine the reliability of his sources. To the extent that data are quantitative the underwriter may utilize statistical methods in his analysis. Subjective data are analyzed by judgment. The result of his analysis may indicate that a particu-

[31] For more detail on sources of information see *Ibid.*, pp. 63–79.

lar applicant (or applicants) does not meet the acceptance standards that have been established. This fact leads to a consideration of the alternatives that may be available in making a decision about an application. Among the alternatives that an underwriter may consider are: (1) various levels of acceptability; (2) policy (contract) modifications; (3) adjustment of rates; and (4) reinsurance.

Under the general heading of acceptability the underwriter may consider a declination or cancellation of a risk or a recision of coverage in the event, say, of a material misrepresentation or the application may be accepted as presented or accepted with reservations. In some instances an application may be made acceptable by altering policy (contract) provisions through the use of deductibles, limiting the perils covered, coinsurance clauses, or requiring specific conditions to be met in regard to maintenance of the premises. Endorsements may also be used as a way of limiting the risk transferred to the insurer. Another alternative to outright declination is the possibility of adjusting rates. This might be done by placing the applicant in a different risk class than was originally contemplated. The fourth alternative listed above is reinsurance. An underwriter may find that a particular application involves a transfer of an amount beyond the retention limits of the insurer. In that case he may be willing to retain part of the risk if the balance can be transferred to a reinsurer.

The third step in the underwriting process is to make a specific decision or to decide among the alternatives. In making the decision the underwriter must keep in mind the principles surrounding risk transfer among which are the need for homogeneity, spread of risk, chance events, avoidance of the catastrophe hazard, and the problems surrounding small losses. He must also consider the need for a profitable book of business on the part of the insurer, the possible loss of other business from the prospective insured, the point of view of the agent or broker who depends on commissions for his livelihood, and the possible effect on public relations of underwriting decisions that may be viewed as incompatible with societal objectives. There is some need for an underwriter to make decisions promptly, since failure to do so may lead to an unnecessary loss for the insurer if an event should occur before a decision has been made on a bound risk or may lead to loss of confidence in the insurer on the part of a producer or client.

The two final steps in underwriting consist of an evaluation of decisions made and the taking of corrective action that might be indicated as a result of the evaluation. Since underwriting is an ongoing process, it is desirable for the underwriter to determine how successful past decisions have been in light of the underwriting objectives of the insurer and to learn from errors that may have been made in the past. It is also important for the underwriter to take corrective action where indicated and this may involve repeating the steps taken in arriving at the original decision.[32]

Underwriting by Line of Insurance

Each line of insurance has its own peculiarities, underwriting needs, and special problems. Policy forms used in the various lines differ in many respects and the coverage provided varies. The knowledge needed for underwriting varies accordingly. No effort will be

[32] For further discussion of these points see *Ibid.*, pp. 81–117.

made here to discuss each line from an underwriting viewpoint. Such knowledge may be obtained by consulting specialized texts on the subject.[33]

Life Insurance

In property and liability insurance underwriting concerns center around the forces that might bring about the destruction of property while in life insurance the concern is about those forces that affect mortality. The function of underwriting in life insurance, then, is primarily to select insureds in such a way that the assumptions as to mortality and other factors used in setting premium rates will be met.

In addition to age and sex the following factors influence mortality:

1. Build, or height and weight and its distribution.

2. Family history — the influence of inherited characteristics.

3. Physical condition or characteristics such as pulse rate, heart sounds, blood pressure, condition of lungs and other organs.

4. Personal history of illnesses and ailments.

5. Occupational accident and health hazards, and the hazards associated with poor environment which is usually dependent on occupation.

6. Habits with respect to alcohol and drugs.

7. Moral standards.

8. Residence or travel in unhealthy or hazardous areas.

9. Aviation hazards. (These may be connected with occupation, travel, or avocation.)

[33] *Ibid.*

10. Avocations

11. Race[34]

In judging an applicant from a mortality viewpoint he/she may be classified as standard, substandard, or superstandard and premiums will be assigned accordingly. Thus, a person whose health may be to some extent impaired may nevertheless be accepted by paying a larger premium than would be required of a standard risk of the same age.

Build, family history, general physical condition, and history of ailments may be grouped under the general heading of physical risk. Underwriting judgments about these items are made from studies that have been conducted over the years about the effect of various physical impairments on mortality. Thus, it is known that overweight, high blood pressure, circulatory ailments, and other factors may bring about higher than average mortality. Data collected on these and other factors have been tabulated in such a way that underwriters can rate (often numerically) departure from a standard set for each item.[35]

Occupational influences on mortality are well known. In addition to the possibility of industrial accidents, there are health hazards such as dusts, poisons, abnormalities of air pressure and temperature, dampness, defective illumination, infections, radiant energy, and repeated motion.[36] Both occupational accidents and diseases are more likely in some types of businesses than in others. A classification of occupations

is available to the underwriter that provides information of a statistical type about the nature of some eleven occupational groups. It has been found that variation as to mortality varies among types of employment within an industry as well as among industrial groups.

Another set of factors influencing mortality may be broadly construed as personal — such factors as finances, habits, and morals. Since life insurance contracts are not contracts of indemnity but fixed obligations to pay the face amount, the underwriter must be concerned about possible speculation on the part of the insured. Thus, the face amount of insurance should bear a reasonable relationship to the loss that might be suffered by the beneficiary. One way to establish this relationship is to investigate the financial position of the insured. Concern about habits and morals derives from problems that may arise from the use of alcohol and other drugs and problems that may evolve from conduct not generally considered a part of the community norm. A fairly large amount of statistical information suggests that immoderate use of alcohol leads to above-average mortality and that persons engaging in immoral activity are susceptible to physical and other problems that may lead to disability and/or death. An underwriter considers information about these items in making decisions about an application.

Items 7, 8, 9, and 10 may be classified as external forces that are likely to influence mortality. Where a person lives may lead to problems with sickness and death, especially if the area where the applicant resides is one where public health standards are not high. Also travel to such areas may be a problem from a health point of view. Means of travel is also a consideration particularly if travel is by air. Although many avocations probably have no great sig-

---

[34] Pearce Shepherd and Andrew C. Webster, *Selection of Risks* (Chicago, Ill.: The Society of Actuaries, 1957).

[35] For detailed discussion about the state of underwriting knowledge for various ailments see *Ibid.*, pp. 13–104.

[36] *Ibid.*, p. 107.

nificance from an underwriting point of view, certain activities may be significant from a mortality viewpoint. Among these are aviation, horse racing, polo playing, mountain climbing, auto racing, and yacht racing. A basic problem is that antiselection may occur because the insured has considerable control over the extent to which an avocation is pursued.

SUMMARY AND CONCLUSIONS

1. Underwriting and rating methods may have a large effect on the ultimate cost of insurance to the insured.

2. The net premium in life insurance is based on mortality and interest only.

3. The cost factors in life insurance are mortality, interest, and expenses, and the gross premium (selling price of the contract) is based on these factors.

4. Basically all insurance premiums consist of one part that provides for the insured's share of loss costs and one part that provides for his (her) share of expenses.

5. Cost factors must be estimated and some fairly difficult problems arise in the process.

6. Rate making in property and liability insurance has objectives similar to those in life insurance but specific methods differ markedly.

7. Use of rating bureaus for the purpose of computing rates is common in property and liability insurance in contrast to life insurance where they are not used.

8. Classification of risks is the first step in the insurance rating process and such systems are more complex in property and liability insurance than in life insurance.

9. Fire insurance rates are of two types: 1) class (or minimum) and 2) specific (or tariff).

10. In casualty insurance, manual rates are computed by using either the loss ratio approach or the pure premium approach.

11. Merit rating is a way of establishing different rates for insureds falling within the same rating classification. These rates may be established through the use of schedules or statistical experience.

12. Underwriting is the process of selecting business for the insurer. It involves securing information, developing alternative courses of action, deciding on the best course, evaluating the selected course of action, and making necessary corrections.

QUESTIONS FOR DISCUSSION

1. Discuss the cost factors in life insurance. What are some of the considerations in pricing nonparticipating contracts as opposed to participating contracts?

2. According to the 1958 C.S.O. mortality table, what is the probability that a person age 35 will die within 2 years? Within 5 years?

3. Assuming the 1958 C.S.O. mortality table, what is the probability that a person age 25 will survive to age 65?

4. Compute the present value of a life annuity due of $12,000 per annum issued to a female aged 45. Assume the annuity table and interest at 3 percent.

5. Compute the net level annual premium for a five year term life insurance contract having a face value of $100,000 issued at age 25. Assume the 1958 C.S.O. mortality table with interest at 3 percent.

6. Compute the net single premium for a whole life insurance contract of face amount $150,000 issued at age 30 to a person age 35. Assume the 1958 C.S.O. mortality table with interest of 3 percent.

7. Contrast rate making in property and liability insurance with that in life insurance.

8. Discuss rate regulation in insurance. Classify the rating laws of the various states according to the type of law, *e.g.*, open competition, file and use, and use and file. What kinds of insurance are subject to rate regulation?

9. Compare the universal mercantile schedule with the analytic system. Which system is the more widely used?

10. Assume the average loss cost for bodily injury liability insurance is $125 per automobile. Assuming credibility of 1 and trend in costs of 10 percent per year, what premium should be charged for a contract covering bodily injury liability insurance if the loss ratio for this type of insurance for the insurer in question is 0.60?

11. Define merit rating and discuss the extent of its use in insurance rate making.

12. Contrast underwriting in property and liability insurance with that in life insurance.

13. List and discuss the factors that affect mortality. Into what classes may an applicant be placed from a mortality viewpoint?

14. Discuss the factors that affect interest rates. What effect do increasing interest rate have on the profitability of life insurers? Property and liability insurers?

18

Mergers, Foreign Operations, and Risk Management

The materials considered in previous chapters of this book have involved problems of risk management that arise in the operation of a single business entity and its subsidiaries, including possible foreign operations. There are situations where the risk manager may be called upon to supervise or offer advice and counsel on foreign risk management and on the particular risk and insurance problems involved in corporate mergers. In some cases these problems overlap because a business firm often expands into world business by means of merging with foreign entities. In both of these areas, special difficulties for the risk manager exist. This chapter discusses risk management as it touches upon mergers of two or more corporations and upon world business problems.

Major parts of this chapter are:

1. Risk management and merger problems

2. Responsibilities of the risk manager in mergers

3. Growth of international operations

4. Political risk

5. World insurance markets

6. Special problems in international risk management

7. Insurance conditions abroad

RISK MANAGEMENT AND MERGER PROBLEMS

The merger of two firms is generally a complex process and this fact is as true for the risk management departments of the merging companies as it is of the firm as a whole. Before the benefits can be achieved it is usually necessary to resolve a number of problems. Among these problems are (1) differing approaches to the concepts of insurance and risk management; (2) role of subsidiaries; and (3) effects of existing programs of property and liability insurance, as well as various employee benefit programs.

Differing Approaches

It does not necessarily follow that two merging companies will each have a risk management department. If the firms are of differing size, the smaller firm may not have anyone designated as a risk manager and whatever policy exists about risk may be the responsibility of the controller or his assistants. It is conceivable that neither firm has recognized risk as a separate function, especially when the firm to be acquired is a foreign company. Even where formal risk departments exist, they may differ dramatically in terms of size and organization. Some firms have highly centralized departments while others operate in a decentralized fashion with risk managers in various plants or divisions. The scope of the departments may also differ, with one department giving the risk manager responsibility for such matters as employee benefits, safety, property and liability insurance, and the other department restricting responsibility to safety and property and liability insurance. The titles of the persons responsible for risk matters may be different in the merging firms, with one title suggesting fairly broad responsibility and the other, limited. The scope and organization of the merging department will need to be determined as a part of the merger plan.

Philosophical differences may emerge also. The merging companies may have opposing views as to the desirability of retention programs, such as self-insurance, in place of relying on transfer as the typical mode of meeting risk. Opinions may also differ on the merits of insurers organized as mutuals compared to those operating as stock companies. In terms of the purchase of insurance, one of the merging firms may have relied fairly heavily on the advice of agents and brokers. The other firm may have preferred direct writers or insurers using exclusive agency systems. Another area in which philosophical differences can arise is in the use of deductibles and excess insurance. Yet another is foreign operations which may also pose risk management problems for merging companies, not only in terms of expropriation but in terms of insurance coverage. Some of these problems may

be resolved through the use of analytical procedures, but others may still be in the realm of tradition and preference.

Role of Subsidiaries

One or both of the parties to the merger may have subsidiaries that may be involved in the merger, although perhaps not at the precise time that the merger of the parent companies takes place. It does not follow that subsidiaries necessarily follow the risk management philosophy and practices of their owners. This fact may lead to additional problems when the merger takes place.

Existing Programs — Property and Liability Insurance and Employee Benefits

Apart from philosophical and organizational differences, when two firms merge, immediate practical problems arise about how to cope with existing insurance contracts and employee benefit programs.

Property and Liability Insurance

Property and liability insurance contracts are legal documents that are very specific about such matters as the name of the insured, the property covered, and other circumstances surrounding the transfer. Typically they cannot be assigned without the consent of the insurer. Decisions will have to be made about the type of coverage to be carried after the merger, as well as about the insurer who will be assuming the risk.

A number of examples of problems that arise with specific coverages may be cited. In workers' compensation certain legal filings must be made with the various areas of operation. These filings will need amending as a result of the merger. In fire insurance it will be necessary to arrange for assignment of contracts, and, as soon as practical, it will be imperative to review coinsurance clauses, property values, possibilities of blanket insurance, and other factors involving the fire insurance contract. Specific attention should also be paid to fire prevention and safety. Other contracts that will need review are various types of liability, fidelity bonds, and business interruption.[1]

Employee Benefits

Employee benefit plans (as was seen in Chapter 11) can be extensive and diverse. Attempting to bring differing plans together often presents some complex problems. Types of plans offered, level of benefits, magnitude of employee and employer contributions, funding media, and other plan characteristics may require considerable discussion and negotiation. Some plans, such as profit sharing, deferred compensation for executives, stock ownership plans, and key man insurance, usually affect relatively small numbers and may not be difficult to adjust in the event of merger. So, too, benefits involving group insurance contracts present no unusual problems, although extensive differences in benefit levels may require adjustment and additional expense. Of the various employee benefit plans pensions probably will require the most attention during merger. They are long-term in character, typically involve large amounts of money, are technically fairly complicated, and involve legal requirements of an increasingly complex sort.[2]

Walker identifies pension problems that will occur before merger and those that will arise after it takes place.[3] Included in the first set are (1) the determination of the characteristics the plan will have after merger and (2) valuation of pension liabilities under the new plan. The second set of problems are described by Walker as mechanical and include decisions on the funding medium, timing of any changes to be made, and meeting the requirements set forth by the Treasury Department for qualified plans.

Determining the characteristics of a new benefits plan will involve an effort to harmonize two benefit structures. Hawn has recommended that a revision in benefit structure should:[4]

1. Keep the acquired organization competitive with regard to both cost of goods sold and the labor market.

2. Maintain the level of benefits enjoyed by the acquired personnel (if consistent with the preceding point).

3. Provide the optimum benefit for the maximum number of employees.

4. Provide the highest return for the dollars spent.

5. Maintain the proper balance between hourly and salaried employees.

6. Anticipate future trends.

---

[1] This list is not complete. The risk manager will need to consider all insurance contracts that may exist at the time of the merger.

[2] See Chapters 12 and 13.

[3] Ralph J. Walker, "Pension Funding and Group Benefits in Merger," *Meeting New Needs in Risk Management* (New York: American Management Association, Insurance Series No. 115, 1957), pp. 9–10.

[4] John L. Hawn, "Fringe Benefit Policy and the Merger," *Corporate Growth Through Merger and Acquisition*, Management Report No. 75 (New York: American Management Association, 1963), p. 154.

7. Permit simple explanation to the employees.

8. Permit efficient administration.

Difficulties may arise in applying these criteria because of differing management philosophies and problems of employee adjustment.

The evaluation of pension liabilities can be crucial in determining the terms of a merger. Extensive liabilities could add considerably to merger costs especially if it is necessary to increase the benefits provided to either the acquired or acquiring group.

RESPONSIBILITIES OF THE RISK MANAGER IN MERGERS

Since merger involves two not previously related risk management departments, consideration must be given early to the administrative responsibilities that must be carried while plans for a new risk management department are being made. Cooper lists three tools for consolidation: "(1) advance notice; (2) a postmerger program; and (3) authority to carry it out."[5] Before the merger there must be an exchange of information and someone should be appointed and given the authority to seek assignment of insurance contracts and to make the required filings for such items as workers' compensation. After the merger selection of a risk manager for the combined department is of first importance. His primary responsibility will be to activate the new program and to facilitate its smooth functioning.

RISK MANAGEMENT IN WORLD BUSINESS

Most large enterprises in the world operate across political boundaries. Handling the risk of foreign operations may present difficult tasks for the risk manager in these enterprises because of differences in conditions affecting risk and insurance abroad. In this chapter an analysis is made of some of these differences, particularly as they affect the transfer of risk to insurers. Special emphasis is given to problems facing the risk manager in the United States who must handle some of the risks in the multinational corporation.

Growth of International Operations

A significant characteristic of most industrial nations in the period after World War II has been the increased involvement in world affairs. Evidence of this is seen in the growth of international communication and trade, the rise in world living standards, the increased interest in economic integration such as has occurred in the various common markets established around the world. Much of this enlargement has been due to the spread of technological know-how and scientific cooperation through facilities of various organizations, both public and private. Much of the economic leadership has been provided by the multinational corporation, whose emergence has been perhaps one of the most dominant factors in business and economic development since World War II.[6] It has been estimated that by 1975

---

[5] James M. Cooper, "Merger Decentralization, and the Insurance Function," in *Meeting New Needs in Insurance Management, Insurance Problems in Mergers*. Insurance Series 115 (New York: American Management Association, 1957) p. 4.

[6] Neil H. Jacoby places the growth of international business as one of the three most important developments affecting corporations since World War II. The other two are advancements in management science and the

approximately 25 percent of the gross national product in the free world (excluding the U.S.) was provided by branches and subsidiaries of U.S. multinational companies.

International investments by multinational companies have necessitated a corresponding growth in the need for adequate insurance protection and other risk-handling methods. Private, long-term investments of U.S. corporations, for example, increased almost five times over the period 1955–73, equivalent to a compound annual growth rate of about 10 percent. Foreign investments in the United States have increased nearly six times over the same period. Total U.S. investments abroad at year end in 1973 totalled over $143 billion, compared to $163 billion of investments by foreigners in the United States.[7] A major reason for this growth in investments abroad by U.S. firms has been the rapid industrial growth of Western Europe and Japan, which are relatively less dependent on imports from the U.S. than before. For example, in the period 1966–71 eight major Western European nations[8] increased their imports from the United States by only 54 percent, compared to nearly 100 percent increase in imports from each other. The combined population of these countries was 253 million people compared to 200 million in the United States.

Total insurance premiums collected throughout the world have increased at an average annual growth

rate of about 9 percent in the period 1950–73.[9] Thus, the rate of growth in insurance premiums has on the whole corresponded fairly evenly with the growth in international investments, although, of course, these growth rates varied greatly from country to country. It is generally true that those areas of the world with the greatest increase in economic growth have also experienced the greatest increase in insurance activity. For example, over the period 1950–73 annual premiums in all major insurance lines have increased at an average annual compound growth rate as follows: Europe, 13.8%; North America, 7.7%; all other countries, 17.9%; total business, 9.3%.[10] Thus, the most rapid rate of increse in insurance exists in those nations, particularly Japan, Mexico, and Argentina, where rapid industrialization has been occurring.

International Risk

Operating in foreign countries is generally perceived to be more risky than domestic operations. Many factors contribute to this. Language, customs, monetary conditions, government, consumer preferences, inflation rates, geography, climate, and legal environment abroad are often relatively unfamiliar to the risk manager. This lack of knowledge of operating environment tends to increase perceived risk. Furthermore, statistics of loss records, loss prevention facilities, and other underwriting information is typically lacking.

Insurance contract language is not uniform across various countries, giving rise to gaps in coverage that may not be anticipated. Distances from foreign

growth of conglomerate enterprise. Neil H. Jacoby, *Corporate Power and Social Responsibility.*

[7] U.S. Department of Commerce, *1975 Economic Report of the President*, p. 35.

[8] Belgium-Luxembourg, Denmark, France, Germany, Ireland, Italy, the Netherlands, and the United Kingdom. From data reported by *Business Europe*, January 19, 1973, p. 21.

[9] Swiss Reinsurance Company, *Sigma*, April 1976, p. 3.

[10] *Ibid.*

areas are such that time lapse prevents or discourages close contact with the foreign corporation and hinders fast decision making. For example, in one large multinational corporation with construction operations in several countries, the risk manager reported that it took a full year of negotiation and preparation to complete the property insurance program for the company. These factors all tend to make the job of the risk manager in large companies quite complex.

In spite of the difficulties, and perhaps because of them, the risk manager's task in foreign operations is increasingly recognized as essential to the development of international business. Without means to handle the risk, foreign operations would be severely handicapped, if not stopped entirely. Foreign opportunities, however, are too large and too important to ignore by most firms of substance. It is doubtful that most modern nations as we know them could survive without international trade and investment. Hence, ways must be found to handle international risk efficiently and effectively.

Political Risk

One of the factors of great importance in contributing to international risk is political risk.[11] Political risk is usually not as an important factor in risk management in the domestic United States, but it should receive careful analysis by those charged with international responsibilities.

Political risk may be defined as that uncertainty stemming from unanticipated and unexpected acts of gov-

[11] S. H. Robock, and K. Simmonds, *International Business and Multi-national Enterprises* (Homewood, Ill.: Richard D. Irwin, 1973), Chapter 15.

ernments or other organizations which may cause loss to the business firm. Both pure and speculative risks are involved. Examples of political losses are (a) take-over of properties or confiscation of assets of the foreign business firm without compensation or with inadequate compensation, (b) damage to property or personnel from revolution, kidnapping, murder, insurrection, riot, or vandalism, (c) governmental interference with the terms of privately negotiated contracts such as imposition of bans on imports of necessary materials, goods, or supplies, (d) bans on remittances of currency in payment of foreign obligations or for dividends to foreign stockholders, (e) discriminatory taxation, and/or (f) requirements that the foreign firm deal exclusively with a governmental agency for given goods or services, such as insurance.

Political risk stems from several factors over which the risk manager may have little direct control. Examples of such factors are opposing political parties each attempting to obtain control of the government by almost any means, opposition by local business groups seeking to overcome or avoid competition by foreign firms, extreme poverty which brings on social unrest and disorder, existence of organized outlaw groups which resort to such means as kidnapping or murder of foreign businessmen, new treaties with other foreign governments requiring different treatment of foreign business interests, and a desire to correct adverse trade balances. For example, when Libya seized assets of British Petroleum Company and its American partner Bunker Hunt in 1971, part of the reason was reported as being in retribution for American support for Israel in the Mid-East conflict and for British complicity in Iranian occupation of Arab lands.

The premier was reported as saying, "The time has come for us to deal America a strong slap on its cool, arrogant face. American policy will cause a disaster to American interests in the region."[12]

Sometimes political risk produces bizarre losses. In Argentina, over 250 kidnappings of U.S. executives by terrorists groups have occurred. For example, in 1973 the Ford Motor Company was forced to pay $1 million to a subversive group in return for a promise that its executives would not be harassed. Similar demands were made against Coca-Cola Export Company, Otis Elevator, Firestone Tire and Rubber Company, and several other large U.S. companies. The funds were to be used to correct adverse social conditions. News media reported that Firestone paid out $3 million for the release of a kidnapped executive; other companies transferred entire executive staffs out of the country.[13] In 1969 a number of U.S.-owned grocery supermarkets were bombed in Argentina when Governor Nelson Rockefeller, of New York, visited that country as a special envoy of President Richard M. Nixon.

In Cuba, when the Castro government swept into power in 1959–60 both domestic and foreign firms alike were confiscated. Similar large scale expropriations have occurred in Mexico, Algeria, Burma, Chile, Egypt, Ghana, Uganda, and Indonesia. Petroleum and other natural resource companies have been especially susceptible to political risk because of the tendency of foreign countries to feel that only nationals should be allowed to exploit basic resources. A study by the U.S. Department of State identified 70 recent situations in noncommunist countries involving losses from political risk.[14] Another example of this was in India, where 42 foreign and 64 domestic insurance companies were nationalized.[15]

Loss Prediction

In spite of the fact that the risk manager may have little direct control over political risk, there is something he can do to help predict loss from political risk and to advise on methods to reduce the probability of loss. Stefan Robock and Kenneth Simmonds have suggested a method of predicting political risk.[16] This method involves four basic steps:

(1) Understand the type of government presently in power, its patterns of political behavior, and its norms for stability.

(2) Analyze the multinational enterprise's own product or operation to identify the political risk most likely to be involved in a given area.

(3) Determine the source of potential political risk. For example, if the risk involves possible restriction on operations, is the source that of local businessmen or political parties?

(4) Estimate the probability of loss and the time span in which the loss may occur.

An example of an application of this method is that of construction of a probability tree. (See Chapter 3.) In this case the risk manager has estimated that a certain property may be confiscated if the radical party is elected to power in the next five years. There is a 30 percent probability that this party

[12] *Atlanta Journal and Constitution,* August 12, 1973, p. 8-A.

[13] *Ibid.,* p. 11-A.

[14] *Nationalism, Expropriation, and Other Takings of United States and Certain Foreign Property Since 1960,* Bureau of Intelligence and Research, U.S. Department of State, November 30, 1971.

[15] *Wall Street Journal,* May 14, 1971, p. 4.

[16] Robock and Simmonds, *International Business,* pp. 370–75.

will be elected, and a 70 percent probability that the conservative party will be elected. If the radicals are elected, the probability of confiscation is 50 percent. If the conservatives are elected the probability of loss is zero. The probability of loss by confiscation is therefore 15 percent (30 percent × 50 percent). Additional types of political risk (other than confiscation) can be similarly treated. The probable dollar loss is obtained by multiplying the expected cash flows for each outcome by the probability of that outcome and calculating the present values of this cash flow. Decisions to make new investments, withdraw existing investment, or take actions to reduce the probability of loss can then be made with greater certainty.

Handling Political Risk

Political risk, like other types of risk, can be managed with traditional tools of risk management: avoidance, transfer, diversification, loss prevention, insurance, and retention. Among the actions the risk manager may recommend to minimize political risk are the following:

(1) *Avoidance.* He may recommend that the firm not make an initial investment at all if the probability of loss is too high. Sometimes this action itself reduces political risk. For example, investment by United States firms in France fell far below the levels in other western European countries during the 1960s when DeGaulle was in power and foreign investment was discouraged. After President Pompidou took office in 1969 this negative policy was changed and active efforts were made to attract U.S. investment in France.[17]

(2) *Transfer.* The risk manager may recommend that ownership in a given investment be shared with local

[17] *Business Week*, September 5, 1970.

interests or with the government. In this way there is less likelihood that loss from physical destruction of assets, or that governmental take-over will occur, since local interests would also suffer along with the foreign owners.

(3) *Diversification and loss prevention.* A firm may diversify in such a way as not to be totally dependent on production in a given country. This may be accomplished by maintaining plants in other countries capable of substituting for plants which may be nationalized in other countries. The very existence of such alternative facilities may help prevent the loss by deterring nationalization in the first place. Petroleum producers have used this technique extensively. In addition, a firm may reduce political risk of take-over by developing a strong marketing system for the product. If the production facilities were nationalized the new owners would realize that they would have no efficient way of disposing of the product, and to develop their own marketing system might not be feasible for a long period of time. For example, assume that a manufacturing firm has a policy of obtaining supplies from a large number of small local producers who usually cannot economically establish their own marketing systems for the final product. These small producers will likely resist any political pressure to take over the manufacturing facilities of the foreign firm because to do so would mean loss of sales.

(4) *Insurance.* The risk manager may recommend insurance against political risk. For example, kidnapping insurance in the case of Argentine kidnappings was reported to be available. A typical policy was alleged to cost 4 percent of the policy amount.[18] In the field of credit risk, insurance is available in

[18] *Business Insurance*, July 16, 1973, pp. 1, 30ff.

three major forms: (a) export credit insurance against loss from failure of foreign buyers to pay for goods or services they have purchased; (b) investment insurance against loss from war, insurrection, revolution, or other acts of foreign governments such as expropriation or confiscation of assets or from inconvertibility of foreign currency; and (c) exchange risk insurance against loss from devaluation or revaluation of currencies.

(a) *Export credit insurance.* Export credit insurance is underwritten in the United States by the Foreign Credit Insurance Association, which represents about fifty private insurers, with the backing of the Export-Import Bank, an agency of the U.S. government. The coverage has been available since 1961. Coverage extends to commercial risk (*e.g.,* the peril insolvency) as well as political risk (*e.g.,* war, revolution, insurrection, confiscation, and inconvertibility of currency). Preshipment coverage is available; this insurance covers loss due to cancellation of orders before the goods are shipped. Normally, about 90 percent of the loss may be insured, and a dollar deductible amount (called the primary loss) applies. Arrangements may be made in which the exporter is given a "discretionary credit limit," under which he may ship to foreign buyers without first obtaining approval from the FCIA; in other cases, prior approval must first be arranged before shipment. The exporter may also obtain credit insurance indirectly through banks, who may obtain Eximbank guarantees against loss from loans extended to the exporter.

Short-term policies (credit terms up to six months) require that the exporter cover all of his sales on a blanket basis. Agricultural commodities may be insured with 98 percent coverage on both commercial and political risks. Medium-term policies (credit terms from six

months to five years) are issued on a case-by-case basis with no requirement that the exporter insure all of his transactions. On these sales the FCIA requires that the exporter obtain a down payment of at least 10 percent. A special combination policy is available under which the exporter may offer overseas dealers "floorplan financing" without a down payment requirement until 270 days have passed. This policy was devised to facilitate sales by liberalizing credit terms at no increased risk to the exporter. A master comprehensive policy is available covering both political and commercial risks on both short-term and medium-term sales. An example of this plan was the issuance in 1973 of a $40 million policy to American Motors Corporation, which covers sales of autos and accessories abroad with 100 percent financing without recourse on American Motors.

The cost of export credit insurance varies according to the country of destination, terms of payments, the exporter's record of credit loss, the amount of deductible assumed, and other factors. Costs may range as high as 2 percent of the invoice value. The charges made cover for the full term of the credit guarantee.

(b) *Investment insurance.* In 1948 the United States government established an investment insurance program to protect the assets of U.S. investors abroad. The program is administered by the Overseas Private Investors Corp. (OPIC). Perils insured include expropriation, nationalization, or confiscation of the foreign investment, war, revolution, and insurrection. In addition, coverage is available against loss from inconvertibility into dollars of profits, royalties, fees, and other income, as well as the original capital investment. Since the inception of the program in 1948, through

1972, about 4,100 specific insurance contracts for a total coverage of nearly $12 billion have been written.

Coverage is available only in specified developing countries. To be eligible for insurance, the country must have signed a bilateral agreement with the United States under which the foreign country recognizes the transfer to the U.S. government of the insured investor's rights, if payment is made under the insurance contract. The country also agrees to submit any conflict arising out of the agreement to arbitration. Although about ninety developing countries have signed such agreements, several of these restrict the agreement in such a way as to limit the scope of coverage available. For example, expropriation insurance is not available in Argentina; protection against war, revolution, and insurrection is not available in Argentina, El Salvador, Guatemala, and Nigeria. Mexico and Uruguay have not signed agreements and no investment insurance is available in those countries.

Only new investments are eligible for investment insurance. Approval for the investment must be given by the host country. Although existing investments may not be insured, coverage is available for expansion, modernization, or development of existing projects. Property insured can include not only physical plant and equipment, but also foreign currency, loans, patents, processes, or technical services. In general, the ownership of the investment must be held by U.S. citizens or by corporations in which U.S. citizens have at least 50 percent ownership. If the investment is sold, the insurance may usually be transferred to the new owner. There is no maximum limit on the amount of coverage, but the term of coverage may not exceed twenty years. In the case of investments through loans, coverage is granted only for the term of the loan, usually not less than three years.

The annual premium for investment insurance depends on the number of perils covered. There is an application fee of $100 for investments of $100,000 or more. The annual premium for inconvertibility is .3 percent; for expropriation, .6 percent; for war, revolution, and insurrection, .6 percent. These fees are the same for all countries. Currently, no variation exists according to the type of investment, although an action was under consideration in 1973 to introduce a schedule of fees which varied according to the nature of the project.

Losses under the investment insurance program have been relatively modest so far. Over the period 1948–72 claims totalled about $6 million, compared to about $160 million of premiums collected. The largest claim paid, excluding claims originating in Chile, was $2.7 million to Indian Head Mills for expropriation of a textile mill it owned in Nigeria.

Under a separate program, OPIC also offers loan guarantees on an all-risk basis to lenders who fund given types of projects. Normally, a project is developed and planned by the investor who then arranges financing from a bank or insurance company. The loan guarantee stipulates that if there is any interruption in the repayment schedule for any reason, the OPIC will respond. The loan, which is usually for five to fifteen years, is covered 100 percent plus interest. To be eligible the investment must be shown to contribute substantially to the economic and social development of the host country. The annual premium for loan guarantees is at least 1.75 percent on the outstanding balance of the loan.

According to a survey by Business International Corporation, a majority of U.S. firms use investment insurance where it is available, although different policies exist on when to insure. For example, in one study of 19 companies, it was found that 11 had no fixed minimum investment amount for which coverage must be taken. Three firms have a $100,000 minimum, one $200,000, two $500,000, one $1 million, and one $2 million.[19]

Following the lead of the United States, several other countries now offer their investors investment insurance somewhat more limited in scope than that offered in the United States. However, in 1973 the European Economic Community's Council of Ministers developed a plan to set up an Office for Private Investment Guarantee (OPIG) with an initial capital of $10.8 million. OPIG, when fully operational, would provide coverage for European-based multinational firms essentially similar to that described above for U.S.-based firms.[20]

(c) *Exchange risk insurance.* Exchange risks can be viewed from two different viewpoints, short term and long term. In some European countries, insurance may be obtained against losses from long-term exchange risk, but short-term protection usually take forms other than insurance.

Exchange risk is the uncertainty of loss arising from devaluation or revaluation of foreign currencies. To illustrate, assume that the multinational firm has a branch operation in France and has bank deposits of $1 million in francs. If

the exchange rate were Ffr 5: $1, this amounts to Ffr 5 million. If the franc is devalued 10 percent in terms of the dollar, the firm's franc holdings are now worth only $910,000, because it now would take 5.5 francs to purchase the $1 instead of 5 francs. According to one study of 109 currencies over the period 1948–69, 96 were devalued at least once, 69 were devalued two or more times.[21] In the event of revaluation (upward), firms holding soft currency suffer losses if they must later convert this to the revalued currency.

Short-term risk. When devaluation threatens losses from short-term exchange, risk can be lessened by minimizing the amounts held in soft currencies (such as cash, accounts receivable, or inventories) or maximizing the amounts represented by debts to others in the soft currency country. Another technique is to speed up payments of dividends or other remittances due to the parent corporation, or to others in hard currency countries. When the risk is revaluation of a foreign currency these techniques should be reversed. Thus, if a company operating in Germany feels that the mark will be revalued, it should minimize its holdings of soft currency (*i.e.*, dollars), maximize its holdings of the hard currency (*i.e.*, marks), and should minimize its local debts payable in hard currency.

The firm may also hedge in the futures market for foreign currencies. If a multinational firm sells goods to a soft currency buyer, agreeing to accept the soft currency in payment within ninety days, it is exposed to loss through devaluation. To protect itself, the firm may sell three months' futures contracts in the soft currency. A futures contract is an agreement to deliver the specified

[19] Business International, Inc., "Investment Guarantees" in *Techniques for Financing,* February 1973.

[20] For details see "EEC to Guarantee Investments in Developing Countries," *Business Europe,* Vol. 13, No. 1 (New York: Business International, January 1973).

[21] "Protecting Foreign Assets," *Financing Foreign Operations* (New York: Business International, 1973).

currency to a buyer at some specified time in the future at a price determined at the time the contract is made. If the currency is later devalued before the expiration of the contract, the seller can purchase the needed currency at a reduced price in order to fulfill his contract. The profit made on this transaction offsets the loss the firm has suffered because he must accept payment for his merchandise in a devalued currency. The hedging transaction thus protects the firm's normal operating margins. Unfortunately, the cost of entering into futures transactions in soft currencies can be excessive. The weaker the currency the higher the cost. For example, in April 1973, it was estimated that if a Swiss exporter wished to obtain forward cover against the dollar (which was weak at the time) he would have to add about 20 percent to his price to cover the costs of hedging.[22] This may make the exporter's prices noncompetitive and sales may be lost.

Long-term risk. Several European countries, France, Austria, Belgium, Germany, Spain, and Switzerland, have adopted exchange risk guarantee programs to handle the long-term risk. The exchange risk guarantee takes effect not sooner than one year after the contract is signed. A normal period is two years. The insured must retain the first 2 or 3 percent of long-term exchange loss. Such contracts are designed to protect the long-term lender or the seller who has agreed to make deliveries well into the future at prices agreed to in advance. If the currency of payment is devalued, the seller or lender is protected against the ensuing loss.

An example of such a program is that adopted by France. Coverage is 100

22 "How Exchange Risk Guarantees Can Safeguard Exporter's Profits," *Business Europe*, Vol. 13, No. 17 (New York: Business International, Inc., January 1973), p. 129.

percent for contracts and payments longer than one year. The annual premium is .648 percent of the outstanding balance. Protection can be extended to the U.S. dollar, the Swiss franc, the yen, and any currency traded on the Paris market except EEC currencies. The insured must bear the first 2.25 percent of any exchange loss. If the seller or lender has purchased the guarantee, he may ordinarily obtain bank funds at an interest cost of .5 percent less than would be the case without the guarantee.

(5) *Retention.* The firm will recognize that not all political risk can be avoided, insured, reduced, or otherwise eliminated. Foreign investments will still be made; the remaining political risks deliberately retained. The analysis of political risk made necessary by employing the other risk-handling methods discussed above, however, will likely be of substantial effect in reducing subjective risk (the degree of uncertainty perceived by the firm's management). Presumably, the opportunities for profit from assuming this residual risk will make the retention worthwhile.

World Insurance Markets

To appreciate fully the problems in efficient handling of risk in worldwide operations it is necessary to recognize that the supply of insurance (referred to as the insurance market) is international in character. A central function of insurance is to obtain as wide and diversified a spread of risk as possible. This spread has been achieved through participation in loss exposures abroad via reinsurance as well as direct writings. Hence, the risk manager should learn what he can about dealing both with domestic as well as foreign (or alien) insurers. This is especially true because of periodic shortages of domestic insurance capacity (see Chap-

TABLE 18–1
International Distribution of Insurance

	Number	Percent of Total
USA and Canada	4,783	45.7
20 European nations	3,932	37.5
18 Latin American nations	805	7.7
18 African countries	202	1.9
14 Asian countries	369	3.5
4 Australian nations	388	3.7
	10,479	100.0

Source: Swiss Reinsurance Company, 1972.

ter 16, Insurance Capacity), the existence of laws restricting the use of non-admitted insurance and the need to obtain the best coverage and service available at the most economic price.

A study by the Swiss Reinsurance Company in 1972, covering 76 nations, revealed the existence of 10,479 insurance companies and 3,200 foreign branches, for a total of 13,700 world insurance offices. The insurance companies were distributed as shown in Table 18–1. By contrast, it was estimated that in 1900 there were only about 1,300 insurers in the world.[23] Thus, the number

of insurance offices has expanded tenfold since 1900, compared to an increase in world population over the same period of slightly over twofold. The United States, while being the largest insurance country in the world (4,698 companies), still has less than half of the total number of insurers in the world. The German market is second (882 companies); Great Britain third (740); and Spain fourth (674).

Division of insurance premiums (in percent of total) in insurance throughout major nations in 1973 is as shown in Table 18–2:[24]

The risk manager may judge from these data the extent to which insurers are specialized in the various lines of coverage in major countries and the importance of these lines. For example, automobile coverage is more important to European insurers, relatively speaking, than it is to North American insurers. Hence, investigation of foreign insurance capacity and terms may be worth the time or trouble it may involve.

Some insurers are more experienced in international coverage than others. As shown in Table 18–3, Great Britain appears to be the leading international insurance country in the world, followed by the United States, France, Switzerland, and Germany, in that order. About 75 percent of all foreign branches are op-

[23] Swiss Reinsurance Company, *Sigma*, October 1972, pp. 1–4.

[24] *Ibid.*, p. 9.

TABLE 18–2
Distribution of Total Insurance Premiums (Percent of Total)

Line of Insurance	Europe	North America	Other Countries
Fire	10.0	10.1	10.2
Automobile	30.2	19.6	20.8
Accident/liability	11.2	26.8	4.4
Marine, aviation	4.2	.7	4.4
Life	30.9	37.9	57.0
All other	13.5	4.9	3.2
Total	100.0	100.0	100.0

Source: Swiss Reinsurance Company, *Sigma*, October 1972.

erated from four countries: Great Britain, United States, France, and Switzerland. Among the nations in which U.S. insurers operate most extensively are Puerto Rico, Canada, Great Britain, Guam, Germany, the Philippines, Japan, India, and the Netherlands. Foreign countries whose insurers are operating in the United States with greatest frequency are: Great Britain (18 insurers); France (4); Canada and Japan (3 each); Hong Kong and Australia (2 each); and the Netheralnds, Switzerland, Brazil, Mexico, New Zealand, and the Philippines (1 each).

Insurance markets are not necessarily located according to population. For example, North America which has about 7 percent of the world's population has the highest density of insurance companies in the world, 22 companies per 1 million of population. Insurance density in Asia, with about a third of the world's population, is the lowest in

TABLE 18–3

Extent of International Insurance
Operations by Country

Country	Number of Countries in Which Insurance Operations are Undertaken	Number of Foreign Branches
Great Britain	58	985
United States	47	703
France	41	308
Switzerland	36	176
Germany	16	93
The Netherlands	18	83
Italy	27	71
Belgium	8	70
Australia	17	62
Canada	17	45
Japan	19	44

Source: Swiss Reinsurance Company, 1972.

the world, about one company for each 1 million persons. The average worldwide density of insurance companies is about 6.4 companies per 1 million of population.[25] Japan has only about 40 domestic insurers, although its population is over 100 million. These data suggest also that insurance is a business which lends itself to the economies of large-scale operations. This topic is taken up below.

Concentration in Insurance

Markets for insurance tend to be highly concentrated with relatively few insurers doing a large proportion of the total business. In 1970, for example, 1.8 percent of the world's insurers wrote 44 percent of the total premium volume. Measured by market shares of the largest companies, concentration is usually much greater elsewhere than in the United States. In the nonlife field, the ten largest insurers wrote about 29 percent of the business in the United States; this compared to 45.5 percent in France, 70.6 percent in Denmark, 79.1 percent in Great Britain, 61.7 percent in Italy, 89 percent in Sweden, 53.1 percent in Germany, 78 percent in Switzerland, 74.4 percent in Japan, and 26.1 percent in Spain. In the United States in life insurance the concentration is much higher than in nonlife insurance; 48.4 percent of the total life insurance premiums are collected by the ten largest insurers. In other countries, too, concentration in life insurance tends to be greater than in nonlife insurance and also much greater than in the United States. For example, the ten largest life insurers in France did 79.1 percent of the business in 1970. In Italy they did 95.5 percent; in Sweden, 98.3 percent; in Japan, 87.4 percent; in Germany, 49 percent; in Great Britain, 56.7 percent; in Switzerland, 94 percent;

[25] *Ibid.*

and in Denmark 85.3 percent. In all but the last four of the nations mentioned the concentration in life insurance has increased over the period 1960–70.[26]

Some of the reasons for having relatively large size and heavy concentration in insurance are: (1) Increased involvement in international operations by insurers usually requires larger units for efficiency. (2) Larger units tend to be more efficient in insurance because of more intensive use of specialists (*e.g.,* actuaries, financial planners), reduced marketing costs (mainly through reduced agency commissions), and use of electronic data processing. (3) It may be difficult to enter some lines of insurance without the advantages of size. For example, mass merchandising (group property and liability insurance) probably would not be profitable without mass processing of applications and premium collections through payroll deduction. This in turn requires substantial investment in electronic data processing equipment, as well as increased marketing effort. Usually the customers for mass merchandising systems are large firms themselves and require insurers to be correspondingly substantial. (4) Larger insurance companies may achieve better distribution of risks and, hence, attain more stable underwriting results. For example, firms diversified internationally may achieve broader geographic and industrial dispersion of risk. Such firms are more likely to be able to offer a continuous supply of coverage at more stable rates than firms not so diversified.

Caveats

The risk manager, recognizing the heavy concentration in the insurance industry, particularly outside the United States, should be aware of possible pit-

26 *Ibid.*

falls in placing coverage internationally. (1) Relative lack of competition may exist among insurance markets abroad. The practice of competitive bidding, common in the United States, may not operate as successfully abroad because of this factor. Direct negotiation with international insurance markets is common. (2) Because economies of scale may not always exist, the risk manager should be aware that he may not always be dealing with the least cost insurer just because it is large. As in manufacturing, and other types of business, large size in insurance may bring on difficulties in communication, increased opposition to change, less flexibility, and lack of individual initiative. As a result, the risk manager may find it preferable to discover and deal with smaller insurers in the market. (3) Large units may not necessarily offer larger capacity than smaller units with adequate reinsurance facilities. For example, large insurance units may desire to concentrate in the so-called mass lines, such as private passenger auto insurance, or residential risks. They may avoid the unusual exposure. The risk manager with hard-to-place exposures should consider carefully the underwriting policies of the large insurer before he commits his firm's business to it, in order to avoid a situation in which he has placed the large profitable line with one insurer who refused to accommodate the smaller or unusual exposure. The risk manager may be faced with great difficulties in placement of the unusual exposure unless he also offers the supplier volume lines as well.

Leading International Insurers and Brokers

Current examples of leading U.S. property-liability insurers operating in foreign areas are ARIA, American International Underwriters (AIU), factory mutual associations, Insurance Company of North America, American Insurance, Great American Insurance, Hartford Fire Insurance, Home Insurance, and Continental National American. Examples of leading life insurers operating abroad are John Hancock, American International Life, Combined Insurance, and Aetna Life Insurance. Perhaps the oldest American international insurance group is AFIA, formerly known as American Foreign Insurance Association. It was formed in 1917 to do business in China. AFIA actually operates as a management organization representing about nine separate insurers. These insurers indicate the extent to which they may be bound for coverage, and AFIA carries out these policies for them in foreign markets. American International Underwriters, formed in 1927, operates similarly to AFIA except that it has greater control over the insurers it represents. AFIA and AIU handle local indigenous business in foreign lands in addition to the business of American firms operating abroad. Because of their long experience in international insurance, these firms are dominant factors in international insurance markets for American firms.

Factory mutuals are represented by two major systems, the Factory Insurance Association (FIA) made up of about forty stock insurers, and the Factory Mutual Association (FMA) representing four mutuals. These organizations accept only accounts which will accept rigid standards of loss prevention activity, i.e., so-called high protection risks. In this regard, factory mutuals also offer engineering services to their customers.

The risk manager should also be familiar with the operations of international insurance brokers, through which contact with insurance markets abroad may be achieved. Important international insurance brokerage firms with branches in most important foreign countries are Marsh and McLennan, Johnson and Higgins, Alexander and Alexander, Frank B. Hall, Reed Shaw Osler, and Fred S. James. These brokerage firms not only represent many of the American insurers operating abroad, but also alien insurers, including insurers chartered in the foreign country other than that in which the exposure to risk is located. Most of the leading brokerage firms offer fairly complete services, including the provision of important underwriting information necessary for proper placement of the risk in the appropriate markets.

SPECIAL PROBLEMS IN INTERNATIONAL RISK MANAGEMENT

Many problems in risk management are the same whether they involve foreign or domestic operations. However, the particular conditions under which international operations are conducted often serve to complicate the risk management functions and special attention to their management is required.[27] Some of these problems have been referred to above. Other major problems are: (1) Risk identification and discovery is complicated by unusual operating conditions abroad, cultural differences, language barriers, special regulatory requirements, etc. (2) Control over risk management procedures is complicated by difficulties in communication with foreign affiliates, lack of trained risk management personnel abroad, different

[27] A detailed treatment of this subject is found in Norman A. Baglini, *Risk Management in International Corporations* (New York: Risk Studies Foundation, 1976).

corporate objectives and procedures between the parent company and the foreign affiliate. (3) The risk manager may lack sufficient authority abroad to see that uniform procedures are carried out throughout the enterprise. For example, the managers of foreign subsidiaries may have established certain procedures which conflict with centralized risk management policy at the home office. (4) Environmental differences require special attention. (These problems are examined in some detail below.) For example, local taxation and regulation over insurance matters may require the company to purchase what is known as unadmitted insurance rather than deal with local insurers. Special arrangements regarding insurance may have to be made because of punitive taxation in a given locality. Problems of foreign exchange, referred to above, compulsory insurance, differences in policy coverage, special hazards, and financial strength of insurers may demand particular risk management procedures unknown in purely domestic risk management problems. For example, captive insurers are frequently employed as useful risk management devices for foreign operations.[28] (See Chapter 6.)

Insurance Conditions Abroad

The risk manager should be aware of the many differences which exist in insurance conditions abroad in order that he may make appropriate adjustments in his planning. An important lesson to be learned from an analysis of these differences is that grave errors will be made if the risk manager assumes that there are no important differences and he can proceed abroad much the same as he does at home. For example, requirements abroad

[28] *Ibid.*, pp. 97–110.

differ regarding insurance regulation, compulsory policies, policy language, exclusions and deductibles, premium taxes, and rates. The major differences in insurance conditions may be grouped under the following headings: unadmitted insurance, compulsory insurance, inflation, regulation, policy coverage, distribution, hazards, and strength of insurers.

Unadmitted Insurance

Although much insurance regulation abroad is less restrictive than U.S. regulation, in some cases it is more restrictive. An important example is in regulation of unadmitted insurance. Unadmitted insurance is coverage on property or other exposures in a given country offered by an insurer who is not admitted to do business in that country. Losses and premiums are usually paid in dollars and the policy language is English. By contrast, admitted insurance is written in the language of the country and premiums and losses are paid in local currency to insurers who are locally licensed. Some nations permit unadmitted insurance; others prohibit it and impose severe penalties for its use. A typical unadmitted insurance policy would be the worldwide liability coverage of a multinational corporation headquartered in the United States and operating abroad. However, in a country such as Brazil which does not permit foreign insurers to operate except under certain circumstances, local insurance must be used. Most South American countries, Mexico, France, Ireland, Japan, Italy, Spain, and Portugal are among the countries which either prohibit unadmitted insurance or severely restrict its use. Unadmitted insurance is often used, in spite of restrictions, for coverage such as liability because of severe coverage limitations which would exist by using local insurers who may not be able to respond to claims in dollars or to foreign claims arising out of a defective article which has been exported.

An example of unadmitted insurance regulation is that of Venezuela, whose law on this subject was passed in 1965. Prior to 1965 firms could insure abroad, although they lost certain tax benefits by so doing. After 1965, insurance contracts written abroad have no status in Venezuelan courts. Policies written must be in admitted insurers, and the premium must have been paid in local currency. The law applies both to insurance on personnel and on property, including ships, aircraft, or other vehicles registered in Venezuela. Losses on unadmitted insurance may not be adjusted in Venezuela. Violators of the law are punishable by heavy fines and loss of license to operate in the country. Unadmitted insurance is permissible only if local insurers cannot underwrite the needed coverage.[29]

Unadmitted insurance laws have brought on a dilemma in multinational firms which prefer unadmitted insurance but are legally unable to utilize such coverage. Admitted insurance may contain limitations in coverage which are not acceptable to the corporation. For example, local liability coverage may not apply in foreign operations which the multinational company requires. Admitted coverage, however, has the advantages of (a) being payable in local currency, (b) being subject to settlement in local courts, (c) providing a better corporate image for the multinational company because of the involvement with local business, and (d) carrying

premiums which are deductible for local income taxes. In many countries (*e.g.,* Mexico) local admitted carriers develop arrangements which permit them to accept otherwise unacceptable risks on terms required by multinational corporations and in turn pass these risks on to reinsurers. These local insurers may be affiliated with foreign insurers. In this way foreign business firms can secure the advantages of admitted insurance without many of the disadvantages.

Compulsory Insurance

Some types of insurance, such as social insurance, automobile insurance, and even fire insurance may be required under local law (*e.g.,* in Brazil). Furthermore, many foreign countries require the use of domestic insurers for certain types of coverage, especially compulsory lines such as workers' compensation or automobile insurance. Increasingly, the laws of a country will require that coverage be placed, directly or indirectly, through a state-owned insurance enterprise. For example, in South America it is common to require reinsurance in a state-owned reinsurance company by domestic insurers. Since the national insurer is in effect a monopoly, insurance tends to operate without price competition. In France most of the large property and liability insurers were nationalized after World War II and today these insurers write about half of all the property-liability business in that country. It is possible that many of the private insurers operating in the international markets may in the future operate mainly through accepting reinsurance from domestically chartered insurers or with state-owned companies.[30]

[29] Joseph Diamond, "Six Countries Review Rules on Nonadmitted Insurers," *The National Underwriter*, January 14, 1966, pp. 42–43.

[30] H. Donald Lindell, "The Nationalistic Trend in International Insurance," *International Insurance Monitor*, January 1972, p. 17.

The risk manager may increasingly be required to place business through state-owned insurers under more inflexible rating and underwriting conditions than existed before.

Regulation

Foreign laws may alter the operation of insurance contracts in ways greatly different from U.S. conditions. For example, negligence of the insured in a fire loss to his own property is not a bar to recovery under the policy in the U.S., but it may so operate in some countries (*e.g.*, Japan). In other countries whose legal systems are based on the Napoleonic Code (Belgium, Egypt, Greece, Italy, Spain, Turkey, Lebanon, and certain African countries) the law may impose liability on an insured if he is negligent in causing a fire which later spreads to a neighbor's property. Coverage should be secured against such liability by the multinational company operating in these countries.

Foreign tax laws may be much more severe in their effect on insurance than is true in the United States. Premium taxes, for example, may range as high as 40 percent (Argentina) compared to 2 or 3 percent in the United States. Unadmitted insurance is advantageous in high premium tax countries. However, the country may not permit a deduction for unadmitted insurance for local income taxes. The risk manager must study the relative tax situation carefully in arranging coverage.

Rate regulation abroad is usually less restrictive than in the United States. Rates and premiums tend to be negotiable and secrecy more prevalent. For example, because of secrecy in business operations, it may not be practicable to offer insurance coverage whose premium is subject to a year end audit,

such as the case of auditing payroll to determine the workers' compensation premium, a common method used in the United States.

Inflation

In many parts of the world, inflation is much more severe than in the United States. In several countries in South America, for example, annual inflation rates of 20 percent or higher are not uncommon. Such rates adversely affect risk management and insurance in many ways. Among the more obvious of these are: (1) Constant increases in the replacement value of insured assets require special attention to the problem of their protection. For example, inflation may cause underinsurance, and may subject the insured to coinsurance penalties in the event of loss. Because compulsory minimum coinsurance clauses and minimum amounts of insurance are common, this latter problem is of special consequence.

For example, in Brazil all corporations are required to purchase fire insurance on assets which at any location exceed 20,000 cruzieros in value. All fire policies must contain at least 70 percent coinsurance clauses. Firms operating in Brazil commonly insure fixed assets at replacement value. A leading brokerage firm in Brazil recommends updating of insured sums during the policy year, with issuance of new policies, since in Brazil policy amounts may not be increased by endorsement.[31]

(2) Premium rates for commercial insurance are increased more than necessary currently because of anticipated increases in the cost of settling future claims. The risk manager must

[31] *Corporate Insurance in Brazil* (Rio de Janeiro; Argos. Companhia de Seguros, 1976), p. 2.

consider the lost investment income on such funds as an additional cost of risk transfer. The problem of analyzing opportunity cost was considered in Chapter 14.

(3) In providing group life and health insurance, as well as group pensions, the risk manager must consider that long-term inflation can make the benefit provisions of these contracts seriously inadequate. Accordingly, various devices must be employed to adjust the benefits according to changing living costs. Pension funds, for example, will probably be invested in different types of assets (such as common stock and real estate) than would be the case without inflation.

(4) Since rapid inflation rates make a country more likely to engage in currency devaluation, exchange restrictions, and import quotas, the risk manager in world business must monitor such conditions so as to be able to anticipate and minimize any resulting loss. For example, a firm may ship goods to a foreign buyer only to have the goods rejected at the entry port because of a sudden imposition of import quotas in the buyer's country. Planning for the resulting loss is the job of the risk manager in world business.

(5) Rapid inflation may bring about inflated insurer loss ratios. This in turn may cause a loss of market capacity, making it difficult or impossible for the risk manager to obtain needed coverage.

Policy Coverage

Insurance coverage abroad varies from domestic coverage for several reasons: regulation, custom, financial size of the insurer, nature of local demand. This discussion here is meant to be il-lustrative of these differences, not a comprehensive listing.[32]

A basic difference is that the policy language will normally be in the language of the foreign nation. Official translations into English may or may not be available. Claims may be payable only in the currency of the foreign nation, and the convertibility of loss proceeds depends on foreign exchange conditions at the time. Requirements in notice and proof of loss are often stricter abroad.

In fire insurance many types of differences exist. In the United Kingdom whose standard fire form is used in many European countries, the policy period may extend up to ten years and usually may not be cancelled except under specific circumstances. The coverage may be restricted so that fire following explosion, windstorm, volcanic eruption, earthquake, etc., is not automatically covered as it is in U.S. forms. Such coverage may be added by endorsement. It is common to require that fire insurance be written with 100 percent coinsurance clauses. It may not be possible to secure blanket coverage or coverages based on the selling price of goods rather than the cost of the goods.

In liability insurance it is necessary to see to it that forms meet basic legal coverage requirements. In Germany, for example, a firm is absolutely liable for contamination of subsoil as

[32] Mark R. Greene, "The Insurance Environment in Foreign Countries," *Risk Management*, February 1973, pp. 17–20. See also AFIA guides to Europe, Asia, and Latin America, published and updated periodically, and Robert Wells, *Sourcebook of International Corporate Insurance and Employee Benefit Management, Vol. 2 Selected Countries of the World, 1968*, AMA Research Study 80, (New York: American Management Association, 1969).

well as surface water, regardless of fault. The German policy covering this risk contains a deductible of 20 percent. The risk manager will recognize that his firm must assume a considerable liability and other ways of handling this risk may be devised. In Japan the auto insurance policy covers only three-fourths of the insured's liability and the insured must adjust his own claims. Many foreign auto policies exclude coverage when the driver is drunk, under the influence of drugs, or driving without a valid license.[33]

In Italy it is required that the insurer must provide three to six months' notice of cancellation for most property insurance coverages. A similar provision applies in Germany. Otherwise, the policies are automatically renewed. Collision insurance on automobiles is not generally available and physical damage coverage is usually limited to fire and theft.

In Germany the law requires advance notice for dismissal of employees, for any cause, including shutdown because of insurable perils. Many firms operating in Germany, accordingly, purchase business interruption insurance which has been designed for this liability.

Distribution

Insurance is almost universally distributed abroad through agency forces in a manner similar to the Independent Agency System in the United States. Argentine law requires the use of an agent or broker, and direct negotiation between the insured and the insurer is prohibited. In many countries, however,

[33] Philip J. Brown, Jr., "The Role of the U.S. Broker in Europe," *International Insurance and Employee Benefit and Pension Management* (New York: American Management Association, 1966), pp. 6–11.

no particular regulations exist to prohibit rebating of agency commissions to the customer as is true in the United States. It is not uncommon for larger clients to be appointed agents for their own accounts, so that all of the commission is earned by the client. In Japan, whose law does not recognize brokers as such, it is customary for the Zaibatsus, or Japanese business combines, to set up their own insurance agencies to deal directly with the insurer. Agents' commissions abroad are often considerably larger than similar commissions in the United States.

Hazards

Some parts of the world are subject to greater hazards, both physical, moral, and morale hazards, than is true in the United States. For example, Japan has a considerable earthquake hazard and since 1966, all fire policies have carried a mandatory earthquake endorsement. Tidal waves and typhoons are a special hazard in Southeast Asia, as well as other areas of the world. Because of lower income levels and different standards of conduct in some parts of the world, fidelity risk is deemed especially important for U.S. firms. Unstable governments, prejudice against foreign firms, and poor law enforcement increases the hazards of writing insurance in many parts of the globe.

Strength of Insurers

An insurance condition abroad that requires special attention by the multinational firm is the financial condition of foreign-based insurers. Many foreign insurers are as large and strong as U.S.-based carriers, but many others are very weak by U.S. standards. Undercapitalization and excessive investments in nonliquid assets such as real estate are common conditions. In Spain, for example, the ratio of premiums written to policyholders' surplus is about twice that of the United States for all insurers operating there.[34] Some countries require insurers to make deposit guarantees and to maintain investments in the countries in which they operate. As one writer states, "This protective legislation led to the rapid growth of a frequently undercapitalized local insurance industry in a great many countries . . . Actually, many of these companies were so grossly undercapitalized and their net retentions so infinitesimal that, in actual practice, they were nothing more than reinsurance brokers."[35] It is, therefore, necessary for the risk manager to examine financial statements of foreign-based insurers with whom he has placed risks to learn of their ability to respond to claims. It is also advisable to investigate the nature and extent of reinsurance facilities of foreign insurers (see discussion of reinsurance below).

Reinsurance

Reinsurance has always been an important mechanism in effecting the transfer of risk from one insurer to another. For example, in 1973 U.S. insurers paid $607 million for foreign reinsurance, and received $471 million from reinsurance sold to foreigners. After adjustment for losses paid and collected, there was a net outflow of $80 million to other countries in 1973.[36]

Through such spreading of losses,

the risk faced by each insurer is lessened and its capacity to underwrite enhanced. In international operations, reinsurance is especially important for several reasons.

First, the ability of many local foreign insurers to accept risk is limited, due to lack of adequate surplus and capital. Second, the existence of unadmitted insurance laws in many foreign countries places a burden on local insurers which they would often be unable to accept without reinsurance. Third, as developed above, international risk is generally higher than domestic risk, and special knowledge of this risk is often provided by experts who work for reinsurance companies. Fourth, it is through the reinsurance mechanism that many governments have enlarged insurance capacity by offering financial guarantees to private insurers who accept particular types of risk that would otherwise not be acceptable. For example, in the United States, the federal government reinsures many types of risks — flood, war, political, and property damage risks in central cities (through F.A.I.R. plans), to mention a few.

In many foreign countries, the government has established reinsurance agencies to share the risks of domestic insurers. In Argentina a state-owned reinsurer, INDER, has a monopolistic position. In some countries, severe restrictions have been placed on the use of foreign reinsurance as a method of conserving foreign exchange. Other arguments used to justify these restrictions include (a) keeping local control over funds collected by insurance companies so that these funds will be used for investment in local industry rather than be repatriated to foreign owners, (b) reducing the number of insurers operating in order to increase the average size of the remaining carriers, and (c) helping

[34] Mark R. Greene, "The Spanish Insurance Industry — An Analysis," *The Journal of Risk and Insurance*, Vol. 39, No. 2 (June 1972), p. 224.

[35] Lindell, "Nationalistic Trend," p. 17.

[36] "Commerce Reports 1973 Reinsurance Transactions," DIBA 74–125. A news release of the U.S. Department of Commerce by James F. Rourke, December 3, 1974.

build up the local insurance industry and to overcome what has been termed unfair competition by foreign insurers.

The movement to restrict the international flow of insurance dollars in world reinsurance markets has centered largely in developing countries, which generally are short of developmental capital. The arguments for restrictions, outlined above, contain many fallacies. Perhaps the most important fallacy is that these restrictions tend to inhibit free trade on which the development of small nations depends. Furthermore, the loss of foreign exchange through reinsurance is in most cases a small portion of the total premiums paid for reinsurance. This follows because most of the premium is returned in the settlement of losses and for administrative costs paid locally. The exchange loss is further reduced by the sale of insurance to foreigners. In many years there will be a net inflow of funds from reinsurance due to large loss settlements. In any event, the economic benefits of a free flow of insurance and reinsurance across political boundaries in encouraging commerce appear to be far greater than the costs.[37]

Types of Agreements

There are two major types of reinsurance agreements in use in international insurance: facultative and automatic. Facultative reinsurance is that type of agreement which is individually arranged and negotiated between insurance companies for each risk. Automatic treaties of reinsurance are those ar-

rangements under which a whole class of risk is shared by the contracting parties on some predetermined basis for sharing premiums and losses.

Two basic types of automatic agreements exist: pro rata and excess of loss. In the former, all premiums and losses are shared in some proportion, e.g., each of ten insurers accepts say 10 percent of the losses and collects 10 percent of the premiums of a given type of business, e.g., commercial fire. Under excess of loss agreements the reinsurer pays losses in excess of some predetermined deductible amount, called a retention, which is paid by the primary insurer. The primary insurer, known as the ceding company, is allowed to keep a certain percentage of the premium to reimburse it for the acquisition expense.

To illustrate reinsurance consider the following example in which three types of reinsurance are in effect: Insurer "D," the ceding insurer, writes a $5 million fire insurance policy on client "C's" factory. The following reinsurance is in effect: $500,000 facultative agreement on the factory with reinsurer "E"; above this amount, "D" retains $1 million of any one fire loss, and cedes $1 million each to four other reinsurers under a pro rata treaty. "D" also has an excess of loss treaty with reinsurer "F" who agrees to pay any of "D's" losses above $250,000 on any one fire. Assume there is a $2 million fire loss to "C's" factory. In the settlement, insurer "E" pays $500,000 under its facultative agreement; under the pro rata treaty, each insurer, including "D," is responsible for one-fifth of the remaining $1,500,000 loss. Since "D's" share is $300,000 under the pro rata treaty, its loss exceeds the $250,000 retention under the excess of loss agreement with insurer "F." Therefore, "F" will pay

[37] For further analysis of this question see, U.S. Chamber of Commerce, *Position Paper on International Insurance and Reinsurance* (Washington: Chamber of Commerce of the U.S., 1972), pp. 33–36.

$50,000 to "D" under this agreement ($300,000 − $250,000 = $50,000).

The advantages of reinsurance to the ceding insurer and to the customer are obvious. The customer obtains a fire policy for $5 million in the above case and may never realize that his insurance company has ceded portions of the liability on to others. The risk manager is spared the inconvenience of shopping the insurance market and attempting to find several insurers willing to accept the risk. The ceding insurer is able to accept a $5 million fire risk, but will not suffer a loss in excess of $250,000 on any one exposure. The ceding insurer is thus able to accommodate for insurance far more customers than it would otherwise. It should be noted that reinsurance agreements take hundreds of different forms and that the above examples are illustrative of only a few major types of agreements.

Employee Benefit Management Abroad

An important problem faced by the multinational corporation is that of arranging competitive compensation systems for employees who work abroad. A significant portion of total compensation is that portion represented by the cost of employee benefits. In many foreign countries, employee benefits form a greater part of total compensation than is true in the United States, particularly if the cost of social insurance is included. Social insurance programs are generally more extensive in developed foreign countries than in the United States. It is a significant part of the responsibility of many risk managers to contribute toward the goal of making employee benefit programs competitive and integrating the benefits

of these programs with the benefits of social insurance plans abroad.

Social Insurance Abroad

The U.S. Social Security Administration has compiled a list of 127 countries in the world with different types of social insurance.[38] The total number of social insurance programs has more than doubled over the period 1940–73. The most common program is that covering work injuries, existing in 125 nations. Other programs and the number of countries sponsoring them are: old age, invalid and survivor programs, 105; sickness and maternity programs, 70; family allowance programs, 65; and unemployment insurance programs, 37.[39]

Some of the main features about social security programs abroad as they affect risk management are: (1) Most countries require the person to have been employed as a prerequisite of obtaining retirement benefits. Only seven countries provide universal pensions regardless of former work status. (2) The tax rate, generally a flat percentage of payroll, supporting these programs is often higher in the U.S. The range is great, between 3 and 30 percent of payroll. (3) It is becoming more common to tie retirement benefits to some cost of living index. Such a provision existed in 14 countries at the time of the survey. (4) Health insurance covering sickness and maternity costs is more often than not nationalized (5) Family allowance programs exist in about half of the countries surveyed; most of these pro-

[38] U.S. Social Security Administration, *Social Security Throughout the World 1969* (Washington, D.C.: U.S. Government Printing Office, 1973).

[39] *Ibid.*

grams require that the family head be working, but a few nations (*e.g.*, France, Luxembourg) cover nonemployed workers as well. Most plans permit workers to receive family allowance in addition to other income benefits.

From the above remarks it may be inferred that privately sponsored employee benefits should be integrated carefully with the social insurance laws of the particular country of operation; no universally applied benefit formula or set of eligibility requirements will be appropriate.

Third Country Nationals

A third country national (TCN) is an employee who is a citizen of one country working for an employer whose citizenship is that of another country and who is working in a country which is not his home country. An example would be a French national working in Italy for a U.S. corporation. The TCN presents a special problem to his employer in the matter of employee benefits because the TCN may not qualify for either his parent company benefit plan nor the social insurance plan in his home country. Since he is often transferred, it is difficult or impractical to include him in a local private plan. Even though he may be required to contribute to a social insurance plan in the country where he works, the chances are that by the time he retires he will have been transferred and will not qualify for these benefits. Usually he will not receive any refund of social insurance taxes he has paid or which have been paid on his behalf.

A sound risk management program in the multinational firm must take into consideration the special problems of the TCN. Special insurance programs for this particular class of em-

ployee will often be indicated. For example, one writer stated:[40]

"Domestic U.S. pension plans are not flexible enough to absorb a great mobility in funds reserved and the 30 percent withholding tax, applicable to benefit paid to non-resident aliens, makes it unattractive to Third Country Nationals. Their needs are best satisfied by creating a central plan completely funded, administered, and managed offshore, making benefit payments not subject to U.S. withholding tax. The creation of an offshore pension plan through a non-U.S.-based insurer allows the employer to provide a total pension benefit formula more adaptable to the various local Social Security plans. It also allows the accumulation and transferability of reserves, when a TCN employee is transferred from one country to another, without interruption in funded pension credits. Another advantage to an offshore fund is the feasibility of paying benefits in more than one freely convertible currency . . ."

Types of Plans

In general, the firm should provide foreign employees, including TCNs, with benefits that are comparable to those provided for domestic employees. These will include group life insurance, group health insurance, disability income insurance, and retirement income plans, as well as the compulsory social insurance coverages such as workers' compensation, unemployment, and the like. A survey taken in 1967 covering 236 U.S. firms operating in 13 foreign countries revealed the following types of plans being provided by the stated percentage of firms surveyed: hospital expense, 35.9 percent; doctor bill, 36.7

[40] Georga A. Abouzeid, "Third Country Nationals," *Contact*, Vol. 22, No. 5 (April 1971), p. 7.

percent; major medical, 15.2 percent; disability income, 35.9 percent; group life, 46.4 percent; accidental death and dismemberment, 61.2 percent; and retirement plan, 51.5 percent.[41] This study revealed that fewer than 20 percent of the surveyed firms differentiated retirement benefits for U.S. nationals and foreign nationals working abroad.

A common method of providing uniformity in retirement plan benefits for employees of the multinational company is to establish a given percentage, say 60 percent, of final average salary as the benefit. To the extent that the employee becomes eligible for social insurance benefits in any country, his employer's contribution is reduced. The employee is relieved of the worry of losing pension rights as he is transferred from one country to another. Such a system has been found to be a powerful tool in attracting TCNs as well

as other employees in working for multinational companies.

In some countries special features of local law need to be given careful attention in developing appropriate employee benefit plans. For example, in Japan the customary term of employment for a worker is lifetime, and a common age for retirement is 55, with lump-sum payment being made in lieu of a lifetime annuity. Private employers will often make special arrangements in Japan for supplementary pension plans payable as an annuity, and will give special emphasis to company welfare plans. In Mexico and in many Latin American countries there are laws requiring the employer to pay special severance allowances to workers according to the length of time he has been with the employer. In some cases the employer is able to substitute a privately funded pension plan for the severance allowance at less cost and with greater benefit to the employee.[42]

[41] Mark R. Greene, "International Levels of Employee Benefits," *Journal of Risk and Insurance*, Vol. 135, No. 1 (March 1968), pp. 1–15.

[42] G. N. Calvert, *Pension Plans for U.S. Companies in Mexico* (New York: Alexander International, undated).

SUMMARY AND CONCLUSIONS

1. International business has grown at a rapid pace since World War II. Insurance to cover the risks involved in this expansion has kept pace. International aspects of risk management require special attention and represent an increasingly important problem area for the modern risk manager.

2. Risks of multinational enterprise are generally conceded to be greater than domestic risks. Political risk constitutes an important source of the international uncertainty. Methods to predict and control political risk exist, but these methods must receive special study for effectiveness. Export credit insurance, investment insurance, and exchange risk insurance are three types of insurance commonly utilized in handling political risk.

3. Foreign sources of insurance present special opportunities for the alert risk manager who is often faced with shortages of insurance capacity at home. Leading international insurance countries in the world are Great Britain, United States, France, and Switzerland. Foreign insurance markets tend to be more highly concentrated than U.S. markets.

4. There are many differences in insurance conditions in the various countries of the world which require constant study and coordination by the risk manager. Important among these differences are insurance regulation, unadmitted insurance, compulsory coverages, policy conditions and coverage, methods of distribution, physical and moral hazards, and financial strength of insurers.

5. Reinsurance is a special characteristic of international insurance. It is doubtful that insurance could be extended to many developing countries of the world requiring risk transfer if it were not for reinsurance, the free market for which is often restricted in the very countries most benefiting by it.

6. Employee benefit management in the international sphere of operations presents many unique problems for the risk manager charged with these responsibilities. These problems center about developing fair and uniform benefits for employees of multinational companies operating in many different nations each with different types of social security programs and legal requirements.

QUESTIONS FOR DISCUSSION

1. For many years gross national product in the United States has been growing at about 5 percent annually. Exports have not increased as a proportion of gross national product and they constitute about 5 percent of the gross national product. In view of these facts, suggest reasons why insurance premiums have increased about 9 percent annually since about 1960.

2. What factors contribute to increasing the level of international risk above that of domestic risk?

3. Give major examples of perils caused by unstable political conditions.

4. The risk manager of a multinational company observes that a particular foreign country in which his firm is building a factory has had a large and growing adverse balance of payments for the previous five years. The inflation rate in this country is averaging 20 percent annually. This has tended to dampen exports and the prospects for improvement are considered poor. In what ways might such a situation increase the degree of political risk? Why?

5. An observer on the foreign operations of Coca-Cola Export Corporation states that Coke's overseas operations produced $140 million in earnings in 1972, or 55 percent of the parent company's total, making its international business more profitable than its domestic business, even though sales abroad still represent about 40 percent of the total. To achieve this growth management was decentralized. The company chairman, J. Paul Austin, was quoted as explaining "If they nationalize the assets they're nationalizing their own people." Nevertheless, the company was forced out of several Arab states for refusing to stop selling in Israel. (a) In your opinion are the greater political risks abroad worth assuming, or should firms confine their operations to low risk local markets? (b) Suggest possible reasons for the belief that decentralization of management is considered a way to handle political risk of nationalization? (c) In what ways is insurance useful in handling political risk? Explain.

6. Why is investment insurance for foreign risks limited to new investment only?

7. A firm sold goods to a buyer in France valued at 6 million French francs. The exchange rate at the time of the sale was 4.94 francs to the dollar, making the sale worth $1,214,575. Later on before the sale was completed the U.S. devalued its currency so that $1 was worth 5.55 francs. (a) How many dollars is the sale worth to the firm after the devaluation? (b) How could the firm have protected itself against this loss in the currency futures market? Explain.

8. A U.S. firm operating in the United Kingdom decided that a devaluation of the pound was likely within six months. It took steps to borrow as much of its current working capital needs as possible from British banks, and increased its notes payable to banks by 10 million pounds. An equivalent amount of dollars were transferred to New York at the exchange rate 2.5 pounds to $1. (a) If the pound is devalued 10 percent, how many pounds can the firm purchase with the dollars it transferred to New York? Show calculations. (b) What method of handling risk does this transaction illustrate? Explain.

9. It is stated that the United States is the largest insurance country but that the United Kingdom is the largest international insurance country in the world. Explain.

10. Suggest possible reasons for the fact that an industrialized nation such as Japan with a population of over 100 million has only about 40 domestic insurers. The United States has over 200 million population, but has 4,698 insurance companies.

11. Judging from the degree of concentration in insurance or other factors would you expect price competition in insurance to be stronger abroad or in the United States? Why?

12. What are the advantages of (a) unadmitted insurance? (b) admitted insurance?

13. What important differences sometimes exist between fire insurance written in the U.S. and fire insurance abroad?

14. In 1970 Lloyds of London paid $8.5 million for the destruction of Arab terrorists of a BOAC airliner. In 1972 Lloyds faced another claim for the loss of a $24 million jumbo jet owned by Japan Air Lines. The plane was skyjacked in Amsterdam and blown up four days later by terrorists in Libya. The primary insurer was Tokyo Marine and Fire Insurance Company, who had ceded 90 percent of the coverage to Lloyds. What does this case illustrate about (a) political risk and its management and (b) world reinsurance?

15. What is the main difference between reinsurance on a facultative basis and reinsurance offered under treaties? Which type is most likely to be used in the reinsurance on jumbo jets? Why?

16. What is the problem of third country nationals? Explain.

17. In 1970 the gross national product of the 18 most important countries in Europe was $740 billion, that of the United States was $970 billion. For the same year the American nonlife companies achieved a premium volume of approximately $42 billion or 4.4 percent of the GNP; the European nonlife insurers, on the other hand, only achieved $66 billion or just over 2 percent of the GNP. The proportion of life business to the GNP was 2.6 percent in the U.S. and 1.4 percent in Europe. The share in world premium volume is over 50 percent of the U.S. and around 25 percent for Western Europe. What conclusions can you draw about the potential for future insurance sales in Europe from these data?

18. The share of real estate invested as a proportion of total assets of life insurers for 1971 was as follows: Italy, 45.4 percent; Switzerland, 20.5 percent; Australia, 14.8 percent; Great Britain, 13.8 percent; West Germany, 13.2 percent; France, 12.4 percent; Belgium, 11.3 percent; Japan, 8.9 percent; Holland, 7.8 percent; Canada and Sweden, 5.4 percent each; Denmark, 4.9 percent; and the United States, 3.1 percent. What do these figures suggest about contrasting management methods in insurance when compared across political boundaries?

19. Discuss the problems that may arise in the area of property and liability insurance when merger occurs. What procedures would you suggest for facilitating a smooth transition?

20. There are those that believe a merger of two firms might well founder because of funding problems associated with pension plans. What are the arguments that might support such a conclusion?

19

Regulation, Government Insurance, and Risk Management

Increasingly, the risk manager is concerned with governmental regulation and participation in insurance. An understanding of the way in which insurance is governed, the ways in which private insurance interacts with public insurance, the regulatory environment, specific rules laid down by regulators, and the general requirements of insurance laws are all part of the necessary knowledge of the modern risk manager. For example, the risk manager may be responsible for seeing that a company-owned insurance subsidiary complies with all applicable laws and that requirements of the Employees' Retirement Income Security Act of 1974 (ERISA) and those of other federal and state laws are observed. The risk manager may also need to deal directly with governmental agencies in purchasing coverage and settling claims.

The major sections of this chapter are:

1. Reasons for regulation
   a. Background
   b. Federal vs. state regulation

2. Areas of regulation

3. Consumerism and insurance

4. Governmental insurance programs

   a. Federal programs
   b. State programs

REASONS FOR REGULATION

Insurance is regulated primarily because it is very closely associated with the public interest. In some respects the insurance industry is similar to a public utility, providing a service which is not considered optional, but rather a necessity for operation of modern business enterprise. Although insurance is not a natural monopoly in the same way that a public utility may be, there are several other good reasons for its regulation.

Complexity

Insurance is effected by a legal contract, which is complex and very often ambiguous. The existence of a large body of insurance law and legal cases involving insurance testify to the fact that frequent recourse to the courts is necessary for interpretation of the insurance agreement, and in settling disputes between parties to insurance contracts. Regulation of contract wording, for example, has become necessary in order to provide some uniformity and to protect the consumer's interest.

Future Performance

Insurance is an agreement under which the insured must pay in advance for a service which is to be performed in the future, depending upon certain conditional events. Safeguarding of the policyholders' funds therefore becomes important. Regulation of the investment of these funds becomes a matter of public interest. The insurer must keep funds on hand sufficient to cover the uncertain expenses and losses in the future. Regulation of the investment of buffer funds therefore becomes significant. Procedures for adjudicating disagreements must be provided by the courts.

Uncertain Costs

Insurance is a service for which the price is set in advance without the full knowledge of the future costs to be paid. Insurers' rates must be regulated so that they are not excessive nor inadequate. Furthermore, the rates must be regulated in such a way that they are fair in that they discriminate properly between insureds with different hazards. Without regulation unrestricted competition might drive rates down below supportable levels for long-run solvency of the insurer. Excessive rates, on the other hand, might encourage unreasonably large profits by those who provide a vital service — a service for which there is no substitute.

BACKGROUND

Prior to about 1850 the private insurance business was essentially unregulated, or at least had no greater degree of regulation than any other type of industry. After 1850, states began to establish departments headed by insurance commissioners. The first states to have some sort of formal regulatory system were New Hampshire, Massachusetts, California, Connecticut, Indiana, Missouri, New York, and Vermont. By 1871 nearly all states had some type of regulation.

In 1868 a U.S. Supreme Court decision, *Paul* v *Virginia*,[1] formally upheld the right of states to regulate insurance. The decision held that insurance was not commerce and, hence, the federal government with its power to oversee interstate commerce had no formal status in regulating insurance. This decision was upheld in subsequent cases until it was reversed in 1944 by the U.S. Supreme Court in Southeastern Underwriters (SEUA) case.[2]

The SEUA case held that 200 stock fire insurers organized in an association violated Sections 1 and 2 of the Sherman Antitrust Act. The fire insurance companies in the case sold over 90 percent of the fire insurance in six southeastern states where they operated. They were able to fix premium rates and agents' commissions, to use boycotts, and to force the buyer to use a certain insurer. Noncomplying insurers were denied reinsurance. Agents' licenses were withdrawn if they represented competing insurers not in the association. Even consumers doing business with nonassociation insurers were threatened with boycotts. The power of Congress to regulate insurance when conducted across state lines was established by the decision.

A major effect of the case was to establish dual state-federal regulations of insurance since states still had jurisdiction over purely intrastate matters. The special federal laws affecting competitive practices in insurance are the

[1] 8 Wall 168, 163 (1868).

[2] 322 U.S. 533.

Sherman Antitrust Act of 1890, the Clayton Act of 1914, the Robinson-Patman Act of 1937, and the Federal Trade Commission Act of 1937. The purpose of these acts is to prevent restraint of free competition, and to prohibit business practices which substantially lessen competition, such as price discrimination, interlocking directorates, and certain stock acquisitions. The Federal Trade Commission is given power to investigate and to restrain unfair trade practices. Among the unfair trade practices and unfair methods of competition are the following: 1) unfair rate discrimination; 2) rebating; 3) use of boycotts, coercion, or intimidation; 4) filing of false financial statements; and 5) false advertising or defamation of persons engaged in insurance. The Federal Trade Commission has been particularly active in prosecuting companies for false advertising in mail order insurance.

Public Law 15

Following the SEUA case, Congress sought to restore some of the formal authority of states to regulate insurance. The result of this deliberation was Public Law 15, also known as the McCarran-Ferguson Act of 1945. The law declared that it was the intent of Congress that state regulation of insurance should continue and that no state law regarding insurance should be affected by federal law unless such law were specifically directed at the business of insurance. Public Law 15 also provided that all of the basic federal antitrust laws (mentioned above) should apply to insurance but with a three-year delay. It also provided that that section of the Sherman Antitrust Act relating to boycotts, coercion, and intimidation should remain fully applicable to the insurance business. Public Law 15 pro-

vides that all applicable federal laws will apply to insurance to the extent that individual states fail to regulate it in those respects. Thereafter all of the states passed a model bill designed to bring state regulation into conformity with the antimonopoly statutes of the federal government, it being the intent of the states to preserve state regulation to the fullest extent possible.

Since 1948, when Public Law 15 first became effective, the federal government has had varying degrees of involvement with the insurance business. Many of the laws which have been passed at the federal level were designed to smooth out the sometimes conflicting state regulation and to strengthen it. Many hearings have been held by Congress, most of which did not result in specific federal regulation, but the effect was to strengthen the resolve of those in charge of state regulation to prevent unacceptable practices. For example, the hearings by the subcommittee on monopoly power (1949), headed by Representative Emanuel Celler of New York, did not result in any specific federal regulation or legislation, but shortly afterward the Federal Trade Commission carried out an extensive campaign to reduce fraud committed in mail order insurance. The Securities and Exchange Commission conducted hearings on the sale of variable annuities and eventually ruled that these instruments were subject to regulation in part by the SEC. This ruling was upheld by the U.S. Supreme Court.[3] Studies of the automobile insurance system conducted in 1970–71 by the U.S. Department of Transportation resulted in a 28-volume report on the economic consequences of automobile accidents, the causes of au-

[3] Securities and Exchange Commission v. Variable Annuity Life Insurance Company of America, 359 U.S. 65 (1959).

tomobile accidents, and the efficiency of insurance as a system of compensating the victims of automobile accidents. Other subjects investigated by congressional hearings covered fields of aviation and ocean marine insurance, rate regulation, alien insurers, insurer insolvency trends, and the problem of the lack of insurance availability. As is discussed below, several important federal laws relating to insurance have been passed.

FEDERAL VS. STATE REGULATION OF INSURANCE

For many years students of insurance both within and without of the insurance industry have argued the question of federal vs. state regulation. As noted above, the present system is dual regulation and it is doubtful that this situation will change significantly in the future.

Criticism of State Regulation

State regulation has been criticized on many grounds: 1) It is not uniform and companies operating across state lines must conform to a welter of different and sometimes conflicting laws. 2) Its effect in correcting weaknesses among insurance companies is diminished because of the fragmentation. Practices that may be prohibited in one state are perhaps not prohibited in another state. Presumably, under state regulation an insurer could be practicing dangerous or unsound practices in one area and not in another; yet the unsound practices would weaken its entire structure. 3) Many types of state laws and rulings have been hastily conceived and ill-advised due to local pressures. Examples have been those laws re-

quiring an insurance company to reinvest within a given state all or a certain proportion of the premiums it collects within that state even though the insurer may not find investments there that are suitable within the company's investment policy.

4) State insurance commissioners tend to be selected with political considerations in mind. Very often the insurance commissioners are drawn from the industry and their decisions might be biased by this fact. 5) The budgets of insurance departments are often too low to carry out the duties required under state law. For example, budgets may not be adequate to permit a full-scale financial examination of each insurer operating within the state every three years as is often required under state law. 6) Bureaucratic delays and cumbersome procedures often prohibit the admission and licensing of insurers to do business within state borders. As a result, insurers wishing to operate nationwide may not be able to accomplish this objective for several years. 7) State laws governing capital and surplus requirements for new insurers may be grossly inadequate. In Arizona, for example, an insurer may be formed for as little as $37,500 in capital and surplus — an amount which is probably too low to permit reasonable financial stability in continued operation. The repeated occurrences of insurer insolvencies bear testimony to this problem.

Federal Regulation

The weaknesses of exclusive federal regulation should not be overlooked. The major advantage of state regulation might be said to be that it permits more flexibility in coping with ever-changing problems. For example, an insurer might test a new contract or rate at a local level — a procedure which might be difficult to accomplish under federal regulation. 2) Federal regulation may tend to be too uniform to meet the varying needs among the states. 3) Exclusive federal regulation of insurance may be objected to on the grounds that it extends the growth of centralization and the growth of federal power over private business — a trend viewed as objectionable by many economic observers.

It seems inevitable, in spite of the above arguments, that the influence of federal regulation and control of insurance will continue to be felt. Congress has not been hesitant to establish nationwide programs meeting unfilled insurance needs, such as crime and flood coverage. The need for greater uniformity in coverage has been increasingly felt, particularly among large companies where risk management is an important function. A very large proportion of total business in the United States is accomplished through firms operating nationally and internationally. In order to service insurance needs, insurers must be able to operate across state and national boundaries with as much uniformity and security as possible.

The problem of variation in state laws establishing funds to protect a policyholder from loss due to insolvency of insurers is a case in point. States usually do not have uniform legal environments. Standards of solvency, effectiveness of financial examinations, and enforcement of solvency regulations vary tremendously. For example, all but three states have passed laws for meeting the insolvency problem. Although these laws were to be patterned after a model bill developed by the National Association of Insurance Commissioners, in practice laws have been quite different. The Missouri statute will illustrate the situa-

tion. In Missouri all insurers writing business there are required to join an association whose purpose is to provide a fund to meet the claims of insolvent insurers.[4] However, several fields of insurance are omitted from the jurisdiction of the association: life, accident and sickness, title, surety, disability, credit mortgage guaranty, and ocean marine insurance. The assessment limitation is placed at 1 percent of direct premiums written within the state instead of 2 percent which was the recommendation of the model bill. Liability for any one claim was limited to $50,000 in spite of the recommendation of the model bill that the limit be $300,000. An insurer's contribution to the central fund for meeting insolvent companies' claims may be deducted from their state premium tax liability. Thus, in effect, the state government is financing the association's obligations. The result is obviously a half-measure in which insureds will receive some protection, but probably not adequate protection. A federal solvency bill which had been proposed for a federal guaranty insurance corporation was forestalled by the passage of state laws which attempt to accomplish the same result. Because of the limitations and variation in these laws, however, it seems clear that a claimant against an insolvent insurer lacks complete assurance that a claim will be met in all the jurisdictions in which the claimant operates.

AREAS OF STATE REGULATION OF INSURANCE

In addition to regulation of insurance in the area of fair competitive practices, state governments presently regulate the insurance business in four major

[4] Section 1, Chapter 375,785 R.S. Missouri.

ways: finance and investments, rates and expenses, sales methods, and contractual provisions.

Finance and Investments

In the area of financial solvency and investment portfolio management, insurance laws of each state are usually quite explicit. State laws set minimum capital and surplus requirements for the commencement of operations. Typically, $500,000 in capital and surplus are required to commence business. For insurers writing every line of insurance, the minimum capital and surplus requirements are considerably higher, and for companies writing only one or two lines of coverage, the requirements may be less. State laws generally license the type of insurance business to be conducted and minimum capital requirements for each type of insurance are stated. It is generally conceded by most students of the subject that many minimum capital requirements are too low. One study, for example, revealed that inadequate capital requirements are responsible for the termination of many new life insurance companies, and that to assure their survival, the present capital requirements for formation must be two, three, or four times as large as at present.[5]

The type of assets in which insurance companies can invest is also closely regulated. In general, life insurance companies are required to restrict their investments mainly to bonds and mortgages, with only the modest provision for equity investments such as real estate, common, and preferred stock. For property and liability insurance companies, states generally allow the invest-

ment in equities of amounts representing the company's capital and surplus. However, those assets representing loss reserves and unearned premium reserves must be invested in fixed-dollar-type investments. State laws also specify how assets are to be valued. For example, bonds and mortgages may be carried on insurers' balance sheets on an amortized cost basis, whereas stocks must be carried at market value. Thus, if the market value of a bond or a mortgage declines because of adverse market conditions or rising interest rates, the true value of the insurer's assets may be overstated. In some extreme cases the insurer may be actually insolvent because of loss of values in bond portfolios, and yet under current regulations the company would be classified as solvent.

Some types of assets, *i.e.*, nonadmitted assets, may not be recognized by state regulators. Thus, assets such as office furniture, office buildings, overdue balances from agents, and others not normally available for meeting obligations due policyholders are not recognized at all, even though they may have cost the insurance company a great deal.

State insurance commissioners are given regulatory authority over the liquidation of an insurer which is determined to be insolvent. Theoretically, insurance commissioners are supposed to prevent insolvencies by periodic examination of insurers (usually at least every three years). Unfortunately, this objective has not been realized in the past because of inefficient procedures for discovering companies which are in financial difficulties.[6] State laws also

[5] E. J. Leverett, Jr., "Paid-In Surplus and Capital Requirements of a New Life Insurance Company," *Journal of Risk and Insurance*, Vol. 38, No. 1 (March 1971), p. 27.

[6] One of the largest insolvencies in recent years, that of the Equity Funding Company, was first reported to regulatory officials by a former employee who was disillusioned by what he felt to be illegal practices within the company.

promulgate the size of various security deposits required for the protection of policyholders. In general, the size of security deposits has been too small in proportion to the volume of business to be of any real protection to the insured.

Regulation of Rates, Reserves, and Expenses

As noted previously, under practically all state laws insurance rates must meet three criteria. The rates must be adequate, not excessive, and not unfairly discriminatory. In about half of the states, advance filings of intended rate schedules must be submitted to the insurance commissioner and approved before use. In most of the other states, a company may use a newly promulgated rate subject to later review and possible reversal by the insurance commissioner. Expense allowances are similarly regulated. For example, in New York the amount of commissions payable to a life insurance agent for the production of life insurance is limited to approximately 50 percent of the first-year premium on ordinary life insurance. Companies chartered in other states and not operating in New York may pay the life insurance agent twice this amount or more. Thus, expense regulation is not uniform.

Not only are rates and expenses regulated, but so are the methods of calculating various insurance reserves. For property and liability insurers there are two major types of reserves — unearned premium reserves and loss reserves. Under statutory requirements, when a new policy is issued, insurers are required to set up a liability reserve for possible return of the advance premiums paid in, known as the unearned premium reserve. As the policy runs its course, unearned premium reserves gradually may be reduced on a pro rata basis. Because the expenses of acquisition of the policy must be paid for in advance and may not be amortized over the life of the policy, each property and liability contract written will show a deficit the moment it is written. This deficit must be taken from surplus. Thus, a company without adequate surplus may not accept new business as rapidly as it may like. The expected profit to be achieved in writing each policy cannot be recognized in accounting until the expiration of the contract. Thus, the effect of statutory requirements in treating the unearned premium reserve is to understate the true profits of a rapidly growing firm and to overstate the true profits of a firm whose business is stable or whose business is declining.

In a similar manner, loss reserves are subject to certain statutory requirements. When claims are reported, the loss is estimated and a reserve established. The true profit of the insurer often may not be determined until it is finally known whether the loss reserves have been correctly stated, understated, or overstated. A conclusion which may be reached regarding the effect of statutory requirements on rates, expenses, and loss reserve accounting is that the true profit status and financial position of the insurer may not accurately be known until the policy period covered by the accounts has expired.

In the field of life insurance, accounting problems similar to those in property insurance arise. Because statutory requirements generally set life insurance accounts on a cash basis rather than an accrual basis, profits and reserves were commonly adjusted by financial analysts for better interpretation. In order to secure greater uniformity in making these adjustments, a basis known as GAAP (Generally Accepted Accounting Principles) was introduced.

GAAP accounting arose out of an investigation by the Committee on Insurance Accounting and Auditing of the American Institute of Certified Public Accountants in 1966. This committee developed an audit guide for stock life insurance companies. Although the final recommendations of this committee have yet to be fully adopted, many life insurers are now reporting their profits and other financial statements on a GAAP basis. For example, under GAAP accounting the expenses necessary to put an insurance policy into effect are amortized over the life of the policy rather than taken out in advance as is required under statutory accounting.[7]

In view of the above comments it seems clear that reported profits of insurers should be interpreted with great caution; they may not accurately reflect the current position of a particular life insurance or property insurance company. However, most studies indicate that the stated profits of insurance companies are not excessive, and are, in fact, smaller than comparable industries in the field of finance. In one evaluation of property and liability insurance companies it was determined that the companies earned an average of 10.39 percent on net worth over the period 1961–73.[8] Fluctuations in earnings

rates, however, were very great, ranging from a high of 26.21 percent in 1972 to a loss of 7.09 percent in 1969.

The relatively poor profit results of insurance companies have had unfortunate implications for the risk manager. For example, because reported profits fluctuate a good deal, management may have had to tighten underwriting requirements and to restrict insurance supply in some years more than might otherwise have been necessary had true information been available about the position of the insurance company's financial status. Restrictions on the supply of insurance in certain years has encouraged the government to enter the private insurance business in one way or another. (See below.)

Furthermore, it has been difficult for the insurance industry to attract new capital through the public issuance of stocks or bonds. Most growth must be financed internally, mainly from investment earnings. In periods when underwriting losses and investment losses coincide, the restrictions on capacity are much greater than normal, thus compounding the problem of insurance availability.

A recent example of this problem is the experience of the Argonaut Insurance Company (controlled by Teledyne Corporation). In 1975 Argonaut began to experience large underwriting losses from writing medical malpractice liability insurance. This type of coverage is characterized by a rather longtime lag between the time premiums are collected

[7] Robert L. Posnak, "Perspectives on Life Insurance Financial Reporting," *Journal of Risk and Insurance*, Vol. 40, No. 1, (March 1973), pp. 7–30. This article provides an accurate and detailed history of how GAAP accounting originated and developed. See also Dale R. Gustafson, "Solving a Risk Theory Problem Under Time Pressure (Life Insurance Adjusted Earnings)," *Journal of Risk and Insurance*, Vol. 41, No. 2, (June 1974), pp. 259–65.

[8] Mark R. Greene, *Risk and Insurance*, 4th ed. (Cincinnati: South-Western Publishing Co., 1977), p. 623. Data were derived from

Best's Aggregates and Averages 1971 (Morristown, N.J.: A.M. Best Co., 1971), pp. 31–32. See also James S. Trieschmann, "Property-Liability Profits: A Comparative Study," *Journal of Risk and Insurance*, Vol. 38, No. 3 (September 1971) pp. 437–53 and Stephen W. Forbes, "Rates of Return in Nonlife Insurance Industry," *Journal of Risk and Insurance*, Vol. 38, No. 3 (September 1971), pp. 409–22.

and the time losses must be paid, due to court delays. Argonaut underwriters reasoned that because of the lengthy delay they could accept a lower-than-average premium for liability insurance making up the anticipated losses by investment earnings on advance premiums collected. Unfortunately, investment losses from a declining stock market and underwriting losses from increasing claim severity occurred at the same time. In January 1975, the company was forced to cancel existing policies and to raise rates very markedly on renewals. For example, in New York the company announced a 200 percent rate increase effective immediately in 1975. Since this move was blocked by the New York Insurance Department, Argonaut officials announced that they would have to cancel the coverage of the New York Medical Society. Because of the underwriting and investment difficulties, officials from the parent corporation began to exercise stricter control over Argonaut's claim settlement policies. Many experienced executives left Argonaut rather than cancel policies on a wholesale basis.[9]

Regulation of Contract Provisions

Most states require that new policy forms be approved before they may be offered to the public. Many types of provisions are specified in the law. For example, life insurance policy provisions such as the incontestable clause, the misstatement of age clause, the nonforfeiture options, and the grace period must be included in words which closely follow legal requirements. A similar situation exists in the field of health insurance and automobile insurance. State laws also require standard

[9] *Wall Street Journal,* January 30, 1975, p. 26.

wording in the field of fire insurance. Both the conditions and stipulations and the insuring clause follow uniform wording throughout the United States (with only minor exceptions in a few states).

Insurance Marketing

Another important control on insurance company operation is maintained through laws regulating insurance marketing practices. For example, as was noted in Chapter 15, agents must be licensed in nearly all states. In some states, agents must pass rigid examinations requiring substantial preparation by successful applicants. In other states, very simple examinations are given which may be passed by a brief review of a booklet designed for that purpose. In some states adjusters and insurance consultants are also licensed. In this way some minimum level of competence is required of those engaged in the distribution process.

Most states have countersignature laws under which property and liability insurance must be signed by a duly authorized agent who is a resident of the state.

Unfair trade practices such as rebating, twisting, and misleading advertising are also prohibited. Antirebating laws prohibit an agent from returning any part of the premium to the policyholder as a way to cut the price or to induce sales. Twisting is a form of misrepresentation under which an agent may cause a policyholder to cancel the contracts with one insurer in order to take out another contract which might be disadvantageous. The insurance commissioners generally have broad powers to prevent unfair trade practices such as those mentioned.

Court decisions also affect insurance field practices. A recent example of this effect is illustrated in the case of a large disability insurance carrier, The Mutual of Omaha.[10] In this case a policyholder's back was injured in a fall from a roof. Under his policy he was entitled to lifetime benefits of $200 a month for disability from an accident, and three months' disability income for sickness. Following the accident the policyholder underwent surgery; the insurer reclassified his disability as a sickness and ended his benefits. The court decided that the insurer's action was with malice, fraud, and oppression against the policyholder. The jury awarded the policyholder $45,600 as compensation due under his policy, $78,000 for mental distress caused by the insurer's actions, and $5 million punitive damages (reduced in a later decision) against the insurer. In addition, the court awarded a judgment against the claim supervisor of the insurer in the amount of $1,000 and against the adjustor settling the claim in the amount of $900. In an appeal, a superior court judge upheld the judgment indicating that the company and its claims adjustors had shown a "total disregard for the rights of the insured."[11] Undoubtedly cases such as this influence claims settlement procedures of many insurers, in addition to the insurer against which action was directed in this case.

Taxation

Revenue from the taxation of insurance has become an important part of many state budgets, and is an additional reason for insurer regulation. Insurers must pay, for example, a tax on gross premium income usually slightly

[10] *Wall Street Journal*, Wednesday, November 27, 1974, p. 7.

[11] *Wall Street Journal*, January 23, 1975, p. 20.

over 2 percent. Insurers must also pay state and federal income taxes on underwriting profits and investment income. It is interesting to observe that only a small proportion of the tax revenue taken in by states (approximately 5 percent) is used for the operation of state insurance departments.

CONSUMERISM AND INSURANCE

From the above discussion of federal and state regulation of insurance, it is clear that much insurance legislation is made to protect the consumer of insurance as much as it is to obtain an orderly operation of the insurance mechanism in society. In recent years consumerism has affected many commodities and services, and insurance is no exception.

Many state and federal laws illustrate the influence of consumerism on insurance. Reference has already been made, for example, to state laws against twisting and rebating. Many state insurance departments have established divisions of complaints in which the consumer may receive independent assistance in such matters as the settlement of claims against insurers.

The Securities and Exchange Commission has established requirements relating to the disclosure of financial information concerning all corporations, including insurance, whose securities are being publicly sold. Laws have been passed in many states restricting the right of insurers to cancel policies. For example, most automobile insurers must now state the reasons for cancellation as one of the policy provisions. Regulations regarding the readability of contracts has been passed. As illustrated in the Mutual of Omaha case cited above, punitive judgments for unfair practices are now being handed down by the courts.

Another example of laws protecting the consumer are statutes on the service and process of unauthorized insurers. Under such statutes, if a policy of insurance is delivered by an unauthorized and unlicensed insurer, the state insurance commissioner is appointed as an attorney-in-fact upon whom legal process may be served if it becomes necessary to bring a legal action against this insurer. In this way a consumer does not have to travel to a distant state in order to bring a legal action. This legislation has been passed as an attempt to control mail order insurance in unlicensed areas.

Pressure on insurance companies to publish more accurate information on the cost of life insurance is another example of the trend toward consumerism. Traditionally, life insurers have issued what has been held to be misleading estimates of the costs of the policies they issue. Misstatements arise over uncertainties in dividend schedules. Also, misleading representations about the cost of life insurance stem from failure of the insurer to consider lost interest which would otherwise have been earned by the insured on the premium invested in the contract. So-called interest-adjusted costs must now be made more generally available to consumers. Various shopping guides to insurance have been published by insurance trade publications, insurance commissioners, and by others.[12] These shopping guides purport to give more accurate and impartial information on insurance costs

[12] See, for example, Pennsylvania Insurance Department, *Shoppers Guide to Term Life Insurance;* Joseph M. Belth, *Life Insurance: A Consumer's Handbook* (Bloomington, Ind.: Indiana University Press, 1973); and National Underwriter Co., *Interest Adjusted Index, Life Insurance Payment and Cost Comparison* (Cincinnati).

than is generally available through the normal marketing channels.

Another example of the consumer movement is in the area of product safety. In 1972 the Consumer Product Safety Act was passed, creating a commission to require notification by manufacturers, distributors, and retailers of any substantial product hazard of which they are aware. Because of the fairly rigid requirements as to product safety, the availability of product liability insurance is importantly affected. By following the doctrine of strict liability the courts have held manufacturers liable to the user for defective manufacturing which causes a loss, even though the manufacturer is not negligent in his operations. Unfortunately, the product safety movement may reduce the supply of public liability insurance to the point that the insurance method of treating this risk is no longer possible.

The passage of no-fault automobile insurance laws in many states is another example of bills designed to protect the consumer. These bills also importantly affect the way insurers operate, shifting many of the claims from third party liability to first party direct compensation basis.

Perhaps the most significant recent piece of legislation reflecting the consumer movement in insurance is the Employee Retirement Income Security Act of 1974 (ERISA). (See Chapter 13.) In this act Congress greatly tightened regulation over private pensions. Minimum standards of vesting, communication to the employee, and plan funding were imposed. A national benefit guarantee corporation was set up to give protection to the retiree against loss in case the employer's pension plan is terminated. The consumerism movement promises to have an even more important influence on insurance in the future than in the past.

GOVERNMENT INSURANCE PROGRAMS

Although the U.S. economy is based upon the concept of free, private, competitive enterprise, both state and federal governmental agencies have always been fairly important influences in the economic effort of the U.S. society. Adam Smith's doctrine in which governments are supposed to confine their activities to such functions as law enforcement, monetary regulation, supervision of transportation, national defense, and public education has largely been ignored in the U.S. Rather, government has been actively involved in many lines of private business, as the builder of public highways, the operator of the postal system, the owner and operator of ships and railroads, and the owner and operator of one of the largest banking systems in the world, to name a few. The government has operated as a partner with private business in many fields, and it operates as a competitor and exclusive agent in other fields. In insurance, governments operate in all three capacities, at both the state and federal level.

Before examining in detail the nature of government participation in the insurance business, it is well to examine the rationalization which underlies this type of effort. There are several basic reasons which may be cited. The government may attempt: 1) to supply markets unfilled by private agencies; 2) to eliminate or reduce selling costs; 3) to administer compulsory insurance programs; and 4) to achieve collateral social purposes. For example, to accomplish the social objective of economic stability unemployment insurance and bank deposit insurance programs were used. A social purpose of the social security program has been the prevention of poverty, particularly among the aged.

An important collateral social purpose of flood insurance was to improve building practices so as to avoid construction in flood plains. Flood insurance also illustrates the rationale of filling demand not met by private insurers.

Federal Government Programs

The size and extent of federal government insurance programs are not widely appreciated. A summary of these programs is presented in Table 19–1. Revenues of all federal programs in 1973 were about $70 billion of which about $60 billion were accounted for by the Social Security (OASDHI) program. By comparison, the income from insurance premiums of all private life insurance companies in that year were approximately $49 billion, and from property and liability companies $41 billion, for a total of $90 billion. Thus, in 1973 major government insurance programs were approximately 44 percent as large as all private insurers combined. This compares to about 42 percent in 1971, 39 percent in 1965, and 25 percent in 1960.[13]

It is interesting that half of all of the 28 programs shown in Table 19–1 were conducted at cash losses, the largest being the programs of unemployment insurance, the Federal Housing Administration, the Agricultural Credit Insurance Fund, and the National Flood Insurance Fund. The largest money-makers are the Federal Deposit Insurance Corporation, Federal Savings and Loan Insurance Corporation, Mutual Mortgage Insurance Fund, and the National Service Life Insurance Fund. The federal programs were expected to earn approximately $.5 billion in 1974, but to

[13] Estimates are in Table 5–1, Greene, *Risk and Insurance* 1st, 2nd, 3rd ed. (Cincinnati: South-Western Publishing Co., 1962, 1968, 1973, respectively).

lose over $1 billion in 1975, largely due to expected depletions in the unemployment trust fund, due to the economic depression which began in late 1974.

The federal government insurance programs may be classified under three headings: 1) those in which the federal government is in a type of partnership with private insurers; 2) those in which the federal government is a competitor with private insurers; and 3) those in which the government is an exclusive agent. Examples of insurance in each of these three groups are:

Partnerships with private insurers
   Federal Flood and FAIR Plans
   Nuclear Energy Liability Pools

Competitor to private insurers
   OASDHI
   Federal Crime Insurance

Governmental exclusive agencies
   Loan Guaranty Programs
   Unemployment Insurance
   War Risk for Aviation and Marine Vessels

Government Partnerships with Private Insurers

Federal Flood Insurance

A good example of a partnership phenomenon between government and private insurance is the program established by the National Flood Insurance Act of 1968 and Flood Disaster Protection Act of 1973. Under these acts were authorized the federal reinsurance of flood risks covered by a consortium of private insurers, the National Flood Insurers Association (N.F.I.A.). Insurance rates are subsidized by the government. Self-sustaining actuarial rates are to be charged eventually. The program is supplemented by a system of requirements under which, to be eligible for coverage,

a community must agree to certain land use standards and protective measures against flood. As of March 31, 1974, 3,364 communities in the U.S. had qualified for flood insurance. Over $7.5 billion of flood insurance was in force.

An important purpose of federal involvement in flood insurance is to help society reduce loss from flood. Among the requirements for eligibility for flood insurance are the following: The community must (a) require building permits for all construction, (b) require that new buildings in a flood zone be so constructed as to be reasonably safe from flooding, (c) require that water and sewer systems be designed to minimize infiltration of flood waters, and (d) in identified flood zones require that new buildings have the lowest flood level elevated above the level of the 100-year flood.[14] The degree of required vigilance in administering land use programs rises with the completeness of flood information available to the community. In some cases the community will be required to refuse building permits for new construction in areas most prone to flood. Communities must give attention to flood warning and emergency preparedness plans.

The N.F.I.A.

An insurer meeting certain qualifications may join the N.F.I.A. and write flood insurance. Among these qualifications the insurer must (a) have assets of at least $1 million, (b) agree to assume a minimum net loss liability of $25,000, and (c) agree to other rules and regulations set down by the N.F.I.A., which assumes responsibility for adjustment and payment of claims for losses. The

[14] Part 1909 General Provisions, Subchapter B, National Flood Insurance Program. Code of Federal Regulations, Title 24, Revised April 1, 1973.

TABLE 19-1
Operating Revenues, Expenses, and Profits (Loss) of Selected Federal Insurance Agencies, 1973–75
(in millions)

	Revenue	1973 (Actual) Expenses	Profit (Loss)	1974 (Estimated) Profit (Loss)	1975 (Estimated) Profit (Loss)
Insured Loan Agencies					
1. Rural Development Insurance Fund	$ 11.3	$ 25.5	$ (14.2)	$ (45.5)	$ (49.9)
2. Agricultural Credit Insurance Fund	55.0	605.8	(550.8)	(229.3)	(184.5)
3. Federal Deposit Insurance Corporation	503.2	51.6	451.6	62.1	64.1
4. Veterans Loan Guaranty Revolving Fund	81.9	103.5	(21.6)	(34.1)	(40.0)
Student Loan Insurance Fund					
5. — Federal Insurance	4.5	23.6	(19.1)	(23.5)	(34.7)
6. — Federal Reinsurance	.8	12.4	(11.6)	(20.6)	(25.3)
7. Federal Savings and Loan Insurance Corporation	352.5	93.6	258.9	276.4	311.5
Federal Housing Administration					
8. — Mutual Mortgage Insurance Fund	360.7	246.3	114.4	110.8	110.9
9. — General Insurance Fund	120.4	332.8	(212.4)	(276.0)	(302.0)
10. — Cooperative Management Housing Insurance Fund	5.8	.9	4.9	3.9	3.5
11. — Special Risk Insurance Fund	77.0	271.4	(194.4)	(257.2)	(324.6)
12. Rural Housing Insurance Fund	37.3	436.6	(399.3)	(332.6)	(351.3)
13. Federal Ship Financing Fund	6.6	1.5	5.1	9.8	14.3
14. Credit Union Share Insurance Fund	13.3	2.7	10.6	11.6	14.2
Subtotal	$1,630.3	$2,208.2	$ (577.9)	$ (744.2)	$ (793.8)
Property Insurance Agencies					
15. Aviation War Risk Insurance Revolving Fund	$ 2.2	$ .05	$ 2.15	$ (.03)	$ (.03)
16. War Risk Insurance Revolving Fund	.13	.07	.06	.03	.03
17. Federal Crop Insurance Corporation	42.0	29.9	12.1	4.2	(4.0)
National Insurance Development Fund					
18. — FAIR (Riot Reinsurance)	7.4	1.4	6.0	6.6	6.8
19. — Crime Insurance	1.3	2.3	(1.0)	(.8)	(.8)
20. National Flood Insurance Fund	1.5	30.2	(28.7)	(34.9)	(64.9)
Subtotal	$ 54.53	$ 63.92	$ (9.39)	$ (24.90)	$ (62.90)

TABLE 19–1 (cont.)

Life Insurance Agencies

21. Service-Disabled Insurance Fund	$ 18.2	$ 31.7	$ (13.5)	$ (15.6)	$ (18.0)	
22. Veterans Reopened Insurance Fund	49.8	48.0	1.8	.7	1.2	
23. Veterans Special Life Fund	61.0	53.0	8.0	8.2	8.7	
24. Servicemen's Group Life Insurance Fund	79.4	79.4	0	0	0	
25. National Service Life Fund	798.0	518.9	279.1	208.4	214.1	
26. U.S. Government Life Insurance Fund	39.1	66.3	(27.2)	(36.7)	(35.7)	
Subtotal	$1,045.5	$ 797.3	$ 248.2	$ 165.0	$ 170.2	
27. Unemployment Trust Fund	$6,690.7	$5,353.8	$1,336.9	$1,100.0	$ (400.0)	
Subtotal, 21–27	$9,421.03	$8,423.22	$ 997.81	$ 495.9	$(1,086.5)	
			(in billions)			
28. OASDHI						
— Old Age and Survivor Insurance Trust Fund	$ 43.6	$ 42.8	$ .8	—	—	
— Disability Insurance Trust Fund	5.9	5.4	.5	—	—	
— Hospital Insurance Trust Fund	8.3	6.8	1.5	—	—	
— Supplemental Medical Insurance Trust Fund	2.9	2.7	.2	—	—	
Total OASDHI	$ 60.7	$ 57.7	$ 3.0	—	—	
GRAND TOTAL, 1–28	$ 70.12	$ 66.12	$ 3.997	—	—	

SOURCE: *Budget of the United States Government*, Fiscal Year 1975, Appendix. Totals may not add precisely, due to rounding.

government determines rates, eligibility, loss control requirements, and provides financial backing.

Currently, the N.F.I.A. will not issue policies with greater coverage than specified maximums: for residences, $70,000; for contents, $10,000; for properties with more than one residence, $200,000; for contents, $20,000; for churches, $200,000 for either building or contents.

It would appear that the current flood insurance program represents a satisfactory partnership between private insurers and the government in a venture where both parties make an important contribution. Both the force of government and the administrative, distribution, and underwriting abilities of private insurers are brought to bear effectively to solve an important national problem in risk management. Private flood insurance was not generally available before the program began because of the catastrophic hazard. Now risk managers may transfer the risk to insurers.

FAIR Plans

Fair Access to Insurance Requirement (FAIR) plans were authorized in 1968 to provide property insurance in central cities where private insurance was in restricted supply. They appear to have operated at a profit to the federal government (see Table 19–1), although private insurers were reported to have sustained an aggregate underwriting loss of $82.6 million on these plans over the period 1968–72.[15]

As of 1975, 33 FAIR plans were operating in 31 states, Washington, D.C., and Puerto Rico. Under the program the federal government reinsures policies written by private insurers in central cities in which standard property insurance coverage is not available at normal rates. About $16.7 billion of coverage was in force as of 1975, most of it in New York, California, Michigan, New Jersey, Pennsylvania, Illinois, and Massachusetts. in 1975, 650,000 new or renewal policies were issued,[16] down from 840,000 in 1972, indicating a reduced need for this coverage facility by the consumer.

Under a FAIR plan the insured pays the standard premium for insurance unless property owned falls below certain minimum underwriting standards, in which case an excess premium may be levied.[17] The insured is entitled to have the property inspected and to receive a statement of what is necessary to bring the property up to given standards. In some cases the insured may receive a grant from the federal government to make the necessary repairs. The grant application may not be turned down because the property is located in riot-prone areas or for other environmental hazards.

Through the federal-private partnership an important social problem, insurance unavailability, was met through FAIR plans. However, it appears that voluntary markets are now gradually being restored and there may no longer be a need for this partnership in the future.

---

[15] *Insurance Facts, 1975*, pp. 23.

[16] *Ibid.*

[17] In a study covering the operation of the Minnesota FAIR plan, about 20 percent of the dwellings and apartment houses were charged standard fire and extended coverage rates, while the most common extra charge was 51 percent of standard rate. For all the dwellings the average charge was 65 percent, and for apartments, 76 percent. Andrew F. Whitman and C. Arthur Williams, Jr. "Fair Plan and Excess Rate Plan Rates in Minnesota," *Journal of Risk and Insurance*, Vol. 38, No. 1 (March 1971), p. 46.

THE FEDERAL GOVERNMENT AS A COMPETITOR TO PRIVATE INSURANCE

The Federal Social Security Act

The largest insurance program operated by the federal government by almost any standard is the OASDHI, which competes directly with private enterprise in the fields of life and health insurance, and pensions. A brief description of each program follows. See, also, discussion of these programs in Chapter 11.

Old Age and Survivors Insurance

This program provides monthly payments to retired workers, their dependents, their survivors, and to certain uninsured persons age 72 or over.

Total benefit payments are expected to rise for four main reasons: 1) Benefits to retired workers and dependents are tied to the cost-of-living index which is rising steadily. 2) Benefits are geared to average wage levels which are rising. 3) The number of retired persons is increasing and their average life expectancy is also increasing. 4) Congress is expected to liberalize future benefit provisions.

Disability Insurance

This program pays disabled workers and dependents a monthly income for long-term disability that is expected to prevent substantially gainful employment for one year or longer. Nearly four million people received these benefits in 1974. The government processes nearly 2 million disability applications each year. A maximum of 1.5 percent of disability benefits has been authorized for vocational rehabilitation services.

Health Insurance

This program is in two parts: 1) hospital insurance, and 2) supplemental medical insurance. Most persons over 65 are covered by these programs. Hospital coverage extends to nursing and other posthospital care, as well as to extended care facilities. It applies also to disabled persons on social security for two years who are under age 65.

Operations

In 1974 total income of OASDHI was approximately $73 billion. Total taxes on payroll were 5.85 percent on the first $14,100 of wages in 1975 and 5.85 percent on the first $15,300 in 1976. In 1973 the total income, including investment income, of all private life insurers in the U.S. was $64.8 billion.[18] Thus, the government's personal insurance program through OASDHI takes in about 53 percent of the total of both programs, public and private. The Social Security Administration estimates that the ratio of payments under federal social insurance programs has risen from 1.9 to 7.3 percent of gross national product in the U.S. over the period 1950–74, an increase of 2.8 times.[19] The ratio of private life insurance and annuity premiums to disposable personal income declined from 5.1 to 3.8 percent over the same period, a decrease of 25 percent.[20] Public preferences apparently are running in favor of social insurance as a way of meeting the needs for life and health insurance.

Through OASDHI and related programs, the federal government has made a major entry into private per-

[18] *1974 Life Insurance Fact Book* (New York: Institute of Life Insurance, 1974), p. 57.

[19] *Social Security Bulletin*, January 1975, p. 12.

[20] *1974 Life Insurance Fact Book*, p. 59.

sonal insurance lines through requiring insurance for floor of protection for (a) old age pension, (b) long-term disability, and (c) hospitalization and medical expense for the aged. Over 90 percent of all workers are covered. In the latter coverage, the protection is nearly complete; it is certainly more than a "floor of protection."

OASDHI operates with a fund smaller than the size of one year's expenditures, which is very small compared to private life insurers. The power of taxation for benefits is a major reason for the modest-sized fund. Large "actuarial" funds are not only unnecessary for a special program, but from an economic standpoint would probably be unwise. Funding these programs to the level necessary under private actuarial standards would require such large tax contributions that private employers would be hurt financially. From a political standpoint, large funds would have their disadvantages as well, since they might tempt Congress to increase benefit levels even more than it has. Over the years OASDHI has operated on a sound basis considering its public nature, but controversy now exists on this point. Some observers argue that taxes may be insufficient to pay future benefits, as presently scheduled. This arises from current projections of a shrinking labor force and a rising proportion of aging persons in the economy.[21]

OASDHI vs. Private Insurance

Although it is not surprising that the compulsory federal social insurance program has grown more rapidly than

[21] See George E. Rejda and R. J. Shepler, "The Import of Zero Population Growth on the OASDHI Program," *Journal of Risk and Insurance*, Vol. XL, No. 3 (September 1973), pp. 313–25.

private insurance programs, these programs still have not absorbed all of the market for private insurance. For example, in December 1973 the average retirement benefit under OASDHI was $166 for retired workers, or about $251 for a worker and a dependent spouse. Clearly, there is an unfilled need for additional pension benefit which could be supplied by private insurers under individual as well as group programs. A similar situation exists for disability insurance beneficiaries. Not only is the OASDHI disability beneficiary receiving modest allowances (comparable to retirement benefits) but the definition of disability under OASDHI is fairly rigid, leaving opportunity for more liberal disability definitions by private insurers. For example, the OASDHI's definition of disability is such that a person must be disabled for five months before drawing benefits. Further, it must be demonstrated that the disability is expected to last at least one year. Private long-term disability insurance can be arranged with waiting periods much shorter than this, and there is no requirement that the disability must last any definite period of time in the future. Finally, widows' benefits under OASDHI averaged only $228 monthly for a widow with one child in 1973. This benefit usually terminates when the child reaches age 18, leaving a black out period until the widow reaches age 60. There is obviously still an opportunity for private insurance to increase the benefit and cover those periods not insured under OASDHI.

Even though OASDHI has not taken over the market for private life and health insurance completely, by any means, a review of historical developments in the program show that Congress has broadened coverage and increased benefits almost every session. If these trends continue, a time may come when private life and health insurance may discover that providing a floor of protection is not the guiding philosophy of OASDHI, but rather the objective of Congress will be to provide adequate protection.

Implications for Risk Management

It seems unlikely that Congress will reverse the trend toward more comprehensive social insurance programs unless considerable political or economic pressure is brought to bear. However, OASDHI is a popular program and no substantial adverse criticism of it has so far made much headway. Perhaps the response most appropriate for risk managers is to develop coverages that build on existing social insurance programs effectively at reasonable cost. If Congress can be convinced that private industry has the talent, ability, and resolution to fill the personal lines market, its eagerness to expand OASDHI may be somewhat diminished.

Federal Crime Insurance

Federal crime insurance which competes directly with private insurance began in 1968 with the passage of the Urban Property Protection and Reinsurance Act of 1968, which also created authority for riot reinsurance and for FAIR plans. The HUD secretary designated the Federal Insurance Administration to carry out its provision. The law stated (Sec. 1231)

(a) The Secretary shall conduct a continuing review of the market availability situation in each of the several States to determine whether or not crime insurance is available at affordable rates either through the normal insurance market or through

a suitable program adopted under State Law.

(b) Upon determining . . . that any time on or after August 1, 1971, a critical market unavailability situation for crime insurance then exists in any State and has not been met through appropriate state action, the Secretary is authorized to make crime insurance available at affordable rates within such State through the facilities of the Federal Government.

The HUD secretary, through the Federal Insurance Administration, conducted surveys of the need for crime insurance at affordable rates. Affordable rate was defined in the act as "such premium rate as the Secretary determines would permit the purchase of a specific type of insurance coverage by a reasonably prudent person in similar circumstances with due regard to the costs and benefits involved." The act specified that due regard should be given to requiring reasonable protective measures to prevent loss. It was determined that ten jurisdictions did not meet the affordability criterion.

The act broke new ground by permitting the federal government to offer coverage formerly handled exclusively by the private insurance market. The Federal Insurance Administration wasted no time in developing plans for federal insurance, and on August 1, 1971, the earliest date permitted by the act, the first policies were made available in nine states and the District of Columbia. Two states, California and Michigan, developed their own crime insurance plans.

Growth

Federal crime insurance appeared to develop slowly. Only burglary and robbery insurance were offered. In the first five months of operation a total of 2,158 residential and 799 commercial policies were written, 77 percent of which were in New York and Massachusetts. Only 14 policies were written in the District of Columbia, and 120 in Ohio.[22] As of June, 1974, however, the program had expanded to five new states (Delaware, Florida, Kansas, New Jersey, and Tennessee) and a total of 16,424 residential and 6,209 commercial policies were in force, 72 percent of which were in New York and Massachusetts. The total number of policies expanded 8½ times over the 2½ years (from 2,657 to 22,633). The most rapid growth in percentage was in Illinois. Yet with only 559 policies in force there, it would appear that the potential market for coverage had hardly been scratched. Furthermore, 194 (or 35 percent) of these policies were residential.

Nationally, 73 percent (16,424 out of 22,633) or all federal crime policies outstanding in June 1974 were residential, in spite of the fact that crime insurance is offered under the homeowners program — the most widely used form of privately insured protection for householders. Nationally, only 22,633 policies are outstanding, among an estimated 11½ million business establishments in the country.[23] In 1972 the federal program collected $1.1 million in premiums, compared to an estimated $130 million of net premiums written by private insurers.[24] It would appear that the market acceptance of federal crime insurance has not been overwhelming and that the main intended beneficiaries, the small business-

men, have in particular not utilized the protection offered.

Barriers to Growth

Several factors may explain the somewhat limited acceptance of federal crime insurance:

(1) Private insurance is still widely available at apparently affordable rates in most areas, even in those states which make federal crime insurance available.

(2) Although standard brokerage commissions (14–16 percent) are paid, federal crime insurance has not been vigorously promoted either by private insurers and agents or by the Federal Insurance Administration. Many high crime areas are not served particularly well by agents.

(3) Federal crime insurance for burglary involves adherence to specific types of loss prevention by insureds and uncertainty as to these requirements and their costs may have hindered the growth of the program. Undoubtedly in many cases when the insured installs the required devices, he becomes an acceptable risk at affordable rates for private insurers and thus may obtain coverage in the private market.

(4) The program had relatively low coverage limits, high rates, and high deductibles. Even though deductibles were reduced in 1974, they are still substantial. Currently, the deductible for residences is $50 (formerly $75) or 5 percent of the loss, whichever is greater. The deductible for commercial firms is 5 percent of the loss, or a dollar amount ranging from $50 to $200 depending on the gross receipts of the firm, whichever is greater.[25]

Coverage limits are $10,000 for residences and $15,000 for commercial

---

[22] *1971 HUD Statistical Yearbook* (Washington, D.C. USGPO, 1972), p. 93.

[23] *Statistical Abstract of the United States, 1973.*

[24] *Insurance Fact Book, 1973* (New York: Insurance Information Institute, 1973), p. 10.

[25] *Federal Register*, 39 F.R. 2361, January 21, 1974.

firms, sold in $1,000 amounts. Rates vary by territory, type of business, and gross receipts. In Miami, Florida, for example, a residence policy premium was $80 for $10,000 of coverage ($40 for $1,000, and $60 for $5,000). A commercial rate for a grocer with annual receipts under $100,000 was $72 for robbery and $60 for burglary for $1,000 of coverage ($120 for both coverages). Coverage of $5,000 would cost $288 for robbery and $240 for burglary, or $480 if both coverages are taken. This premium is 9.6 percent of the policy amount of $5,000, and 12 percent for the $1,000 policy.

However, it is still true that most crime loss in the U.S. is uninsured; a large unfilled potential market exists for crime coverage. If private means are not found to satisfy this market it is possible that the federal crime insurance program may expand, not contract, in the years ahead, particularly if crime rates continue to expand in the future as rapidly as they have in recent years in the past.[26]

EXCLUSIVE AGENCIES

The federal government is an exclusive agent, or nearly so, in several types of insurance. Under the loan guaranty programs listed in Table 19–1, the federal government has almost a monopoly.

[26] For example, crimes against property were estimated by the FBI in 1972 as follows: Robbery, $91 million; burglary, $722 million; larceny of goods, $475 million; embezzlement loss, $2–$3 billion. Yet the total premiums of burglary and theft insurance in 1972 were only $130 million, and fidelity bond premiums were estimated at $200 million. Loss payments, of course, were probably only about 60% of premiums written. Thus, only about 5 percent of burglary and robbery losses were covered, and conservatively, only about 5 percent of fidelity losses were covered. Data from *Insurance Facts, 1973*. Percentages calculated.

Private insurers of a type similar to the Mortgage Loan Guarantee Insurance Corporation (MGIC) offer insurance on loans of certain types, such as conventional mortgages. However, most of the coverage is governmentally controlled.

The government is the only direct insurer of the unemployment, which is considered uninsurable by private insurers due to the catastrophic hazard, difficulty in predicting losses, and control by the potential insured over the occurrence of losses (lack of random occurrence).

The federal government is also the exclusive insurer of the war risk peril for aviation and marine vessels, programs identified in Table 19–1.

It would appear that the insurance programs in which the government operates exclusively tend to be limited in number. Governmental agencies so far prefer to work with private industry in some capacity. Only in cases where private industry will not participate and where a public economic or social problem exists, is the government likely to enter the field of insurance.

STATE GOVERNMENT INSURANCE PLANS

Practically all insurance plans in which state governments are involved are of the competitor or partnership variety (or some combination). Discussed here are workers compensation insurance, temporary disability insurance, the Maryland State Automobile Insurance Fund, and state government property insurance.

Workers' Compensation

Workers' compensation programs, operated at the state level, illustrate the partnership and exclusive agent as well as the competitor aspects of governmental participation in insurance. A partnership program exists in that state law sets up benefit schedules for injured workers and promulgates other insurance conditions, but the insurance of these benefits and the administration of the provisions of the law are left exclusively to private insurers in all but 18 states. The competitor status exists in those 12 states[27] where state-owned funds compete with private insurers in the insurance and administration of the workers' compensation laws. The exclusive agent concept exists in six states[28] when private insurers are not permitted and state-owned funds enjoy the exclusive right to operate in the field. Most Canadian provinces also have exclusive state funds.

State funds have gradually reduced their share of total premium written over the years. For example, during the period 1939–68 losses paid by state funds as a whole declined from 29 to 23 percent of total,[29] where state funds compete with private insurers. In three large industrial states, New York, California, and Michigan, the share of premiums written by state funds stood in 1970 at 20.2, 21.6, and 5.4 percent, respectively, down from 25, 27, and 8 percent, respectively, in 1950.[30] Thus,

private insurers seem to be competing effectively with governmental enterprise in this field.

Federal Intervention

Under the Occupational Safety and Health Act of 1970, a commission was set up to undertake a comprehensive study and evaluation of state workers' compensation laws. The commission published many studies including three volumes of special supplemental studies on the subject.[31] In its report to Congress in July 1972, it concluded that present state compensation laws were not adequate or equitable and recommended that these laws be changed to broaden coverage, liberalize benefits, and improve medical and rehabilitation services. The Commission recommended a three-year period (ending July 1, 1975) for state compliance with the essential recommendations. The result has been substantial liberalization of benefit provisions in workers' compensation laws, and continuing liberalization is expected. For, over the period of 1971–73, 13 states made medical coverage unlimited, ten states made coverage compulsory, 12 states added full occupational disease coverage, and 8 states eliminated numerical exceptions to determine whether employers were required to offer coverage to their employees.[32]

---

[27] Arizona, California, Colorado, Idaho, Maryland, Michigan, Montana, New York, Oklahoma, Oregon, Pennsylvania, and Utah.

[28] Washington (established 1911), Ohio (1912), West Virginia (1913), North Dakota (1919), Nevada (1913), and Wyoming (1915).

[29] A. M. Skolnik and D. N. Price, "Another Look at Workmen's Compensation," *Social Security Bulletin*, October 1970, pp. 3–25.

[30] B. J. Webb, W. R. Bagwell, and B. A. Palmer, "The Profitability of Workmen's Compensation Insurance" in Monroe Berkowitz, Ed. *Supplemental Studies* for the National

Commission on State Workmen's Compensation Laws, Vol. III (Washington, D.C., 1973), p. 239, and Whitman and Williams, "Rates in Minnesota," p. 153.

[31] The National Commission of State Workmen's Compensation Laws, *Workmen's Compensation*, Volumes I, II, III (Washington, D.C.: USGPO, 1973).

[32] Melvin B. Bradshaw, "Workmen's Compensation: Our Unfinished Task," *Risk Management*, May 1974, p. 37.

Temporary Disability Insurance

Another area in which state governmental bodies and private insurers compete in the field of health insurance is that of temporary (nonoccupational) disability income coverage. Under these plans a disabled worker is supposed to receive an income of between one-half to two-thirds of gross wages after a waiting period of 3 to 7 days for a maximum period of between 13 and 26 weeks. However, it is estimated that these plans actually restored only about 34 percent of a worker's total income loss, a ratio that has been fairly level since 1969.[33] Approximately 15 million workers, or about one-fourth of the labor force in 1972, were covered by temporary disability insurance laws, including the railroad program. These laws exist in Rhode Island (1942), California (1946), New Jersey (1948), New York (1949), Puerto Rico and Hawaii (1969). (See discussion in Chapter 11.)

State Funds

In California, New Jersey, and Puerto Rico, state-operated funds exist, but employers are permitted to satisfy the requirement of the law by purchasing acceptable insurance from private insurers, self-insuring, or by negotiating an agreement with a union or employees' association. Coverage is automatic unless the employer presents an acceptable substitute for state insurance.[34] In New York, a state fund operating like a private insurer exists and competes with private underwriters; it does not automatically provide coverage for workers of employers not presenting acceptable plans. In both New York and Hawaii, a special fund exists to pay workers not covered privately. In Rhode Island there is an exclusive state-operated fund. No account is taken of private cash sickness plans, and a covered employer may provide extra benefits if he wishes to do so. In summary, state-operated funds of some type exist in all of the six jurisdictions, but only in Rhode Island is the state fund the only funding method recognized by the law.

Evaluation

Nonoccupational temporary disability insurance has long been an important field for private health insurers. In 1971 over 41 million persons were covered by private insurers under both group and individual policies, which covered 32 million and 12 million persons, respectively; 3 million persons were covered by both individual and group policies. Another 17 million persons were covered by paid sick-leave plans, liability for which the employer assumed or self-insured.[35] Thus, about 75 percent of the work force is covered under private plans. Participation by state insurance agencies in this field under laws in six jurisdictions has been fairly minimal; employers have preferred private insurers over state agencies where they had a choice. No state had established a temporary disability insurance law for 20 years until Hawaii and Puerto Rico passed theirs in 1969. These two laws did not mandate coverage for a state insurance agency, but created funds only for workers who

[33] Daniel N. Price, "Cash Benefits for Short Term Sickness, 1948–1972," *Social Security Bulletin*, January 1974, p. 27.

[34] *Social Security Programs in the United States*, DHEW Publication No. 73–11915 (Washington, D.C.: Social Security Administration, 1973), pp. 88–89.

[35] *1972–1973 Source Book of Health Insurance Data* (New York: Health Insurance Institute, 1973), p. 25.

would not otherwise be insured. This type of insurance appears to be one in which there is little jurisdiction for state government participation, since private insurers usually offer adequate capacity on acceptable terms.

Maryland Automobile Insurance Fund

Governmental participation in automobile insurance has been traditionally restricted to regulation until 1973 when the state of Maryland became the first state to establish an insurance fund (effective January 1, 1973). There, automobile coverage is offered to motorists who have been turned down for coverage in the private market by at least two insurers or whose policies have been cancelled for reasons other than nonpayment of premium. The fund, termed the Maryland Automobile Insurance Fund (MAIF), was established to fill only a residual market for automobile coverage. The assigned risk plan was abolished under the same legislative action, and the MAIF took over the state's unsatisfied judgment fund. The legislature also passed an add-on type of no-fault coverage, called *economic loss*, for $2,500 of medical and disability losses. Liability coverage was made compulsory.[36]

Important among the justifications advanced for the MAIF was the fact that a substantial proportion of Maryland's drivers were insured in the assigned risk plan, even though they had "good records for automobile driving. For example, many families with youthful drivers were assigned risks paying substandard rates, even though they had no record of traffic violations. Thus, industry rating and underwriting procedures were found sufficiently unac-

[36] Sec. 16A Par. 243, Maryland Annotated Code.

ceptable to significant numbers of insureds that political action to create an alternative to private insurance was successfully supported. It is too early to tell where the MAIF will set a new trend toward governmental operation of automobile insurance at the state level. However, it would appear that governmental competition has been found necessary to force changes in the private auto insurance system in Maryland.

State Government Property Insurance

In some states, self-insurance funds for property insurance coverage have been established, indicating still another area in which governmental bodies compete directly with private insurers. According to a study by the author, 22 such funds[37] were in operation in 1975, writing approximately 3–4 percent of total fire and extended coverage insurance on all property in the respective states. In an earlier study by Lester B. Strickler in 1969, 9 states had established funded plans, and 14 states deliberately assumed property risks.[38] The remaining states employed commercial insurance or assumed the risk. Six states had at one time operated self-insurance plans, but later abandoned them.[39]

Perils covered under state plans generally include fire, extended cover-

[37] In the order of size of assets the states were South Carolina, Alabama, North Dakota, Florida, North Carolina, Oregon, Wisconsin, Georgia, Louisiana, Arkansas, Maine, Virginia, Kentucky, Kansas, Maryland, Delaware, Arizona, Tennessee, West Virginia, Pennsylvania and Utah.

[38] Lester B. Strickler, "Funded Self-Insurance for State Buildings & Contents," *Risk Management*, March 1970, p. 61.

[39] Colorado, Iowa, Michigan, Minnesota, New Jersey, and Rhode Island.

age, vandalism and malicious mischief, and sprinkler leakage. In a few states additional perils such as boiler explosion, earthquake, flood, state-owned buildings and contents, and occasionally, state-owned ocean-going research vessels. Usually coverage is similar to that in commercial policies, but some states do not use coinsurance clauses or deductibles. Premiums charged to state agencies commonly fall between 50 and 70 percent of commercial rates. Most state funds purchase reinsurance commercially, so that losses in excess of between $50,000 and $500,000 (depending on the state) are passed on to the commercial market.[40]

[40] Lester B. Strickler, "Funded Self-Insurance," p. 9.

SUMMARY AND CONCLUSIONS

Major conclusions of significance to risk management concerning the role of governments in regulating and participating in insurance may be stated:

1. Almost all aspects of insurance are regulated. A general understanding of the major types of regulation is necessary for an appreciation of the limits as well as the opportunities in conducting insurance operations.

2. Insurance is regulated at both the state and federal levels in the U.S. The role of federal regulation seems likely to expand in the years ahead. Subjects of regulation include rating, selling, accounting, investing, financing, advertising, and contract provisions.

3. The impact of consumerism on insurance has been significant. It has strengthened the position of the insurance buyer in dealing with insurers, and has offered the buyer greater protection against abuse. Its influence will continue to be felt.

4. Both the state and federal governments participate in insurance directly and indirectly, as partners, competitors, and as exclusive agents. The largest federal insurance program is represented by OASDHI, although property insurance programs also exist. State governments are now involved in many kinds of insurance, including workers' compensation, temporary disability, automobile, and state property plans. Increasingly, the risk manager must recognize the limits and extent of these programs by governmental agencies.

QUESTIONS FOR DISCUSSION

1. What justification might exist a) for *any* regulation of insurance and b) for both federal *and* state regulation of insurance?

2. Has insurance always been considered to be interstate commerce? Discuss.

3. What major areas of insurance are regulated? Are there any major areas of insurance which are *not* regulated? Discuss.

4. How has insurance been affected by the consumer movement?

5. "The federal government writes about 44 percent of the insurance business." What five major federal programs account for most of government's participation in the insurance business? What major state programs exist? Discuss.

6. Governments may act as a competitor, or partner to private enterprise, or as an exclusive agent in offering insurance to the public. Which of these statuses is most important in quantitative terms? Explain.

7. Counting state government programs, estimate the percentage of total insurance premiums taken in by the government. To what extent do you believe that this situation amounts to nationalization of the insurance industry in the United States? Discuss.

8. What are the implications for risk management in the rising amount of government involvement in insurance, both as a regulator and as a direct participant? Discuss.

20

Cases in Risk Management

Cases in this chapter are designed to give practice in dealing with broad managerial problems in risk management. Questions at the end of the cases should be considered as suggestive of these problems, not all-inclusive. A suggested procedure to prepare cases is:

1. Identify the major problems. Separate basic (often unstated) problems from apparent problems. Rank problems according to their importance.

2. Separate important facts from irrelevant or unimportant facts or assumptions.

3. Consider alternative solutions or approaches to solutions of the problems identified.

4. Develop lists of advantages and disadvantages of each solution.

5. Rank different solutions in accordance with their value and feasibility.

6. Select the best solution or solutions and defend your choice.

The following cases are presented below:

A. **Bedsole-Gwin Clothing Stores.** Administration and organization of risk management. Insurance program.

B. **Fuqua, Inc. (A).** Organization for risk management and for loss control.

C. **Fuqua, Inc. (B).** Use of a captive insurer.

D. **Kaiser Aluminum & Chemical Corporation.** Organizational considerations in risk management.

E. **Credico, Inc.** Self-insurance. Liability insurance problems.

F. **Calwood Lumber Company (A).** The property and liability risk.

G. **Charles Milton, Sr.** Estate planning.

H. **Southern Saw Service (A).** Retirement planning.

I. **Hawkins Engineering Testing Co.** Employee benefit planning.

J. **Midwest Gas & Oil Co.** Integration of risk management in a merger.

K. **Southern Saw Service (B).** Export credit insurance — foreign risk management.

L. **Kaiser Aluminum & Chemical Corporation Foreign Operations.** Merger problems; foreign operation problems.

Case A

Bedsole — Gwin Clothing Stores

In 1972, Mr. E. B. Gwin, majority stock-holder of Bedsole-Gwin Clothing Stores, was reviewing the risk management program of his newly formed corporation. He was wondering if the new organizational structure should require any new policies or procedures on risk and insurance matters.

Bedsole-Gwin Clothing Stores, incorporated, was founded in early July, 1973, and is the result of the acquisition of three stores formerly held by Bedsole Dry Goods Company, Inc. When Mr. J. L. Bedsole, owner of 80 percent of the stock outstanding in Bedsole Dry Goods Company, Inc., decided to liquidate his holdings, the new corporation was formed for the purpose of acquiring his interest.

The corporation now operates three clothing stores in Alabama. All three carry a complete line of women's, men's, and children's clothes, as well as shoes, baby clothes, piece goods (bolt cloth and sewing accessories), and accessories such as purses and hats.

Mr. Gwin anticipated that no dividends would be declared in the near future, with the profits being used to expand existing stores, remodel existing stores, and acquire other business inter-ests in the corporate name. Bedsole-Gwin plans to expand into other communities now inadequately served by existing retail establishments. This expansion will be into areas where competition with large chain store operations such as Belk's, Sears, and J. C. Penny's will not exist. It is anticipated that in ten years, Bedsole-Gwin Clothing Stores, Inc. will have branch stores in at least 15 Alabama, Florida, and Mississippi communities. It is the ultimate goal of the corporation to have 25 to 50 stores in operation.

PROPERTY EXPOSURES

Buildings

The buildings in all three of the stores are constructed of either masonry block or brick veneer with wooden/steel roofs covered with tar and rock.

There are no sprinkler or burglar alarm systems in any of the stores, although they all conform to state and local requirements for fire extinguisher placement, storage of combustible materials, fire exits, and smoking restrictions.

All stores have sturdy, immovable, fireproof safes which are used to store records of receivables, records of payables, and sufficient cash to carry on business until banking begins (this amount is usually less than $500 in all stores, except for days when the banks are closed; on these days, the amount may exceed $2,000).

All buildings are centrally air-conditioned and heated. The air-conditioning units utilize a cooling tower mounted on the roof of the building, and the units themselves are enclosed and separated from merchandise and any combustible materials. Each unit has a fire extinguisher mounted adjacent to it. Stockrooms are well ventilated, with merchandise arranged away from possible fire hazards, such as heat or electrical wiring.

All entrances are aluminium-framed plate glass doors with a top and bottom deadbolt and double-locking mechanism. The service entrances are steel over oak or pine doors with double-locking deadbolt mechanisms and a 2 × 4 steel-clad crosspiece. All display windows are tempered plate glass and are well lighted all night and on weekends.

In Fairhope, Alabama, the building is free-standing, except for a small jewelry store on one side. This represents no appreciable increase in fire hazard. In Monroeville and Atmore, Alabama, the store buildings are flanked on both sides by buildings of the same general construction. This represents some increased fire hazard, although the buildings are separated by a fire wall. The only real additional hazard is represented by the possibility of water and smoke damage, plus the spread of the fire from one roof to another. Mr. Gwin did not feel that this represented a great deal of hazard, however.

Contents

The merchandise in all three stores is primarily clothing, composed mostly of cotton and synthetic fabrics. There are also shoes, accessories, costume jewelry, and cologne. The clothing is flammable and susceptible to smoke damage. Mr. Gwin felt that since the merchandise is susceptible to water damage, there should be no sprinkler systems in any of the stores because the damage from accidental discharge of a sprinkler system would damage the entire contents of the store.

The fixtures are all of a non-flammable pressboard or masonite construction, although they will ignite at a temperature considerably higher than that of wooden fixtures. The stockroom merchandise (out of season or newly delivered) is stored either in corrugated cardboard boxes or in glass-front storage cases.

Automobiles, Trucks, Airplanes

The company has no automobiles, trucks, or airplanes either owned or leased. Any trips made that require the use of an automobile are made in the personal vehicles of employees making the trip. The company makes no home deliveries.

Equipment

There are three cash registers in each of the stores, along with a receivables posting machine, adding machines, and typewriters. Additionally, each store has an electric price-tag making machine, and an electric steamer to remove wrinkles from stored or newly arrived merchandise. Mr. Gwin felt that none of the equipment listed above would cause more than an inconvenience should it malfunction. All of the cash registers may be manually operated by a hand crank in the event of a power failure, and the likelihood of all the machines in any one store having a mechanical malfunction at the same time is so remote as to be ignored. The functions of all the other machinery can be duplicated by hand.

Inventory

The value of the inventory fluctuates less than 10 percent seasonally, and there are no sharp changes in inventory value.

Values at the three locations are shown in Table A–1. For other values see the financial statements for the company, Appendices A, B, and D.

Accounts Receivable

Records of accounts receivable are kept by hand in all three stores, as are records of payments. The files are kept in a fireproof safe when not in use. There are no computer records or equipment presently in use in any of the stores. Old files are kept for five years in the past, and are stored in boxes in other parts of the stores.

LIABILITY EXPOSURES

Automobiles and Airplanes

The company owns no automobiles or airplanes. When an employee is travelling for the company, he uses his own automobile to provide transportation, and all expenses are reimbursed by the company.

Business Premises and Operations

The floors in all the stores are asphalt tile over a concrete slab, and are usually waxed to a high gloss with a commercial nonslip waxing compound. There has been only one incident of anyone falling in any of the stores, and that involved an elderly lady who had fallen on numerous occasions in other places due to her age.

There are considerable amounts of plate glass in all the stores. Occasionally

TABLE A-1

	Fairhope	Monroeville	Atmore
Inventory	$48,122	$47,367	$39,705
Supplies	400	300	250
Total	$48,522	$47,647	$39,955
Store fixtures and office machinery			
Cost	$47,844	$47,367	$21,560
Less: depreciation	44,736	27,332	15,040
Book Value	$ 3,108	$ 8,820	$ 4,300
Leasehold improvements	0	$14,700	$ 8,600
Less: depreciation	0	5,880	4,300
Book Value	0	$ 8,820	$ 4,300

a small child will run headlong into a plate glass door, not realizing that it is there, but there has been no serious injury or frequent incidence of this to this point in time. The use of glass shelving in some of the fixture displays has been an area of concern for some time. Although no injuries have resulted from broken glass, the shelves are fairly easy to break, and breakage is a more frequent occurrence than is desirable. At this time, consideration is being given to replacing all the shelves outright with plexiglass or wooden shelving.

Care is taken to avoid placing merchandise in such a manner that it could be pulled over or fall onto a customer or a small child. No free-standing fixture is higher than shoulder height, and all fixtures are securely fastened to the floor or weighted in such a manner as to be stable.

There are no public restrooms or water fountains in any of the stores. All fountains are plainly marked "This is NOT a public fountain." Although some customers insist on using both the fountains and the restrooms provided for the employees, the signs are generally effective.

The entrances to stockrooms and storerooms are all plainly marked "Employees Only" and "Do Not Enter." Small children often disregard these notices, but so far there have been no injuries resulting from a child entering a stockroom or storeroom. Thought has been given to locking these doors, but the constant employee traffic through these areas makes this a practical impossibility. No suitable solution has yet been found for this problem.

There are no advertising signs on the outside of any building that could fall and cause any property or personal damage. None of the stores have billboards or roadside signs which could afford any liability of this sort.

Products

Mr. Gwin believes that the company sells no products which could cause personal injury to any of its consumers. He stated that in his opinion the worst possible damage to a consumer would be an allergic reaction to a fabric or a cologne. All merchandise is sold with the express warranty of the manufacturer plus the company's personal guarantee of satisfaction. Cash refunds or credits are given on all merchandise returned for defects. Poorly fitting merchandise may be returned for refund or exchange providing the manufacturer's tags are still intact and there is proof of purchase. Since only brand-name, high quality merchandise is sold by the company, there has been little incidence of defective merchandise. In the past year, though, there has been an increase in the number of returns for defective merchandise, due to the general decline in workmanship of goods. All defective merchandise is returned to the manufacturer for credit against future orders.

The company strives to keep the friendship and good will of the customer, sometimes even to the point of making adjustments where the customer was obviously at fault. The cost of these adjustments are made at the expense of the company.

Contractual

The stores accept no consignment shipments from furriers, jewelers, or clothing designers. All merchandise offered for sale is the property of the company.

Goods in Transit

The stores will not accept delivery on merchandise until it has been inspected in the presence of the common carrier that is responsible for shipping. Claims for damaged merchandise are made directly to the common carrier for damage in transit. All merchandise is shipped F.O.B. the manufacturer's plant, and the company accepts title while the merchandise is in transit. All orders are delivery dated, and if these dates are not met, it is the company's option to accept or return the merchandise. Seasonal merchandise is generally returned if delivery is made more than two weeks after the beginning of the season. Sale and special order merchandise is returned if delivered after the designated sale period. Staple merchandise, such as foundation garments, work clothes, and other nonseasonal merchandise is usually accepted even if delivery is delayed by a considerable period of time.

Employees

The company is liable to the employees for accidents which occur in the line of their responsibility to the company. There have been no incidents of employee injury in the past, and every effort is made to prevent accidents to the employees. Merchandise handling is done with care, and stock men are used to operate the ticket-making machines and steamers and to open shipping crates.

The employees are furnished restrooms, coke machines, and hot coffee on the premises. It is usually the responsibility of the employees in the morning to make coffee before the stores open.

Elevators

There are no elevators of any kind in any of the stores.

PERSONNEL EXPOSURES

Key Men

Mr. Gwin felt that the manager of each store could be considered for key man coverage, but there is enough depth of management talent that each store could continue to function effectively in the absence of any of the managers.

Mr. Gwin believes that since the company is a closely held corporation, with no publicly held stock, there is little need for a buy/sell or cross-purchase agreement. He has personally considered a life policy to cover the amount of the inheritance tax payable in the event of his death, but has not acted so far because he feels that the cost at his age is prohibitive. He also has some doubts about his insurability.

Mr. Gwin's wife, Mrs. E. B. Gwin; son, John M. Gwin; and daughter-in-law, Pamela B. Gwin have cross-willed their ownership interests within the family, so there is no need for a buy/sell agreement or any company held insurance policies to recover the stock in the event of the death of one of the stockholders.

Mr. Gwin stated that all employees, except for the managers of the stores, are "expendable" without any undue hardship on the company. The training for nearly all the positions is approximately four to eight hours on-the-job, so there is no training problem and the positions are easily filled. The company feels, however, that it has an obligation to its employees for long years of service to the firm. Although no formal arrangement exists, the firm is known to "take care of its own." In one particular example, a long-time employee of some twelve years contracted a terminal disease. The firm not only filled in the gaps in his hospitalization where necessary, but also continued his full salary for the duration of his illness, a period of some four months until his death.

INDIRECT LOSS EXPOSURES

Business Interruption

In the event of a business interruption due to fire or hurricane damage, it is expected that six weeks to two months would be the maximum time of interruption. The potential loss from this interruption would be dependent on the time of the fire or hurricane. A fire during the Christmas season, for example, would cause roughly twice the loss that a fire in July would cause.

Assuming that only one store would catch fire in any given time period, the maximum possible business interruption loss would be caused by a fire in the Fairhope store on or about the first week in December. (See Appendix E, page 480.)

Mr. Gwin is of the opinion that business interruption from damage caused by a hurricane is an unlikely occurrence, and possible in the Fairhope store only. There have been "close calls" on several occasions in the past, but so far, no real damage has been caused. Hurricane Camille, which devastated the Mississippi coast in 1969, was within 90 miles of Fairhope. The only threat is wind damage, since the store is high enough off the water to avoid any water damage. Wooden shoring is used to conceal all the windows in the event of a hurricane warning, and the damage from a hurricane would be minimal.

Mr. Gwin stated that he realized that a business interruption, especially during the Christmas season, would be crippling to the corporation in terms of lost profits and continued expenses. However, the idea of business interruption coverage was discarded as being too expensive. It was his opinion that the chances of a business interruption of the magnitude computed was so remote as to be virtually impossible.

Leasehold Interest

All the buildings are leased, and the Atmore and Monroeville stores have done considerable leasehold improving. The leases on all the stores are very valuable to the company, and the Fairhope building, because of its strategic location would be irreplaceable. All leases maintain leasehold in the event of fire. The leasor carries responsibility for fire insurance on the buildings in all cases. Estimated value of the leaseholds are: Fairhope, $50,000; Monroeville, $30,000; and Atmore, $25,000.

INSURANCE PROGRAM

Insurance is currently carried by each store separately. The program for the Fairhope store, presented below, is typical of that existing for other stores. Invitations to bid on the total package of coverage are let by the company to local agents on a store-by-store basis.

(1) Crime Policy. Annual premium, $424.00.
Employee dishonesty
Pilferage, theft, and misrepresentation by employees, either working alone or in collusion with others.
Coverage: $10,000
Loss of money and securities
Robbery, burglary, and accidental loss of legal tender and/or securities within premises.
Coverage: $3,000

Robbery and accidental loss of legal tender and/or securities outside premises.
Coverage: $2,500

Forgery of issued instruments
Check forgery, credit forgery, and illegal credit card usage (not covering the issuance of checks with insufficient funds by legal writer).
Coverage: $10,000

Counterfeit money orders and paper currency
Issuance of counterfeit United States currency, or issuance of counterfeit money order.
Coverage: $1,000

(2) Workers' Compensation. Annual premium, $306.00.
Coverage for occupational accidents and disability
Employer liability limits of coverage: $100,000.
Voluntary medical coverage for each employee
$10,000 per person.

(3) Special Multiperil Policy. Annual Premium, $1,500.
General public liability
Bodily injury to person(s) on premises due to negligence.
Coverage: Bodily injury, $100,000/$300,000
Property damage, $25,000
Plate glass destruction due to negligence.
Coverage: Actual cost of replacement.
Medical payments to persons injured on premises, regardless of negligence.
Coverage: $250.00 per person. $10,000 per accident.

Off premises coverage
Merchandise damaged off premises not more than thirty days.
Coverage: $1,000
Merchandise damaged in transportation under care of salesman.
Coverage: $1,000
Loss of valuable papers through negligence or theft while off premises.
Coverage: $1,000

Merchandise inventory
Damage or destruction of merchandise through natural or man-caused disaster. Reported at cost with allowance for old, obsolete, and unsaleable merchandise.
Coverage: 100 percent
Fixed coverage through destruction by natural or man-caused disaster. Includes debris removal.
Coverage: depreciated cost

(4) Blue Cross/Blue Shield
All regularly employed persons are covered by Blue Cross/Blue Shield for hospitalization and major medical under group policy carried with affiliate companies. Cost is paid by employee.

(5) Group Life Policy
After six months with the company, there is a $2,000 life insurance policy made available to the employee at a premium rate based on salary. The company pays the balance of the premium. An additional $8,000 policy is also made available to be paid entirely by the employee. Cost not available.

TOTAL ANNUAL PREMIUMS, $2,230.00.

QUESTIONS

1. How are the expansion plans of Bedsole-Gwin likely to affect the nature of the risk management task of the corporation?

2. Evaluate the risk management attitudes of Mr. Gwin and the risk and insurance management program of Bedsole-Gwin. What are its strengths and weaknesses?

3. In the light of the new organizational structure, suggest improvements in the risk management program and justify each.

4. Do you agree with the calculation of the potential business interruption loss in the Fairhope store: (See Appendix E.) Compare this estimated loss with the amount of insurance which would be required (at a minimum) in a typical business interruption policy. Discuss.

Bedsole-Gwin
Composite Balance Sheet
December 31, 1972

Assets

Current Assets:

Cash		$182,482.00	
Accounts receivable	$126,465.00		
Less: Bad debt allowance	(8,619.00)		
Net accounts receivable		117,846.00	
Inventory		133,514.00	
Total Current Assets			$433,842.00

Fixed Assets:

Store fixtures	$100,198.00		
Less: Depreciation	(76,509.00)		
Net store fixtures		$ 23,689.00	
Office equipment	$ 16,573.00		
Less: Depreciation	(10,599.00)		
Net office equipment		5,974.00	
Leasehold improvements		23,300.00	
Prepaid insurance		3,168.00	
Total Fixed Assets			56,131.00
Total Assets			$489,973.00

Liabilities and Net Worth

Liabilities:

Trade creditors		$ 12,999.00	
Payroll tax payable		3,783.00	
State tax payable		8,818.00	
Federal and state tax			
Accrued	$(41,863.00)		
Less: Federal and state tax payable	12,601.00		
Net federal and state tax credit		(29,262.00)	
Provision for profit sharing		35,723.00	
Total Liabilities			$ 32,061.00

Net Worth:

Capital stock paid in		$330,000.00	
Surplus undistributed profits		127,912.00	
Total Net Worth			457,912.00
Total Liabilities and Net Worth			$489,973.00

APPENDIX B
Bedsole-Gwin
Composite Profit/Loss Statement, 1972

Gross Sales	$1,459,649.		
Less: Returns and allowances	28,954.		
Net Sales		$1,430,695.	
Cost of Goods Sold		965,735.	
Gross Profit on Sales			$464,960.
Salary Expense:			
Sales personnel	$ 124,706.		
Office personnel	28,078.		
General administrative	27,662.		
Other personnel	18,133.		
Total Salary Expense		$ 198,597.	
Service and General Expense:			
Advertising	20,393.		
Contributions	1,810.		
Travel	1,669.		
Alteration and repair	5,604.		
Store supplies	10,136.		
Employee insurance	4,279.		
Other insurance	8,608.		
Ad Valorem taxes	4,206.		
Social Security taxes	10,560.		
Telephone and telegraph	3,092.		
Postage and stationery	7,739.		
Bad debt allowance	8,066.		
Total Service and General Expense		$ 86,162.	
Plant and Equipment Expense:			
Rent	36,315.		
Utilities	9,894.		
Depreciation allowance	4,014.		
Miscellaneous expense	2,268.		
Total Plant and Equipment Expense		$ 52,491.	
Total Operating Expenses			$337,232.
Net Operating Profit			$127,728.
Other Income	$ 51,455.		
Other Deductions	$ (2,980.)		
Net Additional Income			$ 48,475.
Net Profit Before Taxes			$176,203.

APPENDIX C
Bedsole-Gwin
Percentage Comparison Profit/Loss Statement, 1972

	F'hope	M'ville	Atmore	Total
Gross Sales	102.20	102.10	101.40	102.00
Less Returns and Allowances	(2.20)	(2.10)	(1.40)	(2.00)
Net Sales	100.00	100.00	100.00	100.00
Cost of Goods Sold	66.71	68.36	68.19	67.50
Gross Profit on Sales	33.29	31.64	31.81	32.50
Salaries Expense:				
Sales personnel	8.66	9.60	7.58	8.72
Office personnel	1.88	2.02	2.11	1.96
General administrative	1.56	1.98	2.75	1.93
Other personnel	.76	1.31	2.44	1.27
Total Salaries	12.86	14.91	14.88	13.88
Service and General Expense:				
Advertising	.84	1.62	2.57	1.43
Contributions	.07	.21	.16	.12
Travel	.13	.10	.08	.11
Alterations and repairs	.12	.99	.20	.39
Store supplies	.58	.82	.86	.70
Employee insurance	.21	.34	.45	.30
Other insurance	.53	.68	.68	.60
Ad Valorem taxes	.19	.30	.54	.29
Social Security taxes	.70	.78	.77	.74
Telephone and telegraph	.20	.18	.30	.22
Postage and stationery	.35	.63	.74	.54
Bad debt allowance	.41	.66	.94	.56
Total Service and General	4.33	7.31	8.29	6.00
Plant and Equipment Expense:				
Rent	2.79	2.00	2.75	2.54
Utilities	.45	.90	.99	.69
Depreciation	.11	.28	.68	.28
Miscellaneous	.07	.16	.33	.15
Total Plant and Equipment	3.42	3.34	4.75	3.66
Total Operating Expense	20.61	25.56	27.92	23.54
Net Operating Profit	12.68	6.07	3.88	8.96
Other Income	2.77	4.23	4.65	3.60
Other Deductions	(.41)	–0–	–0–	(.21)
Net Income Before Taxes	15.04	10.30	8.53	12.35

Gross Sales	$730,414.00		
Less: Returns and allowances	15,817.00		
Net Sales		$714,597.00	
Cost of Goods Sold		476,708.00	
Gross Profit on Sales			$237,889.00
Salary Expense:			
Sales personnel	$ 61,884.00		
Office personnel	13,434.00		
General administrative	11,200.00		
Other personnel	5,379.00		
Total Salary Expense		$ 91,897.00	
Service and General Expense:			
Advertising	$ 6,008.00		
Contributions	480.00		
Travel	996.00		
Alteration and repair	844.00		
Store supplies	4,146.00		
Employee insurance	1,504.00		
Other insurance	3,756.00		
Ad Valorem taxes	1,370.00		
Social Security taxes	4,988.00		
Telephone and telegraph	1,452.00		
Postage and stationery	2,882.00		
Bad debt allowance	2,516.00		
Total Service and General Expense		$ 30,942.00	
Plant and Equipment Expense:			
Rent	$ 19,794.00		
Utilities	3,186.00		
Depreciation allowance	800.00		
Miscellaneous expense	659.00		
Total Plant and Equipment Expense		$ 24,439.00	
Total Operating Expense			$147,278.00
Net Operating Profit			$ 90,611.00
Other Income	$ 19,838.00		
Other Deductions	(2,980.00)		
Net Additional Income			$ 16,858.00
Net Profit Before Taxes			$107,469.00

Appendix E
Bedsole-Gwin
Computation of Potential Business
Interruption Loss
Fairhope, Alabama

Estimated profit loss for six weeks' period from December 1 to January 15 of store operation equals 20 percent of the years' projected profits before taxes.

$$.20 \times \$107{,}469.00 = \$21{,}494.00$$

Estimated continued business expenses during a six-week business interruption from December 1 to January 15:

Office and Personnel Expenses	$ 9,750.00
General Administrative Expense	1,400.00
Continued Workmen's Compensation	175.00
Other Insurance Payments	500.00
FCIA Payments	700.00
Continued Rental Payments	2,475.00
Total Continued Expenses	$15,000.00
Estimated Lost Profits	21,494.00
Total Business Interruption Loss for the Period December 1 through January 15:	$36,494.00

Case B

Fuqua Industries, Inc. (A)

In March 1973, Mr. Robert Spencer, Insurance Manager and Vice-President of Fuqua Industries, was contemplating the organizational structure for risk management within his company. Mr. Spencer had just been promoted to the position of Vice-President, having served formerly as Insurance Manager for the company. He felt that control of losses was one of the most important objectives of his work and was considering ways by which losses could be further reduced. He was considering whether the loss control policies of McDonough Power, one of Fuqua's subsidiaries, should be applied generally throughout the company.

BACKGROUND

Fuqua industries is a holding company for some 22 subsidiaries whose activities are mainly in four major divisions: (1) leisure time, (2) transportation, (3) shelter, and (4) agribusiness. Its total sales in 1972 approximated $430 million, and its net operating income was $18 million. (See Appendices A, B, and C.) The corporation manufactures sporting goods, agricultural equipment, marine products, lawnmowers, and snowmobiles. It is also engaged in

theatre and broadcasting operations, owns a transportation company, and is involved in real estate and housing.

The McDonough Power Equipment Company, located in McDonough, Georgia, manufactures lawnmowers and other lawn and gardening equipment. Sales of McDonough products are national, sold through a nationwide network of distributors and 6,000 franchised retail dealers. McDonough products are not exported, although other Fuqua companies are engaged in international business. The McDonough power plant employs about 500 hourly paid employees and 80 salaried personnel.

ORGANIZATION FOR RISK MANAGEMENT

Fuqua's home office organizational structure is considered to be quite formal. Each subsidiary operates as a profit center and is responsible for its own activities, with only modest coordination and direction from the home office. Insurance is an exception to this general rule, however, because most of the insurance activity is consolidated and controlled at the home office. The home office staff consists of only 18 executives. The organizational chart for the company is given in Figure 1.

Mr. Spencer indicated that he had the authority to go directly to any executive in the company concerning any matter relating to insurance or risk management. He reports directly to the Senior Vice President, but has access to the Chairman of the company, Mr. J. B. Fuqua, and the President, Mr. C. L. Patrick. He is equal in rank to the other major executives, such as the Vice-President of Finance, the Comptroller, and the Vice-President of Operations. He has one assistant, Mr. Bill Brown, two secretaries, and four claims people.

When Fuqua Industries acquires a new subsidiary all insurance matters are centralized as soon as possible. Mr. Spencer estimated that centralization has saved the company at least 50 percent of what would have otherwise been the cost of commercial insurance. The company spends approximately $7.5 million a year on insurance and self-insurance, including the cost of operating the insurance department. This figure does not include the cost of all the loss prevention in the subsidiaries, however. The only exception to the general rule of centralization is that the Inter-State Motor Freight Company, one of the largest subsidiaries of Fuqua Industries, performs its own day-to-day administration of its own insurance program, but is supervised by the home office insurance staff.

Fuqua Industries' international operations consist of two plants and a motor freight line in Canada and three plants in Mexico. In those locations the various brokerage firms serve the insurance needs of the company.

Mr. Spencer deals indirectly with the presidents of the various subsidiaries in all insurance matters. Every three years all commercial insurance is put out for competitive bidding, depend-

ing on market conditions. In this activity, Mr. Spencer deals directly with the insurers, negotiating commissions and brokerage fees which will be charged.

The company employs two brokers. One broker handles a premium volume of approximately $2,000,000 and another broker approximately $1.5 million. Mr. Spencer believes that each broker, thus, has enough premium volume to justify giving considerable amounts of attention to the Fuqua insurance problems.

Fuqua Industries had no captive insurer. This matter had been investigated, but it had been decided so far, that it was not advantageous. Mr. Spencer looks upon the insurance department as strictly a service center, not a profit center. However, management is informed regarding the estimated annual savings which the department "produces."

Fuqua Industires uses a considerable amount of self-insurance. Its workers' compensation insurance is completely self-administered. The property insurance program employs an aggregate deductible of $100,000. The top limit on any one loss is $22,000,000. The total value of all property insured is approximately $140,000,000.

Mr. Spencer anticipates that self-insurance will be used more and more each year. The company does not maintain a self-insurance fund, but the $100,000 until it is used up. Once the sessed to all the subsidiaries. As losses occur these are charged against the $100,000 until it is used up. Once the $100,000 is used up the commercial insurance cover attaches. The $100,000 is not invested in securities, but is kept in banks as compensating balances against company loans.

Each subsidiary is charged a certain amount of money for insurance, ac-

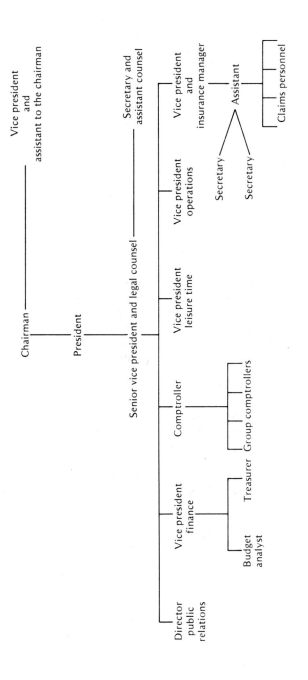

FIGURE 1.

cording to its losses. The "premiums" correspond as closely as possible to the losses reported by each subsidiary. For example, in workers' compensation the subsidiaries are charged a manual premium which is equal to 25 percent of the standard (commercial) premium charged for this insurance. If the subsidiary's losses justify it, rebates are made. Mr. Spencer believes this preserves incentives for the individual plant managers to exercise care in loss prevention.

Pension plans are decentralized according to the needs of each individual subsidiary. Mr. Spencer, however, is considering the possibility of centralizing the pension plans, too. All group life and health is commercial insurance. All claims are paid from the home office. Premiums have been negotiated so that the insurer's overhead (retention) has been reduced to only 4 percent. Thus, about 96 percent of the premiums are returned to Fuqua in loss payments. Because of this factor no dividends are paid upon the group life and health insurance contracts.

The company uses a long-term disability plan, covering salaried workers. This plan has a 90-day waiting period, and restores 60 percent of a person's salary up through age 65. The plan is integrated with benefits for workers' compensation and social security. It offers 24-hour occupational and non-occupational coverage. Mr. Spencer feels that the cost of this plan is quite reasonable and is equal to about .05 percent of payroll.

LOSS CONTROL

Mr. Spencer believes that communication is the largest problem in the organizational strucure of the loss control and insurance program in Fuqua Industries. The company attempts to secure copies of claims monthly from each subsidiary. These claims are computerized and a monthly print-out obtained. Copies are sent to each subsidiary monthly. Mr. Spencer and his assistant, Mr. Brown, travel extensively to each subsidiary, visiting each one at least once and sometimes two or three times yearly. On the trips to the subsidiaries they carry with them a copy of the claims record for the preceding months. Investigation is made as to the reason for claims and other facts surrounding them. One of the reasons for developing their own claims information is the difficulty of securing prompt loss claims information from the insurers. The 22 subsidiaries are located in 26 states at 70 different locations.

Mr. Spencer indicated no particular problems had been encountered yet with the administrators of the Occupational Safety and Health Act of the federal government. The main reason for this is that most of the work of Fuqua Industries is in light industry.

Mr. Spencer's authority is advisory in nature. For example, if he felt that a given plant needed a sprinkler system, he only has the power to advise the president to secure one, and not to order him to do it. Mr. Spencer felt, however, that informal pressure could be applied to the subsidiary president to carry out the advice. Mr. Spencer indicated that occasionally he recommends that given individuals be discharged for failing to carry out risk management policies.

The company does not employ independent agencies to perform loss prevention services, it places considerable emphasis on loss prevention. The company requires that monthly safety meetings be held in each subsidiary and a copy of the minutes be sent to corporate headquarters for inspection. At these meetings the topics for discussion include safety, housecleaning problems, expense allowances, etc. Two or three times a year there is a plant meeting of all employees on safety. Mr. Spencer feels that this policy has paid off in reducing loss claims and in reducing the cost of insurance and self-insurance.

Mr. Spencer indicated that the company did not carry product recall insurance in case it is necessary to recall products to correct safety defects. Neither do they carry officers' and directors' liability insurance, a risk which is assumed. The company has three outside directors.

Mr. Spencer indicated that he attempted to maintain a close rapport with all of the people in the subsidiaries, including plant foremen. Often he is able to obtain directly from such individuals needed information on losses, because of this personal contact. Few written reports are used. Most reports are made by personal contact or by telephone. When written reports are used, they are usually limited to one-page memos. Mr. Spencer feels that this policy is a good one, because it cuts down on paper work.

LOSS PREVENTION AT McDONOUGH POWER COMPANY

Mr. Spencer feels that one of Fuqua's subsidiaries, McDonough Power Company, offers a good illustration of how loss prevention and loss control is handled in Fuqua Industries.

McDonough Power Company produces primarily lawn equipment, such as riding and push-type mowers marketed under the brand name of "Snapper." It is the opinion of the management that their most significant financial losses will occur from suits arising out of product liability. To pro-

tect themselves they carry heavy liability coverage, and also design the mowers to be as safe as practical. The mower decks are strong enough to stop thrown objects and are low enough to keep feet from the blades. The opening which allows cut grass to escape is designed in such a way as to partially deflect and arrest thrown objects. In spite of this, accidents still happen. For example, recently an eight-year-old cut off his foot while using a Snapper riding mower. Mr. Spencer believed that it will cost the company between $8,000 and $10,000 in compensation. Another product safety problem arises with the occasional breakage of mower blades. This problem has been partially solved by changing to softer steel in the blades.

Most power machines are equipped with safety devices which help decrease the danger to the operator. Employees are required to wear safety goggles and steel-reinforced shoes; all routes which forklifts follow in the plant are well marked with painted lines. This precaution helps create employee awareness when they are in traffic lanes. A periodic inspection is made to insure that proper ventilation of the work area is maintained; all machines that produce loud noises above a certain frequency level are soundproofed. A close check is made weekly with a sound measuring device to help control potential auditory damage.

The plant is a large fire-resistant brick- and steel-structured building all on one level. There is no sprinkler system on the premises, but water hoses and fire extinguishers are located at strategic points throughout the plant. All areas where there is increased danger of fire are especially fireproofed. The painting center, for example, is completely sealed from the rest of the factory and uses only fire-resistant, water-based paint.

The grounds at McDonough are protected with a 10-foot fence which surrounds the plant, an alarm system, and a 24-hour guard and watch service. It is believed that this watch service facilitates the detection and control of small fires before they grow.

The management at McDonough recognizes and accepts its responsibility for promoting the safety and well-being of their employees. The following guidelines were developed to help further this end.

I. Responsibility
   A. All management personnel shall accept responsibility for the safety and well-being of employees under their supervision.
   B. Management shall be responsible for providing a safe working environment for all employees.
   C. A safety coordinator shall be appointed.

II. Facilities
   A. Adequate medical and first-aid facilities shall be provided.
   B. Adequate fire protection shall be provided.

III. Activities
   A. Periodic safety meetings shall be conducted.
   B. Periodic inspections shall be conducted in all operations and prompt corrective action shall be taken when unsafe conditions or unsafe actions are noted.
   C. All accidents shall be investigated in order to determine the cause and the action which should be taken to prevent recurrence.

IV. Education
   A continuous program of safety education shall be carried on, to create and maintain the interest of all employees in the prevention of accidents. The use of safety bulletins, posters, films, safety incentives, etc., are recommended.

In carrying out the guidelines for the safety program, management follows several practices: (1) Safety meetings are held every month with risk engineers and all foremen present. Each foreman is quizzed as to why an injured man hurt his foot or cut his arm. Each accident is reviewed with the foreman under whom the victim worked. These men are then told what the accident cost and instructed in means whereby they can prevent future recurrences.

(2) Inspections for unsafe conditions are carried out once a week. Two men, one from the insurance department of Fuqua Industries and one foreman from the plant make a tour of the facility. Each safety hazard is noted and appropriate action taken to correct it. Every week there is a different foreman on the tour. This change is made in order to get a fresh perspective of the hazards and new suggestions to solve them.

(3) When an accident occurs the foreman in charge, as soon as possible, must fill out a written report of the incident. They are required to submit written instead of verbal reports because it better impresses upon the foreman's mind the cause and impact of the injury.

Mr. Spencer feels that McDonough Power Company is not as safe for the employees as it could be. However, he realizes that there is a fine line between safety and hurting production efficiency severely. He expressed hope that a medium between the two has been achieved at McDonough.

All the property at the McDonough Equipment plant is insured at actual cash value, except computer equipment (which is leased). Because there is no insurance coverage provided on accounts receivable, computer tapes, or valuable records, a grandfather computer tape is maintained and stored off the plant premises. This tape is updated weekly and then returned to storage. The records kept on the premises are filed in metal filing cabinets. There is very little money kept on the premises and the loss of money and securities presents a very low loss exposure.

QUESTIONS

1. Should the insurance manager's authority be line or staff? How would you characterize Mr. Spencer's authority in this case? Does he have sufficient power to achieve his goals?

2. Analyze the advantages and disadvantages of centralized authority for risk management in Fuqua Industries. Would you believe that as the firm grows in the future this type of organization will have more or fewer advantages? Why?

3. Assess the effectiveness of organization for loss control and loss prevention activities at McDonough Power Equipment. Can the company afford to spend more on such things as loss prevention? Should McDonough Power Equipment's policies be applied generally throughout the corporation?

4. Which theory of loss prevention, human engineering or physical engineering, do you think is most effective in the long run? Which do you feel receives most emphasis at Fuqua? Discuss.

5. Why does Mr. Spencer feel that communication is so important? Suggest ways by which he may make improvements.

6. Is Fuqua's emphasis on loss control consistent with its use of insurance deductibles?

APPENDIX A

STATEMENT OF CONSOLIDATED INCOME
Fuqua Industries, Inc. & Subsidiaries
Years Ended December 31,
(In $ Thousands)

	Actual 1971	Estimated 1972	Forecast 1973
Net Sales and Revenues	$366,557	$430,000	$484,000
Operating Costs and Expenses	331,072	385,600	431,600
Interest Expense	8,006	8,700	10,000
Total Costs and Expenses	339,078	394,300	441,600
Operating Income Before Taxes	27,479	35,700	42,400
Provision for Income Taxes	13,477	17,700	21,000
Net Operating Income	14,002	18,000	21,400
Extraordinary Item	(3,500)[1]	—	—
Net Income	$ 10,502	$ 18,000	$ 21,400
Earnings Per Common and Common Equivalent Share			
(8,541,000 shares in 1971, 9,500,000 shares in 1972 and 10,000,000 shares[2] in 1973)			
Net Operating Income	$1.59	$1.85	$2.09[2]
Extraordinary Item	(.41)	—	—
Net Income	$1.18	$1.85	$2.09[2]
Earnings Per Common Share Assuming Full Dilution			
(9,731,000 shares in 1971, 9.870,000 shares in 1972 and 10,000,000 shares[2] in 1973)			
Net Operating Income	$1.44	$1.80	$2.09[2]
Extraordinary Item	(.36)	—	—
Net Income	$1.08	$1.80	$2.09[2]

[1] Loss on the sale of a business.

[2] Earnings per share forecast for 1973 does not include shares which may be issued in either stock dividends or in acquisitions.

APPENDIX B
CONSOLIDATED BALANCE SHEET
Fuqua Industries, Inc./December 31,
(In $ Thousands)

	1971	Estimated 1972
ASSETS		
Current Assets		
Cash	$ 13,706	$ 10,200
Accounts Receivable — Net	46,685	57,000
Inventories[1]	75,939	89,000
Prepaid Expenses	2,838	4,000
Total Current Assets	139,168	160,200
Notes Receivable and Other Assets	37,002	36,900
Property, Plant and Equipment — at Cost	158,916	206,166
less: Accumulated Depreciation	(60,145)	(75,166)
Property, Plant and Equipment — Net	98,771	131,000
Motor Carrier and Broadcast Operating Rights	18,497	18,300
Excess of Cost over Net Assets of Businesses Acquired	23,177	24,400
Total Assets	$316,615	$370,800
LIABILITIES AND STOCKHOLDERS' EQUITY		
Current Liabilities		
Accounts Payable and Accrued Liabilities	$ 45,788	$ 58,400
Notes Payable and Current Portion of Long-Term Debt	30,940	34,000
Total Current Liabilities	76,728	92,400
Deferred Income Taxes and Other Deferred Items	12,595	15,600
Capital Funds:		
Long-Term Debt — Parent	31,382	35,000
Long-Term Debt — Subsidiaries	28,834	43,000
Subordinated Debt	45,548	37,800
Stockholders' Equity	121,528	147,000
Total Capital Funds	227,292	262,800
Total Liabilities and Stockholders' Equity	$316,615	$370,800

[1] Inventories include $31 million in 1972 and $28 million in 1971 related to real estate operations.

APPENDIX C
SUMMARY OF OPERATIONS
Fuqua Industries, Inc./Years Ended December 31,
($ Millions)

SALES & REVENUES	1967	1968	1969	1970	1971	Estimated 1972	Forecast 1973
Leisure Time							
Snowmobiles & Lawnmowers	13.9	21.4	30.9	36.9	45.8	56.0	68.0
Sporting Goods	15.9	19.8	24.1	28.3	31.4	37.0	39.0
Marine Products	38.4	49.7	49.5	29.7	34.0	41.0	48.0
Entertainment	24.6	24.5	25.0	26.9	27.1	38.0	45.0
Photographic Finishing	14.1	17.0	19.6	18.1	17.9	21.0	23.0
Total Leisure	106.9	132.5	149.1	139.9	156.2	193.0	223.0
Transportation	66.5	72.0	97.5	113.2	131.0	140.0	147.0
Shelter[1]	26.0	29.7	37.3	39.4	41.6	61.0	74.0
Agri-business	18.1	20.9	21.0	28.9	33.0	36.0	40.0
Total Continuing Operations[2]	217.5	255.1	304.9	321.4	361.8	430.0	484.0
Add: Discontinued Operations	40.8	40.8	43.7	28.5	6.1	—	—
Less: Restatements of Businesses Purchased	36.7	40.8	11.0	5.5	1.3	—	—
Total Sales and Revenues	223.2	255.1	337.6	344.4	366.6	430.0	484.0

APPENDIX C (cont.)
SUMMARY OF OPERATIONS
Fuqua Industries, Inc./Years Ended December 31,
($ Millions)

EARNINGS	1967	1968	1969	1970	1971	Estimated 1972	% of Total	Compound Annual Growth Rate %	Forecast 1973
Leisure Time									
Snowmobiles & Lawnmowers	2.4	4.7	5.8	6.2	7.3	9.7	22%	32%	11.4
Sporting Goods	1.1	2.0	2.9	3.2	3.1	4.1	9	30	4.1
Boats & Boat Trailers	1.0	3.6	3.3	.3	.6	3.3	7	27	4.5
Entertainment	2.5	3.2	4.5	4.2	4.5	6.4	14	16	6.8
Photographic Finishing	1.6	1.8	1.4	1.0	1.7	2.5	6	9	2.9
Total Leisure	8.6	15.3	17.9	14.9	17.2	26.0	58	24	29.7
Transportation	3.6	4.3	6.0	4.5	9.2	10.0	22	23	10.0
Shelter[1]	.3	2.0	5.9	6.2	4.7	2.8	5	56	5.5
Agri-business	3.1	3.0	1.5	3.1	5.3	6.7	15	17	6.9
Total Continuing Operations[2]	15.6	24.6	31.3	28.7	36.4	45.5	100%	23%	52.1
Add: Discontinued Operations	1.7	1.6	.5	1.6	(.8)	(.1)			—
Less: Unallocated Corporate Expenses and Corporate Interest	.9	1.7	3.9	6.2	7.9	9.7			9.7
Less: Restatements of Businesses Purchased	1.2	2.7	.3	1.0	.2	—			—
Income Before Income Taxes	15.2	21.8	27.6	23.1	27.5	35.7		19	42.4
Income Taxes	7.0	11.0	13.6	11.5	13.5	17.7			21.0
Net Operating Income	8.2	10.8	14.0	11.6	14.0	18.0		17%	21.4

[1] Does not include Brigadier Industries since acquisition had not been completed.

[2] Includes all continuing companies for all periods regardless of date of acquisition except that Gulf States Theatres is included only for the periods since June 1, 1972. Gulf States Theatres was only a part of a business complex, and accurate data for prior periods on the theatres is not available.

Case C

Fuqua Industries, Inc. (B)

On January 1, 1976, Fuqua Industries, Inc. began operating an offshore captive insurance company under the name Fuqua Insurance Company Limited. The purpose of the captive was to provide coverage for the liability risk of the subsidiary companies of Fuqua Industries. This move occurred as a reaction to drastic rate increases by property-liability insurers who had suffered large underwriting losses in 1975. Mr. Robert Spencer, vice-president and manager of risk and insurance for Fuqua, was confident that the captive would result in considerable long-run savings to the company.

BACKGROUND

Fuqua Industries, a holding company for about 16 subsidiaries, had net sales in 1974 of $550,719,000 and net operating income of $9,556,000. The corporation manufactures sporting goods, lawn and garden equipment, housing, and marine products. It engages in theater and broadcasting operations and runs a transportation system that extends over 38 states and Canada.

Fuqua employs approximately 15,000 people and operates in 70 locations within the continental United States. Unions exist only within the transportation division and there have been no recent interruptions or strikes.

As of 1976 the company had no international operations; however, plans existed to expand the operations of one subsidiary, the Colorcraft Corporation, into West Germany. Colorcraft engaged in photofinishing and hoped to compete in Europe by offering faster service than was currently available.

LIABILITY INSURANCE

Fuqua maintained the following liability coverages: Primary insurance of general and automotive liability with a million dollar combined single limit of $1,000,-000; excess coverage in the form of an umbrella with dollar limits of $50,000,-000. Deductibles applying were: general liability $50,000 per occurrence; auto liability $25,000 private passenger autos; and $50,000 trucks and tractors. Applicable annual aggregate limits were: other than truck lines $500,000; truck lines (Interstate Motor Freight Co.) $900,000.

Annual premium paid under Fuqua's property-liability policies were as follows:[1]

Workers' compensation (self-insured) — manual premium	$1,250,000
Excess of $100,000 per occurrence insured	80,500
Insured (fronted by commercial insurer and reinsured by the captive)	325,000
General and auto liability (fronted by the commercial insurer and reinsured by the captive)	950,000
Employee dishonesty, depositors' forgery	12,005
Umbrella liability	72,000
Directors' and officers' liability	18,500
Aircraft liability and hull	22,971
Business travel accident	14,500
Property — real and personal	375,000
Boiler and machinery	35,000
Total	$3,155,476

FORMATION OF THE CAPTIVE

Underwriting and investment losses in 1974 and 1975 led commercial property-liability insurers generally to greatly increase premiums. Mr. Spencer determined that in order to maintain existing insurance programs, it would be necessary to pay an additional $700,000 in premium annually. In his opinion Fuqua's loss experience did not justify such an increase. At that point Mr. Spencer directed his broker, Johnson and Higgins, to study the feasibility of forming an offshore captive to be

[1] Automobile physical damage is self-insured and an annual expense of $350,000 is incurred. Total annual expenditures of about $7,500,000 are made for losses and risk management items, of which $3,155,476 are for commercial insurance.

domiciled in Bermuda. The findings indicated that after set-up expenses were met, a cost savings of over $700,000 could be realized, i.e., captive formation would permit continuation of existing insurance programs with no increase in premium. On this basis the captive was formed. It was capitalized at $150,000, with $30,000 held in Bermuda and $120,000 held at the Chemical Bank in New York as a compensating balance for Fuqua Industry's loans.

Currently, the captive is only involved in the liability areas of workers' compensation, general liability, and automobile liability. Fuqua's workers' compensation was already self-insured, except in 13 states. Coverage in these 13 states is put into the captive program. The fronting company for the captive is United Insurance Co. Under this arrangement United receives $309,000 for workers' compensation coverage, keeping 9.8 percent ($30,282) for reinsurance and 17.2 percent ($47,939) for ceding commissions, taxes and assessments. This leaves a balance of $230,779 to be remitted to the captive, Fuqua Insurance Company Limited, in Bermuda. United retains 5 percent of each loss and reinsures 95 percent with Fuqua Insurance Company Limited to $100,000 per occurrence. Any loss in excess of $100,000 is reinsured by the United. Thus, the captive is to accept $95,000 of liability for each occurrence, and 95 percent of all workers' compensation loss.

The general liability and automobile liability coverages are handled with different retention limits. United issues liability policies as needed with a $1 million combined single limit. All liability coverages have a $50,000 deductible. Fuqua pays United $950,000. United keeps 10 percent for reinsurance and 17.2 percent for ceding commission, taxes, and assessments. The balance is remitted to Fuqua Insurance Company Limited in Bermuda. The captive keeps 5 percent participation and reinsures the rest. The breakdown of reinsurance premium is as shown in Table 20C–1.

Companies A, B, C, and D are all large commercial insurers. With the exception of Interstate Motor Freight, all losses are handled by the United. Interstate will continue to handle its own losses within the deductible area. All losses within $50,000 are sent to Fuqua Industries headquarters monthly for reimbursement. Losses that exceed the $50,000 retention level will be submitted to Fuqua Insurance Company, Limited for collection from its reinsurers.

Although Fuqua's captive was

TABLE 20C-1

Percent of Loss Shared Above Retention	Insurance Company	Annual Premium
5%	Fuqua, Ltd.	$ 47,500
10	United	95,000
45	Co. A	427,000
10	Co. B	95,000
20	Co. C	190,000
10	Co. D	95,000
100%		$950,000

domiciled offshore, it insures risks arising within the United States. Mr. Spencer did not favor a domestic captive for three reasons: (1) the required capitalization for a domestic captive was much greater (Colorado the only state in 1976 with special legislation regarding the formation of captive insurers, required minimum capital of $500,000); (2) domestic captives are subject to much more stringent regulation of investments and reserves than offshore captives, and (3) profits of domestic captives are subject to immediate taxation at standard corporate income tax rates.

On the other hand, the Bermuda captive was capitalized at less than Colorado requirements. It possesses greater underwriting flexibility and freedom from state regulation. It enjoys a tax deferral on premium income unless profits are repatriated or unless more than 5 percent of total premiums are derived from domestic risks.

It was Mr. Spencer's observation that the most significant cost advantage related to the captive was that its formation permitted direct negotiation with the reinsurance market. This placed Mr. Spencer in a position to bargain for rates that were much more favorable than those offered by domestic commercial insurers.

Fuqua's financial results for 1972 are presented in Appendices A–D.

QUESTIONS

1. In your opinion, was Fuqua's captive established on a sound basis?

2. Evaluate Mr. Spencer's rationale for establishing the captive.

Losses and Premiums
Interstate Motor Freight System, Subsidiary of Fuqua Industries
6/30/75

Losses within $25,000 self-insured retention

Year	No. of Accidents	Paid	Expense	Reserve	Total
1/73–1/74	1602	339,721	89,200	140,544	569,465
1/74–1/75	1495	265,252	57,832	245,722	568,806
1/75–6/30/75	622	84,377	10,494	154,841	249,712

Prior to 1/1/73, Interstate was on a different accounting system plus their insurance was excess of $5000 B.I. and $10,000 P.D. However, the following information should be helpful.

Year	Gross Revenue	Self-insured Cost	Cost per 100 Revenue
5/70–71	$ 92 million	$413,000	.45/100
5/71–72	103 million	428,000	.42/100
5/72–1/73	73 million	302,000	.41/100

APPENDIX B
Group Performance — Fuqua Industries

The following table shows Fuqua's sales,
revenues and pre-tax earnings by operating groups.

In Millions	1972	1973	1974	1975	1976
Net Sales and Revenues(a):					
Manufacturing and distribution:					
Lawn and garden	$ 36.0	$ 54.9	$ 69.5	$ 51.0	$ 62.5
Sporting goods	31.0	49.7	87.4	90.0	93.3
Shelter	41.9	55.0	55.6	43.1	53.8
Service:					
Entertainment	37.2	46.5	52.3	57.9	46.6
Photofinishing	21.8	26.2	35.5	43.7	52.1
Transportation	140.7	156.6	181.6	194.0	226.8
Total Current Operations	308.6	388.9	481.9	479.7	535.1
Businesses not part of future operations(b)	40.4	47.6	40.6	26.0	.7
Total	$349.0	$436.5	$522.5	$505.7	$535.8
Pre-Tax Earnings(a):					
Manufacturing and distribution(c):					
Lawn and garden	$ 8.9	$ 13.2	$ 11.1	$ 8.8	$ 14.8
Sporting goods	4.3	6.8	5.2	2.4	8.3
Shelter	3.7	5.4	1.8	.8	1.5
Service:					
Entertainment	6.2	6.4	8.3	7.6	7.2
Photofinishing	2.4	3.3	4.0	4.8	4.7
Transportation	10.0	9.7	5.9	(1.1)	8.3
Total Current Operations	35.5	44.8	36.3	23.3	44.8
Businesses not part of future operations(b)	1.9	3.1	(1.0)	(4.5)	(.4)
Unallocated corporate interest and expenses	(9.9)	(11.7)	(15.8)	(25.5)d	(16.2)
Total	$ 27.5	$ 36.2	$ 19.5	$ (6.7)	$ 28.2

(a) Consolidated continuing operations before income taxes, restated for discontinued operations.

(b) Includes results of operations, for the years indicated, of businesses sold and results of real estate development activities substantially completed in 1975.

(c) Most companies in these operating groups were changed to LIFO accounting for inventories in 1974. Income was reduced in 1974 by this change and prior results are not restated.

(d) Includes losses and write-downs described in Notes to Consolidated Financial Statements.

APPENDIX C
Consolidated Balance Sheet
FUQUA INDUSTRIES, INC. AND SUBSIDIARIES
December 31,
In thousands

ASSETS	1976	1975
Current Assets		
Cash	$ 24,640	$ 22,624
Receivables (due Fuqua on credit sales; less allowances for doubtful accounts of $2,361 in 1976 and $4,007 in 1975)	68,105	68.123
Inventories (cost of raw materials, products in process, and finished products)	56,188	65,734
Refundable income taxes	—	5,082
Prepaid expenses (operating expenses which will benefit the coming year)	4,966	4,068
Total Current Assets	153,899	165,631
Notes Receivable (due Fuqua on sales of land and businesses; less allowances for doubtful notes of $4,504 in 1976 and $5,976 in 1975)	13,304	12,636
Investment Property (land and property held for investment)	23,013	17,635
Other Assets (other long-term investments)	10,052	8,476
Property, Plant and Equipment (assets used for the production of products and services)		
Land	15,621	14,288
Buildings and improvements	51,761	57,027
Terminals and improvements — Interstate	22,807	19,359
Trucks, tractors, trailers — Interstate	75,615	71,199
Machinery and equipment	60,142	61,016
Less allowances for depreciation (deduction)	(91,503)	(85,429)
	134,443	137,460
Operating Rights (costs allocated to licenses and operating rights of Fuqua's motor carrier and broadcasting business)	24,912	21,996
Excess of Cost over Net Assets of Business Acquired (including product names, reputation, earning capacity, etc.)	32,159	33,542
TOTAL ASSETS	$391,782	$397,376

APPENDIX C (*cont.*)

LIABILITIES AND STOCKHOLDERS' EQUITY	1976	1975
Current Liabilities		
Accounts payable, accrued expenses and other current liabilities (amounts due currently for materials, services and other expenses)	$ 61,924	$ 55,575
Federal and state income taxes (amounts due currently for income taxes)	12,315	4,579
Subordinated debt	—	22,000
Notes payable and current portion of long-term debt (borrowed funds due within one year)	26,126	24,170
Total Current Liabilities	100,365	106,324
Deferred Income Taxes (Income taxes payable in future years)	15,970	15,658
Long-Term Debt (borrowed funds)		
Parent	41,660	53,359
Interstate	36,209	35,078
Other subsidiaries	15,419	17,865
Subordinated Debt — Parent (borrowed funds subordinate to other debt)	36,283	36,693
Stockholders' Equity (net worth)		
Preference Stock	2,267	2,267
Common Stock	9,851	9,835
Additional capital	54,391	57,965
Retained earnings	92,647	80,805
Treasury stock (deduction)	(13,280)	(18,473)
Total Stockholders' Equity	145,876	132,399
Litigation and Contingencies		
TOTAL LIABILITIES AND STOCKHOLDERS' EQUITY	$391,782	$397,376

Appendix D
FUQUA INDUSTRIES, INC. AND SUBSIDIARIES
Years ended December 31,
In thousands except per share amounts

	1976	1975
Net Sales and Revenues (amounts charged for products and services)	$535,851	$505,719
Costs and Expenses:		
Costs of products and services sold (includes materials, labor, plant overhead, depreciation, etc.)	420,828	403,995
Selling, general and administrative (costs of marketing, management, and depreciation)	74,543	79,734
Interest expense (cost of borrowed funds)	12,239	17,072
Total Costs and Expenses	507,610	500,801
	28,241	4,918
Loss on Disposal of Businesses and Write-Down of Certain Assets	—	11,662
Income (Loss) from Consolidated Continuing Operations before Income Taxes	28,241	(6,744)
Income Taxes (Credit)	14,706	(2,093)
Income (Loss) From Consolidated Continuing Operations	13,535	(4,651)
(Loss) from Unconsolidated Subsidiary	—	(3,939)
Income (Loss) From Continuing Operations	13,535	(8,590)
Discontinued Operations, net of Income Taxes:		
Income (Loss) from operations	33	(9,037)
Gain (Loss) on disposal of business	75	—
	108	(9,037)
Net Income (Loss)	$ 13,643	$(17,627)
Earnings (Loss) per Share of Common Stock:		
Income (Loss) from continuing operations	$ 1.51	$ (1.05)
Discontinued operations	.01	(1.06)
Net Income (Loss)	$ 1.52	$ (2.11)

Case D

Kaiser Aluminum & Chemical Corporation

ORGANIZATIONAL CONSIDERATIONS IN RISK MANAGEMENT

The Organization Planning Department, at the request of the vice-president was asked to come up with recommendations, preferably within the existing organizational structure, which would make possible a more efficient discharging of Kaiser Aluminum & Chemical Corporation's risk managament function.

While Kaiser Aluminum & Chemical Corporation had undergone rapid expansion both in the United States and abroad, and while this expansion was accompanied by repeated examination of and changes in the organizational structure, it was felt that the risk function had not been considered in other than piece-meal fashion. Lines of authority were not clearly established, and with the scattering of operations and the increasingly large investment in widely disposed assets, the problem was definitely in need of attention.

The vice-president made his request of the Organization Planning Department after reviewing the main conflicting views in the literature of the field. He was especially interested, for example, in the ideas of one scholar, to the effect that:

. . . the proper place for the discussion of insurance, at least so far as insurance of capital is concerned, is in the department of production.[1]

He was fully aware of other conflicts; the economies of centralization in risk management and the importance of personal contact and communications with the operating divisions. He, therefore, expected the manager of the Organization Planning Department to report on these matters quite fully, as supporting data to any recommendations.

Kaiser Aluminum & Chemical Corporation's early history started with the formation of Todd-California Shipbuilding Corporation in 1940 to build World War II cargo vessels. It was the creation of Henry J. Kaiser and his associates in the construction industry.

In 1941, under the new company name of the Permanente Metals Corporation, the firm entered the light metals industry to produce magnesium using the carbothermic process. In 1942, a

[1] A. H. Willett, *The Economic Theory of Risk and Insurance* (Homewood, Ill. Richard Irwin, 1951), p. 88.

Reprinted from Stanford business cases, 1962, with permission of the publishers, Stanford University Graduate School of Business, © 1962, by the Board of Trustees, of the Leland Stanford Junior University.

second magnesium plant was built and it employed the silicothermic process. Permanente "Goop," a secret magnesium paste which went into incendiary bombs was developed by the corporation during World War II.

Following termination of hostilities, an entry was made into the primary aluminum industry and by 1960 the corporation was producing about 24 percent of the primary aluminum output of the United States, ranking as the third largest domestic producer of primary aluminum (See financial data in Exhibit 1). Its integrated aluminum operations included the mining and processing of bauxite in Jamaica; the production of alumina from bauxite in Louisiana; the reduction of alumina to aluminum in Louisiana, Washington, and West Virginia; and the fabrication of aluminum and aluminum alloys into a variety of products in California, Illinois, Indiana, Maryland, Ohio, Pennsylvania, Rhode Island, Washington, and West Virginia. The corporation also produced refractories, dolomites and magnesia, and other chemicals.

THE COMPANY'S GROWTH

The rapid expansion of the Kaiser Aluminum & Chemical Corporation was the result of a combination of factors: some internal and contributed by the Kaiser management organization; some external and representing the dynamics of a relatively new industry based on a versatile metal possessing a unique combination of properties. Progress of the Corporation can best be demonstrated by the following simple comparison spanning just over a decade shown in Table 20D–1.

Since its entrance into the aluminum business in 1946, Kaiser Aluminum's growth occurred in three well-defined stages:

The first stage may be described as one of acquisition and general improvement and expansion of original facilities. This stage lasted through June of 1950. During these first four years in aluminum, the Corporation bought the Baton Rouge, La., alumina plant; the Mead and Tacoma reduction plants, and the Trentwood rolling mill in Washington; a rod, bar, wire, and cable plant at Newark, Ohio; and a foil mill at Permanente, California. These plants, together with other miscellaneous facilities, required the expenditure of about $60,000,000.

The second stage of Kaiser Aluminum expansion was ushered in at the time of the Korean crisis. The Corporation was already expanding, but defense requirements added new urgency and new dimensions to that expansion. In a period of three years the company spent $245,000,000 in expanding its produc-

TABLE 20D-1

	1947	1960
Total Assets	$27,890,000	$785,600,000
Property, Plant & Equipment — net	5,360,000	534,430,000
Net Worth	10,990,000	303,980,000
Average number of employees	3,834	18,958
Sales of aluminum products — tons	78,311	465,394
Net Sales	45,420,000	406,570,000
Dividends paid or declared during period '47 through '60	129,620,000	

tive capacity by more than 130 percent. Projects included increased capacity in alumina production and mill fabricating and completion of bauxite mining and shipping facilities in Jamaica.

At the close of the Corporation's second stage of expansion in 1953, all basic operations were integrated, from the mining of bauxite in Jamaica to the manufacture and shipment of a full range of aluminum and mill fabricated products on a national basis.

Stage three, beginning in 1954, was Kaiser Aluminum's largest expansion program to date, requiring expenditure of more than $400,000,000.

The new third stage facilities included a combined aluminum reduction plant and sheet, plate and foil rolling mill located in Ravenswood, West Va., within 500 miles of 70 percent of the nation's aluminum usage; a 430,000-ton alumina plant at Gramercy, La., on the Mississippi River; and new and larger equipment and other facilities at a number of other plant locations, including the Erie, Pa., forging plant, and the Halethorpe, Md., extrusion plant.

In step with the development of its production complex, Kaiser Aluminum built a national sales organization. Warehouses, distributors and jobbers were strategically located and stocked to provide fast, efficient service to thousands of fabricators and consumers of aluminum end products.

Industrial salesmen, from over fifty regional, district and branch offices served the full cross-section of the nation's metalworking industries with all of the corporation's basic aluminum products — pig, ingot, billet, aluminum sheet and plate, extrusions, forgings and mechanical rod, bar and wire. A building products sales organization promoted and sold fabricated products, including standard and Diamond Rib roofing, Shade Screen, aluminum gutters, downspouts and accessories.

An extensive line of aluminum foil and foil products, including industrial, consumer, laminated and processed foil, and a variety of aluminum food containers, was also marketed nationally.

Electrical conductor products, sold through a national sales organization and distributors, included bare and stranded aluminum cable, aluminum conduit, and the widest range of insulated cable in both aluminum and copper available from one source in the United States.

Foreign markets were receiving increasing attention with the establishment of additional Kaiser Aluminum sales offices and sales agents in important world markets and the investigation and selection of promising ventures abroad.

Interests outside of the United States and Jamaica in 1961 included participation, with the Birla interests of India, in the Hindustan Aluminum Corporation, Ltd., which was to construct and operate a 20,000 metric ton aluminum reduction plant in India. Kaiser Aluminum also invested in aluminum reduction facilities in Spain, and was to sponsor a consortium of aluminum producers which would build a primary aluminum plant in Ghana, Africa. In Argentina, a subsidiary, Kaiser Aluminum International, joined with Guillermo Decker S.A. to establish a new corporation for manufacturing a wide variety of aluminum mill products for South American markets. In England, Kaiser Aluminum and Delta Metal Company Ltd., have formed James Booth Aluminum Ltd., for the purpose of producing and selling aluminum-wrought products in that market. Finally, in Australia and New Zealand the Corporation was to join with the

Consolidated Zinc Corporation, Ltd. in the planning of a new and complete aluminum production complex. This $400 million joint venture was scheduled for completion by 1966.

Growing in size and importance was the company's production and sale nationally of a complete line of refractories. These were materials having the capacity to withstand high temperatures and they were used to line industrial ovens, kilns, and furnaces.

Integrated and highly diversified with its own sources of raw materials, the Refractories and Chemicals Division of Kaiser Aluminum & Chemical Corporation was in 1961 among the nation's major producers of refractories, with ten plants located in the United States and Canada.

The expansion and diversification of the company in the refractories industry was enormously accelerated when, in May 1959, Mexico Refractories Company of Mexico, Missouri, was merged with the corporation. This move not only more than doubled the company's dollar volume in refractories, but added new and complementary lines of products and greatly increased sales and service outlets.

Prior to the merger, the company specialized in basic refractories. Its entry into this field began during the early days of World War II when, as Permanente Metals Corporation, the company was producing magnesium, a metal needed vitally for the war effort. To furnish the raw material, a dolomite quarry and plant was established at Natividad, California, and a sea water magnesia plant was constructed at Moss Landing, some 15 miles away.

The Natividad and Moss Landing plants have each undergone two major expansions since the war. In 1946, a basic refractories plant was built adjacent to the magnesia facilities at

Moss Landing. With the growth of the market for basic refractories and increased market penetration by Kaiser products, a second basic refractories plant was build near the center of the eastern market at Columbiana, Ohio. This plant, too, had been expanded twice since starting up in 1956. To supply additional raw material, a second refractory magnesia plant was built at Midland, Michigan, and commenced operation in late 1960. Basic refractories, one of the major growth segments of the industry, now account for about a quarter of all refractories sold.

The merger with the Mexico Refractories Company provided the corporation with facilities to produce and sell a complete line of refractory materials including fireclay, silica, and alumina refractories as well as a number of specialty products. These plants are located at Mexico, Missouri; Niles, Ohio; Frostburg, Maryland; Van Dyke, Pennsylvania; and Bronte, Ont., Canada.

Like Kaiser, Mexico Refractories had been a growing concern, and established a reputation for quality products. The Mexico plant, the largest facility, was established in 1930. It has been expanded many times until 1961 when it had fifteen presses and two lines for making extruded brick by the stiff-mud process.

Kaiser refractory products were sold through a network of sales offices, sales subsidiaries, distributors, and dealers. The Division's three general sales offices were located in Pittsburgh, Pa., Mexico, Mo., and Oakland, Calif., with district offices strategically located to serve customer industries.

In addition to refractories, the Division also handled a variety of special alumina and magnesia products. The alumina products, manufactured at the corporation's Baton Rouge, La., works included calcined, low-soda, tabular, hydrated, and active grades. These special aluminas found a variety of uses in Chemical and petroleum production, as well as for a variety of manufactured items. Magnesia, produced at Moss Landing, was sold primarily to paper processing and chemical industries and was used as a soil sweetner.

Kaiser Aluminum & Chemical Corporation's relationship with Kaiser Industries Corporation is shown in Exhibit 2. Exhibit 3 presents the principal subsidiaries of Kaiser Aluminum and Chemical Corporation.

TABLE 20D-2
Plant Facilities

	Products	Approx. Employment	Annual Cap. Tons
ALUMINUM FACILITIES			
Raw Materials			
Jamaica, W.I.	Bauxite	—	4,100,000
Mulberry, Fla.	Sodium Silicofluoride	10	15,000
Gary, Ind.	Calcined coke	15	N/A
Purvis, Miss.	Calcined coke	15	60,000
Alumina			
Baton Rouge, La.	Alumina	850	850,000
Gramercy, La.	Alumina	600	430,000
	Caustic soda		40,000
	Chlorine		36,000
Reduction			
Chalmette, La.	Primary Alum. Ingot & Billet	2,300	247,500
Mead, Wash.	Primary Alum. Ingot	1,150	176,000
Tacoma, Wash.	Primary Alum. Ingot	N/A	41,000
Ravenswood, W. Va.	Primary Alum. Ingot & Billet	2,900	145,000
(Rolling & Fabricating)	Sheet & Plate		160,000
(Rolling & Fabricating)	Foil		9,150
Rolling & Fabricating			
Los Angeles, Calif.	Food Containers	50	6,000
Permanente, Calif.	Foil	240	9,000
Dolton, Ill.	Extrusions & Conduits	360	24,000
Wanatah, Ind.	Food Containers	95	5,500
Halethorpe, Md.	Extrusions	360	32,000
Belpre, O.	Laminated foil	115	7,300
Newark, O.	Rod, Bar, Wire, Electric cond. cable Billets	1,475	172,000
Erie, Penn.	Forgings	475	6,000
Bristol, R.I.	Ins. wire and cable	1,125	18,000
Trentwood, Wash.	Sheet, Plate, and Rolled tubing	2,100	198,000

TABLE 20D–2 (*cont.*)

	Products	Approx. Employ- ment	Annual Cap. Tons
CHEMICAL & REFRACTORIES FACILITIES			
Moss Landing, Calif.	Refractories		100,000 T
(2 plants)	Magnesia	400	120,000 T
Natividad, Calif.	Dolomite		300,000 T
Frostburg, Md.	Clay refractories	130	24,000,000 bricks
Midland, Mich.	Periclase	35	45,000 T
Mexico, Mo.	Clay refractories	630	55,000,000 bricks
Columbiana, O.	Basic refractories	175	100,000 T
Niles, O.	Clay & silica refractories	120	25,000,000 bricks
Van Dyke, Penn.	Silica refractories	80	12,000,000 bricks
Bronte, Ont.	Refractory mixes	—	—

PLANTS & FACILITIES

The location of the plant facilities of Kaiser Aluminum & Chemical, and the products they were equipped to produce are shown in Table 20D–2 as a supplement to the map presented as Exhibit 4. Exhibit 5 shows the company's sales offices.

SOME ASPECTS OF THE COMPANY'S MANAGEMENT PHILOSOPHY

Kaiser Aluminum and Chemical Corporation's President had recently expressed the overall corporate purpose in these words:

To build a stronger Kaiser Aluminum and Chemical Corporation by increasing the market, earning a larger share of that market, providing greater opportunity for personal achievement, and being the most efficient and profitable company in the industry.

To carry out these objectives, the Corporation had stressed managerial decision making with the least possible amount of interference from above. Managers were granted freedom of action in that they were held for results, not methods. Rapid changes and innovations required management personnel who were capable of making quick, effective decisions. Considerable emphasis was placed on informality among, and ready accessibility to, top executives, and on the need to delegate authority and responsibility.

It was felt that organizational rigidity could hamper management's freedom of action, and consequently, the organization structure was looked upon as a dynamic condition — reflecting the ever-changing nature of the company's growth, operations, and personnel. At managerial and supervisory levels, informal consultations on day-to-day decisions were encouraged. Staff guidance was always available to managers who requested aid. Inasmuch as offices of key executives were located in the same building, they had constant access to each other — a sort of perpetual committee.

The organization into which the risk management function had to be integrated appears as Exhibit 6.

EXHIBIT 1
KAISER ALUMINUM & CHEMICAL CORPORATION
Condensed Consolidated Balance Sheets
as at December 31, 1958–60
(Dollar figures in thousands)

	1960	1959	1958
Assets			
Cash	$ 20,520	$ 21,193	$ 23,779
Receivables (net)	85,651	80,562	61,608
Inventories	120,049	106,566	85,885
Prepayments	4,000	2,907	2,249
Investments and Advances	16,379	5,942	5,354
Property (net)	534,434	565,912	572,068
Deferred charges	4,574	2,894	3,453
Total	$785,607	$785,976	$754,396
Liabilities and Net Worth			
Current Liabilities	$106,537	$ 99,048	$ 82,195
Long-term Obligations	295,943	310,325	319,608
Deferred Federal Income Taxes	79,150	75,850	72,300
Capital Stock and Surplus	303,977	300,753	280,293
Total	$785,607	$785,976	$754,396
Miscellaneous Financial Information			
Net Sales	$406,574	$435,550	$408,559
Net Income	22,771	22,328	25,232

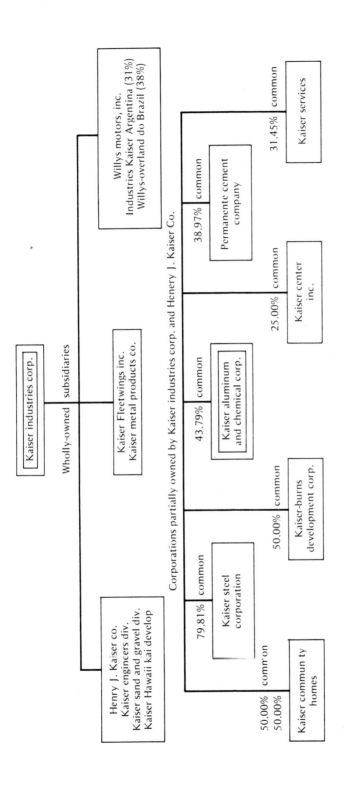

Exhibit 2
Kaiser Industries Corporation Chart
(Principal companies only)

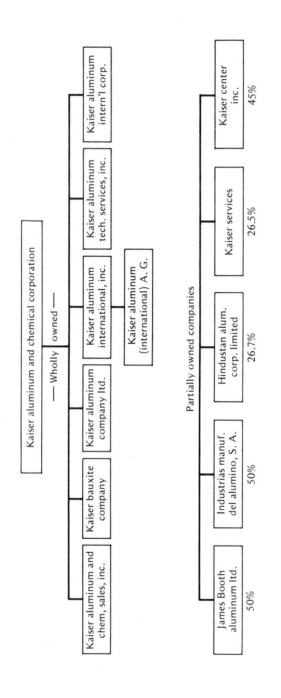

EXHIBIT 3
Chart of Principal Subsidiaries

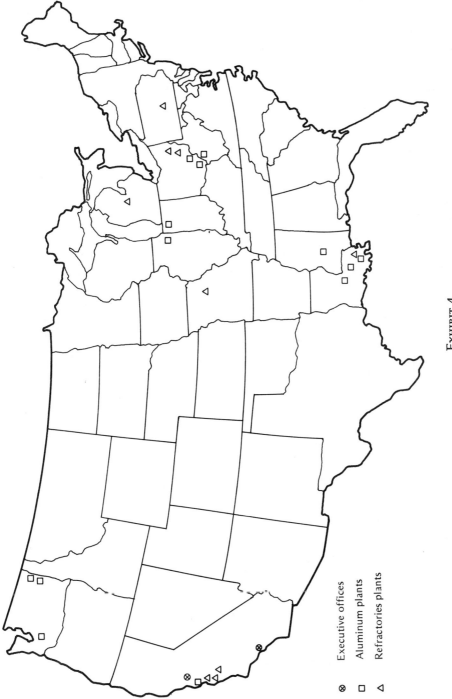

EXHIBIT 4
Plant Locations, Continental U.S.A.

⊗ Executive offices

☐ Aluminum plants

◁ Refractories plants

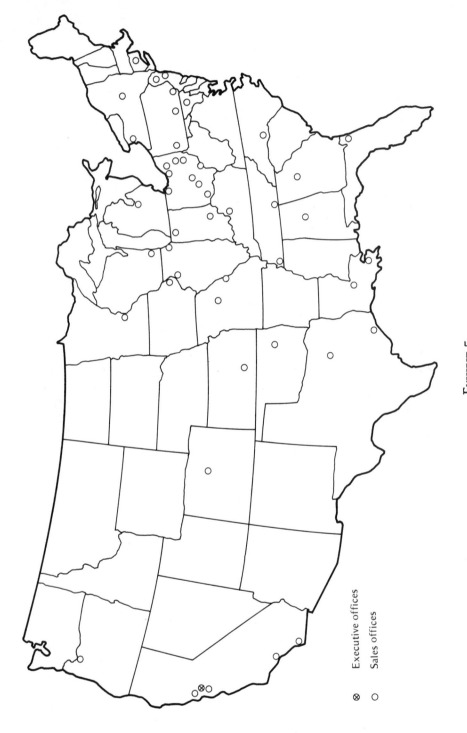

Exhibit 5
Sales Offices, Continental U.S.A.

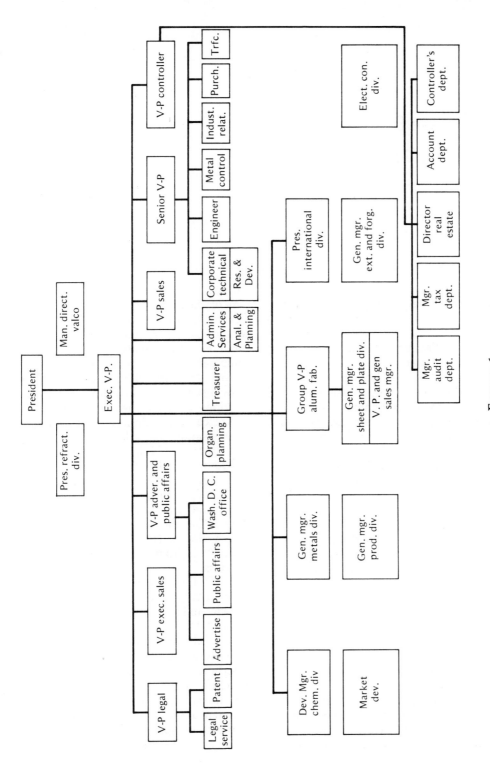

EXHIBIT 6

Headquarters Organization Chart (Approx.)

Case E

Credico Inc.

In the latter part of 1975, Mr. D. E. Rogers, the Director of Insurance of Credico Inc., was facing a serious problem of the errors and omissions insurance of U.S. Engineering Co. (U.S.E.), a subsidiary of Credico Inc. Previous to 1976, Credico Inc. was known as American Credit Companies, consisting of ten wholly owned companies and four divisions. All companies are basically in the information reporting business.

Credico, founded in 1899, presently serves some 63,000 business customers. The corporation maintains offices in over 1,700 locations throughout North America. Working from these locations are some 13,000 employees, over 5,000 of whom are field representatives. Except for the main office in Atlanta, Georgia, and four branches, all office space is leased.

Financial data on Credico and affiliates is given in Appendix A.

OPERATIONS OF U.S. ENGINEERING CO.

U.S.E. has been in business since 1919 serving insurance industry underwriting and engineering departments through providing of underwriting surveys and various safety and loss control services. One of the initial services provided was elevator inspection service to aid the insurance carrier in their evaluation of insured elevator, escalator, and hoisting equipment. Loss control services were offered, through which physical plants were inspected in order to recommend activities directed toward the elimination or control of fire, casualty, workers' compensation, and inland marine losses.

In 1969, U.S.E.'s policy was modified to include direct service to commercial property owners and businessmen. U.S.E., operated on an international basis, and provided service in all fifty states, Canada, and the Caribbean. It had a $6,000,000 revenue of which $350,000 is from the elevator inspection business.

U.S.E. merged with Credico in May 1968, and presently has 31 branch offices, 375 employees, and serves 3,000 customers.

U.S.E. handles about 360,000 underwriting surveys and premium audit reports each year in the following lines: premium audits, loss audits, fire, allied fire lines, liability, surety, burglary, commercial multiperil, ocean marine, workers' compensation, fidelity, glass, boiler & machinery, excess market surveys, elevator & escalators, safety programs and loss control, services to industry and government.

INSURANCE AND RISK MANAGEMENT POLICY OF CREDICO

In order to preserve the corporation's resources, the following policy and guidelines have been set up for the managing of insurance and risks:

1. All risks of loss and need for insurance are to be evaluated from both a single corporation and the entire group of corporations' viewpoint.

2. Conditions and practices which may cause loss are to be eliminated or modified wherever possible.

3. Risks are to be assumed whenever the amount of potential loss would not significantly affect the corporation's financial position.

In determining what constitutes a "significant loss," Credico uses as a guideline a limit of $50,000 in any single occurrence, and a $100,000 annual aggregate.

Exceptions to this guideline are made (a) when insurance is required by law or contractual agreement, (b) when it is desirable to buy special services such as legal defense, claims handling, adjusters, engineering or similar services as a part of an insurance contract, and (c) when the degree of risk compared with the cost of insurance dictates the economic feasibility of purchasing insurance coverage.

4. Risks are insured whenever the amount of loss would be $50,000 or more. Exceptions may be made (a) when cost of insurance compared with the risk indicates purchase of insurance is not financially sound, and (b) when government contracts prohibit the purchase of insurance.

5. Authority and responsibility has been delegated to the director of insurance in (a) purchasing and administration of all corporate insurance programs relating to property, liability, workers' compensation coverages, and the administration and purchasing of employee benefits insurance programs (The employee benefits program is coordinated by the personnel department.); (b) recommendation and selection of insurance sources; (c) developing and implementing risk management programs; (d) working with the legal department in the settlement of liability losses and negotiating and settling other insured or uninsured losses.

6. Insurance is purchased from whatever source thought to be in the best interest of the corporation using the following guidelines:

a) A competitive atmosphere is desired. Continuity of relationships with insurance sources is felt to be advantageous and is maintained unless there is a significant reason for making a change.

b) Selection is based on quality of protection, services provided, and the ultimate cost, in that order.

c) Insurance negotiations are conducted by invitation to selected sources as opposed to open bidding.

All efforts in the insurance and risk management are aimed to complement long-range planning, fulfill legal requirements, and maintain sound relationships with governmental agencies, the public, the insurance industry, and the employees of the company.

Self-Insurance Policy

Credico presently is self-insured in the areas listed below. Deductibles are considered as a form of self-insurance; they are paid out of current income.

1. Branch office fire and extended coverage on furniture and fixtures for all companies.

2. Theft or loss of corporate property for all companies.

3. Property damage liability involving small losses for all companies.

4. Long-term disability of employees in Hawaii.

5. The first $5,000 of loss under comprehensive business liability.

6. The first $25,000 of loss on files (fire and extended coverage).

7. The first $2,500 of loss under errors and omissions liability at Hunnicut.

8. The first $5,000 of loss under general liability of U.S.E. and the first $10,000, errors and omissions on elevator inspections at U.S.E.

   Areas of probable new or additional self-insurance included:

1. New marketing products where minor liability or difficult to place liability is involved — mobile home checks, property and chattel mortgage checks, inventory checks, product recall or pickups, etc.

2. Increasing current deductible amount or including current sizable deductibles.
   a) Debt Reports, Inc. — errors and omissions (currently $25,000 deductible)
   b) Comprehensive business policy (increase from current $5,000)
   c) Auto nonownership liability

3. Workers' compensation for medical cases under $100

4. Furniture in transit policy (claims under $50)

   Areas for long-range analysis of possible self-insurance include:

1. California disability — premiums currently $80,000

2. Workers' compensation in Ohio ($12,000), Washington ($7,200), and Georgia ($24,000). However, the problem here is that the premium expenses are too small, at least at the moment, to justify administrative self-insurance expenses. As insurance has to be limited to the state of operation, self-insurance is even less attractive as it would be if all subsidiaries could be covered under one policy.

Loss Prevention Activity

Personnel completing elevator inspections are full-time salaried employees. Individuals selected for elevator training are carefully screened for previous experience, mechanical ability, and inspection ability. A comprehensive training and qualification program is then administered. To become qualified as an inspector, one must pass a written examination which is based on that of the state of Pennsylvania, acknowledged to be among the most difficult exams in the nation. During the first year, the approved candidate is subject to review of completed reports by corporate headquarters, check rides with a senior elevator inspector, and additional training.

All elevator inspections and training is based on the "American National Standard Safety Code for Elevators, Dumbwaiters, Escalators, and Moving Walks" ANSI.A17.1 and/or the prevailing local codes.

Completed reports are systematically called into corporate headquarters for review as to content, details, wording, and setup. Inspections are completed on standard elevator reporting forms or the forms which might be required by a local authority.

Qualification of Inspectors

U.S.E. seeks to hire men who have had practical experience in elevator inspections; this experience may be with an elevator company or insurance company. Also, people with potential for elevator inspections are specially trained. As to the ANSI-A17.1 Elevator Code, U.S.E. concerns themselves with those parts of the code dealing with inspection, and then as a matter of reference only.

Inspectors are licensed or commissioned in all states and municipalities where there is a requirement that this be done. Wherever states require special qualifications for elevator inspections, U.S.E. inspectors have these qualifications.

Inspection Procedures

Before making an inspection, the inspector secures permission of a building superintendent, plant manager, or whoever may be in charge.

All moving parts and safety devices on the elevator equipment are visibly checked. Inspectors follow the ANSI Code only as it applies to inspections. There is no journal method of checking field inspectors. Inspectors report only on obvious code violations and conditions found during their inspection. Recommendations are discussed with the contact at each location, if available. Inspectors are seldom able to contact members of management who are at a decision level of authority.

Reporting

Reports are returned to the insurance carrier's office within five to ten days after inspection. As U.S.E. finds it the responsibility of the carrier to file reports with the regulatory agencies, they do not do this, unless state or municipal code requires it.

Reports

State and municipal code requirements on reporting each elevator by number are followed. If the elevator has no number, report is made by street number and point of compass. In addition, each report shows the date of inspection. Inspectors discuss recommendations with someone in authority, if possible. The contact's name and title are reported to the customer.

With the exception of new or altered installation, the date of the last load test is seldom available to the inspectors.

ERRORS AND OMISSIONS INSURANCE PROBLEM

As Mr. Rogers stated, "Our people work on their own a great deal of the time, and make numerous reports in Credico's name every day. We try to exercise control as well as we can (see Training and Quality Control — Loss Prevention), but still we face liability exposures in this area.

In connection with the elevator inspection, U.S.E. has had several lawsuit expenses in the past, causing the company some problems. The largest suit was in 1972, when an employee of a company where U.S.E. had inspected the elevator was severely injured when the elevator doors closed on her. Although U.S.E. has a general policy against giving to their customers any hold harmless or indemnity agreement, and assumes no legal liability due to misinformation given by their inspectors, nor for inaccuracies, human error, etc., U.S.E. was held liable by court for $248,000. In the past six years U.S.E. had three lawsuit expenses, totalling $400,000.

In the case of a lawsuit, U.S.E. is usually a codefendant, along with the elevator manufacturer, the owner of the building, the insurance company, the elevator service company and possibly other parties.

Prior to late last year U.S.E. had an errors and omissions and personal liability insurance with a $5 million coverage, a $10,000 deductible carrying a $23,000 annual premium. This included both underlying and umbrella liabilities policies. However, these policies were cancelled by the umbrella carrier; (errors and omissions insurance were excluded from the umbrella policy.)

According to Mr. Rogers, "we are in a situation we don't like to be in, and that is that we are unable to find adequate coverage in the insurance industry for errors and omissions on our elevator inspections. We want to protect ourselves against the catastrophe losses, and as to U.S.E. we feel we haven't adequately done this. As of late last year, we only have $500,000 worth of coverage with a $10,000 deductible and a $40,000 premium for the elevators only! One insurance company offered to give us a second $500,000 layer of coverage, but they want a $34,000 premium. However, that $350,000 worth of elevator business gives us only a normal profit of approximately 10 percent, so there's our profit. The market is just plain scared of any liability coverage in general. The elevator inspection is a specialty type of operation, so the in-dustry doesn't have much to go by as far as determining premiums. The insurance companies are our big customers. Yet, they are the ones that do not want to insure us. So we feel like reinsurers. Although we can get coverage up to $1 million, we feel that it is at a very high price, more so than we can economically stand. Moreover, this summer we have to renegotiate terms, which might be worse than they are now."

Mr. Rogers was considering the following alternatives:

1. Do nothing, and assume the loss above $500,000 if one occurs. This was the action he thought his major competitor took.

2. Accept the quote of a second $500,000 layer of coverage, which would still mean an assumption of losses by U.S.E. over $1 million.

3. Possibly in combination with no. 2, raise the prices of elevator inspections to fund for additional coverage.

4. Go out of the elevator inspection business. However, even though it was only a small revenue item, it did pay for some of the fixed costs. Second, U.S.E. performed a service for the general insurance industry, who were customers in all the other lines. In general, the insurance industry stated that they really needed the service.

5. Try to get some kind of agreement with U.S.E. customers to either hold U.S.E. completely harmless (which probably would not succeed), or to at least perhaps form an agreement with them that they would share in the cost of any loss.

Analyze each of the alternatives as to the liability problem at U.S.E. What should Mr. Rogers do?

Appendix A
Credico

Credico Subsidiaries	Nature of Operations
American Credit Company	Insurance, employment and financial control information for business decisions in the United States and Mexico
American Credit Company of Canada, Ltd.	Insurance, employment and financial control information for business decisions in Canada
Jones, Inc.	Multiple-line independent insurance adjustments
U.S. Engineering Co.	Payroll audits, loss control, and information for commercial property insurance decisions
Medical Data, Inc.	Physical measurements for life and health insurance underwriting
Brown & Associates, Inc.	Property appraisals
Commercial Collection Agency, Inc.	Reports for business and mortgage loan grantors and collection aids in major metropolitan areas
Debt Reports, Inc. of Georgia	Credit reports, collection services and credit card promotions for credit grantors in the United States
Debt Reports of Montreal, Ltd.	Credit reports, collection services and credit card promotions for credit grantors in Canada
Debt Reports Marketing Services, Inc.	Credit card solicitations and promotional programs for credit grantors
Quick Printing & Distributing	Commercial printing and distribution
Market Research Service	Full service market research
Card Services	Recovery of lost, stolen, or cancelled credit cards for credit grantors
Telesystems Division	Motor vehicle records, teleprocessing, and rapid communications

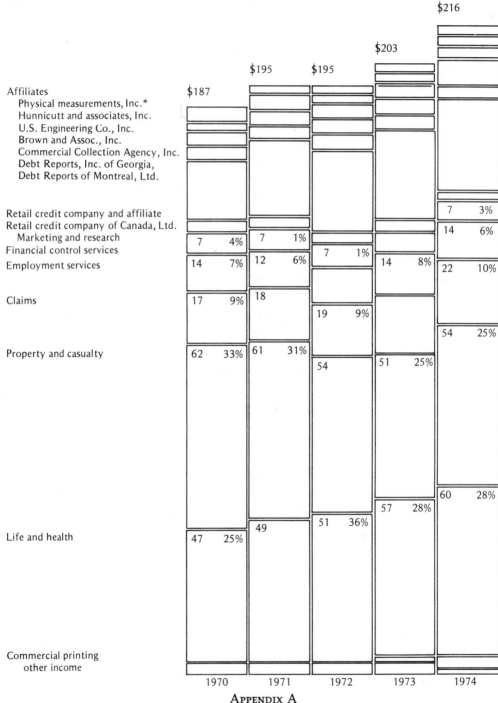

APPENDIX A
Credico Revenues

Five Year Summary of Operations

In thousands of dollars	1974	1973	1972	1971	1970
Total revenue	$215,874	$203,238	$195,262	$194,826	$187,011
Costs and expenses	202,927	189,136	177,802	175,626	167,996
Income before taxes, extraordinary item and cumulative effect of change in accounting	12,947	14,102	17,460	19,200	19,015
Provision for income taxes	6,209	6,595	8,273	9,376	9,485
Income before extraordinary item and cumulative effect of change in accounting	6,738	7,507	9,187	9,824	9,530
Extraordinary item	—	—	—	211	—
Cumulative effect on prior years of change in accounting for lawsuit expense	—	—	(240)	—	—
Net income	6,738	7,507	8,947	10,035	9,530
Dividends paid	6,308	6,344	6,382	6,369	6,364
Per share of stock:					
Income before extraordinary item and cumulative effect of change in accounting	2.14	2.37	2.86	3.05	2.96
Extraordinary item	—	—	—	.06	—
Cumulative effect on prior years of change in accounting for lawsuit expense	—	—	(.07)	—	—
Net income	2.14	2.37	2.79	3.11	2.96
Net income per dollar of revenue	.031	.037	.046	.052	.051
Dividends:					
Per share of stock	2.00	2.00	2.00	2.00	2.00
Percent of net income	94%	85%	71%	63%	67%

A. Lawsuit expense. 1972 net income of $2.79 is net of the cumulative effect on prior years of change in accounting for lawsuit expense, net of applicable income taxes. Pro forma per share net income if the cumulative effect of $.07 were applied retroactively would be $2.86 in 1972 and $3.04 in 1971.

B. Interest expense. Interest expense was $614,000 for 1974, $207,000 for 1973, $162,000 for 1972 and $178,000 for 1971. Interest expense was immaterial for the year ended December 31, 1970.

C. Per share data. Net income per share of common stock is based upon the weighted average number of shares outstanding during each year plus shares issued in 1972 and 1970 poolings of interest transactions. Cash dividends per share of common stock are based upon the number of shares actually outstanding at the end of each dividend period.

Revenue Distribution and Profitability

Revenue In thousands of dollars	1974 Amount	1974 % of Total	1973 Amount	1973 % of Total	1972 Amount	1972 % of Total	1971 Amount	1971 % of Total	1970 Amount	1970 % of Total
American Credit Company and American Credit Company an Canada, Ltd. Information for business decisions to aid:										
Life and health insurance companies in the evaluation of risks	$ 59,276	28%	$ 56,389	28%	$ 51,693	26%	$ 49,495	26%	$ 47,243	25%
Property and casualty insurance companies in the evaluation of risks	53,561	25	50,415	25	54,180	28	60,677	31	61,533	33
Insurance companies in the settlement of claims	22,384	10	20,134	10	18,575	9	18,191	9	16,964	9
Various commercial, financial, and insurance companies in the selection of personnel	13,761	6	13,835	7	12,005	6	12,075	6	14,091	7
Businesses with financial control in the granting of credit, collection of debts, retrieval of credit cards, and other financial areas	6,798	3	7,176	3	7,375	4	7,448	4	6,819	4
Business and governmental bodies with marketing and research services	2,994	1	1,752	1	1,404	1	1,513	1	1,754	1
Commercial printing services	971	1	434	—	—	—	—	—	—	—
Total revenue American Credit Company and American Credit Co. of Canada, Ltd.	159,745	74	150,135	74	145,232	74	149,399	77	148,404	79

In thousands of dollars	1974 Amount	1974 % of Total	1973 Amount	1973 % of Total	1972 Amount	1972 % of Total	1971 Amount	1971 % of Total	1970 Amount	1970 % of Total
Debt Reports, Inc. of Georgia and Debt Reports of Montreal, Ltd. Other affiliates	31,330	15	30,380	15	28,885	15	26,875	14	21,798	12
Commercial Collection Agency, Inc.; Jones, Inc.; Medical Data, Inc.; U.S. Engineering Co.; Brown & Associates, Inc.	24,386	11	22,223	11	20,509	11	18,017	9	16,136	9
Other income (Preferred stock dividends and other interest income)	413	—	500	—	636	—	535	—	673	—
Total revenue	$215,874	100%	$203,238	100%	$195,262	100%	$194,826	100%	$187,011	100%

Income before Provision for Income Taxes
In thousands of dollars

	1974 Amount	1974 % of Total	1973 Amount	1973 % of Total	1972 Amount	1972 % of Total	1971 Amount	1971 % of Total	1970 Amount	1970 % of Total
American Credit Company and American Credit Company of Canada, Ltd.	$ 10,718	83%	$ 12,150	86%	$ 13,124	75%	$ 16,030	83%	$ 16,859	89%
Debt Reports, Inc. of Georgia and Dept Reports of Montreal, Ltd.	1,255	10	826	6	2,725	16	1,538	8	1,164	6
Other affiliates	561	4	626	4	975	6	1,097	6	319	2
Other income	413	3	500	4	636	3	535	3	673	3
Total income before provision for income taxes	$ 12,947	100%	$ 14,102	100%	$ 17,460	100%	$ 19,200	100%	$ 19,015	100%

Note: Corporate staff costs are carried by American Credit Company and are not allocated to affiliated companies.

Stock Prices and Dividends

	High	Low	Dividend
1973			
First Quarter	33⅜	29⅞	.50
Second Quarter	31	24½	.50
Third Quarter	26⅜	20	.50
Fourth Quarter	23⅜	15¾	.50
1974			
First Quarter	20¼	17¼	.50
Second Quarter	18⅞	17½	.50
Third Quarter	18¾	14½	.50
Fourth Quarter	15¾	12⅛	.50

Case F

Calwood Lumber Company

"Disaster planning potentially can have a bad effect on the balance between optimism and pessimism in the business leader," said Timothy Burr, president of the Calwood Lumber Company, to Woodward Sawyer the company's treasurer. "It essentially is a defensive and depressing pastime. It has many of the appearances of constructive work but

Reprinted from Stanford business cases, 1977, with permission of the publishers, Stanford University Graduate School of Business, © 1977, by the Board of Trustees of the Leland Stanford Junior University.

its direct result is seldom a bold decision of the type which inspires subordinates, potential investors, or one's customers. Nevertheless, disaster planning is a necessary requirement of this type of business. In making a disaster plan I think the executive continually must sustain an objective view. He must review periodically the actual chances that disaster will occur without becoming overburdened with pessimism. What I am trying to say Woody, is that I want you to undertake a risk analysis for the firm. Your analysis will be the first step in our drawing up a complete disaster plan. As a start you may want to review these industry statistics (Exhibits 1 and 2) that I have compiled."

BACKGROUND

The Calwood Lumber Company, a California company, was incorporated in 1951 with a net worth of $12,000. The company stock was divided among 13 shareholders. Mr. Burr, the principal operating officer, held 80% of the stock.

The Calwood Company primarily was in the wholesale lumber business. Its lumber business was threefold: 1) processing of green lumber; 2) wholesaling; and 3) brokerage. In the early stages of the company's existence it was engaged only in wholesaling and brokerage. The wholesaling operation involved purchasing lumber for inventory from processing mills and reselling it to retailers and at times to other wholesalers. Inventoried lumber was kept either at the company's warehouse in Eureka or aboard rail cars. The lumber on rail cars was a sort of moving inventory which hopefully could be sold at a good price by virtue of its being in the right place at the right time. The company's brokerage activity essentially was a trading operation in which an attempt was made to buy lumber from one source and sell it to another at a profit. Knowledge of market conditions for lumber obviously was important to the success of this operation as evidenced by the company's $30,000 annual outlay for telephone and telegraph service.

The company entered the lumber-processing business in 1959 when Mr. Burr rented a small planing mill in another sector of Eureka and purchased about $50,000 in machinery and equipment. There the company converted rough green lumber into finished boards which were then air dried and later sold.

Assisting Mr. Burr in running the firm in 1960 were Sawyer, the treasurer, a sales manager, six salesmen, three office girls, ten yard men, and fifteen men at the mill.

From its modest beginning in 1951, the Calwood Company's net worth reached a peak in 1959 of $175,000. Heavy losses in 1960 reduced the net worth by $45,000. Company financial statements are presented as Exhibits 3, 4, and 5.

The main warehouse and company offices were located on a ten-acre site owned by Mr. Burr and leased to the company. The firm also had a planing mill. The firm owned 50 acres of rural land outside of Eureka valued at $520 per acre, which was being held for future expansion.

In 1954, the company started a subsidiary trucking company with a net investment of $1,500. The trucking company, which was organized to deliver lumber sold by the parent company, had a net worth of $70,000 in 1960. The financial statements of the two operations were not consolidated.

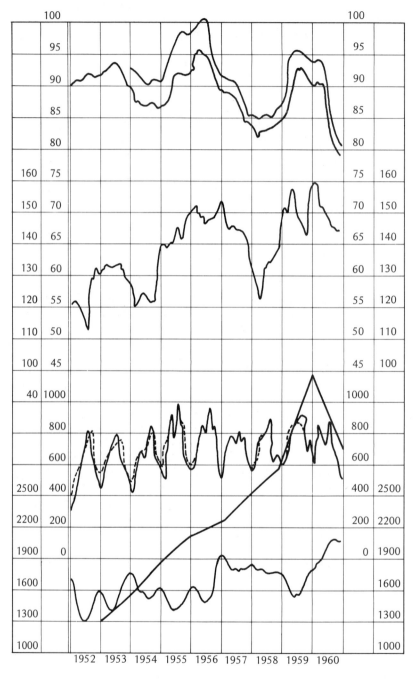

EXHIBIT 1

Exhibit 2
CALWOOD LUMBER COMPANY
Consumption and Utilization
Lumber Consumption

	Building and Construction[1]	Boxes and Crating[2]	Industrial[3]	Railroad[4]	Export[5]	Total Consumption[6]	Softwood Lumber[6]	Hardwood Lumber[6]
	(Million Board Feet)							
1929	20,137	4,645	4,230	3,622	3,197	35,831	28,905	6,926
1930	13,820	4,038	3,255	3,052	2,352	26,517	21,475	5,042
1931	9,672	3,358	2,290	2,059	1,701	19,080	15,434	3,646
1932	6,469	2,425	1,425	1,641	1,156	13,116	10,647	2,469
1933	8,135	2,549	1,613	1,582	1,281	15,160	12,385	2,775
1934	7,969	2,661	1,670	1,832	1,349	15,481	12,774	2,707
1935	10,898	3,221	2,150	1,732	1,313	19,314	16,086	3,226
1936	14,012	3,664	2,518	2,156	1,284	23,634	19,824	3,810
1937	14,613	4,003	2,760	2,287	1,443	25,106	21,062	4,044
1938	13,667	3,840	2,542	1,478	977	22,504	19,180	3,324
1939	16,637	4,054	2,754	1,889	1,104	26,438	22,392	4,046
1940	20,357	4,295	2,994	1,929	972	30,547	26,169	4,378
1941	22,876	5,142	3,820	2,396	693	34,927	28,995	5,932
1942	25,958	9,138	4,742	2,209	463	42,510	34,555	7,955
1943	15,744	14,142	4,956	2,108	310	37,260	29,157	8,103
1944	11,920	15,241	4,706	2,145	360	34,372	26,401	7,071
1945	13,708	11,714	3,811	1,886	435	31,554	23,996	7,558
1946	20,910	5,724	4,482	1,757	648	33,521	25,766	7,755
1947	21,898	4,907	4,701	1,790	1,352	34,648	27,451	7,197
1948	25,571	3,993	4,378	1,962	647	36,551	28,976	7,575
1949	24,349	3,777	4,086	1,448	667	34,327	28,628	5,699
1950	30,879	4,291	4,842	1,609	518	42,139	34,664	7,475
1951	26,797	4,510	4,683	1,572	998	38,560	31,522	7,038
1952	28,372	4,690	4,771	1,582	735	40,150	32,795	7,355
1953	27,025	4,414	4,903	1,713	644	38,699	31,305	7,394
1954	28,628	4,092	4,465	1,276	723	39,184	32,608	6,576
1955	30,877	4,208	4,558	1,445	844	41,932	33,451	8,481
1956	29,563	4,537	4,915	1,446	767	41,228	33,346	7,882
1957	25,885	4,011	4,348	1,294	811	36,349	30,234	6,115
1958	26,704	4,235	4,587	890	728	37,144	30,833	6,311
1959*	29,003	4,344	4,707	1,002	788	40,644	34,242	6,402
1960*	27,261	4,094	4,436	1,050	861	37,702	31,391	6,311

* Subject to revision.

SOURCES:

[1] N.L.M.A. estimates based on reports of construction activity. Includes all construction except by railroads.

[2] N.L.M.A. estimates based on trend of merchandise movements and other indicators.

[3] N.L.M.A. estimates, includes lumber consumed in the manufacture of furniture, caskets, handles, motor vehicles, and other products, as well as the contruction of railroad cars by private car builders.

[4] Includes sawed cross ties and rough and finished lumber for buildings, car construction and repairs in railroad shops, and maintenance of way, structure, and equipment. Data are derived from reports of Association of American Railroads.

[5] Includes sawed timber, boards, planks and scantlings, flooring, box shook and railroad ties. Exports are reported by Bureau of the Census, U.S. Department of Commerce.

[6] Quarterly Reports of Lumber Survey Committee to Secretary of Commerce.

EXHIBIT 3
CALWOOD LUMBER COMPANY
Balance Sheet
Dec. 31, 1958–60

CURRENT ASSETS	1960	1959	1958
Cash	$ 18,342	$ 22,134	$ 15,948
Securities	962	962	962
Accounts receivable	222,152	241,716	227,180
Allowance for bad debts	(21,502)	(229)	(7,892)
	$200,650	$241,487	$219,288
Notes receivable			4,581
Lumber inventory (lower of cost or market)	349,214	389,303	95,935
Auto inventory			1,500
Prepaid expense	6,790	7,442	2,606
Deposits and advances to suppliers			15,373
Estimated refund of federal income taxes	21,236		
TOTAL CURRENT ASSETS	$597,194	$661,328	$356,193
PROPERTY, PLANT, AND EQUIPMENT			
Land	$ 2,272	$ 2,272	$ 2,272
Delivery equipment	8,290	8,853	8,853
Office equipment	9,235	9,235	8,948
Machinery and equipment	85,174	74,035	18,234
Rental dwelling	3,369	3,369	3,369
	$108,340	$ 97,764	$ 39,406
Less accumulated depreciation	51,593	30,569	22,224
	56,747	67,195	17,182
Leasehold improvements	55,107	54,742	48,220
Less accumulated amortization	14,174	10,946	7,844
	$ 40,933	$ 43,796	$ 40,376
OTHER ASSETS			
Investments	$ 1,500	$ 1,500	$ 1,500
Organization costs	1	1	1
	$696,374	$773,819	$417,525

CURRENT LIABILITIES	1960	1959	1958
Notes payable to bank (secured by A/R)	$264,925	$271,175	$187,960
Notes payable to bank (unsecured)		25,000	5,000
Notes payable on demand	63,998	39,000	—
Accounts payable	138,806	141,629	45,284
Contracts payable			787
Accrued payroll	5,931	8,536	1,845
Withheld and accrued payroll taxes	6,848	17,515	6,246
Accrued sales taxes	749	962	256
Federal income taxes payable		6,289	7,252
Long-term debt due within one year	18,260	18,054	1,848
TOTAL CURRENT LIABILITIES	$499,517	$528,160	$256,478
LONG-TERM DEBT	$ 86,204	$ 88,960	$ 45,827
Less amount due within one year	18,260	18,054	1,848
TOTAL LONG-TERM DEBT	$ 67,944	$ 70,906	$ 43,979
STOCKHOLDERS' INVESTMENT			
Capital stock	$ 78,903	$ 78,903	$ 36,000
Earnings retained in business	50,010	95,850	81,068
TOTAL SHAREHOLDERS' INVESTMENT	128,913	174,753	117,068
	$696,374	$773,819	$417,525

Exhibit 4

CALWOOD LUMBER COMPANY
Statement of Net Earnings, 1958–60

	1960	1959	1958
SALES	$2,768,860	$3,249,854	$3,281,824
COST OF SALES — Lumber			
Inventory, beginning of year	67,194	95,936	383,736
Purchases	2,458,284	3,004,297	2,540,213
Freight in	74,047	73,988	114,494
Commissions	9,706	7,824	7,227
Planer Costs		113,556	201,492
	$2,609,231	$3,295,601	$3,247,162
Less inventory, end of year	95,935	383,736	348,239
	$2,513,296	$2,911,865	$2,898,923
GROSS PROFIT	$ 255,564	$ 337,989	$ 382,899
SELLING, GENERAL, AND ADMINISTRATIVE EXPENSES	224,164	304,192	335,024
NET PROFIT FROM OPERATIONS	$ 31,400	$ 33,797	$ 47,875
OTHER EXPENSES			
Cost or market adjustment for the year			87,838
Discounts allowed	$ 39,617	$ 50,865	$ 55,262
Interest	13,593	19,993	28,451
	$ 53,210	$ 70,858	$ 171,551
OTHER INCOME			
Discounts earned	$ 42,496	$ 45,381	$ 47,101
Miscellaneous	2,982	9,600	9,266
Proceeds received in excess of fire loss		3,063	
Gains on sale of fixed assets			233
	$ 45,478	$ 58,044	$ 56,600
OTHER EXPENSES — NET	$ 7,732	$ 12,814	$ 114,951
NET EARNINGS (LOSS) BEFORE FEDERAL TAXES	$ 23,668	$ 20,983	$ (67,080)
PROVISION FOR FEDERAL TAXES	7,200	6,200	
ESTIMATED REFUND OF FEDERAL TAXES			21,240
NET EARNINGS (LOSS)	$ 16,468	$ 14,783	$ (45,840)

EXHIBIT 5
CALWOOD LUMBER COMPANY
Selling, General, and Administrative Expenses
1958–60

	1960	1959	1958
Advertising	$ 2,705	$ 2,349	$ 2,032
Automobile	2,830	2,895	1,337
Legal	630	958	1,825
Accounting	1,268	995	845
Depreciation	21,458	14,667	10,340
Doubtful Accounts	12,570	11,721	4,987
Dues and Subscriptions	11,984	6,173	2,895
Fuel	4,578	3,345	3,202
Insurance	26,921	16,438	3,899
Maintenance	5,662	8,441	7,143
Rent	4,800	4,800	1,200
Salaries	156,585	166,326	132,299
Taxes — Payroll	6,878	6,246	—
Taxes and Licenses	13,830	6,352	6,449
Telephone and Telegraph	29,160	29,475	28,738
Travel	3,730	3,486	3,275
Utilities	663	1,333	502
Claims	7,093	4,090	3,632
Donations	65	205	—
Supplies	11,898	10,655	9,558
Workers' Compensation Expense	9,616	3,039	6
Miscellaneous	—	3	—
Directors' Fees	100	200	—
	$335,024	$304,192	$224,164

Case G

Planning the Estate of Charles Milton, Sr.[1]

In early August 1966, Mr. I. Peter Chancellor, an agent of the Protective Life Insurance Company, called on Charles Milton, Sr., one of the partners in the Milton Development Company. Chancellor had been referred to Mr. Milton by a former client, a close friend of Milton's, for whom Chancellor had performed an estate analysis a few months before. Though wary of any insurance man who might try to place unneeded insurance on him, Mr. Milton agreed to the interview on the strength of his friend's referral. Chancellor was well aware of Mr. Milton's substantial position in the community, both social and financial: He owned a construction company in partnership with his son; he was intimately involved in many joint-venture construction projects with other contractors; and his cash and borrowing positions at the local bank were judged to be excellent. Chancellor surmised, and rightly, that Mr. Milton's large estate might be in need of a complete estate plan, much like that performed for Milton's referror.

After hearing Chancellor's introductory remarks, Mr. Milton became convinced that an estate analysis might be worthwhile. He was especially attracted by Chancellor's reference to conservation of dollars which the plan could provide. Like most independent businessmen, Mr. Milton was anxious to preserve for his heirs as much of his accumulated wealth as he could. His only son was already involved in the principal business of the family and Mr. Milton believed that it was time that some sort of plan be worked out whereby the affairs of the family, including the business, could be carried on smoothly in the event of his death.

Mr. Milton, after considerable thought, consented to allow Chancellor to perform the analysis. In consultations with Milton himself and with Milton's lawyer and accountant, Chancellor established the total size of the Milton estate, including business interests, personal assets such as cash and furnishings, and other assets like securities, real property, insurance, etc. A summary of these assets, along with information on titles, is presented in Exhibit 1.

He also requested personal information on Mr. Milton's family. He

Reprinted from Stanford business cases, 1965, with permission of the publishers, Stanford Graduate School of Business, © 1965 by the Board of Trustees of the Leland Stanford Junior University.

[1] This case was prepared for Dr. Oscar Serbein by Jack Lowe of the Stanford Graduate School of Business, and in cooperation with the Connecticut General Life Insurance Company.

found that Mr. Milton had three children, one son and two daughters, and a wife still living. The ages are as shown in Table 20G–1.

Chancellor further inquired whether Mr. Milton had considered the problem of distribution of assets in the event of death. Mr. Milton said that he had, and on the advice of his lawyer, had drawn up wills for both him and his wife. Brief summaries of these wills are included as Exhibit 2.

Chancellor asked Mr. Milton to make an estimate of what it would cost Mrs. Milton to live if he died. The figure which Mr. Milton settled on was $1,000 a month.

Chancellor was also interested in a $40,000 land holding which Milton had told him about. Milton specified that it consisted of nonincome-producing property, and that at one time he had considered putting it in trust, but had not done so.

Chancellor pursued his line of questioning to his own specialty, life insurance. He found that Mr. Milton had one $27,000 policy on his life, with a double indemnity rider in case of accidental death. There was no insurance on Mrs. Milton, and the couple's accident and health insurance consisted of a small Blue Cross policy.

Mr. Milton had also mentioned several small business interests, which he called "partnerships" (shown in Exhibit 1 as "Garden Company," "Loan Company," etc.). In reality, these assets

represented what was left of several joint ventures entered into in the past by Mr. Milton and other contractors. He was slowly liquidating these remaining assets since, as a rule, they were not income-producing.

After 1½ hours of intensive questioning, Chancellor thanked Mr. Milton, and informed him that a complete analysis of his estate would be ready in two weeks. He also indicated that he would keep in touch with Mr. Milton's attorney and accountant, since without their cooperation and consultation, Chancellor's work would be useless.

Back in his office, Chancellor mulled over the information which he had received concerning Milton's affairs. Several aspects of the present estate concerned him: First, Mr. Milton's wife, a pleasant but unexceptional woman, was named executrix of his will. Chancellor had seen from experience that appointment of a wife as executrix usually resulted in a delay in the processing of an estate due simply to grief resulting from the husband's death. Second, the division of Mr. Milton's share in the construction partnership among so many heirs appeared to Chancellor to endanger the profitable continuation of this business. Third, the titling of the following assets in joint tenancy was clearly unwise, since one-half of the total would be taxed *both* in Mr. Milton's and his wife's estates:

Real Estate	$12,000
Bonds	500
Cash	38,000
	$50,500

Fourth, Chancellor felt that the $27,000 insurance on Mr. Milton's life was inadequate in view of the size of his estate (and the resulting size of estate taxes

TABLE 20G–1

	Age	
Mr. Milton	62	
Mrs. Milton	62	
Son	28	Unmarried
Daughter	32	Married, 2 children
Daughter	31	Married, 2 children

and settlement costs). Fifth, Chancellor saw a real need for guaranteeing, through a contractual arrangement, the son's right to continue the business unmolested by inheritance worries.

With these observations in mind, Chancellor went to work on a detailed examination of every phase of Mr. Milton's personal finances. He first computed estate costs as the Milton's will

TABLE 20G–2

Mr. Milton	If He Dies First Wife Will Have	If He Dies Second His Heirs Will Have
Executors' commissions & Attorney's fees	$ 9,000	$ 5,972
Miscellaneous expenses	1,380	780
Accrued income taxes	5,000	10,000
Accrued property taxes	540	540
Current bills	500	500
Expenses of last illness & burial	1,500	1,500
Federal estate tax	23,331	21,173
California inheritance tax	2,688	2,415
	$43,939	$42,880
Liquidity in sight:		
Stocks	$14,000	
El Segundo sale	28,000	
Loan Company sale	12,500	
Cash[1]		$38,000
Insurance	27,000	3,021
	$81,500	$41,021
Balance to be raised	—	$ 1,859

Mrs. Milton	If She Dies First Husband Will Have	If She Dies Second Heirs Will Have
Executors' fees and Attorney's Fees	$ 6,140	$ 7,108
Miscellaneous expenses	813	1,006
Accrued taxes		800
Current bills		250
Expenses of last illness and burial	1,500	1,500
Federal estate tax	27,661	33,053
California inheritance tax	2,853	4,353
	$38,967	$48,070
Liquidity in sight:		
Cash	$ —	$38,000
	$38,967	$ 9,432

[1] See p. 533, Note 5.

now stood. This is shown in Table 20G–2.

From these calculations it was evident to Chancellor that a real liquidity problem existed for Mr. and Mrs. Milton. In Mr. Milton's case, his fairly liquid position was the result of a very recent sale of his El Segundo and Loan Company property; and, as can be seen, if he were to die first, the $38,000 cash held in joint tenancy could not be used to pay his estate costs.[2] In Mrs. Milton's case, the liquidity need was even more obvious, especially if she were to die first.

Using the same figures, Chancellor calculated on a percentage basis, the shrinkage to be undergone by the Milton estate upon both their deaths. This is shown in Table 20G–3. Mr. Chancellor felt that such shrinkage was excessive.

Next Mr. Chancellor examined the figure of $1,000 per month which Mr. Milton had set as a minimum monthly income for his wife. Chancellor knew that it would be hard to reach this objective, given the present provisions of the Milton estate. To arrive at an estimate of expected income from properties and sources other than Social Security and insurance, Chancellor applies an annual three percent return after taxes to income-producing assets. He did not include proceeds from the business operation, since in his eyes these returns were highly uncertain (Table 20G–4).

[2] See below, Note 5.

If Mr. Milton's objectives were to be realized, Chancellor had to come up with some method of supplementing Mrs. Milton's income by $400 to $500 per month.

Before designing a solution to Mr. Milton's estate problems, Mr. Chancellor outlined the main areas of weakness in the present Milton estate:

1. Both wills are inadequate, especially in the appointment of executors.
2. Joint ownership of certain assets can result in:
   (a) Double taxation of the same assets
   (b) Possible payment of long-term capital gains tax on those assets growing in value.
3. The present life insurance policy is inadequate and improperly utilized.
4. After reinvestment of presently liquid funds (cash from the sale of El Segundo and Loan Company property), the estate will again be faced with a serious liquidity problem.
5. If the wife predeceases, there will be almost no liquid funds to pay estate costs, unless Mr. Milton releases his portion of the cash held in joint tenancy, or unless the cash is divided into separate property. Otherwise, it will be frozen for several weeks by inheritance tax appraisers.
6. No assurance exists that the business can or will be continued for the benefit of the family, or in its best interest.

TABLE 20G–3

	Husband's Estate	Wife's Estate	Total	Percentage
Gross Estates:	$378,121	$ 4,000	$382,121	100.0%
	43,950	48,070	92,020	24.1
Costs:		NET	$290,318	75.9%

TABLE 20G–4

Monthly Income	Until She Reaches 65	After 65
Guaranteed Income (Social Security and Life Insurance)	$ 160	$ 234
Other Income from the estate	213	213
Income from wife's assets	128	128
	$ 501	$ 575
Minimum objective:	$1,000	$1,000
Additional needs:	$ 499	$ 425

7. In the event of Mr. Milton's death, under present circumstances, Mrs. Milton could not count on the minimum income considered necessary by Mr. Milton.

Chancellor then proceeded to work out a solution which would conserve dollars for the Milton heirs, preserve the liquidity of the estate, and meet the income needs of Mrs. Milton in the event of her husband's death.

EXHIBIT 1

Assets	Current Gross Values	How Titled	Type of Property
Residence	$ 20,000	Wife	Comm. Property
Other Real Estate	12,000	Jt. Wife	″ ″
Personal Effects	2,500	Own	″ ″
Securities (Common Stocks)	14,400	Own	″ ″
Savings Bonds	500	Jt. Wife	″ ″
Cash	38,000	Jt. Wife	″ ″
Land Company	15,500	Own	″ ″
Homes Company — Joint Ventures with other businessmen or partners	14,000	Own	″ ″
Loan Company	12,000	Own	″ ″
Garden Company	15,000	Own	″ ″
Life Insurance	27,000	Own	″ ″
Automobile	1,200	Own	″ ″
Other Property	40,000	Own	″ ″
El Segundo	28,000	Own	″ ″
Partnership with Son	135,000	Own	″ ″
Certificate of Deposit	3,021	Own	″ ″
Total Net Estate	$378,121		
Assets in Wife's Name			
Jewelry and Furs	$ 4,000		Separate Property
Total Gross Estate	$382,121		

EXHIBIT 2

CURRENT WILL OF MR. MILTON:

1. Payment of funeral expense, costs of administration, etc. from Mr. Milton's own interest in community property.

2. Bequest to wife of all household furniture, personal effects, and automobiles. These are to be subtracted from Mr. Milton's separate property and his half of community property, the remaining items constituting his share of the net family estate. If Mrs. Milton dies within 6 months of Mr. Milton, the aforementioned articles to be divided equally among the children.
   a) Net Family Estate is equal to 100 percent of all enumerated properties *except* Mrs. Milton's separate property. Therefore, Mr. Milton's one-half of community property can be termed "one-half of net family estate."

3. Bequest to wife of Mr. Milton's net estate, consisting of community, joint, insurance, and other property excepting only wife's separate property.
   a) "Net Value" of the estate is gross value of enumerated properties less claims for mortgages, funeral, and administration expense, but *not* considering federal and estate inheritance taxes. "Value" shall be the federal taxation figure or fair market value as of valuation dates if no federal tax figure is available.

4. If wife survives one year, bequest of residuary estate is trust with income to wife for life. The trust shall be testamentary. At wife's death, the estate is to be divided, and distributed to children as per stirps.

5. All federal estate, inheritance, and succession taxes are payable out of the "residuary estate" if they cannot be paid out of the taxable estate.
   a) "Residuary estate" consists of Mr. Milton's one-half of community property, plus her separate property, both of which are exempt from tax at Mr. Milton's death.

6. Executrix: wife Anne. Also contingent executrix named; son, Charles, Jr.

CURRENT WILL OF MRS. MILTON:

1. Numbers 1, 3, 5 are the same as Mr. Milton's only in reverse.

2. Bequest to husband, if surviving wife 6 months, residence, household and personal effects; otherwise to children per stirps.

4. Trustee: Husband, Charles Milton.

6. Executor: Husband, Charles Milton. Contingents also named in both cases.

QUESTIONS

1. Work out a comprehensive solution to the problems discovered by the life insurance agent. Try to coordinate all assets: Personal Business, Real Estate, and Insurance. Your solution should involve a revised will, trust agreements, and changes in titling of property. You should be able to save as much as 10 percent in final estate settlement costs.

2. What was the purpose of the proposal that the $40,000 in "other property" be placed in trust? Of what particular value are trust agreements in a case such as this? What specific trust or trusts should be set up for the Milton estate?

3. Should there be a sale of life insurance? If so, on whom? How much?

Case H

Southern Saw Service, Inc. (A)

In May 1973, Mr. Robert Haege, treasurer of Southern Saw Service, Inc., received a report from the John Hancock Mutual Life Insurance Company, Actuarial Division, concerning the company's retirement program, the Deposit Administration Contract No. 438 GAC, for year ending February 28, 1973. A copy of the report is attached as Exhibit 1. Mr. Haege was uncertain as to what the company should do about the current level of the unfunded past service liability. Last year the company had paid no premium on the deposit administration

contract because of a decline in profits. The company also wished to negotiate additional bank loans for capital expansion and wished to present as favorable a balance sheet as possible to potential lenders. The unfunded past service liability had reached $665,554. The normal cost (cost for currently earned benefits under the plan) was running nearly $75,000 a year. Under the contract the Southern Saw Service, Inc. was supposed to make an annual payment of at least 75 percent of the normal cost, or approximately $56,000 a year. Normal cost had risen 11 percent in the previous year because of increased salaries.

Financial information on the company is given in Exhibits 1–3.

THE RETIREMENT PLAN

The retirement plan adopted by the Southern Saw Service, Inc. began in 1957. It covers all eligible employees who have completed one year of service and who are under age 60. Formal retirement age is 65, but with the consent of the company the employee may continue working until age 70. The employee may retire as early as age 55 with a reduced retirement income.

An employee's pension is based on his average annual salary for the ten years preceding his retirement. The formula provides an income equal to .773 percent of the first $6,600 of annual earnings plus 1¼ percent of earnings in excess of the $6,600 multiplied by the number of credited years of service excluding the first year. An example of how this benefit formula operates for a person whose average earnings were $7,800 during his last ten years with the company and whose total years of service is 37 years, would be calculated as follows:

.773 percent of $6,600	$51.00
1.25 percent of $1,200	15.00
Total	$66.00
Times years of service	× 36 years
Total annual benefit	$2,376.00
Total monthly benefit	$ 198.00

In addition, the employee is entitled to Social Security benefits. The company's retirement plan together with Social Security benefits is expected to provide about 80 percent of the employee's average earnings during his last ten years with the company.

The employee's rights are vested after 15 years of service and upon having reached age 55. If the employee dies before retirement, no pension benefits are payable.

In a retirement booklet distributed to all employees, the company states, "The insurance company does not guarantee the sufficiency of the retirement annuity fund to purchase the retirement annuities described in the contract. When you retire the amounts are then withdrawn from this fund to purchase a retirement annuity which is guaranteed by the insurance company for as long as you live . . . Should the plan be modified or discontinued before future service annuities have been purchased for 10 years into the plan, retirement annuities already purchased on behalf of certain higher paid employees may be reduced in order to meet the requirements of the United States Treasury Department."

The Southern Saw Service has the policy of paying the premium on Medicare Insurance for employees and spouses if the employee has had 25 years of service or more. For employees with 15 to 25 years of service the Medicare premium is carried for the employee only.

In addition, group life insurance is continued on behalf of all employees during retirement in an amount equal to one-half of the coverage given while the employee was working.

THE DEPOSIT ADMINISTRATION PLAN

The Southern Saw Service has adopted a deposit administration plan in order to give the company maximum flexibility in the management of its retirement program. Mr. Haege was not sure what were the full implications of the Actuary's report. (Exhibit 1)

QUESTIONS

1. In view of the company's current financial position do you feel that suspension of payments in 1972 was warranted? Why?

2. Why might the plan be disqualified by IRS unless payments are resumed?

3. What are the financial implications of the unfunded past service liability? When, if ever, should the company pay off this liability?

EXHIBIT 1

May 14, 1973

Mr. Robert H. Haege, Treasurer
Southern Saw Service, Inc.
Box 11000
Atlanta, Georgia 30310

Group Annuity Contract # 438 GAC

Dear Mr. Haege:

We have completed our annual actuarial valuation of your pension plan funded through John Hancock Deposit Administration Contract No. 438 GAC, for the plan year ending February 28, 1973. The valuation is based upon 130 active employees.

The attached exhibits display the results of the valuation, as described below.

> Exhibit A Development of the unfunded past service liability as of February 28, 1973.
>
> Exhibit B Development of normal cost for the year commencing March 1, 1973.
>
> Exhibit C Alternative recommended payments for the year commencing March 1, 1973.
>
> Exhibit D Analysis of fund experience for the sixteenth plan year.
>
> Exhibit E Schedule of estimated fund withdrawals.
>
> Exhibit F Statement of funding method and actuarial assumptions.

Normal cost has increased this year by 11 percent over last year's level of $67,053 primarily as the result of the large actuarial losses sustained as the result of increased salaries.

It is again necessary to point out the hazards of continued funding at a rate below the minimum recommended payment:

> 1. Possible plan disqualification by the I.R.S.;
> 2. Possible future fund inadequacy.

We have examined the rate of expected withdrawals from the fund for retirements expected to occur on normal retirement dates in the next five years, and determined that the fund will continue to be adequate to provide for such withdrawals in this period, provided contributions are made at least at the rate specified in recommended payment "B" (Exhibit C). It should be noted, however, that this prediction will not necessarily hold true if substantial numbers of early retirements occur, or if a payment less than that recommended is made. If either of these eventualities is foreseen, we will be glad to reexamine expected fund adequacy, upon request.

Very truly yours,
/s/ Arthur D. Davis, A.S.A.
Actuarial Associate

Group Annuity Contract # 438 GAC
Exhibit A

Development of Unfunded Past Service Liability as of February 28, 1973

1.	(a) Unfunded past service liability on March 1, 1972	$577,420
	(b) Interest at 4% on (a) from March 1, 1972 to February 28, 1973	23,097
	(c) Sum of (a) and (b)	600,517
2.	(a) Normal cost assumed due March 1, 1972	67,503
	(b) Interest at 4% on (a) from March 1, 1972 to February 28, 1973	2,700
	(c) Sum of (a) and (b)	70,203
3.	(a) Contributions applicable to the plan year ending February 29, 1972	5,000
	(b) Interest at 4% on (a) from receipt	166
	(c) Sum of (a) and (b)	5,166
4.	Unfunded Past Service Liability as of February 28, 1973	$665,554
	1(c) + 2(c) − 3(c)	

Group Annuity Contract #438 GAC
Exhibit B

Development of Normal Cost for year commencing March 1, 1973

1.	Present value of total liability as of March 1, 1973	$ 1,787,986
2.	Assets available as of March 1, 1973 to meet liability in (1)	318,253
3.	Unfunded past service liability as of March 1, 1973	665,554
4.	Present value of benefits to be funded through future normal costs (1) − (2) − (3)	804,179
5.	Present value of future compensation as of March 1, 1973	13,670,973
6.	Accrual rate (4) + (5)	.0588
7.	Annual covered payroll as of March 1, 1973	1,270,640
8.	Normal cost assumed due March 1, 1973 (6) × (7)	$ 74,714

Group Annuity Contract #438 GAC
Exhibit C

Alternative Recommended Payments for the year commencing March 1, 1973

A. *Maximum Recommended Payment*

1. Normal cost assumed due March 1, 1973	$ 74,714
2. Estimated Administrative Charge	0
3. 10% of Largest 10% Base	66,555
4. Total payment (1) + (2) + (3)	$141,269

B. *Minimum Recommended Payment*

1. Normal cost assumed due March 1, 1973	$ 74,714
2. Estimated Administrative Charge	0
3. Interest at 4% on the unfunded past service liability	26,622
4. Total payment (1) + (2) + (3)	$101,336

C. *Contractual Minimum*

1. 75% of Normal Cost	$ 56,036

The Largest 10% Base was computed in accordance with Example D-1 given in the Bulletin on Sections 23 (p) (1) (A) and (B) of the Internal Revenue Code, dated June 1, 1945. Supporting data detailing its computation will be furnished upon request.

Group Annuity Contract #438 GAC
Exhibit D

Analysis of fund experience for the sixteenth plan year

Source of Gain (Loss)	Amount of Gain (Loss)
Mortality and turnover other than expected	$ 24,995
Interest earnings other than expected	4,158
Postponed retirements	(2,797)
Withdrawals for annuities different from expected	9,359
Changes in objectives due to salary increases	(122,943)
Net Gain (Loss)	$(87,228)

Under the Attained Age Normal Cost Method the above gains and losses respectively reduce or increase the present value of benefits to be funded through future normal costs, and are thereby spread over all future normal cost payments. The analysis displayed above is therefore given for your information only, as an indication of the extent to which fund experience has followed the predictions made in the funding assumptions.

Group Annuity Contract #438 GAC
Exhibit E

Schedule of Estimated Fund Withdrawals and Estimated Deposit
Administration fund balances for the Five-Year Period commencing
March 1, 1973 and ending February 28, 1978

Year	Assumed Employer Contribution	Estimated Withdrawal	Estimated Balance
1974	$101,336	$246,858	$182,579
1975	101,336	19,090	273,757
1976	101,336	62,027	324,795
1977	101,336	16,510	424,293
1978	101,336	48,176	495,477

The above estimates are based upon the funding assumptions stated in Exhibit F.

Group Annuity Contract #438 GAC
Exhibit F

Funding Method

Attained Age Normal Cost Method, as described in Part III of the bulletin on Sections 23 (p) (1) (A) and (B) of the Internal Revenue Code, dated June 1, 1945.

Funding Assumptions

Mortality before and after retirement: The Group Annuity Table for 1951 (Males) projected by Scale C to 1959 and set back one year for males and six years for females.

Interest before and after retirement: 4% per annum.

Expenses: 5% of gross contributions.

Normal Retirement Age: Contractual.

Computation of Final Average Salary Benefits: Projections based upon current earnings.

Salary Scale: Salaries assumed to remain at current levels.

Exhibit 2

Comments on the Balance Sheet

A summary of the financial condition at June 30, 1973, and a comparison with a summary of the financial condition at June 30, 1972, are presented in the following table:

	June 30, 1973	June 30, 1972	Increase + Decrease −
Current Assets:			
Cash	$ 143,126.83	$ 184,688.05	$ 41,561.22−
Trade Accounts Receivable	313,908.38	286,137.61	27,770.77+
Miscellaneous Accounts Receivable	16,044.05	14,769.24	1,274.81+
Inventories	841,833.77	744,374.36	97,459.41+
Total Current Assets	$1,314,913.03	$1,229,969.26	$ 84,943.77+
Current Liabilities:			
Notes Payable	$ 168,915.00	$ 182,658.25	$ 13,743.25−
Trade Accounts Payable	93,329.33	103,990.53	10,661.20−
Accounts Payable — Employees	11,251.13	11,045.39	205.74+
Income Taxes Payable	21,208.91	21,523.89	314.98−
Withholding Tax Deductions	16,673.42	20,392.16	3,718.74−
Accrued Liabilities	75,684.71	72,656.57	3,028.14+
Total Current Liabilities	$ 387,062.50	$ 12,266.79	$ 25,204.29−
Working Capital	$ 927,850.53	$ 817,702.47	$110,148.06+
Investments in Subsidiary Companies	364,592.00	346,453.09	18,138.91+
Property, Plant, and Equipment — Net	894,029.48	789,521.73	104,507.75+
Cash Value of Life Insurance	154,657.00	138,058.00	16,599.00+
Patents and License — Net	1,305.00	2,584.00	1,279.00−
Total	$2,342,434.01	$2,094,319.29	$248,114.72+
Long-term Liabilities	619,393.65	517,092.85	102,300.80+
Stockholders' Equity	$1,723,040.36	$1,577,226.44	$145,813.92+
Current Ratio	3.40 to 1	2.98 to 1	

EXHIBIT 2 (*cont.*)

NOTES PAYABLE — BANK — PAYMENTS
DUE WITHIN ONE YEAR — $152,000.00:
NOTES PAYABLE — BANK — PAYMENTS
DUE AFTER ONE YEAR — $569,503.26:

The total indebtedness to the Fulton National Bank is evidenced by three notes: one for $1,000.00 dated August 19, 1965, payable on demand and secured by seven life insurance policies owned by Southern Saw Service, Inc., on the life of E. A. Anderson; one for an original amount of $740,000.00, payable quarterly and secured by a bill of sale to secure debt on all machinery, equipment, furnishings and certain land and buildings owned by Southern Saw Service, Inc., on which there was an unpaid balance of $444,000.00, payable in 12 quarterly payments of $37,000.00 each, beginning July 5, 1973; and one for $276,503.26, drawn against a temporary line of credit in the amount of $400,000.00, which will expire December 31, 1973. The drawings against the $400,000.00 line of credit are being used to pay off certain loans and for the construction of a new office building. On completion of the office building, or by December 31, 1973, this $400,000.00 temporary line of credit will be combined with the unpaid balance of the $740,000.00 loan. The new loan will be for a period of 5 years and payable in twenty quarterly installments. Interest on the $740,000.00 note is at 1½% above prime rate, on the temporary line of credit at 1¾% above prime rate, and on the $1,000.00 note at 8%.

That part of the above loans due within one year from June 30, 1973, (assuming a consolidation of the $400,000.00 temporary line of credit with the unpaid balance of the $740,000.00 term loan) in the approximate amount of $152,000.00 is presented on the Balance Sheet, Exhibit A, as a current liability; the balance of $569,503.26 is shown thereon as a long-term liability.

Under the provisions of the loan agreement, working capital is to be maintained in an amount not less than $600,000.00, capital expenditures may not exceed $75,000.00 per year without prior written approval of the bank, and total bonuses as extra compensation may not exceed $10,000.00, nor may any dividends be paid without prior written approval of the bank. There are also certain other limitations and restrictions enumerated in the loan agreement.

Capital additions for the year under review amounted to $190,313.00, which amount was not in excess of the $400,000.00 temporary line of credit authorized by the bank for the construction of a new office building, etc. During the current year, approximately $58,000.00 was paid on the new office building under construction the total cost of which is estimated to be approximately $286,000.00.

Bonuses for the year under review amounted to $34,693.00, which amount was not in excess of the $37,000.00 special authorization by the bank.

NOTES PAYABLE — OTHERS — PAYMENTS
DUE WITHIN ONE YEAR — $16,915.00:
NOTES PAYABLE — OTHERS — PAYMENTS
DUE AFTER ONE YEAR — $49,890.39:

Exhibit 3
Comments on Operations

A summary of the results of operations for the year ended June 30, 1973, and a comparison with a summary of the results of operations for the year ended June 30, 1972, are presented in the following table:

	Year Ended 6/30/73	Year Ended 6/30/72	Increase + Decrease −
Gross Income	$4,311,733	$4,107,760	$203,973+
Cost of Sales and Service	2,167,261	1,973,832	193,429+
Gross Profit	$2,144,472	$2,133,928	$ 10,544+
Selling and Collection Expense	767,512	715,916	51,596+
Balance	$1,376,960	$1,418,012	$ 41,052−
General and Administrative Expense	946,731	932,154	14,577+
Operating Profit	$ 430,229	$ 485,858	$ 55,629−
Other Income	34,051	24,691	9,360+
Total	$ 464,280	$ 510,549	$ 46,269−
Other Deductions	152,537	105,448	47,089+
Net Income Before Income Taxes and Income from Subsidiaries	$ 311,743	$ 405,101	$ 93,358−
Income Taxes	181,655	204,420	22,765−
Net Income Before Income from Subsidiaries	$ 130,088	$ 200,681	$ 70,593−
Net Income from Subsidiaries	26,793	60,932	34,139−
Net Income — Note 1	$ 156,881	$ 261,613	$104,732−
Net Income Per Share	$ 6.28	$ 10.46	

EXHIBIT 3 (cont.)

The percentages that each of the items in the foregoing summary of operations bears to the amounts of gross income for the respective years are presented in the following table:

	Year Ended 6/30/73	Year Ended 6/30/72	Increase + Decrease −
Gross Income	100.00%	100.00%	0.
Cost of Sales and Service	50.26	48.05	2.21+
Gross Profit	49.74%	51.95%	2.21−
Selling and Collection Expense	17.80	17.43	.37+
Balance	31.94%	34.52%	2.58−
General and Administrative Expense	21.96	22.69	.73−
Operating Profit	9.98%	11.83%	1.85−
Other Income	.79	.60	.19+
Total	10.77%	12.43%	1.66−
Other Deductions	3.54%	2.57	.97+
Net Income Before Income Taxes and Income from Subsidiaries	7.23%	9.86%	2.63−
Income Taxes	4.21	4.98	.77−
Net Income Before Income from Subsidiaries	3.02%	4.88%	1.86−
Net Income from Subsidiaries	.62	1.48	.86−
Net Income — Note 1	3.64%	6.36%	2.72−

Note 1.   For comparative purposes only, the above statement of income for the year ended June 30, 1972, has been restated to include Net Income from Subsidiaries.

Case I

Hawkins Engineering Company

The year 1975 was rather severe for Hawkins Engineering Testing Company (HEC). Gross fees were down sharply from the previous year and expenses were up as a result of the increasing cost of operations. HEC's professional employees are the firm's greatest asset since its product is in the form of services. The result of turnover of engineers is very costly to the firm not only in terms of retraining and rehiring expense, but also in terms of the possible loss of clients.

HEC believes it has a comprehensive program of employee benefits which it must maintain in order to attract and hold high quality personnel. The risk manager of HEC, Mr. Robert T. Haley, has as one of his responsibilities the administration of the employee benefit program. One of the problems facing Mr. Haley during early 1976 is what to do about employee benefit cost. (See Appendix B.) Robert Haley feels that as a result of decreased net income in 1975 and a possible recurrence in 1976 that one of his chief responsibilities is to control the cost of the employee benefit program. However, Mr. Haley realizes that turnover of professional employees can lead to adverse consequences for the firm.

BACKGROUND

Hawkins Engineering Company is a privately owned professional corporation. HEC was founded by the late Fredrick C. Hawkins. Upon the death of Mr. Hawkins, the Hawkins' interest was purchased by the professional and administrative employees. Mr. Hawkins' name has been retained out of respect for his abilities, his contributions, and his reputation as a pioneer in the quality control testing field.

The corporation has around $9 million dollars in assets mostly consisting of accounts receivables, buildings, and office equipment. There are no significant items of debt on the corporate balance sheet; and HEC obtains the majority of its capital from employee stock purchases. HEC has around 544 employees. (See Appendix C.) From 1970 to 1975 employees were projected to reach 800. Since 1975 was a low profit year, the corporation was forced to lay off many of its employees.

HEC has basically three operations which are as follows: geotechnical engineering, construction services, and environmental sciences. The major portion of its fees are derived from geotechnical engineering. This consists of two services: (1) soil testing and engineering of a site on which a project is to be constructed, and (2) once the construction is underway, quality control of building materials to make sure they measure up to desired specifications. In advance of major construction, HEC's engineers study various foundation plans and determine locations where soil samples will be extracted. Drillers extract a core soil sample from the selected locations. These samples are then tested in HEC's laboratories by the company's technicians. The test results are then interpreted by engineers who analyze the ability of the soil to safely support planned structures. The engineers also make recommendations on the type of foundation that might be required, as well as building materials to be used on the job.

As favorable construction sites become more and more scarce, the problems of construction engineering become more and more necessary and complex. Soil conditions for supporting several large construction projects become a challenging problem to engineering firms. New engineering techniques are continuously being developed to enable new construction without endangering existing buildings. The corporation takes a great deal of pride in its reputation for quality service and its high caliber personnel.

THE RISK MANAGEMENT PROGRAM

Mr. Haley believes there is no formal risk management policy for the firm. (See Appendix D — Organizational Chart.) The responsibility is on his shoulders to manage the firm's risk. Mr. Haley believes his functions as a risk manager to be unique due to the nature of HEC's product and its personnel. Two important duties consist of (1) handling the property-liability exposure of the firm, and (2) administering the firm's employee benefit program. The latter takes up the majority of his time.

Property-liability Exposure

HEC has thirteen branch offices in cities throughout the southeast. All real property is covered up to $2,811,200 with a 90 percent coinsurance requirement. The coverage is on an all-risk basis which includes buildings, contents, and improvement and betterments (see Appendix E for complete property-liability insurance program and Appendix F for loss report).

The liability exposure is handled through commercial insurance, assumption, and transfer. As well as having a $1 million umbrella liability policy, HEC has $4 million excess umbrella liability coverage. However, the umbrella policies do not cover for professional errors and omissions. Therefore, the major problem concerns professional liability. Although the corporation has a professional liability policy which covers up to $1 million with a $250,000 deductible, Mr. Haley feels that HEC is grossly underinsured in this area. Mr. Haley claims the reason for the $250,000 deductible is one of necessity due to the high cost of the coverage, $58,050 annually, which compares to that of malpractice insurance for physicians. The officers of the corporation share Mr. Haley's opinion that the cost of any better coverage is prohibitive. Consequently, HEC is intentionally assuming the catastrophic loss from professional mistakes. HEC carries professional liability coverage primarily because a few clients ask for the coverage to be provided. Competition is such that in order to get a job certain factors enter into the client's decision. Mr. Haley describes these as follows: (1) price, (2) ability to provide quality professional services, and (3) financial stability. This last factor, financial stability, is evidenced by financial assets and appropriate liability insurance coverage. However, the risk manager believes that even with inadequate professional liability coverage the firm has not lost any business in the past due to this factor.

The risk manager transfers as much of the liability exposure as possible. The firm does not typically consult an attorney on contractual matters. It is Mr. Haley's job to read most of the contracts the firm enters into. Every attempt is made to transfer or avoid contractual liability, but in order to compete for jobs, HEC is forced to assume liability it would rather avoid. As Mr. Haley says, "We get stuck with every type of hold harmless agreement imaginable."

Employee Benefit Program

The second area and most important area of concern of the risk manager consists of administering the employee benefit program. The professional employees in the firm are engineers that have acquired highly technical and specialized knowledge. It has been mainly through their efforts that HEC has been successful. There is concern on the part of top management that turnover of key employees could cost the firm millions of dollars in fees through loss of clients as well as the cost associated with rehiring and retraining individuals to serve as replacements. Turnover of the younger employee presents a similar problem. Young engineers are hired directly out of college at competitive salaries. According to Mr. Haley, begin-

ning engineers can expect to earn a starting salary of around $14,000 annually. The associated training cost is estimated around $10,000 the first year. After working a few years engineers are often hired away by competing firms or go out on their own as independent consultants. HEC has attempted to make its firm attractive so as to retain its employees. The corporation also provides job stability in times of economic down turn. In 1972 there was a shortage of qualified engineers, but in 1973 and 1974 an excess developed. This new environment in the job market has made a broad comprehensive benefit program very attractive. Mr. Haley indicates that the salary range for a senior independent consultant may vary from $50,000 to $60,000 annually. An experienced counterpart with HEC would earn around $40,000. HEC offers a variety of employee benefits (see Appendix B) such as comprehensive life and health coverage, dental insurance, vacation pay, pension plan, long- and short-term disability income, and so forth. Mr. Haley believes that the corporation's position is one of providing the professional employee with incentive to stay by offering him something he cannot get on his own.

Appendix B lists employee benefits cost for 1973 and estimated cost for 1976. The costs are stated as a percentage of regular pay as well as their aggregate cost to the firm. The risk manager is faced with the problem of controlling employee benefit cost. From 1973 all employee benefits have increased 21 percent from 26.9 percent to 32.45 percent of regular pay. The net income for the firm has declined significantly from the 1973 level. Gross fees, however, have only fluctuated slightly. The major problem has been operating expenses for the firm. Due to its nature of operation, HEC has been unable to pass on much of its increases in operating cost. Competition in a period of a declining construction industry has been severe. HEC depends on big jobs which require large numbers of qualified personnel. Therefore, most of its operating expenses consist of payroll (41 percent of estimated 1976 figures). Fees from 1973 to 1976 represents a 15 percent increase. However, operating expenses over the same period are expected to increase 25 percent. The result is an estimated net income of 5.5 percent of gross fees in 1976 as compared to 8.5 percent in 1973.

In analyzing the reasons for the increasing cost of employee benefits the significant increases can be explained. Group life and health increases have come about by the effect of inflation on hospital and medical cost. The pension plan's annual cost has increased due to the effects of ERISA (Employee Retirement Income Security Act of 1974). Employees of HEC have an average age of 32 to 35 which has resulted in earlier vesting than under the 1973 plan. Payroll taxes (FICA and UCI) have increased due to the wage base increasing to $15,300. The corporation instituted a dental plan in 1975 in order to be more competitive in hiring new employees.

Mr. Haley faces several alternative ways to reduce employee benefit cost, but feels that of all the benefits provided the dental plan and group life and health plan offers the largest sources of potential savings. It is obvious that other employee benefits would be either impractical or impossible to reduce or eliminate. For example, payroll taxes and workers' compensation would be difficult to reduce. Certain benefits such as employee development, vacation pay, holiday pay, and excused time pay are also difficult to take away from employees once provided.

THE DENTAL PLAN

On March 1, 1975, the company added a dental plan as an extra benefit for their employees. The reason given by Mr. Haley was top management felt that to attract and hold qualified employees a dental plan would be a competitive fringe benefit. The risk manager was able to obtain reasonable rates from Prudential. The plan cost the firm around $54,000 annually. Appendix G shows a letter from the regional group manager indicating the monthly premium. The loss ratio for the first nine months ran around .53 percent. Mr. Haley says that HEC's first year experience will be about the same.

Several problems have come about since the initiation of the dental plan. The program has been one of constant complaint from employees. These complaints run along three lines: (1) errors have been made in a number of claim payments, (2) claims were paid correctly but with certain dental work excluded (see Appendix H for analysis of dental claims), and (3) insurance carrier takes too long to pay claims. Mr. Haley claims that in the Atlanta area dentists are performing unnecessary services which are not covered in the plan (see Appendix I for exclusions).

The risk manager feels that due to the problems in the Prudential Dental Plan the employees do not perceive the plan as a benefit. Mr. Haley also feels that the dental plan is of no good to HEC unless it can be made to be more of a benefit to the employees. For this reason and for the purpose of reducing employee benefit cost, Mr. Haley is considering self-insuring HEC's dental insurance. His reasoning is as follows: (1) The 53 percent loss ratio is extremely low for the first year. These claims indicate that the employees did not have the typical higher costing deferred dental problems that usually accompany the initiation of a dental insurance plan. The reason probably being the HEC employees have exceptional dental health, and (2) insurance carrier actuaries figure that a 20 percent buffer fund will be sufficient to cover any excess claims. For these reasons Mr. Haley has made cost comparisons between a self-insurance plan and the insured plan. He estimates that self-insurance might cost $42,444 annually, saving $11,556 a year. This estimate was derived from carrier's experience (Table I–1).

Mr. Haley indicates that these comparisons represent the minimum savings he feels are possible, however, he realizes that some risks are involved due to his basing the self-insurance program on only one year of experience.

LIFE AND HEALTH INSURANCE PLAN

The cost of life and health insurance has risen 22.3 percent since 1973 irrespective of a decrease in employment (see Appendix J). The loss ratio can be seen to run about 82 percent. Annual premiums in 1976 are expected to be $250,000. Mr. Haley believes that it is not feasible to self-insure the life and health program. The plan is self-rated and HEC presently handles the administration. In order to evaluate the decision the following analysis was made (Table I–2).

The risk manager has concluded that the problem of cutting cost in the life and health insurance plan has two possible solutions:

(1) Increase the cost to the employee by

    a. Employee contributions
    b. Employees paying all of the dependent coverage

(2) Reduce the benefit

    a. Increase the deductible
    b. Reduce the coinsurance percentage

Mr. Haley believes that the second method of reducing the benefit would be the least objected to by the employees. His reasons are due to the fact that HEC professional employees are highly compensated and can easily afford the extra expense. Under the present coverage the most that an employee would ever have to pay is $700. There is a flat $100 deductible, 80 percent coinsurance up to the first $1,000, then 90 percent coinsurance up to

TABLE I-1

	$ of Premium	Cost
Annual premium: $54,000		
Losses	53	$28,620
Administrative Cost	15	8,100
Contingency (20% of 53%)	10.6	5,724
	78.6%	$42,444
Savings	21.4%	$11,556

TABLE I-2

Self-Insurance Cost:

Claims	$205,000
Administration Expense	20,000
Excess Major Medical	20,000
Georgia Premium Tax 2 Percent	5,000
	$250,000

Insurance Cost:

Insurance Premium	$250,000
NO SAVINGS	–0–

$4,000, and finally 100 percent coverage up to $50,000 per employee. The following presents a comparison of the associated cost involved with each alternative.

I. Increasing the cost to the employee:

Presently HEC pays as follows:

Employee Cost	$ 79,000
Dependent Cost	53,950
Administration Expense	25,000
	$157,950

A. Alternative #1:

Let the employee pay for 25% of the employee cost. Savings over present plan: $19,750

B. Alternative #2:

Let the employee pay for the total dependent cost. Savings over present plan: $53,950

II. Reduce the benefits:

A. Alternative #3:

1. Increase the deductible to $100 per person instead of $100 per family per year. Savings: $20,000.
2. Employee pays first day in hospital. Savings: $5,000.
3. Separate $50 deductible for prescription drugs. Savings: $5,000.
4. Separate $200 deductible on maternity benefits. Savings: $4,000.

Total Possible Savings: $34,000

B. Alternative #4 — Reduce coinsurance percentage

Presently, the plan provides:

	Employee Pays
$100 deductible then plan pays:	$ 100
80 percent of first $1,000	200
90 percent the next $4,000	400
100 percent over $5,000	–0–
Total Maximum Paid by Employee:	$ 700

Alternative #4:

$100 deductible plan pays:	$ 100
80 percent of first $5,000	1,000
100 percent over $5,000	–0–
Total Amount Paid by Employee:	$ 1,100
Savings:	$12,000

A comparison of savings under the four possible alternatives follows:

Effect on Employee Benefit Cost:

Alternative #1	$19,750
Alternative #2	53,950
Alternative #3	34,000
Alternative #4	12,000

Mr. Haley favors alternative #3 or #4. He feels that the employees will object less to either of these actions.

QUESTIONS

1. Should HEC reduce employee benefit costs? Analyze each alternative and its possible effects on the company.

2. Should the risk manager try to find out the attitudes and opinions of the employees about possible reduction of employee benefits? How?

3. Should Mr. Haley self-insure the dental plan? Why or why not?

4. How much should the company carry in general liability limits? In professional liability limits? How much should the deductible be in each case? Give reasons.

APPENDIX A
Comparative Income Statements 1973–74

| | (figures in 1,000) | | |
	1973	1974	1976
Gross Fees	$14,700	$18,400	$14,500
Operating Expenses	12,197	15,535	14,100
Operating Income	2,503	2,865	400
Net Income*	$ 1,251	$ 1,428	$ 200
	(Expressed in percent of Gross Fees)		
Gross Fees	100.0%	100.0%	100.0%
Operating Expenses	83.0%	84.0%	97.0%
Operating Income	17.0%	16.0%	3.0%
Net Income*	8.5%	8.0%	1.5%

* 50% tax bracket assumed.

APPENDIX B
Employee Benefit Costs

| | 1973 | | 1976 | |
	Cost	Percentage of Regular Pay	Cost	Percentage of Regular Pay
Workers Compensation	$ 31,100	.55	$ 78,608	1.12
Group Life and Health	123,524	2.18	157,900	2.26
Pension	190,490	3.36	300,000	4.28
Employee Development	329,984	5.81	406,700	5.81
Long and Short Term Disability	23,896	.04	35,000	.05
Payroll Taxes (FICA and UCI)	335,672	5.91	630,900	9.01
Holiday Pay	173,105	3.05	213,500	3.05
Vacation Pay	212,362	3.75	262,500	3.75
Excused Time Pay	107,328	1.89	132,300	1.89
Dental	—	—	54,000	.08
	$1,527,531	26.91%	$2,271,458	32.45%

APPENDIX C
Personnel

By Type of Skill

Administrative	113
Chemical Engineers	1
Civil Engineers	11
Construction Inspectors	155
Draftsmen	9
Ecologists	6
Economists	1
Geologists	13
Hydrologists	6
Oceanographers	1
Soil Engineers	104
Construction Materials Engineers	38
Physicists	1
Metallurgists	1
Drillers	84
Total	544

By Geographical Area

Atlanta, Ga. (Corporate)	40
Gainesville, Ga.	77
Greenville, S.C.	73
Houston, Texas	69
Nashville, Tenn.	20
Marietta, Ga.	1
Athens, Ga.	28
Charlotte, N.C.	76
Orlando, Fla.	1
Gainesville, Fla.	14
Raleigh, N.C.	3
Tampa, Fla.	11
Washington, D.C.	38
Birmingham, Ala.	38
Norfolk, Va.	55
Total	544

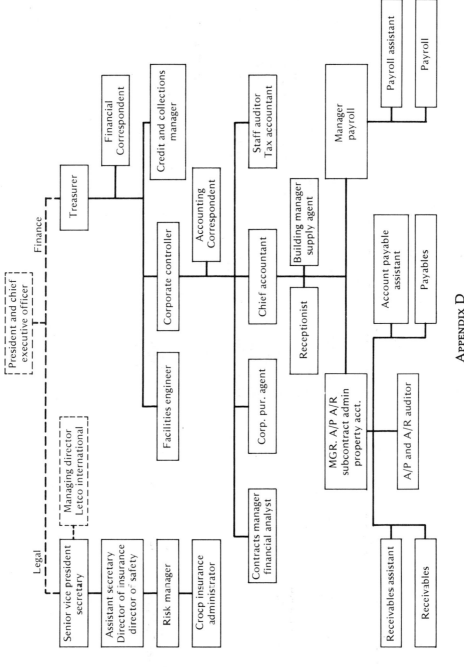

APPENDIX D

APPENDIX E

Policy Name	Policy Number	Policy Term	Amount/Limit	% Coins	Premium	Comments
Workers' Compensation and Employers' Liab.	1417-00-052816	1/1/76 to 1/1/77	Statutory. In 21 States. $100,000. Additional Medical in 2 Limited States		$ 78,594. Subject to Audit	Extension of Employers' Liability to the 6 monopolistic state fund states. Foreign Coverage — state of hire benefits. Maritime Coverage — Type I and Type II. U.S. Longshoremen's & Harbor Workers' (USL&H), Broad Form All States, Voluntary Compensation, Extended Protection and 60 days notice endorsements. 1.23 Experience Mod.
Comprehensive General Liability	1427-00-052816	1/1/76 to 1/1/77	Bodily Injury $300,000. 300,000. Property Damage $100,000. 100,000. (PD has $250. deductible per occurrence)		$ 25,775. Subject to Audit	Blanket Contractual Liability. 60 days notice. Personal Injury with employee exclusion deleted. Owned, Hired, & Nonowned watercraft coverage. Broad Form Additional Insureds endorsement. Limited Insureds for specific operations. Limited Insureds for specific locations. World Wide Coverage, Broad Form Property Damage, Employees as additional insureds, & Modified notice of an occurrence.

Insurance Coverage Abstract   For: Hawkins Engineering Company   Date: 1/1/76

Policy Name	Policy Number	Policy Term	Amount/Limit	% Coins	Premium	Comments
Comprehensive Auto Liability & Physical Damage	1427-02-052816	1/1/76 to 1/1/77	Bodily Injury $300,000. 300,000. Property Damage $100,000. (PD has $250. deductible per occurrence) Minimum P.I.P.		$ 65,105. Subject to Audit	Physical Damage on Fleet Automatic basis with $250. Deductible Collision on 1972 and later models and $100. Deductible Comprehensive all units. Liability includes blanket hired, owned and non-owned coverage. Broad Form Additional Insureds endorsement. Office trailers are included on this policy. Hired & Non-owned Liability is Worldwide. 60 Days notice.

All of the Workers' Compensation premium and the first $20,000. Bodily Injury and the first $20,000. Property Damage Liability premiums for the Ccmprehensive General and Comprehensive Auto policies are included in a one year Retrospective Plan D. There are no loss limitations in this plan.

APPENDIX E (continued)

Insurance Coverage Abstract		For: Hawkins Engineering Company				Date: 1/1/76
Policy Name	Policy Number	Policy Term	Amount/Limit	% Coins	Premium	Comments
Manufacturers Output Policy including Contractors' Equipment Floater	1467-00-052816	1/1/76 Until Cancelled	Real Prop. $2,811,200. Personal Prop. $ 708,500. Contractors Equipment $ 975,000. Improve. & Better. $ 251,000. Extra Expense $ 100,000. Blanket (40-30-30 basis) $500. Ded. Per Occurrence	90%	$20,000.	All-risks coverage on schedule of 31 locations for contents, buildings, improvements and betterments. $15,000. on buildings, contents or improvements at miscellaneous unnamed locations. Schedule of $7,116. watercraft and motors. $100,000. flood coverage on contractors equipment. Replacement cost basis on buildings. ACV basis on contents and equipment. $25,000. Worldwide extension on equipment. $50,000. extension on rented equipment. Broad Form Additional Insureds. Owner-Additional Insureds at 3 locations. Waiver of subrogation—blanket basis. Excludes property of employees and property (other than contractors equipment) while in transit.
Schedule Crime	1453-00-052816	1/1/73 Until Cancelled	$ 250,000. Employee Dishonesty $ 250,000. Forgery of Issued Instruments		$ 1,685.	Broad Form Additional Insureds and ERISA endorsements for "Pension Plan for All Employees of Hawkins Engineering Company."
Professional Liability	AE 450387	12/20/75 to 12/20/76	$1,000,000. per occurrence and aggregate. $250,000. Ded.		$58,050.	Professional Errors and Omissions protection. Retroactive to 1/1/71, Worldwide coverage, prior acts exclusion, 30 days notice.

Insurance Coverage Abstract					For: Hawkins Engineering Company		Date: 1/1/76
Policy Name	Policy Number	Policy Term	Amount/Limit	% Coins	Premium	Comments	
Aircraft Liability and Hull	AIR 028190	One Year	$6,000,000. combined single limit for BI, PD including passengers		$ 1,431.	Includes $25,000. All-risks Hull coverage with no deductible and $2,500. each person medical payments. Blanket Broad Form Hired and Nonowned Liability	
Umbrella Liability	1437-04-052816	1/1/76 to 1/1/77	$1,000,000. per occurrence and aggregate		$ 1,985.	Excess of Comprehensive General and Auto Liability and of Employers' Liability with $10,000. retention for occurrences not covered by them.	
Excess Umbrella	M-831051	8/1/75 to 1/1/77	$4,000,000. per occurrence and aggregate		$ 2,129.	Catastrophe Liability protection excess of the $1,000,000. Umbrella.	

APPENDIX E
Property Liability Cost Summary

Insurance Coverage	Premium
Workers' Compensation & Employers' Liability	$ 78,594
Comprehensive General Liability	25,775
Comprehensive Auto Liability & Physical Damage	65,105
Manufacturers Output Policy including Contractors' Equipment Floater	20,000
Schedule Crime	1,685
Professional Liability	58,050
Aircraft Liability & Hull	1,431
Umbrella Liability	1,985
Excess Umbrella	2,129
Other	506
Total	$255,335

APPENDIX F

February 4, 1976

TO: Branch and Regional Managers
FROM: Safety Director
SUBJECT: *1975 Loss Report*
    Enclosed are the loss reports for 1975 and comparison of losses for 3 years.

(1) Workers' Compensation Branch	1973	1974	1975
Atlanta, Ga.	$ 743	$ 3,107	$ 1,809
Charlotte, N.C.	1,306	276	82
Greenville, S.C.	16,891[1]	16,161[4]	8,102[6]
Houston, Texas	404	3,886	6,244
Washington, D.C.	440	16,989[5]	396
Norfolk, Va.	20,515[3]	4,338	3,034
Athens, Ga.	477	1,507	43
Tampa, Fla.	892	117	45
Birmingham, Ala.	10,971[2]	2,611	1,740
Gainesville, Fla.	—	—	183
Nashville, Tenn.	—	—	65
Atlanta, Ga.	0	0	15
Company Totals	$52,639	$48,992	$21,758

[1] Loss of arm on drill rig.
[2] Back Injury.
[3] Truck Accident.
[4] Fall off scaffolding.
[5] Truck Accident.
[6] Car Accident.

(2) Motor Vehicle Experience

Branch	1973	1974	1975
Atlanta, Ga.	$ 7,010	$ 1,192	$ 4,636
Charlotte, N.C.	2,369	10,267	2,945
Greenville, S.C.	391	8,633	16,527[1]
Houston, Texas	500	3,954	7,044
Washington, D.C.	263	3,199	438
Norfolk, Va.	954	2,679	1,920
Athens, Ga.	0	0	335
Tampa, Fla.	582	2	0
Birmingham, Ala.	8,023	179	266
Gainesville, Fla.	—	—	157
Nashville, Tenn.	—	—	0
Company Totals	$20,092	$30,105	$34,268

[1] Car Accident 3/16/75.

(3) General Liability Experience

Branch	1973	1974	1975
Atlanta, Ga.	0	$ 1,000	0
Charlotte, N.C.	0	0	0
Greenville, S.C.	0	$10,000	0
Houston, Texas	$3,339	0	0
Washington, D.C.	0	0	0
Norfolk, Va.	0	500	143
Athens, Ga.	0	0	0
Tampa, Fla.	0	0	0
Birmingham, Ala.	0	0	288
Gainesville, Fla.	—	—	0
Nashville, Tenn.	—	—	0
Company Totals	$3,339	$11,500	$431

APPENDIX G
Memorandum

December 30, 1975

To: HEC
From: Insurance Company Manager

As we discussed, enclosed are the Group Insurance Benefit Payment Listings which were somehow not referred to your personal attention. Henceforth, a monthly listing will be prepared and sent to you.

I understand the March 1, 1975, listing was sent directly to your attention and enclosed are the following items:

June 1, 1975	Policy year to date listing Claims	$ 7,469.24
September 1, 1975	Policy year to date listing Claims	15,201.49
Loss ratio—53%		

Perhaps it might be helpful to you to review the Monthly Group Premium Reports:

March 1, 1975	$4,864.65
April 1, 1975	4,773.21
May 1, 1975	4,818.06
June 1, 1975	4,888.98
July 1, 1975	4,614.92
August 1, 1975	4,554.39
September 1, 1975	4,529.61
October 1, 1975	4,513.80
November 1, 1975	4,531.74

Please let me know if I can assist you further in any way.

APPENDIX H
Dental Analysis

Hawkins Engineering Company

Number of Claims Paid Correctly	479
Number of Claims with Errors	39
Total Claims	519
Claims paid correctly but with exclusions	107
Incorrect Claims	39
Total Claims with Errors and Exclusions	146
Ratio of Total Claims Paid to Claims with errors and exclusions	28%
Total Exclusions	$5,409.50
Approximate Benefit (70%) (for 3 quarters)	$3,786.65
Pro Rate to 1 year	$5,048.88

APPENDIX I

Exclusion Under Dental Expense Insurance

In the case of an individual whose Dental Expense Insurance starts more than 31 days after that individual becomes eligible to be insured, services received during the first year the insurance is in effect will not be covered. But this exclusion does not apply to a service made necessary by an accident occurring while the individual is insured. The insurance does not cover:

1. A service or supply not included in the "List of Dental Services" except under the conditions explained in "What the Insurance Covers."

2. Anything not furnished by a dentist, except X-rays ordered by a dentist, and services by a licensed dental hygienist under the dentist's supervision; anything not necessary or not customarily provided for dental care.

3. Services (a) furnished by or for the U.S. Government, or (b) furnished by or for any other government unless payment is legally required, or (c) to the extent provided under any governmental program or law under which the individual is, or could be, covered.

4. An appliance, or modification of one, where an impression was made before the patient was covered; a crown, bridge or gold restoration for which the tooth was prepared before the patient was covered; root canal therapy if the pulp chamber was opened before the patient was covered.

5. A crown, gold restoration, or a denture or fixed bridge or addition of teeth to one, if the work involves a replacement or modification of a crown, gold restoration, denture, or bridge installed less than five years before.

6. A denture or fixed bridge involving replacement of teeth extracted before the individual was covered, unless it also replaces a tooth that is extracted while covered, and such tooth was not an abutment for a denture or fixed bridge installed during the preceding five years.

7. Services due to an accident related to employment or disease covered under workers' compensation or similar law.

8. Replacement of lost or stolen appliances; appliances or restorations for the purpose of splinting, or to increase vertical dimension or restore occlusion.

9. Orthodontics (a program to straighten teeth); dental care of a congenital or developmental malformation; services for cosmetic purposes unless made necessary by an accident occurring while covered. Facings on molar crowns or pontics are always considered cosmetic.

10. Any portion of a charge for a service in excess of the reasonable and customary charge (the charge usually made by the provider when there is no insurance, not to exceed the prevailing charge in the area for dental care of a comparable nature, by a person of similar training and experience).

11. Expenses applied toward satisfaction of a deductible under the Dental Expense Insurance.

APPENDIX J
Hawkins Engineering Company
Group Life and Health Experience
Self-Rated Contract

Year	Earned Premium	Paid Claims	Estimated Unpaid Liabilities	Total Incurred Claims	Loss Ratio %
1966	$ 29,302.03	$ 24,770.90	$ 3,250.38	$ 28,021.28	95.6%
1967	41,176.33	29,534.18	(120.86)	29,413.32	71.4%
1968	60,105.34	46,753.55	13,566.83	60,320.38	100.4%
1969	66,284.66	35,679.97	(5,057.06)	30,622.91	46.2%
1970	75,639.39	57,259.95	10,004.72	67,264.67	88.9%
1971	89,364.28	66,846.63	(200.00)	66,646.63	74.6%
1972	129,428.10	69,892.03	18,661.86	88,553.89	68.4%
1973	196,957.79	111,665.47	76,696.01	188,361.48	95.6%
1974	234,218.87	178,758.54	13,621.04	192,379.58	82.1%
1975	240,839.00	—	—	196,907.00	81.8%
Total	$1,163,315.70	—	—	$948,491.14	81.5% (Average)

Case J

Midwest Gas and Oil Company

Early in 1962, as negotiations for the addition of New England Petroleum Ltd. to the Midwest Gas and Oil Company

Reprinted from Stanford business cases, 1962, with permission of the publishers, Stanford University Graduate School of Business, © 1962, by the Board of Trustees of the Leland Stanford Junior University.

were nearing completion, Ralph Warren (the latter concern's risk manager) was asked by the treasurer Jim Loffmask to submit a detailed plan for integrating the insurance aspects of New England Petroleum with Midwest's program. In that New England did not maintain an insurance department, the entire postmerger philosophy would become the responsibility of Mr. Warren.

NEW ENGLAND PETROLEUM LTD.

New England Petroleum Ltd., a marketing company with almost 5,000 employees was incorporated in Massachusetts. It operated through 9,200 retail outlets almost equally distributed across six eastern states. Only a third of these stations were company owned. Most recent net sales figures were in the neighborhood of $507 million. (Other financial information is provided in Appendix A.)

The firm's insurance program was run quite informally, handled primarily by the company's legal counsel William Hall, though the board of directors became involved when major changes in coverage were contemplated.

In the area of workers' compensation, New England was a self-insurer in all six states. However, self-insurance was not resorted to in the case of public liability and the following policies were in effect:

1) Scheduled automobile liability (covers vehicles of commission agents and hired vehicles in addition to those owned by the firm) with $100,000 all-inclusive limits. This is an annually written contract.

2) Products liability with aggregate limits of $1 million for the company and $500,000 for agents. Limits per accident are $10,000 and $50,000 respectively. This is a three-year contract with about two years left to run.

3) Garage liability (paid for by dealers) with limits of $50,000/$1,000,000/$15,000; and involving annual renewal.

4) Aviation liability coverage to take care of New England's two aircraft. Public liability limits are $1,000,000/$600,000/$100,000, while passenger liability is $1 million per seat. There is also provision for medical payments. This contract is written on an annual basis.

5) Comprehensive general and automobile liability, used as excess coverage, with a maximum limit of $20 million. This is also a one-year contract.

In property insurance, the company is a self-insurer to the extent of $200,000. In excess of that amount there is a fire contract with extended coverage. Boiler and machinery insurance (direct loss only) is carried at eleven locations. Both the fire and boiler policies have three years to run.

In dishonesty insurance, the company is a self-insurer except for a blanket position bond with each employee covered for $10,000, a commercial blanket excess bond for $100,000, and a depositors' forgery bond with a twelve month discovery period after expiration and $50,000 insurance on both incoming and outgoing instruments. All are issued annually.

Group benefits include health insurance for 100 key employees, paid for entirely by the company. Indemnity for loss-of-time amounts to 60 percent of salary after a 26-week waiting period. Benefits are for up to 104 consecutive weeks in event of sickness or total disability. The usual loss of limbs, sight, or life benefits are also included. No provision is made for medical or hospital expenses.

All employees receive ten days sick leave with full pay for each year's service, up to maximum of twenty-six weeks. In addition, there are provisions for a contributory-trusteed-annuity plan. Both employer and employee contribute 4 percent of gross income, with vesting after twenty years or at age sixty-five.

MIDWEST GAS AND OIL COMPANY

Midwest Gas and Oil, a large integrated company with 45,000 employees and sales approaching $3 billion, operates in all fifty states of the U.S. and several foreign countries. Loosely speaking, the company can be called a self-insurer; though no funding is involved, reserves are set up, and appear on the balance sheet (see Appendix B).

All insurance is handled by a risk manager, attached to the treasurer's department and reporting directly to the treasurer. The treasurer bypasses the vice-president in charge of finance and reports directly to the chairman of the board. The aforementioned vice-president is, however, chairman of the insurance committee which includes the treasurer. Major decisions involving insurance are communicated to the board but for the purposes of information only. While the risk manager is responsible for most matters involving insurance, employee benefits and workers' compensation are handled by the benefits and safety divisions of the personnel department respectively.

Midwest self-insures workers' compensation in states where it is both legally permissible and where it has a sufficient concentration of employees. This policy also applies offshore on drilling platforms. It should be noted that the company has very few employees in Alaska, Alabama, Georgia, Kentucky, Mississippi, Vermont, and Virginia.

With public liability, the company is self-insured up to $1 million both on land and offshore, and for both bodily injury and property damage. This is also the case with P. & I. liabilities in connection with the ownership and operation of tankers. Excess insurance, written on an occurrence basis and in the form of a $19 million single-limit comprehensive general and automobile liability policy, is contracted for. This mode of coverage also applies to the firm's thirty aircraft. No provision is made for any coverage to extend to commission agents or service station dealers.

In the case of property insurance, Midwest is self-insured up to $2 million against fire and extended perils plus flood, earthquake, and transportation. While no coverage is provided for wells, the plants, equipment, drilling platforms, and tankers are covered in this manner. Excess coverage offshore is on an all-risks basis while coverage ashore is limited to fire and the extended coverage endorsement, plus vandalism and malicious mischief.

Though limited amounts of boiler and machinery insurance are carried so as to get inspection service, no provision is made for business interruption, plate glass, or dishonesty losses. Surety bonds are purchased because of the legal requirement, and a depositor's forgery bond with $50,000 insurance on both incoming and outgoing instruments is carried.

Group benefits are fairly extensive and include:

1) Life insurance of up to the equivalent of two years salary — depending on length of service, plus an additional year if killed on the job. Employees can, at their own expense, arrange for the equivalent of one year's salary as a supplement.

2) A contributory trusteed annuity plan, with 5 percent of gross income being

set aside by both employer and employee. Vesting occurs after twenty-five years or at retirement age. This program can be expanded by a stock purchase plan to which the company makes contributions.

3) Hospital and medical payments benefits are purchased by the company for employees. There is a $50 aggregate annual deductible along with 20 percent coinsurance. The employee can purchase coverage for his dependents under the same contract.

4) Sick leave is provided by the company, building up to twenty-six weeks at full pay plus twenty-six weeks at half pay after ten years of service.

APPENDIX A
New England Petroleum Ltd.
Balance Sheets as at December 31
(in thousands)
of dollars

	1961	1960
Current Assets:		
Cash	$ 16,000	$ 17,300
Short-term investments[1]	1,100	1,000
Accounts Receivable (net)	33,160	32,000
Inventories	17,600	18,580
Prepaid Insurance	401	420
Misc.	339	300
Total Current Assets	$ 68,600	$ 69,600
Fixed Assets:		
Land	$ 6,200	$ 6,000
Plant and Equipment	115,600	98,400
Allowances for Depreciation	41,800	38,500
Total Assets	$148,600	$135,500
Current Liabilities:		
Accounts Payable	$ 23,100	$ 17,100
Accrued Taxes	20,600	20,400
Total Current Liabilities	$ 43,700	$ 37,500
Capital Stock & Surplus:		
Capital Stock	$ 20,000	$ 20,000
Capital Surplus	1,400	1,400
Earned Surplus	82,400	75,600
Reserve for contingencies — fire, flood, etc.	1,100	1,000
Total Liabilities and Net Worth	$148,600	$135,500

[1] See Reserve for contingencies.

APPENDIX B
Midwest Gas and Oil Company
Consolidated Balance Sheets as at December 31
(in thousands of dollars)

	1961	1960
Current Assets:		
Cash	$ 109,100	$ 101,000
Short-term investments	137,900	138,000
Receivables (net)	317,900	310,500
Inventories	216,400	201,000
Misc.	4,500	4,500
Total Current Assets	$ 785,500	$ 745,000
Prepaid Charges	23,100	21,900
Investments	116,400	91,100
Properties, Plant, & Equipment	4,152,500	3,834,000
Allowances for depreciation & depletion	1,112,500	1,100,000
Total Assets	$3,965,000	$3,592,000
Current Liabilities:		
Accounts Payable	$ 301,700	$ 256,000
Accrued Taxes	108,300	101,600
Current Portion of debt	2,400	2,400
Total Current Liabilities:	$ 412,400	$ 360,000
Reserves — Insurance	$ 31,600	$ 30,100
Long-term Debt	207,500	209,400
Shareholders' Equity:		
Preferred Stock	$ 131,100	$ 130,000
Common Stock	504,500	504,500
Capital Surplus	76,000	76,000
Earned Surplus	2,601,900	2,482,000
Total Liabilities and Equity	$3,965,000	$3,592,000

Case K

Southern Saw Service (B)

In 1971, Mr. Carlos Martel, sales manager, and Mr. Robert Haege, treasurer, Southern Saw Service, were considering the policy of credit risk in the international operations of the firm. The policy of the firm had been to sell on open account in most cases, with terms of credit up to 90 days. No credit insurance was currently being purchased for either domestic or export sales. Recently, a representative of the Foreign Credit Insurance Association (FCIA) had contacted Mr. Martel about the possibility of taking out short-term export credit insurance under a master policy.

CREDIT MANAGEMENT POLICIES

Merchandise sales of the company are handled through a subsidiary, the Atlanta Saw Company. Exports are billed in U.S. dollars in order to avoid the risk of fluctuations in value of foreign currencies. Export sales had been good. In the first six months of 1973 exports rose from 25 percent to 45 percent of total sales. In the first nine months of 1973 exports were 42 percent of total sales. Management has the objective of greatly increasing exports in the future.

Bad debt losses have been very modest, averaging perhaps .4 percent of sales. For example, bad debt losses in 1972 were slightly over $17,000 on sales of $2,286,000 for the Southern Saw Company and under $800 for the Atlanta Saw Company on sales of $892,000. One reason for the low level of bad debts in the Southern Saw Company is traceable to their policy of only leasing saws and saw equipment to customers. In this way the company maintains a close contact with all customers. In the case of export sales, the company seeks at least three commercial references together with the name of the customer's bank. These references are obtained from international banks or from Dun and Bradstreet. If the references are satisfactory, shipment is made on open account; otherwise, on sight draft or cash against documents. The company feels that open account credit is a stimulus to sales and represents good business. For the last five years the company has suffered only one relatively severe bad debt loss amounting to $6,000. This loss stemmed from a customer in Puerto Rico who had originally sought an exclusive distributorship. This request was refused, since it is not the policy of Atlanta Saw Company to grant exclusive distributorships. The customer pressed again later on for an exclusive distributorship, but was refused again. The customer simply refused to pay for his current account.

Mr. Haege investigated the possibility of bringing legal action in Puerto Rico but found that it was extremely difficult to do so. The company engaged two lawyers in an attempt to collect the debt and they still have not succeeded although the debt is over three years old.

As of November 14, 1973, the company's four largest account balances were as follows: $28,100, $20,500, $17,500, and $7,500. Most of these accounts are on 90-day credit terms. Mr. Haege believed that no undue risk was presented by these accounts. When the export business first began, the company worked with a large local bank which had an arrangement with the FCIA to insure all export credit sales of the firm. One of the difficulties with this arrangement was that the bank would only approve what the company considered safe accounts. Mr. Haege believed that the doubtful accounts on which coverage was needed were routinely refused. Another difficulty with the arrangement was the bookkeeping. "We didn't know where we stood at any one time," stated Mr. Haege. If a customer desired credit beyond the discretionary limit it might or might not be approved. The greatest difficulty, though, was the uncertainty in learning at any one moment the exact status of coverage. This uncertainty delayed shipments and caused customer ill will. When export credit insurance was dropped, the company took over the risk itself. Mr. Haege did not believe that there was much trouble in getting a credit report. They normally used their local bank, the Fulton National Bank, which was able to obtain a report within three weeks. Occasionally, Dun and Bradstreet and the U.S. Department of Commerce World Trade Data services were used, but credit reports through these agencies sometimes took as long as three months.

THE EXPORT CREDIT INSURANCE PROPOSAL

Under the terms of the master policy of export credit insurance, the exporter is granted 90 percent coverage on bad debt losses against commercial and 95 percent against political risks. The credit manager would have a discretionary credit limit whereby he could ship to customers, up to a limit, without obtaining prior approval from the F.C.I.A., thus speeding up the credit-granting process. The policy would have a deductible roughly equal to expected or normal bad debt losses in the exporter's business. The premium would depend on the size of the deductible, the credit terms, and the degree of risk attached to the foreign country in which the goods were sold.

In the case of Southern Saw Service, for example, the policy would be issued on a whole turnover basis, covering all of the company's export sales. However, on medium term credit sales (180 days to 5 years), the F.C.I.A. would permit the exclusion from coverage of large well-rated accounts considered to carry little risk. The discretionary limit would be set so that it would include 80 percent of the exporter's orders. If 50 percent of all orders were under, say, $5,000, and 80 percent were under $10,000, the discretionary limit might be set at $10,000. An order under $10,000 would be shipped with coverage applying without prior approval of the F.C.I.A. The deductible would be about equal to the discretionary limit, or $10,000. Before the company could ship under a discretionary limit, it would have to be able to show that it had at least two current satisfactory credit reports on the buyer (available from international banks, Dun and Bradstreet, or the U.S. Department of Commerce).

TABLE J–1

Terms of Sale	A Country	D Country
	(Rate per $100 of Sales)	
1. Irrevocable letter of credit or cash vs. documents	$.21	$ .56
2. Sight draft up to 30 days	.27	.72
3. Open account credit 1–90 days	.44	1.16
4. Open account credit 91–180 days	.54	1.42

The premium on a policy with a $10,000 deductible would depend on terms of sale and on the risk attached to the market in which the sales take place. Markets (countries) are rated A through D, according to risk. A sample of rates might be shown in Table J–1.

Under the master policy the Southern Saw Service's sales would be analyzed and a composite rate would be charged on all sales. For example, if half of all sales were in A countries and half were in D countries, on sight draft terms the composite rate applying to all sales would be $.495 per $100 of invoice value ($.27+$.72/2). Claims would take about 10 days to process. A claim can be filed once the account is at least 90 days past due.

However, Mr. Martel believed that the firm can handle the export credit risk satisfactorily by good credit management procedures. His shipments were of relatively small unit value (averaging about $1,000) and were widely dispersed geographically. Considerable care was taken to check out customers before orders were shipped. An example of this was a customer from Nigeria (Animawun & Sons), as shown in a letter dated May 18, 1971 (Exhibit 1). Mr. Martel answered the letter (see Exhibit 2) on May 25, 1971, and received a further reply and order (Exhibit 3) on June 11 together with a draft for $15,000. Mr. Martel discovered through his bank that no record could be found of the existence of the "International Bank of Nigeria, Ltd." He wrote to Animawun & Sons on June 22, 1971 (Exhibit 4) and received a reply on July 8, 1971 (Exhibit 5). Mr. Martel did not ship the goods and heard no further from the customer. He believed that this case was somewhat typical of other similar cases he had experienced in which buyers attempted to secure merchandise using methods of questionable honesty.

QUESTIONS

1. Evaluate the methods of international risk management used by Mr. Martel illustrated in this case in the light of risks faced by the firm.

2. To what extent is the formation of Atlanta Saw itself a method of risk management? Discuss.

3. Should Southern Saw Service use export credit insurance? Why or why not?

EXHIBIT 1

ANIMAWUN & SONS

Importers Exporters & General Merchants

(Registered in Nigeria)

****

Head Office

17, Iwade Street,

Lagos-Nigeria, W. A.

18th May . . . . . . 197. . 1 . . .

Our Ref. . . . . AS/71 . . . .

Your Ref. . . . .

Messrs: Southern Saw Service Inc.,

1594 Evans Drive, S.W.,

Atlanta, Georgia, U.S.A.

Dear Sir,

Re: Hand Saws

    We obtained your name and address through the American Register of Exporters and Importers Directory that you are one of the leading Manufacturer and exporter of the above mentioned items.

    Therefore, kindly send us your full catalogues together with your prices by the coming air mail express together with other necessary particulars about your business.

    For your information, we are one of the leading and the best importer of Nigeria, specialized on the above mentioned goods, and we are willing to work with your House.

    Kindly give us an immediate reply to this letter and comply with the requests therein so that we shall book our order immediately when we receive the catalogues, we shall book our order in large quantities, therefore we want an immediate reply.

Yours faithfully,

ANIMAWUN & SONS

/s/ . . . .

Director

Exhibit 2

May 25, 1971
Animawun & Sons
17, Iwade Street
Lagos-Nigeria, W. A.

Dear Sirs:

Your gracious letter of May 18 has been referred to us by the addressee, our parent company Southern Saw Service, Inc. Since Southern Saw Service is only a rental and service organization and our company deals strictly in the sale of the same products, we are pleased to answer your inquiry.

We are enclosing a copy of our current catalog which is presently under revision. You may use the information and prices therein until July 1st, at which time we anticipate that we will incorporate some changes in format and certain price increases. The catalog contains the prices suggested for retail (FOB Atlanta) and you, as a distributor, would be allowed a 30% discount on these. The only exception is the Special Volume Parts price list which lists net prices that are proportional to volume.

Terms for payment are upon presentation of pro-forma invoice prior to shipment of the goods or through letter of credit in our favor through the Fulton National Bank, Atlanta, Georgia. Shipping charges will be added to the cost of the goods ordered.

We will be anxious to hear from you when you have had an opportunity to study our catalog and appraise the acceptability that our products may enjoy in your country. Please let us know if we can answer any questions or be of assistance in any way.

We look forward to serving you soon.

Sincerely yours,

Carlos Martel, Jr.
Sales Engineer

CM/bh

Encl.

IMMEDIATE ACTION PLEASE
ANIMAWUN & SONS
/s/   Director

Exhibit 3
ANIMAWUN & SONS
Importers Exporters & General Merchants
(Registered in Nigeria)
****

Head Office
17, Iwade Street,
Lagos-Nigeria, W. A.

Our Ref.......AS/71.........

Your Ref....................

11th June, ...197.....1..

Messrs: Atlanta Saw Company,
Box 11000,
1594 Evans Drive
Atlanta, Georgia 30310, U.S.A.

Dear Sir,

RE: A SHIPMENT OF HAND SAW WITH FRAMES & BLADES
(HACK SAW)

We acknowledge the receipt of your letter together with your catalogues of 25th May, 1971, contents of which was carefully noted with same we give many thanks.

Furthermore, we are confirming our first order, sample order today for prompt shipment and delivery by sea (STEAMER).

To meet the great demands and the requirements of our customers in this country, we are now giving you our first trial order in accordance with the request of our customers.

SHIPMENTS

ORDER: HAND SAW FRAMES AND BLADES.

Quantity:- 500 pieces

Sizes- All sizes available in the stock are requested.

Packing:- Strongly packed in wooden cases.

Mark: A & S., 17, IWADE STREET LAGOS NIGERIA, should be written or executed on the body of the packages.

We hope you would effect prompt shipment of the goods as quickly as possible to enable same to meet the general demands and requirements of our customers without any prolongation over the delivery.

In pursuance of this, we enclosed here with our bill of exchange Draft No. 0086 of 11th June, 1971 for an amount of US$15.000.00 (FIFTEEN THOUSAND US DOLLARS) to cover the quantities booked.

p.t.o.

The above mentioned order must be executed as quickly as possible and the enclosed Draft No. 0086 must be officially rubberstamped and duly

Exhibit 3 cont.

signed by you and the draft must be attached with the ORIGINAL shipping documents and invoices bearing 15 DAYS DRAFT ACCEPTANCE with the enclosed draft and send them to our Bank immediately when the shipment of the goods is Executed.

Moreover, you are requested to comply with every instructions without any hinderance to avoid any unnecessary delay.

Please make it urgently, after your shipment of this order now in progress you are requested to send to us cable of shipment date, name of the steamer and copies of the shipping documents for notification to our address directly.

Please if you receive any communication from our area, direct them to us.

Thanking you for co-operation and hoping to receive your order confirmation next week by cable, stating date of definate shipment.

We are,

Your faithfully,
ANIMAWUN & SONS
/s/ _____ Director

No. $\frac{D}{2}$ 0086

Amount US$15.000.00
11th June, 19 71

D/A

At 15-DAYS sight pay this Bill of Exchange (FIRST unpaid) to the order of Messrs Atlanta Saw Company, Box 11000, U.S.A.

the sum of FIFTEEN THOUSAND US DOLLARS ONLY

payable at collecting Bank drawing rate for demand draft on London value which place to account as advised

Through International Bank of Nigeria Ltd.

ANIMAWUN & SONS
Yakubu Gowon Street, Lagos.
/s/ _____ Director

Animawun & Sons,
For a/c of 17, Iwade Street, Lagos, Nigeria

Reverse side of draft:

TERMS: This draft is momentarily negotiable for payment with the attachment of our Original shipping documents, duly and officially endorsed by us on the payment terms of 15/30 days D/A sight as indicated overleaf.

EXHIBIT 4

June 22, 1971
Animawun & Sons
17, Iwade Street
Lagos-Nigeria, W. A.

Gentlemen:

Thank you for your letter of June 11, your first order for 500 handsaws contained therein, and the bill of exchange for US $15,000 attached thereto.

Upon receipt of your correspondence, we consulted with our bank, to insure that we followed the proper procedure in handling your bill of exchange. They informed us that your country is presently enduring foreign exchange problems under which availability of a clearance for importing foreign products and thus expending foreign currency is very limited. Our bank therefore suggested that if you do have a clearance, that you should request your bank to telex our Fulton National Bank of Atlanta, Georgia, USA, and notify them that the required clearance is available to you. We regret that we will have to temporarily delay your order until we receive a favorable communication from your bank.

We are very anxious to have you use our products, therefore we hope to clarify this matter promptly so your shipment can be dispatched.

Sincerely yours,

Carlos Martel, Jr.
Sales Engineer

CM/cm

EXHIBIT 5

ANIMAWUN & SONS
Importers Exporters & General Merchants
(Registered in Nigeria)
****

Head Office
17, Iwade Street,
Lagos-Nigeria, W. A.

Our Ref...... AS/71 ....   8th July, ...197..1...
Your Ref...................

Attention *CARLOS MARTEL, Jr*
(Sales Engineer)

Messrs:- Atlanta Saw Company,
Division of Southern Saw Service Inc.,
Box 11000, Atlanta, Georgia 30310.,
U.S.A.

Dear Sir,

We acknowledge receipt your letter dated 22nd June, 1971, contents of which was carefully noted and understood, with same we give many thanks.

Upon receipt of your letter, and on the surface of the contents therein, we consulted our banker, and have discussion with them, and we are being told by our BANKER that we should write you back, and tell you that, since you have the BILL OF EXCHANGE with you and you go through the "INSTRUCTION" at the bank of the "DRAFT" the CLEARANCE is available on the schedule DAYS in the DRAFT.

"FOR US AND TO THE ORDER OF MESSRS: ATLANTA SAW COMPANY
BOX 11000, U.S.A.

Note:-   PAYMENT GUARANTEE:

"WE HEREBY ENGAGE OURSELVES AND GUARANTEE" TO THE HOLDERS OF THIS BILL OF EXCHANGE (DRAFT) THAT IMMEDIATE REIMBURSEMENT AMOUNT ON THIS DRAFT WILL BE RELEASED AND MADE PAYABLE IN ACCORDANCE WITH THE NIGERIA EXCHANGE CONTROL ORDINANCE WITH ALL RELEVANT SHIPPING DOCUMENTS AND BILLS OF LADING, CUSTOM INVOICES, COMMERCIAL INVOICES, INSURANCE CERTIFICATE, CERTIFICATE OF ORIGIN AND PACKING LIST, EACH OF THESE DOCUMENTS IN QUADRUPLICATE ARE SENT DIRECTLY TO US THROUGH OUR BANKERS:

INTERNATIONAL BANK OF WEST AFRICA NIGERIA LTD
YAKUBU GOWON STREET,
LAGOS.
/2.....

Exhibit 5 cont.

-----2-----

We therefore beg your House not to disapoint us before our customers, who are awaiting to see the quality of your articles.

Please, before the shipment, kindly send us, "One Sample" by air parcel post through our post office, Lagos, for more advertisement to our customers, moreover, you are requested to comply with every "INSTRUCTIONS" without any hinderance to avoid unnecessary delay.

Thanking you for co-operation, and hoping to receive your order of confirmation next week by Cable, stating date of shipments and the name of the steamer.

> We are,
> Yours faithfully,
> ANIMAWUN & SONS
> /s/   Director

Case L

Kaiser Aluminum & Chemical Corporation

FOREIGN OPERATIONS

In early 1958 the controller of Kaiser Aluminum and Chemical was preparing to report to the executive vice-president on how the firm's continuing expansion

Reprinted from Stanford Business cases, 1961, with permission of the publishers, Stanford University Graduate School of Business, © 1961, by the Board of Trustees of the Leland Stanford Junior University.

into international operations would affect the controller's division.

The problem of uncertainties surrounding overseas operations was considered especially deserving of attention. The controller was concerned with the whole spectrum of risk, but particularly with the role of insurance in risk management. He had previously given considerable thought to such matters as language barriers and rapport, confiscation, expropriation, restrictions on the placing of insurance, taxation of insurance claims, convertibility of currency, war and insurrection, depreciation of currencies and coinsurance, differences in policy forms and coverage, servicing, financial strength of the insurer, general legal problems, public relations, and price. He had at the time asked the corporations's insurance manager to gather pertinent information by investigating potential problems at their source.[1]

So as to appreciate more fully the problem of foreign insurance and its demands, the financial officer asked his insurance manager to submit a report that would evaluate the perils likely to be faced in the firm's international operations, and outline the necessary coverages. In addition to such risk analysis, attention was to be given in a separate section of the report to actual placing of the coverage, including the feasibility of self-insurance, and the services of the Export-Import Bank. Finally, the advisability of operating on a decentralized basis was to be considered.

A short time later, but prior to receiving the complete report requested, the controller was faced with another problem of insurance, this one requiring an immediate decision.

Negotiations for sale of both pure and foundry aluminum ingots were being carried on with several European concerns, including the Netherlands firm of Van den Berg, Wouda, and Grilk with offices on the outskirts of the

Hague. In view of the difficulty in securing shipping exactly as required, below-deck freight space was engaged on the MS Oslofjord to Rotterdam and arrangements were made to have the goods stored in a bonded warehouse while sales on the continent were being finalized. If this manner, prompt delivery could be assured — a necessity in view of competition — and payments of import duties avoided or deferred as the case may be. It was a virtual certainty that but a few days storage would be involved.

The warehouseman had contacted the company and indicated his willingness to arrange for all necessary insurance, including cargo insurance with a warehouse-to-warehouse clause. The insurance manager was asked for a decision as to whether the company should accept the warehouseman's offer to arrange insurance, along with some specific details on the required coverage, terms, and conditions to be insisted upon if the offer was to be accepted.

GENERAL HISTORY OF KAISER ALUMINUM & CHEMICAL CORPORATION

Kaiser Aluminum & Chemical Corporation's early history started with the formation of Todd-California Shipbuilding Corporation in 1940 to build World War II cargo vessels. It was the creation of Henry J. Kaiser and his associates in the construction industry.

In 1941 under the new company name of the Permanente Metals Corporation, the firm entered the light metals industry to produce magnesium using the carbothermic process. In 1942 a second magnesium plant was built and it employed the silicothermic process. Permanente "Goop," a secret magnesium paste which went into incendiary

---

[1] The insurance department, which handled all of Kaiser Aluminum & Chemical's insurance, consisted of stenographic help plus four others besides the manager. Even should the function of risk management remain a centralized program, expansion outside of the United States, as projected, would call for addition of at least one staff member (ignoring stenographic and clerical help).

bombs was developed by the Corporation during World War II.

Following termination of hostilities, an entry was made into the primary aluminum industry.[2] This was the result of a lease in 1946, and subsequent purchase from the government in 1949, of an alumina plant at Baton Rouge, Louisiana; a reduction plant at Mead, Washington, and a rolling mill at Trentwood, Washington. In 1946, the corporation also increased its participation in the industrial chemical and refractory field through purchase of the refractory business of Permanente Cement Company.

In 1947, the government-owned reduction plant at Tacoma, Washington, was acquired as were initial options on bauxite reserves in Jamaica. The government-owned rod and bar mill at Newark, Ohio, was purchased in 1949 and later equipped to produce wire and cable. Also in 1949, a foil mill was installed at Permanente, California.

In May 1951, the Corporation leased from the government an extension plant near Baltimore, Maryland. A government-owned magnesium plant at Manteca, California, built and operated by the Corporation during World War II, was operated for the government from June 1951 to July 1953.

From 1950 to 1954, the Corporation completed a major program of expansion which included the construction of a primary aluminum plant at Chalmette, Louisiana; the installation of facilities to aid the development of bauxite reserves in Jamaica; the adoption and enlargement of its Baton Rouge, Louisiana, alumina plant to process Jamaican, as well as other bauxite, and the installation of addi-

tional primary capacity at its aluminum plants in the Northwest. The Corporation's primary aluminum capacity was increased during this period from 133,000 tons to 428,000 tons annually.

Late in 1954, a major expansion program with a total estimated cost in excess of $400 millions was embarked on. Most important of the new facilities under this program was the construction of a fully integrated reduction plant and sheet and foil rolling mill at Ravenswood, West Virginia. Also included in the expansion were a new alumina and caustic-chlorine plant at Gramercy, Louisiana; an additional potline at the Chalmette, Louisiana, reduction plant; extrusion plants at Halethorpe, Maryland, and Dolton, Illinois;[3] a forge plant at Erie, Pennsylvania; a wire and cable plant at Bristol, Rhode Island; construction of foil-processing facilities at Wanatah, Indiana, and Belpre, Ohio, and various other facilities. This expansion program was completed in 1959 and increased the Corporation's production capacity for primary aluminum to 609,500 tons annually.

On May 1, 1959, to augment its refractory line, the Mexico Refractories Company was merged into the Corporation in exchange for 300,000 shares of common stock and 150,000 4¾% cumulative convertible preference shares ($100 par) of Kaiser Aluminum & Chemical Corporation. In 1959, the corporation entered into various agreements for either the production or fabrication of aluminum in India, Spain, the Republic of Ghana, Argentina, and Great Britain. Specifically, the firm expanded its international interest to include participation, with local interests, in Hindustan Aluminium Coporation, Ltd., which will operate a 20,000 metric ton aluminum reduction plant in central

---

[2] Firm name was changed to the Permanente Metals Corporation in 1941 and to Kaiser Aluminum & Chemical Corporation in 1949.

[3] The latter now leased with option to purchase.

India. The corporation has also invested in aluminum reduction facilities in Spain and sponsored a consortium of aluminum producers for the establishment of a primary aluminum plant in the Republic of Ghana. In Argentina, the corporation joined with Guillermo Decker S.A., a major manufacturer on nonferrous metal products, to establish a new corporation for the manufacture of a wide variety of aluminum mill products for South American markets.

In early 1960, negotiations were completed with Delta Metal Company, Ltd., an English firm, for a one-half interest in the ownership of James Booth Aluminium, Ltd., a fabricating company with substantial aluminum facilities. A new 148-inch hot rolling mill, one of the largest in Western Europe, is being in-stalled at the James Booth plant in Birmingham. The most outstanding event of 1960 for the long-term point of view of the firm was, however, its joining with The Consolidated Zinc Corporation, Ltd. in the planning of a new and complete aluminum production complex in Australia and New Zealand. This $550 million joint venture is scheduled for completion by 1966.

Exhibits 1 and 2 summarize Kaiser Aluminum's financial statements for 1958–60. Exhibits 3, 4, and 5 present organization charts which show the relationships of: Kaiser Aluminum and Kaiser Industries; the subsidiaries that make up the Kaiser Aluminum and Chemical Corporation; and the administrative departments within Kaiser Aluminum.

EXHIBIT 1
Kaiser Aluminum & Chemical Corporation
Condensed Consolidated Balance Sheets
as of December 31, 1958–60
(Dollar figures in thousands)

Assets	1960	1959	1958
Cash	$ 20,520	$ 21,193	$ 23,779
Receivables (net)	25,657	80,562	61,608
Inventories	120,049	106,566	85,885
Prepayments	4,000	2,907	2,249
Investments and Advances	16,379	5,942	5,354
Property (net)	534,434	565,912	572,068
Deferred Charges	4,574	2,894	3,453
Total	$785,607	$785,976	$754,396
Liabilities & Net Worth			
Current Liabilities	$106,537	$ 99,048	$ 82,195
Long-term Obligations	295,943	310,325	319,608
Deferred Federal Income Taxes	79,150	75,850	72,300
Capital Stock and Surplus	303,977	300,753	280,293
Total	$785,607	$785,976	$754,396

EXHIBIT 2
Kaiser Aluminum & Chemical Corporation
Consolidated Earnings Summations
(Dollar figures in thousands)

| | Year Ended December 31 | | |
	1960	1959	1958
Net Sales	406,574	$435,550	$408,559
Income before Federal Income Tax, Interest, Depreciation, & Depletion	91,705	94,566	90,962
Interest on Long-term Obligations	12,932	13,177	13,266
Depreciation & Depletion[1]	46,303	44,561	35,980
Provision for Federal Income Tax	6,400	11,618	10,534
Provision for Deferred Federal Income Tax	3,300	2,882	5,950
Net Income	22,771	22,328	25,232
Earned Surplus at End of Period	$136,814	$132,318	$118,956

Per Share Common Stock Data

	1960	1959	1958
Earnings after Preferred Dividends	$ 1.20	$ 1.17	$ 1.43
Cash Dividend	$ 0.90	$ 0.90	$ 0.90
Net Tangible Assets	$13.35	$13.04	$12.84
Price Range	$54⅞–32	$65–37	$47¾–23
Common Stock Outstanding	$15,015,932	$15,012,662	$14,702,234

[1] Amounts shown for depreciation and depletion are less than amounts computed for federal income tax purposes.

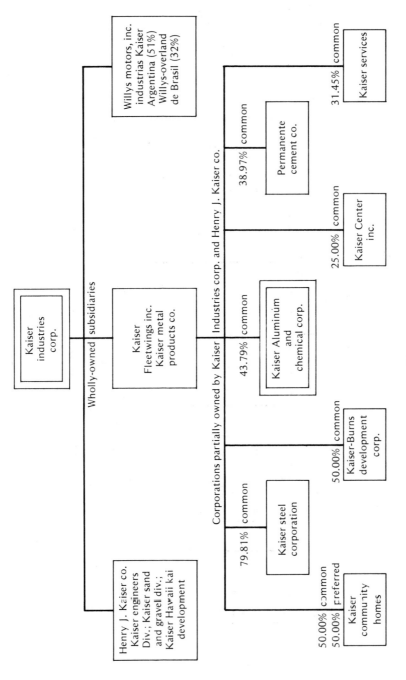

Kaiser industries corp.

Wholly-owned subsidiaries

Henry J. Kaiser co.
Kaiser engineers
Div.; Kaiser sand
and gravel div.;
Kaiser Hawaii kai
development

Kaiser
Fleetwings inc.
Kaiser metal
products co.

Willys motors, inc.
industrias Kaiser
Argentina (51%)
Willys-overland
de Brasil (32%)

Corporations partially owned by Kaiser Industries corp. and Henry J. Kaiser co.

50.00% common
50.00% preferred

Kaiser
community
homes

79.81% common

Kaiser steel
corporation

50.00% common

Kaiser-Burns
development
corp.

43.79% common

Kaiser Aluminium
and
chemical corp.

25.00% common

Kaiser Center
inc.

38.97% common

Permanente
cement co.

31.45% common

Kaiser services

Exhibit 3

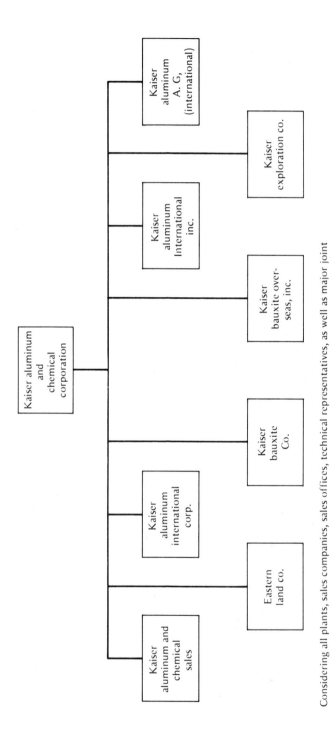

Considering all plants, sales companies, sales offices, technical representatives, as well as major joint ventures, Kaiser Aluminum and Chemical Corporation itself, or its subsidiaries operate in the following countries:

Argentina	Brazil	Germany	Great Britain	Italy	Netherlands	Venezuela
Australia	Canada	Chana	India	Japan	New Zealand	Spain
						Switerland

EXHIBIT 4

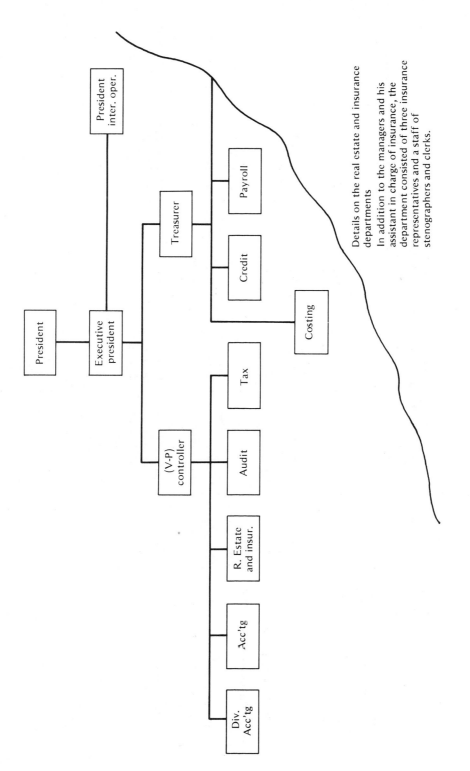

Details on the real estate and insurance departments

In addition to the managers and his assistant in charge of insurance, the department consisted of three insurance representatives and a staff of stenographers and clerks.

President
inter. oper.

President

Executive
president

Treasurer

(V-P)
controller

Payroll

Credit

Costing

Tax

Audit

R. Estate
and insur.

Acc'tg

Div.
Acc'tg

Exhibit 5

APPENDIX

Sample of Foreign Insurance Requirements, as of June 1961

	Argentina	Brazil	Ghana	India	Japan	Venezuela
Is unadmitted insurance prohibited?						
Fire	Yes	Yes	No	Yes	Yes	Yes
Auto & General Liability	Yes	Yes	No, except auto	Yes	Yes	Yes
Marine	Yes	Yes, except imports	No	Yes	Yes, except imports	Yes
Workers' Compensation	Yes	Yes	No	Yes	Yes	Yes
May dollar policies be written locally?	Yes, if $ premiums	No	Yes	No	Yes, except auto liability	No
What insurance has to be placed with government or other monopoly?	None directly	Workers' compensation	None	Work. Comp. in larger centers	Workers' compensation	Work. Comp. in 12 cities
Compulsory insurance if any.	None	Fire insurance on fixed & movable properties over $27,500. Goods in transit over $5,500 against "Road Risks."	Auto liability or else a deposit	Auto liability	Auto liability workers' compensation	Auto liability workers' compensation

Is there a workers' compensation act?	Yes	Yes	Yes	Yes	Yes
Have injured employees alternate rights of action?	Yes	No	Yes, where negligence	Yes	No
Must compulsory automobile insurance be with a local company?	n/a	n/a	Yes	No	No
What are "Road Act" limits of responsibility?	n/a	n/a	Unlimited	With some exceptions unlimited	Maximum $840–death $280–injury	30-30-20 thousand Bs.

Appendices

Appendix A Bibliography

RISK MANAGEMENT

Agents and Buyer's Guide. Cincinnati, Ohio: National Underwriter Co., Annually.

Alderson, Wroe and Green, Paul E. *Planning and Problem Solving in Marketing.* Homewood, Ill.: Richard D. Irwin, Inc., 1964.

Allen, Everett T., Jr., Melone, Joseph J., and Rosenbloom, Jerry S. *Pension Planning,* 3rd ed. Homewood, Illinois: Richard D. Irwin, 1976.

Allen, T. C., and Duvall, R. M. *A Theoretical and Practical Approach to Risk Management. New York:* The American Society of Insurance Management, 1971.

Analysis of Workmen's Compensation Laws, Washington, D.C.: United States Chamber of Commerce, annually.

Arrow, K. J. *Essays in the Theory of Risk Bearing.* Chicago: Markham Publishing Co., 1971.

Athearn, James L. *General Insurance Agency Management.* Homewood, Ill.: Richard D. Irwin, 1965.

Baglini, Norman A. *Risk Management in International Corporations.* New York: Risk Studies Foundation, 1976.

Burtelson, Edwin L. and others. *Health Insurance Provided through Individual Policies,* 2nd Ed. Chicago: Society of Actuaries, 1968.

Belth, Joseph M. *Life Insurance: A Consumer's Handbook.* Bloomington: Indiana University Press, 1973.

Berin, Barnet N. *Fundamentals of Pension Mathematics,* Revised Edition. Chicago: Society of Actuaries, 1972.

Best, A. M. *Fire and Casualty Aggregates and Averages.* Oldwick, N.J.: A. M. Best Co. annually.

Best's Insurance Reports (Property-Casualty). Oldwick, N.J.: A. M. Best and Company, annually.

Best's Insurance Reports (Life and Health). Oldwick, N.J.: A. M. Best and Company, annually.

Best's Key Rating Guide Property and Liability. Oldwick, N.J.: A. M. Best & Co., annually.

Bickehaupt, David I. *General Insurance,* Ninth Edition. Homewood, Ill.: Richard D. Irwin, 1974.

Birren, James E. *The Psychology of Aging.* Englewood Cliffs, N.J.: Prentice-Hall, 1964.

Black, K. *Group Annuities.* Philadelphia: University of Pennsylvania Press, 1955.

Borch, Karl Henrik. *The Economics of Uncertainty.* Princeton, N.J.: Princeton University Press, 1968.

————. *The Mathematical Theory of Insurance.* Lexington, Massachusetts: D. C. Heath & Co., 1974.

Brosterman, Robert. *The Complete Estate Planning Guide.* New York: New American Library, 1970.

Carter, Robert L. *Handbook of Risk Management.* Middlesex, England: Kluwer-Harrap, Rembrandt House, 1976.

Casey, W. J. *Estate Planning,* vol. 1. New York: Institute for Business Planning, 1971.

————. *Estate Planning,* vol. 2. New York: Institute for Business Planning, 1973.

————. *Estate Planning Ideas,* vol. 3. New York: Institute for Business Planning, 1977.

Cooper, Robert W. *Investment Return and Property-Liability Insurance Rate-making.* Homewood, Illinois: Richard D. Irwin, 1974.

Cunnion, J. D. *How to Get Maximum Leverage from Puts and Calls.* Larchmont, N.Y.: Business Reports, 1966.

Denenberg, H. S., et al. *Risk and Insurance,* 2nd ed. Englewood Cliffs, N.J.: Prentice-Hall, 1974.

Dewey, John. *The Quest for Certainty.* New York: G. P. Putnam's Sons, Capricorn Books Ed., 1960.

Dominge, Charles C., and Lincoln, Walter O. *Building Construction as Applied to Fire Insurance,* 4th ed. Philadelphia: Spectator, 1949.

Eilers, Robert D., and Crowe, Robert M. eds. *Group Insurance Handbook.* Homewood, Ill.: Dow Jones-Irwin, 1965.

Elliott, Curtis M. and Vaughan, Emmett J. *Fundamentals of Risk and Insurance.* New York: John Wiley and Sons, 1972.

Employee Benefits 1975. Washington, D.C.: Chamber of Commerce of the United States, 1975.

Factory Mutual Engineering Division. *Handbook of Industrial Loss Prevention.* New York: McGraw-Hill Book Co., 1959.

Fire, Casualty, and Surety Bulletins, 3 vols. Cincinnati: National Underwriter Company.

Freedman, Warren. *Richards on the Law of Insurance.* New York: Baker Voorhis and Co., 1952.

Frisch, Robert A. *The Magic of E.S.O.T.: The Fabulous New Instrument of Corporate Finance.* Rockville Center, N.Y.: Farnsworth Publishing Co., 1975.

Fuchs, Victor. *Essays in the Economics of Health and Medical Care.* New York: National Bureau of Economic Research, 1972.

The Future and Changing Role of Corporate Insurance as Seen by the Risk/Insurance Managers: An Attitudinal Survey Sponsored by *Time* in cooperation with the Risk Insurance Management Society, 1975.

Gaines, Jr., Price (Editor). *Interest Adjusted Index.* Cincinnati, Ohio: National Underwriter Co.

Gordis, Philip. *Property and Casualty Insurance.* Indianapolis: Rough Notes Co., annually.

Goshay, Robert C. *Corporate Self-Insurance and Risk Management Plans.* Homewood, Ill.: Richard D. Irwin, 1964.

Greene, Mark R., Pyron, H. Charles, Manion, U. Vincent, and Winklevoss, Howard. *Early Retirement: A Survey of Company Policies and Retirees' Experiences.* Eugene, Oregon: University of Oregon, 1969.

————, and Swadener, Paul. *Insurance Insights.* Cincinnati, Ohio: South-Western Publishing Co., 1974.

————. *Preretirement Counseling, Retirement Adjustment, and the Older Employee.* Eugene, Oregon: University of Oregon, 1969.

————. *Risk and Insurance Management,* 2nd ed. Washington: U.S. Government Printing Office. Small Business Administration, SBMS No. 30, 1970.

————. *A Primer on Quantitative Methods.* New York: Risk and Insurance Management Society, 1977.

————. *Risk Aversion Insurance and the Future.* Bloomington, Ind.: Graduate School of Business, Indiana University, 1971.

————. *Risk and Insurance,* 4th ed. Cincinnati, Ohio: South-Western Publishing Co., 1977.

————. *The Role of Employee Benefit Structures in Manufacturing Industry.* Eugene, Oregon: University of Oregon, 1964.

Greenough, William C., and King, F. P. *Pension Plans and Public Policy.* New York: Columbia University Press, 1976.

Gregg, D. W., and Lucas, V. B., eds. *Life and Health Insurance Handbook,* 3rd ed. Homewood, Illinois: Richard D. Irwin, 1973.

The Growing Job of Risk Management. New York: American Management Association, 1972.

Hammond, J. D. *Essays In The Theory of Risk and Insurance.* Glenview, Illinois: Scott Foresman and Co., 1968.

Harnett, Bertram. *Responsibilities of Agents and Brokers.* New York: Matthew Bender, 1975.

Hardy, C. O. *Risk and Risk Bearing.* Chicago: University of Chicago Press, 1923.

————. *Readings in Risk and Risk Bearing.* Chicago: University of Chicago Press, 1924.

Head, George L. *Insurance to Value.* Homewood, Ill.: Richard D. Irwin, 1971.

Heinrich, H. W. *Industrial Accident Prevention,* 4th ed. New York: McGraw-Hill Book Co., 1959.

Hetherington, Robert W., Hopkins, Carl E., and Roemer, Milton I. *Health Insurance Plans: Promise and Performance.* New York: John Wiley and Sons, Inc., 1975.

The Hold Harmless Agreement. Cincinnati, Ohio: The National Underwriter Co., 1968.

Holtom, Robert B. *Underwriting Principles and Practices.* Cincinnati, Ohio: The National Underwriter Co., 1973.

Howard, W. M. *Cases on Risk Management.* New York: McGraw-Hill Book Co., 1967.

Huebner, S. S. and Black, Kenneth, Jr. *Life Insurance,* 9th ed. Englewood Cliffs, N.J.: Prentice-Hall, Inc., 1976.

Insurance Facts. New York: Insurance Information Institute, Annually.

Jordan, C. W. *Life Contingencies,* 2nd ed. Chicago, Illinois: Society of Actuaries, 1967.

Kenney, Roger. *Fundamentals of Fire and Casualty Strength.* Dedham, Mass.: Roger Kenney, 1957.

Knight, F. H. *Risk, Uncertainty and Profit.* Boston and New York: Houghton-Mifflin Co., 1921.

Kulp, C. A. *Casualty Insurance,* 3rd ed. New York: Ronald Press, 1956.

Life Insurance Fact Book. New York: American Council of Life Insurance, annually.

Long, John D., and Gregg, Davis W., eds. *Property and Liability Insurance Handbook.* Homewood, Illinois: R. D. Irwin, 1965.

Loss and Expense Ratios–Insurance Expense Exhibits. Albany: New York Insurance Department, annually.

Magee, J. H. and Serbein, O. N. *Property and Liability Insurance,* 4th ed. Homewood, Ill.: Richard D. Irwin, Inc., 1967.

MacDonald, Donald L. *Corporate Risk Control.* New York: The Ronald Press Co., 1966.

McCormick, Ray C. *Coverages Available.* Indianapolis, Ind.: Rough Notes Co., 1976.

McDonald, M. E. *Reciprocity Among Private Multiemployer Pension Plans.* Homewood, Illinois: Richard D. Irwin, Inc., 1975.

Marshall, Robert A. *Life Insurance Company Mergers and Consolidations.* Homewood, Illinois: Richard D. Irwin, 1972.

Mehr, Robert I. and Cammock, Emerson. *Principles of Insurance,* 6th ed. Richard D. Irwin, Inc., 1976.

Mehr, Robert I., and Hedges, Robert A. *Risk Management — Concepts and Applications.* Homewood, Ill.: Richard D. Irwin, 1974.

Milne, W. D. *Factors in Special Fire Risk Analysis.* New York: Chilton Co., 1959.

Municipal Risk Management: A Risk Management and Insurance Handbook. Cincinnati: Society of Chartered Property and Casualty Underwriters, 1971.

Munnell, Alicia H. *The Future of Social Security.* Washington, D.C.: The Brookings Institution, 1977.

National Board of Fire Underwriters. *Building Codes, Their Scope and Aims.* New York: The Board, 1957.

1975 Study of Industrial Retirement Plans, Including Analysis of Complete Programs Recently Adopted or Revised. New York: Bankers Trust Co., 1975.

Mowbray, A. H., Blanchard, R. H. and Williams, Jr., C. A. *Insurance, Sixth Edition.* New York: McGraw-Hill Book Co., 1969.

Olson, Douglas. *Insolvencies Among Automobile Insurers.* Washington, D.C.: U.S. Government Printing Office, 1970.

Patterson, Edwin W. *Essentials of Insurance Law,* 2nd ed. New York: McGraw-Hill Book Co., 1957.

Petersen, Daniel C. *Techniques of Safety Management.* New York: McGraw-Hill Book Co., 1971.

Pfeffer, Irving and David R. Klock. *Perspectives on Insurance.* Englewood Cliffs, New Jersey: Prentice-Hall, Inc., 1974.

Pfenningstorf, Werner. *Legal Expense Insurance.* Chicago: American Bar Foundation, 1975.

Pickrell, J.F. *Group Disability Insurance.* Homewood, Illinois: Richard D. Irwin, 1958.

Pomerony, Felix, Ramsey, Gordon P., Steinberg, Richard M. Pensions an *Accounting and Management Guide,* New York: The Ronald Press Co., 1976.

Reed, Prentice B. and Thomas, Paul I. *Adjustment of Property Losses.* Third Edition, New York: McGraw-Hill Book Co., 1969.

The Regulation of Mass Marketing in Property and Liability Insurance. Milwaukee: National Association of Insurance Commissioners, 1971.

Risk Analysis Questionnaire. New York: American Management Association, 19—.

Rosenbloom, Jerry S. *A Case Study in Risk Management.* New York: Appleton-Century-Crofts, 1972.

Sample Insurance Policies (Property and Liability). N.Y.: Insurance Information Institute, 1977.

Schmidt, J. W. and Taylor, R. E. *Simulation and Analysis of Industrial Systems.* Homewood, Illinois: Richard D. Irwin, 1970.

Seal, Hilary L. *Stochastic Theory of a Risk Business.* New York: John Wiley and Sons, 1969.

Serbein, O. N. *Paying for Medical Care in the United States.* New York: Columbia University Press, 1953.

Shepherd, Pearce, and Webster, Andrew C. *Selection of Risks.* Chicago: The Society of Actuaries, 1957.

Shopper's Guide to Pennsylvania Automobile Insurance: Some Key Premium Comparisons for Beginning Your Search for the Best Automobile Insurance Bargain, rev. ed. Harrisburg, Pennsylvania: Pennsylvania Insurance Department, 1972.

Snider, H. W., ed. *Risk Management.* Homewood, Illinois: Richard D. Irwin, 1964.

Society of Chartered Property and Casualty Underwriters, Georgia Chapter, *Risk Management in Building Construction.* Cincinnati, Ohio: National Underwriter Co., 1977.

Spurr, W. A. and Bonini, Charles P. *Statistical Analysis for Business Decisions.* Homewood, Illinois: Richard D. Irwin, Inc., 1967.

Stephenson, G. T. and Wiggins, N. A. *Estates and Trusts,* 5th ed. Englewood Cliffs, New Jersey: Prentice-Hall, Inc., 1973.

Study Kit for Students of Insurance. Chicago: American Mutual Alliance, 1977.

Tibbitts, Clark, and Donahue, Wilma. *Social and Psychological Aspects of Aging.* New York: Columbia University Press, 1962.

Tisdell, C. A. *The Theory of Price Uncertainty, Production and Profit.* Princeton: Princeton University Press, 1968.

Title Insurance Companies. Stanford, Connecticut: Philo Smith, Landstreet and Co., 1969.

Vance, William R. *Handbook on the Law of Insurance,* 3rd ed. Edited by Buist M. Anderson. St. Paul: West Publishing Company, 1951.

Von Neuman, John and Morgenstern, Oskar. *Theory of Games and Economic Behavior.* Princeton: Princeton University Press, 1944.

Watson, Donald, and Homan, D. *Insurance and Risk Management for Small Business.* Washington, D.C.: Small Business Administration, 1963.

Weese, Samuel H. *Non-Admitted Insurance in the United States.* Homewood, Ill.: Richard D. Irwin, 1971.

White, Edwin H., and Chasman, Herbert. *Business Insurance,* 4th ed. Englewood Cliffs, N.J.: Prentice-Hall, 1974.

White, E. H., ed. *Fundamentals of Federal Income Estate and Gift Taxes,* Indianapolis, Ind.: The Research and Review Service of America, Inc. (most recent edition).

Who Writes What in Life and Health Insurance. Cincinnati, Ohio: National Underwriter Co., annually

Willett, A. H. *The Economic Theory of Risk and Insurance.* Philadelphia: University of Pennsylvania Press, 1951.

Williams, C. Arthur, Jr., and Heins, Richard M. *Risk Management and Insurance,* 3rd ed. New York: McGraw-Hill Book Co., 1976.

Winklevoss, Howard E. *Pension Mathematics:* with *Numerical Illustrations.* Homewood, Ill.: Richard D. Irwin, Inc., 1977.

Appendix B Summary of the Employee Retirement Income Security Act (ERISA)

The Employee Retirement Income Security Act of 1974 is a complex document that establishes a legal framework for governing the conduct of those persons and organizations responsible for developing and maintaining employee benefit and pension plans. Interpretive documents are still being issued, and it will be some time before a complete understanding of the law will be achieved by those most affected by it. The paragraphs that follow are intended to provide a fairly comprehensive summary of the principal features of this legislation.

PROTECTION OF EMPLOYEE BENEFIT RIGHTS

The protection of employee benefit rights is accomplished by the establishment of rules regarding reporting and disclosure, participation and vesting, funding, fiduciary responsibility, and administration and enforcement.

Reporting and Disclosure

The administrators of employee benefit plans, including pension plans, are required to submit reports to participants and beneficiaries of the plans and to the Secretary of Labor. The reports to the beneficiaries and participants are (1) a summary plan description and (2) a copy of statements and schedules (within 210 days after the close of the fiscal year), which include such information as assets and liabilities of the plan "aggregated by categories and valued at their current value, and the same data displayed in comparative form for the end of the previous fiscal year of the plan."[1] Also, there must be a "statement of receipts and disbursements during the preceding twelve-month period aggregated by general sources and applications."[2] If a participant or beneficiary so requests in writing, the plan administrator must provide a statement giving the total benefits accrued and the "nonforfeitable pension benefits, if any, which have accrued, or the earliest date on which benefits will become nonforfeitable."[3] Another section of the law provides that

each administrator required to register under section 6057 of the Internal Revenue Code of 1954 shall, before the expiration of the time prescribed for such registration,

[1] Public Law 93-406, 93rd Congress, H.R. 2 (September 2, 1974), p. 15.

[2] *Ibid.*

[3] *Ibid.*

furnish to each participant described in subsection (a) (2) (c) of such section, an individual statement setting forth the information with respect to such participant required to be contained in the registration statement required by section 6057 (a) (2) of such Code.[4]

The reports that must be filed with the Secretary of Labor are: (1) a summary plan description; (2) a plan description; (3) a statement of modifications and changes in the plan; (4) an annual report; and (5) terminal and supplementary reports. The type of information that must be included in these reports is set forth in the Act.

Space does not permit a detailed consideration of all of the details on reporting and disclosure that are contained in the Act. As an example of the kind of information required, consideration will be given to some of the requirements for annual reports that must be published by every employee benefit plan and filed with the Secretary of Labor and made available to participants.

For all employee benefit plans the following types of information must be provided:

1. "A statement of assets and liabilities of the plan aggregated by categories and valued at their current value, and the same data displayed in comparative form for the end of the previous fiscal year of the plan;

2. A statement of receipts and disbursements during the preceding twelve-month period aggregated by general sources and applications;

3. A schedule of all assets held for investment purposes aggregated and identified by issuer, borrower, or les-

[4] *Ibid.*, p. 21.

sor, or similar party to the transaction (including a notation as to whether such party is known to be a party in interest), maturity date, rate of interest, collateral, par or maturity value, cost, and current value;

4. A schedule of each transaction involving a person known to be party in interest, the identity of such party in interest and his relationship or that of any other party in interest to the plan, a description of each asset to which the transaction relates; . . .

5. A schedule of all loans or fixed income obligations which were in default as of the close of the plan's fiscal year or were classified during the year as uncollectible. . . .

6. A list of all leases which were in default or were classified during the year as uncollectible; . . .

7. If some or all of the assets of a plan are held in a common or collective trust maintained by a bank or similar institution or in a separate account maintained by an insurance carrier or a separate trust maintained by a bank as trustee, the report shall include the most recent annual statement of assets and liabilities of such common or collective trust, and in the case of a separate account or a separate trust, such other information as is required by the administrator in order to comply with this subsection.

8. A schedule of each reportable transaction. . . ."[5]

[5] *Ibid.*, pp. 15–16. A "reportable transaction" is defined in the law. An example would be "a transaction involving an amount in excess of 3 percent of the current value of the assets of the plan." The omissions in 4,5,6, and 8 above are of some of the details involved in the reporting of the items discussed.

In addition to the financial information just described the administrator is required to furnish:

1. "The number of employees covered by the plan.

2. The name and address of each fiduciary.

3. Except in the case of a person whose compensation is minimal (determined under regulations of the Secretary) and who performs solely ministerial duties (determined under such regulation), the name of each person (including but not limited to any consultant, broker, trustee, accountant, insurance carrier, actuary, administrator, investment manager, or custodian who rendered services to the plan or who had transactions with the plan) who received directly or indirectly compensation from the plan during the preceding year for services rendered to the plan or its participants, the amount of such compensation, the nature of his services to the plan or its participants, his relationship to the employer or the employees covered by the plan, or the employee organization, and any other office, position, or employment he holds with any part in interest.

4. An explanation of the reason for any change in appointment of trustee, accountant, insurance carrier, enrolled actuary, administrator, investment manager, or custodian.

5. Such financial and actuarial information as the Secretary may find necessary or appropriate."[6]

For employee pension plans, with a few exceptions, *e.g.*, profit-sharing plans, the annual report must include a

6 *Ibid.*, p. 17.

complete actuarial statement containing the following type of information:

1. "The date of the plan year, and the date of the actuarial valuation applicable to the plan year for which the report is filed.

2. The date and amount of the contribution (or contributions) received by the plan for the plan year for which the report is filed and contributions for prior plan years not previously reported.

3. The following information is applicable to the plan year for which the report is filed: the normal costs, the accrued liabilities, and identification of benefits not included in the calculation; a statement of the other facts and actuarial assumptions and methods used to determine costs, and a justification for any change in actuarial assumptions or cost methods; and the minimum contribution required under section 302 (Minimum Funding Standards).

4. The number of participants and beneficiaries, both retired and non-retired, covered by the plan.

5. The current value of the assets accumulated in the plan, and the present value of the assets of the plan used by the actuary in any computation of the amount of contributions to the plan required under section 302 and a statement explaining the basis of such valuation of the present value of the assets.

6. The present value of all the plan's liabilities for nonforfeitable pension benefits allocated by the termination priority categories as set forth in section 4044 of this Act (Allocation of Assets), and the actuarial assumptions used in these computa-

tions. The Secretary shall establish regulations defining (for purposes of this section) 'termination priority categories' and acceptable methods, including approximate methods, for allocating the plan's liabilities to such termination priority categories.

7. A certification of the contribution necessary to reduce the accumulative funding deficiency to zero.

8. A statement by the enrolled actuary
   (A) that to the best of his knowledge the report is complete and accurate, and
   (B) the requirements of section 302(c) (3) (relating to reasonable actuarial assumptions and methods) have been complied with.

9. A copy of the opinion required by subsection (a) (4).

10. Such other information regarding the plan as the Secretary may by regulation require.

11. Such other information as may be necessary to fully and fairly disclose the actuarial position of the plan."[7]

The administrator of the plan is required to engage an enrolled actuary[8] who will prepare the materials required by the actuarial report and who will give an opinion as to whether the contents of the report are reasonable and represent his best estimate of anticipated experience under the plan.

An insurance company or similar organization may be required to file a report if "some or all of the benefits

[7] Ibid., pp. 17–18.

[8] Under Title III of the Act, the Secretary of Labor and the Secretary of the Treasury are required to establish a Joint Board for the Enrollment of Actuaries. An "enrolled actuary" is a person who has been enrolled by this board.

under the plan are purchased from and guaranteed" by such insurer or organization. Among the items that are to be included are such matters as premium rates, total premiums received, approximate number of persons covered by each class of benefits, and total claims paid.

Participation and Vesting

Restrictive eligibility requirements and lack of vesting can operate to deny benefits to participants. The Act seeks to minimize this possibility by establishing participation and vesting requirements that apply with minor exceptions to all employee pension plans.

Minimum Participation Standards

No employer may establish an eligibility requirement for participating in a plan that requires a period of service on the part of the employee extending beyond the later of the date on which the employee becomes age 25 or the date on which he has completed 1 year of service. Some exceptions are made to this general requirement. For plans that give employees a right to 100 percent of their accrued benefits (including nonforfeitability at the time the benefit accrues) after no more than 3 years of service, the 1-year service requirement may be changed to 3 years. In the case of educational institutions meeting the definitions and requirements specified in the Internal Revenue Code and that have benefit plans specifying that "each participant having at least 1 year of service has a right to 100 percent of his accrued benefit under the plan" and that also specifies the benefit is "nonforfeitable at the time such benefit accrues," age 30 may be substituted for age 25. In general no pension plan may exclude an employee who has reached a specified age unless the plan is a defined benefit or defined target plan and the employee has reached an age that "is not more than 5 years before the normal retirement age under the plan."[9]

Minimum Vesting Standards

The Act requires that each pension plan contain a provision stating that "an employee's right to his normal retirement benefit is nonforfeitable upon the attainment of normal retirement age. In addition there must be a statement that an employee's rights in the accrued benefits determined by his own contributions are nonforfeitable. It is also necessary to specify the employee's rights to his employer's contribution. This requirement is satisfied if the plan meets the specifications of 1, 2, or 3 below.[10]

1. An employee who has at least 10 years of service has a nonforfeitable right to 100 percent of his accrued benefit derived from employer contributions.

2. An employee who has completed at least 5 years of service has a nonforfeitable right to a percentage of his accrued benefit derived from employer contributions which percentage is not less than the percentage determined in Table 1.

3. A participant who is not separated from the service, who has completed at least 5 years of service, and with respect to whom the sum of his age and years of service equals or exceeds

TABLE 1

Years of Service	Nonforfeitable Percentage
5	25
6	30
7	35
8	40
9	45
10	50
11	60
12	70
13	80
14	90
15 or more	100

45, has a nonforfeitable right to a percentage of his accrued benefit derived from employer contributions determined under Table 2.

The requirements specified in item 3 are modified by an additional provision that states that vesting requirements will not be met by item 3 above "unless any participant who has completed at least 10 years of service has a nonforfeitable right to not less than 50 percent of his accrued benefit derived from employer contributions and to not less than an additional 10 percent for each addi-

TABLE 2

If years of service equal or exceed	and sum of age and service equals or exceeds,	then the nonforfeitable percentage is
5	45	50
6	47	60
7	49	70
8	51	80
9	53	90
10	55	100

tional year of service thereafter."[11] In addition to stating minimum vesting standards, the Act states the situations under which an accrued benefit shall not be treated as forfeitable and the rules for computing the years of service that are to be used in determining the nonforfeitable percentage. The Act also provides that "a pension plan may allow for nonforfeitable benefits after a lesser period and in greater amounts than are required" by the standards stated above.

As a part of the discussion of participation and vesting, the Act provides rules relating to benefit accrual requirements and the joint and survivor annuity requirement. The need for rules about accrual requirements arises largely out of situations where an employee separates from service to an employer before reaching retirement age. Although the rules specified in the Act are too detailed for consideration here, they serve to safeguard accumulations for both defined benefit and fixed contribution plans. The joint and survivor annuity requirement is stated as follows: "If a pension plan provides for the payment of benefits in the form of an annuity, such plan shall provide for the payment of annuity benefits in the form having the effect of a qualified joint and survivor annuity . . . The term 'qualified joint and survivor annuity' means an annuity for the life of the participant with a survivor annuity for the life of his spouse which is not less than one-half of, or greater than, the amount of the annuity payable during the joint lives of the participant and his spouse and which is the actuarial equivalent of a single annuity for the life of the participant."[12]

[11] *Ibid.*

[12] *Ibid.*, Sec. 205 (a) and 205f (3).

Funding

With a few exceptions specified in the Act[13] employee pension benefit plans must meet certain minimum funding standards. Each plan must establish and maintain a funding standard account. This account must be charged for a plan year with the sum of the following items:

1. "The normal cost of the plan for the plan year.

2. The amounts necessary to amortize in equal annual installments (until fully amortized) —
   a. in the case of a plan in existence on January 1, 1974, the unfunded past service liability under the plan on the first day of the first plan year to which this part applies, over a period of 40 plan years,
   b. in the case of a plan which comes into existence after January 1, 1974, the unfunded past service liability under the plan on the first day of the first plan year to which this part applies, over a period of 30 plan years (40 plan years in the case of a multiemployer plan,
   c. separately, with respect to each plan year, the net increase (if any) in unfunded past service liability under the plan arising from plan amendments adopted in each year, over a period of 30 plan years (40 plan years in the case of a multiemployer plan,
   d. separately, with respect to each plan year, the net experience loss (if any) under the plan, over a period of 15 plan years (20 plan years in the case of a multiemployer plan), and

[13] See 301 (a).

e. separately, with respect to each plan year, the net loss (if any) resulting from changes in actuarial assumptions used under the plan, over a period of 30 plan years,

3. The amount necessary to amortize each waived funding deficiency . . . for each prior plan year in equal annual installments (until fully amortized) over a period of 15 plan years, and[14]

4. The amount necessary to amortize in equal annual installments (until fully amortized) over a period of 5 plan years an amount credited to the funding standard account under part 4 of the next paragraph."

The credits to be made to the funding standard account are:

1. "The amount considered contributed by the employer to or under the plan year.

2. The amount necessary to amortize in equal annual installments (until fully amortized)
   a. Separately, with respect to each plan year, the net decrease (if any) in unfunded past service liability under the plan arising from plan amendments adopted in such year, over a period of 30 plan years (40 plan years in the case of a multi-employer plan)
   b. Separately, with respect to each plan year, the net experience gain (if any) under the plan, over a period of 15 plan years (20 plan years in the case of a multiemployer plan), and

c. Separately, with respect to each plan year, the net gain (if any) resulting from changes in actuarial assumptions used under the plan, over a period of 30 plan years.

3. The amount of the waived funding deficiency . . . for the plan year, and

4. in the case of a plan year for which the accumulated funding deficiency is determined under the funding standard account if such plan year follows a plan year for which such deficiency was determined under the alternative minimum funding standard, the excess (if any) of any debt balance in the funding standard account (determined without regard to this subparagraph) over any debit balance in the alternative minimum funding standard account."[15]

A plan shall be regarded as having met the minimum funding standard as of the end of the plan year if it does not have an accumulated funding deficiency, by which is meant that the "total charges to the funding standard for all plan years" must not exceed the total credits.

Another item related to the funding standard account is that the "account (and items therein) shall be charged or credited — with interest at the appropriate rate consistent with the rate or rates of interest used under the plan to determine costs."[16] The Act also provides that "normal costs, accrued liability, past service liabilities, and experience gains or losses shall be determined under the funding method used to determine costs under the plan."[17]

[14] By "waived funding deficiency" is meant "the portion of the minimum funding standard — for a plan year waived by the Secretary of the Treasury and not satisfied by employer contribution." Public law 93–406, p. 45.

[15] Ibid., pp. 41–42.

[16] Ibid., p. 43.

[17] Ibid.

Under minimum funding standards the Act also refers to the valuation of a plan's assets. The general requirement is that the plan's assets be determined "on the basis of any reasonable actuarial method of valuation which takes into account fair market value and which is permitted under regulations prescribed by the Secretary of the Treasury." The Act also provides that the "value of a bond or other evidence of indebtedness which is not in default as to principal or interest may, at the election of the plan administrator, be determined on an amortized basis running from initial cost of purchase to par value at maturity or earliest call date." The election must take place in accordance with regulations published by the Secretary of the Treasury and can be revoked only with the Secretary's consent.[18]

In the case of business hardship it may not be possible in some years for an employer to meet the minimum funding standard. The Act permits the Secretary of the Treasury to waive the requirements of the minimum standard for a plan year, subject to certain limitations, if substantial business hardship would be incurred if the usual contributions to the plan were to be made. Among the items to be considered in determining hardship are: "(1) the employer is operating at an economic loss; (2) there is substantial unemployment or underemployment in the trade or business and in the industry concerned; (3) the sales and profits of the industry concerned are depressed or declining; and (4) it is reasonable to expect that the plan will be continued only if the waiver is granted." The Act also provides for an alternative minimum funding standard in any plan year for plans "that require contributions in all years

[18] Ibid.

not less than those required under the entry age normal funding method may maintain an alternative minimum funding standard account for any plan year."[19] The requirements for the alternative standard are set forth in the law.

Fiduciary Responsibility

The Act requires that employee benefit plans, including pension plans, be in writing and that the formal document establishing the plan name one or more fiduciaries "who jointly or severally shall have authority to control and manage the operation and administration of the plan."[20] Every employee benefit plan is required to: "(1) provide a procedure for establishing and carrying out a funding policy and method consistent with the objectives of the plan and requirements of this title; (2) describe any procedure under the plan for the allocation of responsibilities for the operations and administration of the plan . . . ; (3) provide a procedure for amending such plan, and for identifying the persons who have authority to amend the plan; and (4) specify the basis on which payments are made to and from the plan."[21] All assets of the plan must be held in trust by one or more trustees, with a few exceptions, among which are that assets consisting of insurance contracts with qualified insurers or deposits with insurers need not be held in trust.

Subject to some restrictions, such as not letting the assets of the plan inure to the benefit of the employer, a fiduciary must discharge his responsibil-

[19] Ibid., p. 45.

[20] There are a few relatively minor exceptions to the requirement for naming a fiduciary.

[21] Ibid., p. 47.

ities to the plan "solely in the interest of the participants and beneficiaries" and must conduct himself as a prudent man and must "diversify the investments of the plan so as to minimize the risk of large losses, unless under the circumstances it is clearly prudent not to do so." He must also perform in accordance with the documents and instruments governing the plan "insofar as such document and instruments are consistent with the provisions of this title."[22]

A fairly substantial section of the Act referring to fiduciaries is devoted to a discussion of prohibited transactions and exemptions from prohibited transactions. Examples of prohibited transactions are: "(1) sale or exchange, or leasing, of any property between the plan and a party in interest; (2) lending of money or other extension of credit between the plan and a party in interest; (3) furnishing of goods, services, or facilities between the plan and a party in interest; (4) transfer to, or use by or for the benefit of, a party in interest, of any assets of the plan; or (5) acquisition, on behalf of the plan, of any employer security or employer real property in violation" of the sections of the Act prescribing the rules for such acquisition. One such rule is the 10 percent limitations "with respect to acquisition and holding of employer securities and employer real property." Another prohibited transaction is that a fiduciary shall not "deal with the assets of the plan in his own interest or for his own account." An example of an exemption from a prohibited transaction is: "Any loans made by the plan to parties in interest who are participants or beneficiaries of the plan if such loans (A) are available to all such participants and

beneficiaries on a reasonably equivalent basis, (B) are not made available to highly compensated employees, officers, or shareholders in an amount greater than the amount made available to other employees, (C) are made in accordance with specific provisions regarding such loans set forth in the plan, (D) bear a reasonable rate of interest, and (E) are adequately secured."[23] Every fiduciary, with some exceptions, is required to be bonded with the amount of the bond "fixed at the beginning of each fiscal year of the plan." The amount of the bond "shall not be less than 10 per centum of the amount of funds handled."[24]

Administration and
Enforcement

This section of the law specifies criminal penalties for certain types of violations and states the rules under which a civil action may be brought. It also provides statements about claim procedures, investigative authority of the Secretary, and other items of an essentially administrative sort. Of interest is the establishment of an advisory council and provisions for research and studies relating to pension plans. The council has the title Advisory Council on Employee Welfare and Pension Benefit Plans. It consists of 15 members appointed by the Secretary. Three of these members must be from employee organizations, 3 shall represent employers, and 3 shall come for the general public. One member each shall be selected from the fields of insurance, corporate trusts, actuarial counseling, investment counseling, investment management, and accounting.

[22] *Ibid.*, p. 49.

[23] *Ibid.*, pp. 51–56.
[24] *Ibid.*, p. 60.

TITLE II — AMENDMENTS TO THE INTERNAL REVENUE CODE RELATING TO RETIREMENT PLANS

Title II has two subtitles: Subtitle A, Participation, Vesting, Funding, Administration, etc.; and Subtitle B, Other Amendments to the Internal Revenue Code Relating to Retirement Plans. Subtitle A contains the amendments to the Internal Revenue Code necessary to bring its requirements for a qualified plan into conformity with Title I of ERISA. Thus, much of the material found in Subtitle A has already been discussed.

Subtitle B contains a number of sections dealing with tax matters. Of special interest is the section increasing the maximum amount that is deductible for self-employed persons who have set up pension plans and the new section providing deductions for individuals who have retirement savings plans. For the self-employed the new maximum shall not exceed $7,500 or 15 percent. In the case of individuals who have retirement plans that qualify under this section the amount that is deductible is "15 percent of the compensation includible in gross income for such taxable year or $1,500 whichever is less."[25]

TITLE III — JURISDICTION, ADMINISTRATION, ENFORCEMENT; JOINT PENSION TASK FORCE, ETC.

Title III has three subtitles: Subtitle A, Jurisdiction, Administration, and Enforcement; Subtitle B, Joint Pension Task Force; and Subtitle C, Enrollment of Actuaries. Subtitle A provides a statement of procedures in connection with determination letters provided by

[25] *Ibid.*

the Secretary of the Treasury stating whether a pension, profit-sharing, or stock bonus plan meets the requirements of the Internal Revenue Code. It also provides procedures relating to continued compliance. Subtitle B establishes a Joint Pension Task Force and provides for other studies. The Joint Pension Task Force is charged with the responsibility of reporting within 24 months after the date of enactment of ERISA. The law specifies some 5 areas to be reviewed by the Task Force. One of these areas, for example, is "the effects and desirability of the Federal preemption of state and local law with respect to matters relating to pension and similar plans." The other studies relate to retirement plans "established and maintained or financed (directly or indirectly) by the government of the United States, by any state (including the District of Columbia) or political subdivision thereof, or by any agency or instrumentality of the foregoing." Among the matters to be studied are existing fiduciary standards; necessity for federal legislation in regard to such plans; and adequacy of such items as participation, vesting and financial arrangements. A second area of study relates to "protection for employees under federal procurement, construction, and research contract or grants."

Subtitle C provides for the establishment of a Joint Board for the Enrollment of Actuaries. The Board has the responsibility for determining standards and qualifications for actuaries working with plans covered under the Act. After January 1, 1976, the standards include "(1) education and training in actuarial mathematics and methodology as evidenced by (A) a degree in actuarial mathematics or its equivalent from an accredited college or university, (B) successful completion of an examination in actuarial mathematics and methodology to be given by the Joint Board, or (C) successful completion of other actuarial examinations deemed adequate by the Joint Board and (2) an appropriate period of responsible actuarial experience."[26]

TITLE IV — PLAN TERMINATION INSURANCE

There are four subtitles that make up Title IV. They are Subtitle A, Pension Benefit Guaranty Corporation; Subtitle B, Coverage; Subtitle C, Terminations; and Subtitle D, Liability. This title and its subtitles undertake to guarantee that benefits will be paid in the event a plan covered under the title is in default or terminated. A principal provision of the title is the establishment of a Pension Benefit Guarantee Corporation within the Department of Labor. The purposes stated for the corporation are "(1) to encourage the continuation and maintenance of voluntary private pension plans for the benefit of their participants; (2) to provide for the timely and uninterrupted payment of pension benefits to participants and beneficiaries under plans to which this title applies, and (3) to maintain premiums established by the corporation — at the lowest level consistent with carrying out its obligations under this title."[27]

The corporation is governed by a board of directors made up of the Secretaries of Commerce, Labor and Treasury with the Secretary of Labor as chairman. The routine business of the Corporation is taken care of by the execu-

tive director of the corporation. There is a seven-member advisory committee appointed by the president, which advises on "policies and procedures relating to the appointment of trustees in plan termination proceedings; investment of monies; whether plans being terminated should be liquidated immediately or continued in operation under a trustee; and on other issues as requested by the corporation."[28] One of the major purposes of the Pension Benefit Guarantee Corporation is to establish termination insurance. Three programs are provided for by the Act. One is an insurance program guaranteeing basic retirement benefits; a second is a program to cover employers' contingent liability that may come about if plans are terminated with insufficient assets; and the third is a discretionary program that would insure nonbasic benefits.

Termination procedures are provided for in the Act. Termination may take place voluntarily in situations where an employer wishes to discontinue a plan or involuntarily when the Pension Benefit Guarantee Corporation institutes proceedings. This may take place when some violation has occurred or when losses in the plan raise serious questions about solvency. Regardless of the reason for the termination, assets must be allocated according to the provisions of the Act.[29]

---

[26] *Ibid.*, p. 174.

[27] *Ibid.*, p. 176.

[28] Harold C. Krogh, "An Analysis of Plan Termination Insurance, Employee Retirement Income Security Act of 1974," Paper delivered before the Annual Meeting of the American Risk and Insurance Association, Boston, Mass., August 17, 1976.

[29] For further discussion, see *Ibid.*

Appendix C
Unified Rate Schedule for
Estate and Gift Taxes

If the amount with respect to which the tentative tax to be computed is:	The tentative tax is:
Not over $10,000	18% of such amount.
Over $10,000 but not over $20,000	$1,800 plus 20% of the excess of such amount over $10,000.
Over $20,000 but not over $40,000	$3,800 plus 22% of the excess of such amount over $20,000.
Over $40,000 but not over $60,000	$8,200 plus 24% of the excess of such amount over $40,000.
Over $60,000 but not over $80,000	$13,000 plus 26% of the excess of such amount over $60,000.
Over $80,000 but not over $100,000	$18,200 plus 28% of the excess of such amount over $80,000.
Over $100,000 but not over $150,000	$23,800 plus 30% of the excess of such amount over $100,000.
Over $150,000 but not over $250,000	$38,800 plus 32% of the excess of such amount over $150,000.
Over $250,000 but not over $500,000	$70,800 plus 34% of the excess of such amount over $250,000.
Over $500,000 but not over $750,000	$155,800 plus 37% of the excess of such amount over $500,000.
Over $750,000 but not over $1,000,000	$248,300 plus 39% of the excess of such amount over $750,000.
Over $1,000,000 but not over $1,250,000	$345,800 plus 41% of the excess of such amount over $1,000,000.
Over $1,250,000 but not over $1,500,000	$448,300 plus 43% of the excess of such amount over $1,250,000.
Over $1,500,000 but not over $2,000,000	$555,800 plus 45% of the excess of such amount over $1,500,000.
Over $2,000,000 but not over $2,500,000	$780,800 plus 49% of the excess of such amount over $2,000,000.
Over $2,500,000 but not over $3,000,000	$1,025,800 plus 53% of the excess of such amount over $2,500,000.

If the amount with respect to which the tentative tax to be computed is:	The tentative tax is:
Over $3,000,000 but not over $3,500,000	$1,290,800 plus 57% of the excess of such amount over $3,000,000.
Over $3,500,000 but not over $4,000,000	$1,575,800 plus 61% of the excess of such amount over $3,500,000.
Over $4,000,000 but not over $4,500,000	$1,880,800 plus 65% of the excess of such amount over $4,000,000.
Over $4,500,000 but not over $5,000,000	$2,205,800 plus 69% of the excess of such amount over $4,500,000.
Over $5,000,000	$2,550,800 plus 70% of the excess over $5,000,000.

Appendix D
Commissioners 1958 Standard
Ordinary Mortality Table Based on
Data for the Period 1958-1954

Age	Deaths Per 1,000	Expecta-tion of Life (Years)	Age	Deaths Per 1,000	Expecta-tion of Life (Years)
0	7.08	68.30	28	2.03	43.08
1	1.76	67.78	29	2.08	42.16
2	1.52	66.90	30	2.13	41.25
3	1.46	66.00	31	2.19	40.34
4	1.40	65.10	32	2.25	39.43
5	1.35	64.19	33	2.32	38.51
6	1.30	63.27	34	2.40	37.60
7	1.26	62.35	35	2.51	36.69
8	1.23	61.43	36	2.64	35.78
9	1.21	60.51	37	2.80	34.88
10	1.21	59.58	38	3.01	33.97
11	1.23	58.65	39	3.25	33.07
12	1.26	57.72	40	3.53	32.18
13	1.32	56.80	41	3.84	31.29
14	1.39	55.87	42	4.17	30.41
15	1.46	54.95	43	4.53	29.54
16	1.54	54.03	44	4.92	28.67
17	1.62	53.11	45	5.35	27.81
18	1.69	52.19	46	5.83	26.95
19	1.74	51.28	47	6.36	26.11
20	1.79	50.37	48	6.95	25.27
21	1.83	49.46	49	7.60	24.45
22	1.86	48.55	50	8.32	23.63
23	1.89	47.64	51	9.11	22.82
24	1.91	46.73	52	9.96	22.03
25	1.93	45.82	53	10.89	21.25
26	1.96	44.90	54	11.90	20.47
27	1.99	43.99	55	13.00	19.71

Age	Deaths Per 1,000	Expectation of Life (Years)	Age	Deaths Per 1,000	Expectation of Life (Years)
56	14.21	18.97	83	139.38	4.89
57	15.54	18.23	84	150.01	4.60
58	17.00	17.51	85	161.14	4.32
59	18.59	16.81	86	172.82	4.06
60	20.34	16.12	87	185.13	3.80
61	22.24	15.44	88	198.25	3.55
62	24.31	14.78	89	212.46	3.31
63	26.57	14.14	90	228.14	3.06
64	29.04	13.51	91	245.77	2.82
65	31.75	12.90	92	265.93	2.58
66	34.74	12.31	93	289.30	2.33
67	38.04	11.73	94	316.66	2.07
68	41.68	11.17	95	351.24	1.80
69	45.61	10.64	96	400.56	1.51
70	49.79	10.12	97	488.42	1.18
71	54.15	9.63	98	668.15	.83
72	58.65	9.15	99	1,000.00	.50
73	63.26	8.69			
74	68.12	8.24			
75	73.37	7.81			
76	79.18	7.39			
77	85.70	6.98			
78	93.06	6.59			
79	101.19	6.21			
80	109.98	5.85			
81	119.35	5.51			
82	129.17	5.19			

Appendix E Asset-Exposure Analysis*

The Asset-Exposure Analysis is intended as an additional guide to Risk Managers. In it, Assets are divided into Physical — real, personal and miscellaneous property – and Intangible, in an attempt to allow the Risk Manager to review *all* assets, whether or not they may properly be considered insurable.

Exposures are broken down into three areas — Direct, Indirect or Consequential and Third Party Liabilities. Again, the purpose is to cover all fortuitous exposures to loss of assets or earning power, even to including some exposures which are somewhat speculative in nature.

This Asset-Exposure Analysis should be used in conjunction with other check-lists and questionnaires. It is not a crutch but hopefully an additional stimulus to a logical and systematic interpretation of *all* exposures to loss, the basis of risk management. Effective loss control, risk assumption and risk transfer can only come after the most thorough and searching exposure analysis and risk evaluation.

This check-list is part of a continuing American Management Association program to develop improved tools for the Risk Manager. The Insurance Division welcomes any constructive and/or critical comments and suggestions.

Asset-Exposure Analysis
List 1 — Assets

A. *Physical Assets:*

  1. *Real Property*

    a) Buildings

1) Under construction	6) Garages & Hangars
2) Owned or leased	7) Dwellings — Farms
3) Manufacturing	8) Tanks, Towers & Stacks
4) Offices	9) Wharfs & docks
5) Warehouses	10) Pipes & wires (above ground)

    b) Underground Property

1) Cables and wires	4) Mines and shafts
2) Tanks	5) Wells, ground water
3) Shelters, caves, tunnels	6) Piping & pipelines

    c) Land

1) Improved	2) Unimproved

* Reprinted by permission of the publisher from *Risk Analysis Guide to Insurance and Employee Benefits* by A. E. Pfaffle and Sal Nicosia, © 1977 by AMACOM, a division of American Management Associations. All rights reserved.

2. *Personal Property* (on and off premises & in transit)

    a) Equipment and Machinery

        1) Machines and tools

        2) Dies, jigs, molds, castings

        3) Boilers and pressure vessels

            (a) Fired vessels — steam & hot water boilers

            (b) Unfired vessels —

        4) Mechanical electrical equipment (transformers, generators, motors, fans, pumps, compressors)

        5) Engines — diesel, gasoline, steam

        6) Meters and gauges

        7) Turbines — steam, gas, water

        8) Conveyors and lifts, trams, elevators.

    b) Furniture and fixtures

    c) Electronic Data Processing equipment

    d) Improvements and betterments

    e) Stock — supplies, raw materials, goods in process, finished goods

    f) Fine Arts — antiques, paintings, jewelry, libraries

    g) Safety equipment — instruments, apparel, alarms, installations

    h) Valuable Papers

        1) Blueprints

        2) Formulae

        3) Accounts Receivable

        4) Patents & copyrights

        5) Titles and deeds

        6) Tapes, cards, discs, programs

        7) Own securities — negotiable & non-negotiable

        8) Other corp. securities

        9) Cash (indicate currency)

3. *Miscellaneous Property*

    a) Vehicles (including contents)

        1) Commercial

        2) Private passenger

        3) Contractors equipment (licensed)

        4) Warehouse equipment

    b) Aircraft

        1) Missiles & satellites

        2) Lighter-than-air

        3) Aircraft — jet, piston, fixed-wing, rotary wing

    c) Animals

    d) Antennae

    e) Crops, gardens, lawns.

    f) Fences

    g) Firearms

    h) Nuclear & radioactive property — isotopes, tracers, reactors, cyclatrons, accelerators, bevatrons.

    i) Promotional displays — signs, models, plates, handbills, exhibits

    j) Recreational facilities — parks, gyms, lakes, cafeterias.

    k) Watercraft (including contents) — boats, yachts, barges, ships, submersibles, buoys, drilling rigs.

B. *Intangible Assets*

(Assets not necessarily shown on Balance Sheet or Earnings Statement)

1. *External Assets*

   a) Markets
   b) Resource availability

1) Suppliers	4) Public utilities
2) Transportation	5) Public protection
3) Employees (full-time & temporary)	

   c) Communications — telephone, teletype, television, radio, newspaper
   d) Locational — climate, political, economic & social stability, currency convertibility
   e) Counsel & specialists — legal architecture, accounting, insurance, real estate, general management, marketing, advertising, banking

2. *Internal Assets*

   a) Research and development
   b) Goodwill and reputation
   c) Financial

1) Credit cards	6) Royalties and Rents
2) Credit lines (rec'd.)	7) Leasehold interest
3) Insurance	8) Ownership of stock
4) Customer credit	9) Company foundations (non-profit)
5) Emp. Benefit Program	10) Tax loss carry-forward

   d) Personnel (employees and executives)

   1) Education and training
   2) Experience
   3) "Key" employees

   e) Rights

   1) Mineral & oil rights (above, underground & offshore)
   2) Air rights
   3) Patents and copyrights
   4) Royalty agreements
   5) Distribution agreements
   6) Manufacturing rights

List 2 — Exposures to Loss

A. *Direct Exposures:*

   1. *Generally uncontrollable and unpredictable*

      a) Electrical disturbance: lightning, burnout, sun spots, power surge, demagnetization of tapes
      b) Falling Objects: aircraft, meteors, missiles, trees
      c) Land movement: earthquake, volcano, landslide, avalanche
      d) Sound & shock waves: sonic boom, vibration, water hammer
      e) Subsidence: collapse, settlement, erosion

f) War, insurrection, rebellion, armed revolt, sabotage

g) Water Damage: flood, rising waters, flash flood, mudslide tidal waves (tsunami), geyser, ground water, sprinkler leakage, sewer back-up

h) Weight of ice, snow

i) Windstorm: Typhoon, hurricane, cyclone, tornado, hailstorm, rain, dust, seche, sandstorm

2. *Generally controllable or predictable*

a) Breakage of glass: other fragile items

b) Breakdown: malfunction of part, lubricant, etc.

c) Collision: on and off premises: watercraft, aircraft, vehicles

d) Contamination: liquid, solid, gaseous, radioactive, pollution

e) Corrosion: wear, tear, abuse, poor maintenance

f) Employee negligence

g) Explosion and implosion

h) Failure of environmental control: temperature, humidity pressure

i) Fauna: animals, rodents, insects, pests

j) Fire

k) Installation and construction hazards: dropping

l) Intentional destruction: jettison, backfiring, etc.

m) Perils of sea: pirates, rovers, barratry, etc.

n) Physical change: shrinkage, evaporation, color, mildew, expansion, contraction

o) Rupture, puncture of tank, vessel

p) Smoke damage, smudge

q) Spillage, leakage, paint spray

r) Structural defects, crane or elevator fall

s) Transportation: overturn, collision

t) Unintentional error: employee, computer, counsel

u) Vegetation

v) Vandalism, malicious mischief, defacing of property

w) Riots, civil disorders, strikes, boycotts, curfews

3. *Primarily financial in nature*

a) Employee dishonesty — forgery, embezzlement, larceny

b) Expropriation — nationalization, seizure, exercise of eminent domain, confiscation.

c) Fraud, forgery, theft, burglary, robbery

d) Invalidity of deed, title, patent, copyright

e) Inventory shortage: mysterious disappearance, loss or mislaid property

f) Obsolescence

B. *Indirect or Consequential Exposures:*

a) All direct exposures as they affect:

1) Suppliers	4) Transportation (personnel and property)
2) Customers	5) Employees
3) Utilities	

b) Extra expense: rentals, communication, product, etc.

c) Concentration of assets

  d) Change in style, taste, desire
  e) Bankruptcy: employee, executive, supplier, customer, counseler
  f) Disruption of educational system (racial, political, economic)
  g) Economic fluctuation: inflation, recession, depression
  h) Epidemic, disease, plague
  i) Increased replacement cost, depreciation
  j) Invasion of copyright, patent
  k) Loss of integral part of set, pair, group
  l) Loss of rights resulting from records destruction
  m) Managerial error in:

     1) pricing, marketing   6) political predictions
     2) distribution   7) investments
     3) production   8) dividend declaration
     4) expansion   9) tax filing
     5) economic predictions

  n) Recall of product
  o) Spoilage

C. *Third Party Liabilities* (Compensatory and Punitive Damages)

  1. Aviation Liability

     a) Owned and leased aircraft
     b) Non-owned: officers and employees licensed
     c) Grounding and sistership liability

  2. Athletic

     a) Sponsorship of teams, recreational facilities, etc.

  3. Advertiser's and Publisher's Liability

     a) As agents
     b) Libel, slander, defamation of character
     c) Media used: radio, TV, newspaper, samples, exhibits

  4. Automobile Liability

     a) Operation of vehicles: owned and non-owned
     b) Loading and unloading
     c) Dangerous contents: flammables, explosives

  5. Contractual Liability

     a) Purchase agreements
     b) Sales agreements
     c) Lease agreements: real or personal property
     d) Performance or service
     e) Loans, mortgages, notes
     f) Hold Harmless clauses
     g) Surety agreements

  6. Easements

     a) In gross
     b) Appurtenant
     c) Positive or negative under common law
     d) Rights to access to light, water, drainage, support

7. Employer's Liability
    a) Workers' Compensation or similar laws
    b) Federal Employees Liability Act
    c) Common Law
    d) U.S. Longshoreman's and Harbor Workers Act
    e) Jones Act
    f) Defense Bases Act
    g) Outer Continental Shelf Act
    h) Unemployment Compensation
    i) Discrimination in employment

8. Fringe Benefits Plans Liability
    a) Pensions, trusts, profit sharing plans, investments
    b) Insured: life, accident, health, etc.
    c) Credit unions

9. Malpractice Liability — Errors and Omissions
    a) Medical: doctors, nurses, specialists
    b) Lawyers
    c) Engineers
    d) Trustees of pension plans
    e) Patent infringement

10. Ordinary Negligence
    a) Of employees
    b) Of agents
    c) Of invited or uninvited guests
    d) Of contractor or subcontractor
    e) Failure to provide safety equipment, warnings, etc.
    f) Inadequate enforcement of regulations
    g) Improper preparation of food

11. Non-ownership Liability
    a) Leased real or personal property
    b) Bailee's liability
    c) Employee's use of vehicle, aircraft, watercraft

C. *Third Party Liabilities*
    12. Owner's Liability
        a) Attractive nuisance
        b) Invited guests
        c) Trespassers (false arrest)
        d) Rights of others: riparian, mineral, light, air, view, lateral support, easements, part walls, licenses, drainage, eminent domain

    13. Products Liability (each product sold, distributed, made)
        a) Implied warranty
        b) Express warranty
            1) by agents: sales, advertising or general
            2) by employees
            3) of merchantability

    4) of suitability or fitness for use
    5) of title
    6) by sample

14. Protective Liability

    a) Industrial contractors hired
    b) Construction or demolition

15. Railroad Liability

    a) Sidetract agreements
    b) Right of way
    c) Grade crossings

16. Director's and Officer's Liability (stockholder derivative suits)

17. Watercraft Liability

    a) Ownership, leased, operation
    b) Types: boats, yachts, ships, submersibles

Appendix F
Some Mathematical Formulas

Computation of the present value of a life annuity due of $1 payable annually to a person aged X.

Let $\ddot{a}_x$ = symbol for present value of a life annuity due of $1 payable annually to a person aged X.

l_x = number of persons alive at age X according to the mortality table selected for use in the computation.

$v^n = (1 + i)^{-n}$ when n = years and i = interest rate assumed.

$$\ddot{a}_x = \$1 + \$1\,\frac{l_{x+1}}{l_x}\,v + \$1\,\frac{l_{x+2}}{l_x}\,v^2 + \ldots$$

to end of mortality table.

$$= \frac{\$1 \cdot l_x + \$1 \cdot l_{x+1}\,v + \$1 \cdot l_{x+2}\,v^2 + \ldots}{l_x}$$

$$(1)$$

Multiply numerator and denominator of (1) by v^x obtaining

$$\ddot{a}_x = \frac{\$1 \cdot v^x l_x + \$1 \cdot v^{x+1} l_{x+1} + \$1 \cdot v^{x+2} l_{x+2} + \ldots}{v^x l_x}$$

Let $D_x = v^x l_x$

Then $$\ddot{a}_x = \frac{D_x + D_{x+1} + D_{x+2} + \ldots}{D_x}$$

Let $N_x = \sum_{t=0}^{w-x-1} D_{x+1}$, where w = upper limit on age in the mortality table.

Then, $$\ddot{a}_x = \frac{N_x}{D_x}$$

Index